OXFORD MONOGRAPHS IN INTERNATIONAL LAW

GENERAL EDITOR: PROFESSOR IAN BROWNLIE CBE, QC, FBA
Chichele Professor of Public International Law in the University of
Oxford and Fellow of All Souls College, Oxford.

THE INTERNATIONAL COVENANT ON ECONOMIC, SOCIAL, AND CULTURAL RIGHTS

D0220915

OXFORD MONOGRAPHS IN INTERNATIONAL LAW

General Editor: Professor Ian Brownlie CBE, QC, FBA, Chichele Professor of Public International Law in the University of Oxford and Fellow of All Souls College, Oxford.

The aim of this series of monographs is to publish important and original pieces of research on all aspects of public international law. Topics which are given particular prominence are those which, while of interest to the academic lawyers, also have important bearing on issues which touch the actual conduct of international relations. None the less the series is wide in scope and includes monographs on the history and philosophical foundations of international law.

RECENT TITLES

The International Covenant on Economic, Social, and Cultural Rights

A Perspective on its Development

MATTHEW C. R. CRAVEN

CLARENDON PRESS · OXFORD

Oxford University Press, Great Clarendon Street, Oxford OX2 6DP

Oxford New York

Athens Auckland Bangkok Bogota Bombay Buenos Aires
Calcutta Cape Town Dar es Salaam Delhi Florence Hong Kong Istanbul
Karachi Kuala Lumpur Madras Madrid Melbourne Mexico City
Nairobi Paris Singapore Taipei Tokyo Toronto Warsaw

and associated companies in
Berlin Ibadan

Oxford is a trade mark of Oxford University Press

Published in the United States
by Oxford University Press Inc., New York

© Matthew Craven 1995

First published 1995
Issued in paperback (will corrections) 1998

All rights reserved. No part of this publication may be reproduced,
stored in a retrieval system, or transmitted, in any form or by any means,
without the prior permission in writing of Oxford University Press.
Within the UK, exceptions are allowed in respect of any fair dealing for the
purpose of research or private study, or criticism or review, as permitted
under the Copyright, Designs and Patents Act, 1988, or in the case of
reprographic reproduction in accordance with the terms of the licences
issued by the Copyright Licensing Agency. Enquiries concerning
reproduction outside these terms and in other countries should be
sent to the Rights Department, Oxford University Press,
at the address above

British Library Cataloguing in Publication Data
Data available

Library of Congress Cataloging in Publication Data
Craven, Matthew C. R.
The International Covenant on Economic, Social, and Cultural
Rights: a perspective on its development / Matthew C. R. Craven.
p. cm.
Includes bibliographical references.
1. International Covenant on Economic, Social, and Cultural Rights
(1966) 2. Human rights. I. Title.
K3238.31966.C73 1995
341.4'81—dc20   94-46610
ISBN 0–19–825874–7
ISBN 0–19–826788–6 (Pbk)

Printed in Great Britain
on acid-free paper by
Bookcraft Ltd., Midsomer Norton, Avon

Editor's Preface

This work originated as a doctoral thesis prepared at the University of Nottingham. It provides an exhaustive account of the International Covenant on Economic, Social and Cultural Rights, and makes a substantial contribution to the existing literature.

The subject-matter of the Covenant extends to some areas of notorious complexity, including trade union rights, the right to strike and closed shop agreements. Other topics of interest examined are the concept of discrimination, the right to housing and the right to food. The whole extended family of Covenant-related topics is examined with scholarly care and appropriate candour. A particular feature of the work is its meticulous documentation.

The *Oxford Monographs* series now includes four significant studies in the field of human rights.

IAN BROWNLIE.

All Souls College,
OXFORD.

23rd February 1995.

Preface

I AM indebted to a great number of people for the part they have played, whether directly or indirectly, in the production of this book. My main debt of gratitude in terms of its content goes to the supervisors of my Ph.D. thesis, Professors David Harris and Michael Gunn, both of whom surpassed their nominal duties as supervisors. I should also thank in that respect my examiners, Dr Nigel White and Professor Rosalyn Higgins, whose comments were very useful. As regards my work in Geneva, I must thank the individual members who sit on the Committee on Economic, Social, and Cultural Rights whose work comprises the raw material from which this book is developed, and especially Professors Philip Alston and Bruno Simma, for their advice and assistance.

On a personal level, in the years that it has taken me to complete this book I have relied heavily upon the support of family and friends; I must thank in that regard my mother and father, Oriole and Michael Craven, who have consistently encouraged me in my work. Finally, and most importantly, I am ever endebted to Janet Morrison, who has in countless different ways provided the necessary support and understanding to help me through what, at times, has seemed a long and painful process.

Preface to the Paperback Edition

Since 1995, when this book was first published, there have been a number of developments of note in relation to the work of the UN Committee on Economic, Social and Cultural Rights. In the broader context, although the protection of economic, social and cultural rights remains a secondary concern for most States, it has been increasingly the subject of attention in the work of the UN Commission on Human Rights and its Sub-Commission. Issues of child labour, forced evictions, and involuntary resettlement, for example, have all achieved a prominence in recent years in a way that had previously only been the case with instances of torture and inhuman treatment. Similarly, although not necessarily arising in the terminology of human rights, the themes and concerns that fall within the purview of the Covenant have been the subject of discussion at several international conferences such as the 1995 World Summit for Social Development in Copenhagen.[1]

At a regional level, there has also been some progress in recent years. In Europe, a revised European Social Charter has been adopted, and an Additional Protocol for the receipt of group communications has been signed (although it has yet to enter into force).[2] Similarly, the League of Arab States has adopted the Arab Charter on Human Rights which includes the full range of human rights, including a number of economic, social and cultural rights, within a single text.[3] As far as Africa is concerned, the African Commission has begun to consider communications relating to economic, social and cultural rights in the Charter and has, on occasion, taken a remarkably strong stance.[4] The situation in the Americas, by contrast, has not been quite as positive. The 1988 Additional Protocol to the Inter-American Convention on Human Rights in the Area of Economic, Social and Cultural Rights (the Protocol of San Salvador)[5] still awaits sufficient ratifications to enter into force, and the I/A Commission has yet to begin dealing with economic and social rights in a consistent and satisfactory manner.[6]

---

[1] Report of the World Summit for Social Development, 6–12 March 1995, UN Doc. A/CONF.166/9 (1995).

[2] European Treaty Series, No. 158.

[3] 15 September 1994. 4 I.H.R.R. (1997) 850.

[4] See e.g., Union Interafricaine des Droits de l'Homme v. Zaire, Communication No. 100/93, 4 I.H.R.R. (1997) 89, paras. 47–48.

[5] OAS, Treaty Series, No. 69.

[6] See generally, Craven M., 'The Protection of Economic, Social and Cultural Rights under the Inter-American System of Human Rights', in *The Inter-American System of Human Rights*, Harris D. and Livingstone S. (1998) 289.

The International Covenant on Economic, Social and Cultural Rights

Over the past three years the number of States parties to the International Covenant has risen to 135 with the recent inclusion of Chad (9 September 1995), Kuwait (21 August 1996), Kyrgyzstan (7 January 1995), Namibia (28 February 1995), Sierra Leone (23 November 1996) and Uzbekistan (28 December 1995) Annex 1-XIII of the UK-Chinese Joint Declaration suggests that the ICESCR will remain in force as regards Hong Kong. The modalities of reporting, however, have yet to be made clear. On ratification, Kuwait made two interpretative declarations and reserved its position in relation to one article. In its interpretative declarations, Kuwait took the view that the equality/non-discrimination provisions in articles 2(2) and 3 should be interpreted as being exercised within the limits set by Kuwaiti law, and that the right to social security in article 9 should be interpreted as applying only to Kuwaiti nationals.[7] It further reserved its position as regards the application of article 8(1)(d) which guarantees the right to strike. The position adopted with respect to articles 8 and 9 is unfortunate, but clearly defensible. The same cannot be said for the 'interpretative declaration' adopted in relation to articles 2(2) and 3 which appears to deny any possible incompatibility of Kuwaiti law with obligations assumed under the Covenant.

The UN Committee on Economic, Social and Cultural Rights

The Committee has continued to meet for two sessions of three weeks each year taking the total, at the end of December 1997, to seventeen sessions. Its working methods have largely remained the same. The membership of the Committee is now as follows: Ade Adekuoye, Mahmoud Ahmed, Philip Alston (Chairperson), Ivan Antanovich, Virginia Bonoan-Dandan, Dumitru Ceausu, Oscar Ceville, Abdessatar Grissa, Maria de los Angeles Jimenez Butragueno, Valeri Kouznetsov, Jaime Marchan Romero, Ariranga Pillay, Kenneth Rattray, Walid Sadi, Philippe Texier, Nutan Thapalia, Javier Wimer Zambrano.

The Reporting Procedure

Compliance with the reporting procedure has not improved dramatically despite the Committee's efforts to deal with the problem (for example by considering the situation of non-reporting States and revising its reporting guidelines[8]). A total of 19 States parties have failed to submit a single report in the past ten years[9]—a list which notably includes Greece—and the quality

---

[7] E/C.12/1993/3/Rev.2, at 15.
[8] Report of the Committee's Fourteenth and Fifteenth Sessions, UN Doc. E/1997/22, at 13, para. 22, UN ESCOR, Supp. (No. 2) (1997). E.g., Guinea, (May 1996).
[9] E/C.12/1997/6.

of reports remains generally mediocre. At the same time, the Committee has been faced with a growing backlog of reports which has not only led it to request an extraordinary third session in 1998, but also induced it to reconsider its procedures in relation to the reporting system as a whole. As regards the latter, the Committee is currently considering moving from a system of comprehensive periodic reports, to one in which States are asked to report on a brief list of issues identified in advance by the Committee.[10] How far this reform will remain consistent with the principles enunciated in the Committee's first General Comment, however, remains to be seen.

As regards the current operation of the reporting procedure, the Committee has continued its established practice of adopting concluding observations following the consideration of State reports. These have improved the quality of the debate and have concentrated the Committee's mind on matters of importance. In recent years the Committee has continued to be concerned with matters such as poverty,[11] malnutrition,[12] discrimination,[13] lack of housing[14] or forced evictions,[15] restrictions on the right to join and form trade unions or to strike,[16] child labour,[17] the exploitation of foreign workers,[18] the absence of proper labour regulation,[19] and inadequate wages.[20] It has also continued to indicate where it considers a situation to be clearly inconsistent with the terms of the Covenant.

The Committee has adopted further procedures in relation to the follow-up of issues that remained unresolved during the constructive dialogue. It now issues a document detailing what additional information remains to be provided by States parties following the discussion, and providing a

---

[10] E/C.12/1997/CRP.1/Add. 1, at 4–5.

[11] See e.g., Concluding Observations on the report of Colombia, E/C.12/1995/12; the Russian Federation, E/C.12/1/Add. 13 (1997) para. 14.

[12] See e.g., Concluding Observations on the report of the Russian Federation, E/C.12/1/Add. 13 (1997) paras. 23–24.

[13] See e.g., Concluding Observations on the report of Mauritius, E/C.12/1995/14, para. 10; Ukraine, E/C.12/1995/15, paras. 15, 16; Algeria, E/C.12/1995/17, paras. 16–17; Paraguay, E/C.12/1/Add. 1 (1996) paras. 9–10; Spain, E/C.12/1/Add. 2 (1996) para. 17; Zimbabwe, E/C.12/1/Add. 12 (1997) para. 10; Libyan Arab Republic, E/C.12/1/Add. 15 (1997) para. 13; the Russian Federation, E/C.12/1/Add. 13 (1997) paras. 15–16; Peru, E/C.12/1/Add. 14 (1997) paras. 15–17.

[14] See e.g., Concluding Observations on the report of Algeria, E/C.12/1995/17, para. 20; El Salvador, E/C.12/1/Add. 4 (1996) para. 21.

[15] See e.g., Concluding Observations on the report of Zimbabwe, E/C.12/1/Add. 12 (1997) para. 13; Peru, E/C.12/1/Add. 14 (1997) para. 26.

[16] See e.g., Concluding Observations on the report of Paraguay, E/C.12/1/Add. 1 (1996) paras. 12–13; El Salvador, E/C.12/1/Add. 4 (1996) para. 19; Libyan Arab Republic, E/C.12/1/Add. 15 (1997) para. 13; Zimbabwe, E/C.12/1/Add. 12 (1997) para. 11; Peru, E/C.12/1/Add. 14 (1997) para. 19.

[17] See e.g., Concluding Observations on the report of Paraguay, E/C.12/1/Add. 1 (1996) para. 15; El Salvador, E/C.12/1/Add. 4 (1996) para. 12; Zimbabwe, E/C.12/1/Add. 12 (1997) para. 12; Peru, E/C.12/1/Add. 14 (1997) para. 23.

[18] See e.g., Concluding Observations on the report of the Libyan Arab Republic, E/C.12/1/Add. 15 (1997) paras. 15–16.

[19] See e.g., Concluding Observations on the report of Guatamala, E/C.12/1/Add. 3 (1996) para. 18; the Russian Federation, E/C.12/1/Add. 13 (1997) para. 18.

[20] See e.g., Concluding Observations on the report of Paraguay, E/C.12/1/Add. 1 (1996) para. 11; Peru, E/C.12/1/Add. 14 (1997) para. 18.

deadline for the receipt of that information.[21] Following the precedent set in relation to Panama the Committee has again sent an expert group to undertake an on-site visit to a State party by way of follow-up. On this occasion, its concern was the situation in the Dominican Republic in which there had been several reported instances of mass forced evictions. As in the earlier case, the expert group reported back to the Committee which adopted a report on the situation at its session in December 1997.

The Optional Protocol

Perhaps the development of greatest significance in the work of the Committee is its adoption of a draft Optional Protocol for the receipt of individual and group communications. The draft was finally adopted at the Committee's fifteenth session in 1996[22] after a lengthy period of deliberation involving the consideration of a series of four separate reports drafted by Professor Alston.[23] The draft Optional Protocol has yet to be considered by the UN Commission on Human Rights and remains in preliminary form.

Whilst the project of drafting an Optional Protocol might yet be one of the most significant initiatives undertaken by the Committee, its inception has not been auspicious. During the debate within the Committee it soon became clear that the draft could not be adopted by consensus. In fact one member of the Committee—Mr Grissa—was adamantly opposed to the proposal of an Optional Protocol in any form, and insisted that his name not be associated with it. As a result, although a single draft Protocol was completed, it was adopted only by majority decision and, as the commentary makes clear, a number of issues remain to be decided by the Commission on Human Rights if it eventually takes hold of the matter. This is clearly unfortunate. If the Committee, as an independent group of experts, is unable to agree upon a definitive text, it would appear unlikely that States will take up the matter with enthusiasm within the political organs of the UN.

As it stands, the current text of the draft Optional Protocol envisages that any individual or group claiming to be (or acting on behalf of) a victim of a violation by a State party of any of the rights recognized within the Covenant, should be entitled to submit a written communication to the Committee.[24] The receivability and admissibility of a communication would

---

[21]   See e.g., E/C.12/1997/7.
[22]   E/CN.4/1997/105. For the discussion see, E/C.12/1996/SR.44–49, 54.
[23]   E/C.12/1991/WP.2, E/C.12/1992/WP.9, E/C.12/1994/12, and E/C.12/1996/CRP.2/Add. 1. The Committee was encouraged in its efforts by the World Conference on Human Rights. Paragraph 75 (Part II) of the Vienna Declaration and Programme of Action 'encourage[d] the Commission on Human Rights, in cooperation with the Committee on Economic, Social and Cultural Rights, to continue the examination of optional protocols to the International Covenant on Economic, Social and Cultural Rights'.
[24]   Draft article 2.

be determined by standard clauses such as those found in the First Optional Protocol to the International Covenant on Civil and Political Rights.[25] Thus, among other requirements, communications would have to be well-founded, and applicants would be required to exhaust all available domestic remedies. If the application is deemed admissible, the Committee would proceed to examine the application on its merits, together with any written submissions provided by the State concerned. In the absence of a friendly settlement, the Committee would then adopt a set of 'views' as to the State's compliance with its obligations under the Covenant which would be transmitted to the author and the State concerned, together with any recommendations it considers appropriate.[26]

Whilst much of the draft Protocol follows that of the ICCPR, there are a number of notable differences. First, and foremost, the draft envisages the possible receipt of both individual and group communications. On this point the draft also differs from the Additional Protocol to the European Social Charter which restricts communications to groups, rather than individuals. Secondly, specific provision is made for the adoption of interim measures of protection in cases where 'a preliminary study gives rise to a reasonable apprehension that the allegations, if substantiated, could lead to irreparable harm'.[27] Thirdly, no provision is made for the resolution of inter-state disputes—although this was a matter that the Committee thought might be considered by the Commission on Human Rights. Fourthly, in line with its policy under the reporting procedure, the Committee would not be restricted in its reliance upon information provided by the parties concerned (the individual or the State). It would be entitled to have use of 'all information made available to it' including 'information obtained from other sources'.[28] Fifthly, as part of its examination of a communication, the Committee would be entitled to visit the territory of the State concerned provided, of course, that the State agrees.[29] Finally, in line with the practice of the Human Rights Committee, the Committee would, in cases where it was of the view that a violation had taken place, recommend that the State party take specific measures to remedy the violation and prevent its recurrence,[30] and would subsequently invite the State concerned to discuss what measures had been taken.[31]

Two interesting issues arose in discussions prior to the adoption of the draft Protocol. The first was whether communications had to refer exclusively to violations of rights recognized in the Covenant, or whether they could refer, more broadly, to non-compliance with obligations. The latter approach was adopted by an expert meeting convened in Utrecht in 1995 on the basis that not every failure to comply with obligations under the

---

[25] Draft article 3. [26] Draft article 7. [27] Draft article 5.
[28] Draft article 7(1). [29] Draft article 7(3). [30] Draft article 8.
[31] Draft article 9.

Covenant would constitute a violation of a right.[32] The Committee took the view that the 'violations approach' would be the best not least because, if otherwise, it would include matters such as compliance with the reporting procedure.

The second point of debate was whether or not the communications procedure should cover the whole range of rights within the Covenant, or whether it should be restricted (or open to restriction) to selected rights. Here, a majority of the Committee preferred the comprehensive approach although a significant minority did favour the possibility of States selecting which rights should be governed by the procedure. One point of difficulty arising from the adoption of a comprehensive approach was that it would necessarily include the right to self-determination in article 1 of the Covenant—a matter which caused some apprehension among members of the Committee. The Committee, therefore, took the view that it would only consider communications in relation to article 1 insofar as they concerned economic, social or cultural aspects of self-determination. The civil and political dimensions of the right would remain matters for the Human Rights Committee.

General Comments

Since the last edition of this book was written, the Committee has adopted a further three General Comments by way of clarifying the nature of State obligations assumed in relation to the Covenant. General Comment No. 5 concerned 'persons with disabilities',[33] No. 6 the 'economic social and cultural rights of older persons',[34] and No. 7 the question of forced evictions.[35] In line with its stated policy, these general comments may be regarded as an attempt by the Committee to flesh out its understanding of the obligations undertaken by States in relation to the Covenant. The emphasis of the General Comments, however, are clearly different. On the one hand, the General Comment on Forced Evictions has been driven by the Committee's experience of dealing with such issues under the reporting procedure and represents an extension of its earlier General Comment on the Right to Housing. The other two Comments, by contrast, are not so much concerned with the Committee's own experience, but make extensive reference to norms established in other fora.

---

[32] See Coomans F. and Hoof G. (eds), The Right to Complain about Economic, Social and Cultural Rights: Proceedings of the Expert Meeting on the Adoption of an Optional Protocol to the International Covenant on Economic, Social and Cultural Rights (1995).

[33] E/C.12/1994/13.

[34] E/C.12/1995/16/Rev. 1.

[35] E/C.12/1997/4. The Committee also has a number of draft General Comments awaiting adoption which concern: the domestic application of the Covenant; the right to health; ensuring gender equality in the implementation of economic, social and cultural rights; the right to food; the right to education; cultural rights. See UN Doc. E/C.12/1997/CRP.1/Add. 1.

GENERAL COMMENT NO. 5
Persons with disabilities
(Eleventh session, 1994), UN Doc. E/C.12/1994/13 (1994).*

1. The central importance of the International Covenant on Economic, Social and Cultural Rights in relation to the human rights of persons with disabilities has frequently been underlined by the international community.[1] Thus a 1992 review by the Secretary-General of the implementation of the World Programme of Action concerning Disabled Persons and the United Nations Decade of Disabled Persons concluded that 'disability is closely linked to economic and social factors' and that 'conditions of living in large parts of the world are so desperate that the provision of basic needs for all—food, water, shelter, health protection and education—must form the cornerstone of national programmes'.[2] Even in countries which have a relatively high standard of living, persons with disabilities are very often denied the opportunity to enjoy the full range of economic, social and cultural rights recognized in the Covenant.

2. The Committee on Economic, Social and Cultural Rights, and the working group which preceded it, have been explicitly called upon by both the General Assembly[3] and the Commission on Human Rights[4] to monitor the compliance of States parties to the Covenant with their obligation to ensure the full enjoyment of the relevant rights by persons with disabilities. The Committee's experience to date, however, indicates that States parties have devoted very little attention to this issue in their reports. This appears to be consistent with the Secretary-General's conclusion that 'most Governments still lack decisive concerted measures that would effectively improve the situation' of persons with disabilities.[5] It is therefore appropriate to review, and emphasize, some of the ways in which issues concerning persons with disabilities arise in connection with the obligations contained in the Covenant.

3. There is still no internationally accepted definition of the term 'disability'. For present purposes, however, it is sufficient to rely on the approach adopted in the Standard Rules of 1993, which state:

'The term "disability" summarizes a great number of different functional limitations occurring in any population . . . People may be disabled by physical, intellectual or sensory impairment, medical conditions or mental illness. Such impairments, conditions or illnesses may be permanent or transitory in nature.'[6]

4. In accordance with the approach adopted in the Standard Rules, this General Comment uses the term 'persons with disabilities' rather than the older term

---

* Adopted at the 38th meeting, on 25 November 1994.
[1] For a comprehensive review of the question, see the final report prepared by Mr Leandro Despouy, Special Rapporteur, on human rights and disability (E/CN.4/Sub.2/1991/31).
[2] See A/47/415, para. 5.
[3] See para. 165 of the World Programme of Action concerning Disabled Persons, adopted by the General Assembly by its resolution 37/52 of 3 December 1982 (para. 1).
[4] See Commission on Human Rights resolutions 1992/48, para. 4 and 1993/29, para. 7.
[5] See A/47/415, para. 6.
[6] Standard Rules on the Equalization of Opportunities for Persons with Disabilities, annexed to General Assembly resolution 48/96 of 20 December 1993 (Introduction, para. 17).

'disabled persons'. It has been suggested that the latter term might be misinterpreted to imply that the ability of the individual to function as a person has been disabled.

5. The Covenant does not refer explicitly to persons with disabilities. Nevertheless, the Universal Declaration of Human Rights recognizes that all human beings are born free and equal in dignity and rights and, since the Covenant's provisions apply fully to all members of society, persons with disabilities are clearly entitled to the full range of rights recognized in the Covenant. In addition, insofar as special treatment is necessary, States parties are required to take appropriate measures, to the maximum extent of their available resources, to enable such persons to seek to overcome any disadvantages, in terms of the enjoyment of the rights specified in the Covenant, flowing from their disability. Moreover, the requirement contained in article 2(2) of the Covenant that the rights 'enunciated . . . will be exercised without discrimination of any kind' based on certain specified grounds 'or other status' clearly applies to discrimination on the grounds of disability.

6. The absence of an explicit, disability-related provision in the Covenant can be attributed to the lack of awareness of the importance of addressing this issue explicitly, rather than only by implication, at the time of the drafting of the Covenant over a quarter of a century ago. More recent international human rights' instruments have, however, addressed the issue specifically. They include the Convention on the Rights of the Child (art. 23); the African Charter on Human and Peoples' Rights (art. 18(4)); and the Additional Protocol to the American Convention on Human Rights in the Area of Economic, Social and Cultural Rights (art. 18). Thus it is now very widely accepted that the human rights of persons with disabilities must be protected and promoted through general, as well as specially designed, laws, policies and programmes.

7. In accordance with this approach, the international community has affirmed its commitment to ensuring the full range of human rights for persons with disabilities in the following instruments: (a) the world Programme of Action concerning Disabled Persons, which provides a policy framework aimed at promoting 'effective measures for prevention of disability, rehabilitation and the realization of the goals of "full participation" of [persons with disabilities] in social life and development, and of "equality" ';[7] (b) the Guidelines for the Establishment and Development of National Coordinating Committees on Disability or Similar Bodies, adopted in 1990;[8] (c) the Principles for the Protection of Persons with Mental Illness and for the Improvement of Mental Health Care, adopted in 1991;[9] (d) the Standard Rules on the Equalization of Opportunities for Persons with Disabilities (hereinafter referred to as the 'Standard Rules'), adopted in 1993, the purpose of which is to ensure that all persons with disabilities 'may exercise the same rights and obligations as others'.[10] The Standard Rules are of major importance and constitute a particularly

---

[7] World Programme of Action concerning Disabled Persons (see note 3 above), para. 1.

[8] A/C.3/46/4, annex I. Also contained in the Report on the International Meeting on the Roles and Functions of National Coordinating Committees on Disability in Developing Countries, Beijing, 5–11 November 1990 (CSDHA/DDP/NDC/4). See also Economic and Social Council resolution 1991/8 and General Assembly resolution 46/96 of 16 December 1991.

[9] General Assembly resolution 46/119 of 17 December 1991, annex.

[10] Standard Rules (see note 6 above), Introduction, para. 15.

valuable reference guide in identifying more precisely the relevant obligations of States parties under the Covenant.

I. GENERAL OBLIGATIONS OF STATES PARTIES

8. The United Nations has estimated that there are more than 500 million persons with disabilities in the world today. Of that number, 80 per cent live in rural areas in developing countries. Seventy per cent of the total are estimated to have either limited or no access to the services they need. The challenge of improving the situation of persons with disabilities is thus of direct relevance to every State party to the Covenant. While the means chosen to promote the full realization of the economic, social and cultural rights of this group will inevitably differ significantly from one country to another, there is no country in which a major policy and programme effort is not required.[11]

9. The obligation of States parties to the Covenant to promote progressive realization of the relevant rights to the maximum of their available resources clearly requires Governments to do much more than merely abstain from taking measures which might have a negative impact on persons with disabilities. The obligation in the case of such a vulnerable and disadvantaged group is to take positive action to reduce structural disadvantages and to give appropriate preferential treatment to people with disabilities in order to achieve the objectives of full participation and equality within society for all persons with disabilities. This almost invariably means that additional resources will need to be made available for this purpose and that a wide range of specially tailored measures will be required.

10. According to a report by the Secretary-General, developments over the past decade in both developed and developing countries have been especially unfavourable from the perspective of persons with disabilities:

'. . . current economic and social deterioration, marked by low-growth rates, high unemployment, reduced public expenditure, current structural adjustment programmes and privatization, have negatively affected programmes and services . . . If the present negative trends continue, there is the risk that [persons with disabilities] may increasingly be relegated to the margins of society, dependent on ad hoc support.'[12]

As the Committee has previously observed (General Comment No. 3 (Fifth session, 1990), para. 12), the duty of States parties to protect the vulnerable members of their societies assumes greater rather than less importance in times of severe resource constraints.

11. Given the increasing commitment of Governments around the world to market-based policies, it is appropriate in that context to emphasize certain aspects of States parties' obligations. One is the need to ensure that not only the public sphere, but also the private sphere, are, within appropriate limits, subject to regulation to ensure the equitable treatment of persons with disabilities. In a context in which arrangements for the provision of public services are increasingly being privatized

---

[11] See A/47/415, passim.   [12] Ibid., para. 5.

and in which the free market is being relied on to an ever greater extent, it is essential that private employers, private suppliers of goods and services, and other non-public entities be subject to both non-discrimination and equality norms in relation to persons with disabilities. In circumstances where such protection does not extend beyond the public domain, the ability of persons with disabilities to participate in the mainstream of community activities and to realize their full potential as active members of society will be severely and often arbitrarily constrained. This is not to imply that legislative measures will always be the most effective means of seeking to eliminate discrimination within the private sphere. Thus, for example, the Standard Rules place particular emphasis on the need for States to 'take action to raise awareness in society about persons with disabilities, their rights, their needs, their potential and their contribution'.[13]

12. In the absence of government intervention there will always be instances in which the operation of the free market will produce unsatisfactory results for persons with disabilities, either individually or as a group, and in such circumstances it is incumbent on Governments to step in and take appropriate measures to temper, complement, compensate for, or override the results produced by market forces. Similarly, while it is appropriate for Governments to rely on private, voluntary groups to assist persons with disabilities in various ways, such arrangements can never absolve Governments from their duty to ensure full compliance with their obligations under the Covenant. As the World Programme of Action concerning Disabled Persons states, 'the ultimate responsibility for remedying the conditions that lead to impairment and for dealing with the consequences of disability rests with Governments'.[14]

II. MEANS OF IMPLEMENTATION

13. The methods to be used by States parties in seeking to implement their obligations under the Covenant towards persons with disabilities are essentially the same as those available in relation to other obligations (see General Comment No. 1 (Third session, 1989)). They include the need to ascertain, through regular monitoring, the nature and scope of the problems existing within the State; the need to adopt appropriately tailored policies and programmes to respond to the requirements thus identified; the need to legislate where necessary and to eliminate any existing discriminatory legislation; and the need to make appropriate budgetary provisions or, where necessary, seek international cooperation and assistance. In the latter respect, international cooperation in accordance with articles 22 and 23 of the Covenant is likely to be a particularly important element in enabling some developing countries to fulfil their obligations under the Covenant.

14. In addition, it has been consistently acknowledged by the international community that policy-making and programme implementation in this area should be undertaken on the basis of close consultation with, and involvement of, representative groups of the persons concerned. For this reason, the Standard Rules recom-

---

[13] Standard Rules (see note 6 above), Rule 1.
[14] World Programme of Action concerning Disabled Persons (see note 3 above), para. 3.

mend that everything possible be done to facilitate the establishment of national coordinating committees, or similar bodies, to serve as a national focal point on disability matters. In doing so, Governments should take account of the 1990 Guidelines for the Establishment and Development of National Coordinating Committees on Disability or Similar Bodies.[15]

III. THE OBLIGATION TO ELIMINATE DISCRIMINATION ON THE GROUNDS OF DISABILITY

15. Both de jure and de facto discrimination against persons with disabilities have a long history and take various forms. They range from invidious discrimination, such as the denial of educational opportunities, to more 'subtle' forms of discrimination such as segregation and isolation achieved through the imposition of physical and social barriers. For the purposes of the Covenant, 'disability-based discrimination' may be defined as including any distinction, exclusion, restriction or preference, or denial of reasonable accommodation based on disability which has the effect of nullifying or impairing the recognition, enjoyment or exercise of economic, social or cultural rights. Through neglect, ignorance, prejudice and false assumptions, as well as through exclusion, distinction or separation, persons with disabilities have very often been prevented from exercising their economic, social or cultural rights on an equal basis with persons without disabilities. The effects of disability-based discrimination have been particularly severe in the fields of education, employment, housing, transport, cultural life, and access to public places and services.

16. Despite some progress in terms of legislation over the past decade,[16] the legal situation of persons with disabilities remains precarious. In order to remedy past and present discrimination, and to deter future discrimination, comprehensive anti-discrimination legislation in relation to disability would seem to be indispensable in virtually all States parties. Such legislation should not only provide persons with disabilities with judicial remedies as far as possible and appropriate, but also provide for social-policy programmes which enable persons with disabilities to live an integrated, self-determined and independent life.

17. Anti-discrimination measures should be based on the principle of equal rights for persons with disabilities and the non-disabled, which, in the words of the World Programme of Action concerning Disabled Persons, 'implies that the needs of each and every individual are of equal importance, that these needs must be made the basis for the planning of societies, and that all resources must be employed in such a way as to ensure, for every individual, equal opportunity for participation. Disability policies should ensure the access of [persons with disabilities] to all community services'.[17]

18. Because appropriate measures need to be taken to undo existing discrimination and to establish equitable opportunities for persons with disabilities, such

[15] See note 8 above.   [16] See A/47/415, paras. 37–38.
[17] World Programme of Action concerning Disabled Persons (see note 3 above), para. 25.

actions should not be considered discriminatory in the sense of article 2(2) of the International Covenant on Economic, Social and Cultural Rights as long as they are based on the principle of equality and are employed only to the extent necessary to achieve that objective.

IV. SPECIFIC PROVISIONS OF THE COVENANT

A. Article 3—Equal rights for men and women

19. Persons with disabilities are sometimes treated as genderless human beings. As a result, the double discrimination suffered by women with disabilities is often neglected.[18] Despite frequent calls by the international community for particular emphasis to be placed upon their situation, very few efforts have been undertaken during the decade. The neglect of women with disabilities is mentioned several times in the report of the Secretary-General on the implementation of the World Programme of Action.[19] The Committee therefore urges States parties to address the situation of women with disabilities, with high priority being given in future to the implementation of economic, social and cultural rights-related programmes.

B. Articles 6–8—Rights relating to work

20. The field of employment is one in which disability-based discrimination has been prominent and persistent. In most countries the unemployment rate among persons with disabilities is two to three times higher than the unemployment rate for persons without disabilities. Where persons with disabilities are employed, they are mostly engaged in low-paid jobs with little social and legal security and are often segregated from the mainstream of the labour market. The integration of persons with disabilities into the regular labour market should be actively supported by States.

21. The 'right of everyone to the opportunity to gain his living by work which he freely chooses or accepts' (art. 6(1)) is not realized where the only real opportunity open to disabled workers is to work in so-called 'sheltered' facilities under substandard conditions. Arrangements whereby persons with a certain category of disability are effectively confined to certain occupations or to the production of certain goods may violate this right. Similarly, in the light of principle 13(3) of the Principles for the Protection of Persons with Mental Illness and for the Improvement of Mental Health Care,[20] 'therapeutical treatment' in institutions which amounts to forced labour is also incompatible with the Covenant. In this regard, the prohibition on forced labour contained in the International Covenant on Civil and Political Rights is also of potential relevance.

---

[18] See E/CN.4/Sub.2/1991/31 (see note 1 above), para. 140.
[19] See A/47/415, paras. 35, 46, 74 and 77. [20] See note 9 above.

22. According to the Standard Rules, persons with disabilities, whether in rural or urban areas, must have equal opportunities for productive and gainful employment in the labour market.[21] For this to happen it is particularly important that artificial barriers to integration in general, and to employment in particular, be removed. As the International Labour Organisation has noted, it is very often the physical barriers that society has erected in areas such as transport, housing and the workplace which are then cited as the reason why persons with disabilities cannot be employed.[22] For example, as long as workplaces are designed and built in ways that make them inaccessible to wheelchairs, employers will be able to 'justify' their failure to employ wheelchair users. Governments should also develop policies which promote and regulate flexible and alternative work arrangements that reasonably accommodate the needs of disabled workers.

23. Similarly, the failure of Governments to ensure that modes of transportation are accessible to persons with disabilities greatly reduces the chances of such persons finding suitable, integrated jobs, taking advantage of educational and vocational training, or commuting to facilities of all types. Indeed, the provision of access to appropriate and, where necessary, specially tailored forms of transportation is crucial to the realization by persons with disabilities of virtually all the rights recognized in the Covenant.

24. The 'technical and vocational guidance and training programmes' required under article 6(2) of the Covenant should reflect the needs of all persons with disabilities, take place in integrated settings, and be planned and implemented with the full involvement of representatives of persons with disabilities.

25. The right to 'the enjoyment of just and favourable conditions of work' (art. 7) applies to all disabled workers, whether they work in sheltered facilities or in the open labour market. Disabled workers may not be discriminated against with respect to wages or other conditions if their work is equal to that of non-disabled workers. States parties have a responsibility to ensure that disability is not used as an excuse for creating low standards of labour protection or for paying below minimum wages.

26. Trade union-related rights (art. 8) apply equally to workers with disabilities and regardless of whether they work in special work facilities or in the open labour market. In addition, article 8, read in conjunction with other rights such as the right to freedom of association, serves to emphasize the importance of the right of persons with disabilities to form their own organizations. If these organizations are to be effective in 'the promotion and protection of [the] economic and social interests' (art 8(1)(a)) of such persons, they should be consulted regularly by government bodies and others in relation to all matters affecting them; it may also be necessary that they be supported financially and otherwise so as to ensure their viability.

27. The International Labour Organisation has developed valuable and comprehensive instruments with respect to the work-related rights of persons with disabilities, including in particular Convention No. 159 (1983) concerning

---

[21] Standard Rules (see note 6 above), Rule 7.
[22] See A/CONF.157/PC/61/Add. 10, p. 12.

vocational rehabilitation and employment of persons with disabilities.[23] The Committee encourages States parties to the Covenant to consider ratifying that Convention.

C. Article 9—Social security

28. Social security and income-maintenance schemes are of particular importance for persons with disabilities. As stated in the Standard Rules, 'States should ensure the provision of adequate income support to persons with disabilities who, owing to disability or disability-related factors, have temporarily lost or received a reduction in their income or have been denied employment opportunities'.[24] Such support should reflect the special needs for assistance and other expenses often associated with disability. In addition, as far as possible, the support provided should also cover individuals (who are overwhelmingly female) who undertake the care of a person with disabilities. Such persons, including members of the families of persons with disabilities, are often in urgent need of financial support because of their assistance role.[25]

29. Institutionalization of persons with disabilities, unless rendered necessary for other reasons, cannot be regarded as an adequate substitute for the social security and income-support rights of such persons.

D. Article 10—Protection of the family and of mothers and children

30. In the case of persons with disabilities, the Covenant's requirement that 'protection and assistance' be rendered to the family means that everything possible should be done to enable such persons, when they so wish, to live with their families. Article 10 also implies, subject to the general principles of international human rights law, the right of persons with disabilities to marry and have their own family. These rights are frequently ignored or denied, especially in the case of persons with mental disabilities.[26] In this and other contexts, the term 'family' should be interpreted broadly and in accordance with appropriate local usage. States parties should ensure that laws and social policies and practices do not impede the realization of these rights. Persons with disabilities should have access to necessary counselling services in order to fulfil their rights and duties within the family.[27]

31. Women with disabilities also have the right to protection and support in relation to motherhood and pregnancy. As the Standard Rules state, 'persons with disabilities must not be denied the opportunity to experience their sexuality, have

---

[23] See also Recommendation No. 99 (1955) concerning vocational rehabilitation of the disabled, and Recommendation No. 168 (1983) concerning vocational rehabilitation and employment of persons with disabilities.

[24] Standard Rules (see note 6 above), Rule 8, para. 1.

[25] See A/47/415, para. 78.

[26] See E/CN.4/Sub.2/1991/31 (see note 1 above), paras. 190 and 193.

[27] See the World Programme of Action concerning Disabled Persons (see note 3 above), para. 74.

sexual relationships and experience parenthood'.[28] The needs and desires in question should be recognized and addressed in both the recreational and the procreational contexts. These rights are commonly denied to both men and women with disabilities worldwide.[29] Both the sterilization of, and the performance of an abortion on, a woman with disabilities without her prior informed consent are serious violations of article 10(2).

32. Children with disabilities are especially vulnerable to exploitation, abuse and neglect and are, in accordance with article 10(3) of the Covenant (reinforced by the corresponding provisions of the Convention on the Rights of the Child), entitled to special protection.

E. Article 11—The right to an adequate standard of living

33. In addition to the need to ensure that persons with disabilities have access to adequate food, accessible housing and other basic material needs, it is also necessary to ensure that 'support services, including assistive devices' are available 'for persons with disabilities, to assist them to increase their level of independence in their daily living and to exercise their rights'.[30] The right to adequate clothing also assumes a special significance in the context of persons with disabilities who have particular clothing needs, so as to enable them to function fully and effectively in society. Wherever possible, appropriate personal assistance should also be provided in this connection. Such assistance should be undertaken in a manner and spirit which fully respect the human rights of the person(s) concerned. Similarly, as already noted by the Committee in paragraph 8 of General Comment No. 4 (Sixth session, 1991), the right to adequate housing includes the right to accessible housing for persons with disabilities.

F. Article 12—The right to physical and mental health

34. According to the Standard Rules, 'States should ensure that persons with disabilities, particularly infants and children, are provided with the same level of medical care within the same system as other members of society'.[31] The right to physical and mental health also implies the right to have access to, and to benefit from, those medical and social services—including orthopaedic devices—which enable persons with disabilities to become independent, prevent further disabilities and support their social integration.[32] Similarly, such persons should be provided with rehabilitation services which would enable them 'to reach and sustain their optimum level of independence and functioning'.[33] All such services should be

---

[28] Standard Rules (see note 6 above), Rule 9, para. 2.
[29] See E/CN.6/1991/2, paras. 14 and 59–68.
[30] Standard Rules (see note 6 above), Rule 4.
[31] Ibid., Rule 2, para. 3.
[32] See the Declaration on the Rights of Disabled Persons (General Assembly resolution 3447 (XXX) of 9 December 1975), para. 6; and the World Programme of Action concerning Disabled Persons (see note 3 above), paras. 95–107.
[33] Standard Rules (see note 6 above), Rule 3.

provided in such a way that the persons concerned are able to maintain full respect for their rights and dignity.

G. Articles 13 and 14—The right to education

35. School programmes in many countries today recognize that persons with disabilities can best be educated within the general education system.[34] Thus the Standard Rules provide that 'States should recognize the principle of equal primary, secondary and tertiary educational opportunities for children, youth and adults with disabilities, in integrated settings'.[35] In order to implement such an approach, States should ensure that teachers are trained to educate children with disabilities within regular schools and that the necessary equipment and support are available to bring persons with disabilities up to the same level of education as their non-disabled peers. In the case of deaf children, for example, sign language should be recognized as a separate language to which the children should have access and whose importance should be acknowledged in their overall social environment.

H. Article 15—The right to take part in cultural life and enjoy the benefits of scientific progress

36. The Standard Rules provide that 'States should ensure that persons with disabilities have the opportunity to utilize their creative, artistic and intellectual potential, not only for their own benefit, but also for the enrichment of their community, be they in urban or rural areas. . . . States should promote the accessibility to and availability of places for cultural performances and services . . .'.[36] The same applies to places for recreation, sports and tourism.

37. The right to full participation in cultural and recreational life for persons with disabilities further requires that communication barriers be eliminated to the greatest extent possible. Useful measures in this regard might include 'the use of talking books, papers written in simple language and with clear format and colours for persons with mental disability, [and] adapted television and theatre for deaf persons'.[37]

38. In order to facilitate the equal participation in cultural life of persons with disabilities, Governments should inform and educate the general public about disability. In particular, measures must be taken to dispel prejudices or superstitious beliefs against persons with disabilities, for example those that view epilepsy as a form of spirit possession or a child with disabilities as a form of punishment visited upon the family. Similarly, the general public should be educated to accept that persons with disabilities have as much right as any other person to make use of restaurants, hotels, recreation centres and cultural venues.

---

[34] See A/47/415, para. 73.
[35] Standard Rules (see note 6 above), Rule 6.
[36] Ibid., Rule 10, paras. 1–2.
[37] See A/47/415, para. 79.

GENERAL COMMENT NO. 6
The economic, social and cultural rights of older persons
(Thirteenth session, 1995), UN Doc. E/C.12/1995/16/Rev. 1 (1995).*

I. INTRODUCTION

1. The world population is ageing at a steady, quite spectacular rate. The total number of persons aged 60 and above rose from 200 million in 1950 to 400 million in 1982 and is projected to reach 600 million in the year 2001 and 1.2 billion by the year 2025, at which time over 70 per cent of them will be living in what are today's developing countries. The number of people aged 80 and above has grown and continues to grow even more dramatically, going from 13 million in 1950 to over 50 million today and projected to increase to 137 million in 2025. This is the fastest growing population group in the world, projected to increase by a factor of 10 between 1950 and 2025, compared with a factor of six for the group aged 60 and above and a factor of little more than three for the total population.[1]

2. These figures are illustrations of a quiet revolution, but one which has far-reaching and unpredictable consequences and which is now affecting the social and economic structures of societies both at the world level and at the country level, and will affect them even more in future.

3. Most of the States parties to the Covenant, and the industrialized countries in particular, are faced with the task of adapting their social and economic policies to the ageing of their populations, especially as regards social security. In the developing countries, the absence or deficiencies of social security coverage are being aggravated by the emigration of the younger members of the population and the consequent weakening of the traditional role of the family, the main support of older people.

II. INTERNATIONALLY ENDORSED POLICIES IN RELATION TO OLDER PERSONS

4. In 1982 the World Assembly on Ageing adopted the Vienna International Plan of Action on Ageing. This important document was endorsed by the General Assembly and is a very useful guide, for it details the measures that should be taken by Member States to safeguard the rights of older persons within the context of the rights proclaimed by the International Covenants on Human Rights. It contains 62 recommendations, many of which are of direct relevance to the Covenant.[2]

---

* Adopted at the 39th meeting of the thirteenth session, on 24 November 1995.
[1] Global targets on ageing for the year 2001: a practical strategy. Report of the Secretary-General (A/47/339), para. 5.
[2] Report of the World Assembly on Ageing, Vienna, 26 July–6 August 1982; (United Nations publication, Sales No. E.82.I.16).

5. In 1991 the General Assembly adopted the United Nations Principles for Older Persons which, because of their programmatic nature, is also an important document in the present context.[3] It is divided into five sections which correlate closely to the rights recognized in the Covenant. 'Independence' includes access to adequate food, water, shelter, clothing and health care. To these basic rights are added the opportunity for remunerated work and access to education and training. By 'participation' is meant that older persons should participate actively in the formulation and implementation of policies that affect their well-being and share their knowledge and skills with younger generations, and should be able to form movements and associations. The section headed 'care' proclaims that older persons should benefit from family care, health care and be able to enjoy human rights and fundamental freedoms when residing in a shelter, care or treatment facility. With regard to 'self-fulfilment', the Principles [state-sic] that older persons should pursue opportunities for the full development of their potential through access to the educational, cultural, spiritual and recreational resources of their societies. Lastly, the section entitled 'dignity' states that older persons should be able to live in dignity and security and be free of exploitation and physical or mental abuse, should be treated fairly, regardless of age, gender, racial or ethnic background, disability, financial situation or any other status, and be valued independently of their economic contribution.

6. In 1992, the General Assembly adopted eight global targets on ageing for the year 2001 and a brief guide for setting national targets. In a number of important respects, these global targets serve to reinforce the obligations of States parties to the Covenant.[4]

7. Also in 1992, and in commemoration of the tenth anniversary of the adoption of the Vienna International Plan of Action by the Conference on Ageing, the General Assembly adopted the Proclamation on Ageing in which it urged support of national initiatives on ageing so that older women are given adequate support for their largely unrecognized contributions to society and older men are encouraged to develop social, cultural and emotional capacities which they may have been pre- vented from developing during breadwinning years; that families are supported in providing care and all family members encouraged to cooperate in caregiving; and that international cooperation is expanded in the context of the strategies for reaching the global targets on ageing for the year 2001. It also proclaimed the year 1999 as the International Year of Older Persons in recognition of humanity's demographic 'coming of age'.[5]

8. The United Nations' specialized agencies, especially the International Labour Organization, have also given attention to the problem of ageing in their respective fields of competence.

---

[3] General Assembly resolution 46/91 of 16 December 1991, 'Implementation of the International Plan of Action on Ageing and related activities', annex.
[4] Global targets on ageing for the year 2001: a practical strategy (A/47/339), chaps. III and IV.
[5] General Assembly resolution 47/5 of 16 October 1992, 'Proclamation on Ageing'.

III. THE RIGHTS OF OLDER PERSONS IN RELATION TO THE INTERNATIONAL COVENANT ON ECONOMIC, SOCIAL AND CULTURAL RIGHTS

9. The terminology used to describe older persons varies considerably, even in international documents. It includes: 'older persons', 'the aged', 'the elderly', 'the third age', 'the ageing', and, to denote persons more than 80 years of age, 'the fourth age'. The Committee opted for 'older persons' (in French, 'personnes âgée's; in Spanish, 'personas mayores'), the term employed in General Assembly resolutions 47/5 and 48/98. According to the practice in the United Nations' statistical services, these terms cover persons aged 60 and above (Eurostat, the statistical service of the European Union, considers 'older persons' to mean persons aged 65 or above, since 65 is the most common age of retirement and the trend is towards later retirement still).

10. The International Covenant on Economic, Social and Cultural Rights does not contain any explicit reference to the rights of older persons, although article 9 dealing with 'the right of everyone to social security, including social insurance', implicitly recognizes the right to old-age benefits. Nevertheless, in view of the fact that the Covenant's provisions apply fully to all members of society, it is clear that older persons are entitled to enjoy the full range of rights recognized in the Covenant. This approach is also fully reflected in the Vienna International Plan of Action on Ageing. Moreover, insofar as respect for the rights of older persons requires special measures to be taken, States parties are required by the Covenant to do so to the maximum of their available resources.

11. Another important issue is whether discrimination on the basis of age is prohibited by the Covenant. Neither the Covenant nor the Universal Declaration of Human Rights refers explicitly to age as one of the prohibited grounds. Rather than being seen as an intentional exclusion, this omission is probably best explained by the fact that, when these instruments were adopted, the problem of demographic ageing was not as evident or as pressing as it is now.

12. This is not determinative of the matter, however, since the prohibition of discrimination on the grounds of 'other status' could be interpreted as applying to age. The Committee notes that while it may not yet be possible to conclude that discrimination on the grounds of age is comprehensively prohibited by the Covenant, the range of matters in relation to which such discrimination can be accepted is very limited. Moreover, it must be emphasized that the unacceptableness of discrimination against older persons is underlined in many international policy documents and is confirmed in the legislation of the vast majority of States. In the few areas in which discrimination continues to be tolerated, such as in relation to mandatory retirement ages or access to tertiary education, there is a clear trend towards the elimination of such barriers. The Committee is of the view that States parties should seek to expedite this trend to the greatest extent possible.

13. Accordingly, the Committee on Economic, Social and Cultural Rights is of the view that States parties to the Covenant are obligated to pay particular attention to promoting and protecting the economic, social and cultural rights of older persons. The Committee's own role in this regard is rendered all the more important by

the fact that, unlike the case of other population groups such as women and children, no comprehensive international convention yet exists in relation to the rights of older persons and no binding supervisory arrangements attach to the various sets of United Nations principles in this area.

14. By the end of its thirteenth session, the Committee and, before that, its predecessor, the Sessional Working Group of Governmental Experts, had examined 144 initial reports, 70 second periodic reports and 20 initial and periodic global reports on articles 1 to 15. This examination made it possible to identify many of the problems that may be encountered in implementing the Covenant in a considerable number of States parties that represent all the regions of the world and have different political, socio-economic and cultural systems. The reports examined to date have not provided any information in a systematic way on the situation of older persons with regard to compliance with the Covenant, apart from information, of varying completeness, on the implementation of article 9 relating to the right to social security.

15. In 1993, the Committee devoted a day of general discussion to this issue in order to plan its future activity in this area. Moreover, it has, at recent sessions, begun to attach substantially more importance to information on the rights of older persons and its questioning has elicited some very valuable information in some instances. Nevertheless, the Committee notes that the great majority of States parties' reports continue to make little reference to this important issue. It therefore wishes to indicate that, in future, it will insist that the situation of older persons in relation to each of the rights recognized in the Covenant should be adequately addressed in all reports. The remainder of this General Comment identifies the specific issues which are relevant in this regard.

IV. GENERAL OBLIGATIONS OF STATES PARTIES

16. Older persons as a group are as heterogeneous and varied as the rest of the population and their situation depends on a country's economic and social situation, on demographic, environmental, cultural and employment factors and, at the individual level, on the family situation, the level of education, the urban or rural environment and the occupation of workers and retirees.

17. Side by side with older persons who are in good health and whose financial situation is acceptable, there are many who do not have adequate means of support, even in developed countries, and who feature prominently among the most vulnerable, marginal and unprotected groups. In times of recession and of restructuring of the economy, older persons are particularly at risk. As the Committee has previously stressed (General Comment No. 3 (1990), para. 12), even in times of severe resource constraints, States parties have the duty to protect the vulnerable members of society.

18. The methods that States parties use to fulfil the obligations they have assumed under the Covenant in respect of older persons will be basically the same as those for the fulfilment of other obligations (see General Comment No. 1 (1989)). They include the need to determine the nature and scope of problems within a State through regular monitoring, the need to adopt properly designed policies and pro-

grammes to meet requirements, the need to enact legislation when necessary and to eliminate any discriminatory legislation and the need to ensure the relevant budget support or, as appropriate, to request international cooperation. In the latter connection, international cooperation in accordance with articles 22 and 23 of the Covenant may be a particularly important way of enabling some developing countries to fulfil their obligations under the Covenant.

19. In this context, attention may be drawn to Global Target No. 1, adopted by the General Assembly in 1992, which calls for the establishment of national support infrastructures to promote policies and programmes on ageing in national and international development plans and programmes. In this regard, the Committee notes that one of the United Nations Principles for Older Persons which Governments were encouraged to incorporate into their national programmes is that older persons should be able to form movements or associations of older persons.

V. SPECIFIC PROVISIONS OF THE COVENANT

Article 3—Equal rights of men and women

20. In accordance with article 3 of the Covenant, by which States parties undertake 'to ensure the equal right of men and women to the enjoyment of all economic, social and cultural rights', the Committee considers that States parties should pay particular attention to older women who, because they have spent all or part of their lives caring for their families without engaging in a remunerated activity entitling them to an old-age pension, and who are also not entitled to a widow's pension, are often in critical situations.

21. To deal with such situations and comply fully with article 9 of the Covenant and paragraph 2(h) of the Proclamation on Ageing, States parties should institute non-contributory old-age benefits or other assistance for all persons, regardless of their sex, who find themselves without resources on attaining an age specified in national legislation. Given their greater life expectancy and the fact that it is more often they who have no contributory pensions, women would be the principal beneficiaries.

Articles 6 to 8—Rights relating to work

22. Article 6 of the Covenant requires States parties to take appropriate steps to safeguard the right of everyone to the opportunity to gain a living by work which is freely chosen or accepted. In this regard, the Committee, bearing in mind that older workers who have not reached retirement age often encounter problems in finding and keeping jobs, stresses the need for measures to prevent discrimination on grounds of age in employment and occupation.[6]

---

[6] See ILO Recommendation 162 (1980) concerning Older Workers, paras. 3–10.

23. The right 'to the enjoyment of just and favourable conditions of work' (Covenant, art. 7) is of special importance for ensuring that older workers enjoy safe working conditions until their retirement. In particular, it is desirable, to employ older workers in circumstances in which the best use can be made of their experience and know-how.[7]

24. In the years preceding retirement, retirement preparation programmes should be implemented, with the participation of representative organizations of employers and workers and other bodies concerned, to prepare older workers to cope with their new situation. Such programmes should, in particular, provide older workers with information about: their rights and obligations as pensioners; the opportunities and conditions for continuing an occupational activity or undertaking voluntary work; means of combating detrimental effects of ageing; facilities for adult education and cultural activities, and the use of leisure time.[8]

25. The rights protected by article 8 of the Covenant, namely, trade union rights, including after retirement age, must be applied to older workers.

Article 9—Right to social security

26. Article 9 of the Covenant provides generally that States parties 'recognize the right of everyone to social security', without specifying the type or level of protection to be guaranteed. However, the term 'social security' implicitly covers all the risks involved in the loss of means of subsistence for reasons beyond a person's control.

27. In accordance with article 9 of the Covenant and the provisions concerning implementation of the ILO social security conventions—Convention No. 102 concerning Social Security (Minimum Standards) (1952) and Convention No. 128 concerning Invalidity, Old-Age and Survivors' Benefits (1967)—States parties must take appropriate measures to establish general regimes of compulsory old-age insurance, starting at a particular age, to be prescribed by national law.

28. In keeping with the recommendations contained in the two ILO Conventions mentioned above and Recommendation No. 162, the Committee invites States parties to establish retirement age so that it is flexible, depending on the occupations performed and the working ability of elderly persons, with due regard to demographic, economic and social factors.

29. In order to give effect to the provisions of article 9 of the Covenant, States parties must guarantee the provision of survivors' and orphans' benefits on the death of the breadwinner who was covered by social security or receiving a pension.

30. Furthermore, as already observed in paragraphs 20 and 21, in order fully to implement the provisions of article 9 of the Covenant, States parties should, within the limits of available resources, provide non-contributory old-age benefits and other assistance for all older persons, who, when reaching the age prescribed in national legislation, have not completed a qualifying period of contribution and are not entitled to an old-age pension or other social security benefit or assistance and have no other source of income.

---

[7] Ibid., paras. 11–19.
[8] See ILO Recommendation 162 (1980) concerning Older Workers, para. 30.

Article 10—Protection of the family

31. On the basis of article 10, paragraph 1, of the Covenant and recommendations 25 and 29 of the Vienna International Plan of Action on Ageing, States parties should make all the necessary efforts to support, protect and strengthen the family and help it, in accordance with each society's system of cultural values, to respond to the needs of its dependent ageing members. Recommendation 29 encourages Governments and non-governmental organizations to establish social services to support the whole family when there are elderly people at home and to implement measures especially for low-income families who wish to keep elderly people at home. This assistance should also be provided for persons living alone or elderly couples wishing to remain at home.

Article 11—Right to an adequate standard of living

32. Of the United Nations Principles for Older Persons, principle 1, which stands at the beginning of the section relating to the independence of older persons, provides that: 'Older persons should have access to adequate food, water, shelter, clothing and health care through the provision of income, family and community support and self-help'. The Committee attaches great importance to this principle, which demands for older persons the rights contained in article 11 of the Covenant.

33. Recommendations 19 to 24 of the Vienna International Plan of Action on Ageing emphasize that housing for the elderly must be viewed as more than mere shelter and that, in addition to the physical, it has psychological and social significance which should be taken into account. Accordingly, national policies should help elderly persons to continue to live in their own homes as long as possible, through the restoration, development and improvement of homes and their adaptation to the ability of those persons to gain access to and use them (recommendation 19). Recommendation 20 stresses the need for urban rebuilding and development planning and law to pay special attention to the problems of the ageing, assisting in securing their social integration, while recommendation 22 draws attention to the need to take account of the functional capacity of the elderly in order to provide them with a better living environment and facilitate mobility and communication through the provision of adequate means of transport.

Article 12—Right to physical and mental health

34. With a view to the realization of the right of elderly persons to the enjoyment of a satisfactory standard of physical and mental health, in accordance with article 12, paragraph 1, of the Covenant, States parties should take account of the content of recommendations 1 to 17 of the Vienna International Plan of Action on Ageing, which focus entirely on providing guidelines on health policy to preserve the health of the elderly and take a comprehensive view, ranging from prevention and rehabilitation to the care of the terminally ill.

35. Clearly, the growing number of chronic, degenerative diseases and the high hospitalization costs they involve cannot be dealt with only by curative treatment. In this regard, States parties should bear in mind that maintaining health into old age requires investments during the entire life span, basically through the adoption of healthy lifestyles (food, exercise, elimination of tobacco and alcohol, etc.). Prevention, through regular checks suited to the needs of the elderly, plays a decisive role, as does rehabilitation, by maintaining the functional capacities of elderly persons, with a resulting decrease in the cost of investments in health care and social services.

Articles 13 to 15—Right to education and culture

36. Article 13, paragraph 1, of the Covenant recognizes the right of everyone to education. In the case of the elderly, this right must be approached from two different and complementary points of view: (a) the right of elderly persons to benefit from educational programmes; and (b) making the know-how and experience of elderly persons available to younger generations.

37. With regard to the former, States parties should take account of: (a) the recommendations in principle 16 of the United Nations Principles for Older Persons to the effect that older persons should have access to suitable education programmes and training and should, therefore, on the basis of their preparation, abilities and motivation, be given access to the various levels of education through the adoption of appropriate measures regarding literacy training, life-long education, access to university, etc.; and (b) recommendation 47 of the Vienna International Plan of Action on Ageing, which, in accordance with the concept of life-long education promulgated by the United Nations Educational, Scientific and Cultural Organization (UNESCO), recommends informal, community-based and recreation-oriented programmes for the elderly in order to develop their sense of self-reliance and the community's sense of responsibility. Such programmes should enjoy the support of national Governments and international organizations.

38. With regard to the use of the know-how and experience of older persons, as referred to in the part of the recommendations of the Vienna International Plan of Action on Ageing dealing with education (paras. 74–76), attention is drawn to the important role that elderly and old persons still play in most societies as the transmitters of information, knowledge, traditions and spiritual values and to the fact that this important tradition should not be lost. Consequently, the Committee attaches particular importance to the meassage contained in recommendation 44 of the Plan: 'Educational programmes featuring the elderly as the teachers and transmitters of knowledge, culture and spiritual values should be developed'.

39. In article 15, paragraphs 1 (a) and (b), of the Covenant, States parties recognize the right of everyone to take part in cultural life and to enjoy the benefits of scientific progress and its applications. In this respect, the Committee urges States parties to take account of the recommendations contained in the United Nations Principles for Older Persons, and in particular of principle 7: 'Older persons should remain integrated in society, participate actively in the formulation and implementation of policies that directly affect their well-being and share their knowledge and skills with younger generations'; and principle 16: 'Older persons

should have access to the educational, cultural, spiritual and recreational resources of society'.

40. Similarly, recommendation 48 of the Vienna International Plan of Action on Ageing encourages Governments and international organizations to support programmes aimed at providing the elderly with easier physical access to cultural institutions (museums, theatres, concert halls, cinemas, etc.).

41. Recommendation 50 stresses the need for Governments, non-governmental organizations and the ageing themselves to make efforts to overcome negative stereotyped images of older persons as suffering from physical and psychological disabilities, incapable of functioning independently and having neither role nor status in society. These efforts, in which the media and educational institutions should also take part, are essential for achieving a society that champions the full integration of the elderly.

42. With regard to the right to enjoy the benefits of scientific progress and its applications, States parties should take account of recommendations 60, 61 and 62 of the Vienna International Plan of Action and make efforts to promote research on the biological, mental and social aspects of ageing and ways of maintaining functional capacities and preventing and delaying the start of chronic illnesses and disabilities. In this connection, it is recommended that States, intergovernmental organizations and non-governmental organizations should establish institutions specializing in the teaching of gerontology, geriatrics and geriatric psychology in countries where such institutions do not exist.

GENERAL BIBLIOGRAPHY ... [omitted]

GENERAL COMMENT NO. 7
The right to adequate housing (Art. 11(1) of the Covenant) forced evictions
UN Doc. E/C.12/1997/4 (1997).

1. In its General Comment No. 4 (1991), the Committee observed that all persons should possess a degree of security of tenure which guarantees legal protection against forced eviction, harassment and other threats. It concluded that forced evictions are prima facie incompatible with the requirements of the Covenant. Having considered a significant number of reports of forced evictions in recent years, including instances in which it has determined that the obligations of States parties were being violated, the Committee is now in a position to seek to provide further clarification as to the implications of such practices in terms of the obligations contained in the Covenant.

2. The international community has long recognized that the issue of forced evictions is a serious one. In 1976, the United Nations Conference on Human Settlements noted that special attention should be paid to 'undertaking major clearance operations should take place only when conservation and rehabilitation are not feasible and relocation measures are made'.[1] In 1988, in the Global Strategy for Shelter to the Year 2000, adopted by the General Assembly in its resolution 43/181, the 'fundamental obligation [of Governments] to protect and improve houses

---

[1] Report of Habitat: United Nations Conference on Human Settlements, Vancouver, 31 May–11 June 1976 (A/CONF.70/15), chap. II, recommendation B.8, para. C(ii).

and neighbourhoods, rather than damage of destroy them' was recognized.[2] Agenda 21 stated that 'people should be protected by law against unfair eviction from their homes or land'.[3] In the Habitat Agenda Governments committed themselves to 'protecting all people from, and providing legal protection and redress for, forced evictions that are contrary to the law, taking human rights into consideration; [and] when evictions are unavoidable, ensuring, as appropriate, that alternative suitable solutions are provided'.[4] The Commission on Human Rights has also indicated that 'forced evictions are a gross violation of human rights'.[5] However, although these statements are important, they leave open one of the most critical issues, namely that of determining the circumstances under which forced evictions are permissible and of spelling out the types of protection required to ensure respect for the relevant provisions of the Covenant.

3. The use of the term 'forced evictions' is, in some respects, problematic. This expression seeks to convey a sense of arbitrariness and of illegality. To many observers, however, the reference to 'forced evictions' is a tautology, while others have criticized the expression 'illegal evictions' on the ground that it assumes that the relevant law provides adequate protection to the right to housing and conforms with the Covenant, which is by no means always the case. Similarly, it has been suggested that the term 'unfair evictions' is even more subjective by virtue of its failure to refer to any legal framework at all. The international community, especially in the context of the Commission on Human Rights, has opted to refer to 'forced evictions' primarily since all suggested alternatives also suffer from many such defects.

4. The term 'forced evictions' as used throughout this General Comment is defined as the permanent or temporary removal against their will of individuals, families and/or communities from the homes and/or land which they occupy, without the provision of, and access to, appropriate forms of legal or other protection. The prohibition on forced evictions does not, however, apply to evictions carried out by force in accordance with the law and in conformity with the provisions of the International Covenants on Human Rights.

5. The practice of forced evictions is widespread and affects persons in both developed and developing countries. Owing to the interrelationship and interdependency which exist among all human rights, forced evictions frequently violate other human rights. Thus, while manifestly breaching the rights enshrined in the Covenant, the practice of forced evictions may also result in violations of civil and political rights, such as the right to life, the right to security of the person, the right to non-interference with privacy, family and home and the right to the peaceful enjoyment of possessions.

6. Although the practice of forced evictions might appear to arise primarily in heavily populated urban areas, it also takes place in relation to forced population

---

[2] Report of the Commission on Human Settlements on the work of its eleventh session, Addendum (A/43/8/Add. 1), para. 13.

[3] Report of the United Nations Conference on Environment and Development, Rio de Janeiro, 3–14 June 1992, Volume I (A/CONF.151/26/Rev. 1 (vol. I), annex II, Agenda 21, chap. 7.9(b).

[4] Report of the United Nations Conference on Settlements (Habitat II) (A/CONF.165/14), annex II, The Habitat Agenda, para. 40(n).

[5] Commission on Human Rights resolution 1993/77, para. 1.

transfers, internal displacement, forced relocations in the context of armed conflict, mass exoduses and refugee movements. In all of these contexts, the right to adequate housing and not to be subject to forced evictions may be violated through a wide range of acts or omissions attributable to States parties. Even in situations where it may be necessary to impose limitations on such a right, full compliance with article 4 of the Covenant is required so that any limitations imposed must be 'determined by law only in so far as this may be compatible with the nature of these rights [i.e. economic, social and cultural] and solely for the purpose of promoting the general welfare in a democratic society'.

7. Many instances of forced evictions are associated with violence, such as evictions resulting from international armed conflicts, internal strife and communal or ethnic violence.

8. Other instances of forced evictions occur in the name of development. They might be carried out in connection with conflict over land rights, development and infrastructure projects, such as the construction of dams or other large-scale energy projects, with land acquisition measures associated with urban renewal, housing renovation, city beautification programmes, the clearing of land for agricultural purposes, unbridled speculation in land, or the holding of major sporting events like the Olympic Games.

9. In essence, the obligations of States parties to the Covenant in relation to forced evictions are based on article 11.1, read in conjunction with other relevant provisions. In particular, article 2.1 obliges States to use 'all appropriate means' to promote the right to adequate housing. However, in view of the nature of the practice of forced evictions, the reference in article 2.1 to progressive achievement based on the availability of resources will rarely be relevant. The State itself must refrain from forced evictions and ensure that the law is enforced against its agents or third parties who carry out forced evictions (as defined in para. 3 above). Moreover, this approach is reinforced by article 17.1 of the International Covenant on Civil and Political Rights which complements the right not to be forcefully evicted without adequate protection. That provision recognizes, inter alia, the right to be protected against 'arbitrary or unlawful interference' with one's home. It is to be noted that the State's obligation to ensure respect for that right is not qualified by considerations relating to its available resources.

10. Article 2.1 of the Covenant requires States parties to use 'all appropriate means', including the adoption of legislative measures, to promote all the rights protected under the Covenant. Although the Committee has indicated in its General Comment No. 3 (1990) that such measures may not be indispensable in relation to all rights, it is clear that legislation against forced evictions is an essential basis upon which to build a system of effective protection. Such legislation should include measures which (a) provide the greatest possible security of tenure to occupiers of houses and land, (b) conform to the Covenant and (c) are designed to control strictly the circumstances under which evictions may be carried out. The legislation must also apply in relation to all agents acting under the authority of the State or who are accountable to it. Moreover, in view of the increasing trend in some States towards their Government greatly reducing their responsibilities in the housing sector, States parties must ensure that legislative and other measures are adequate to prevent and, if appropriate, punish forced evictions carried out, without appropriate safeguards, by private persons or bodies. States parties should therefore

review relevant legislation and policies to ensure that these are compatible with the obligations arising from the right to adequate housing and to repeal or amend any legislation or policies that are inconsistent with the requirements of the Covenant.

11. Women, children, youth, older persons, indigenous people, ethnic and other minorities, and other vulnerable individuals and groups all suffer disproportionately from the practice of forced eviction. Women in all groups are especially vulnerable given the extent of statutory and other forms of discrimination which often apply in relation to property rights (including home ownership) or rights of access to property or accommodation and their particular vulnerability to acts of violence and sexual abuse when they are rendered homeless. The non-discrimination provisions of Articles 2.2 and 3 of the Covenant impose an additional obligation upon Governments to ensure that, where evictions do occur, appropriate measures are taken to ensure that no form of discrimination is involved.

12. Whereas some evictions may be justifiable, such as in the case of the persistent non-payment of rent or of damage to rented property without any reasonable cause, it is incumbent upon the relevant authorities to ensure that those evictions are carried out in a manner warranted by a law which is compatible with the Covenant and that all the legal recourses and remedies are available to those affected.

13. Forced eviction and house demolitions as a punitive measure are also inconsistent with the norms of the Covenant. Likewise, the Committee takes note of the obligations enshrined in the Geneva Conventions of 1949 and Protocols thereto of 1977 concerning prohibitions on the displacement of the civilian population and the destruction of private property as these relate to the practice of forced eviction.

14. States parties shall ensure, prior to carrying out any evictions, and particularly those involving large groups, that all feasible alternatives are explored in consultation with affected persons, with a view to avoiding, or at least minimizing, the need to use force. Legal remedies or procedures should be provided to those who are affected by eviction orders. States parties shall also see to it that all individuals concerned have a right to adequate compensation for any property, both personal and real, which is affected. In this respect, it is pertinent to recall article 2.3 of the International Covenant on Civil and Political Rights which requires States parties to ensure 'an effective remedy' for persons whose rights have been violated and the obligation upon the 'competent authorities (to) enforce such remedies when granted'.

15. In cases where eviction is considered to be justified, it should be carried out in strict compliance with the relevant provisions of international human rights law and in accordance with general principles of reasonableness and proportionality. In this regard it is especially pertinent to recall General Comment No. 16 by the Human Rights Committee, relating to article 17 of the International Covenant on Civil and Political Rights, which states that interference with a person's home can only take place 'in cases envisaged by the law'. The Committee observed that the law 'should be in accordance with the provisions, aims and objectives of the Covenant and should be, in any event, reasonable in the particular circumstances'. The Committee also indicated that 'relevant legislation must specify in details the precise circumstances in which such interferences may be permitted'.

16. Appropriate procedural protection and due process are essential aspects of all human rights but are especially pertinent in relation to a matter such as forced evictions which directly invokes a large number of the rights recognized in both the International Covenants on Human Rights. The Committee considers that the

procedural protections which should be applied in rel⁻.ıon to forced evictions include: (a) an opportunity for genuine consultation with those affected; (b) adequate and reasonable notice for all affected persons prior to the scheduled date of eviction; (c) information on the proposed evictions and where applicable, on the alternative purpose for which the land or housing is to be used, to be made available in reasonable time to all those affected; (d) especially where groups of people are involved, Government officials or their representatives to be present during an eviction; (e) all persons carrying out the eviction to be properly identified; (f) evictions not to take place in particularly bad weather or at night unless the affected persons consent otherwise; (g) provision of legal remedies; and (h) provision, where possible, of legal aid to persons who are in need of it to seek redress from the courts.

17. Evictions should not result in rendering individuals homeless or vulnerable to the violation of other human rights. Where those affected are unable to provide for themselves, the State party must take all appropriate measures, to the maximum of its available resources, to ensure that adequate alternative housing, resettlement or access to productive land, as the case may be, is available.

18. The Committee is aware that various development projects financed by international agencies within the territories of State parties have resulted in forced evictions. In this regard, the Committee recalls its General Comment No. 2 (1990) which states, inter alia, that 'international agencies should scrupulously avoid involvement in projects which, for example . . . promote or reinforce discrimination against individuals or groups contrary to the provisions of the Covenant, or involve large-scale evictions or displacement of persons without the provision of all appropriate protection and compensation. Every effort should be made, at each phase of a development project, to ensure that the rights contained in the Covenant are duly taken into account'.[6]

19. Some institutions, such as the World Bank and the Organization for Economic Cooperation and Development (OECD) have adopted guidelines on relocation and/or resettlement with a view to limiting the scale and human suffering associated with the practice of forced eviction. Such practices often accompany large-scale development projects, such as dam-building and other major energy projects. Full respect for such guidelines, insofar as they reflect the obligations contained in the Covenant, is essential on the part of both the agencies themselves and by States parties to the Covenant. The Committee recalls in this respect that statement in the Vienna Declaration and Programme of Action to the effect that: 'while development facilitates the enjoyment of all human rights, the lack of development may not be invoked to justify the abridgement of internationally recognized human rights' (Part I, para. 10).

20. In accordance with the guidelines for reporting adopted by the Committee, State parties are requested to provide various types of information pertaining directly to the practice of forced evictions. This includes information relating to (a) the 'number of persons evicted within the last five years and the number of persons currently lacking legal protection against arbitrary eviction or any other kind of eviction', (b) 'legislation concerning the rights of tenants to security of tenure, to protection from eviction' and (c) 'legislation prohibiting any form of eviction'.[7]

[6] E/1990/23, annex III, paras. 6 and 8(d).
[7] E/C.12/1990/8, annex IV.

21. Information is also sought as to 'measures taken during, inter alia, urban renewal programmes, redevelopment projects, site upgrading, preparation for international events (Olympics and other sporting competitions, exhibitions, conferences, etc.) "beautiful city" campaigns, etc. which guarantee protection from eviction or guarantee rehousing based on mutual consent, by any persons living on or near to affected sites'.[8] However, few States parties have included the requisite information in their reports to the Committee. The Committee, therefore, wishes to emphasize in this regard the importance it attaches to the receipt of such information.

22. Some States parties have indicated that information of this nature is not available. The Committee recalls that effective monitoring of the right to adequate housing, either by the Government concerned or by the Committee, is not possible in the absence of the collection of appropriate data and would request all States parties to ensure that the necessary data is collected and is reflected in the reports submitted by them under the Covenant.

[8] Ibid.

Contents

Abbreviations

AC	Appeal cases
AJCL	American Journal of Comparative Law
AJIL	American Journal of International Law
Am. Uni. L Rev.	American University Law Review
Bull. Czech. L	Bulletin of Czech Law
Bull. HR	Bulletin of Human Rights
BYIL	British Yearbook of International Law
Cal. West ILJ	California Western International Law Journal
Can. HRY	Canadian Human Rights Yearbook
Can. YIL	Canadian Yearbook of International Law
CAT	Committee Against Torture
CEDAW	Committee on the Elimination of Discrimination Against Women
CERD	Committee on the Elimination of All Forms of Racial Discrimination
CESCR	Committee on Economic, Social, and Cultural Rights
CLJ	Cambridge Law Journal
CMLR	Common Market Law Reports
Col. HRLR	Columbia Human Rights Law Review
Columb. J Trans. L	Columbia Journal of Transnational Law
Conv. EDAW	Convention on the Elimination of All Forms of Discrimination Against Women
Cornell ILJ	Cornell International Law Journal
DREComHR	Decisions and Reports of the European Commission on Human Rights
ECHR	European Convention on Human Rights and Fundamental Freedoms
ECOSOC	Economic and Social Council of the UN
EHRR	European Human Rights Review
ESC	European Social Charter
ESCOR	Economic and Social Council Official Records
Eur. Ct. HR	European Court of Human Rights

FAO	Food and Agriculture Organization
Fem. L St.	Feminist Legal Studies
GA	General Assembly
GAOR	General Assembly Official Records
GCHQ	Government Communications Headquarters
GDP	Gross Domestic Product
Ger. YIL	German Yearbook of International Law
GNP	Gross National Product
Harv. LR	Harvard Law Review
Harv. Hum. Rts. J	Harvard Human Rights Journal
Howard LJ	Howard Law Journal
HRC	Human Rights Committee
HRJ	Human Rights Journal
HRLJ	Human Rights Law Journal
HRO	Human Rights Organisation
Hum. Rts. Q	Human Rights Quarterly
Hum. Rts. J	Human Rights Journal
Hum. Rts. LJ	Human Rights Law Journal
IBRD	International Bank for Reconstruction and Development (World Bank)
ICCPR	International Covenant on Civil and Political Rights
ICERD	International Convention on the Elimination of All Forms of Racial Discrimination
ICESCR	International Covenant on Economic, Social, and Cultural Rights
ICJ	International Court of Justice
ICJ Rep.	International Court of Justice Reports
ICJ Rev.	International Commission of Jurists Review
ICLQ	International and Comparative Law Quarterly
ILM	International Legal Materials
ILO	International Labour Organization
ILR	International Law Reports
IMF	International Monetary Fund
Ind. JIL	Indian Journal of International Law
Ind. LJ	Industrial Law Journal
Ind. LR	Industrial Law Review
Int. Lab. Conf.	International Labour Conference
Iowa LR	Iowa Law Review
Isr. YHR	Israeli Yearbook of Human Rights

JICJ	Journal of the International Commission of Jurists
Jnl. of Philosophy	Journal of Philosophy
Liv. LR	Liverpool Law Review
McGill LJ	McGill Law Journal
Mel. Uni LR	Melbourne University Law Review
MLR	Modern Law Review
Neth. Yrbk. IL	Netherlands Yearbook of International Law
Neth. ILR	Netherlands International Law Review
NGO	Non-Governmental Organizations
NQHR	Netherlands Quarterly of Human Rights
ODA	Overseas Development Administration
Oklahoma LR	Oklahoma Law Review
Osg. HLJ	Osgoode Hall Law Journal
PCIJ	Permanent Court of International Justice
PQLI	Physical Quality of Life Index
Proc. Am. Soc. IL	Proceedings of the American Society of International Law
RBDI	Revue Belge de Droit International
Rutgers L Rev.	Rutgers Law Review
Santa Clara LR	Santa Clara Law Review
SAYIL	South African Yearbook of International Law
Scand. Stu. L.	Scandinavian Studies in Law
Tex. ILJ	Texas International Law Journal
UDHR	Universal Declaration on Human Rights
UKTS	United Kingdom Treaty Series United Nations
UN ESCOR	United Nations Economic and Social Council Official Records
UN GAOR	United Nations General Assembly Official Records
UNDP	United Nations Development Programme
UNESCO	United Nations Educational, Scientific and Cultural Organization
Uni. HR	Universal Human Rights

UNICEF	United Nations International Children's Emergency Fund (United Nations Children's Fund)
UNRISD	United Nations Research Institute on Social Development
UNTS	United Nations Treaty Series
Vand. LR	Vanderbilt Law Review
Virg. JIL	Virginia Journal of International Law
WHO	World Health Organization
Wisc. LR	Wisconsin Law Review
Yale JIL	Yale Journal of International Law
Yrbk. ILC	Yearbook of the International Law Commission
Yrbk. Eur. L.	Yearbook of European Law

Table of Cases

INTERNATIONAL CASES

THE NETHERLANDS

UK

US

Table of Agreements, Charters, Committees, Conventions, Declarations, Resolutions, Recommendations and Treaties

Introduction

The International Covenant on Economic, Social, and Cultural Rights (ICESCR)[1] entered into force on 3 January 1976, following the deposit of the 35th instrument of ratification.[2] Together with the International Covenant on Civil and Political Rights (ICCPR)[3] and the Universal Declaration on Human Rights (UDHR)[4] it forms part of the 'International Bill of Rights'[5] which was intended to form the basis of freedom, justice, and world peace following the Second World War. Despite the ambition of the United Nations to secure the foundations of the new world order upon a respect for human rights, it took nearly twenty years to finalize the text of the Covenant. A further decade lapsed before the Covenant entered into force and yet another before the Covenant was provided with a supervisory body that was worthy of the name.

Despite its age, the Covenant should rightly be regarded as a relatively 'new' human rights instrument. Until 1986, it existed only as a textual reference point subject to the speculative claims of both its proponents and detractors. Its terms required clarification and its system of implementation reconstructing. In short, it needed the nurture of a committed and active supervisory body to be brought to life. The creation of the UN Committee on Economic, Social, and Cultural Rights, composed as it was of independent experts, was the initiative needed to make this possible.[6]

Since its inheritance of the supervisory role in 1986, the Committee has begun to reinvigorate the Covenant by developing a meaningful system of supervision and generating a clearer understanding of the terms of the Covenant. As at June 1994, the Committee has held ten sessions, reviewed 82 State reports, held a number of in-house discussions, and adopted four general comments. The system of periodic reporting has been changed beyond all recognition and is probably the most advanced of its kind. Similarly, in terms of the substantive guarantee, the Committee has begun the important, but lengthy, process of normative development.

The main purpose of this study is to outline and evaluate the development of the Covenant as a human rights treaty guarantee both in terms of its substance and its procedure. The introductory chapter traces the roots of

[1] 993 UNTS 3 (1966). The text is to be found in App. I.
[2] As at 30 June 1994, the Covenant has been ratified, or acceded to, by 129 States. *See* UN Doc. E/C.12/1994/2. For a list of States Parties, see App. III.
[3] 999 UNTS 171. (1966).
[4] GA Resn. 217 A (III), (10 Dec. 1948), 3 UN GAOR, Resns., Pt. 1, at 71 (1948).
[5] *See* Marie J.–B., 'Les Pactes Internationaux Relatifs aux Droits de l'Homme Confirment-ils l'Inspiration de la Declaration Universelle?' (1970) 3 *HRJ* 397.
[6] ECOSOC Resn. 1985/17, UN ESCOR, Supp. (No.1), at 15 (1985).

economic, social, and cultural rights, considers their nature as 'human rights', and outlines the process of codification following the end of the Second World War. An attempt is made to evaluate the Covenant as it stands in terms of the degree to which it might contribute to the international protection of economic, social, and cultural rights. Chapter 2 addresses the emergence, role, and working methods of the Committee as a human rights supervisory body. Particular consideration is given to the Committee's development of the reporting system and the prospect of establishing formal or informal mechanisms for the receipt of individual or group complaints. The third chapter could be described as the backbone of the study, in that it discusses the nature and scope of State obligations under the Covenant. The terms of article 2(1), which are unique to the Covenant, are initally examined in the light of certain theoretical models which have been used to describe State obligations. The chapter goes on to describe and analyse the methodology adopted by the Committee, examine how it has been exercised in practice, and assess it for its consistency and efficacy.

As the title of the study suggests, the main purpose is to provide a perspective on the development of the Covenant. As such, while the work only focuses on the development of a selected number of rights or articles, it attempts to address the issues in depth and to draw some broad conclusions. Those articles that are dealt with here are article 2(2) (and to a lesser extent article 3) relating to non-discrimination and equality, article 6 concerning the right to work, article 7 regarding the right to just and favourable conditions of work, article 8 concerning rights related to trade unions, and article 11 concerning the right to an adequate standard of living and, in particular, the rights to food and housing. The choice of articles addressed reflects a number of concerns. The major consideration was the need to concentrate upon those articles which had been developed most coherently by the Committee. In the early stages of its work, the Committee mainly dealt with reports relating to articles 6 to 9 which became the initial focus for analysis. Since then, however, it has concentrated on other articles, in particular article 11 upon which it has adopted a General Comment, and which is therefore analysed here. Additional considerations that influenced the choice of articles include the amount of international case law available on the subject area (plentiful in the case of non-discrimination and the right to join trade unions), how well the norms have been developed in other fora such as the ILO (articles 6, 7, and 8 being cases in point), and the need to include examples of provisions that are not subject to progressive implementation (as in article 8).

In each chapter dealing with a substantive article, the first section will deal with the *travaux préparatoires* of the article concerned which provide an idea of the intended scope and meaning of the provisions and raise a number of issues that are still pertinent today. The second section of each chapter outlines the manner in which the Committee has developed the relevant provisions through its consideration of State reports. In each case an attempt has been made to outline the direction in which the Committee appears to be moving, assess the appropriateness or sufficiency of its approach, and, on occasions, make suggestions as to alternative strategies.

A number of points should be made about the methodology of this work. According to article 31 of the Vienna Convention on the Law of Treaties[7] (which is generally reflective of customary international law), treaties are to be interpreted according to their ordinary meaning in their context and in the light of their object and purpose. Although a certain amount may be gained from a textual analysis of the Covenant, the obscure and imprecise nature of many of its terms frequently leaves important questions unanswered. That the object and purpose of the Covenant, as a human rights treaty, is to be taken into account means that its terms are to be interpreted in a manner favourable to the individual and that, in particular, limitations and restrictions on rights are to be construed narrowly. However, this does not resolve all the problems or ambiguities that arise from a textual interpretation.

According to article 32 of the Vienna Convention, the *travaux préparatoires* may be used as a supplementary means of interpretation that may be resorted to, in order to confirm an interpretation adopted under article 31, or to determine the meaning of a provision where the initial interpretation is ambiguous or manifestly absurd. In the case of the Covenant, the terms of the *travaux préparatoires* are particularly relevant in that its provisions are generally open-textured and capable of conflicting interpretations. Indeed as the drafting spanned nearly twenty years, the *travaux* provide a particularly rich source of material and give a detailed indication of the intentions of the drafters. For that reason, it was considered useful for a summary of the *travaux* to be provided in the case of all the substantive articles.[8] In many cases the *travaux* reinforce an approach adopted under a literal reading of the Covenant and clarify some of the more obscure elements of the text. They are, however, only a limited form of material (indeed often being contradictory) which should only be seen to supplement, rather than replace, an interpretation offered by a textual reading of the Covenant.

The most important element of this study is the work of the Committee

---

[7] Vienna Convention on the Law of Treaties 1969, 1155 UNTS 331.

[8] Summaries of the *travaux préparatoires* are not provided with respect to all parts of this study as in some cases they have been extensively explored in other literature (e.g. with respect to implementation and non-discrimination). The pertinent parts of the *travaux* are nevertheless referred to in such cases.

on Economic, Social, and Cultural Rights. As a matter of treaty interpretation it should be recognized that, in the absence of a body mandated with making binding interpretations of the Covenant, it is primarily for the States themselves to interpret the Covenant in their relations *inter se*. However, the Committee, in its position as the primary supervisory body, acts as a 'clearing centre' for the divergent interpretations of the Covenant offered by States parties and is best placed for establishing the common agreement of States as to the interpretation of the Covenant.[9] Its views, therefore, may be said to have considerable legal weight and indeed may ultimately serve to direct and shape the practice of States in applying the Covenant, such that the agreement of States is developed over time.

The Committee's role in the development of the Covenant is of particular importance for two main reasons. First, in contrast to the position with respect to most other international treaties, human rights treaties are not so much reciprocal agreements dependent for their force upon mutual acceptance, but rather 'unilateral' or 'objective' undertakings which require some process of 'collective enforcement'.[10] The Committee is essentially charged with that task. Secondly, human rights treaty norms by their nature are phrased in such a general manner that further development and normative clarification are necessary. This is nowhere more apparent than in the case of the ICESCR which suffers, not merely from the generality of its norms, but also from the fact that there is little national or international case law relating to economic, social, and cultural rights that might assist in the process of 'normative development'.

In terms of its development of the norms within the Covenant, the Committee on Economic, Social, and Cultural Rights does not have the same opportunities to consider and pronounce upon specific aspects of the treaty as other bodies, such as the Human Rights Committee (HRC), which operate 'complaints' procedures. Rather, the Committee has been confined to developing its understanding of the terms of the Covenant in the generalized and unspecific process of reviewing State reports. Much of this material is provided by the comments and questions of the Committee members during their 'constructive dialogue' with State representatives. Although often contradictory and lacking specificity, the comments and questions of individual Committee members do frequently gain the concurrence of other members and may provide quite a clear indication of the approach of the Committee or at least demonstrate its principal concerns.

The most coherent and detailed information on the position of the Committee is provided by its general comments. These usually amount to bold interpretative statements made by the Committee reflecting the experience

---

[9] *See e.g.* Meron T., *Human Rights Law-Making in the United Nations* (1986) at 10.
[10] *See e.g. Ireland* v. *United Kingdom*, Eur. Ct. HR, Series A., Vol. 25, Judgment of 18 January 1978, 2 EHRR 25.

it has gained during the process of considering State reports. As at June 1994, however, the Committee has only concluded four such General Comments and therefore other sources of information need to be relied upon. The next best source of material is to be found in the Committee's 'concluding observations' which, while not prescribing precise standards, do offer good insights into the approach and assumptions of the Committee. For example, the concluding observations frequently indicate when the Committee considers a State to have fallen short of compliance with its obligations under the Covenant and generally refer to those matters that are of concern to the Committee. Occasional reference will also be made to the Committee's 'general discussions' which are intended to provide an opportunity for members of the Committee and other experts to air their views on a particular subject, and to the Committee's 'reporting guidelines' which were drafted to assist States parties to produce adequate reports. In each case, although the material does not provide a concrete indication of the Committee's approach, it does suggest what issues are of importance to it, and provides a tentative indication of what the Committee assumes to be the content of the Covenant's provisions.

I

Economic, Social, and Cultural Rights and their Codification

I. INTRODUCTION

Prior to 1945, international law was generally not concerned with how States treated individuals within their own borders. Such matters were regarded as being within the domestic jurisdiction of each State. Exceptions did exist in the cases of slavery,[1] humanitarian intervention,[2] the treatment of aliens,[3] minorities,[4] and the laws of war,[5] but they were spasmodic,[6] limited in scope,[7] and largely political rather than idealistic in motivation.[8] Following the Second World War, however, the international human rights movement was born. As a reaction to events prior to and during the Second World War, the allies, and later the international community as a whole, came to the belief that the establishment of the new world order should be based upon a commitment to the protection of human rights and fundamental freedoms. Accordingly the protection of human rights was declared to be one of the purposes of the United Nations (UN), and the UN Charter imposed certain obligations upon member States to that end.[9]

Since 1945, a large number of human rights treaties have been adopted

---

[1] *E.g.* Convention to Suppress the Slave Trade and Slavery 1926, 60 UNTS 253.

[2] *See* Hall W., *A Treatise on International Law* (4th ed., 1895), 302–9; Lillich R., 'Forcible Self-Help, by States to Protect Human Rights', (1967) 53 *Iowa LR* 325; Akehurst M., 'Humanitarian Intervention', in Bull H. (ed.), *Intervention in World Politics* (1980), 93–118; Teson F., *Humanitarian Intervention* (1988).

[3] *See generally* Amerasinghe C. F., *State Responsibility for Injury to Aliens* (1967); Borchard E., *The Diplomatic Protection of Aliens Abroad* (1915); Sohn L. and Buergenthal T., *International Protection of Human Rights* (1973), 23–236.

[4] *See generally* Thornberry P., *International Law and the Rights of Minorities* (1991), 25–54. For the League of Nations system, *see* Sohn and Buergenthal, *ibid.* at 213–335.

[5] For history *see* Draper G., 'The Geneva Conventions of 1949' (1965), 114 *Hague Recueil* 63.

[6] Luard E., 'The Origins of International Concern over Human Rights', in Luard E. (ed.), *The International Protection of Human Rights* (1967), 7, at 14.

[7] The minority treaties only applied to certain States—they did not establish universal norms; similarly humanitarian law only established reciprocal undertakings.

[8] Henkin L., 'Introduction', in Henkin L. (ed.), *International Bill of Rights* (1982), 1, at 5.

[9] Arts. 1, 55, and 56, United Nations Charter (1945), 1 UNTS xvi. Other relevant human rights provisions in the Charter include arts. 13, 62(2), 68, and Chs. XI and XII. *See generally* Humphrey J., 'The UN Charter and the Universal Declaration of Human Rights', in Luard E. (ed.), *The International Protection of Human Rights* (1967), 39.

both at a universal[10] and a regional level.[11] The centrepiece of the UN human rights strategy has been the International Bill of Rights consisting of the Universal Declaration of Human Rights (UDHR),[12] the International Covenant on Civil and Political Rights (ICCPR),[13] and the International Covenant on Economic, Social, and Cultural Rights (ICESCR).[14] Although the UDHR remains an important 'standard of reference'[15] in the development of national and international human rights norms, the two Covenants expand and define its terms and establish legal obligations to which States may bind themselves. As the Covenants have gained broader acceptance in the international community and as their respective supervisory systems have been developed, they have begun to figure more largely in the international protection of human rights.

Each Covenant deals with a separate category of rights (civil and political rights on the one hand, and economic, social, and cultural rights on the other) and each provides for a separate implementation procedure. That it was decided to draft two separate treaties instead of a single composite instrument is largely a reflection of the perception developed during the drafting of the Covenants that the two categories of rights were different in nature, origin, and significance. These differences were considered such that it would not be practical, and certainly not politically acceptable, for a single treaty to be drafted containing all the rights to be found in the UDHR. Before addressing the detail of the drafting process, consideration will be given to the real and assumed characteristics of economic, social, and cultural rights as a particular species of human rights.

II. ECONOMIC, SOCIAL, AND CULTURAL RIGHTS

Economic, social, and cultural rights, as embodied in the text of the ICESCR (which includes *inter alia* the rights to work, to fair conditions of employment, to join and form trade unions, to social security, housing, health, education, and culture), have formed an integral part of the inter-

[10] The most significant include: International Convention on the Elimination of All Forms of Racial Discrimination (1966) 60 UNTS 195; International Covenant on Economic, Social, and Cultural Rights (1966) 993 UNTS 3; International Covenant on Civil and Political Rights (1966) 999 UNTS 171; Convention on the Elimination of All Forms of Discrimination Against Women (1979), (1980) 19 ILM 33; UN Convention Against Torture and Other Cruel, Inhuman, or Degrading Treatment (1984), (1985) 24 ILM 535; UN Convention on the Rights of the Child (1989), (1989) 28 ILM 1456.

[11] The most significant include: European Convention on Human Rights and Fundamental Freedoms (1953) 213 UNTS 221; European Social Charter (1961) 529 UNTS 89; American Convention on Human Rights (1969) 9 ILM 673; African Charter on Human and People's Rights (1981) 21 ILM 59.

[12] GA Resn. 217 A (III), 3 GAOR, Pt. 1, Resns., 71 (1948).   [13] 999 UNTS 171.

[14] 993 UNTS 3. The text is to be found in App. I.   [15] Humphrey, *supra*, n. 9, at 51.

nationally recognized catalogue of human rights as developed since 1945.[16] Apart from the Covenant itself, recognition of economic, social, and cultural rights may be found in the UDHR (articles 22–8), the Convention on the Elimination of All Forms of Racial Discrimination (article 5), the Convention on the Elimination of All Forms of Discrimination Against Women (article 1), the Convention on the Rights of the Child,[17] and the Convention on the Rights of Migrant Workers.[18] Significant expression is also given to economic, social, and cultural rights at a regional level in the European Social Charter[19] (of the Council of Europe) which is the only other international human rights instrument dedicated solely to the protection of such rights.

That economic, social, and cultural rights have been identified as a discrete category of human rights is most usually explained in terms of their distinct historical origin. Economic, social, and cultural rights are frequently termed 'second generation' rights, deriving from the growth of socialist ideals in the late nineteenth and early twentieth centuries[20] and the rise of the labour movement in Europe.[21] They contrast with the 'first generation' civil and political rights associated with the eighteenth-century Declarations on the Rights of Man,[22] and the 'third generation' rights that encompass the rights of 'peoples' or 'groups', such as the right to self-determination and the right to development.[23] In fact the reason for making a distinction between first and second generation rights could be

---

[16] Economic, social, and cultural rights could be said to be an expression of Roosevelt's idea of 'freedom from want'. *See The Public Papers and Addresses of Franklin D. Roosevelt: War and Aid to Democracies, 1940* (1941), 284–5. The US Secretary of State, Stettinius, later commented that freedom from want encompassed the right to work, the right to social security, and the right to opportunity for advancement, *US Dept. of State Bulletin* (1945), Vol. XII, 928–9. Roosevelt himself mentioned the right to a useful and remunerative job, the right to earn enough to provide adequate food and clothing, the right to a decent home, and the right to education, *Congressional Record* (1944), Vol. 90, Pt. 1, 78 Cong. 2nd Sess., at 57.

[17] Those rights include the right to the enjoyment of the 'highest attainable standard of health' (art. 24); the right of the child to benefit from social security (art. 26); the right of the child to an adequate standard of living (art. 27); the right of the child to education (art. 28); the right of a child to culture (arts. 30 and 31); the right to protection from exploitation (arts. 30 and 31).

[18] These include the right to social security (art. 27), the right to medical care (art. 28), the right of access to education (art. 30), the right to respect for their cultural identity (art. 31).

[19] *Supra*, n. 11.

[20] *See e.g.* Szabo I., 'Historical Foundations of Human Rights and Subsequent Developments', in Vasak K. and Alston P. (eds.), *The International Dimensions of Human Rights* (1982), 11; Weston B., 'Human Rights' (1984) 6 *Hum. Rts. Q 257. Cf.* Marshall T., *Class, Citizenship, and Social Development* (1964), at 105.

[21] For the effect of the emerging labour movement *see* Ghebali V.–Y., *The International Labour Organisation: A Case Study on the Evolution of UN Specialized Agencies* (1989), 1–16; Follows J., *The Antecedents of the International Labour Organization* (1951).

[22] *See generally* Henkin L., *The Rights of Man Today* (1979).

[23] *See generally* Alston P., 'A Third Generation of Solidarity Rights: Progressive Development or Obfuscation of International Human Rights Law?' (1982) 29 *Neth. ILR* 307; Marks S., 'Emerging Human Rights: A New Generation for the 1980s' (1981) 33 *Rutgers L Rev.* 435.

more accurately put down to the ideological conflict between East and West pursued in the arena of human rights during the drafting of the Covenants. The Soviet States, on the one hand, championed the cause of economic, social, and cultural rights, which they associated with the aims of the socialist society. Western States, on the other hand, asserted the priority of civil and political rights as being the foundation of liberty and democracy in the 'free world'.[24] The conflict was such that during the drafting of the International Bill of Rights the intended treaty was divided into two separate instruments which were later to become the ICCPR and the ICESCR.[25]

The fact of separation has since been used as evidence of the inherent opposition of the two categories of rights. In particular, it has led to a perpetuation of excessively monolithic views as to the nature, history, and philosophical conception of each group of rights and has contributed to the idea that economic, social, and cultural rights are in reality a distinct and separate group of human rights. Of greater concern, however, is that despite the clear intention not to imply any notion of relative value by the act of separating the Covenants,[26] it has nevertheless reinforced claims as to the heirarchical ascendance of civil and political rights.[27] Although within the UN there is now almost universal acceptance of the theoretical 'indivisible and interdependent' nature of the two sets of rights,[28] the reality in practice is that economic, social, and cultural rights remain largely ignored.[29] As the Committee on Economic, Social, and Cultural Rights has pointed out, the reality is that:

the international community as a whole continue to tolerate all too often breaches of economic, social and cultural rights which, if they occurred in relation to civil and political rights, would provoke expressions of horror and outrage and would lead to concerted calls for immediate remedial action. In effect, despite the rhetoric, violations of civil and political rights continue to be treated as though they were far more serious, and more patently intolerable, than massive and direct denials of economic, social and cultural rights.[30]

[24] Gros Espiel H., 'The Evolving Concept of Human Rights: Western, Socialist and Third World Approaches', in Ramcharan B. (ed.), *Human Rights Thirty Years After the Universal Declaration* (1979), 41.

[25] *See generally* Humphrey J., *Human Rights and the United Nations—A Great Adventure* (1984), at 107.

[26] Preamble to GA Resn. 543 (VI).

[27] *See e.g.* Abram (USA), E/CN.4/Sub.2/1992/SR.24, at 6, paras. 19–21.

[28] *See* Proclamation of Teheran, art. 13, GA Resn. 32/130, (16 Dec. 1977), 33 UN GAOR, Resns., Supp. (No. 45), at 150 (1977); GA Resn. 41/128, art. 6(2), (4 Dec. 1986), 41 UN GAOR, Resns., Supp. (No. 53), at 186 (1986).

[29] Alston P., 'The Importance of the Inter-play between Economic, Social and Cultural Rights, and Civil and Political Rights', UN Doc. A/CONF.157/PC/66/Add. 1, at 25–26, para. 13. For the view that economic, social, and cultural rights have come to dominate the work of the UN *see* Abram M., 'Human Rights and the United Nations: Past as Prologue' (1991) 4 *Harv. Hum. Rts. J* 69.

[30] Statement to the World Conference, UN Doc. E/1993/22/, at 83, para. 5.

The picture is even less promising at the national level. In the majority of States, economic, social, and cultural rights are almost entirely absent from the common discourse on human rights. Even in those States where economic and social rights are constitutionally enacted or where the ICESCR forms part of domestic law,[31] national courts have relied upon the oversimplified characterization of economic and social rights as 'non-justiciable' rights, with the result that they have rarely given them full effect.[32] In turn, the lack of national case law directly related to economic, social, and cultural rights has itself perpetuated the idea that those rights are not capable of judicial enforcement.

The scepticism with which economic and social rights are currently considered generally rests upon two basic assertions: first, that human rights derive from a 'natural law' pedigree which is concerned with individual autonomy and freedom, and provides a justification for civil and political rights but not for economic, social, and cultural rights.[33] The latter, being 'second' rather than 'first' generation rights are seen to derive from a distinct source and have a different, even conflicting, theoretical rationale. The second basic assertion is that economic, social, and cultural rights lack the essential characteristics of universality and absoluteness which are the hallmarks of human rights properly so-called and have therefore 'debilitated, muddied, and obscured' the notion of human rights.[34]

With respect to the first assertion, it is commonly held that human rights have their direct source in the natural rights philosophy of the eighteenth century and from there an indirect source to natural law dating back to the philosophy of the Greeks.[35] One of the principal hallmarks of the natural rights theory was its individualism,[36] and its emphasis on personal autonomy and freedom from State interference.[37] Indeed it was the perceived 'atomistic' or 'egoistic' nature of the philosophy that so enraged its later

---

[31] *See e.g.* Argentina, E/C.12/1990/SR.18, at 4, para. 14; Ecuador, E/C.12/1990/SR.39, at 2, para. 6; Afghanistan, E/C.12/1991/SR.4, at 4, para. 21; Costa Rica, E/C.12/1990/SR.38, at 15, para. 85; Weitzel, E/C.12/1990/SR.33, at 8, para. 29; Mexico, E/C.12/1990/SR.6, at 4, para. 15.

[32] *See e.g.* Weitzel (Luxembourg), E/C.12/1990/SR.33, at 8, para. 29. *See generally* Craven M., 'The Domestic Application of the International Covenant on Economic, Social and Cultural Rights' (1993) 40 *Neth. ILR.* 367.

[33] Minogue K., 'The History of the Idea of Human Rights' in Laquer W. and Rubin B. (eds.), *The Human Rights Reader* (1989) 3, at 13–14.

[34] Cranston M., 'Human Rights Real and Supposed', in Raphael D. (ed.), *Political Theory and the Rights of Man* (1967), 43.

[35] *See generally* Lauterpacht H., *International Law and Human Rights* (1950); Vincent R., *Human Rights and International Relations* (1986), 19–36; Waldron J., 'Natural Rights in the Seventeenth and Eighteenth Centuries' in Waldron J. (ed.), *Nonsense upon Stilts* (1987), 7; Tuck R., *Natural Rights Theories: Their Origin and Development* (1979).

[36] The three characteristics of the natural rights theory are said to be its rationalism, individualism, and radicalism. *See* d'Entrèves A., *Natural Law: An Introduction to Legal Philosophy* (1970), 51–63.

[37] *See generally* Macpherson C., *The Political Theory of Possessive Individualism* (1962); Shapiro I., *The Evolution of Rights in Liberal Theory* (1986).

critics.[38] The philosophy of radical individualism, particularly as developed later by Nozick,[39] conceives of rights in negative terms (as negative liberties[40]), justifying principally a limited range of civil rights. Under this approach, economic, social, and cultural rights not only fall outside the scope of human rights but also, in so far as they require an element of wealth redistribution, they represent an unjustified interference in individual liberty.[41]

There are a number of objections that might be made to this thesis. First, it is by no means universally agreed that the natural law tradition did in fact provide a coherent philosophical basis for the modern notion of human rights.[42] To assert that the rights expressed in the Universal Declaration were inspired solely by the philosophy of Hobbes or Locke is little more than mere speculation and indeed might lend force to claims of cultural relativism.[43] In reality, it is likely that the International Bill of Rights was drafted 'not because . . . [States] had agreed on a philosophy, but because they had agreed, despite philosophical differences, on the formulation of a solution to a series of moral and political problems'.[44] Human rights, in this sense, is a name given to 'plural and divergent ideologies',[45] such that a search for an immutable or universal foundation is bound to fail.[46]

Secondly, even if one were to accept the basic assertion that human rights have their roots in the natural rights philosophies of the seventeenth and eighteenth centuries one is not left with a coherent picture of which rights might accordingly be justified. While the philosophies of Hobbes and Locke are often interpreted as providing the basis for only a limited range of civil rights,[47] Locke does refer extensively to the right to private property which is, if anything, an economic or social right.[48] Similarly, the later eighteenth century philosophies and texts do not confine themselves solely to civil

---

[38] Marx K., 'On the Jewish Question' in *Collected Works III* (1975), at 162.

[39] Nozick R., *Anarchy, the State and Utopia* (1974).

[40] *Cf.* Berlin I., 'Two Concepts of Liberty' in Berlin I., *Four Essays on Liberty* (1969), 129.

[41] Nozick, *supra*, n. 39, at 167–74.   [42] *See* d'Entrèves, *supra*, n. 36, at 17.

[43] *See generally* Donnelly J., 'Cultural Relativism and Universal Human Rights' (1984) 6 *Hum. Rts. Q* 400; Teson F., 'International Human Rights and Cultural Relativism' (1985) 25 *Virg. JIL* 868; Renteln A., 'The Unanswered Challenge of Relativism and the Consequences for Human Rights' (1985) 7 *Hum. Rts. Q* 514.

[44] Mckeon R., 'The Philosophical Bases and Material Circumstances of the Rights of Man', in UNESCO Symposium, *Human Rights Comments and Interpretations* (1949), 37. *See also* Fields B. and Wolf-Deiter N., 'Human Rights as a Wholistic Concept' (1992) 14 *Hum. Rts. Q* 1; Morsink J., 'The Philosophy of the Universal Declaration' (1984) 6 *Hum. Rts. Q* 309.

[45] Vincent, *supra*, n. 35, at 1.

[46] This does not necessarily undermine the utility of speaking of 'rights', *see* Lomasky L., *Persons, Rights and the Moral Community* (1987), 13.

[47] *See* MacPherson C., 'Natural Rights in Hobbes and Locke' in Raphael D. (ed.), *Political Theory and the Rights of Man* (1967), 4.

[48] For the view that the philosophy of Locke serves to justify both 'positive' and 'negative' rights *see* Donnelly J., *Universal Human Rights in Theory and Practice* (1989), 88–106.

rights. Recognition is given, for example, not only to political rights,[49] but also to a number of social and economic rights.[50]

Ultimately, one might concede that human rights are a species of natural right (as is implied by the terms of the UDHR),[51] but that is only to say that they must be deduced from human nature rather than from custom or from law;[52] it does not stipulate a particular historical pedigree or that they should be conditioned by the liberal overtones of eighteenth century doctrines of natural rights.[53] Modern 'natural rights' theories vary enormously and may be identified as such only in so far as they are all based upon some morally relevant characteristic of human nature or the human condition. For example, the notions of practical reasonableness,[54] moral autonomy,[55] human needs,[56] human dignity,[57] equality,[58] equal respect,[59] or human development[60] have all been utilized as bases for rights theories. The range of rights to which each theory gives recognition depends entirely upon the theory of nature that has been adopted. As Donnelly points out, there is nothing inherently limited about the natural rights approach as, although it specifies the source and form of human rights, 'the content is provided by the particular theory of human nature that one adopts'.[61]

[49] The French Declaration of 1789, e.g., tempered its liberalism with a commitment to democratic principles such as no taxation without consultation (art. 14) and popular participation in law-making (art. 6). The Declaration on the Rights of Man and the Citizen 1789, reprinted in Waldron J. (ed.), *Nonsense upon Stilts* (1987), 26.

[50] Thomas Paine refers in 'The Rights of Man' to the rights to employment and social assistance. Paine T., *The Rights of Man*. *See generally* Raphael D., 'Human Rights Old and New' in Raphael D. (ed.), *Political Theory and the Rights of Man* (1967), 57; Henkin L., 'Economic–Social Rights as 'Rights': A United States Perspective' (1981) 2 *Hum. Rts. LJ* 223; Siegel R., 'Socioeconomic Human Rights: Past and Future' (1984) 7 *Hum. Rts. Q* 257; Palley C., *The United Kingdom and Human Rights* (1991), 56–68.

[51] Art. 1 UDHR reads: 'All human beings are born free and equal in dignity and rights.' This is clearly not a statement of fact, but a meta-ethical assertion as to the nature of humanity.

[52] MacPherson, *supra*, n. 47, at 14.

[53] An alternative 'teleological' or 'social justice' approach seeks to justify human rights by reference to their instrumental value in achieving certain social goals. *See e.g.* Beitz C., 'Human Rights and Social Justice', in Brown P. and MacLean D. (eds.), *Human Rights and US Foreign Policy* (1979), 45. In the final analysis, such theories will inevitably rest upon certain deontological assumptions as to the organization of an 'ideal society' and may therefore differ only marginally from other 'natural rights' theories.

[54] Finnis J., *Natural Law and Natural Rights* (1980), 34–41.

[55] *See e.g.* Raz J., 'Right-Based Moralities' in Waldron J., *Theories of Rights* (1992), 182; Lomasky, *supra*, n. 46, at 51–83.

[56] Lewis J., 'On Human Rights' in UNESCO, *Human Rights Comments and Interpretations* (1949), 54; Bay C., 'Self-Respect as a Human Right: Thoughts on the Dialectics of Wants and Needs in the Struggle for Human Community' (1982) 4 *Hum. Rts. Q* 53.

[57] McDougal M., Lasswell H., and Chen L., *Human Rights and World Public Order* (1980), 376–8. Gewirth A., *Human Rights: Essays on Justification and Applications* (1982), at 7.

[58] Vlastos G., 'Justice and Equality' in Waldron J. (ed.), *Theories of Rights* (1992), 41.

[59] Dworkin R., *Taking Rights Seriously* (1976).

[60] O'Manique J., 'Universal and Inalienable Rights: A Search for Foundations' (1990) 12 *Hum. Rts. Q* 465.

[61] Donnelly J., 'Human Rights as Natural Rights' (1982) *Hum. Rts. Q* 391, at 399.

Two general forms of justification for economic, social, and cultural rights may be identified. The first views them as being essential conditions for the full enjoyment of civil and political rights.[62] It is argued that the ideals of freedom or moral autonomy can only be made meaningful if the individual also enjoys a certain degree of material security;[63] freedom of expression, for example, has little importance to the starving or homeless. This is a limited form of justification as material security only has an instrumental value and is relevant only in so far as it contributes to individual freedom. The second, and fuller, form of justification views economic, social, and cultural rights as inherently valuable considerations irrespective of what they contribute to the enjoyment of civil and political rights. For example, such rights may be considered universal human rights in so far as they relate to fundamental elements of the individual's physical nature, whether that be their physical needs[64] or their ability to enjoy social goods.[65]

The second principal argument against economic, social, and cultural rights is that, unlike the traditional category of civil and political rights, they are neither universal nor categorical and therefore lack the essential characteristics of human rights.[66] Human rights are said to be universal in so far as they are ascribed to every individual by virtue of their humanity rather than as a result of their position or role in society.[67] Economic, social, and cultural rights, it is argued, fail the test of universality in that they only refer

MacDonald comments in this vein: 'natural rights are the conditions of a good society. But what those conditions are is not given by nature or mystically bound up with the essence of man and his inevitable goal, but is determined by human decisions': MacDonald M., 'Natural Rights', in Waldron J. (ed.), *Theories of Rights* (1984), 21, at 34.

[62] As Shue argues: 'No one can fully, if at all, enjoy any right that is supposedly protected by society if he or she lacks the essentials for a reasonably healthy life': Shue H., *Basic Rights* (1979), at 24–5.

[63] *See* Berlin, *supra*, n. 40, at 122–34; Waldron J., *Liberal Rights* (1993), 4–10; Raphael, *supra*, n. 50, at 64.

[64] Bay C., 'A Human Rights Approach to Transnational Politics' (1979) 1 *Uni. Hum. Rts*, 29.

[65] *See e.g.* Gewirth A., *Human Rights: Essays on Justification and Applications* (1982), 7.

[66] Wasserstrom identifies four characteristics of human rights: they are universal (i.e. held by everybody); they are possessed equally; they are possessed by persons as persons (i.e. without regard to institutional membership); they are assertable claims against the whole world. Wasserstrom R., 'Rights, Human Rights, and Racial Discrimination' (1964) 61 *Jnl. of Philosophy* 628, at 631–2. Fried argues that the primary consideration of human rights is that they are 'categorical moral entities such that violation . . . is always wrong'. From this, he concludes that human rights must always be immediately practicable. Fried C., *Right and Wrong* (1978), 108–13. Cranston identifies three characteristics of human rights as international moral rights: they must be universal, fundamental, and practicable: Cranston, *supra*, n. 34, at 49–51.

[67] The notion of universality is sometimes attached to duties. Hart, e.g., distinguishes between 'general rights' or rights *in rem*, and 'special rights' or rights *in personam*. Hart H., 'Are there any Natural Rights?', in Waldron J. (ed.), *Theories of Rights* (1984), 77, at 84–8. This distinction is lost in the international law of human rights, however, as the State is always considered to be the primary duty-holder.

classes of people.[68] For example, the right to social security is a right that may be claimed only by people fulfilling the requisite criterion of need. The same criticism, however, may be directed towards a number of civil and political rights (like the right to a fair trial or the right to vote), which only apply to individuals in certain socially defined situations (when accused or when old enough). The point is that all such rights are universal in the sense that they apply (at least potentially) to everyone; it is just that the exercise of those rights is related to the particular circumstances in which individuals find themselves.[69]

Another particular characteristic of human rights is that they are of such fundamental importance that no one may be deprived of them 'without a grave affront to justice'.[70] Cranston argues, referring in particular to the right to holidays with pay,[71] that economic and social rights lack that element of paramountcy. Rather, they are mere 'liberality and kindness' embodied in 'moral ideals' which cannot be immediately realized.[72] The simple response is that even if it is conceded that the right to paid holidays is not ultimately fundamental, the same cannot be said with respect to other economic or social rights such as the rights to food or housing. Indeed those rights might in some circumstances be said to be more important than other civil and political rights such as the right to vote.[73]

The thrust of Cranston's argument, however, goes to another more important point. Rights, he argues, are such important interests, they 'must be respected here and now'.[74] Whereas that is the case with respect to civil and political rights which are 'negative' and defined in terms of non-interference, economic and social rights are by their nature 'positive' rights demanding the provision of resources, such as health, education, or welfare which cannot be realized immediately. As Fried commented:

It is logically possible to treat negative rights as categorical entities. . . . Positive rights, by contrast, cannot as a logical matter be treated as categorical entities because of the scarcity limitation. It is not just that it is too costly to provide a subsistence diet to the whole Indian subcontinent in time of famine—it may simply be impossible.[75]

---

[68] Cranston, *supra*, n. 34, at 51.

[69] *e.g.* the fact that convicted prisoners are deprived of a number of rights does not mean that those rights are no longer 'universal'. *See generally* Donnelly J., *The Concept of Human Rights* (1985), 12.

[70] Cranston, *supra*, n. 34, at 51. Fried comments similarly that rights are 'categorical moral entities such that violation of a right is always wrong': Fried, *supra*, n. 66, at 108.

[71] Art. 24 UDHR.   [72] Cranston, *supra*, n. 34, at 52–3.

[73] As has been pointed out Cranston's comparison is 'no more valid than choosing a very bright yellow and a very dull red to demonstrate that yellow is brighter than red': Okin S., 'Liberty and Welfare: Some Issues in Human Rights Theory' in Pennock J. and Chapman J. (eds.), *Human Rights, Nomos XXIII* (1981), 242.

[74] Cranston, *supra*, n. 34, at 53.   [75] Fried, *supra*, n. 66, at 113.

This argument relies upon two assertions: first that economic and social rights, unlike civil and political rights, are not 'absolute' in that they are dependant upon the existence of sufficient resources and can only be implemented progressively.[76] Secondly, only those rights that are capable of immediate implementation qualify as human rights.

While it appears that certain economic and social rights are contingent for their implementation upon the existence of sufficient resources, it is not necessarily appropriate categorically to differentiate their implementation from that of civil and political rights.[77] On the one hand, it is clear that several economic and social rights, such as the right to join and form trade unions, are primarily rights of non-interference. It is in fact possible to identify duties of forbearance with respect to most economic and social rights.[78] On the other hand, it would be wrong to suggest that civil and political rights themselves are entirely negative or free of cost. The right to a fair trial, for example, assumes the existence and maintenance of a system of courts.[79] Similarly, the protection of civil and political rights at an inter-individual level necessitates the operation of a police force and a penal system.[80] As Shue notes, it would be 'either fatuous or extraordinarily scholastic' to maintain that civil and political rights, such as freedom from torture, can be ensured merely through an increase in restraint.[81] In fact, as Shue points out, most human rights can be seen to impose three core obligations upon States: the duty to avoid depriving, the duty to protect from deprivation, and the duty to aid the deprived.[82] When viewed in such a light, differences between rights, or between groups of rights, become merely a matter of emphasis.

The second assertion which lies at the heart of Fried's approach is that

---

[76] This argument is most fully developed by Bossuyt who, noting that civil rights require *l'abstention de l'État* and economic and social rights *l'intervention de l'État*, concludes that whilst the former were invariable and absolute, the latter are dependent upon State resources and therefore relative or contingent considerations. He goes on to point out that while civil and political rights can be applied immediately, totally, and universally, economic and social rights are to be applied progressively over time and to selective portions of the population. Bossuyt M., 'La Distinction juridique entre les droits civils et politiques et les droits économiques, sociaux et culturels' (1975) 8 *Hum. Rts. LJ* 783, at 790; Bossuyt M., *L'Interdiction de la discrimination dans le droit international des droits de l'homme* (1976), 193–202. *Contra*, Van Hoof G., 'The Legal Nature of Economic, Social and Cultural Rights: A Rebuttal of Some Traditional Views', in Alston P. and Tomasevski K. (eds.), *The Right to Food* (1984), 97.

[77] Bossuyt, *ibid.* 790.   [78] *See e.g.* Shue, *supra*, n. 62, at 35–45.

[79] For positive obligations in the context of the ECHR *see Airey*, Eur. Ct. HR, Series A, Vol. 32, 9 Oct. 1979, 2 EHRR 305; *Marckx*, Eur. Ct. HR, Series A., Vol. 31, 13 June 1979, 2 EHRR 330. *See generally* Berenstein A., 'Economic and Social Rights: Their Inclusion in the European Convention on Human Rights. Problems of Formulation and Interpretation' (1981) 2 *Hum. Rts. LJ* 257.

[80] *See generally* Plant R., *Modern Political Thought* (1991), 270–1.

[81] Shue H., 'Rights in the Light of Duties' in Brown P. and MacLean D. (eds.), *Human Rights and US Foreign Policy* (1979), 65, at 69.

[82] *See generally* Shue, *supra*, n. 62, at 51–64.

one cannot speak of the individual possessing a 'right' if they are not able to 'claim' or 'enforce' it as such. Stoljar explains:

You cannot have a right unless it can be claimed or demanded or insisted upon . . . Rights are thus performative-dependent, their operative reality being their claimability; a right one could not claim, demand, ask or enjoy or exercise would be a vacuous attribute.[83]

One response to this might be that in so far as economic and social rights have been given recognition in international law, the individual has a basis for making a strong moral or political claim against the State, especially where that State is party to the ICESCR. What appears to be suggested, however, is that rights are dependent upon the existence of specific legal remedies.[84] While this might ring true in national legal systems, it is difficult to reconcile this approach with the theory of international human rights. It has to be accepted that an appeal to human rights is important principally when national law remedies are unavailable or inadequate; it is in fact an appeal to the adjustment of national law and practice. The appeal is not necessarily vitiated by the absence of specific international remedies open to the individual. Indeed the nature of international law is such that the question of enforceability has never been conclusive as to the existence of international rights or duties.

In the final analysis, there are no really convincing arguments either for denying economic, social, and cultural rights the status of human rights or for maintaining absolute distinctions between them and civil and political rights. Certainly differences between rights might be identified in terms of their historical recognition, philosophical justification, or emphasis in implementation but rarely in any coherent or categorical manner. Indeed it should be borne in mind that the identification of economic, social, and cultural rights as a discrete and separate group of rights was principally a result of the ideological rivalry between East and West during the drafting of the International Bill of Rights.

III. THE INTERNATIONAL COVENANT ON ECONOMIC, SOCIAL, AND CULTURAL RIGHTS

A The Drafting of the Covenant

The decision was made in 1947 to draft an 'International Bill of Rights' consisting of three documents: a non-binding declaration of a general na-

---

[83] Stoljar S., *An Analysis of Rights* (1984), 3–4.
[84] *See e.g.* Vierdag E., 'The Legal Nature of the Rights Granted by the International Covenant on Economic, Social and Cultural Rights' (1978) 9 *Neth. ILR* 69.

ture, a convention of more limited scope, and a document of methods of implementation. The newly-created Commission on Human Rights quickly completed the text of the non-binding declaration which, after considerable revision,[85] was adopted by the General Assembly on 10 December 1948 as the Universal Declaration of Human Rights.[86] Although the underlying philosophy of the UDHR has been criticized as being primarily 'western' and 'liberal', with a preference for civil and political rights,[87] it does give recognition to a number of economic, social, and cultural rights.[88]

In 1948, the Commission on Human Rights was requested by the General Assembly to give priority to the preparation of a draft Covenant on human rights and measures of implementation.[89] At its fifth session[90] the Commission began to examine a draft Covenant comprising a range of civil and political rights. It also considered a number of suggestions as regards implementation procedures including, *inter alia*, the proposed establishment of an International Court of Human Rights.[91] Despite opposition from the USSR, a majority of the Commission agreed upon the necessity of some form of international supervision with the possibility of inter-State petitions. Opinion was divided, however, over the issue of individual complaints procedures. In light of continuing disagreements, the Commission decided to transmit the draft Covenant, together with a number of pro-

---

[85] The Third Committee alone sat for 81 meetings and considered 168 amendments before it adopted the UDHR.

[86] GA Resn. 217 A (III), (10 Dec. 1948), 3 UN GAOR, Resns. Pt. 1, at 71 (1948). It was adopted by 48 votes to 0 with 8 abstentions (Byelorussia, Czechoslovakia, Poland, USSR, Saudi Arabia, Ukraine, S. Africa, and Yugoslavia).

[87] There was seemingly an intention to maintain a distinction between the civil and political rights which form the first 20 arts., and economic, social, and cultural rights which lie at the end. This was apparent in the rejection of a joint amendment to art. 3, to include a reference to social and economic security. Similarly the discussion on the form of art. 1 suggests that much emphasis was placed on an 18th-century concept of human rights. *See* Morsink, *supra*, n. 44; Dowrick F., 'Introduction', in *Human Rights—Problems, Perspectives and Texts* (1979), 1.

[88] Tolley notes that there were three ideological forces in competition. First the Western States preferred a minimum list of strictly enforceable civil and political rights; secondly the Eastern Bloc States championed economic, social, and cultural rights with State implementation and concomitant duties; lastly, the Latin American States, having recently completed their Bogota Declaration, wished to incorporate a maximum catalogue of rights including the economic, social, and cultural components. Tolley H., *The UN Commission on Human Rights* (1987), at 21–2. However Humphrey comments in this respect: 'The legislative history of the Declaration shows that, while there was deep disagreement on how they [the provisions] should be implemented, there was substantial agreement on the stated objectives': Humphrey, *supra*, n. 25, at 74.

[89] GA Resn. 217 E (III), *supra*, n. 86; ECOSOC Resn. 191 (VIII), (9 Feb. 1949), 8 UN ESCOR, Resns. Supp. (No. 1), at 7 (1949).

[90] UN Doc. E/1371, 9 UN ESCOR, Supp. (No. 10) (1949).

[91] Other proposals included: a special commission with authority to receive petitions from individuals; a panel of experts to review inter-State complaints on an *ad hoc* basis; a commission within each State and a conciliation committee mandated with the review of individual petitions with final recourse to the International Court of Justice. *Ibid.* Annex III.

posed additional articles (including certain economic, social, and cultural rights) and a questionnaire on implementation, to States for their comments.[92]

At its sixth session[93] in 1950 the Commission continued with its consideration of the draft Covenant, but decided that as additional time was needed to discuss economic, social, and cultural rights and consult the specialized agencies concerned,[94] it would be best to adopt an initial draft Covenant limited to civil and political rights with a view to adopting further Covenants on other rights at a later stage.[95] It therefore resolved to begin drafting a separate Covenant on economic, social, and cultural rights at its next session in 1951. In terms of implementation, the Commission had decided upon the establishment of a permanent human rights committee with provision for inter-State (but not individual[96]) complaints.[97] As, however, the Commission had decided to deal with economic, social, and cultural rights separately, it appears that this procedure was to operate exclusively with respect to civil and political rights.

To resolve something which had become a matter of some contention, ECOSOC requested the General Assembly to make a policy decision as to the desirability of including articles on economic, social, and cultural rights in the draft Covenant.[98] After a long and acrimonious debate, the General Assembly declared *inter alia* that 'the enjoyment of civil and political freedoms and of economic, social, and cultural rights are interconnected and interdependent'. As such the Commission was to include in the draft Covenant 'a clear expression of economic, social, and cultural rights in a manner which relates them to the civil and political freedoms proclaimed by the draft Covenant'.[99] The decisions of the Assembly were accordingly discussed by ECOSOC which then transferred them to the Commission and invited the specialized agencies to participate in the Commission's work regarding economic, social, and cultural rights.[100]

---

[92] *Ibid.* Annex I.

[93] UN Doc. E/1681, 11 UN ESCOR, Supp. (No. 5) (1950).

[94] The Commission was in possession at this time of the survey of activities of UN organs and specialized agencies in matters within the scope of arts. 22 to 27 of the Universal Declaration. UN Doc. E/CN.4/364 (1950).

[95] E/CN.4/SR.377–9, 11 ESCOR (377–9 mtgs.) (1950). It actually referred to 'economic, social, cultural' and 'political' rights; the suggestion being that the draft convention only dealt with civil rights.

[96] The suggestion for NGO petitions was rejected by 7 votes to 4 with 3 abstentions; that of individuals by 8 votes to 3 with 3 abstentions.

[97] *Supra*, n. 93.

[98] ECOSOC Resn. 303 I (XI), (9 Aug. 1950), 11 UN ESCOR, Resns. Supp. (No. 1), at 29 (1950).

[99] GA Resn. 421 (V), Sect. E, (4 Dec. 1950), 5 UN GAOR, Resns. Supp. (No. 20), at 42 (1950).

[100] ECOSOC Resn. 349 (XII), (25 Feb. 1951), 12 UN ESCOR, Resns. Supp. (No. 1), at 8 (1951).

[101] UN Doc. E/1992, 13 UN ESCOR, Supp. (No. 9) (1952).

At its seventh session in 1951,[101] the Commission held a lengthy discussion spanning six meetings on the question of including articles on economic, social, and cultural rights.[102] Various draft proposals were considered[103] leading to the adoption of fourteen articles on economic, social, and cultural rights and two separate 'umbrella clauses' concerning obligations and limitations.[104] Despite the General Assembly's instructions, the Commission continued to treat economic, social, and cultural rights as a distinct category of rights and proceeded to draft a number of articles outlining a system of State reporting under UN supervision,[105] intended to appertain solely to economic, social, and cultural rights.[106] Faced with the unwieldy prospect of having a 'covenant within a covenant'[107] (in the sense of having two separate implementation systems), ECOSOC was forced to request the General Assembly to reconsider its decision and allow the draft Covenant be divided into two separate instruments.[108]

In the following year, the General Assembly's Third Committee conducted an extended debate on the draft Covenant.[109] After deciding not to take on the drafting of the Covenant itself,[110] the Third Committee adopted a joint amendment[111] directing the Commission to draft two separate Covenants. This decision was reaffirmed by the General Assembly which, in a complete reversal of its original position, requested the Commission:

To draft two Covenants on human rights . . . , one to contain civil and political rights and the other to contain economic, social and cultural rights, in order that the General Assembly may approve the two Covenants simultaneously and open them at the same time for signature, the two Covenants to contain, in order to emphasize

---

[102] The discussion was conducted during the Commission's 203 to 208 meetings. Opposition to the inclusion of economic, social, and cultural rights was such that members of the Commission even questioned whether it was technically bound by decisions of the General Assembly.

[103] The proposals of governments and the specialized agencies are to be found in UN Doc. E/CN.4/AC.14/2 and Add. 1–5, (1951).

[104] The inclusion of the umbrella clauses (*ibid.* Annex 1, pt. III, draft arts. 19 and 32) showed that the Commission was determined to maintain a distinction between the categories of rights even if forced to deal with them in the same convention.

[105] For a discussion of the rejected ILO proposal *see* Ch. 2, text accompanying nn. 38–40.

[106] Much of the discussion centred around the role of the specialized agencies in the reporting process, suggesting that it was tailor-made for economic, social, and cultural rights, E/CN.4/SR.218, 237–8, 241–3, 236–7 (1951). Similarly the question whether the petition procedure should apply to only the civil and political rights was to be decided at a later stage, *ibid.* Annex 1, pt. IV.

[107] Humphrey, *supra*, n. 25, at 144.

[108] ECOSOC Resn. 384 (XIII), (29 Aug. 1951), 13 UN ESCOR, Resns. Supp. (No. 1), at 35 (1951). UN Doc. E/2152, at 36, 13 UN ESCOR, Supp. (No. 1) (1952).

[109] UN Docs. A/C.3/SR.358–72, 387–411, 6 UN GAOR, C.3, (358–72 and 387–411 mtgs.) (1952).

[110] See the report of the Committee. UN Doc. A/C.3/559, 6 UN GAOR, C.3, Annexes (Ag. Item 29), at 4 (1951).

[111] Joint amendment proposed by Belgium, India, Lebanon, and USA: UN Doc. A/C.3/L.184/Rev. 1 (1951).

the unity of the aim in view and to ensure respect for and observance of human rights, as many similar provisions as possible.[112]

On the basis of that decision, the Commission was therefore asked to revise the draft articles on economic, social, and cultural rights, taking into consideration the views of governments, NGOs, and the specialized agencies.[113]

In accordance with the decision of the General Assembly, the Commission spent most of its eighth session[114] drafting two separate Covenants. It produced a draft article on self-determination but was unable to consider the questions of implementation, reservations, or the inclusion of a federal State clause. Similarly, at its ninth session,[115] the Commission only had time to consider certain articles on civil and political rights. It was unable to discuss new additional articles, such as that concerning the right to property, for inclusion in the draft Covenant on Economic, Social, and Cultural Rights. However, the Commission did conclude its consideration of the Covenant at its tenth session in 1954[116] following the redrafting of the articles on periodic reporting and the adoption of a federal State clause. It was noted that the draft Covenants, as completed by the Commission,[117] 'represented a broad compromise between differing political, economic, and cultural opinions and, while not ideal, should be regarded as fairly satisfactory'.[118]

The draft Covenants were duly referred to the General Assembly for consideration at its ninth session.[119] After a general discussion, the Assembly requested further observations from States, specialized agencies and non-governmental organizations, and resolved that the Third Committee should discuss the drafts article by article 'with a view to their adoption at the earliest possible date'.[120]

The Third Committee began its discussion of the draft Covenants by considering the Preambles and the right to self-determination (article 1 of each Covenant) at the Assembly's tenth session.[121] The Committee continued by discussing the obligations provision (article 2) of the draft Cov-

---

[112] GA Resn. 543 (VI), (5 Feb. 1952), 6 UN GAOR, Resns. Supp. (No. 20), at 36 (1952). The majority in this decision was relatively small: 29 votes to 25 with 4 abstentions.

[113] GA Resn. 544 (VI), (5 Feb. 1952), 6 UN GAOR, Resns. Supp. (No. 20), at 36 (1952).

[114] UN Doc. E/2250, 13 UN ESCOR, Supp. (No. 4) (1952).

[115] The 9th session of the Commission was held from 7 Apr. to 30 May 1953. UN Doc. E/2447, 16 UN ESCOR, Supp. (No. 8) (1953).

[116] UN Doc. E/2573, 18 UN ESCOR, Supp. (No. 7) (1954).

[117] The final version of the Commission's draft Covenants is to be found in UN Doc. E/2447, *supra*, n. 115, Annex I.

[118] UN Doc. A/2808 and Corr. 1, 9 UN GAOR, C.3, Annexes (Ag. Item 28), at 10, para. 30 (1954).

[119] UN Docs. A/C.3/SR.557–86, 9 UN GAOR, C.3, (557–86 mtgs.) (1954).

[120] GA Resn. 833 (IX) Sect. 4, (4 Dec. 1954), 9 UN GAOR, Resns. Supp. (No. 21), at 20 (1954).

[121] UN Doc. A/3077, 10 UN GAOR, C.3, Annexes (Ag. Item 28), 30–40 (1955).

enant on Economic, Social, and Cultural Rights, but resolved to postpone the adoption of that article until the other rights in Part III of the Covenant had been discussed. At the General Assembly's eleventh session[122] the Third Committee accordingly addressed itself to the substantive articles which it completed in the following session.[123] The Committee then spent the next four sessions discussing the correlative provisions (articles 6–26) of the draft Covenant on Civil and Political Rights.[124]

It was not until the General Assembly's seventeenth session that the Third Committee resumed its consideration of the draft Covenant on Economic, Social, and Cultural Rights.[125] After considerable discussion on the nature of the obligations incumbent upon the States parties with regard to economic, social, and cultural rights, article 2 was finally adopted.[126] Articles 3 to 5 followed, all being adopted unanimously, without amendment, and with minimal discussion.[127] The substance of the Covenant on Economic, Social, and Cultural Rights was thus virtually completed in 1962.[128]

The Third Committee continued to discuss the measures of implementation at its next session[129] and again in 1966. At this late stage the USA and Italy put forward amendments providing for the establishment of an expert committee to review the State reports.[130] These were largely based upon the measures recently adopted for the International Convention on the Elimination of All Forms of Racial Discrimination.[131] The majority resisted the US proposal on the ground that it would unduly restrict ECOSOC's discretion as the main supervisory body and that it would encroach upon the work of the specialized agencies in the area of economic, social, and cultural rights. In the light of the disagreement the proposals were subsequently

[122] UN Doc. A/3525, 11 UN GAOR, C.3, Annexes (Ag. Item 31), 2–22 (1956).
[123] UN Doc. A/3764, 12 UN GAOR, C.3, Annexes (Ag. Item 33), 1–15 (1957).
[124] UN Doc. A/4045, 13 UN GAOR, C.3, Annexes (Ag. Item 32) (1958); UN Doc. A/4299, 14 UN GAOR, C.3, Annexes (Ag. Item 34) (1959); UN Doc. A/4625, 15 UN GAOR, C.3, Annexes (Ag. Item 34) (1960–1); UN Doc. A/5000, 16 UN GAOR, C.3, Annexes (Ag. Item 35) (1961–2).
[125] UN Doc. A/5365, 17 UN GAOR, C.3, Annexes (Ag. Item 43), 6–17 (1962).
[126] *Ibid.* 13. Art. 2 was adopted by 51 votes to 4 with 33 abstentions. An indication of the controversy is demonstrated by the fact that art. 2 para. 3 was adopted by the narrow margin of 41 votes to 38 with 12 abstentions.   [127] *Ibid.*
[128] For the draft Covenant on Economic, Social, and Cultural Rights as adopted at this stage *see* UN Doc. A/5929 Annex, 20 UN GAOR, C.3, Annexes (Ag. Item 65), 4–7 (1966).
[129] UN Doc. A/5655, 18 UN GAOR, C.3, Annexes (Ag. Item 48), 14–25 (1963).
[130] For the US proposal *see* A/C.3/SR.1401, at 9–10, paras. 13–14 (1966). It proposed that the reports should be considered by a 'Committee on Economic, Social, and Cultural Rights' consisting of independent experts elected by States parties. It is considered that the independence of the proposed Committee, and the fact it would have drawn on expert individuals from States parties and not ECOSOC as a whole, were matters that recommended the proposal, *see* Alston P., 'The United Nations' Specialized Agencies and Implementation of the International Covenant on Economic, Social and Cultural Rights' (1979) 18 *Columb. J Trans. L* 91.
[131] GA Resn. 2106 (21 Dec. 1965), 20 UN GAOR, Supp. (No. 14) (1965); 660 UNTS 195.

withdrawn before going to the vote. It was specifically recognized nevertheless that the withdrawal of the amendments would not prevent ECOSOC establishing in future 'such other Commissions as may be required for the performance of its functions'.[132] This might include the establishment of such an expert committee if it was considered necessary for the administration of the reporting system.[133]

Following final agreement on the terms of implementation and the adoption of a late amendment to article 11, the text of the International Covenant on Economic, Social, and Cultural Rights was finally completed. Together with the International Covenant on Civil and Political Rights and its Optional Protocol, the Covenant was adopted and opened for signature by the General Assembly on 16 December 1966.[134] It entered into force following the deposit of the 35th instrument of ratification on 3 January 1976.

B The Covenant and its Significance as a Human Rights Guarantee

The text of the Covenant comprises of a preamble and thirty-one articles divided into five parts. The Preamble, which is almost identical to that in the ICCPR, clearly places the Covenant in the context of the UN Charter. It recalls the human rights obligations imposed on States by the Charter, and notes that they form the basis of 'freedom, justice, and peace in the world'. It is implied that the terms of the Covenant form a partial definition of those Charter obligations. The Preamble also attempts to provide an ethical basis for the rights in the Covenant declaring that they are founded in the 'inherent dignity of the human person'. In that vein it also makes note of the duties owed by the individual to other individuals and to the community to which they belong.

Part I of the Covenant, which comprises solely article 1, proclaims the right of all peoples to self-determination including the right freely to pursue their economic, social, and cultural development and freely to dispose of their natural wealth and resources. Part II of the Covenant (articles 2–5), outlines the general clauses that apply to all the substantive provisions in Part III, including clauses relating to general obligations (article 2(1)), non-discrimination (article 2(2)), equal rights for men and women (article 3), and general limitations (articles 4 and 5). It is notable that no provision is made for derogation from the rights in the Covenant in time of public emergency.

Part III (articles 6–15) constitutes the heart of the Covenant, outlining

---

[132] Art. 68 UN Charter.
[133] *Cf*. Rumbos (Venezuela), A/C.3/SR.1399, at 126, para. 12 (1966).
[134] GA Resn. 2200 (XL), (16 Dec. 1966), 21 UN GAOR, Resns. Supp. (No. 16), at 49 (1966).
On the drafting of the ICCPR *see* McGoldrick D., *The Human Rights Committee* (1991), 3–43.

the rights to be protected which include broadly the right to work (article 6), the right to fair conditions of employment (article 7), the right to join and form trade unions (article 8), the right to social security (article 9), the right to protection of the family (article 10), the right to an adequate standard of living (article 11), the right to health (article 12), the right to education (article 13), and the right to culture (article 15).

Part IV of the Covenant outlines the main elements of the system of supervision. Unlike the ICCPR, it does not provide for the receipt of individual or State complaints, but rather envisages a system in which States are required to submit periodic reports to the UN on the measures adopted and the progress made in achieving the observance of the rights in the Covenant. Those reports are then scrutinized by the Economic and Social Council of the UN (ECOSOC) and the Commission on Human Rights. Provision is made for the involvement of the UN specialized agencies who are entitled to submit reports to ECOSOC on the matters falling within the scope of their activities. Part IV also includes a rather tangential saving clause which provides that nothing in the Covenant should be interpreted 'as impairing the inherent right of all peoples to enjoy and utilize fully and freely their natural wealth and resources'. The intention of this provision appears to have been to ensure that developed States did not interfere excessively, by means of the supervision system, in the utilization of natural resources within developing countries.

Part V contains the final provisions relating to the modalities of ratification and entry into force of the Covenant. Under article 26, the Covenant is open for signature by any State member of the UN, members of the specialized agencies, or State party to the Statute of the ICJ. Other States which have been so invited by the UN General Assembly may also become party to the ICESCR. Although a number of reservations or objections have been made to this clause, it no longer appears to be of significance given the broad, and almost universal, membership of the United Nations. Of more significance is article 28, which provides that the provisions of the Covenant extend to all parts of federal States 'without any limitations or exceptions'. In addition, Part V includes article 27 which governs the entry into force of the Covenant, article 29 the process of amendment, and article 31 the authoritative languages.

The ultimate test for the Covenant as a human rights guarantee is the degree to which it can contribute to the international protection of human rights. As at February 1994, it has been ratified or acceded to by 126 States (with relatively few reservations) from all geographical areas representing a range of social, political, and legal systems.[135] Apart from the European Social Charter (ESC),[136] which is limited to the European context, the

---

[135] *See* UN Doc. E/C.12/1994/2.
[136] *See generally* Harris D., *The European Social Charter* (1986), 192–9.

Covenant is the only international human rights instrument that deals extensively with economic, social, and cultural rights. Of the other universal human rights instruments, a number do make reference to economic, social, and cultural rights[137] but generally the range of protection for economic, social, and cultural rights is limited in its scope.

The protection given to economic rights is broad, but general. Article 7, for example, recognizes the right to equal remuneration for work of equal value, rather than just the more restrictive equal pay for equal work. Similarly, article 8 provides not only for the right to join and form trade unions, but also for the right of trade unions to function freely, and the right to strike. However it is with respect to social and cultural rights that the Covenant stands out. In addition to the rights to social security and the protection of the family, it refers to the rights to education, to cultural life, and to health. Indeed, more significantly, it gives specific recognition to the rights to food and housing which do not find comparable enactment elsewhere.

Further, the Covenant, like the ICCPR is notable in that concrete recognition is given to the right of self-determination. The inclusion of a provision on self-determination in both Covenants was secured despite considerable disagreement during the drafting process.[138] The fact that it did not prevent signature or ratification of the Covenant[139] is perhaps only a reflection of the perception that in its 'external form' it was confined to the colonial context.[140] Leaving aside the difficulty of defining a 'people' for the purpose of self-determination,[141] it may be questioned whether the inclusion of a right of 'peoples' in the context of a human rights treaty concerned primarily with the position of individuals was entirely appropriate.[142] It may be rationalized, nevertheless, as a necessary recognition of the context in which the realization of rights within the Covenant is to take place.[143] In that light article 1 of the ICESCR, despite being textually

---

[137] *See above* text accompanying nn. 16–17.

[138] *See generally* Morphet S., 'Article 1 of the Human Rights Covenants: Its Development and Current Significance', in Hill D. (ed.), *Human Rights and Foreign Policy* (1989), 67; Cassese A., 'The Self-Determination of Peoples', in Henkin L. (ed.), *International Bill of Rights* (1981), 92; and 'Political Self-Determination—Old Concepts and New Developments' in Buergenthal T. (ed.), *Human Rights, International Law and the Helsinki Accord* (1979), 137.

[139] On the UK 'understanding' in this respect, *see* Schwelb E., 'The United Kingdom Signs the Covenants on Human Rights' (1969) 18 *ICLO* 457.

[140] This appeared to be the view of the Soviet States at the time, *see* Tunkin G., *Theory of International Law* (1974), 60–9.

[141] *See* Emerson R., 'Self-Determination' (1966) 60 *Proc. Am. Soc. IL* 135, at 136. For conflicting views *see* Chen L.–C., 'Self-Determination as a Human Right' in McDougal H. *et al.* (eds.), *Human Rights and World Public Order* (1986), 198; Falk R., 'The Rights of Peoples' in Crawford J. (ed.), *The Rights of Peoples* (1988), 17.

[142] Sieghart comments that human rights are 'precisely the rights that the individual may invoke against the claims of those who exercise power over him, and which they only too often assert in the name of the people': Sieghart P., *The Lawful Rights of Mankind* (1986), 164.

[143] On such a contextual approach *see* Van Boven T., 'The Relation Between Peoples' Rights and Human Rights in the African Charter' (1986) 7 *HRLJ* 183.

identical to article 1 of the ICCPR, could be construed as giving recognition to a right to economic, rather than political, self-determination. As such, it would have significant parallels with the notion of a 'right to development'.[144]

Of those rights that might be clearly defined as 'economic', 'social', or 'cultural' rights, the only obvious absence from the Covenant is the right to property. A draft article based upon article 17 of the Universal Declaration of Human Rights had been put forward for inclusion in the Covenant[145] but disagreement over the issues of expropriation and compensation meant that agreement upon a text was never possible.[146] Further unsuccessful proposals that were also briefly considered include the rights to water and transport.[147] A more significant failing of the Covenant, especially when compared with the ESC, is that it does not identify those groups which might be considered to need special protection. Specific reference is only made to the position of women and children. Ideally, one might have hoped that mention would be made to the position of aliens, migrant workers,[148] the elderly,[149] and those with physical or mental disabilities.[150] However, it would be wrong to suppose that the Covenant fails to offer any protection in that respect. The rights to which the Covenant refers are the rights of 'everyone'; the only limit *ratione personae* is to be found in article 2(3) which permits 'developing States' to determine the extent to which they would guarantee the economic rights to non-nationals. In any case, it is arguable that the particular concerns of these groups may best be dealt with by specific international instruments that address the issues in detail.

While the Covenant benefits from an impressive scope, it suffers from the excessive generality of its terms even when compared with the ESC. For example, whereas the ESC has three articles dealing with the right to social security,[151] the Covenant merely has the briefest of statements.[152] The amount of detail to be included in the provisions of the Covenant was the subject of much debate in the drafting of the Covenant. Although it was noted that more general wording could leave the way open to conflicting and subjective interpretations,[153] generally phrased provisions were often

---

[144] Declaration on the Right to Development 41/128; 41 UN GAOR; Resns, Supp. (No. 53), at 186 (1986).

[145] Proposal of the US: UN Doc. E/CN.4/L.313 (1949).

[146] Although the constituent parts of the Sub-Committee proposal were agreed upon, the text as a whole was rejected by 7 votes to 6 with 5 abstentions.

[147] *See above* Ch. 8, text accompanying nn. 40–50.

[148] Cf. Art. 19, European Social Charter.

[149] It was argued during the drafting of art. 9 that the rights of the elderly should be provided for in a separate convention. *See e.g.* Mehta (India), E/CN.4/SR.282, at 10 (1952).

[150] *Cf.* Art. 15, European Social Charter.

[151] The European Social Charter provides for the right to social security (art. 12), the right to social and medical assistance (art. 13), and the right to benefit from social welfare services (art. 14).

[152] Art. 10.   [153] *See e.g.* Shoham-Sharon (Israel), A/C.3/SR.728, at 235, para. 1 (1957).

preferred in order to avoid restricting the scope of the articles[154] and preventing conflict with the standards established by the specialized agencies (particularly the ILO).[155]

The generality and breadth of the Covenant's terms could be said to contribute to its longevity by providing scope for a dynamic interpretation of its provisions. Nevertheless, it does place a heavy burden on the supervisory body whose central role inevitably becomes one of developing and defining the content of the norms. Although the drafters clearly envisaged a continuing process of standard–setting (whether under the auspices of the ILO or otherwise[156]), the fact that this must take place after ratification leaves the way open to conflicts in interpretation that might ultimately undermine the implementation process as a whole. The degree to which this may be avoided ultimately depends upon the skill and commitment of the supervisory body.

Similar comments may be made as regards the level of protection afforded by the Covenant. Unlike the ICCPR which requires States to 'respect and ensure' the rights recognized,[157] article 2(1) of the ICESCR merely obliges States 'to take steps . . . with a view to achieving progressively the full realization of the rights'.[158] The terms of article 2(1) reflect the belief held during the drafting of the Covenant that the implementation of economic, social, and cultural rights could only be undertaken progressively, as full and immediate realization of all the rights was beyond the resources of many States. It may, nevertheless, be criticized not only for allowing States excessive leeway in the implementation of their obligations, but it also fails to take into account those provisions that may be implemented immediately.

The protection afforded by the terms of the Covenant is also undermined, to some extent, by textual inconsistencies and the lack of clarity in a number of its provisions. Three examples serve to illustrate this point. First, in terms of the reach of article 2(1), it only appears to operate with respect to the rights 'recognized' in the Covenant. While the majority of articles begin with the phrase 'The States Parties . . . recognize the right of everyone', articles 3 and 8 use the term 'ensure', and articles 13(3) and 15(3) use the term 'respect'. Similarly, there is no reference to rights at all in article 10 or 14. It is open to interpretation whether the general terms of article 2(1) apply with respect to those provisions. Secondly, the Covenant, unlike other international human rights instruments, possesses no dero-

---

[154] *See e.g.* opposition to the proposal to include a partial definition of art. 9, Simarsian (USA), E/CN.4/SR.282, at 13 (1952); Juvigny (France), *ibid.*

[155] *See e.g.* Elliot (UK), A/C.3/SR.710, at 143, para. 26 (1956); *see also* Pickford (ILO), E/CN.4/SR.282, at 8 (1952).

[156] This is indicated in particular by the inclusion of art. 8(3) which refers to ILO Convention No. 87.

[157] Art. 2(1) ICCPR.   [158] Art. 2(1) ICESCR.

gation provision. It appears that the drafters perceived article 2(1) to be sufficiently flexible to dispense with the necessity of a derogation clause. However, lack of a derogation clause does lead to the possibility of inconsistencies arising where, for example, a State may legitimately derogate from its obligation to ensure the right to join and form trade unions (article 22 of the ICCPR) by virtue of article 4 of the ICCPR, but may not do so under the terms of the ICESCR. Finally, article 8(3) which makes reference to the guarantees laid down in ILO Convention No. 87, introduces confusion into the protection offered by the Covenant by creating different levels of obligation. For those States parties that are also party to the ILO Convention, article 8 has to be read as embodying, as a minimum, the standards of that Convention. For the rest, the terms of article 8 stand on their own and therefore might be deemed to have a significantly different interpretation.

While none of these matters poses insuperable problems, they could potentially affect the significance or effectiveness of the guarantee in so far as they provide scope for conflicts over matters of interpretation to arise. As suggested above, this ultimately places considerable emphasis upon the role of the body charged with supervising the implementation of the Covenant. As far as the text of the Covenant is concerned, the position is not promising. There is no single body which clearly has central responsibility for supervision; no body has the ability to interpret the Covenant in a manner that binds States parties; the implementation of the Covenant is by means of State reports which only provide for a general and unfocused means of supervision. The position is quite different in practice, however; the Committee on Economic, Social, and Cultural Rights, as this study will show, has developed its procedures and practices in an innovative and dynamic manner such that it now stands out among the international human rights committees.

Although the work of the Committee is undoubtedly central to the development of the Covenant and its status in the international community, the significance of the Covenant to individuals within States is more likely to be affected by the terms of domestic law and the availability of local remedies. In this dimension, the ability of individuals to rely upon the terms of the Covenant in domestic court proceedings is of vital importance.[159] Generally, in order for the Covenant to have 'direct applicability', it either has to be positively adopted (whether automatically or by incorporation) into domestic law or form part of domestic law by virtue of expressing rules of customary international law.[160]

---

[159] *See generally* Craven M., 'The Domestic Application of the International Covenant on Economic, Social and Cultural Rights' (1993) 40 *Neth. ILR* 367.

[160] *See* Sørensen M., 'Obligations of a State Party to a Treaty as Regards Municipal Law', in Robertson A. (ed.), *Human Rights in National and International Law* (1968), 11.

As far as the former is concerned, the Covenant does form part of domestic law in a number of States.[161] However, there is precious little evidence of its being relied upon in domestic legal procedings let alone providing a cause of action. For the most part, this is a result of the widespread perception that economic, social, and cultural rights are not 'justiciable' and therefore not suitable for or capable of being invoked by domestic courts.[162] To speak of economic, social, and cultural rights as being non-justiciable *per se* is to suffer under a general misconception. The question whether a court has jurisdiction to consider a particular issue depends not only upon the nature of the issue itself, but upon an understanding of the constitutional role and function of the court concerned; this may, and indeed does, vary from State to State. Certainly, some courts are not in a position to dictate on issues of central government expenditure, but it is wrong to assume that the only dimension of economic, social, and cultural rights is to embody claims to financial resources. As suggested above, each right also embodies a duty of non-interference: the right to housing, for example, includes a right not to be arbitrarily evicted from one's home. Such elements are ideally suited to judicial determination in most countries.

The second manner in which the Covenant could have significance in domestic law is if its terms were considered to be expressive of rules of customary international law.[163] This is of great significance not merely because it would provide a basis for judicial scrutiny but because it would also bind States that are not formally party to the Covenant. Although claims are frequently made as to the status of the UDHR as a whole (including a number of economic, social, and cultural rights) being expressive of customary international law,[164] they would appear to exaggerate the position.[165] It is arguable that certain international labour standards have become part of general international law in the form of 'general principles of law recognized by civilized nations',[166] but for the most part the

---

[161] *See e.g.* Afghanistan, E/C.12/1991/SR.4, at 4, para. 21; Costa Rica, E/C.12/1990/SR.38, at 15, para. 85; Ecuador, E/C.12/1990/SR.39, at 2, para. 6; Luxembourg, E/C.12/1990/SR.33, at 8, para. 29.

[162] *See e.g. The State of the Netherlands* v. *LSVB [The National Union of Students]*, Sup. Ct., 14 Apr. 1989, AB (1989), *cited in* (1990) 21 *Neth. Yrbk. IL* 369; *D. Hoogenraad* v. *Organization for Pure Research in the Netherlands*, Sup. Ct., 20 Apr. 1990, (1990) Rvdw No. 88, *cited in* (1991) 22 *Neth. Yrbk. IL* 376. *See generally* Van Dijk P., 'Domestic Status of Human Rights Treaties and the Attitude of the Judiciary—The Dutch Case', in Nowak M. *et al.* (eds.), *Progress in the Spirit of Human Rights* (1988), 634.

[163] *See* Cassese A., 'Modern Constitutions and International Law' (1985) 192 *Hague Recueil* 335, at 368–70.

[164] *See e.g.* Sohn L., 'The New International Law: Protection of the Rights of Individuals Rather than States' (1982) 32 *Am. Uni. L Rev.* 1.

[165] *See* Alston P., 'Labour Rights Provisions in US Trade Law: "Agressive Unilateralism"?' (1993) 15 *Hum. Rts. Q* 1, at 13.

[166] *See* Meron T., *Human Rights and Humanitarian Norms as Customary Law* (1989), 98.

norms within the Covenant remain binding only as regards States parties. This is only likely to change if national and international bodies adopt a more considered and principled approach to economic, social, and cultural rights.

2

The System of Supervision

I. INTRODUCTION

As Sieghart pointed out, the concept of a human rights treaty is something of an anomaly.[1] In accordance with the horizontal nature of international law[2] the large majority of treaties contain reciprocal obligations under which compliance by one State party is a condition for another State party to be bound by the terms of the treaty in their relations *inter se*.[3] Human rights treaties, however, are not premised upon the mutuality of State obligations; rather, they are intended to create a legal order in which States make binding unilateral commitments to protect the basic rights of all individuals within their jurisdiction. As was noted by the European Court of Human Rights, the European Convention (as a human rights treaty):

comprises more than mere reciprocal engagements between contracting States. It creates, over above a network of mutual bilateral undertakings, objective obligations which . . . benefit from a 'collective enforcement'.[4]

Although it is possible to identify reciprocal State interests in ensuring the enjoyment of human rights, not least in so far as they contribute to international peace and security,[5] the fact that human rights treaties essentially entail unilateral commitments means that other States parties cannot be relied upon to ensure compliance.[6] The institution of international super-

---

[1] Sieghart P., *The Lawful Rights of Mankind* (1986), 92–3.

[2] Henkin L., 'The International Bill of Rights: The Universal Declaration and the Covenants', in Bernhardt R. and Jolowicz J. (eds.), *International Enforcement of Human Rights* (1985), 1, at 8.

[3] Brierly J., *The Law of Nations* (6th ed., 1963), 62; Morgenthau H., *Politics among Nations* (5th ed., 1973), 290.

[4] *Ireland* v. *United Kingdom*, Eur. Ct. HR, Series A, Vol. 25, judgment of 18 Jan. 1978, 2 EHRR 25.

[5] *Cf.* Preamble, UDHR.

[6] The fact that inter-State complaints systems have rarely been utilized is testament to the lack of commitment on the part of States to concern themselves with the human rights situation in other States. Henkin explains: 'While in legal principle every state party is a promisee and entitled to request compliance by any other state party, ordinarily no other state has any interest in doing so and is especially reluctant to demand compliance or threaten sanctions for violation at the expense of its friendly relations and diplomatic capital': Henkin, *supra*, n. 2, at 8. *Cf.* Bilder R., 'Rethinking International Human Rights: Some Basic Questions' (1969) 2 *Hum. Rts. J* 557, at 569–74. Leary recognizes: 'Reciprocity has traditionally been the most important enforcement mechanism in international law. It fails to function, however, when States do not perceive their own immediate interests as threatened by another State's non-compliance with international law': Leary V., *International Labour Conventions and National Law* (1982), 17.

visory mechanisms through the creation of human rights committees has become the accepted form of effecting compliance with human rights treaty obligations.

At a superficial level the main function of such supervisory bodies is to ensure compliance with the relevant treaty obligations. What this entails and how it is to be achieved, however, requires more consideration.[7] Three basic functions of the supervisory process in relation to human rights may be identified. First, clarifying and developing the standards that are to be applied. Secondly, assessing the degree to which States parties are actually acting in conformity with their obligations. Thirdly, taking either remedial or preventive action to ensure compliance. These have been termed respectively the 'creative', the 'review', and the 'correction' functions of supervision.[8] The degree to which emphasis is given to each of these functions and the method by which they are exercised varies according to the type of system of supervision.

Two main forms of supervisory (or implementation) systems exist on the international plane: the reporting system and the petition system. Each of these is thought to have its own theoretical and practical basis. Reporting systems, being the most common[9] and least politically sensitive method of supervision,[10] require States to submit periodic reports on the domestic implementation of the rights within the treaty concerned. Generally, the reports are considered by a supervisory body entitled to review them and make general recommendations.

Reporting systems are dependant, to a large extent, upon the good faith of the States concerned.[11] They are reliant upon the provision of accurate and relevant information by States parties and the supervisory body is mandated purely with the function of assisting and advising the States parties. Reporting systems are therefore considered as

[7] *Cf.* Alston P., 'Appraising the United Nations Human Rights Regime' in Alston P. (ed.), *The United Nations and Human Rights: A Critical Appraisal* (1992), at 1.

[8] Van Dijk P. and Rood J., 'Function and Effectiveness of Supervision in an Economically Interdependent World' in Van Dijk P. *et al.* (eds.), *Restructuring the International Economic Order: The Role of Law and Lawyers* (1987), 135, at 144.

[9] Currently there are 7 universal human rights instruments that impose reporting obligations: the International Convention on the Elimination of All Forms of Racial Discrimination (1965), the International Convention on the Elimination of All Forms of Discrimination Against Women (1979), the International Covenant on Civil and Political Rights (1966), the International Covenant on Economic, Social, and Cultural Rights (1966), the Convention on the Suppression and Punishment of the Crime of Apartheid (1973), the UN Convention Against Torture and Other Cruel, Inhuman, or Degrading Treatment or Punishment (1984), the International Convention on the Rights of the Child (1989), and the International Convention on the Protection of the Rights of Migrant Workers and Members of their Families. In addition, the ILO, UNESCO, and the WHO all have periodic reporting provisions on matters that relate to human rights.

[10] Buergenthal T., 'Implementing the UN Racial Convention' (1977) 12 *Tex. ILJ* 187, at 189.

[11] Schoenberg H., 'The Implementation of Human Rights by the United Nations' (1977) 7 *Isr. YHR* 22, at 37.

mechanisms for fact finding[12] and more specifically the 'verification'[13] or the 'promotion' of human rights in contrast to the protective functions of a petition system.[14] Such a comparison has led many commentators to criticize reporting systems as being 'state centred',[15] 'ineffective',[16] and 'self-contradictory'.[17]

Petition systems, on the other hand, are generally considered the most effective means for the protection of human rights. They involve the receipt of communications from individuals or States parties[18] alleging violations of the treaty concerned.[19] The supervisory body takes on a 'quasi-judicial' function[20] in interpreting the convention and making decisions or recommendations on the merits of each case. As regards the individual com-

[12] Lippman M., 'Human Rights Revisited: The Protection of Human Rights Under the International Covenant on Civil and Political Rights' (1980) 10 *Cal. West ILJ* 450, at 486–7; Vasak comments more specifically that reporting systems fall half way between the functions of information and investigation: Vasak K., 'The Distinguishing Criteria of Institutions' in Vasak K. and Alston P. (eds.), *The International Dimensions of Human Rights* (1982), 215, at 218.

[13] Tumanov V., 'International Protection of Human Rights: Soviet Report' in Bernhardt R. and Jolowicz J. (eds.), *International Enforcement of Human Rights* (1985), 21, at 23.

[14] For a definition of the two opposed functions *see* Vasak, *supra*, n. 12, at 216.

[15] Mower A., 'The Implementation of the UN Covenant on Civil and Political Rights' (1977) 10 *Hum. Rts. J* 271, at 285; Capotorti F., 'The International Measures of Implementation Included in the Covenants on Human Rights', in Eide A. and Schou A. (eds.), *International Protection of Human Rights* (1968), 131, at 147.

[16] Schoenberg, *supra*, n. 11, at 37.

[17] Vasak considers that the lack of a court gives the process a conciliatory character which 'suggests that, despite their sacred and inviolable nature, human rights can be "negotiated" ': Vasak, *supra*, n. 12, at 220.

[18] The inter-State complaints facility is not as effective, probably as a result of the unwillingness of States to sacrifice their good relations with other States for the sake of human rights. Leary, *supra*, n. 6, at 17. *See generally* Leckie S., 'The Inter-State Complaint Procedure in International Human Rights Law: Hopeful Prospects or Wishful Thinking?' (1988) 10 *Hum. Rts. Q* 249.

[19] The main universal human rights treaties that possess petition systems are: the International Covenant on Civil and Political Rights (under its Optional Protocol); the UN Convention Against Torture and Other Forms of Cruel, Inhuman, and Degrading Treatment (art. 22); the International Convention on the Elimination of All Forms of Racial Discrimination (art. 14); the Apartheid Convention; and the Convention on the Rights of Migrant Workers and Their Families (art. 77). As regards petition systems in general *see* Cancado Trinidade A., 'Co-existence and Co-ordination of Mechanisms of International Protection of Human Rights' (1987) 202 *Hague Recueila*; Tardu M., *Human Rights: The International Petition System* (1985).

[20] There might be objections to the use of the term 'quasi-judicial' as it was never the intention for any of the UN human rights monitoring bodies to be considered 'courts'. It has been commented that the Human Rights Committee, when operating under its Optional Protocol, is 'neither a court nor a body with a quasi-judicial mandate'. However it is admitted that it does perform functions similar to those of the European Commission of Human Rights and 'applies the provisions of the Covenant and Optional Protocol in a judicial spirit': de Zayas A., Möller J., and Opsahl T., 'Application of the International Covenant on Civil and Political Rights under the Optional Protocol by the Human Rights Committee' (1985) 28 *Ger. Yrbk. IL* 9, at 11. It is considered, however, that the CESCR has begun to exercise quasi-judicial functions in the context of the reporting system. *See below* text accompanying nn. 176–83.

plaints system, which is generally optional for States parties,[21] the procedure may also be seen to provide the victim of a violation with an international 'remedy' where a domestic remedy is unforthcoming. Although the supervisory body may not necessarily have the power to enforce its decision, this will not always be decisive as to its impact.[22]

It is often assumed, probably as a result of over-simplified analogies with domestic law, that the only really effective mechanism for supervision is the petition procedure. However, when analysed in terms of the essential functions of a supervision, such a conclusion is not beyond doubt. First, in terms of the review function, whereas the petition procedure allows for an in-depth analysis of particular situations, it cannot compare with the breadth and scale of action that takes place under the various reporting mechanisms. It has been noted that even in those cases where petition systems are operative, the reporting system has formed the mainstay of supervision[23] in providing an essential form of continuous monitoring. This is partly due to the limited number of States that have agreed to be bound by the petition systems (which are generally optional), but also because the specific procedures for the receipt and consideration of complaints (including extensive admissibility criteria[24]), mean that they are not always readily accessible to the disadvantaged who might be the victims of violations.[25]

Secondly, in terms of the correction function, both systems ultimately depend for their effectiveness upon the force of national and international pressure. Petition procedures are generally accompanied by greater public

[21] However the American Convention on Human Rights (1969), 1144 UNTS 123, has a compulsory individual petition procedure (art. 44).

[22] For changes in the domestic situation related to the work of the Human Rights Committee, *see* Report of the Human Rights Committee, 45 UN GAOR, Supp. (No. 40), Vol. II, Annex XII, at 207–11 (1990); Cohn C., 'The Early Harvest: Domestic Legal Changes Related to the Human Rights Committee and the Covenant on Civil and Political Rights, (1991) 13 *Hum. Rts. Q* 295.

[23] *See generally* Fischer D., 'International Reporting Procedures', in Hannum H. (ed.), *Guide to International Human Rights Practice*, (1984), 165. Such a point has been noted by Robertson with regard to the ICCPR: Robertson A., 'The Implementation System: International Measures', in Henkin L. (ed.), *The International Bill of Rights* (1981), 332, at 341. *See also* with respect to the ILO, Leary, *supra*, n. 6, at 18.

[24] For the operation of the Optional Protocol of the ICCPR in particular, *see* McGoldrick D., *The Human Rights Committee* (1991), 120–246; Ghandi P., 'The Human Rights Committee and the Right of Individual Petition' (1986) 57 *BYIL* 201; Prounis O., 'The Human Rights Committee: Toward Resolving the Paradox of Human Rights Law' (1985/6) 17 *Col. HRLR* 103; Brar P., 'The Practice and Procedures of the Human Rights Committee Under the Optional Protocol of the International Convention on Civil and Political Rights' (1985) 25 *Ind. JIL* 506; de Zayas A. *et al.*, *supra*, n. 20.

[25] Alston cites in particular: (i) ignorance of the existence of an applicable international procedure; (ii) a lack of time and/or resources; (iii) the physical impossibility of lodging a complaint; (iv) the difficulty of demonstrating sufficient individual, as opposed to general community, standing to justify lodging a complaint; and (v) the assumption that the international body in question is unlikely to stand in favour of the victim in a given situation. Alston P., 'Discussion Note', UN Doc. E/C.12/1991/WP.2, at 8, para. 26 (1991).

interest and therefore could be said to be more effective in 'the mobilization of shame'. However, it cannot be maintained that the principal objective is to condemn and alienate States.[26] Supervisory bodies may play a much more constructive role in assessing the situation and advising countries as to possible remedial action.[27] Indeed petition procedures themselves require a certain amount of co-operation from States parties that might disintegrate if it were thought that the burdens of participation outweighed the benefits.

Additionally, it is often easy to overlook the importance of the promotional or preventive aspects of implementation. This has been most clearly pointed out by the Committee in its General Comment No. 1 of 1989.[28] According to the Committee, the reporting process has a number of objectives at its heart, namely that the State concerned should undertake to monitor and evaluate its own performance by conducting a thorough review of the degree to which the rights are enjoyed by all sections of the population. In doing so it should stimulate public scrutiny of government policy in the areas concerned and pinpoint difficulties and shortcomings in the existing arrangements. Higgins remarks, in this regard, that the reporting process can be a very 'salutary exercise' for States in which failure to comply with substantive obligations is often 'inadvertent'.[29] Such considerations support the idea that reporting systems should form the basis of any supervisory mechanism, to be supplemented by petition systems where possible and appropriate. Accordingly, the 'promotion' of human rights could be said to be 'the first, and the necessary, stage leading to protection'.[30]

Finally, in terms of the creative function of supervision, it is clear that petition systems are particularly effective mechanisms for the elaboration of standards for application in specific cases. In comparison, the process of reviewing State reports does not give rise to similar opportunities for the specification of the norms in the treaty concerned. There has been a tendency, however, among supervisory bodies to adopt a distinct interpretative role in the guise of 'general comments'. Although still lacking in the specificity offered by a petition system the use of General Comments does give the supervisory body an opportunity to develop a general understanding of the norms within the treaty concerned.

[26] As Mower commented: 'The cardinal objective is to gain, for individuals and groups, the most complete enjoyment of rights which can possibly be obtained, not to find and punish 'criminal' governments': Mower, *supra*, n. 15, at 285.

[27] *See* Gaer F., 'First Fruits: Reporting by States under the African Charter on Human and Peoples' Rights' (1992) 10 *NQHR* 29, at 31.

[28] General Comment No. 1, UN ESCOR, Supp. (No. 4), Annex III, at 87–9, UN Doc. E/1989/22 (1989).

[29] Higgins R., 'Some Thoughts on the Implementation of Human Rights' (1989) *Bull. HR* 60, at 63.

[30] *Ibid. See also* Vasak who comments: 'If an international body for the promotion of human rights is successful, it cannot help but assume the task of protection': Vasak, *supra*, n. 12, at 218.

II. BACKGROUND TO THE COMMITTEE'S ESTABLISHMENT

A The Drafting of the Implementation System

During the drafting of the Covenant, there was considerable disagreement as to the nature of the implementation procedure that should accompany the substantive articles. At one stage or another, three forms of supervision were mooted: the possibility of supervision through a petition procedure; supervision by the specialized agencies; and supervision by an expert committee specifically set up for that purpose.[31]

1 A Petition Procedure

Despite the fact that the draft Covenant was divided into two separate texts over the question of implementation,[32] the discussion over whether the Human Rights Committee procedure should apply to economic, social, and cultural rights continued. Two proposals were submitted at the Commission's tenth session for the application of such a procedure to selective economic, social, and cultural rights in specific circumstances.[33] It was argued that certain rights could be subjected to the Human Rights Committee procedure immediately and others as and when they 'become enforceable'.[34] Accordingly it was proposed that States should have the option to accept the jurisdiction of the Human Rights Committee of the ICCPR with respect to certain economic, social, and cultural rights. In cases where there was an overlap in competence with the specialized agencies the Committee would defer to the authority of the agency concerned.[35]

However doubts were expressed about the capability of the Committee to exercise its quasi-judicial functions with regard to rights that were of a programmatic nature.[36] The suggestions were opposed by the specialized agencies in particular, who considered that such a procedure would only

---

[31] *See also* Alston P., 'Out of the Abyss: The Challenges Confronting the New U.N. Committee on Economic, Social and Cultural Rights' (1987) 9 *Hum. Rts. Q* 332, at 335–40 (henceforth 'Abyss'); and 'The Committee on Economic, Social and Cultural Rights', in Alston P. (ed.), *The United Nations and Human Rights: A Critical Appraisal* (1992), 473, at 475–9.

[32] *See above* Ch. 1, text accompanying nn. 80–127.

[33] For the French proposal *see* UN Doc. E/CN.4/L.338, 18 ESCOR, Supp. (No. 7), UN Doc. E/2573, para. 216 (1954). It was suggested that the States parties might be given the opportunity of accepting the Human Rights Committee's complaints procedure for specific economic, social, or cultural rights as they so desired. Such a procedure would be subject to reciprocal agreement by the States concerned.

[34] *Ibid.* 124, para. 42.   [35] *Ibid.* 124, paras. 42–5.

[36] Not only was it considered that there was a lack of criteria to evaluate state compliance, it was argued that: 'Complaints relating to that covenant could only refer to insufficient programmes in the attainment of certain goals and it would be impossible for the committee to determine what the rate of progress in any particular case should be': UN Doc. A/2929, 10 UN GAOR, C.3, Annexes (Ag. Item 28), Pt. II, at 124, para. 41 (1955).

lead to duplication of work and that in any case they were technically better qualified to implement economic, social, and cultural rights.[37] In the face of such opposition the suggestions were withdrawn before being taken to vote.

2 The Specialized Agencies

Being somewhat jealous of its technical and formal jurisdiction the ILO proposed the creation of an implementation system in which the ILO itself would review the State reports.[38] Ultimately this was rejected in favour of a Secretariat draft proposing the submission of periodic State reports to the United Nations with reference of relevant extracts to the specialized agencies.[39]

Although the co-operation of the specialized agencies is clearly of considerable importance,[40] in terms of their knowledge and technical expertise, to the implementation of the Covenant, it would have been inappropriate for one of them to take on the central supervisory role. First, as not all States parties are members of the relevant specialized agencies, the UN would still have to develop its capabilities in those areas. Secondly, a divergence both in standards and implementation systems would emerge between members and non-members of the competent specialized agencies. This would undermine both the universality of the rights and the reciprocity of obligations with the Covenant. Thirdly, and most importantly, no single specialized agency could competently undertake supervisory duties with respect to the whole of the Covenant without extending its existing mandate.

3 An Expert Committee

Following earlier unsuccessful proposals to create a specialized Committee to supervise the implementation of economic, social, and cultural rights,[41] two last-minute proposals were made in 1966. On the one hand, the USA proposed the establishment of a committee of independent experts to oversee the implementation similar to the model created for the Convention on the Elimination of all Forms of Racial Discrimination.[42] Simultaneously,

---

[37] UN Doc. A/2929, 124, para. 40.   [38] UN Doc. E/CN.4/AC.14/1 (1951).

[39] The Secretariat plan for implementation was inspired by the technical assistance programme and 'the idea that it was better to help governments to fulfil their obligations than to penalise them for violations': Humphrey J., *Human Rights and the United Nations—A Great Adventure* (1984), at 143.

[40] *See generally* Alston P., 'The UN Specialised Agencies and Implementation of the International Covenant on Economic, Social and Cultural Rights' (1979) 18 *Colum. J Trans. L* 79; Samson K., 'Human Rights Co-ordination within the UN System' in Alston P. (ed.), *The United Nations and Human Rights: A Critical Appraisal* (1992), 620, at 629–30.

[41] *See* Alston (Abyss), *supra*, n. 31, at 355–8.

[42] A/C.3/L.1360, para. 1., *in* UN Doc. A/6546, 21 UN GAOR, C.3, Annexes (Ag. Item 62) at 10, paras. 13–14 (1966). It proposed that the reports should be considered by a 'Committee

Italy proposed the creation of *ad hoc* committees elected by ECOSOC.[43] Both proposals were based upon the premise that ECOSOC would not have the time or the expertise to examine the reports adequately[44] and would not properly represent the States parties.[45] However, the suggestions were withdrawn at the General Assembly Third Committee's 1401st meeting when it became apparent that there was insufficient support.[46]

In the light of the discussion within the Third Committee it is clear that some form of compromise solution could have been achieved. The fact that no attempt was made at compromise was a reflection of the political situation at that time. In 1966, the Socialist States were still suspicious of any international means of implementation, the African States were disillusioned with 'expert bodies' in the light of the ICJ's recent decision in the *South West Africa Cases*,[47] and the Western States had little political interest in economic, social, and cultural rights. Essentially there was no 'champion' to push for strong implementation procedures for the draft Covenant on Economic, Social, and Cultural Rights.

However, the rejection of the proposals did not necessarily rule out the possibility of the subsequent creation of an expert committee. Schwelb comments:

It appears, however, that the fact that the Italian amendment was withdrawn would not prevent the Council, which is the master of its own procedure (Art. 72 of the Charter) and which is empowered to set up 'such other commissions as may be required for the performance of its functions' (Art. 68 of the Charter) from establishing a subsidiary body to study and report to it on the information transmitted by governments under the Covenant.[48]

Although there was insufficient political will to endorse the creation of an expert committee in 1966, it was clear that 'the door was not irretrievably closed'.[49]

4 The Result

The final intentions of the drafters as regards the provisions on implementation are quite obscure. States parties are required to submit reports 'in

on Economic, Social, and Cultural Rights' consisting of independent experts elected by States parties. It is considered that the independence of the proposed committee and the fact it would have drawn on expert individuals from States parties rather than ECOSOC, were matters that recommended the proposal, see Alston, *supra*, n. 40, at 91–2.

[43] *Ibid.* 11, paras. 18 and 24.
[44] *See e.g.* MacDonald (Canada), UN Doc. A/C.3/SR.1399, at 128, para. 28 (1966).
[45] *See e.g.* Capotorti (Italy), UN Doc. A/C.3/SR.1397, at 120, para. 32 (1966).
[46] UN Doc. A/C.3/SR.1401, para. 19; *ibid.* para. 21.   [47] [1966] *ICJ Rep.* 6.
[48] Schwelb E., 'Some Aspects of the Measures of Implementation of the International Covenant on Economic, Social and Cultural Rights' (1968) 1 *HRJ* 363, at 367. In particular *see e.g.* Mr Richardson (Jamaica), A/C.3/SR.1401, at 142, para. 26 (1966).
[49] Alston, *supra*, n. 31, at 479.

stages', in accordance with a programme to be established by ECOSOC after consultation with the States parties and the specialized agencies concerned.[50] The reports should indicate the 'measures . . . adopted' and the 'progress made' in achieving observance of the rights within the covenant.[51] They may additionally indicate the factors and difficulties affecting the degree of fulfilment of the obligations.[52] Such reports are to be submitted to the Secretary-General, who is required to transmit copies of them to ECOSOC 'for consideration',[53] and copies of their relevant parts to the specialized agencies in so far as they relate to their responsibilities.[54] Where information has already been submitted to a specialized agency it is sufficient to refer thereto.[55] Arrangements may be made for the specialized agencies to report to ECOSOC on the progress made in achieving the observance of the rights within the Covenant including particulars of relevant decisions and recommendations adopted by their competent organs.[56] ECOSOC may also transmit the State reports to the Commission on Human Rights 'for study and general recommendations or, as appropriate, for information'.[57] Any such recommendation submitted by the Commission is open to comment by the specialized agencies and the States parties.[58]

Finally ECOSOC may submit 'from time to time' to the General Assembly reports and recommendations 'of a general nature', together with a summary of the information received from the States parties and the specialized agencies.[59] It may also bring to the attention of other organs of the UN or specialized agencies concerned with furnishing technical assistance any matters that may help those bodies decide what measures are likely to contribute to the effective progressive implementation of the Covenant.[60]

The system outlined in the Covenant is thus unclear as to the nature, purpose, or degree of supervision to be given and as to the extent to which the bodies mentioned should involve themselves. First although ECOSOC is mandated with the 'consideration' of the State reports, the Commission on Human Rights may similarly 'study' the reports and make general recommendations. It is not clear on the face of it which body has the primary responsibility for undertaking supervision. Given that the Commission is a subsidiary body of ECOSOC it might be assumed that it would play the most significant role.

Secondly, although many assumptions may be made about the nature of reporting systems generally, the Covenant itself only provides for the submission of reports and their consideration. The periodicity, form, and specific content of those reports are left open, as is the nature of the

---

[50] Art. 17(1).   [51] Art. 16(1).   [52] Art. 17(2).   [53] Art. 16(2)(a).
[54] Art. 16(2)(b).   [55] Art. 17(3).   [56] Art. 18.   [57] Art. 19.   [58] Art. 20.
[59] Art. 21.   [60] Art. 22.

consideration undertaken. The most significant limitation however is that States parties are only obliged to submit reports on the measures adopted and the progress made in achieving observance of the rights; any further participation in the consideration of the reports is purely voluntary. Moreover, ECOSOC may only submit recommendations to the General Assembly; it is in no way empowered to make decisions binding on States parties.

B The Sessional Working Group

As noted above, ECOSOC has considerable discretion in the conduct undertaken in the consideration of reports.[61] Accordingly, following the entry into force of the Covenant on Economic, Social, and Cultural Rights on 3 January 1976, ECOSOC undertook to consider the best means to supervise its implementation. Although there appears to have been considerable support for the idea that the Commission take on a central role in the supervisory process,[62] the Council adopted an alternative strategy.

In Resolution 1988 (LX) of 11 May 1976 ECOSOC laid down the implementation procedures that were to accompany the Covenant. It created a three-stage, biennial reporting process with a cycle of six years. For the first stage States would be required to submit reports on the rights covered by articles 6 to 9. Two years later, States would be required to report on articles 10 to 12, and two years following that on articles 13 to 15. The reports were to be forwarded by the Secretary-General to ECOSOC which would be 'assisted' in its consideration of the reports by a sessional working group (the Working Group). The specialized agencies were also to receive the State reports as appropriate and could submit their own reports in response and have representatives take part in the proceedings of the Working Group.[63]

---

[61] As Sohn commented: 'The Covenant does not specifically foresee the establishment of a specialist Working Group charged with responsibility for scrutinising reports submitted by the States Parties and the specialised agencies. That responsibility is vested in the Council itself which, in turn, must exercise its own discretion as to the most appropriate arrangements for ensuring effective supervision': Sohn L., 'The Role of the United Nations Organs in Implementing the International Covenant on Economic, Social and Cultural Rights', Background Paper (1985), at 39–40.

[62] *See* Alston, *supra*, n. 31, at 483. He comments: 'The Commission's already overcrowded agenda, its reluctance to take economic, social and cultural rights very seriously, and the undoubted need for specialist expertise in monitoring such rights would all seem to confirm the wisdom of that approach now that a committee of independent experts has been given the principal responsibility'.

[63] See ECOSOC Resn. 1988 (LX), 11 May 1976, *found in* UN Doc. E/C.12/1989/4, at 3 (1988). *See generally* Ramcharan B., 'Implementing the International Covenants on Human Rights' in Ramcharan B. (ed.), *Human Rights: Thirty Years After the Universal Declaration* (1978), 159, at 163–5.

The initial plans for a sessional working group were criticized for having insufficient provision for the consideration of the reports by persons of the requisite expertise[64] and for making no provision for enlisting the services of the Commission on Human Rights.[65] Notwithstanding such objections ECOSOC formally created the 'sessional working group' in Decision 1978/10 of 3 May 1978.[66] Much of the discussion that preceded the decision was concerned with the composition and membership of the working group while its actual role in the consideration of the reports was left unclear.[67] The rather haphazard way the working group began was indicative of how it continued.[68] Following a review of its operation, it was renamed the sessional working group of governmental experts and its members were elected for three years from nominees put forward by States parties to the Covenant. The change did not seem to have any significant effect on the work that the group produced. The barrage of criticism that has been directed at the working group in both its forms can be summarized as follows:

(a) The examination of reports was superficial.[69] In particular it was marked by poor quality of questioning[70] and political disagreement.[71]

(b) The working group failed to establish standards for the evaluation of reports[72] or an effective procedure.[73]

(c) The working group reports were purely procedural, giving little indication of the substance of the reports or discussion.[74] Neither did they indicate any conclusions or recommendations.[75]

---

[64] Massip (Canada), UN Doc. E/SR.1999, at 71, para. 16, 60 UN ESCOR, (Ag. Item 4) (1976).

[65] *See e.g.* Sucharipa (Austria), *ibid.* at 72, para. 19.

[66] ECOSOC Decn. 1978/10 (3 May 1978), *in* UN Doc. E/C.12/1989/4, at 6 (1988).

[67] *See e.g.* Ramcharan, *supra*, n. 63, at 169. The French representative commented in the discussion: 'The form and composition of the sessional working group would be determined by the nature of the tasks entrusted to it and could therefore be determined only after the methods of work and the procedure for considering reports had been established': UN Doc. E/1978/SR.9, para. 5.

[68] *See generally* Sohn, *supra*, n. 61, 1–66; Commentary, 'Implementation of the International Covenant on Economic, Social and Cultural Rights: ECOSOC Working Group' (1981) 27 *ICJ Rev.* 26; Alston (Abyss), *supra*, n. 31, at 340–2; Westerveen G., 'Towards a System for Supervising States' Compliance with the Right to Food' in Alston P. and Tomasevski K. (eds.), *The Right to Food* (1984), 119; Mower G., *International Cooperation for Social Justice* (1988), 31.

[69] Commentary, *ibid.* 35.

[70] *See e.g.* Yakolev (USSR), who seems to respond to the questions of other members of the working group rather than pose questions himself, E/1985/WG.1/SR.9, at 6, paras. 29–30.

[71] *See e.g.* Altercations between Texier (France) and Yakolev (USSR) over the Polish report, E/1986/WG.1/SR.26, at 2–4; and between Yakolev (USSR) and Hoppe (Denmark) over the restrictions on Solidarnosc in Poland, E/1986/WG.1/SR.27, at 7–8.

[72] Westerveen, *supra*, n. 68, at 125.   [73] Sohn, *supra*, n. 61, at 45.

[74] Alston (Abyss), *supra*, n. 31, at 342. *See e.g.* the comments of: Walkate (Netherlands), E/1981/SR.15, para. 90; Bell (Canada), E/1981/SR.15, para. 98.

[75] Westerveen, *supra*, n. 68, at 314; Fischer, *supra*, n. 23, at 175.

(d) There was continual dispute over the participation of the specialized agencies.[76]

(e) The State representatives presenting the reports were often not sufficiently qualified to answer the questions of the working group[77] (members often presenting the reports themselves).

(f) Disagreements within regional caucuses led to difficulty in filling its fifteen seats.[78]

(g) The attendance of the working group members was poor,[79] and there was excessive use of alternates.[80]

(h) The initial one year tenure of the members, and the later high turnover of members led to a lack of continuity and consistency.[81]

(i) State reports were considered too quickly owing to the lack of time available to the Group.[82]

(j) The working group was handicapped by the lack of publicity.[83]

(k) The working group was not even-handed in its consideration of State reports.[84]

(l) The working group's discussions often ignored the broader context in which the realization of economic, social, and cultural rights operates.[85]

(m) The working group was insufficiently supported by the Secretariat.[86]

(n) The lack of technical expertise on the part of States parties and the absence of sufficiently detailed reporting guidelines led to a poor level of compliance with the reporting obligations.[87]

The general dissatisfaction with the effectiveness of the working group as a supervisory body, combined with the increasing emphasis being placed upon economic, social, and cultural rights in the UN and a more conciliatory stance on the part of the Eastern European States,[88] all combined to put fresh impetus into the creation of a truly independent committee of experts. However, although the decision to create the committee indicated

---

[76] Commentary, *supra*, n. 68, at 36 and 38. It was finally agreed that the representatives of the specialized agencies should be able to make general statements but not pose questions to State representatives.

[77] *Ibid.* 35.

[78] Sohn notes that two members were lacking in 1984, one member in 1983, and two members in 1982: Sohn, *supra*, n. 61, at 42.

[79] One member noted that there was rarely more than ten members present at one time. Texier (France), E/1985/WG.1/SR.19, para. 17.

[80] Alston (Abyss), *supra*, n. 31, at 341.   [81] Sohn, *supra*, n. 61, at 43.

[82] Initially the working group only had a two-week session. After 1980 this was extended to three weeks. *See* Commentary, *supra*, n. 68, at 37.

[83] *Ibid.* 33.

[84] Certain States e.g. were given considerably harsher treatment. Indeed the working group actually refused to ask questions of the Chilean report in the light of its general human rights abuses: *ibid.* 38.

[85] Alston (Abyss), *supra*, n. 31, at 342.   [86] Sohn, *supra*, n. 61, at 35.

[87] *Ibid.* at 39.   [88] *See* Alston (Abyss), *supra*, n. 31, at 345–9.

the possibility of a fresh start, it was clear that the form of supervision would remain largely the same.

The Committee on Economic, Social, and Cultural Rights did not so much replace the working group as inherit and develop the existing system. ECOSOC Resolution 1985/17, under which the Committee was formally established, states merely that the working group shall be 'renamed' the Committee on Economic, Social, and Cultural Rights.[89] Similarly paragraph (h) of the same resolution states that the procedures and methods of work established previously for the working group continue to remain in force in so far as they are not superseded by that resolution.[90] More importantly, there was no substantial re-evaluation of the basic system of supervision such as to give effect to articles 19–21. The Committee merely inherited the existing procedures of the working group (such as the 'constructive dialogue' approach to the consideration of reports), which it has attempted to undertake in a more effective manner.

III. THE COMMITTEE ON ECONOMIC, SOCIAL, AND CULTURAL RIGHTS[91]

A The Composition of the Committee

The Committee on Economic, Social, and Cultural Rights, was created in ECOSOC Resolution 1985/17,[92] paragraph (b) of which reads:

(b) The Committee shall have 18 members who shall be experts with recognized competence in the field of human rights, serving in their personal capacity, due consideration being given to equitable geographical distribution and to the representation of different forms of social and legal systems, to this end, 15 seats will be equally distributed among the regional groups, while the additional three seats will be allocated in accordance with the increase in the total number of States parties per regional group;

---

[89] ECOSOC Resn. 1985/17, para. (a), UN ESCOR, Supp. (No. 1), at 15, UN Doc. E/1985/85, (1985).

[90] *Ibid.*

[91] *See generally* Alston P. and Simma B., 'First Session of the UN Committee on Economic, Social and Cultural Rights' (1987) 81 *AJIL* 747; Alston P. and Simma B., 'Second Session of the UN Committee on Economic, Social and Cultural Rights' (1987) 82 *AJIL* 603; Craven M. and Dommen C., 'Making Way for Substance: The Fifth Session of the Committee on Economic, Social and Cultural Rights' (1991) 9 *NQHR* 93; Simma B., 'The Implementation of the International Covenant on Economic, Social and Cultural Rights', in Matscher F. (ed.), *The Implementation of Economic, Social and Cultural Rights* (1991), 75; Leckie S., 'An Overview and Appraisal of the Fifth Session of the UN Committee on Economic, Social and Cultural Rights' (1991) 13 *Hum. Rts. Q* 539.

[92] ECOSOC Resn. 1985/17, *supra*, n. 89.

1 The Appointment of Members

Under ECOSOC resolution 1985/17 paragraph (c) members of the Committee are elected by ECOSOC by secret ballot from a list of nominees submitted by States parties.[93] The first elections took place in 1986 when eighteen members were elected for a term beginning on 1 January 1987. Whereas the regular term of office is four years,[94] the necessity of instituting a staggered membership meant that the President of the Council chose by lot the names of nine members whose terms were to expire at the end of two years.[95] Accordingly half the membership is renewed every second year.[96] Elections have been held every other year since 1988 at each of which ECOSOC elected nine members for a term of office of four years.

The fact that members of the Committee are elected for four-year terms and that elections are staggered allows the Committee an element of continuity.[97] Indeed, ten members of the original Committee are still members as of June 1994, two of whom were actually members of the Committee's predecessor, the working group.[98] It is apparent, particularly in the light of the experience of the original working group, that changes in membership can be disruptive in terms of the Committee's efficient functioning.[99] Long terms of membership promote stability through allowing the development of inter-personal relationships which can help to avoid unnecessary friction. More importantly, it assists consistency and promotes the development of expertise by the individual Committee members that is so essential to the effective analysis of State reports.

2 Representation and Distribution of Membership

Paragraph (b) of ECOSOC resolution 1985/17 stipulates that in the election of the experts 'due consideration' should be given to 'equitable geographical distribution and to the representation of different forms of social and legal systems'. Although the Committee members are undoubtedly appointed as independent experts,[100] this provision appears to ensure that the interests of States are represented in a general manner through social and cultural affiliation.

From the point of view of the Committee, it is entirely suitable that membership should span geographical areas and represent different legal and social forms in that otherwise its expertise would be seriously diminished. The formula devised for the Committee stipulates that fifteen seats

---

[93] *Ibid.*   [94] *Ibid.* para. (c)(i).
[95] *Ibid.* para. (c)(iii).   [96] *Ibid.* para. (c)(ii).
[97] Members of the HRC, CEDAW, CAT are all elected for 4 years.
[98] In comparison, the Human Rights Committee has experienced some problems of continuity, *see* Nowak M., 'UN Human Rights Committee: Comment' (1990) 11 *HRLJ* 139.
[99] *See above* text accompanying n. 81.   [100] *See below*, text accompanying n. 116.

shall be distributed equally among the five regional groups (Africa, Asia, Eastern Europe, Latin America, and Western Europe) and that the additional three seats be allocated according to the increase in the total number of States parties per regional group. It has been argued, however, that this formula is unduly inflexible.[101] Its emphasis on ideological groupings not only means that valid and relevant criteria for membership (such as ensuring a spread of expertise across the relevant disciplines) are ignored, but also places an unwarranted significance on the representation of States parties.

It must be admitted that the composition of the Committee does seem to fulfil, to a large extent, the three criteria of representation (geographical, legal, and social distribution). As far as the regional distribution is concerned, it has three members from each of the regional groups with the extra members going to Africa, Western Europe, and Latin America.[102] The range of legal systems found on the international plane are generally well represented with a mixture of common law and civil systems and a variety of constitutional forms with different philosophies. Similarly, there is a fairly wide representation of differing social structures, although stronger representation from central and southern Africa would be beneficial.

Nevertheless, from the point of view of expertise, it is important that the Committee is composed of experts spanning the areas of concern within the Covenant. It is certainly true that there is a need for people with local knowledge of the various geographical areas and of the different social and legal systems of States parties, but the demands of knowledge and expertise within the Committee are considerably wider. Given that the Committee is in the best position to determine its needs as regards the expertise of its members, a more flexible arrangement in which the Committee could have greater control over membership would be appropriate.

The existing arrangement, especially in so far as it refers to ensuring the representation of States parties, reflects the misplaced idea that the experts are still representatives of States. The fact that members are elected from nominees of the States parties, despite leaving open the faint possibility of experts being elected from nationals of non-States parties,[103] re-emphasizes the unwillingness of States parties to abandon the control previously held over membership of the working group.[104]

---

[101] Alston (Abyss), *supra*, n. 31, at 349.

[102] *See* UN Doc. E/1992/20. For a list of the different groupings for the purposes of elections *see* Hovet T. and Hovet E., *A Chronology and Fact Book of the United Nations 1941–1985* (7th ed., 1986), 310. On political groupings generally *see* Petersen M., *The General Assembly in World Politics* (1986), 290–7; Bailey S., *The General Assembly of the United Nations. A Study of Procedure and Practice* (1960), 21–40.

[103] As Alston comments, 'although there appears to be nothing to prevent the nomination of an individual who is not a national of a State party, there have been no precedents and the chances of election would probably be slight': Alston (Abyss), *supra*, n. 31, at 349.

[104] Whereas the Western States considered that the working group should consist of mem-

3 The Expert Nature of the Committee

ECOSOC resolution 1985/17 requires that the Committee be composed of 'experts with recognized competence in the field of human rights'. The expertise of the membership is of importance not only in as far as it relates to the ability of the Committee to assess the State reports[105] but also in that it lends to the credibility of the Committee in the eyes of States parties.[106] It should be remembered that the willingness of States parties to produce high quality reports is directly related to the quality of the supervision undertaken by the Committee.[107]

Although the working group was supposedly composed of competent members or experts, the quality of analysis shown in the consideration of State reports was manifestly poor.[108] The Committee, on the other hand, has demonstrated an ability to draw out and evaluate some of the finer issues in the reports and has made a certain amount of progress in further defining the substance of the guarantee.[109] Individual members have occasionally fallen short in their legal analysis,[110] but there is demonstrably a core of expertise within the Committee that maintains a high standard of work.

Even so, it is apparent that the Committee does not possess expertise in all the subject areas encompassed by the Covenant. It was noted by one Committee member that 'the Covenant's scope was so broad that the

bers of ECOSOC, the East European States argued that membership of the working group should be limited to States parties to the Covenant. *See generally* Ramcharan, *supra*, n. 63, at 165–7. UN Docs. E/1978/SR. 5, 9, and 12, UN ESCOR (Ag. Item 5) (1978). *Cf.* ECOSOC Decn. E/1978/10, paras. (a) and (c), *supra*, n. 66, and ECOSOC Resn. 1982/33, (6 May 1983), *in* UN Doc. E/C.12/1989/4, at 11 (1988).

[105] As Mower said with respect to the HRC: 'Since a body like this is an aggregate of individuals, the attitudes and competence of individual members become matters of not little significance for the Covenant's effectiveness': Mower G., 'Organizing to Implement the UN Civil/Political Rights Covenant: First Steps by the Committee' (1978) 3 *Hum. Rts. Rev.* 122, at 123. The point is equally relevant with respect to the CESCR.

[106] The Netherlands representative commented in ECOSOC: 'The requirement that members of the Group should be experts in the matter to which the State reports related was of great importance. If reporting States hesitated to submit reports or did not submit reports at all because they believed that they would be discussed by a less than competent group of individuals, the monitoring function of the Council would be undermined': Mr Walkate (Netherlands), E/1981/SR.15, para. 92 (1981).

[107] *See e.g.* Dormenval A., 'UN Committee Against Torture: Practice and Perspectives' (1990) 8 *NQHR* 26, at 32.

[108] *See above*, text accompanying n. 77. One commentator has pointed out that with the exception of Norway and USSR, States were represented by members of the permanent missions whose 'technical preparation was poor', with the result that the questions asked were generally superficial. Fischer, *supra*, n. 23, at 175.

[109] The discussion undertaken on art. 11 illustrates both of these points. *See* E/C.12/1990/SR. 22–3.

[110] e.g. a curious argument was used by one member who suggested that France was in violation of its obligations under the Covenant with respect to art. 9 notwithstanding an explicit reservation on the question. Alvarez Vita, E/C.12/1989/SR.12, at 12, para. 61.

Committee could not hope to find among its members experts in housing, discrimination, nutrition, and all the other subjects involved in economic, social, and cultural rights'.[111] Although it clearly would not be possible for the Committee to have members with expertise in every conceivable area, the fact that the vast majority of current members have a predominantly legal background may be criticized.[112] As a legal entity, the Covenant certainly requires a supervisory body with legal expertise, but it is doubted, given the need for wider knowledge particularly as regards the rights to food, housing, clothing, and health, that the current emphasis on legal expertise is appropriate. Indeed, in so far as the strictly 'legal' functions of the Committee are limited, there is scope for the inclusion of more non-lawyers within its ranks without prejudicing its ability to function effectively. To extend this process further, it is submitted at the Committee should undertake to advise ECOSOC of the nature of the experts it wishes to be appointed at the next election in 1994.

Nevertheless, as was pointed out, the Committee could not hope to have expert members from every field covered by the Covenant. It is, and always will be, dependent upon the use of external advice and technical expertise in its consideration of reports. Ideally this would be the type of support provided to the Committee by the Secretariat.[113] In the absence of such a role being played by the Secretariat, the Committee will have to look towards greater participation by the specialized agencies,[114] and to the use of consultants on an *ad hoc* basis during the consideration of the reports. Such consultants, if used, would deal with issues of a specific nature that may arise in the occasional report.

4 The Independence of the Committee

ECOSOC resolution 1985/17 stipulates in paragraph (b) that the members should serve 'in their personal capacity'.[115] Moreover, rule 13 of the Rules of Procedure provides that members of the Committee make a solemn declaration to undertake their duties 'impartially and conscientiously'.[116] It is clear from the experience of the working group that such independence is crucial to the effective functioning of the Committee. It might be argued that since the reporting system is primarily intended not for making judicial determinations of compliance, but rather for assisting States in the implementation of the rights within the Covenant, an insistence on the independence and impartiality of the Committee members is largely

[111] Alston, E/C.12/1990/SR.22, at 3, para. 12.
[112] *See generally* UN Docs. E/1992/20 and Add. 1 and 2, E/1990/46 and E/1988/46.
[113] *See below*, text accompanying nn. 451–63.
[114] *See below*, text accompanying nn. 321–46.
[115] ECOSOC Resolution 1985/17, *supra*, n. 89, para. (c).
[116] Rules of Procedure as approved by ECOSOC, *in* UN Doc. E/C.12/1990/4/Rev. 1.

misplaced.[117] However, even if the form of judicial impartiality that is essential to those bodies that operate a petition system is not strictly necessary, it is nevertheless debilitating for the Committee to be subjected to the political pressures that attend those organs composed of State representatives.

As the terminology used in the ECOSOC resolution is the same as that in article 28(3) of the ICCPR, it is to be assumed that the Committee should operate in the same independent manner as the Human Rights Committee (HRC), whatever their differences in role. However, the fact that members should act in their personal capacities does not mean in itself that they are entirely free from State control. As noted above, State parties retain significant influence over the election of the members of the Committee, both by the fact that they nominate the candidates and by the necessary political 'trade-offs' that accompany the distribution of seats. Indeed the decision by the Eastern Bloc countries to withdraw their nominee for the Committee at its first session illustrates the political bargaining that enters into the election process.[118] In a similar case, an attempt, albeit unsuccessful, was made to enforce an 'understanding' made during the election process that the *rapporteur* for the second session should be an expert from an Eastern European country.[119]

Moreover it is clear that many members of the Committee have been, and continue to be, government officials and civil servants.[120] Robertson argues that in relation to the Human Rights Committee such a situation is entirely inappropriate. He comments that:

it not only makes it difficult for the members to devote the necessary time and attention, but also makes it less likely that they can perform their functions 'impartially'. The task of the Committee is difficult and delicate and is not aided by subjecting any of its members of political pressures that are inevitable if Committee members are, or are seen as, representing governments.[121]

---

[117] Capotorti, speaking solely from a textual analysis of the ICESCR, noted that although in theory an independent committee of experts was most suitable for human rights treaty supervision, 'as the States reports on economic, social, and cultural questions must also help to promote international cooperation, especially in the field of technical assistance, the Economic and Social Council is still the best qualified organ for this kind of "implementation" of the Covenant': Capotorti, *supra*, n. 15, at 136.

[118] *See* the comment of Sviridov, E/C.12/1987/SR.2, at 3, para. 15.

[119] *See* Sviridov, E/C.12/1987/SR.25, at 2, para. 6.

[120] *E.g.* Mr Rattray is the Solicitor-General of Jamaica; Mr Alvarez Vita is a minister in the Diplomatic Staff of Peru; Mr Fofana is the Avocat Général of Guinea; Mrs Ider is the head of the Department of Legal Affairs of Mongolia; Mr Ceausu is the Romanian Ambassador to Norway; Mr Marchan Romero is an Ambassador for Ecuador. Other members hold various government or civil service posts.

[121] Robertson, *supra*, n. 23, at 338; Galey comments that the fact that members of CEDAW often hold official posts gave rise to 'serious questions as to the extent they can or do serve in their personal capacity independent of governments', Galey M., 'International Enforcement of Women's Rights' (1984) 6 *Hum. Rts. Q* 463, at 478. Such a consideration has also been noted in the Committee itself, *see* Texier, E/C.12/1988/SR.23, at 7, para. 60.

Robertson goes on to argue that this should be established as a matter of principle, and that the Committee members should be permanent salaried staff of the UN.[122] Although it is certainly necessary that members be free from government control, it is doubtful that such a proposition is realistic, especially given the financial constraints under which the UN is currently operating.[123] Indeed it is arguable that Committee members in fact benefit from the knowledge that derives from links with their State.[124] A more modest proposal would be to prohibit future Committee members from being in the direct employment of their State[125] and in the meantime to ensure that every member has adequately declared their interests and responsibilities.

In practice, members of the Committee have consistently stressed their independence before State representatives[126] and there is little evidence of them allowing political affiliations to compromise their role in examining State reports. There is an unofficial agreement, self-imposed on the whole, that an expert from the State whose report is being considered should not participate in the discussion.[127] Interventions in such cases have occurred only when that expert considered that the Committee would benefit from his or her specialist knowledge.[128] More often than not, any conflict within the Committee has related to regional rather than State affiliations, reflecting not so much the interference of States parties, but rather the personal views of the members concerned.

The one area of concern, however, has been the degree of absenteeism experienced by the Committee that may be directly related to the responsibilities of the members. Since its first session, at least one member on average has failed to attend the session (in the seventh session two members were absent) and another two have attended only part.[129] In addition to the casual absences from particular sessions this represents quite a significant problem. Although average attendance must be about twelve or thirteen

[122] Robertson, *Supra*, 339.
[123] The Committee has requested ECOSOC to authorize the payment of an honorarium for each member, but this cannot be considered to be a salary. *See* UN Doc. E/1994/23, UN ESCOR, Supp. (No. 3), 68, para. 349 (1994).
[124] McGoldrick D., *The Human Rights Committee* (1991), at 43.
[125] This would exclude in particular the participation of ambassadors and other civil servants. However, it would raise certain problems of interpretation, e.g. where a university professor was employed in a public institution financed directly by the State.
[126] e.g., following the Chilean representative's reference to the 'Australian representative', it was pointed out that members of the Committee were experts acting in an individual capacity and should be referred to by name or by any other neutral expression. *See* Alston, E/C.12/1988/SR.16, at 3, para. 6.
[127] *See e.g.* consideration of the report of Germany at which Simma was present but to which he made no contribution: E/C.12/1987/SR. 19–20.
[128] *See e.g.* the intervention of Rattray in the consideration of the Jamaican report, E/C.12/1990/SR.21, at 5, para. 21.
[129] Those who are frequently absent include Mr Rattray, Mr Alvarez Vita, and Mr Marchan Romero, all of whom have official government posts.

members, on a number of occasions it falls well below this level. Indeed it was commented at the Committee's third session that much of the Committee's work would not have been possible had the quorum rule of twelve members (Rule 32 of the Rules of Procedure) been strictly enforced.[130] How far such absences are due to official State business is unclear,[131] but it is notable that those members who are seemingly independent have good records of attendance.[132] It is clearly important for the Committee to maintain the quality of its work. This may well be prejudiced by the continuing shortage of members especially if the Committee is forced to take decisions that are technically *ultra vires* as not fulfilling the quorum rule.[133]

B The Status of the Committee

At a theoretical level, the sovereign equality of States dictates that the supervision of any treaty obligations should be undertaken exclusively by those States that are party to the agreement. However, the effective supervision of human rights demands that the body mandated with its implementation should be independent of the States parties. The Covenant, by appointing ECOSOC as the primary organ responsible for the implementation of the Covenant, appears to reflect this need for independence.[134] Nevertheless, the decision to involve ECOSOC in the supervisory process seems to have been made on the assumption that supervision would only involve the provision of technical assistance rather than any form of critical examination.

A debate over the control of the States parties arose during the determination of membership of the working group. It was argued on the one hand that members of the group could be elected from any member of ECOSOC whether or not they were party to the Covenant.[135] On the other hand it was contended that members had to be elected from those members of ECOSOC who were also States parties.[136] This issue was never entirely resolved and, as noted above, the position is no clearer in respect to the Committee itself.[137]

---

[130] *See* Alston, E/C.12/1989/SR.23, at 6, para. 41. Notably the 7th session was also started without the necessary quorum, Alston, E/C.12/1992/SR.1, at 2, para. 5.

[131] The absences of Mrachkov in 1990 and Ceausu in 1993 were specifically cited as being due to State business.

[132] One may cite in particular Mr Alston and Mr Simma.

[133] Dormenval criticizes non-attendance and argues that '[o]ne's agreement to serve as an expert entails the moral duty not to undermine the authority of the Committee one serves on': Dormenval, *supra*, n. 107, at 34.

[134] Although a number of States in ECOSOC are parties to the Covenant, there are also a significant number which are not.

[135] *See above*, n. 104.

[136] Yugoslavia, E/SR.1999, at 5, 60 UN ESCOR (Ag. Item 4) (1976); USSR, *ibid.* 6.

[137] *See above*, text accompanying nn. 103–4.

Although States parties are responsible for the nomination of members of the Committee, it is clear that the Committee as a whole is primarily a United Nations organ. The Committee was established as a subsidiary organ of ECOSOC and as such derives all its authority from, and is responsible to, that body. The interests of the States parties are represented here only in so far as they are taken up by ECOSOC. To this extent the Committee differs quite significantly from other human rights committees.

The obvious benefit of being a subsidiary organ of ECOSOC is that the Committee maintains a significant degree of autonomy from the States parties. Financially speaking, being sponsored by the UN,[138] the Committee has not been subject to the problems faced by other committees that were supported by the States parties themselves.[139] Rather, it is financed exclusively by the United Nations. A further benefit of being a UN organ rather than a treaty body is that alterations of procedure merely require the authorization of ECOSOC—there is no need to amend the text of the Covenant itself. This has enabled the Committee, while working within the broad parameters of the ECOSOC resolutions that created it, to develop its working methods in an unprecedented manner.

Although free from strict textual constraints, the mandate of the Committee is essentially an indirect one. It operates 'to assist the Council' in the consideration of State reports, rather than being directly responsible itself.[140] There is potential here for a conflict of competence to arise, similar to that experienced by the Committee of Independent Experts to the European Social Charter *vis-à-vis* the Governmental Committee.[141] In practice, however, the work of the Committee has drawn little interest from ECOSOC, and only in a few cases has it sought the approval of ECOSOC for the adoption of its working methods.[142]

---

[138] Although the Committee on Economic, Social, and Cultural Rights developed late in the day, it was somewhat fortunate that the earlier proposals for a Committee submitted by the USA and Italy did not come to fruition. Both those proposals envisaged the States parties taking primary responsibility for financing the Committee which would be set up independently of ECOSOC. UN Doc. A/6546, at 10–13, 21 UN GAOR, Annexes (Ag. Item 62) (1966).

[139] For comment on the financial position of CERD *see* Bernard-Maugiron N., '20 Years After: 38th Session of the Committee on the Elimination of Racial Discrimination' (1990) 8 *NQHR* 395. With respect to CAT *see* Dormenval, *supra*, n. 107, at 28. Recently amendments to both ICERD and the Convention Against Torture have been adopted and the Secretary General has been requested to take the appropriate measures for financing the Committees from the regular UN budget, GA Resn. 47/111, para. 9, 47 UN GAOR, Resns. (1992).

[140] *See* Alston, *supra*, n. 31, at 488–9.

[141] The recent Amending Protocol has sought to address the overlap in roles between the two bodies, *see* Harris D., 'A Fresh Impetus for the European Social Charter' (1992) 41 *ICLQ* 659, at 662–4.

[142] These include: the adoption of the Committee's Rules of Procedure E/1989/22, at 74, paras. 333–4 (1989); the ability of NGOs to submit information to the Committee, E/1987/28, at 49, paras. 312–3 (1987); and the creation of a 'blacklist' of non-reporting States, Report of the Committee's Fifth Session, UN Doc. E/1991/23, at 68, para. 264 (1991).

The Committee is also somewhat more vulnerable than other committees to the extent that it is permanently subject to sea changes within ECOSOC upon which it is entirely dependent for its existence. The fragility of the whole implementation system was in fact apparent when it was made clear during the drafting of the Covenant that it was legally impossible for the treaty to impose any obligations on the UN with regard to implementation.[143] However this vulnerability does not seem to have manifest itself in any way as yet. During the recent financial crisis in the United Nations, for example, the Committee was one of the few institutions that was left unaffected.

C Working Methods of the Committee

1 Rules of Procedure

Draft provisional rules of procedure, prepared by the Secretary-General taking into account the relevant resolutions and decisions of ECOSOC and the practice and procedure of other human rights treaty bodies and amended by members of the Committee, were accepted on a provisional basis at the Committee's third session.[144] An amendment was made to the rules at the Committee's fourth session and they were finally approved by ECOSOC in decision 1990/251 prior to the Committee's fifth session.[145]

Although the Committee is nominally a subsidiary of ECOSOC and therefore subject to the rules of procedure of that body, by adopting its own set of rules of procedure it has asserted some form of independence that is entirely appropriate with its role in the supervision of the Covenant. Nevertheless, how far the Committee may go down this road is not clear. For example, the decision to allow an NGO without consultative status to present an oral report to the Committee (albeit 'off the record'[146]) may well be considered technically *ultra vires* in so far as it is not envisaged within the rules of ECOSOC itself. It is considered, however, that given that ECOSOC is not prohibited from adopting such a procedure, the fact that it has not done so itself does not necessarily bar subsidiary organs from taking up that procedure.[147] The crucial test for the Committee will be whether or not the procedure is challenged within ECOSOC. If not, the adoption of the Committee's report in 1994 will amount to a tacit endorsement of the

---

[143] UN Doc. A/2929, *supra*, n. 36, at 119, para. 16. This is the reason the Covenant does not instruct ECOSOC but rather uses the term 'may', as in arts. 18 and 19.
[144] E/C.12/1989/SR.22, at 5, para. 24.
[145] ECOSOC Decn. 1990/251, (10 Oct. 1990), UN ESCOR, Resns. (1990).
[146] *See* Alston, E/C.12/1993/SR.3, at 9–10, para. 56.
[147] *Cf. Certain Expenses of the United Nations Case* [1962] *ICJ Rep.* 151.

Committee's decision to allow NGOs to present oral reports to it in plenary session.

2 *Frequency and Duration of Sessions*

ECOSOC Resolution 1985/17 paragraph (d) provides that the Committee should meet annually for a period of up to three weeks.[148] That the phrase 'up to' might be interpreted as precluding the possibility of longer sessions has been explicitly negatived by rule 1 of the Rules of Procedure which includes the phrase 'or as may be decided by the Economic and Social Council . . . taking into account the number of reports to be examined by the Committee'.[149] It is specifically open for the Committee, when it has a sufficient backlog of reports, to request either an extra session or longer sessions.

There is no doubt that the Committee is disadvantaged when compared with the Human Rights Committee, which meets for nine weeks per year (three three-week sessions) and has an additional three weeks for working groups. Even including the one week meeting for its pre-sessional working group, the Committee on Economic, Social, and Cultural Rights meets for only a third of that time.[150] However, the Human Rights Committee has additional tasks to undertake with the Optional Protocol and the amount of time spent on considering equivalent reports is almost the same.[151] Generally, the Committee spends about eight days considering twelve reports (or four global reports), which gives it an average of one global report every two days. In comparison to CERD or CEDAW this is an inordinate amount of time.[152]

Two competing concerns are apparent here: on the one hand the recent financial crisis within the UN has stressed the need for efficient and productive reporting systems; on the other hand it is necessary for the committees concerned to maintain a high standard of supervision and that

[148] The sessional working group initially only had a two week session per annum. It was clear *ab initio* that this would be inadequate for the effective supervision of the reporting mechanism. *See e.g.* Mr Pastinen (Finland), UN Doc. E/1979/SR.14, para. 61, ESCOR (Ag. Item 4) (1979).

[149] *Supra*, n. 116, at 1.

[150] However it is worth noting that CEDAW, under art. 20 of the Discrimination against Women Convention, only has two weeks per annum. A proposal has been made to amend the Convention to give the Committee adequate time, *see* E/CN.6/1993/CRP.2, Annex 1, para. 6(b).

[151] *Contra*, Alston P., 'Effective Implementation of International Instruments on Human Rights Including Reporting Obligations Under International Instruments on Human Rights', UN Doc. A/44/668 at 41, para. 101. However this report, in comparing the amount of time spent on the consideration of each report by different committees did not take into consideration the fact that the Committee on Economic, Social, and Cultural Rights used to consider 3 state reports in place of a single 'global report'.

[152] CERD, e.g., considered 26 reports in 14 working days.

inevitably takes time. Thus, it has been noted that the unduly short amount of time spent by CERD in examining reports is 'simply pointless'.[153] The Committee has in fact taken a number of innovative procedural steps such as the imposition of time limits, in order to expedite the consideration of reports.[154] It is unlikely, given the breadth and sheer volume of information that is presented before the Committee, that it will be able to shorten the time required for each report in any significant manner. It has been correctly noted that the only way forward for the Committee in the long run is for its sessions to be extended when a significant backlog of reports builds up.[155]

So far, requests by the Committee for extra or longer sessions have met with some success. At its first session, after a debate when it was considered quite widely that it would need two three-week sessions per annum,[156] it was proposed that its sessions should be extended to four weeks, given the financial problems facing the UN.[157] This ECOSOC did not approve. The Committee has, however, managed to gain authorization to hold a pre-sessional working group meeting prior to its plenary sessions, which has eased some of the work load. In addition, following specific requests from the Committee,[158] ECOSOC has allowed the Committee to hold an extra-ordinary session in 1990, 1993, and 1994. It was made clear, both by the Committee and ECOSOC, that the provision of extra sessions was a temporary expedient aimed at enabling the Committee to deal with the long standing backlog of reports.[159] Although in 1990 the extra session did assist the Committee to deal with the existing backlog, the 1993 session was less of a success. The short notice given to States combined with the late receipt of the pre-sessional working group questions meant that a number of States were unprepared and withdrew at the last moment. There is clearly an argument here for institutionalizing the extra session on a regular basis (for example, biennially) so that arrangements may be made sufficiently in advance. The current situation is also unsatisfactory from a long-term perspective. As and when the record of reporting improves, a three-week session per annum will be far from adequate.[160] In such a situation not only

---

[153] Higgins R., 'The United Nations: Still a Force for Peace', subsequently corrected to 'The United Nations: Some Questions of Integrity' (1989) 52 *MLR* 1, at 19.

[154] *See below* text accompanying nn. 266–75.

[155] *See* Alston, E/C.12/1990/SR.7, at 7, para. 31.

[156] *See e.g.* Rattray, E/C.12/1987/SR.23, at 5, para. 21.

[157] Report of the Committee's First Session, UN Doc. E/1987/28, at 50, para. 314, UN ESCOR, Supp. (No. 17) (1987).

[158] Report of the Committee's Second Session, UN Doc. E/1988/14, at 59, para. 346 and 61 para. 356, UN ESCOR, Supp. (No. 4) (1988). Draft Decision I, Report of the Committee's Sixth Session, UN Doc. E/1992/23, at 1, UN ESCOR, Supp. (No. 3) (1992). Draft Decision I, Report of the Committee's Eighth Session, E/1994/23, *supra*, n. 123, at 7.

[159] *Ibid*. The Committee envisages having to hold two permanent sessions in the near future, E/C.12/1993/CRP.1/Add. 3, at 9, para. 29.

[160] It is estimated that it would take the Committee 10 years to review all the outstanding

will it be impossible to predict whether or not ECOSOC will actually grant an extra session but also it is unlikely that an occasional extraordinary session will be sufficient.

3 Consensus Decision-Making

Rule 46 of the Committee's Rules of Procedure states that:

Decisions of the Committee shall be made by a majority of the members present. However, the Committee shall endeavour to work on the basis of the principle of consensus.[161]

In principle, with its present quorum standing at twelve,[162] the Committee may make a decision with the concurring votes of seven members. It is clear from the phrase 'of the members present' (as opposed to those voting), that abstentions are not sufficient to endorse a decision.[163] As with many other human rights committees the emphasis is on working through consensus. There is the possibility that an attempt to work by consensus 'is liable to water down the moral principles to a lowest common denominator' and restrict the power to make decisions at all.[164] However, its use is important in maintaining a cohesiveness and a sense of common purpose within the Committee that will be reflected in its work. Moreover, the use of voting in important decisions not only deprives them of a certain amount of authority, but might encourage political disagreements within the Committee.

In practice the Committee has not resorted to the vote as yet and has maintained a unified approach to all its problems.[165] At the same time, there is little evidence that any of its decisions have been weakened as a result of working by consensus. It is of course important that the Committee retain the ability to take decisions by majority to ensure its power to act in the face of a power of 'veto' (which is implicit in a consensus decision-making process), and to preserve the freedom of conscience and independence of action for each member.[166]

---

reports if they were submitted. *See* Alston P., 'Effective Implementation of International Instruments: Interim Report', UN Doc. A/CONF.157/PC/62/Add.11/Rev.1, at 45. It is commented: 'One of the most problematic aspects of the current situation is that the treaty bodies actually rely very heavily upon the continuing delinquency of a great number of States parties in order to be able to fulfil their obligations within the meeting time currently at their disposal.'

[161] Rule 46, Rules of Procedure, *supra*, n. 116, at 15.   [162] Rule 32, *ibid.* 12.
[163] This contrasts with the position under CERD, *see* Das K., 'United Nations Institutions and Procedures Founded on Conventions on Human Rights and Fundamental Freedoms' in Vasak K. and Alston P. (eds.), *The International Dimensions of Human Rights* (1982), 303, at 309.
[164] Robertson, *supra*, n. 23, at 340.
[165] The collaborative nature of the Committee's work was only upset once, when Professor Grissa threatened to resign during the Tenth Session.
[166] *See* Mower, *supra*, n. 105, at 124.

4 Publicity

Publicity is of prime importance to the Committee both in assisting it in its work and in the realization of the rights in general. From the Committee's point of view, publicity of its work would attract the attention of relevant NGOs and specialized agencies and stimulate their participation. It would also increase awareness of issues relating to economic, social, and cultural rights, thus raising the status of the Committee from that of a poor relation to the HRC.[167] This might, in particular, serve to ecourage ECOSOC to allow the Committee extra time to consider reports and might ultimately stimulate interest in an optional protocol. As far as the Committee is concerned, however, the primary function of publicity is to promote the full realization of the rights in the Covenant. As it has made clear, one of the main aims of the reporting process is to stimulate awareness and debate at a national level. Thus States are expected to make their reports available to the public at the domestic level.[168] The Committee has also encouraged States to undertake activities to foster greater knowledge and awareness of the terms of the Covenant through, for example, the training of officials[169] and the translation of the Covenant into local languages.[170]

In order to give greater publicity to its own work, the Committee regularly makes copies of its annual reports and summary records available for public scrutiny. It has also undertaken a number of initiatives such as holding its meetings in public, and organizing conferences for NGOs and the press. In that vein, members of the Committee have committed themselves to giving the Covenant greater publicity in their personal capacity, whether through attending conferences or publishing articles.[171] Recognizing that such activities are inevitably limited in their effect, the Committee has pushed for greater efforts to be taken by the UN in terms of publicity. In particular, the Committee has asked for both a bibliography of published materials on the Covenant[172] and a brochure on the work of the Committee[173] to be published. It has also recommended that the text of its annual report and summary records, available in English, French, and Spanish, be distributed as widely as possible by the UN Information Office. Thus far, the Secretariat has only produced a sketchy bibliography and a brief 'fact sheet' which has not satisfied the Committee's demand for a 'detailed and informative analysis' of its work to be produced and made widely available.[174]

---

[167] *See e.g.* Alston, E/C.12/1990/SR.3, at 10, para. 63.
[168] *See* Simma, E/C.12/1988/SR.22, at 8, para. 56.
[169] Concluding observations on the Canadian report, E/C.12/1993/5, at 5, para. 29.
[170] Concluding observations on the New Zealand report, E/C.12/1993/13, at 3, para. 16.
[171] E/1988/14, *supra*, n. 158, at 65, para. 372.   [172] *Ibid.* 65, para. 372.
[173] Report of the Committee's Fourth Session, UN Doc. E/1990/23, at 75, paras. 301–2, UN ESCOR, Supp. (No. 3) (1990).
[174] E/1992/23, *supra*, n. 158, at 97, para. 375.

In absence of effective Secretariat backing, the efforts of the Committee to increase the awareness and status of the Covenant and its work will be fairly limited. It is worth noting, however, that publicity will develop when the Committee shows itself to be an effective and useful supervisory body. In particular, it is arguable that the most effective method of generating publicity would be the institution of an optional protocol allowing the Committee to receive and consider individual complaints.[175]

D The Role of the Committee

Primarily, the Committee is merely required to 'assist' ECOSOC in the 'consideration' of reports under the reporting system. While being posited as an alternative to a petition system overseen by an expert committee, the precise nature of that 'consideration' seems to have been assumed by the drafters of the Covenant as being self-evident. No attempt has been made then or since to establish the precise role of the supervisory body in considering reports under such a system.

It is arguable that the decision of ECOSOC to create a committee composed of independent experts signifies its intention that the body should assume some form of quasi-judicial role in the supervisory process. If the role of the supervisory organ was principally to aid States in the implementation of their obligations under the Covenant, particularly by stimulating international co-operation and assistance, it would be most effectively performed by ECOSOC as an inter-governmental body.[176] However, the delegation of its authority to a committee of independent experts can only suggest that some independent form of evaluation is intended in the supervision of State reports.

The Committee has, nevertheless, been rather cautious of taking up a 'quasi-judicial' role. The Committee has emphasized that it sees itself as entering into a 'constructive dialogue' in the reporting process whereby State representatives are asked to appear before it to undertake a mutually beneficial discussion regarding the degree to which the State concerned has fulfilled its obligations under the Covenant. Members of the Committee have stressed, almost unanimously in the past, that the Committee is not a 'court'[177] and therefore should not sit in judgment over States or condemn

---

[175] *See below* text accompanying nn. 471–94.

[176] Capotorti, speaking solely from a textual analysis of the ICESCR, noted that although in theory an independent committee of experts was most suitable for human rights treaty supervision, 'as the States reports on economic, social and cultural questions must also help to promote international cooperation, especially in the field of technical assistance, the Economic and Social Council is still the best qualified organ for this kind of 'implementation' of the Covenant': Capotorti, *supra*, n. 15, at 136. It has also been suggested that an independent Committee would only be necessary if complaints from individuals or States were contemplated, Mr Dombo (Ghana), UN Doc. A/C.3/SR.1401, at 141, para. 15 (1966).

[177] *See e.g.* Mrachkov, E/C.12/1987/SR.4, at 7, para. 26.

them for non-compliance with their obligations.[178] Rather, it is thought that the Committee should play a facilitative role in assisting States in their realization of the rights,[179] especially through filtering requests for international co-operation[180] and technical assistance,[181] and providing States with advice. In particular, it has been felt that the Committee should play the role of a 'catalyst' in encouraging States to make it possible for national organizations to participate in the implementation of the rights.[182]

In fact the Committee has done little to characterize itself as a body capable or willing to facilitate or provide technical assistance and advice. Rather it has developed its role in ways that point more towards the assumption of quasi-judicial functions. In particular, it has undertaken to receive information from NGOs, asserted its authority as the central supervisory body to interpret the Covenant, and has adopted the procedure of making 'concluding comments' or 'observations' of a State-specific nature on each report considered. In most recent cases this has involved making comments as to whether or not the State concerned was acting in conformity with its obligations under the Covenant.[183]

E The Reporting Programme

1 The Obligation to Report

Article 16(1) of the Covenant reads:

The States Parties to the present Covenant undertake to submit in conformity with this part of the Covenant reports on the measures which they have adopted and the progress made in achieving the observance of the rights recognized herein.

The submission of reports by the States parties is clearly central to the integrity of the reporting system and failure to report constitutes a violation of a State's obligations under the Covenant. However it has often been recognized that compliance with reporting obligations is generally poor.[184] The current experience of the Committee on Economic, Social, and Cultural Rights is that fourteen States have not submitted a single report in ten years and seventy-two reports are overdue from sixty-two States parties.[185] While not being the worst record when compared with other human rights

---

[178] *See* Alston, E/C.12/1987/SR.4, at 3, para. 8; Rattray, E/C.12/1987/SR.4, at 11, para. 43; Badawi El Sheikh, E/C.12/1988/SR.2, at 7, para. 35.

[179] *See e.g.* Mrachkov, E/C.12/1987/SR.4, at 7, para. 26.

[180] *See e.g.* Taya, E/C.12/1988/SR.20, at 4, para. 13.

[181] *See* Alston, E/C.12/1988/SR.20, at 5, para. 20.

[182] *See* Alston, E/C.12/1987/SR.4, at 3, para. 8.

[183] *See below* text accompanying nn. 414-7.

[184] Schoenberg noted with respect to the history of the periodic reporting system that it was one of 'limited and shallow participation': Schoenberg, *supra*, n. 11, at 25.

[185] UN Doc. E/1994/23, *supra*, n. 123, at 87-92.

committees,[186] it is certainly not encouraging.[187] Members of the Committee have identified a number of reasons for such a record. First, it is evident that the production of reports requires a certain amount of internal organization[188] and expertise on the part of States which presents problems for developing countries.[189] Secondly, given the vast quantity and range of information required, developing States may not dispose of sufficient personal and economic resources to provide the necessary data.[190] This is a particularly acute problem for those States that are party to a number of different human rights treaties in that they may well be overburdened by reporting requirements.[191] Thirdly, the original set of guidelines were complicated, general, and difficult to apply.[192]

The Committee has responded to the poor record of reporting in two different ways. On the one hand, it has consistently recommended that States that experience problems in drafting reports should seek the assistance of the Secretary-General and particularly the Centre for Human Rights.[193] In the light of the poor response to that endeavour it has also suggested that the Under-Secretary-General for Human Rights should approach each State party that has not submitted such a report, and request that it indicate whether assistance is required.[194]

On the other hand, the Committee has also taken a more adversarial stance. It is undoubtedly true that it cannot rely entirely on the good faith of the States parties. As one commentator noted, even wealthy Western States are often late in submitting their reports.[195] Thus the Committee has requested that the Secretary-General send reminders to States from which reports are overdue,[196] and records the level of compliance in its annual report to ECOSOC. At its fifth and sixth sessions, the Committee

[186] Both CERD and CEDAW have greater numbers of overdue reports, *see* Alston, *supra*, n. 160, at 44.

[187] Both CERD and CEDAW have also had particular problems in this regard. One difficulty in establishing the exact position of reporting under the Covenant has been the move from a triennial reporting system to one in which reports are due once every 5 years. *See below*, text accompanying nn. 212–22.

[188] *See* Alvarez Vita, E/C. 12/1990/SR.7, at 9, para. 52.

[189] *See* Konate, E/C. 12/1987/SR.22/Add. 1, at 3, para. 5; *see also* Nowak, *supra*, n. 98, at 142. It is notable that of the countries that have failed to submit a report for over 6 years the majority are smaller African States.

[190] *See e.g.* Simma, E/C. 12/1989/SR.18, at 8, para. 45. It has also been noted that Federal States have problems with the collection of information, *see* Concluding observations of the Canadian report, E/C.12/1993/5, at 3, para. 11.

[191] Alston, *supra*, n. 160, at 50–5; Report of Meeting of Chairpersons of Human Rights Treaty Bodies, UN Doc. A/39/484, (1984) and UN Doc. A/44/135, paras. 46–100 (1989).

[192] *See* Rattray, E/C.12/1987/SR.22/Add.1, at 4, para. 9; *see also* Sohn, *supra*, n. 61, at 39.

[193] E/1990/23, *supra*, n. 173, at 76, para. 304. *See e.g.* Concluding observations on the report of Kenya, E/C.12/1993/6, at 5, para. 23.

[194] *Ibid.* 68, para. 265.

[195] *See* Higgins, *supra*, n. 153, at 18. Belgium, for example, only came round to submitting a report 10 years after ratification.

[196] E/C.12/1987/SR.23, at 4, para. 14.

drafted a decision for adoption by ECOSOC naming those States that had failed to submit a single report for over a decade.[197] The endorsement of each decision by ECOSOC is notable in so far as it specifically names the States concerned and notes that advisory services were available from the Centre for Human Rights to assist them in the preparation of their reports.[198]

Although both Iceland and Uruguay quickly submitted their reports before the first draft decision was adopted by ECOSOC, members of the Committee did not consider this mechanism to have been entirely success-ful.[199] As far as the Committee was concerned, further action was needed. It noted that the continuing failure to report risked 'bringing the entire super-visory procedure into disrepute'[200] in so far as it gave the non-reporting States an immunity from supervision not enjoyed by other States.[201] Ac-cordingly, following the example of CERD,[202] the Committee adopted the procedure of scheduling for consideration the situation in respect of those States whose initial or periodic reports are significantly overdue whether or not a report has been received.[203] If a report was not then submitted, the Committee resolved to consider the situation in the State concerned in the light of all available information.[204] This procedure was put into effect at the Committee's eighth session where it scheduled for consideration the situation in Belgium, Suriname, Kenya, and Lebanon.[205] Although this de-cision had an immediate effect on Belgium and Suriname, both of whom submitted reports at later sessions,[206] it has been forced to consider the situation in a number of States, such as Kenya, in the absence of a report and without the presence of a State representative.

In those cases where there is no report for the Committee to work upon, nor a representative to address, one member of the Committee has to take responsibility for acting as a country *rapporteur* by compiling a report (or draft concluding observations) on the issues of importance with reference

---

[197] *Cf.* E/1991/23, at 68, para. 264 (1991).

[198] ECOSOC Decn. 1992/260, ESCOR, at 134 (1992). It has to be noted that there is nothing in the terms of the Covenant itself that specifically allows the Council to make State-specific recommendations of this kind. The fact that many States parties to the Covenant are also members of ECOSOC, however, gives considerable force to such an interpretation of its powers.

[199] *See e.g.* Mratchkov, E/C.12/1991/SR.24, at 11, para. 86.

[200] Report of the Committee's Seventh Session UN Doc. E/1993/22, at 184, para. 242 (1993).

[201] *Ibid. See also* Report of the Meeting of Chairpersons of Human Rights Treaty Bodies, UN Doc. A/47/628, para. 71.

[202] Houshmand, E/C.12/1991/SR.24, at 10, para. 80.

[203] E/1992/23, *supra*, n. 158, at 99, para. 382(b).

[204] E/1993/22, *supra*, n. 200, at 64, para. 245.

[205] Alston, E/C.12/1992/SR.6, at 9, para. 42. The position with respect to four other States (Mali, Mauritius, Guinea, and Gambia) was scheduled for consideration at the Committee's tenth session, E/C.12/1993/CRP.1, at 6, para. 19.

[206] *See* UN Doc. E/1990/5/Add.15 (Belgium) and E/1990/5/Add.20 (Suriname). Kenya also subsequently submitted a report: E/1990/5/Add.17.

to all available information. In certain cases, the procedure has undoubtedly been successful—where the rapporteur has researched widely upon the issue and has identified a number of matters of concern to the Committee. It is apparent, nevertheless, that the procedure raises certain problems. First, the preparation of a country report of this nature is undoubtedly both difficult and time-consuming. The quality of the report will depend significantly upon the expertise of the Committee member and upon the quantity and quality of information available on the State under consideration. Alternative strategies here might be to send an expert to the country concerned on a fact-finding mission or to request the Secretariat to draft a State report.

The second problem is that if States perceive that the Committee will continue to undertake its supervisory role without the participation of State reports, they might take this as a signal that it is unnecessary to submit reports at all. However, it is not always in the interest of States not to submit a report, as without one the Committee would be forced to draw its conclusions from information provided by NGOs and the press. That information tends, by its nature, to be more critical of the social and economic position in the country concerned. As the Committee pointed out, 'non-submission of reports and non-appearance before the Committee deprives a government of . . . [the] possibility to set the record straight'.[207]

The third problem relates to the competence of the Committee to institute such a procedure. If the Committee's mandate is read strictly, it is only entitled to assist ECOSOC in the consideration of State reports. This does not give it the right to consider the situation of States in the absence of a report any more than it can consider the situation of a State not party to the Covenant. It is arguable, however, that, as a logical inference from the terms of article 21, ECOSOC does have the authority to consider the progress made in implementation in absence of a State report.[208] In so far as the Committee has taken up this role it may be deemed to be *ultra vires* as regards ECOSOC's internal procedure, but not substantively *ultra vires* with respect to the supervision process as a whole.[209] Even then, given the

---

[207] E/C. 12/1993/6, at 2, para. 3.

[208] Art. 21 provides that ECOSOC may submit reports to the General Assembly *inter alia* on the 'measures taken and the progress made in achieving general observance of the rights recognised in the present Covenant'. There is no indication that the report has to be confined to information received from States parties.

[209] *See The Certain Expenses Case, supra,* n. 147. There it was argued that the expenses incurred by the UN operations in the Congo were not 'expenses of the organisation' as they were authorized by the General Assembly rather than the Security Council. The court, in negativing this proposition commented: 'If the action was taken by the wrong organ, it was irregular as a matter of that internal structure, but this would not necessarily mean that the expense incurred was not an expense of the Organisation. Both national and international law contemplate cases in which the body corporate or politic may be bound, as to third parties, by an *ultra vires* act of an agent': *Id.,* at 168.

need to ensure the integrity and effectiveness of the supervision system, a teleological interpretation of the Commitee's duty to assist ECOSOC would suggest that the procedure was legitimate.

It is considered that the Committee had no choice but to take a strong stance on non-reporting. The alternatives, such as considering three or four periodic reports together,[210] or altering the cycle of submission according to the actual date of submission, could only be counter-productive. The Committee has in fact resolved that it will not, except in exceptional cases, allow States to defer the submission of subsequent reports where the initial report was submitted late as that 'would amount to rewarding States for the tardy submission of a previous report'.[211] In that there is a positive correlation between the effectiveness of the reporting system and the extent to which States parties take their reporting obligations seriously, the Committee's approach here is undoubtedly correct.

2 *The Periodicity of Reports*

Article 17(1) reads:

The States Parties to the present Covenant shall furnish their reports in stages, in accordance with a programme to be established by the Economic and Social Council within one year of the entry into force of the present Covenant after consultation with the States Parties and the specialized agencies concerned.

During the drafting of the Covenant a proposal was made that the periodicity of reports should be set in the text itself.[212] It was fortuitous that the amendment, which provided for the submission of reports every two years, was not adopted, as it is unlikely that such a schedule would have been realistic either for the States concerned or the supervisory body. Such was the position of CERD which, despite the textual requirement of bi-annual reports, has now adopted a four-yearly cycle. It is clear that the solution adopted for the Covenant was appreciated for its flexibility and the amount of discretion given to ECOSOC.[213]

Following the requirements of article 17(1) the Secretary General carried out consultations with the States parties and the specialized agencies and came to the decision that the States parties should report on an annual basis over a period of six years.[214] This proposal was modified by ECOSOC in May 1976 which established a three-stage, biennial reporting process within

---

[210] Bernard-Maugiron, *supra*, n. 139, at 396.
[211] E/1994/23, *supra*, n. 123, at 80, para. 361.
[212] Proposed Amendment of Italy, UN Doc. A/C.3/L.1358, para. 3.
[213] UN Doc. A/6546, at 14, para. 44, 21, UN GAOR, C.3, Annexes (Ag. Item 62) (1966).
[214] UN Doc. E/5764, at 5, para. 24, 60 UN ESCOR, Annexes (Ag. Item 4) (1976).

a six year cycle.[215] This was the system inherited initially by the Committee.

Although the three-part reporting system was justified on the basis of the interest of the specialized agencies in the area it became clear that the agencies were never likely to perform the role which was initially envisaged for them. Equally, given the need to ease the burden of reporting on States parties and facilitate the task of the Committee,[216] it was no longer considered suitable for the rights to be separated into discrete categories.[217] Accordingly, following the recommendation of the Committee at its second session, ECOSOC decided that States parties would be requested to submit a single report within two years of the entry into force of the Covenant and thereafter at five-yearly intervals.[218]

On the whole it is difficult to assess the effect of the new five-yearly periodicity on the quality of supervision. Although it has resolved not to receive any further triennial reports after 1 January 1995,[219] the Committee is still in an interim period in which it is considering certain reports from the old reporting cycle. Moreover, the problem of non-reporting tends to overshadow any consideration of the time-scale in which reports become due. Certainly as a rationalizing measure, it is more efficient in terms of time and energy for a single global report to be provided. Whether a five-yearly periodicity is better than a four-yearly or a seven-yearly periodicity, for example, remains to be seen.

An interesting development in the work of the Committee is its apparent move towards requesting *ad hoc* reports in cases of grave concern. Initially in the case of the Dominican Republic,[220] and later with respect to the Philippines,[221] the Committee has undertaken to request a specific report on matters that have been brought to its attention by NGOs outside the specific time-scale of the reporting system. In the case of the Philippines, the Committee declared that the information before it was 'sufficient to give rise to concern that violations are occurring and that future measures might amount to further violations of the obligations contained in the Covenant'.[222] It therefore requested the government to provide a response

---

[215] ECOSOC Resn. 1988 (LX), 11 May 1976. See above text accompanying n. 63. The periodicity for second and subsequent reports was extended by ECOSOC to nine years in 1985. ECOSOC Decn. 1985/132, UN ESCOR, Supp. (No. 1), at 42 (1985).

[216] *See e.g.* Rattray, E/C.12/1988/SR.21, at 3, para. 10.

[217] E/1988/14, *supra*, n. 158, at 58, para. 339; *See e.g.* Alston, E/C.12/1988/SR.21, at 3, para. 7, where it was argued that the right to an adequate standard of living could be linked with the right to social security or with the right to work.

[218] ECOSOC Resn. 1988/4, (24 May 1988), *in* E/C.12/1989/4, at 30 (1988). Although art. 17(1) requires the submission of reports in 'stages' it was considered that the term 'stages' referred to the periodicity of content. *See e.g.* Konate, E/C.12/1988/SR.21, at 4, para. 14.

[219] E/1994/23, *supra*, n. 123, at 72, para. 363.

[220] *See below*, text accompanying nn. 386–8.

[221] *See* E/1994/23, *supra*, n. 123, at 74, para. 374.   [222] *Ibid.*

to the information as soon as possible. Although the Philippines were due to submit a report on articles 10 to 12, one can only assume that the Committee would have made the request whatever the reporting situation. If that is the case, the Committee has established an important precedent for being able to request *ad hoc* reports with respect to situations which give rise to serious concern.

3 The Content of Reports

As indicated above, it is clear from the *travaux préparatoires* that the term 'programme' was to signify a programme for the timing, form, and substance of the reports submitted to ECOSOC.[223] Indeed, in the Third Committee, this view prevailed over the idea that the States parties themselves should determine the content of the reports. The latter proposal was rejected, quite rightly, on the basis that wide divergences in the form and content of the reports would arise and that the reports would soon 'degenerate into vehicles of propaganda'.[224]

States are required to report under article 16 on the 'measures which they have adopted and the progress made in achieving the observance on the rights recognized'.[225] As in article 2(1) there is an implicit question mark over how, and to what extent, the reporting obligation extends to those rights in the Covenant that are not 'recognized'. Although this question was raised by the Secretary-General in 1956,[226] no explanation was given in the drafting process that followed. The practice of the Committee, reinforced by the acquiesence of the States parties, indicates that it is understood that reports are required on all the rights in the Covenant on the same basis.

This reflects the general approach of the Committee in which it has interpreted its powers in accordance with the object or purpose of the implementation system as a whole, rather than confine itself to a strictly literal reading of Part IV of the Covenant. Thus the reporting guidelines show no signs that the Committee wishes to confine the information contained in the reports to that indicating the 'measures adopted' or the 'progress made'. Rather, the Committee has taken the view that all States parties are obliged to submit all information necessary for it to make a proper evaluation of the extent to which they comply with their obligations under the Covenant.

---

[223] UN Doc. A/2929, *supra*, n. 36, at 118, para. 12.
[224] UN Doc. A/6546, *supra*, n. 213, at 14, para. 45. *In particular see* Mr Richardson (Jamaica), UN Doc. A/C.3/SR.1401, at 143, para. 46 (1966).
[225] The ICCPR contains a substantially similar format in art. 40 where States parties 'undertake to submit reports on the measures they have adopted which give effect to the rights recognized herein and on the progress made in the enjoyment of those rights'.
[226] UN Doc. A/2929, *supra*, n. 36, at 117 para. 5.

Under article 17 States parties should indicate the 'factors and difficulties' affecting the degree of fulfilment of the rights.[227] Alston has described
the problem of persuading States to be open about the difficulties encountered in implementing the Covenant as the 'principal dilemma' facing
the Committee.[228] In one case, a State objected to the requirement that
States should indicate the difficulties experienced in the realization of the
rights. It argued that the Covenant used the term 'may' which indicated that
reporting on the difficulties experienced was optional.[229] The Committee
responded that:

it would make a mockery of the Covenant and distort its very spirit to suppose that
it only obliged States to report on the positive aspects of developments; that would
also mean disregarding the preparatory work and the international follow-up of the
Covenant.[230]

This conclusion appears to have been accepted by the State concerned.
That it is important for States to report on the problems encountered is
conditioned by the assumption that no State will consistently apply the
Covenant without problems,[231] and that the Committee has a role to play in
facilitating technical assistance.

The Committee has frequently received reports that are brief, generalized, incomplete,[232] or out of date.[233] They have impeded the process of
considering pertinent issues by the fact that the representative has had to
compensate for the inadequacies of the written report in the oral presentation before the Committee. To some extent the unsatisfactory nature of
the reports has been a result of the poor quality of the original reporting
guidelines and the difficulties experienced by States parties in drafting
them. More evidently, however, the reports show a general lack of commitment or concern with economic, social, and cultural rights.

The Committee, for its part, has been extremely active in trying to
improve the methodology and content of the reporting process. In its first
General Comment, the Committee stressed that reporting was not merely a
'procedural matter designed solely to satisfy each State Party's formal
obligation to report to the appropriate international monitoring body'.[234] It

[227] Nowak, in noting that the Torture Convention does not explicitly ask for information on
the progress made or the factors and difficulties experienced in implementation, comments
that: 'it is implicit in any efficient reporting procedure that States parties shall submit all
information relevant to the implementation of its international obligations, including both
positive and negative developments': Nowak, *supra*, n. 98, at 498.
[228] Alston P., 'Implementing Economic, Social and Cultural Rights: The Functions of the
Reporting Obligations' (1989) *Bull HR* 5.
[229] Walkate (Netherlands), E/C.12/1989/SR.15, at 9, para. 56.
[230] Alston, E/C.12/1989/SR.15, at 15, para. 87.   [231] Alston (Abyss), *supra*, n. 31, at 360.
[232] *See e.g.* Concluding observation on report of Luxembourg, Neneman, E/C.12/1990/
SR.36, at 8, para. 31. Concluding observation on report of Iran, E/C.12/1993/7, at 1, para. 2.
[233] *See e.g.* Concluding observations on report of Germany, E/C.12/1993/17, at 1, para. 2.
[234] General Comment No. 1, *supra*, n. 28, at 87, para. 1.

thereafter outlined a number of different objectives that the reporting process was intended to promote. It is perhaps correct to say that even if the Committee only manages to induce States to report in a full and timely manner, that in itself will be a considerable achievement. Whether or not the Committee should set its sights so low, it is clear that poor reporting is a matter that will not be overcome in a short space of time. Accordingly, the Committee has also taken a number of steps towards improving the quality of State reports.

In line with its right to control the content of State reports, the Committee has adopted a set of reporting guidelines to ensure that the principal issues are dealt with in a 'methodical and informative manner'.[235] These 'general guidelines' were adopted at the Committee's fifth session to replace the existing guidelines drafted by the Secretary-General following a ECOSOC resolution in 1976.[236] The old guidelines were considered too general and rendered out of date by the new reporting periodicity.[237] In addition to reflecting the developments in the substantive content of the rights, the Committee hoped to ease the reporting burden on States by simplifying the guidelines and providing a consolidated general section to be used in all human rights reporting systems.[238]

During the drafting of the guidelines, two points of view presented themselves: on the one hand it was felt that the guidelines should be shorter rather than longer, taking into account States' ability to provide detailed reports in the light of their being at present overburdened by reporting obligations[239] and the ability of the Committee to cope with the voluminous reports that might result.[240] On the other hand it was argued that detailed reporting guidelines were necessary to elicit more precise responses and to enable States to have a clearer idea of what was required.[241] Ultimately, the Committee opted to draft a more complete and detailed set of guidelines. This was undoubtedly the correct choice; the guidelines show a good understanding of the central issues pertaining to each right, avoid the necessity of asking for basic factual information, and enable the Committee to pinpoint

---

[235] E/1992/23, *supra*, n. 158, at 7, para. 22.

[236] ECOSOC Resn. 1988 (LX), (11 May 1976), *in* UN Doc. E/C.12/1989/4, at 3 (1988). A compilation of these guidelines is to be found in E/1991/23, Annex IV, *supra*, n. 142, at 88–110.

[237] E/1990/23, *supra*, n. 173, at 73, para. 288.

[238] The meeting of chairpersons recommended that an agreement should be made as to a consolidated introductory section for all human rights reports covering matters such as the size and organization of the country and its legal and judicial system: Alston, E/C.12/1989/SR.1, at 10, para. 47.

[239] *See e.g.* Neneman, E/C.12/1990/SR.15, at 11, para. 56. One member noted that if the guidelines were made too complicated, States whose statistical services were not sufficiently developed might be deterrred from reporting at all. Neneman, E/C. 12/1987/SR.23, at 3, para. 11.

[240] *See e.g.* Neneman, E/C.12/1989/SR.23, at 11, para. 90; Mrachkov, E/C.12/1989/SR.3, at 5, para. 14.

[241] *See e.g.* Sparsis, E/C.12/1990/SR.47, at 6, para. 20.

the crucial issues more effectively. As was pointed out, those States that lack the requisite bureaucratic organization to draft a report could always request technical assistance from the UN[242] which would in fact undertake to prepare the initial 'country profile' if the State party so wished.[243] That the new guidelines have been relatively effective is apparent in the most recent reports submitted to the Committee which show a considerable improvement in quality.[244]

It has become apparent, nevertheless, that there is a need for a re-evaluation of the reporting process. In order to deal with issues in reasonable depth, it has been necessary for the Committee to request States to provide greater amounts of detailed information. This in turn has meant that reports have been increasingly lengthy[245] and the Committee's task in assimilating all the material that much more difficult. The fundamental problem is that the reporting guidelines are universal and not tailored to the specific problems of a particular country. Much of the information supplied is therefore unnecessary as far as the Committee's supervision is concerned.

While considering possible future strategies, the suggestion was made at the Committee's eighth session that in the case of periodic reports, instead of submitting another full report, States should be requested to address a small number of specific issues that the Committee considers to be of particular concern.[246] These issues would be identified by the pre-sessional working group working on the basis of a 'country analysis' prepared by the Secretariat and any relevant NGO information.[247] The benefit of such a procedure would be to allow the Committee to undertake a more detailed analysis of specific situations and would incidentally reduce the reporting burden of States parties. While an interesting proposal, the success of the procedure would turn upon the Committee's ability to identify in advance the issues of concern and therefore upon the receipt of information from non-governmental sources and the co-operation of the Secretariat, neither of which may be relied upon in great measure. It would also run counter to the express purpose of the reporting system, namely, to ensure that a comprehensive review of State policy and practice is undertaken at the domestic level.

F Consideration of State Reports

The technique adopted by the Committee in the consideration of State reports is one of conducting a 'constructive and mutually rewarding dia-

---

[242] *See e.g.* Konate, E/C.12/1990/SR.47, at 8, para. 29.

[243] *See* Alston, E/C.12/1989/SR.23, at 12, para. 93.

[244] *e.g.* the report of New Zealand, E/1990/5/Add.5; the report of Canada, E/1990/6/Add.3; the report of Australia, E/1990/7/Add.13.

[245] The report of Australia on arts. 13–15 alone is 111 pages long. *Ibid.*

[246] Alston, E/C.12/1993/SR.17, at 12, para. 66.   [247] *Ibid.* 13, para. 70.

logue'[248] with State representatives. Representatives of the reporting States 'are entitled, and indeed are strongly encouraged, to be present at the meetings of the Committee when their reports are examined'.[249] The Committee describes the procedure undertaken in its report:

30. . . . The representative of the State party was invited to introduce the report by making brief introductory comments and introducing any written replies, or otherwise responding orally, to the list of issues drawn up by the pre-sessional working group. A period of time was then allocated to enable the representatives of the specialized agencies to provide the Committee with any observations relevant to the report under consideration. During the same period, members of the Committee were invited to put questions and observations to the representative of the State party. A further period of time, preferably not on the same day, was then allocated to enable the representative to respond, as precisely as possible, to the questions asked. It was generally understood that questions that could not adequately be dealt with in this manner could be the subject of additional information provided to the Committee in writing.

The final phase of the Committee's examination of the report consists of the drafting and adoption of the Committee's concluding observations . . . Within a day or so of the completion of the dialogue with the State party's representatives, the Committee will set aside a thirty-minute period, in closed session, to enable its members to express their preliminary views. The member with primary responsibility in relation to the State party concerned will then prepare, with the assistance of the secretariat, a draft set of concluding observations for consideration by the Committee . . . At a later stage, the Committee then discusses the draft, again in private session, with a view to adopting it by consensus.

The concluding observations are formally adopted in public session on the final or penultimate day of the session. As soon as this occurs they are considered to have been made public. They are then forwarded to the State party concerned and included in the Committee's report. If it so wishes, the State party may address any of the Committee's concluding observations in the context of any additional information that it provides to the Committee.[250]

1 Theoretical Underpinnings of the Constructive Dialogue

The constructive dialogue is primarily intended to allow the Committee to enter into a mutually beneficial dialogue regarding the degree to which the State concerned has fulfilled its obligations under the Covenant, without the necessity of formal declarations of compliance or non-compliance.[251]

[248] E/1993/22, *supra*, n. 200, at 14, para. 32.
[249] *Ibid.* 9, para. 31. Rule 62 of the Rules of Procedure provides: 'Representatives of the reporting States are entitled to be present at the meetings of the committee when their reports are examined. Such representatives should be able to make statements on the reports submitted by their States and reply to questions which may be put to them by the members of the Committee': *supra*, n. 116, at 14.
[250] E/1994/23, *supra*, n. 123, at 16, paras. 32–4.
[251] *See e.g.* Robertson, *supra*, n. 23, at 344.

There are a number of benefits of such an approach. First, in so far as representatives provide answers to the issues of concern it allows the Committee to make a more precise analysis of the problems and intricacies of the situation.[252] Secondly, it gives the Committee an opportunity to offer informal suggestions and recommendations based on their wide experience in the field.[253] Thirdly, it avoids the type of confrontation that may occur with governments following formal declarations of non-compliance.[254]

2 *Effectiveness of the Approach*

As Nowak comments, 'the efficiency of the procedure depends however primarily on the willingness of States' representatives to get down to the problems and engage in a constructive dialogue with the Committee'.[255] Despite the problem of postponements,[256] the constructive dialogue approach has been a relatively successful experience for the Committee. It has not suffered, for example, the problems of the HRC with the refusal of certain States to participate in the process.[257] Indeed, in general the participation of States has been good and a number of the discussions detailed and informative.

However the unwillingness of certain States to participate in good faith has presented the Committee with a number of problems. Despite the fact that the approach is supposedly one of mutual benefit, the Committee is often faced by representatives that are either inept, consummately evasive, or disarmingly open.[258] The Committee has consistently emphasized the desirability of States parties' reports to be presented by experts in the fields concerned.[259] Unfortunately, a certain number of States continue to dispatch representatives who do not possess sufficient experience or knowledge to be able to answer the questions of the Committee in a proficient manner.[260] The Committee has adopted the policy of naming the representatives of the States concerned in Annex V of its annual reports, presumably with a view to indicating which States take the reporting process seriously. In addition, it was suggested at the Committee's sixth session that the Committee should make clear that delegations composed solely of a single Ambassador would in most cases be inadequate.[261]

---

[252] Das, *supra*, n. 163, at 258.   [253] *Ibid.*   [254] Fischer, *supra*, n. 23, at 168.

[255] Nowak, *supra*, n. 98, at 201.   [256] *See below*, text accompanying nn. 308–14.

[257] *See* 'Human Rights Committee: Commentary' (1978) 20 *ICJ Rev.* 25. This has not, however, been an enduring problem for the HRC, *see* McGoldrick, *supra*, n. 24, at 82.

[258] *See e.g.* Grissa, E/C.12/1993/SR.11, at 2, para. 3.

[259] *See e.g.* Mratchkov, E/C.12/1991/SR.10, at 9, para. 46; *Cf.* E/1988/14, *supra*, n. 158, at 62, para. 362.

[260] *See e.g.* Concluding observation on the report of Mexico, Alston, E/C.12/1990/SR.11, at 7, para. 40.

[261] *See* Alston, E/C.12/1991/SR.10, at 9, para. 48.

Although this remains a problem, to a large extent States have provided more than one person in their delegations and have displayed a considerable amount of expertise.[262] It is considered that the Committee should look towards the presence of larger delegations with broad expertise. Inevitably, questions generally cover a large range of subjects that are not necessarily the responsibility of any single person in the government administration. Thus, unlike bodies dealing with civil and political rights, the presence of the Minister of Justice alone, for example, would not be adequate.[263]

It is not merely the expertise of the State delegation that is of concern, but also its willingness to participate constructively in the dialogue. It is not uncommon for the Committee to be confronted by diplomats who evade answering the questions posed.[264] On occasions the Committee has adopted a more flexible approach to the dialogue in which the representative is asked to answer each question as it arises instead of waiting until all the questions had been asked. In the case of Iran, for example, this produced a much more effective form of dialogue in which individual members of the Committee were able to pursue their points until they had elicited an adequate response.[265] There is some doubt whether such a procedure would work successfully in the case of other States where knowledge within the Committee would be less broad-based, but it is considered that it is the form of dialogue to which the Committee should aspire.

The fact that the Committee has only a single three-week session per annum also places a certain pressure on the constructive dialogue in terms of time.[266] The tendency of State representatives to present their reports at great length[267] and of members of the Committee to duplicate their questions[268] has stimulated the Committee to place time limits on the various sections of the Constructive dialogue.[269] It was thus decided at the Committee's fourth session that, in line with the practice of the HRC, up to three meetings would be used to consider a report. Within that time-scale, one to two hours would be set aside for the state party representative to introduce the report and to respond to the list of written questions. Three hours would be given to questions from members of the Committee followed by a further three hours for replies by the State party. Finally, up to one hour on

---

[262] *See e.g.* the list of State delegates which participated in the Committee's 6th session. E/1992/23, Annex V, *supra*, n. 158, at 139–141.

[263] *Cf.* Gaer, *supra*, n. 27, at 38.

[264] *See e.g.* Representative of Colombia, E/C.12/1990/SR.13–14.

[265] E/C.12/1993/SR.8.

[266] It has been noted that lack of time has also seriously affected the operation of CEDAW, *see* Burnes A., 'CEDAW's Tenth Session' (1991) 3 *NQHR* 340.

[267] *Cf.* Higgins, *supra*, n. 153, at 19.   [268] *Cf.* Dormenval, *supra*, n. 107, at 32.

[269] The suggestion was first made at the Committee's 1st session that, in order to expedite the Committee's procedure, it might adopt the practice of the specialized agencies and set time-limits on statements. Sparsis, E/C.12/1987/SR.23, at 5, para. 23.

a subsequent day would be set aside for concluding observations by members of the Committee.[270] It is clear from the Committee's practice, however, that these time limits are primarily 'indicative', relating more to the need to fulfil its schedule than to engender more accurate and concise responses from the State representative. At its most recent sessions for example, there is little evidence that these limits have been strictly imposed. Although there is certainly a need for the Committee to maintain a degree of flexibility in the process to allow for real dialogue to take place,[271] the Committee still needs to exercise some control over those State representatives that spend an excessive amount of time discussing irrelevant issues.[272]

Several other possibilities for expediting the questioning process have been discussed, such as limiting the Committee to a single set of questions,[273] and limiting the oral questions to those members not members of the pre-sessional working group.[274] It is considered that, in accordance with the idea of setting up a dialogue, the Committee should maintain its ability to ask further questions on issues that have not been adequately addressed. Despite the limits of time and the necessity of allowing all the members of the Committee to ask questions at some stage, it should not be necessary that the members of the Committee generally, or of the pre-sessional working group in particular, be restricted from asking further questions when required. This is the case even if there should result some duplication in the questions asked.[275]

One of the major problems with the questioning process is that the questions tend to be general and unfocused.[276] Little attention is paid to the actual text of the Covenant and quite often questions are asked as to matters that appear to have only indirect relevance to the rights concerned. One method of ensuring more specific and informed questions would be to introduce a form of division of labour within the Committee, like that

---

[270] E/1994/23, *supra*, n. 123, at 17, para. 37.

[271] *See e.g.* Simma, E/C.12/1991/SR.10, at 11, para. 54.

[272] *See e.g.* Nanjira (Kenya), E/C.12/1994/SR.12, at 5–6, para. 17.

[273] *See* Jimenez Butragueno, E/C.12/1989/SR.8, at 11, para. 63.

[274] *See* Simma, E/C.12/1989/SR.8, at 11, para. 62.

[275] The Committee commented in the report of its second session: 'It was noted, however, that some duplication was both inevitable and desirable and that it would not be appropriate to seek to limit the type of issues which Committee members might wish to raise': E/1988/14, *supra*, n. 158, at 59, para. 345.

[276] As Alston noted: 'Regarding the process of questioning . . . the only way to elicit detailed and focused responses from the Governments concerned was to begin by asking very specific questions. A general question inevitably gave rise to a standard response whereas a specific one, requesting facts and figures which were generally available to the Government, led to targetted and meaningful dialogue. Similarly, a precise question based on information in the Committee's possession would yield an explicit confirmation or denial, as the case may be. In any case the question and the Government's recorded answer would constitute a tangible contribution to the international debate': Alston, E/C.12/1991/SR.10, at 5, para. 25.

instituted in other fora,[277] in which members of the Committee would be assigned responsibility for questions in certain areas.[278] Although this might discourage members from asking questions on issues outside their area of responsibility,[279] it would encourage individual members to become specialists in their designated areas and thus engender a greater specificity in questioning. An additional benefit would be to enable the Committee to identify those areas in which it requires further specialist input in future years.

3 The Pre-Sessional Working Group

In response to a request by the Committee,[280] ECOSOC in Resolution 1988/4 authorized the creation of a pre-sessional working group[281] whose principal task (although it had no fixed mandate and could undertake a variety of tasks[282]) would be 'to identify in advance the questions which might most usefully be discussed with the representatives of the reporting States'.[283] By doing so, it was thought that it would improve the efficiency of the system and facilitate the task of States parties by providing advance notice of the issues that might arise in the examination of reports.[284] The establishment of the pre-sessional working group was a logical step in the work of the Committee[285] given the diverse range of issues covered, their complexity, and the need for precise and detailed information. It has also been noted that, by removing the element of surprise, the chances of an altercation between the State concerned and the Committee have been reduced.[286]

Accordingly a pre-sessional working group composed of five members, appointed by the Chairman with due regard for a balanced geographical distribution, has met for five days prior to all of the Committee's recent sessions. Following a request by the Committee at its fourth session, ECOSOC approved the holding of the working group's session at a time one to three months prior to the Committee's session,[287] despite the additional (if only marginal) cost. The change in schedule was aimed at allowing sufficient time for the list of questions to be translated into the appropriate language, the transmission of the list to the capital concerned and the preparation of adequate responses by the relevant State party. It

---

[277] *Cf.* Alston, E/C.12/1988/SR.2, at 3, para. 8.
[278] e.g. within the Committee of Independent Experts to the European Social Charter.
[279] *See e.g.* Rattray, E/C.12/1988/SR.22, at 4, para. 24.
[280] E/1988/14, *supra*, n. 158, at 60, para. 348.
[281] ECOSOC Resn. 1988/4, *supra*, n. 218, at 31, para. 10.
[282] *See* Alston, E/C.12/1989/SR.1, at 7, para. 36.
[283] E/1993/22, *supra*, n. 200, at 12, para. 23.
[284] E/1988/14, *supra*, n. 158, at 62, para. 361.
[285] E/1993/22, *supra*, n. 200, at 13, para. 24.
[286] *See* Rattray, E/C.12/1987/SR.4, at 11, para. 4.
[287] ECOSOC Decn. 1990/252, (25 May 1990).

would also allow greater time for the translation and dissemination of the list of issues to Committee members.[288] Since then, the Committee has perceived a need for more time to be given to the States concerned.[289] Working on the assumption that it would continue to hold two sessions annually, the Committee decided that the working group should meet for five days immediately prior to each session but should deal with matters relating to the following session.[290] While this has clear advantages in terms of cost,[291] it is dependent upon the Committee being given a permanent second session each year.

Each member of the working group is assigned a particular report, or reports, taking into consideration the preferred areas of expertise.[292] He or she is then required to make a particularly detailed study of the report and draw up, with the assistance of a file of information provided by the Secretariat[293] and by NGOs, a draft list of the issues which appear to be important for consideration by the working group as a whole. The final list of issues is then transmitted to the permanent delegations of the relevant States together with a copy of the Committee's most recent report and a note indicating that the list of questions is 'not intended to be exhaustive' and 'should not be interpreted as limiting or in any other way prejudging the type and range of questions which members of the Committee might wish to ask'.[294]

Certain operating problems have been identified with regard to the pre-sessional working group. At the Committee's fourth session, following Luxembourg's request for additional time to prepare its responses in light of the number of questions put before it, it became apparent that there was a need to streamline the list of issues drawn up by the working group.[295] Although it was noted in that case that the length of the list of issues was partly a reflection of the poor quality of the report,[296] the matter arose again at the Committee's ninth session. There it was pointed out that streamlining was required not so much to limit the number of questions *per se*, but rather to ensure that the questions posed were 'precise and clearly focused'.[297] The need for greater precision has also led the Committee to recommend that States should provide written, rather than merely oral, replies to the list of questions.[298]

Nowak considers that the consequences of the use of the pre-sessional working group by the HRC has been 'to protract rather than streamline the procedure, and the hope for more controlled exchange of views and infor-

---

[288] E/1989/22, *supra*, n. 142, at 75, para. 338.
[289] *See e.g.* Rattray, E/C.12/1991/SR.10, at 9, para. 44.
[290] E/1994/23, *supra*, n. 123, at 73, para. 371.   [291] *Ibid.*   [292] *Ibid.* 15, para. 27.
[293] *Ibid.* 15, para. 28.   [294] E/1993/22, *supra*, n. 200, at 13, para. 27.
[295] *See* Alston, E/C.12/1990/SR.12, at 1, para. 2.
[296] *See* Simma, E/C.12/1990/SR.12, at 1, para. 4.
[297] E/1994/23, *supra*, n. 123, at 72, para. 365.   [298] *Ibid.* at para. 367.

mation between States representatives and members of the Committee has not materialised yet'. He goes on to assert that it is only the oral questions that really stimulate 'a spontaneous and critical discussion'.[299] However, it must be stressed that for the CESCR the work of the pre-sessional working group is an important element in extending what would otherwise be a brief and unsatisfactory dialogue. The fact that the process is more protracted is really of concern only in so far as it is a drain on the financial resources of the UN which, in the case of the pre-sessional working group, is marginal.

From the point of view of supervising State compliance with the obligations under the Covenant, a sustained dialogue will enable greater specificity and more accurate evaluation. In addition it would be inaccurate to maintain that the Committee does not, by use of the working group, exercise more control over the exchange of views. The pre-sessional working group in theory enables the Committee to direct the constructive dialogue to those issues of greatest concern. It has to be said, nevertheless, that the Committee's consideration of reports has not improved dramatically since the operation of the pre-sessional working group. The questions asked in plenary sessions appear to be equally general, and it is still rare for the Committee to enter into a detailed debate about the issues that have arisen. The main function of the working group, as indicated above,[300] has been as a means of ensuring that the Committee is provided with all the information requested by the reporting guidelines. It is considered that the full potential of the pre-sessional working group will only be realized once States have undertaken to report in a full and accurate manner, and when the Committee has access to sufficient alternative sources of information that problem areas may be identified at an early stage in the constructive dialogue process. Until that time the working group will function in its present limited manner.

Outside the operation of the constructive dialogue, the Committee has also been able to use the pre-sessional working group to undertake a number of tasks that would otherwise consume the Committee's own precious working time.[301] In particular, the working group has been mandated with:

(i) the allocation of time limits in the consideration of State reports;[302]
(ii) considering the transitional arrangements for the extension of the reporting periodicity to five years;[303]
(iii) making a preliminary study of the draft general guidelines;[304]

---

[299] Nowak, *supra*, n. 98, at 201.　　[300] *See above*, text accompanying n. 283.
[301] For the work of the pre-sessional working group at the Committee's 6th session, *see* Texier, E/C.12/1991/SR.1, at 7–8, paras. 36–8.
[302] E/1989/22, *supra*, n. 142, at 2, para. 13.　　[303] E/1989/22, *ibid.* 2, para. 13.
[304] *See* Simma, E/C.12/1990/SR.1, at 6, para. 37.

    (iv) considering how to deal with supplementary reports containing additional information and formulating comments and recommendations on them;[305]

    (v) examining draft general comments;[306]

    (vi) drawing up a list of issues to be addressed during the general discussion.[307]

4 Non-Appearance before the Committee

A recurring problem for the Committee has been the continual deferral by States parties of the consideration of their reports after they have been scheduled in the Committee's work. At the Committee's eighth session, for example, five States asked at the last minute to postpone the consideration of their reports until the following Committee session.[308] Such postponements, particularly when requested at the last minute, have a debilitating effect on the work of the Committee. They disrupt the Committee's schedule of work, waste valuable conference time, and may render nugatory the work undertaken by the pre-sessional working group. Equally, deferrals may significantly inconvenience specialized agencies, NGOs, and other interested parties that had planned their activities on the assumption that the report would be presented.[309] In so far as the Committee is attempting to encourage the participation of such organizations, this is particularly unfortunate.

The Committee adopted decisions at both its fifth[310] and seventh sessions[311] in which it stressed that deferrals should only be sought in extreme circumstances and that in appropriate cases (following the example of the HRC[312]) it might 'proceed with the examination of a report despite a request by a State party for a deferral'.[313] As the evidence of later sessions showed, such decisions did not meet with much success. Thus, at its eighth session, the Committee decided to amend its rules of procedure and establish that once a State party has agreed to the scheduling of its report for consideration by the Committee, the Committee will proceed with the

---

[305] UN Doc. E/1990/23, *supra*, n. 173, at 3, para. 11. Prior to the 4th session the pre-sessional working group considered the additional reports received from the Netherlands, France, and Zaïre.

[306] E/1993/22, *supra*, n. 200, at 13, para. 29.

[307] E/1994/23, *supra*, n. 123, at 67, para. 343.

[308] The Committee was forced to suspend its session for 3 days as a result: *ibid.* 75, paras. 345–6.

[309] *Ibid.* 67, para. 346.   [310] E/1991/23, *supra*, n. 142, at 9, para. 35.

[311] E/1993/22, *supra*, n. 200, at 65, para. 247.

[312] The HRC has occasionally considered state reports without the representative being present (it first did this in 1983 at its 20th session with the report of Guinea). 'Human Rights Committee: Commentary' (1984) 33 *ICJ Rev.* 39. Nowak M., 'UN Human Rights Committee: Survey of Decisions given up till 1984' (1984) 5 *HRLJ* 199, at 200.

[313] E/1993/22, *supra*, n. 200, at 65, para. 248.

examination of that report at the scheduled time, with or without the representative of the State party.[314]

Although this procedure might mean that States will dispense with the need to attend the Committee's meetings (it being clear that they are under no obligation to attend), it seems a clear and sensible arrangement given the problems encountered at the Committee's eighth session. States are likely to recognize quite quickly that if the Committee does proceed with the consideration of the report, non-attendance is unlikely to benefit them. Without explanations being provided by the State, it is far more likely that the Committee will make adverse findings on the evidence before it.[315] Indeed the Committee has been able to claim some limited success for the procedure in that, at its tenth session, no States asked to withdraw at the last minute.

5 Sources of Information

Perhaps the most crucial factor in the success of any reporting procedure is the extent to which the supervisory body has access to information other than that provided by the State concerned.[316] If reliance is placed merely upon the information provided by the State, it is the State that controls the terms of discussion by raising or avoiding issues at will. 'Alternative' sources of information provide the Committee with a necessary foil to evaluate the State reports and contribute towards a more balanced assessment of the actual situation in a given country. Additionally, in that such information may contain allegations regarding violations of the Covenant upon which the Committee may rely in making its evaluation of the report, the provision of alternative information can operate in a manner similar to that of a petition.[317]

In reality States never have a complete monopoly over the information available to a Committee: Committee members will inevitably bring with them information they have gathered generally as experts in their fields. Nevertheless, in a number of Committees this is the extent to which reference may be made to alternative sources of information. As has been noted, there has been a reluctance on the part of monitoring bodies to institutionalize the receipt of information from other sources upon the false premise that it is necessarily less accurate.[318]

---

[314] E/1994/23, *supra*, n. 123, at 68, para. 347.
[315] Alston, E/C.12/1993/SR.14, at 10, para. 50.
[316] The Committee makes the following comment in its annual report: 'The Committee has consistently noted that access to all relevant sources of information pertaining to economic, social and cultural rights was essential in order to enable it to discharge its monitoring functions effectively': E/1992/23, *supra*, n. 158, at 100, para. 384.
[317] *See* in relation to CERD, Buergenthal, *supra*, n. 10, at 202.
[318] Alston, *supra*, n. 31, at 496.

There are a number of benefits to be gained from allowing a supervisory committee open access to alternative sources of information. First, it removes from individual members the burden of seeking relevant information informally and allows for more consistent and greater amounts of information to be available. Secondly, it allows the Committee as a whole to assess the relevance and accuracy of the information provided. Thirdly, it provides NGOs with a permanent and formal mechanism through which they might present their concerns which might encourage greater participation. Finally, it allows for the involvement of the Secretariat which might actively seek information on the Committee's behalf.

The text of the Covenant itself makes scant reference to the use of alternative sources of information. Although the specialized agencies may submit reports to ECOSOC 'on the progress made in achieving the observance of the provisions of the present Covenant falling within the scope of their activities',[319] nothing is said about the possibility of their participating in the consideration of the reports or of any other bodies submitting information to ECOSOC. The Committee, however, in stressing the importance of alternative information in enabling it to discharge its monitoring functions effectively, has taken the unprecedented step of officially inviting 'all concerned bodies and individuals to submit relevant and appropriate documentation to it'.[320] The basis for this step and the various forms of information received will be addressed below.

(a) The Specialized Agencies

As noted above, the Covenant makes specific reference to the possibility of the specialized agencies reporting to ECOSOC in the supervisory process. Indeed, that all but two articles in Part IV of the Covenant refer in some manner to the specialized agencies, emphasizes the important role envisaged for them during the drafting of the Covenant.[321]

Although there was considerable textual support for the participation of the specialized agencies in the consideration of State reports, following the entry into force of the Covenant, attempts were made to minimize their input. A number of States (particularly the USSR) opposed the consideration of the agencies' reports and attempted to prevent them from commenting on State reports, or speaking within the working group.[322] The result was that the ILO, at least, ceased to prepare special reports for the working group.

Although it is clearly unfortunate that the agencies were actively discouraged from participating in the supervision of the reports, two important

---

[319] Art. 18, ICESCR.   [320] E/1992/23, *supra*, n. 158, at 100, para. 386.
[321] *See above*, text accompanying nn. 38–40, and 50–60.
[322] *See generally* Samson, *supra*, n. 38, at 635–7. For an overview of the ILO experience *see* 'Impact of ILO Policies on the UN', ILO Doc. GB.225/IO/3/3, 16–22 (1984).

points were raised about the form of their participation. First, it is apparent that the agencies may receive copies of the relevant parts of State reports,[323] and may submit reports 'on the progress made',[324] but it is open to question whether they are entitled to comment specifically upon the reports of States parties. Ramcharan argues that, whereas the *travaux préparatoires* were 'inconclusive' on the point, at the end of the Council discussion 'there was a clear agreement among all representatives that the specialized agencies could not comment on the reports of States Parties'.[325]

It is considered that this is not the most obvious inference to be drawn from the text of the Covenant. It leaves the specialized agencies in the curious position of being able to utilize the information in the State reports to draw up their own reports under article 18, but not being able to refer to the State reports *per se*. The Committee has not actively sought to clarify this issue. In practice the ILO has undertaken to submit reports 'on the results of the operation of various ILO supervisory procedures in the fields covered by the Covenant'.[326] The reports do not make specific reference to the State reports, nor do they attempt to make a separate evaluation of the implementation of the Covenant.[327] On the other hand, the last report submitted by UNESCO, despite being less comprehensive and more general than the ILO reports, does make reference to the State reports, indicating matters that have not been dealt with and discrepancies in data.[328] As no mention has been made of this development it is assumed that it is satisfactory to all concerned.

The second issue that was raised in the working group concerned the active participation of the agencies in the oral discussion of the reports. Although the Covenant does not refer to the possibility of the specialized agencies assisting ECOSOC in the consideration of reports, the Council expressly authorized representatives of the agencies to 'take part in the proceedings of the Working Group'.[329] Samson argues that the attempt to prevent the representatives from speaking 'would have been contrary not only to the terms of the Council Resolution establishing the Working Group and to the Rules of Procedure of the Council, which were expressly applicable, but to the relationship agreements between the UN and the specialized agencies'.[330]

The Committee has in its Rules of Procedure specifically endorsed the right of specialized agencies to participate in the debate on State reports

---

[323] Art. 16(2)(b).   [324] Art. 18.   [325] Ramcharan, *supra*, n. 63, at 159.

[326] UN Doc. E/1992/4, at 1 (1991). The reports of the ILO to the Committee are to be found in documents: E/1987/59 (1986); E/1988/6 (1987); E/1989/6 (1988); E/1990/9 (1989); E/1991/4 (1990); E/1992/4 (1991); E/1993/4 (1992); E/1994/5 (1993).

[327] *See* Dao (ILO), E/C.12/1988/SR.2, at 5, para. 21.

[328] *See e.g.* Comments of UNESCO on the reports of Argentina, the Philippines, and Ecuador, UN Doc. E/1990/8 (1989).

[329] ECOSOC Resn. 1988 (LX), *supra*, n. 236, at 5.   [330] Samson, *supra*, n. 38, at 637.

within the Committee. Rule 68 states that representatives of specialized agencies 'may make statements on matters falling within the scope of the activities of their respective organizations in the course of the discussion by the Committee of the report of each State party to the Covenant'.[331] Amendments made at the fourth session of the Committee in the light of its established practice make it clear that this rule does not impede the representatives from making specific comments as appropriate.[332]

It is clear that not all specialized agencies are directly involved in the matters covered by the Covenant. Only a limited number participated in the drafting of the Covenant, and an inter-agency consultation in 1976 elicited interest only from the ILO, WHO, UNESCO, and the FAO.[333] Although the provisions of the Covenant certainly do not limit the participation to these specialized agencies, there is no correlative power for the Committee to demand co-operation. The Committee has recently noted the importance of economic, social, and cultural rights in the work of the international financial institutions.[334] As such it has read the reference in article 22 to specialized agencies as including, in addition to the above four agencies, the World Bank (IBRD) and the IMF.[335]

A differentiation might be made between co-operation with the ILO, for example, and co-operation with the financial institutions such as the IMF. Whereas the former can contribute directly to the elucidation of standards within the Covenant, the latter is relevant only in so far as aid provided, or the terms and conditions upon which it is based, may affect the economic, social, and cultural rights of the population concerned.[336] Accordingly it might be concluded that the financial institutions have little part to play in the supervisory role of the Covenant.[337] However, given the possible utility of statistical indicators in the Committee's supervisory functions,[338] the financial institutions and other UN organs might have a significant role to play in providing the Committee with an idea of the current level at which certain rights are enjoyed and the progress made over time.[339] The Committee, recognizing the vast information resources of the financial institu-

---

[331] Rules of Procedure, *supra*, n. 116, at 21.

[332] E/1990/23, *supra*, n. 173, at 74, para. 293.

[333] Sohn, *supra*, n. 61, at 32–3.   [334] E/1990/23, Annex III, *supra*, n. 173, at 86–9.

[335] *Ibid*. 86, para. 2.

[336] *See* Harris D., 'Commentary by the Rapporteur on the Consideration of States Parties' Reports and International Co-operation' (1987) 9 *Hum. Rts. Q* 147, at 153.

[337] The term supervision here is intended to exclude the provision of technical assistance (art. 22), to which the Committee's General Comment No. 2 was directed.

[338] *See* the general discussion at the Committee's 6th session, E/1992/23, Chap. VII, *supra*, n. 158, at 81–6. paras. 332–51.

[339] For the potential role of the World Bank in the implementation of the right to food, *see* Van Hoof G. and Tahzib B., 'Supervision with Respect to the Right to Food and the Role of the World Bank', in de Waart P., Peters P., and Denters E. (eds.), *International Law and Development*, 317 (1988). Alston comments: 'the position with respect to the right to food or the right to education in a given country would be described in infinitely more detail and in a far more informative way in internal reports regularly prepared by the World Bank, the FAO,

tions, resolved to request the World Bank (together with UNESCO, UNICEF, and UNDP) to provide the Committee with all country-specific information relating to the implementation of economic, social, and cultural rights.[340]

As the Committee noted in its General Comment No. 2, 'the attendance by representatives of the appropriate United Nations bodies at its first four sessions has, with the notable exceptions of ILO, UNESCO, and WHO, been very low. Similarly, pertinent materials and written information had been received from only a very limited number of agencies'.[341] Even though representatives of the specialized agencies frequently speak enthusiastically about the possibilities of co-operation,[342] there is little evidence of that becoming a reality. At the Committee's first nine sessions, only the ILO has attended every session. UNESCO has attended eight sessions, the WHO six, and the FAO only two.[343] Similarly, whereas the ILO has submitted written information almost every session, UNESCO has submitted only two reports and the FAO and WHO have as yet submitted no written information to the Committee. Even the ILO, which has by far the best record, has limited itself to providing the Committee with the relevant extracts of ILO supervisory procedures and appears to have abandoned its practice of addressing each State as it presents its report.

The possible reasons for the poor record of participation are diverse. One may surmise that it is a result, in part at least, of the hostility shown by the working group to the specialized agencies. Other reasons include the more general inability of the UN and the agencies to co-operate successfully[344] and the traditional concern that involvement in human rights would politicize the work of the agencies and prejudice their future effectiveness. It is curious that the Committee has not made a concerted effort to encourage the agencies concerned to resume the form of participation that they were willing undertake in 1976. At that stage the ILO, for example, resolved to entrust the Committee of Experts on the Application of Conventions and Recommendations with the task of examining the State reports and other available information on the implementation of the Covenant.[345] It is considered that ideally this is the level of co-operation that the Committee should look towards.

UNICEF, and other agencies than in the reports submitted to the Committee by the States themselves': Alston, *supra*, n. 31, at 500.

[340] E/C.12/1993/CRP.1/Add.3, at 12, para. 37.

[341] General Comment No. 2, UN Doc. E/1990/23, Annex III, at 86–7, para. 4, UN ESCOR, Supp. (No. 3) (1990). As of 1994, the Committee continued to lament its 'inability to obtain consistent access to important and directly relevant documentation prepared by various United Nations Agencies', UN Doc. E/1994/23, *supra*, n. 123, at 84, para. 375.

[342] *See e.g.* Pinet (WHO), E/C.12/1992/SR.11, at 10, para. 44. Cf. Bonev (UNDP), E/C.12/1992/SR.1, at 3, para. 17.

[343] More recently the UNDP and IMF have made appearances before the Committee.

[344] *See* Samson, *supra*, n. 38, at 669–70.   [345] *Ibid.* 636.

It has been suggested that the best way to use the experience of the specialized agencies was not necessarily through asking them for information or requesting them to attend the Committee meetings, but rather by members of the Committee making their own inter-disciplinary studies to obtain the necessary information themselves.[346] Although this would certainly allow the Committee to tailor the substance and form of the information received from such sources to suit its own needs and would help develop the personal expertise of the Committee members, it is a rather poor substitute for full participation by the agencies themselves. It is also doubtful that the Committee members themselves would be willing or able to take on that task given the limited amount of time available to them in sessions.

(b) Non-Governmental Organizations

The participation by NGOs in the work of the Committee is the most significant and perhaps the most controversial aspect of the supervision system as currently operated. The Covenant itself makes no reference to the participation of NGOs in the supervisory process. However, as ECOSOC has primary responsibility for considering State reports, it is arguable that supervision should take place in accordance with the Council's normal rules of procedure. According to ECOSOC Resolution 1296 (XLIV),[347] NGOs are, according to their consultative category, entitled to submit written statements and make oral presentations to the Council.[348] It would appear, therefore, that a limited form of NGO participation in the consideration of State reports under the Covenant may be accommodated.

However, at the Committee's first session, the question of NGO participation sparked a heated debate.[349] It was argued by those who opposed the provision of NGO material, that the Council decisions governing the work of the Committee provided only for the attendance of NGOs.[350] Further, the later and more specific Council resolutions took legal precedence over the earlier general resolution allowing for the participation of NGOs in the work of the Council.[351] On the other hand, it was argued that NGO material was essential to the work of the Committee and that there was nothing in the Council's later resolutions that ruled out the possibility of the submission of that material.[352] The question was eventually referred

---

[346] *See* Alston, E/C.12/1989/SR.2, at 7, para. 32.

[347] ECOSOC Resn. 1296 (XLIV) (1968).

[348] *See generally* Chiang P., *Non-Governmental Organisations at the United Nations* (1981).

[349] *See* Alston and Simma, *supra*, n. 91, at 752.

[350] ECOSOC Resn.1984/9, (24 May 1984), *in* UN Doc. E/C.12/1989/4, at 16 (1988).

[351] *See* Sviridov, E/C.12/1987/SR.24, at 9, para. 64; Mratchkov, *ibid.* 10, para. 67.

[352] *See e.g.* Simma, E/C.12/1987/SR.24, at 10, para. 66; Rattray, *ibid.* 10, para. 69.

to ECOSOC which, in Resolution 1987/5,[353] resolved the issue by formally inviting NGOs to submit to it 'written statements that might contribute to full and universal recognition and realization of the rights in the Covenant'.[354] Interestingly enough, this is not restricted to NGOs with consultative status to ECOSOC.

In general, NGO participation is limited to the submission of written statements; NGOs may not participate in the Committee's dialogue with States parties. NGOs do, however, have certain limited opportunities to contribute orally in the Committee's work. First, it is clear that individual NGO representatives may participate in their capacity as experts in the Committee's general discussions.[355] Secondly, NGOs may submit relevant oral information to the pre-sessional working group.[356] Thirdly, and most significantly, it was decided at the Committee's eighth session that the first afternoon of each of the Committee's sessions would be set aside to hear information from NGOs which is of direct relevance to its consideration of reports during that session.[357]

While the primary objective of the new procedure for allowing oral presentations by NGOs is undoubtedly to foster wider participation by developing the official channels of communication, it also has the benefit of placing such participation on a more 'transparent basis'.[358] In particular, it goes some way to address the concern of States which have felt themselves to be disadvantaged by the fact that they have not had access to NGO information upon which the Committee has relied in its questions.[359] To avoid the procedure being undermined by political confrontation between NGOs and States, the Committee requires that the information should focus on the provisions of the Covenant, be of direct relevance to matters under consideration by the Committee, be reliable, and not be abusive.[360] Although such guarantees are appropriate given the adversarial nature of many NGO communications, it is unclear how the Committee will enforce them without prior scrutiny of the information. If prior scrutiny does take place, it is difficult to see why the information should subsequently be presented orally to the Committee.

The institutionalization of mechanisms for the submission of NGO information has a number of advantages over the informal process undertaken

---

[353] ECOSOC Resn. 1987/5 (26 May 1987), *in* UN Doc. E/C.12/1989/4, at 27 (1988).
[354] *Ibid.* para. 6.   [355] *See below*, text accompanying nn. 430–42.
[356] Rule 69.2, Rules of Procedure, *supra*, n. 116, at 21.
[357] Rule 69.3, *ibid.* This procedure was operated at the Committee's 9th and 10th sessions.
[358] *Ibid.*
[359] *See e.g.* Comments of Panama, Simma, E/C.12/1993/SR.3, at 4, paras. 12–13. Cf. Alston, E/C.12/1993/SR.3, at 8, para. 42. The Committee stresses that where information is referred to by any member of the Committee, it should be made available to the State party, E/1994/23, *supra*, n. 123, at 78, para. 354.
[360] Rule 69.3, Rules of Procedure, *supra*, n. 116, at 21.

by other Committees[361] not least because it should stimulate greater NGO involvement in the work of the Committee.[362] However, the experience of the Committee thus far has not been promising; only a handful of NGOs have participated in any one session and the number of written statements submitted to the Committee has been low. This poor response has not been due to any lack of enthusiasm on the part of the Committee. Indeed in many cases (such as in the reports of Iran, the Dominican Republic, Panama, Italy, and Canada) the Committee has relied heavily upon detailed NGO information in adopting its conclusions.[363] Indeed, in the case of Canada, the Committee was criticized for its 'uncritical acceptance of certain assertions' put forward by NGOs.[364] The fact that the Committee is prepared to rely upon NGO information is extremely encouraging. It suggests that, if developed in a more systematic manner, the receipt of NGO information might at some time in the future become assimilated to a form of informal petition system.

The major obstacles to creative NGO participation in the work of the Committee seem to relate to a lack of sufficient publicity and to the geographical and structural constraints regarding the nature of the organizations working within the sphere of economic, social, and cultural rights. The relevant NGOs can be classified as either international 'development' NGOs, which direct and promote technical and material aid to 'underdeveloped' countries, or national 'voluntary organizations' which deal with concerns such as welfare rights and housing and which operate purely in the domestic field. Neither category of organization naturally draws upon the work of human rights bodies, nor would it necessarily have consultative status in ECOSOC. Conversely, the existing human rights NGOs have shown a distinct reluctance to become involved with the promotion of economic, social, and cultural rights.[365]

That there is little homogeneity in the types of organizations that might successfully contribute to the Committee's work suggests that there is no single method to encourage greater participation. Beyond the ever-important question of publicity, the most critical factor will be the degree to which

---

[361] Members of CERD and HRC, e.g., have access to non-governmental information only in their positions as experts, *see* Del Prado J., 'United Nations Conventions on Human Rights: The Practice of the Human Rights Committee and the Committee on the Elimination of Racial Discrimination in Dealing with Reporting Obligations of States Parties' (1985) 7 *Hum. Rts. Q* 492, at 500. However, under rules 62(1) and (2) of its Rules of Procedure, CAT may receive NGO material. *see* Zoller A.–C., 'UN Committee against Torture' (1989) 7 *NQHR* 210 at 251.

[362] Informal mechanisms also prevent the Committee members from using the information other than in asking questions of representatives. *See* Buergenthal, *supra*, n. 10, at 205.

[363] *See* E/1991/23, *supra*, n. 142, at 64, para. 249.   [364] E/C.12/1993/SR.26, at 13, para. 58.

[365] *See* Tomasevski K., *Development Aid and Human Rights* (1989), 113–16. It has also been suggested that NGOs are uncertain about what information they should collect and how to obtain it, *see* Steiner H., *Diverse Partners: Non-Governmental Organisations in the Human Rights Movement* (1991).

the Committee 'is capable of yielding satisfactory returns' to the input of time and effort by the NGO concerned.[366] It should be noted, however, that if NGO participation is premised upon such grounds, the Committee will be pushed towards taking up a more adversarial stance with an emphasis on identifying 'violations' of the Covenant.

(c) Institutional Mechanisms

In order to institutionalize the receipt of information the Committee has requested the Secretariat to establish a separate file containing 'all available information' on each of the States parties whose reports are 'currently pending consideration'.[367] The Committee has stipulated in particular that the files should include information taken from the reports of other human rights Committees, relevant information from the specialized agencies (such as the ILO, WHO, UNESCO, UNDP, and UNICEF[368]) and any other relevant documentation submitted to the Secretariat for inclusion in the file.[369] Although the files are specifically created for States parties whose reports are 'currently pending consideration', the files are maintained 'on a continuing basis'.[370] It is clear that relevant information may be submitted to the Secretariat at any time, but that a Secretariat 'file' will only be created when that State's report is 'pending consideration' by the Committee and thus will only be available to the Committee at that time. Although there were continuing complaints about the inadequate amount of information in the files at the Committee's seventh[371] and eighth sessions,[372] it appears that the situation is improving.[373]

The high priority placed upon independent sources of information by the Committee is also reflected in its decision to appoint 'liason officers' from the Committee to follow any pertinent work of other human rights bodies (in particular CEDAW, CERD, CAT, and HRC) and report to the Committee at the beginning of each session.[374] This decision appears to be a response to the increasing regularity with which other Committees are dealing with matters that fall within the scope of economic, social, and cultural rights.[375]

In addition the Committee has persisted in its demand for the creation of a 'human rights resource room' for use by members of all of the human rights committees, equipped with documents and statistical information from the UN bodies, regional human rights organizations, and

---

[366] Alston, *supra*, n. 31, at 502.   [367] E/1993/22, *supra*, n. 200, at 68, para. 261.
[368] E/1994/23, *supra*, n. 123, at 74, para. 375.
[369] E/1992/23, *supra*, n. 158, at 100–1, para. 386.
[370] *Ibid.* 101, para. 387.   [371] E/1993/22, *supra*, n. 200, at 68, paras. 261–2.
[372] E/1994/23, *supra*, n. 123, at 69, para. 352.   [373] *Ibid.* 72, para. 367.
[374] E/1990/23, *supra*, n. 173, at 75, para. 298. *Cf.* Alston, E/C.12/1991/SR.24, at 6, para. 53.
[375] e.g., the decisions taken by the HRC under art. 26 ICCPR concerning social security.

non-governmental organizations.[376] Although this proposal has been reiterated by members of the Committee since its third session and endorsed by the Meeting of Chairpersons of the Human Rights Treaty Bodies, the Secretariat has yet to take any action.

6 Follow-up Action

Unlike the practice of the HRC, it was decided early on in the Committee's work that 'it would not be fair to reject a report presented by a State party on the grounds that it did not comply with the general guidelines'.[377] It was therefore considered that States should be given the opportunity to provide additional information to the Committee at a later stage. Additional information may also be requested by the Committee where questions are left unanswered by the State concerned or where the response is inadequate. More often than not, either a request for, or an offer of, additional information will be made at some stage in the consideration of the State report. It has become so frequent that, at the fifth session, every State that appeared before the Committee was either asked, or offered, to provide additional information. Although reliance upon additional information might just be a function of the poor quality of State reports (which should improve with the new guidelines), if it continues it will place a heavy burden on the Committee which is already overloaded with reports.

The Committee adopted a procedure at its fifth session to deal will additional information in which the pre-sessional working group reviewed the information which was then subject to a discussion in plenary at which a representative of the State was invited to attend.[378] Subsequent practice, however, highlighted a number of problems with the procedure.[379] Not least was the fact that State representatives were sometimes requested to attend a meeting at which the Committee merely declared its satisfaction with the additional information provided. The matter was accordingly comprehensively reviewed at the Committee's seventh session where it outlined a number of possible courses of action that might be taken. First, the Committee might merely request that certain issues be dealt with in the State party's next periodic report.[380] Secondly, it might note the State party's intention to provide additional information in writing in response to questions posed by members of the Committee.[381] Thirdly, it might specifically request that information be provided to it within six months to be con-

---

[376] Alston, E/C.12/1989/SR.1, at 10, para. 48; Simma, E/C.12/1990/SR.29, at 7, para. 28.
[377] E/1988/14, *supra*, n. 158, at 62, para. 360.
[378] E/1991/23, *supra*, n. 142, at 70, paras. 274–7.
[379] *See e.g.* E/C.12/1993/SR.15, at 5, paras. 19–23.
[380] *e.g.* Concluding observations on report of Australia, E/C.12/1993/9, at 4, para. 19.
[381] *e.g.* Concluding observations on report of Nicaragua, E/C.12/1993/14, at 3, para. 10.

sidered by the pre-sessional working group.[382] The working group would then have the choice of taking note of the information, adopting specific concluding observations in response to that information, requesting more information, or recommending that the matter be taken up by the Committee at its next session. Finally, in 'urgent' cases, the Committee may request information to be provided within a given time limit of, for example, two or three months. There, it would be the responsibility of the chairperson and the members of the bureau to decide whether the information is adequate and to take appropriate action.[383]

Although, for the main part, additional information will be requested by the Committee following its consideration of a report in order to clarify the situation with respect to a particular issue,[384] this will not always be the case. The Committee notes that additional information might also be requested 'where, in the process of examination of a State party's report, the Committee considers that further information is required in order to enable it to conclude the process'.[385] The crucial difference between these circumstances is that, whereas in the former case an additional report is requested purely as a matter of information, in the latter case, the Committee has not formally concluded its consideration of the situation. This means that that Committee may continue to monitor a situation and may undertake to comment upon, or discuss, matters that have arisen since its original consideration of the State report.

The principal case in point was that of the Dominican Republic which had been requested by the Committee to submit additional information to it in time for its sixth session. Following the State's failure to submit an additional report, the Committee noted that in the meantime it had received information from 'several sources' which 'if accurate, would give rise to serious concern on the part of the Committee'.[386] The Committee thus requested the Dominican Republic 'to suspend any actions which are not clearly in conformity with the provisions of the Covenant, and . . . to provide additional information to [the Committee] as a matter of urgency'.[387] Although ambiguous, the overt implication of this request was that the Committee expected additional information to be provided as to the new situation over and above that already requested at its previous session. It appears now that the Committee believed that it had not completed its consideration of the report of the Dominican Republic and could, therefore, continue to monitor the situation as it developed.[388]

When considered in the light of the Committee's approach with respect

---

[382] *Ibid.* para. 9.   [383] E/1993/22, *supra*, n. 200, at 65–6, para. 251.
[384] *Ibid.* 65, para. 249.   [385] *Ibid.*
[386] E/1992/23, *supra*, n. 158, at 79, para. 330.   [387] *Ibid.*
[388] It is worth noting that such a point was actually made at that time, *see* Alston, E/C.12/1991/SR.15, at 4, para. 13.

to the Philippines,[389] the Dominican Republic case appears to be an example where the Committee has asserted its authority to request information or reports *ad hoc* as to situations of grave concern.[390] Certainly, in so far as the Committee, through ECOSOC, has authority to establish a system for the submission of reports, it may undertake to create a mechanism of reporting in such situations. Such a system could, if developed further, eventually operate as an alternative to an official complaints mechanism as recently discussed by the Committee.

Thus far, although the Committee has made numerous requests for additional information, the response of States has been patchy. A number of States such as the UK and Mexico have been requested to provide the Committee with such information and as yet have failed to do so. The Committee will have to establish a procedure to deal with such a situation. It would be appropriate as a start if the Secretariat were to provide the Committee with an outline of which States have been requested to provide additional information and which have not yet done so, and send the appropriate reminders.[391] The Committee may also consider taking action along the lines of the HRC where, if the additional information is submitted promptly and fully, the Committee will, if appropriate, defer the date for the submission of the State party's next report.

Where the Committee has been in receipt of additional information, it has often merely declared that it is satisfied with the additional information provided by the State and has required no further action to be taken.[392] In other cases, however, it has considered it appropriate to adopt a number of conclusions. It appears that the purpose of such conclusions is to point out issues that have not been adequately dealt with[393] and to identify matters of continuing concern to the Committee.[394] The conclusions drafted on the information supplied by Zaïre, in particular, are detailed and well considered, take into account the arguments presented by the State, and make a useful evaluation of areas of concern to the Committee.[395]

The Committee is clear, however, that in terms of obtaining the information necessary to fulfil its functions, the provision of additional information might not be adequate. Accordingly, it has developed the practice that in extraordinary circumstances, where there is sufficient cause for concern and no alternative approach is available, it will request the State party

---

[389] *See above*, text accompanying nn. 221–2.

[390] This may be seen to parallel the procedure adopted by the HRC to review the situation following the disintegration of Yugoslavia. See UN Doc. A/48/40 at 212–14, 48 UNGAOR, Supp. (No. 40) (1994).

[391] This is a procedure adopted by CAT. UN Doc. CAT/C/SR.38, paras. 10–11.

[392] *e.g.* Additional information of France, Alston, E/C.12/1993/SR.15, at 4, para. 12.

[393] Observations adopted on the additional information of Panama, E/1993/22, *supra*, n. 200, at 52–6, para. 197.

[394] *e.g.* observations on the additional information of Zaïre, E/1992/23, *supra*, n. 158, at 77, para. 328(c).   [395] *Ibid.* 75–8, para. 328.

concerned to accept a mission consisting of one or two members of the Committee. The on-site visit will have the dual function of collecting specific information for the Committee to monitor the situation and of assisting the Committee in exercising its functions in relation to articles 22 and 23 of the Covenant (advising on the provision of technical assistance). The Committee would then adopt a set of conclusions on the report of the representatives.[396]

The Committee has made such an offer on two occasions, first in relation to the Dominican Republic and secondly with respect to Panama.[397] In each case, the Committee's initiative was endorsed by ECOSOC 'subject to the acceptance of the Committee's offer by the State party concerned'.[398] Neither State has accepted the offer nor appears likely to do so.[399] They have, however, agreed to send a representative to the Committee to report on the situations at issue.[400]

7 *The Concluding Observations*

As from its second session, the Committee has adopted the practice of making 'concluding observations' or 'comments' on the State reports at the end of the constructive dialogue. The precise nature and purpose of the concluding observations, however, has been the subject of a certain amount of confusion on the part of the Committee members. It would appear that they evolved as part of the 'constructive dialogue' and represent a stage in the continuing process of 'consideration'. As such they do not represent the 'suggestions and recommendations of a general nature' mandated by ECOSOC to assist it in undertaking its responsibilities in articles 21 and 22 of the Covenant.[401]

It was noted at all of the Committee's early sessions that the concluding observations were often inconsistent,[402] imprecise,[403] and an 'unsatisfactory reflection of the Committee's proceedings'.[404] This was partly due to the political climate in which the Committee was working, which made it difficult for the Committee to agree upon a stronger formulation.[405] A decision

---

[396] E/1994/23, *supra*, n. 123, at 18, paras. 40–1.
[397] Alston, E/C.12/1992/SR.16, at 5, para. 25.
[398] e.g. ECOSOC Decn. 1992/261, 32 ESCOR, Supp. (No. 3), at 134 (1992).
[399] *See* summary of Simma on the reaction of Panama, E/C.12/1993/SR.3, at 2–4, paras. 2–16.
[400] Alston, E/C.12/1994/SR.1, at 4, para. 17; E/C.12/1994/SR.7, at 13, para. 66.
[401] ECOSOC Resolution 1985/17 para. (f), *supra*, n. 89, at 21.
[402] *See* Alston, E/C.12/1988/SR.23, at 6, para. 57.
[403] *See* Neneman, E/C.12/1988/SR.23, at 7, para. 58.
[404] Alston, E/C.12/1989/SR.24, at 5, para. 38.
[405] *See* Alston, E/C.12/1991/SR.10, at 5, para. 27. CEDAW e.g., briefly introduced the procedure of adopting concluding comments but discontinued it after failing to come to agreement about the statement. *See* Byrnes A., 'The "Other" Human Rights Treaty Body: The Work of the Committee on the Elimination of Discrimination against Women' (1989) 14 *Yale JIL* 1, at 21.

to delay the formulation of concluding observations for at least a day following the consideration of the report concerned only partially tackled the problem; there still remained considerable confusion within the Committee itself as to their nature and purpose.[406]

The matter was subject to discussion at the Committee's sixth session and a number of criteria for formulating concluding observations were adopted.[407] They broadly related to the extent to which the oral and written reports were satisfactory[408] and to the need for follow-up action.[409] At its following session, however, the Committee decided that greater emphasis needed to be placed upon the extent to which the State concerned had ensured the realization of the rights in the Covenant.[410] It resolved that the concluding observations should follow a common structure and should provide an 'authoritative statement' as to the Committee's views on the implementation of the Covenant by the State concerned.[411]

The concluding observations adopted by the Committee since 1993 follow the same structure as those of other human rights committees. They include an introduction, a section on progress made, another on factors and difficulties faced, one on the principal subjects of concern, and a final section including suggestions and recommendations addressed to the State party.[412] These new concluding observations, while by no means perfect, represent an important improvement both in terms of the level of detail provided and in the quality of assessment.[413] If they continue to improve in the same manner, they will probably become the single most important element in the Committee's work as regards the development of norms within the Covenant.

That the Committee has expressly declared its willingness to make evaluations as to State performance in implementation merely reflects its current practice. It does, however, go some way to clarify the perceived role of the Committee. For some time the Committee was in the paradoxical situation of seeking to avoid the impression that it was passing judgement on the performance of a given State, while evidently being forced to move in that direction by the theoretical and practical considerations of efficacy.[414] This point of view had led Committee members to argue, rather ambiguously,

---

[406] *See generally* E/C.12/1990/SR.31, at 6–13.

[407] E/1992/23, *supra*, n. 158, at 99–100, para. 383.

[408] The Committee had previously rejected proposals either that the concluding observations should indicate whether the reports were satisfactory or that they should identify which questions had not been answered satisfactorily. For the various proposals *see* Wimer Zambrano, E/C.12/1989/SR.22, at 9, para. 65; Alvarez Vita, E/C.12/1989/SR.22, at 5, para. 33.

[409] *Ibid.*   [410] E/1993/22, at 68, para. 263.   [411] E/1993/22, at 69, para. 265.

[412] The exact format of the concluding observations was subject to review at the Committee's 10th session, *see* E/C.12/1994/SR.6, at 9–12, paras. 47–69.

[413] *See e.g.* Concluding observations on the report of Iran, E/C.12/1993/7.

[414] For the open contradictions of the previous situation *see* Alston, *supra*, n. 151, at 48–9, paras. 123–5.

that the Committee's role was to undertake an 'assessment' of the State reports, which would not mean expressing criticism or making a judgement, but rather 'including an observation in the Committee's report'.[415] That the Committee has now undertaken to make substantive evaluations of State reports will undoubtedly contribute considerably to its perceived effectiveness.[416] As has been noted, the willingness of the Committee to question States parties' compliance 'serves only to strengthen the value of the body, as well as to convey a clear sense of independence and the desire to carry out its mandate effectively'.[417]

The extent to which the Committee is able to make accurate and detailed assessments of compliance, however, will inevitably be a function of the quantity and quality of information available to it. As Capotorti notes:

a specific recommendation presumes an accurate verification of the circumstances . . . Thus, whenever examination of reports is superficial . . . the only possible outcome consists in general recommendations: and these have the function of means for political pressure, rather than of true instruments for supervising the observance of agreements.[418]

In the absence of a consistent and plentiful supply of information it remains to be seen whether the Committee is able to produce accurate and useful assessments of performance in every case. In any event, it would be wise for the Committee to proceed with a certain amount of caution to ensure that it does not undermine the co-operative nature of the constructive dialogue.

8 General Comments

In response to an invitation addressed to it by ECOSOC in paragraph 9 of Resolution 1987/5,[419] the Committee decided to begin, as from its third session, to prepare general comments on the various articles and provisions of the Covenant 'with a view to assisting the States Parties to fulfil their reporting obligations'.[420] Although article 21 of the Covenant refers to the possibility of ECOSOC making recommendations of a general nature to the General Assembly, the Committee's assumed power bears little relation to that provision. Rather, the Committee's authority to make such comments derives from its mandate to assist ECOSOC in the consideration of the State reports. Whether or not this could be said to be a power implied by

---

[415] Texier, E/C.12/1989/SR.13, at 14, para. 71.

[416] Buergenthal correctly notes that the effectiveness of the reporting procedure 'depends ultimately upon the willingness of the Committee to . . . make a formal determination that a State Party has not discharged its obligations under the Convention,': Buergenthal, *supra*, n. 10, at 201.

[417] Leckie, *supra*, n. 91, at 547.   [418] Capotorti, *supra*, n. 15, at 138.

[419] *Supra*, n. 353.   [420] E/1988/14, *supra*, n. 158, at 63, para. 367.

the terms of the Covenant, it is evident that no States have objected to such an interpretation.

As the Committee has stressed, the purpose of the General Comments is to assist the States parties in fulfilling their reporting obligations. More explicitly the Committee aims with its General Comments:

to make the experience gained so far through the examination of these reports available for the benefit of all States parties in order: to assist and promote their further implementation of the Covenant; to draw the attention of the States parties to insufficiencies disclosed by a large number of reports; to suggest improvements in the reporting procedures and to stimulate the activities of the States parties, the international organizations and the specialized agencies concerned in achieving progressively and effectively the full realization of the rights recognized in the Covenant.[421]

The method by which the Committee adopts its general comments was made clear at its second session. Any member of the Committee may put forward a draft general comment for consideration by the Committee in plenary. Once adopted, it is included in the Committee's annual report to ECOSOC and is brought to the attention of the General Assembly. Texts are also transmitted to States parties by the Secretary-General. Any comments from States parties or the specialized agencies are to be brought to the attention of the Committee at its following session.[422]

As has been evident in the practice of the HRC, the use of General Comments is an important mechanism for developing the jurisprudence of a Committee in a way that is not possible in individual comments on State reports. Not only does it provide a means by which jurisprudence may be generated at a faster rate (which is particularly important for a Committee in the early stages of its development), but it is also a means by which members of the Committee may come to an agreement by consensus as to an interpretation of a specific provision without facing the difficult issue of addressing individual States.

Thus far the Committee has adopted four General Comments at its third, fourth, fifth, and sixth sessions.[423] The first three General Comments were directed primarily at outlining the foundations of the reporting system and laying down an analytical framework for the future generation of right-specific jurisprudence. The first deals with the nature of the reporting system, the second with international measures of technical assistance, and

---

[421] E/1993/22, *supra*, n. 200, at 19, para. 49.

[422] E/1988/14, *supra*, n. 158, at 64, para. 370.

[423] General Comment No. 1, (E/1989/22, annex III); General Comment No. 2, (E/1990/23, annex III); General Comment No. 3, (E/1991/23, annex III), and General Comment No. 4, (E/1992/23, annex III). A further two General Comments on the Rights of the Elderly and the Rights of Persons with Disabilities are nearing completion.

the third with the general obligations embodied in article 2(1). Each one has contributed to a general understanding of the Committee's work and has been warmly received.[424] The most recent, and perhaps most important General Comment thus far, has been on the right to housing in article 11— its first General Comment on a substantive article.

The Committee makes clear that the role of General Comments is overtly descriptive: to convey a sense of the existing jurisprudence of the Covenant as viewed by the Committee.[425] However, in its fourth General Comment, the Committee has taken a more constructive approach. In outlining the essential qualitative elements of the right to housing in article 11, it could hardly be said that the Committee was merely describing its current practice or that it was merely reflecting the information collected from State reports.[426] Instead, the Committee has used the General Comment as a means of developing a common understanding of the norms by establishing a prescriptive definition. By doing so, the Committee appears to be asserting its authority to exercise an interpretative function *in abstracto*, rather than confining that function to its particular role in the consideration of State reports.

Although the Committee's interpretations of the Covenant are not binding *per se*, it is undoubtedly true that they have considerable legal weight. In the absence of an authoritative procedure for settling divergences of opinion over the interpretation of the Covenant, it is for the States parties to construe the Covenant for themselves. Individual States may put forward their own interpretations of the Covenant's provisions but such interpretations are by no means authoritative and may be rejected by other States. In fact States have rarely made direct statements regarding the meaning of Covenant provisions. The only real indication as to an agreement by States of a particular interpretation of the Covenant is to be found where there is a significant degree of concurrence in State practice. The relevant State practice is to be found not merely in how the States undertake to realize the rights, but also in their participation in the supervisory processes of Covenant. As Meron commented:

the Committee may be competent to interpret the Convention insofar as required for the performance of the Committee's functions. Such an interpretation *per se* is not binding on States parties, but it affects their reporting obligations and their internal and external behaviour. It shapes the practice of States in applying the

---

[424] *See e.g.* comments by Martenson on General Comment No. 2, E/C.12/1990/SR.36, at 2–3, paras. 6–7.

[425] E/1993/22, *supra*, n. 200, at 19, para. 49. It is clear nevertheless that the General Comments will not be confined to the substantive rights in the Covenant, General Comments Nos. 1 and 2 thus reflect the broader terms of the Committee's mandate.

[426] General Comment No. 4 was produced as the result of extensive co-operation with NGOs, one of which drafted the initial version.

Convention and may establish and reflect the agreement of the parties regarding its interpretation.[427]

Indeed, the endorsement by ECOSOC and the General Assembly (in which significant numbers of States parties participate) of the Committee's annual report gives considerable weight to the Committee's interpretation.[428]

Given the fact that the terms of the Covenant are particularly vague and the general absence, on the national or international plane, of an understanding of the content of the rights, there is a necessity for the Committee to attempt to fill the void. Until it does so, economic, social, and cultural rights will remain, in the minds of many, general aspirations which bind States in only a non-specific manner. The Committee does not benefit by having a petition system in which general principles may be established, and the 'constructive dialogue' is a most unsatisfactory means of developing jurisprudence. Considerable importance must be placed, therefore, upon the use of General Comments to develop a broad understanding of the norms within the Covenant. Once it has created a qualitative framework outlining the general scope and content of each of the rights, the Committee will be in a far better position to utilize the reporting procedure effectively.

Unfortunately, despite the urgency with which the Committee needs to develop its jurisprudence, it has only succeeded in producing one General Comment for every two sessions.[429] This record needs to be improved. Ideally, it would be for the Secretariat to produce draft comments for discussion and adoption by the Committee. In the absence of sufficient Secretariat resources or motivation to take on such a role, the Committee should look to other means by which the production of General Comments may be increased. In the near future, consideration could be given to sacrificing the constructive, but less productive, general discussion in favour of adopting additional General Comments.

9 *The General Discussion*

At the Committee's second session it was felt that a general discussion would be useful to its work. One member commented in presenting the idea to the Committee that:

---

[427] Meron T., *Human Rights Law-Making in the United Nations* (1986), at 10. He was speaking specifically about CERD, but his analysis is still pertinent in the context of the Committee.

[428] Tomuschat similarly argues that the HRC, by the fact of its independence and impartiality, is 'the best suited meeting point and clearing centre for diverging interpretations' of the ICCPR put forth by States with different ideological standpoints. Tomuschat C., 'National Implementation of International Standards on Human Rights' (1984/5), *Can. HRY* 31, at 36.

[429] The Committee has had several draft general comments in circulation for some years without being adopted *e.g.* UN Doc. E/C.12/1993/WP.26.

the reporting process was designed to encourage States parties to reflect on their general policies with respect to economic, social and cultural rights and on the issues raised by the members of the Committee. However, at no time did the Committee try to synthesize all the information put before it and to understand all the implications of specific rights. It could do so by earmarking one day in each session, perhaps in the third week, for such a discussion. That discussion would be based on the reports of States parties over the previous 10 years and focus on interesting practices and experiences in different countries and economic and social systems with regard to the right under consideration. It would be facilitated by inputs from relevant specialized agencies, but would not focus upon or criticise specific reports by States parties . . . No elaborate conclusions need be drafted.[430]

It was commented, in addition, that the Committee would establish a 'common assessment of the criteria relating to the observance of the Covenant' and would 'lay the foundations of its future work' by providing for the 'concrete expression of the Covenant on an increasingly uniform basis'.[431] In addition it would facilitate the exchange of experience among States and develop a better understanding of the content and implications of different rights.[432]

It has become the practice of the Committee to devote one day at each session to a general discussion of one specific right or a particular aspect of the Covenant 'in order to develop in greater depth its understanding of the relevant issues'.[433] Since its third session the Committee's general discussions have focused on right to adequate food,[434] the right to housing,[435] the use of economic and statistical indicators pertaining to the work of the Committee,[436] the right to take part in cultural rights,[437] the rights of the ageing and the elderly,[438] the right to health,[439] and the use of social safety nets.[440]

In the discussion the Committee has sought to draw widely on the available expertise which may assist its work. In particular it has invited special *rapporteurs* from the Sub-Commission on Prevention of Discrimination and the Protection of Minorities, experts from relevant NGOs and representatives of the specialized agencies (ILO, FAO, WHO, UNESCO) and other UN organs (UNDP, UNRISD, and the UN Centre for Human Settlements). In order to facilitate the attendance of experts the Committee has also recommended that ECOSOC set aside money for travel and accomodation.[441] The discussions have highlighted issues of importance, allowed the Committee to address broader issues that are not directly

---

[430] Alston, E/C.12/1988/SR.22, at 5, para. 30.
[431] Rattray, E/C.12/1988/SR.22, at 5, para. 31.
[432] E/1988/14, *supra*, n. 158, at 60, para. 349.   [433] *Ibid.*
[434] UN Docs. E/C.12/1989/SR.20–1.   [435] UN Docs. E/C.12/1990/SR.22–3.
[436] UN Docs. E/C.12/1991/SR.20–1.   [437] E/C.12/1992/SR.17–18.
[438] E/C.12/1993/SR. 13–14.   [439] E/1994/23, *supra*, n. 123, at 56–65.
[440] E/C.12/1994/SR.20.   [441] Draft Decision III, E/1994/23, *supra*, n. 123, at 8.

related to its examination of State reports and have served to develop the relationship between the Committee and other interested bodies. It is particularly notable that the participation of NGOs has been considerably greater at such discussions than in other stages of its work.

It was considered by several members at the Committee's third session that the general discussion (on the right to food) might be expected to provide the basis of a draft General Comment in future.[442] However, only in the case of the right to housing has the general discussion actually borne fruit. The general criticism may be made that, although the general discussions are undoubtedly useful, they are not entirely productive. The Committee has adopted the practice of summarizing the outline of the general discussions in its annual report, but such outlines give little indication of any common agreement. It is considered that, given the lack of time available to the Committee, emphasis should be placed upon using its time in a productive manner. In particular it could look to the establishment, at the end of the debate, of a number of general principles that demonstrate common agreement. It would also be appropriate for the Committee to make it a policy that a general comment be drafted following all of its general discussions. If agreement on such a draft is not possible, that might signify the need to discuss the matter further.

10 Technical Assistance

The Covenant specifically envisages the use of technical assistance in the implementation of the rights within the Covenant. Article 22 reads:

The Economic and Social Council may bring to the attention of other organs of the United Nations, their subsidiary organs and specialized agencies concerned with furnishing technical assistance any matters arising out of the reports referred to in this part of the present Covenant which may assist such bodies in deciding, each within its field of competence, on the advisability of international measures likely to contribute to the effective progressive implementation of the present Covenant.

The provision of technical assistance forms part of 'a range of possible international action' envisaged by article 23 intended to address the external international constraints that might be seen to impede the full realization of the rights.

Essentially, with the wide definition of technical assistance, these provisions throw open the concern of the Committee to all action taken within the United Nations that may affect the economic, social, and cultural rights of a given population. The Committee has emphasized this point by identifying a large number of bodies to which it feels itself capable of directing its

---

[442] E/1989/22, *supra*, n. 142, at 73, para. 330.

recommendations including *inter alia* the UNDP, UNICEF, IMF, IBRD, ILO, UNESCO, FAO, and the WHO.[443]

The Committee has looked in two main directions in its recommendations regarding technical assistance. First, it has made certain recommendations to institutions concerned with development activities to the effect that consideration should be given at all times to the impact of economic policies on the economic, social, and cultural rights of the population.[444] The concern of the Committee centres upon the need to ensure that assistance programmes do not negatively affect the enjoyment of economic, social, and cultural rights. It must be recognized however that, by the terms of article 22, this is a somewhat limited goal. Essentially what is required is the specific direction of technical assistance towards the realization of the rights.

Secondly, the Committee has recommended action to be taken by the Secretariat to assist developing States in complying with their reporting requirements through, for example, the establishment of training courses.[445] As the provision of advisory services is technically outside the competence and capabilities of the Committee itself, the Committee's interest has been to make recommendations to the Secretariat. Accordingly, following the invitation of the Under-Secretary-General, the Committee outlined its suggestions for the development of the advisory services programme[446] with regard to the Covenant. In particular it suggested the provision of:

(a) technical assistance in reviewing national legislation, or drafting appropriate legislative or other instruments as necessary as preparation for the possible ratification of the Covenant;

(b) technical assistance in the preparation of an initial report, including monitoring of the situation with respect to the enjoyment of the rights;

(c) assistance to enable a State party to send an expert to present the report to the Committee, where it would otherwise be unable to do so.[447]

The Committee has also stressed that note should be made of article 23 of the Covenant which provides for the holding of regional and technical meetings for the purpose of consultation and study organized in conjunction with the governments concerned. It concluded that 'every effort should be made to ensure that economic, social and cultural rights are, wherever possible, on the agenda of all regional and other training courses, workshops and seminars'.[448]

[443] General Comment No. 2 (1990), *supra*, n. 423, at 86, para. 2.
[444] *Ibid*. 86–9.   [445] *See below* text accompanying n. 459.
[446] The advisory services programme was created by GA Resn. 926 (X), (1955). It has four basic functions: the provision of advisory services by experts; the awarding of fellowships and sholarships; the holding of international seminars; and the organization of regional or national training courses.
[447] E/1989/22, *supra*, n. 142, at 76, paras. 343–5.   [448] *Ibid*.

It is clear that the UN programme of technical assistance compares rather poorly with that undertaken by the ILO.[449] Where assistance has been provided, little attention has been paid to economic, social, and cultural rights.[450] The principal problem facing the Committee is that it has no authority to provide technical assistance or require that be provided. All it is capable of doing is passing on requests for technical assistance to the Secretariat or other bodies concerned and hope that they might be taken up. It has not been helped in this regard by the failure of States to indicate themselves what assistance they require.

G The Role of Other Bodies in the Committee's Work

1 The Secretariat

Given the range and complexity of issues confronting the Committee the need for strong secretariat assistance is paramount.[451] In contrast to the rather ambiguous relationship that the HRC has with the Secretariat (as it is not a United Nations Body *per se*) the Committee has no such problems. As an expert group of a UN organ, the Secretariat is automatically responsible for its servicing. As such the Secretariat is required to provide the Committee with 'the necessary staff and facilities for the effective performance of its functions'.[452] It is required, *inter alia*, to send reminders to States parties that have failed to report,[453] to provide a compilation of statistics relevant to the Committee's work,[454] to establish and maintain files of information on each of the States parties,[455] to assist the pre-sessional working group in drafting the list of issues to be submitted to States parties and preparing a detailed analysis for each country,[456] and to bring the suggestions and recommendations of the Committee to the attention of States parties.[457] The Secretariat must also ensure that adequate publicity is given to the work of the Committee,[458] and must provide

---

[449] *See* Leary V., 'Lessons from the Experience of the International Labour Organization', in Alston P. (ed.), *The United Nations and Human Rights: A Critical Assessment* (1992), 580, at 589–60.

[450] Alston, E/C.12/1994/SR.1, at 6, para. 23. *See generally* Secretariat Paper, E/C.12/1994/WP.9.

[451] Sohn, *supra*, n. 61, at 35.

[452] ECOSOC Resn, 1985/17, para. (g), *supra*, n. 89, at 21. For the working group *see* ECOSOC Decision 1979/43, para. 15, (11 May 1979), *in* UN Doc. E/C.12/1989/4, at 8. ECOSOC Resn.1982/33, para. (e), (6 May 1982), *ibid.* 13.

[453] ECOSOC Decision 1979/43, para. 14, 11 May 1979.

[454] ECOSOC Resn.1987/5, para. 13, 26 May 1987.

[455] E/1990/23, *supra*, n. 173, at 75, para. 298.

[456] E/1994/23, *supra*, n. 123, at 69, para. 352.

[457] ECOSOC Resn. 1984/9, *supra*, n. 350, para. 8.

[458] ECOSOC Resn. 1987/5, *supra*, n. 454, at para. 12.

advisory services to assist States parties in discharging their reporting obligations.[459]

In practice, as appears to be endemic within the UN human rights system,[460] the support given to the Committee by the Secretariat has been extremely limited. The Committee has been serviced by a single member of the Centre of Human Rights, who has also had duties with respect to other human rights committees.[461] Thus far, beyond the production of a very limited bibliography, virtually no research or other analytical work has been undertaken by the Secretariat on behalf of the Committee. Equally, little has been done to ensure that the work of the Committee is given adequate publicity.

As has been noted elsewhere, the Committee's effectiveness would be greatly enhanced by proper Secretariat support. Ideally, the Secretariat would undertake functions, in addition to those outlined above, such as the production of draft General Comments and other analytical reports, the collection and compilation of information both from official and unofficial sources (such as NGOs) on the situation in each of the States parties, the identification of inadequacies in State reports and issues that deserve further consideration, and the provision of advice and assistance to States parties as to how they might further the enjoyment of the rights.[462] This would require, as the Committee has noted, the Secretariat to be both strengthened and restructured to 'ensure the availability of competent researchers to assist the Committee in its endeavours'.[463]

2 The Economic and Social Council

On the basis that the Committee is mandated with assisting ECOSOC in the consideration of State reports, it might be assumed that ECOSOC itself would take some part in the evaluation process much like the ILO Conference Committee on the Application of Conventions and Recommendations.[464] To that end, the Committee is asked to include in the report on its activities a summary of its consideration of the reports submitted by States parties to the Covenant.[465]

---

[459] *See above*, text accompanying nn. 193–4.

[460] *See* Report of the Meeting of Chairpersons, A/47/628, at 7–8.

[461] Recently, additional helpers have been provided by the Secretariat, Alston, E/C.12/1993/SR.22, at 6, para. 35.

[462] E/1994/23, *Supra*, n. 123, at 73, para. 372.   [463] *Ibid*. 69, para. 353.

[464] The report of the ILO Committee of Experts is considered by the Conference Committee on the Application of Conventions and Recommendations. It chooses the most important cases that arise and asks the government for explanations. The replies form the basis of a discussion within the Conference Committee and in particularly serious disputes a procedure for 'direct contact' exists whereby a representative of the Director General undertakes a discussion, in the country concerned, with the governmental authorities.

[465] ECOSOC Resn. 1985/17, *supra*, n. 89.

In practice ECOSOC does little more than take note of the Committee's report. Indeed, it was decided after the Committee's third session that in future the reports of the Committee would be discussed not by ECOSOC in plenary, but by its Social Council[466] which has no provision for summary records.[467] In justifying such action, it was noted that even if ECOSOC did not consider the report in plenary, it was referred to the General Assembly Third Committee where the report was given substantive consideration.[468]

Although it was noted with disappointment that ECOSOC took little interest in the report of the Committee,[469] it was stressed that ECOSOC should not be encouraged to pronounce on any substantive matters which were rightly in the exclusive domain of the Committee.[470] To the extent that the Council should not take over those functions adopted by the Committee this decision is undoubtedly correct. By the same token, it cannot be maintained that ECOSOC has no role in the implementation process. It is, after all, the Council that is empowered with making general recommendations to be submitted to the General Assembly. Any conclusions drawn by the Committee following the consideration of State reports become the responsibility of ECOSOC when the report is adopted. This would suggest that the Council has a direct interest in considering the report in some depth. From the point of view of the Committee, it is clearly better if the Council, which has direct control over its resources, is aware of all its issues and concerns.

H The Future: An Optional Protocol?

Despite the fact that proposals for a petition procedure relating to economic, social, and cultural rights were specifically rejected during the drafting of the Covenant, at the Committee's most recent sessions the debate has been revived. The Committee has undertaken several discussions on the possibility of drafting an optional protocol to the Covenant on Economic, Social, and Cultural Rights to provide for some form of individual or group complaints mechanism. Whereas in earlier sessions the debate generally ended with the conclusion that it was 'too early' to consider realistically the possibility of such a system,[471] at its seventh session in 1992 the Committee formally proposed that an optional protocol should be drafted and adopted. With that in mind, it included a discussion paper on the matter in its report of the seventh session.[472]

---

[466] *See* Houshmand, E/C.12/1990/SR.1, at 10, para. 70.
[467] *See* Badawi El Sheikh, E/C.12/1990/SR.3, at 7, para. 45.
[468] *See* Houshmand, E/C.12/1990/SR.3, at 9, para. 59.
[469] *See* Simma, E/C.12/1990/SR.3, at 9, para. 55.
[470] *See* Alston, E/C.12/1990/SR.3, at 9, para. 56.
[471] *See e.g.* Rattray, E/C.12/1990/SR.4, at 5, para. 17.
[472] E/1993/22, *supra*, n. 200, at 87–108.

During the discussions at the sixth and seventh sessions, there was general agreement that the institution of an optional protocol would be a beneficial development both in terms of increasing the status of the Covenant and the Committee,[473] and in terms of improving the degree of protection offered. The four main issues of debate, however, related to the form that the optional protocol would take, namely, who should have access to the procedure, what rights should be covered by the procedure, what procedural rules should apply, and what outcomes would be envisaged by the procedure.[474]

First, although certain doubts were expressed about the effectiveness of providing for inter-State complaints,[475] it was generally considered that such an option should not be ruled out.[476] At the same time it was decided that an inter-State procedure 'could not be considered to be a satisfactory substitute for an individual or collective complaints procedure'.[477] Although a range of possibilities was discussed,[478] considerable support was expressed for the procedure to be open to both individual and group complaints.[479] Certainly, in order to maximize the opportunities for the procedure, providing for individual complaints would be extremely desirable. As was pointed out, there is no evidence that such a possibility would necessarily lead to a flood of complaints.[480] Providing for group complaints would also be useful in so far as the problem is of a general structural nature or the right specifically collective,[481] but wider concerns may often be addressed through the medium of individual 'test' cases.

Secondly, the Committee considered a number of options as to the range of rights in the Covenant to which the optional protocol procedure would be applicable.[482] Although there was some support for the idea that the procedure be limited to a select number of rights,[483] a 'maximalist approach' was preferred in which the procedure would apply to all the rights in the Covenant.[484] In order not to exclude prematurely the possibility of well-founded petitions, this appears to be the best solution. One may question,

---

[473] *See e.g.* Konate, E/C.12/1991/SR.13, at 10, para. 51; Bonoan-Dandan, E/C.12/1991/SR.14, at 14, para. 67.

[474] *See* Alston, E/C.12/1992/SR.11, at 2, para. 2.

[475] *See e.g.* Simma, E/C.12/1991/SR.14, at 13, para. 61.

[476] *See e.g.* Mratchkov, E/C.12/1992/SR.11, at 8, para. 28.

[477] 'Towards an Optional Protocol to the International Covenant on Economic, Social and Cultural Rights' (Optional Protocol), in UN Doc. E/1993/22, *supra*, n. 200, at 98, para. 52.

[478] *Ibid.* 99–102, paras. 54–67.   [479] *See e.g.* Simma, E/C.12/1992/SR.11, at 5, para. 12.

[480] Optional Protocol, *supra*, n. 477, at 99, para. 56.

[481] Although economic, social, and cultural rights are often incorrectly characterized as 'group rights', art. 8(1)(b) which speaks of the right of trade unions to establish national federations or confederations is perhaps the only clear case other than the right to self-determination in art. 1.

[482] Optional Protocol, *supra*, n. 477, at 102–4, paras. 68–79.

[483] *See* Simma, E/C.12/1991/SR.14, at 13, para. 62.

[484] *See* Alston, E/C.12/1992/SR.11, at 11, para. 50.

however, in the light of the practice of the HRC, whether it would be appropriate for the right to self-determination in article 1 to be subject to a petition procedure. Nevertheless, as has been pointed out, it would remain open for the Committee to exclude, through the operation of procedural safeguards, matters which are 'appropriately determined only by the domestic political processes'.[485]

Thirdly, there was general agreement that the principal procedural rules that normally apply to petition procedures should apply. Accordingly, conditions would be placed upon the right of petition *ratione temporis*, *materiae*, *personae*, and *loci* in the same way as they apply to the Optional Protocol to the ICCPR. Similarly, there would be rules requiring the exhaustion of domestic remedies and preventing the duplication of procedures or abuse of the right to petition.[486] The one proposal of interest was that the individual would not have to be a 'victim' *per se*, but rather would merely have to demonstrate that a 'detriment' had been suffered. As was argued, this would be more appropriate given the collective dimension of the remedies that would be sought,[487]especially if the right of petition was limited to individuals.

Finally, in terms of outcome, it was considered that the views of the Committee should simply be forwarded to the State party concerned. In addition, however, it was argued that given 'the nature of many of the issues likely to be raised', provision should be made for the friendly settlement of complaints.[488] Although this would have the advantage of making the procedure less confrontational, the Committee would have to retain the right to consider the situation where the settlement is clearly inadequate. If otherwise the State might avoid dealing with a group situation by compensating the individual complainant.

It is considered that the creation of a system of individual or NGO complaints is an attractive proposition for a number of reasons.[489] First and formost, such a system, if operated effectively, would vastly increase the level of national and international awareness of both the Covenant and the Committee. This in turn may encourage better reporting and more participation by NGOs, stimulate the institution of domestic remedies, and generate greater support for the work of the Committee (including more sessions and Secretariat involvement).

Secondly, the insititution of a complaints mechanism would enable the Committee to increase the effectiveness of the supervision system in a way not possible otherwise. Not only would it provide an additional means of supervision bringing extra force to bear on recalcitrant States, it would provide the Committee with the ability to develop the normative content of the rights in a specific and tangible manner. As Alston has noted with respect to the HRC:

---

[485] Optional Protocol, *supra*, n. 477, at 103, para. 71.   [486] *Ibid*. 104–6, paras. 80–90.

[487] *Ibid*. 105, para. 85.   [488] *Ibid*. 106, para. 92.   [489] *Ibid*. 91–3, paras. 20–5.

the collected 'views' of the Committee based on individual cases are of much greater value in shedding light on the meaning of the various rights formulations than either the Committee's General Comments or the insights generated by its examination of State reports.[490]

Contrary to the general perception of petition systems, their value lies not so much in the degree to which they operate as corrective or remedial mechanisms, but rather in the specificity they provide to the norms allowing States to appreciate in advance the precise type of action required of them.[491]

The principal argument against the creation of a petition system relating to economic, social, and cultural rights has been, and remains, the idea that they are essentially non-justiciable. More specifically, it is argued that, given the promotional nature of the rights and the generality of their terminology, it would be impossible for a supervisory body to decide whether or not a State is acting in conformity with its obligations under the Covenant. As was suggested during the drafting of the Covenant, complaints 'could only refer to insufficient programmes in the attainment of certain goals and it would be impossible for the committee to determine what the rate of progress in any particular case should be'.[492]

It is coming to be accepted that it is no longer valid to characterize economic, social, and cultural rights as exclusively 'promotional' or entirely non-justiciable. There is increasing evidence of economic, social, and cultural rights being the subject of international petitions.[493] As far as the Committee is concerned, it has already gone some way to identifying rights and obligations within the Covenant that require immediate implementation and therefore would traditionally be suited to judicial determination. In particular, it has mentioned article 3 (equal rights for men and women), article 7(a)(i) (equal remuneration for work of equal value), article 8 (trade union rights), article 10(3) (protection of children from exploitation), article 13(2)(a) (free and compulsory primary education), article 13(3) (respect for parental choice in education), article 13(4) (right to establish and direct educational institutions), article 15(3) (freedom of scientific research and creative activity).[494] In addition, the Committee has indicated that those

---

[490] *Ibid.* 94, para. 31.

[491] As Vasak notes, petition systems operate not so much to present a remedy for the individual or group, but to prevent the reoccurrence of that situation: Vasak, *supra*, n. 12, at 216.

[492] UN Doc. A/2929, *supra*, n. 36, at 124, para. 41.

[493] One may cite the recent case law of the HRC and CERD. It should also be noted that the Migrant Workers Convention and UNESCO operate petition systems in the field of economic, social, and cultural rights. Moreover, the Inter-American system has recently adopted a protocol allowing for individual petitions on economic, social, and cultural rights, and there is evidence that a system might be established under the European Social Charter, *see* Harris D., 'A Fresh Impetus for the European Social Charter' (1992) 41 *ICLQ* 659, at 673–4.

[494] *See* General Comment No. 3 (1990), *in* UN Doc. E/1990/23, Annex III, at 84, para. 5.

aspects of rights that involve State abstention would similarly be capable of immediate implementation. A number of examples could be: freedom from forced labour (article 6(1)), freedom from arbitrary dismissal (article 6), and freedom from arbitrary eviction (article 11). Such arguments suggest that there is, in fact, a justiciable core to every human right and indeed that it would be theoretically possible to operate a petition system with respect to economic, social, and cultural rights.

More importantly, however, it is considered that the problems associated with the operation of a petition system in relation to general or progressive rights are overstated. In theory, whether or not a provision is worded generally or is subject to progressive implementation, there is nothing to prevent a body with the necessary interpretative powers from making a decision as to the compliance of a State with its obligations. The decision might be a difficult one to make, but that is a different question. The justiciability of a particular issue depends, not upon the quality of the decision, but rather upon the authority of the body to make the decision. *Prima facie* then, in so far as the Committee is given the authority to assume a quasi-judicial role over the rights in the Covenant those rights will be justiciable. It is clear, nevertheless, that in order to maintain its credibility, the Committee would have to concern itself with the quality of the decisions made. Given the difficulty of establishing either the precise conditions of deprivation or the direct responsibility of States, the Committee will have to allow the States a margin of appreciation. Although this will mean concentrating upon overt or manifest violations of the Covenant, it does not entirely deprive the procedure of merit.

It is clear that the precise terms and conditions under which a complaints mechanism might operate will have to be established and agreed upon by the States parties. It will be for the Committee, however, to act as the spur to encourage any such action to be taken. For the Committee effectively to push through the institution of such a mechanism itself, it will have to demonstrate the necessity and advisability of such a development. The primary means by which it might do so is through developing its existing supervisory role in a way that shows the potential of a complaints mechanism.

IV. CONCLUSION

It is undoubtedly the case that in the relatively short period of time that the Committee on Economic, Social, and Cultural Rights has been charged with monitoring the implementation of the Covenant, it has transformed the supervision system beyond recognition. The Committee's work has been marked by a series of procedural reforms, undertaken swiftly and with relative ease, that places it in the position of having one of the most developed and potentially effective reporting mechanisms of all the human rights supervisory bodies. Notably, the Committee has undertaken to receive both written and oral information from non-governmental organizations, has adopted the procedure of making State-specific concluding observations following its consideration of State reports, conducts general discussions with experts from other fields and organizations, and drafts General Comments to further an understanding of the normative content of the rights in the Covenant and the reporting obligations.

That the Committee has been able to undertake such far-reaching procedural reforms is partly a reflection of the nature of its mandate. Essentially the Committee is charged with assisting the Economic and Social Council with the consideration of State reports. Unlike other human rights committees, the CESCR is not constrained by specific textual provisions in the treaty, it receives its authority from, and is primarily responsible to, ECOSOC. ECOSOC itself is authorized merely to 'consider' State reports. Its approach has been to interpret this mandate in a wide sense, allowing the Committee considerable leeway in its development of procedural initiatives.

The success of the Committee in its reform process is more significantly a reflection of the friendly and co-operative relations between its members. On no occasion has it been necessary to take decisions other than by consensus, nor has there been any lasting disagreement between Committee members. Effectively, much work is conducted informally with compromises and agreements being made out of session. The formal cohesiveness of the Committee is, to a large extent, a reflection of the amount of informal work that takes place. Having said that, the development of the Committee's work has been pushed forward by a small number of members. Others, while not being opposed to the direction in which the Committee is moving, have not tended to contribute as fully as they might. This is fortuitous in the sense that it allows a greater unity of purpose, but it also means that the work load becomes disproportionately spread. One might also speculate on the possibly disastrous scenario in which certain of the more active members are not re-elected to the Committee in future.

Notwithstanding the success of its reforms, the Committee still faces a number of problems in developing the effectiveness of the supervision process. In particular one might note the continuing inadequacy of the State reports, the failure on the part of a large number of States to report in a timely manner, and the disruption of the process of supervision by States failing to appear before the Committee. The Committee has taken a number of radical steps to rectify these problems, such as scheduling for consideration the situation in those States that have not submitted a report in ten years, or limiting the possibility of deferring the consideration of

State reports. Whether or not they will have an effect on the compliance of States with their reporting obligations remains to be seen. A further problem of an enduring nature is the fact that the Committee only has a single annual session of three weeks' duration for the consideration of State reports. Although ECOSOC has been responsive in providing the Committee with extra *ad hoc* sessions, the problem is only likely to get worse as reporting becomes more consistent. There is a clear need, not least to give the Committee some form of parity with the Human Rights Committee, for it to have a permanent extra session each year.

The largest problem facing the Committee, however, is posed by the substance of the Covenant itself. The breadth of subjects covered by the Covenant, combined with the lack of case law (whether national or international) in certain vital areas such as health and nutrition, mean that significant importance has to be placed upon the Committee's 'creative' or 'interpretative' functions. That it has undertaken to draft General Comments to develop an understanding of the normative content of the rights is a useful development in this respect. However, there is no doubt that the Committee lacks the support of a skilled and committed Secretariat prepared to produce analytical reports and provide other necessary assistance. Thus far, the Secretariat not only has failed to provide the form of support that ideally would be expected of it, but it has done little to assist the Committee in taking up those tasks itself. The failure of the Secretariat to have any imput into the Committee's substantive work stands out in this respect.

Although the Committee's procedural reforms have been directed at increasing its effectiveness as a supervisory body, they initially lent its work a certain duplicity. The reforms placed the Committee in the position whereby it was theoretically capable of making substantive evaluations of the degree of State compliance with the obligations under the Covenant, but the Committee itself preferred to characterize its role as one of monitoring and facilitating the provision of technical advice and assistance. Even if this were a desirable position to adopt, it is clear that the Committee's technical abilities are limited, and States have not tended to look to it for advice or assistance. This question has, however, been resolved in so far as the Committee has adopted the responsibility of making quasi-judicial determinations as to States' compliance with their obligations under the Covenant. As has been argued, this was an almost inevitable development.

Having adopted a quasi-judicial stance in its consideration of State reports, the Committee appears to be moving inexorably closer to the creation of an unofficial complaints mechanism. Under its current working procedures, it is now conceivable that the Committee, in response to the submission of information from NGO sources, may request the State concerned to submit and *ad hoc* report on the situation and, having considered the report, make an assessment as to State's compliance. Although this suggests that the reporting mechanism has exciting prospects, in the light of the present lack of established standards, minimal NGO participation, and insufficient information, it is considered that the Committee should act with a certain amount of caution.

The extent to which the reporting system is developed along the lines outlined will ultimately depend upon the outcome of the proposed institution of an official complaints mechanism in the form of an optional protocol. Such a procedure, if instituted, would undoubtedly represent the single most important development in the history of the Covenant. It is clear that a complaints system would be a useful and beneficial development, not merely in terms of increasing the level of supervision, but in so far as it would assist in the normative development of the Covenant and would raise the status of the Covenant as a human rights instrument. That there might be certain difficulties in establishing criteria to guide decision-making as regards the more generally stated and progressive rights should not be overstated. Indeed, as a complaints systems would be the most effective mechanism for defining State obligations in a specific and concrete manner, the generality of the norms alone should not stand in the way of such a development. It is important, therefore, that the Committee continues to discuss the issue and to encourage States to take the matter further by, for example, drafting an appropriate text.

3
State Obligations

Article 2(1)
Each State Party to the present Covenant undertakes to take steps, individu-
ally and through international assistance and co-operation, especially eco-
nomic and technical, to the maximum of available resources, with a view to
achieving progressively the full realization of the rights recognized in the
present Covenant by all appropriate means, including particularly the adop-
tion of legislative measures.

I. INTRODUCTION

Article 2(1) could be described as the linchpin of the ICESCR. It describes the duties incumbent upon States parties in the realization of the rights contained in the Covenant, an understanding of which is of critical importance both as to the substance and implementation of the Covenant as a whole. Quite appropriately the Committee has produced a General Comment on the subject of article 2(1) which has formed the basis for the Committee's approach to the Covenant in general.

II. THE NATURE OF THE OBLIGATIONS

The most striking feature of the Covenant as a human rights guarantee is the nature of the obligations undertaken by States as regards the implementation of the rights. Unlike other human rights instruments, States are not required immediately to guarantee the rights, but rather they may implement them over time depending upon the availability of necessary resources. Although the terms of article 2(1) have often led commentators to describe economic, social, and cultural rights themselves as being 'progressive in nature', there is nothing inevitable about the formula adopted. Certainly, the full realization of some of the rights presumes the availability of sufficient economic resources, but one only need to look as far as the European Social Charter to find a radically different solution to that question. By the same token, the failure of many States fully to implement economic, social, and cultural rights can often be more clearly attributed to a lack of political will than any matter of resource scarcity.

Before examining the specific terminology of article 2(1), consideration will be given to the general nature of the obligations within the Covenant. Two particular methods of analysis have been mentioned in the Committee's work: one centering upon obligations of conduct and result, the other upon obligations to respect, protect, and fulfil.

A Obligations of Conduct and Result

Article 2(1) has often been interpreted as imposing 'obligations of result' rather than 'obligations of conduct' upon the States parties.[1] An 'obligation of conduct' as understood by the International Law Commission is one where an organ of the State is obliged to undertake a specific course of conduct, whether through act or omission, which represents a goal in itself. It is to be contrasted with an 'obligation of result' which requires a State to achieve a particular result through a course of conduct (which again can be by act or omission), the form of which is left to the State's discretion.[2] Although these are basically neutral, descriptive terms, to conceive of the Covenant as merely imposing obligations of result is to deprive it of any serious content. As the terms of article 2(1) make clear, the result, namely the full realization of the rights, only has to be achieved in a progressive manner. If States had total discretion as to the means employed to that end, there would be little basis upon which to judge whether or not they were acting in good faith.

Nevertheless, a closer examination shows that the difference between the two forms of obligation is not as great as first appears. In cases of obligations of conduct, there will often be an objective towards which that conduct is aimed. Similarly, obligations of result will invariably require a specific course of action.[3] One is left with the impression that the classification of a particular obligation within one category or the other will rest primarily upon the amount of emphasis or specificity given to either the requisite conduct or result. The terms of article 2(1) are particularly ambiguous in this respect. Although emphasis is placed on the result, namely 'the full realization of the rights', there are plenty of indications within article 2(1) and the substantive articles themselves as to what steps are to be taken.

As the Committee has noted,[4] article 2(1) is perhaps best explained as

---

[1] Report of the International Law Commission (1977) 2 *Yrbk. ILC* 20, para. 8.

[2] *Ibid.* 11–30.

[3] This was readily recognized by the International Law Commission which commented that 'every international obligation has an object or, one might say, a result . . . [c]onversely, every international obligation, even if it is of the type called an obligation "of result", requires of the obligated State a certain course of action'. *ibid.* 13, para. 8.

[4] General Comment No. 3 (1990), UN Doc. E/1991/23, Annex III, UN ESCOR, Supp. (No. 3), at 83 (1991). *See also* Türk, E/C.12/1990/SR. 21, at 4, para. 7.

incorporating a mixture of the two types of obligation.[5] For example, article 6, which provides for the right to work, requires steps to be taken towards the achievement of full employment (an obligation of result), but also prohibits forced labour (an obligation of conduct).[6] Additionally, to the extent that the rights within the Covenant are not capable of immediate fulfilment, States are required to undertake certain obligations of conduct with a view to their progressive achievement. For example, while article 12 provides for the recognition of the right to health, paragraph 2 of that article outlines the 'steps to be taken' including *inter alia* the 'prevention, treatment, and control of epidemic, endemic, occupational, and other diseases'.

The distinction between obligations of conduct and result is complicated by the fact that some of the specified 'steps' may also be seen to be independent norms imposing separate obligations of result. Article 6(2), for example, provides that the steps to be taken in the realization of the right to work 'shall include technical and vocational guidance and training programmes'. It would not be distorting the sense of the Covenant to suggest that vocational guidance should be provided as of right as a partial definition of the right to work.[7]

In the face of the indeterminate and conditional nature of the results to be achieved, the Committee has tended to concentrate upon obligations of conduct. In doing so, it has gone some way towards outlining certain principles that should govern States' conduct in the implementation of the rights. In its early stages of work, the Committee concentrated upon the procedural adequacy of State action. Its initiatives centred, specifically, upon the establishment of norms associated with the reporting requirement of States parties under article 16.[8] Theoretically the obligations incumbent upon States under article 16 are distinct from those found in article 2(1), in that they relate to the supervision process as opposed to the substantive realization of the rights. However, in so far as the domestic implementation of the Covenant may be facilitated by the reporting process, this differentiation loses much of its force. Accordingly, a convergence between the procedural and substantive obligations may be identified, conditioned

---

[5] *See e.g.* Alston P. and Quinn G., 'The Nature and Scope of States Parties' Obligations under the International Covenant on Economic, Social and Cultural Rights' (1987) 8 *Hum. Rts. Q* 156, at 165.

[6] *See below*, Ch. 5.

[7] *See* Trubeck D., 'Economic, Social and Cultural Rights in the Third World: Human Rights Law and Human Needs Programs' in Meron T. (ed.), *Human Rights in International Law: Legal and Policy Issues* (1984), 205.

[8] Art. 16 ICESCR requires States parties to submit reports on the measures adopted and the progress made in achieving observance of the rights recognized in the Covenant. Cf. General Comment No. 1, UN Doc. E/1989/22, Annex III, UN ESCOR, Supp. (No. 4), at 87–9 (1989).

primarily by an approach that emphasizes the process or conduct of State action rather than the result achieved.[9]

Although the approach of the Committee at this stage is legitimate it must not be lost from sight that the objective of the State obligation is clearly stated in article 2(1), namely the 'full realization of the rights recognized' in the Covenant. The compliance of a State with its obligations ultimately is to be measured not merely by compliance with some notion of 'due process', but by the degree to which it has achieved the full realization of the rights.[10]

B Obligations to Respect, Protect, and Fulfil

The second method of analysis adopted by members of the Committee[11] has been to view the obligations in terms of the tripartite typology utilized by a number of commentators. According to the tripartite typology, all human rights entail three forms of State obligation, *viz.* the obligations to respect, protect, and fulfil.[12] The 'obligation to respect' requires the State to abstain from interference with the freedom of the individual. The 'obligation to protect' refers to the duty on the State to prevent other individuals from interference with the rights of the individual. The 'obligation to fulfil' requires the State to take the necessary measures to ensure the satisfaction of the needs of the individual that cannot be secured by the personal efforts of that individual.[13]

[9] Thus a member of the Committee referred to obligations of conduct by way of reassuring the State party concerned that the arts. did not have to be implemented immediately *in full. See* Alston, E/C.12/1988/SR.13, at 5, para. 19.

[10] This has to some extent been recognized by members of the Committee. See, e.g., the comment of Miss Taya in which she recognized that attention should be paid to the 'ideal situation' in the achievement of economic, social, and cultural rights: E/C.12/1990/SR.4, at 2, para. 2.

The International Law Commission commented in this regard that 'there is a breach by a State of an international obligation requiring it to achieve, by means of its own choice, a specified result if, by the conduct adopted, the State does not achieve the result required of it by that obligation': *supra*, n. 1, at 11. Art. 21(1).

[11] *See e.g.* Simma, E/C.12/1990/SR. 21, at 8, para. 28. Although there is considerable concurrence in the Committee as to the utility of this method of analysis, there appear to remain a few doubts. It was commented, e.g., at the Committee's 4th session that there was 'no consensus within the Committee as to the very nature of economic, social and cultural rights': Alston, E/C.12/1990/SR.4, at 10, para. 49.

[12] The tripartite typology of obligations is to be found in Mr Eide's presentation on the Right to Food at the Committee's General Discussion at its Third Session: E/C.12/1989/SR.20. *Cf also* Eide A., *Right to Adequate Food as a Human Right* (1989).

[13] Some typologies have an additional 4th part: the duty to promote. *See* Van Hoof G., 'The Legal Nature of Economic, Social and Cultural Rights: A Rebuttal of Some Traditional Views', in Alston P. and Tomasevski K. (eds.), *The Right To Food* (1985), 97. Shue speaks of a duty to aid which describes 'having to go back and make up for failures in respect and protection': Shue H., 'The Interdependence of Duties', in Alston P. and Tomasevski K. (eds.), *The Right To Food* (1985), 85, at 86. At an earlier stage he characterized the three obligations

This approach not only provides a detailed analytical framework in which a clearer understanding of State obligations in the context of human rights may be achieved,[14] but also serves to counteract some of the traditional assumptions that tended categorically to distinguish economic, social, and cultural rights from civil and political rights.[15] To the extent that the obligations to respect, protect, and fulfil are all to be found to some greater or lesser extent in every human right, it is not possible to speak of economic, social, and cultural rights as being solely 'positive' any more than it is to consider civil and political rights as being merely 'negative'.

1 The Obligation to Respect

It is clear that in certain circumstances, economic, social, and cultural rights require State 'abstention' or 'restraint'. This is most apparent with regard to those rights that are considered to be of immediate application. Thus as the implementation of the rights relating to trade unions in article 8(1) require no substantial economic input on the part of the State they may therefore be put into effect without delay merely through the exercise of State restraint.[16] The same can be said of those articles that refer to individual 'freedom' or 'liberty'. For example, article 13(3) speaks of the 'liberty of parents ... to choose for their children schools, other than those established by the public authorities'.[17] The State here is obliged merely to refrain from placing obstacles in the way of parents wishing to exercise this right.

The State is also more generally required to refrain from acts which would serve to deprive individuals of their rights under the Covenant. It has been commented that 'a systematic deprivation of certain sectors of the community through the action of the State would obviously constitute a violation of the rights derived from the Covenant'.[18] Thus a law in Zaïre that

as those to forbear, protect, and aid. Shue H., 'Rights in the Light of Duties', in Brown P. and Maclean D. (eds.), *Human Rights and U.S. Foreign Policy* (1979), 65, at 76.

[14] It would appear that the obligations to respect and protect tend to fall into the category of obligations of conduct. The obligation to fulfil relates more closely to an obligation of result.

[15] A common contention subsists that whereas civil and political rights require 'State abstention', economic, social, and cultural rights require 'State action': *see e.g.* Bossuyt M., 'La Distinction juridique entre les droits civils et politiques et les droits economiques, sociaux et culturels' (1975) 8 *HRLJ* 783, at 790.

[16] *See e.g.* Sparsis, E/C.12/1989/SR.12, at 4, para. 21. That art. 8 also imposes a positive obligation on States to protect the exercise of the right (e.g. through prevention of arbitrary dismissal) is indicated by the use of the word 'ensure' in that art. Cf. Buergenthal T., 'To Respect and Ensure: State Obligations and Permissible Derogations' in Henkin L. (ed.), *The International Bill of Rights* (1981), 72, at 77. Art. 15(1)(a), which refers to the right of everyone to take part in cultural life, could also be seen as a matter for State restraint.

[17] Art. 13(4) also refers to the liberty to establish such schools. The same principle could apply to the references to 'freedoms' in arts. 6(2) and 15(3).

[18] Rattray, E/C.12/1990/SR.20, at 11, para. 48. *See also* Tomasevski K., *Development Aid and Human Rights* (1989), 126.

required married women to request their husbands' permission either to work outside the home or to open an individual bank account[19] was rightly criticized by the Committee as being a violation of article 6 of the Covenant.[20]

Additionally, it would be appropriate to say that even where States are required to take positive action to realize the rights in the Covenant, they should do so in a manner that preserves the individual's freedom of action. As has been explained by one member of the Committee:

> One of the principles underlying the Covenant was to secure full development of the human personality, something that called for the element of free choice in the exercise of the rights set forth ... [therefore] a fine balance had to be maintained between protective conditions and the need to make sure that they did not inhibit the development of the human personality.[21]

Accordingly, although the achievement of economic and social rights entails significant government intervention, any such action must ultimately preserve the freedom and dignity of the individual.

2 The Obligation to Protect

The obligation to protect the individual's rights from violation by third parties similarly crosses the border between civil and political and economic, social, and cultural rights.[22] Such an obligation implies the 'horizontal effectiveness' of rights, often known as *Drittwirkung der Grundrechte*. As a concept, *Drittwirkung* has had considerable recognition both in national[23] and international case law.[24] However, we are concerned here not so much with the ability of the individual to 'enforce' his or her fundamental rights against another individual as, in absence of a petition procedure, that is primarily a question of national law,[25] but rather with the correlative State

[19] Art. 3(c) Zaïrian Labour Code. E/1986/3/Add.7, at 2.

[20] *See e.g.* Texier, E/C.12/1988/SR.17, at 6, para. 36. The same might be said for the eviction of 15,000 families from their homes by the Dominican Republic authorities: *see* UN Doc. E/1991/23, at 64, para. 249, UN ESCOR, Supp. (No. 3) (1991).

[21] Rattray, E/C.12/1987/SR.13, at 6, para. 24.

[22] The obligation to protect in the field of civil and political rights would seem to require as a minimum the provision of an effective police force and justice system. The problem that many jurists have with the concept of the obligation to protect is that it not only confers positive obligations upon States with regard to civil and political rights, but also that the extent of such an obligation is unclear. *See* Sieghart P., *The Lawful Rights of Mankind* (1986), 90–1.

[23] Starck C., 'Europe's Fundamental Rights in their Newest Garb' (1982) 3 *HRLJ* 103, at 111. The Netherlands mentioned to the Committee that its legal system envisages the horizontal effectiveness of certain human rights provisions: E/C.12/1989/SR.15, at 10, para. 59.

[24] *See e.g.* Van Dijk P. and Van Hoof G., *Theory and Practice of the European Convention on Human Rights* (2nd ed. 1990), 16–20; Drzemczewski A., *European Human Rights Convention in Domestic Law: A Comparative Study* (1983), 199–228; Buergenthal, *supra*, n. 16, at 77.

[25] On the possibility of the 'direct effect' of the ICESCR, *see* Craven M., 'The Domestic Application of the International Covenant on Economic, Social and Cultural Rights' (1993) 40 *Neth ILR* 367.

obligations that accompany a recognition of the horizontal effect of the rights.

There is no indication that the drafters of the Covenant expressly intended the rights to have horizontal effect. However, that no mention was made of this aspect of State obligations is not conclusive. There has to be an overriding assumption, given that the drafters were committed to ensuring the fundamental rights of every individual, that States would be under an obligation to protect the rights of the individual against violation by others.

Indeed, the question of horizontal effectiveness is of particular importance in the field of economic, social, and cultural rights. In the context of article 7, for example, if State obligations were limited to ensuring that public employees enjoyed fair conditions of work, the right would be largely deprived of effect (especially in the case of 'mixed' or 'market' economies). Similar considerations also apply to the right to work (article 6), the right to housing (article 11), and in certain circumstances, the rights to health (article 12), and education (article 13). It must be assumed that where the State is not in a position to ensure the rights itself, it must regulate private interactions to ensure that individuals are not arbitrarily deprived of the enjoyment of their rights by other individuals.

Recognition of an obligation to protect can be found in the Covenant itself. First, it is clear that the rights pertain to 'everyone'. It would be contrary to this clearly worded obligation if a State were to declare, for example, that it could only secure the right to strike for those who worked in the public sector.[26] It is obvious that action must be taken for all sectors of the population.[27] Secondly, article 10(3) expressly stipulates that 'children and young persons should be protected from economic and social exploitation' and that certain practices should be punishable by law. There is a clear recognition here that the responsibility of the State goes beyond the actions of itself or its agents, to positive protection of the individual from third party violations. A similar reference is made in article 13(3) and (4) to the role that the State may take in establishing minimum standards in private educational establishments. Although not stated in terms of an obligation, such provisions seem to envisage a role for the State in which obligations over individual relations are not outside the scope of its responsibility.

The Committee has both expressly and impliedly established an obligation upon States parties to protect the individual's interests against third party interference. It has shown particular concern over the operation of the rights in the private sphere, especially as regards employment. Ques-

---

[26] *See* Marchan Romero, E/C.12/1989/SR.10, at 7, para. 34. His question implied that the right to strike had to be secured in the private sphere.

[27] This is also conditioned by the provision of art. 2(2) whereby the State is under an obligation to take measures in a non-discriminatory fashion.

tions have been asked *inter alia* about the employment of women,[28] the right to strike,[29] retirement ages,[30] and the provision of pensions[31] in the private sector.[32] As a corollary the Committee has looked towards the enactment of legislation as a means of regulation of the private sector,[33] the effective enforcement of those conditions,[34] and the establishment of mechanisms for the settlement of any private disputes.[35] The clearest example of the Committee's approach arose in the case of Iran. There the Committee expressed concern over the implications of the issue of *fatwahs* on creative freedom. The Committee noted in its concluding observations:

While appreciating that *fatwahs* are issued by the religious authorities and not by the State organizations *per se*, the question of State responsibility clearly arises in circumstances in which the State does not take whatever measures are available to it to remove clear threats to the rights applicable in Iran in consequence of its ratification of the Covenant.[36]

The Committee is thus clear that the realm of State responsibility extends not only to the acts of agents of the State but also those of third parties over whom the State has or should have control.

3 The Obligation to Fulfil

The obligation to fulfil is central to the realization of economic, social, and cultural rights, and is the principal concept upon which the terms of article 2(1) were built. As was clear in the drafting of the Covenant,[37] in contrast to the ICCPR,[38] States would not commit themselves to the immediate full

---

[28] *See e.g.* Butragueno, E/C.12/1989/SR.8, at 8, para. 46.

[29] *See e.g.* Marchan Romero, E/C.12/1989/SR.10, at 7, para. 34.

[30] *See e.g.* Butragueno, E/C.12/1988/SR.10, at 8, para. 41.

[31] *See e.g.* Simma, E/C.12/1989/SR.15, at 3, para. 9.

[32] The Committee has also concerned itself with other aspects of the private sector like tenants' rights. *See e.g.* Sparsis, E/C.12/1988/SR.13, at 14, para. 83; Mrachkov, E/C.12/1988/SR.10, at 7, para. 27.

[33] *e.g.* the enactment of a Labour Code, *see* Texier, E/C.12/1987/SR.5, at 5, para. 22.

[34] *e.g.* the provision of a Labour inspectorate and sanctions for enforcement of minimum conditions of work. *See* Simma, E/C.12/1988/SR.5, at 7, para. 29; Taya, E/C.12/1988/SR.12, at 8, para. 34; Sparsis, E/C.12/1990/SR.10, at 14, para. 82.

[35] *See e.g.* Sparsis, E/C.12/1988/SR.7, at 5, paras. 30–1.

[36] Concluding observations on report of Iran, E/C.12/1993/7, at 3, para. 7.

[37] *See above*, Ch. 1, text accompanying nn. 157–8.

[38] Art. 2(1) of the ICCPR requires States parties to 'respect and to ensure' the rights. It is apparent from the practice of the European Court of Human Rights that civil and political rights may entail certain positive obligations upon States (beyond those relating to the protection of individuals) such as the establishment of a court system and the provision of effective remedies. *See e.g.* the right to legal aid, *Airey* v. *Ireland*, Eur Ct. HR, Series A, Vol. 32, judgment of 9 Oct. 1979, (1979–80) 2 EHRR 305; the provision of legal safeguards to allow a child's integration in its family, *Marckx* v. *Belgium*, Eur. Ct. HR, Series A, Vol. 31, judgment of 13 June 1979, (1979–80) 2 EHRR 330. *See also* Berenstein A., 'Economic and Social Rights: Their inclusion in the European Convention on Human Rights. Problems of Formulation and

realization of economic, social, and cultural rights. Accordingly, the wording of article 2(1) was specifically drafted to reflect the need to allow for greater flexibility in the fulfilment of the rights in the Covenant. The intricacies of the obligation to fulfil as reflected in article 2(1) will be dealt with in the following sections.

III. 'UNDERTAKES TO TAKE STEPS'

The fundamental obligation in the ICESCR is for the States parties to 'take steps' towards the realization of the rights contained therein. The phrase 'undertakes to take steps' itself, however, merely reflects the general rule of international law,[39] requiring States to take the necessary action to execute the provisions of the Covenant. The precise nature of that commitment, however, is to be drawn from the other phrases within article 2(1). As is apparent from the discussion above, the phrase 'undertakes to take steps' may refer either to obligations of conduct or obligations of result according to its context.[40]

It has been argued that since the phrase 'to take steps' was considered an alternative to 'ensure' or 'guarantee' in the preparatory work, it has progressive overtones.[41] An analysis of the phrase as used in other international instruments, however, does not seem to bear out this conclusion. An obligation to take 'steps' or 'measures'[42] is to be found in article 2(2) of the ICCPR and in article 2(1) of the Convention against Torture and Other Cruel, Inhuman, or Degrading Treatment or Punishment.[43] As both of these instruments require immediate implementation,[44] the phrase itself can not be deemed to hold progressive connotations.

Interpretation' (1981) 2 *HRLJ* 257. The provision of legal remedies is specifically envisaged by art. 2(3)(a) ICCPR which requires each State party 'to ensure that any person whose rights or freedoms . . . are violated shall have an effective remedy'.

[39] *See The Case Relative to the Exchange of Greek and Turkish Populations under the Lausanne Convention VI*, PCIJ (1925), Series B, No. 10, at 20. The PCIJ advised that a 'State which has contracted valid international obligations is bound to make in its legislation such modifications as may be necessary to ensure the fulfilment of the obligations undertaken'.

[40] *See above*, text accompanying n. 4.

[41] *See* Alston and Quinn, *supra*, n. 5, at 165.

[42] Whereas the term 'measures' appears to be a narrower concept than that of 'steps', implying merely legal action, the terms were used interchangeably. Whereas the English version of the phrase is 'to take steps', the Spanish is 'to adopt measures' (*a adopter medidas*) and the French 'to act' (*s'engager à agir*). *See* General Comment No. 3, *supra*, n. 4, at 83, para. 2.

[43] GA Resn. 39/46, (26 June 1987), 39 UN GAOR, Supp. (No. 51), at 197 (1984); 24 ILM 535.

[44] With regard to the Torture Convention *see* Boulesbaa A., 'The Nature of the Obligations Incurred by States under Article 2 of the UN Convention Against Torture' (1990) 12 *Hum. Rts. Q* 53, at 80.

While the obligation 'to take steps' does not make any stipulations as to the manner of implementation, it is not entirely redundant. As noted above, it signals the immediate assumption of legal commitments by the States parties upon ratification.[45] The Committee has commented:

while the full realization of the relevant rights may be achieved progressively, steps towards that goal must be taken within a reasonably short time after the Covenant's entry into force for the States concerned.[46]

It appears to be considered that all States, whether developing or developed, will need to take specific measures following ratification of, or accession to, the Covenant. Lack of resources in itself would not allow States to defer indefinitely taking the necessary action to give effect to the obligations under the Covenant.

IV. 'BY ALL APPROPRIATE MEANS'

In so far as the full realization of the rights within the Covenant represents an obligation of result, States have a degree of discretion in the conduct they pursue to that end.[47] Thus in principle a State may choose between legislative, administrative, judicial, social, educational, or other methods to undertake the realization of the rights.[48] Given the variety of economic, social, and legal systems that exist among the States parties to the Covenant, and their different levels of development, it is natural that the approach of each State will vary according to the circumstances in which it finds itself. The Committee has commented that:

the phrase 'by all appropriate means' must be given its full and natural meaning. While each State party must decide for itself which means are the most appropriate under the circumstances with respect to each of the rights, the 'appropriateness' of the means chosen will not always be self-evident. It is therefore desirable that States parties' reports should indicate not only the measures that have been taken but also the basis on which they are considered to be the most 'appropriate' under the

[45] Robertson comments in contrast that the Covenant 'does not set out obligations which contracting parties are required necessarily to accept immediately': Robertson A., *Human Rights in the World* (3rd ed., 1992), 230.

[46] General Comment No. 3, *supra*, n. 4, at 83, para. 2. This conclusion was incidentally one which had been drawn in para. 16 of the influential Limburg Principles which declares that: 'All States Parties have an obligation to begin immediately to take steps towards full realization of the rights contained in the Covenant': (1987) 9 *Hum. Rts. Q* 122, at 125. *See also* Eide's address to the Committee where he took this view: E/C.12/1989/SR.20, at 5, para. 14.

[47] It was certainly the view of a number of governments during the drafting of the Covenant that this would be the case. Yugoslavia remarked that the text should 'require governments to undertake to do everything to promote those rights, it being left to each to choose the measures it would adopt for the purpose': E/CN.4/AC.14, at 16 (1951).

[48] General Comment No. 3, *supra*, n. 4, at 85, para. 7.

circumstances. However, the ultimate determination as to whether all appropriate measures have been taken remains one for the Committee to make.[49]

During its discussion of General Comment No. 3, one member stressed that the Committee could not require States to demonstrate why the measures taken were the most appropriate, as that was a task for the Committee itself to undertake.[50] However, the text of the General Comment does suggest that the States parties should make the initial decision as to what measures are considered appropriate. It appears that the Committee, quite correctly, considers that it is not in a position to prescribe to each State party the steps to be taken. In effect, the Committee appears to give States parties a 'margin of discretion'[51] in deciding the appropriate course of action to be taken. Nevertheless, as the final sentence of the General Comment makes clear, the Committee does have a residual power to assess whether or not the measures taken were the most appropriate in the circumstances.[52]

The two main limits upon the exercise of State discretion in determining what measures are to be taken are the requirements found in the text of the Covenant itself and the stipulations of the Committee to that end. Each will be dealt with in turn below.

A Textual Requirements

As a result of the somewhat confused method of drafting, some of the substantive provisions of the Covenant contain details of the steps to be taken in implementation.[53] Thus articles 6(2), 11(2), 12(2), 13(2), and 15(2) all contain some indication of the methods by which the State should realize the rights. Article 13(2)(a), for example, stipulates that primary education should be made compulsory and freely available to all, as a method by which the right to education should be realized. Although in some cases the steps are stated to be merely illustrative,[54] the Committee has emphasized that they are nevertheless mandatory.[55]

---

[49] General Comment No. 3, *supra*, n. 4, at 84, para. 4.

[50] *See* Konate, E/C.12/1990/SR.46, at 10, para. 48.

[51] *Cf.* the 'margin of appreciation' doctrine operated in the context of limitations under the European Convention on Human Rights: *see* Van Dijk and Van Hoof, *supra*, n. 24, at 585–606; MacDonald R., 'The Margin of Appreciation in the Jurisprudence of the European Court of Human Rights' in *International Law and the Time of its Codification: Essays in Honour of Robert Ago* (1987), 187; O'Donnell T., 'The Margin of Appreciation Doctrine: Standards in the Jurisprudence of the European Court of Human Rights' (1982) 4 *Hum. Rts. Q* 474.

[52] *See e.g.* Alston, E/C.12/1990/SR.48, at 8, para. 40.

[53] During the drafting process it was not decided until 1951 to include a general 'umbrella' clause on economic, social, and cultural rights which is now found in art. 2(1): E/CN.4/SR.233, at 21 (1951). Prior to this, some representatives had felt that the role of the State should be defined in each art. *See e.g.* Chile (Santa Cruz), E/CN.4/SR.216, at 22 (1951). *Generally*, UN Doc. A/2929, para. 19, 10 UN GAOR, Annexes (Ag. Item 28), Pt. II (1955). The articles however were not amended sufficiently to conform entirely to the final view.

[54] *e.g.* arts. 6(2), 12(2), and 15(2) all state that the steps taken 'shall include' those stipulated.

[55] An example is the Committee's criticism of Zaïre with regard to art. 13(2)(a): E/C.12/1988/SR.17.

Of the possible steps that are to be taken, article 2(1) itself expresses a preference for legislative measures, the nature of which will be discussed below.[56] That legislative measures are specifically mentioned suggests that they are therefore 'the most normal and appropriate for achieving the purposes of the Covenant in question'.[57] Indeed, a similar provision in the ICCPR[58] has been described as imposing a 'conditional' obligation of conduct.[59]

B Committee Requirements

Beyond the question of specific rights-related comments as to the means for the fulfilment of the rights,[60] the Committee has laid down some general methodological requirements for implementation and has outlined certain substantive considerations that also have to be taken into account.

1 Methodological Requirements

In its General Comment No. 1, the Committee outlined seven 'objectives' to be served by the reporting procedure.[61] Some of these can be seen as having evolved into preconditions for the effective realization of the rights recognized in the Covenant. As a first step, States are obliged to monitor and evaluate the actual situation with regard to the enjoyment of each right within their jurisdiction.[62] In particular, attention must be paid to the proportion of citizens that do not enjoy a specific right[63] and to those specific sectors of the population that appear to be vulnerable or disadvantaged.[64]

---

[56] *See* text accompanying nn. 114–27.

[57] International Law Commission, *supra*, n. 1, at 21, para. 8. It also comments that the expression of a preferred means of implementation is entirely consistent with an obligation of result as there is no obligation to take this course of action.

[58] Art. 2(2) ICCPR reads: '[E]ach State Party . . . undertakes to take the necessary steps . . . to adopt such legislative or other measures as may be necessary to give effect to the rights recognised in the present Covenant.'

[59] Schachter O., 'The Obligation to Implement the Covenant in Domestic Law' in Henkin L. (ed.), *The International Bill of Rights* (1981), 311.

[60] Such comments will be dealt with in subsequent chapters. *See below*, Chs. 5–8.

[61] *Supra*, n. 8.

[62] In its General Comment No. 1 the Committee stated that the first objective of the reporting process was 'to ensure that a comprehensive review is undertaken with respect to national legislation, administrative rules and procedures, and practices in an effort to ensure the fullest possible conformity with the Covenant'. Similarly the second objective 'is to ensure that a State party monitors the actual situation with respect to each of the rights'. *Ibid*. 88, para. 2. *See also* Concluding observations on report of Lebanon, E/C.12/1993/10, at 2, para. 9.

[63] *See e.g.* Concluding observations of report of New Zealand, E/C.12/1993/13, at 3, para. 15.

[64] Concluding observations of report of Australia, E/C.12/1993/9, at 3, para. 16. In its General Comment No. 1, the Committee commented that in order to monitor the situation adequately 'special attention [should] be given to any worse-off regions or areas and to any specific groups or subgroups which appear to be particularly vulnerable or disadvantaged': *supra* n. 8, at 88, para. 3. The Committee has long held that the 'principal concern' of the ICESCR is the position of the vulnerable and disadvantaged. *See* Alston, E/C.12/1987/SR.3, at 3, para. 10.

Concentration on aggregate national statistics, such as per capita GNP, is inadequate as it fails to reflect the position of the marginalized sectors of the population.[65] In practice, reports that fail to identify and analyse the relative position of such disadvantaged sectors of the population have been criticized.[66]

Given the somewhat vague and general wording of certain provisions in the Covenant, such as 'an adequate standard of living' or 'adequate food, clothing, and housing', an essential step in the realization of the rights is for these provisions to be defined more closely. It has been the policy of the Committee to demand that States parties establish national 'yardsticks' or 'benchmarks' by which it may evaluate the domestic situation.[67] In the words of one Committee member, he 'failed to see how a State could meet the obligation specified in article 11 of the Covenant . . . if it had not itself decided what might be regarded as an adequate standard of living, in other words if it had not established what the poverty threshold was'.[68] The use of such indicators must be seen as an essential part of government policy-making whereby problem areas can be targeted and priorities established.[69]

The necessity of utilizing national indicators, as opposed to international ones, is justified primarily by the variety of social and economic contexts in which the rights operate.[70] However, although it may be appropriate for

[65] *See e.g.* Alston, E/C.12/1987/SR.7, at 9, para. 42; General Comment No. 1. *supra*, n. 8, at 88, para. 3.

[66] *e.g.* Concluding remarks on the report of Argentina, Report of the Committee's Fourth Session, E/1990/23, at 64, para. 254, UN ESCOR, Supp. (No. 3) (1990); and Philippines, E/C.12/1990/SR.11, at 11, paras. 40–1. This is also suggested by the requirement under art. 17 that States indicate the factors and difficulties encountered in fulfilling the obligations under the Covenant. *See* Alston, E/C.12/1987/SR.12, at 8, para. 34. This is by no means confined to developing States. *See* Comments of the Committee on the Netherlands report, E/C.12/1987/SR.5–6.

[67] In its General Comment No. 1 the Committee decided that an objective of the reporting process was: 'to provide a basis on which the State Party itself, as well as the Committee, can effectively evaluate the extent to which progress has been made towards the realization of the obligations contained in the Covenant. For this purpose, it may be useful for States to identify specific benchmarks or goals against which their performance in a given area can be assessed. Thus, for example, it is generally agreed that it is important to set specific goals with respect to the reduction of infant mortality, the extent of vaccination of children, the intake of calories per person, the number of persons per health care provider, etc.': Such bench-marks would seem to include both qualitative and quantitative data. General Comment No. 1, *supra*, n. 8, at 89, paras. 6–7. *See also* references to a poverty threshold: Butragueno, E/C.12/1989/SR.3, at 7, para. 28; Alston, E/C.12/1990/SR.2, at 11, para. 65; *ibid.* SR.21, at 7, para. 22.

[68] Sparsis, E/C.12/1989/SR.17, at 8, para. 35.

[69] *See* General Comment No. 1 where the Committee stated: 'While monitoring is designed to give a detailed overview of the existing situation the principal value of such an overview is to provide the basis for the elaboration of clearly stated and carefully targeted policies, including the establishment of priorities which reflect the provisions of the Covenant': *supra*, n. 8, at 88, para. 4.

[70] The Committee has commented that in many areas 'global bench-marks are of limited use, whereas national or other more specific bench-marks can provide an extremely valuable indication of progress': General Comment No. 1, *ibid.* 89, para. 6.

States to be given a margin of discretion in determining the level at which a national benchmark should be set, it may be questioned whether national standards should be the sole criterion for assessment. To allow the indicators for assessment to vary from country to country may undermine the universal nature of the rights[71] and may ultimately give States parties the power to decide the extent of their own obligations.[72]

With this in mind, the Committee explicitly stipulated that it 'cannot accept their (States') national indicators as a general criterion for international assessment'.[73] In practice, it has questioned national qualitative and quantitative data on the basis of that received from international and non-governmental sources. National bench-marks are used not so much as a definitive means of assessment, but rather as an indication of whether the State party is taking its international obligations seriously. The success of this strategy, however, is crucially dependent upon access to reliable alternative sources of information against which the State reports may be balanced.[74] In the absence of such information, the State bench-marks may provide the only basis on which assessment may be made.

The next stage in implementation is for the States parties to establish a coherent policy to overcome the problems encountered and to make sufficient progress in the realization of the rights. This is envisaged specifically in article 14 which establishes that those States parties that do not have free and compulsory primary education for all should adopt a plan for the progressive implementation of this obligation. It could be said that the provision of article 14 merely spells out the obligations implicit in the other articles.[75] Thus a member of the Committee commented with respect to article 11:

[71] Bossuyt argues that economic, social, and cultural rights differ from their civil and political rights counterparts by the fact that they are variable, and dependant upon the resources of the country concerned. Bossuyt, *supra*, n. 15, at 790.

[72] *See* Alston, E/C.12/1989/SR.3, at 3, para. 7. He comments that such a conclusion 'would deprive the obligations set forth in the Covenant of any real significance, and there would be no point in having a monitoring procedure or an international supervisory body'. Tomuschat has similarly concluded that 'each State Party is entitled to suggest an interpretation which it believes to reflect the meaning of the provision concerned. There is no power for a state to determine unilaterally the legal substance of an ambiguous text': Tomuschat C., 'National Implementation of International Standards on Human Rights' (1982) *Can. HRY* 31, at 36.

[73] E/C.12/CRP.1/Add. 10, at 5. Oddly enough this sentence was altered (by mistake it appears) in the final copy of the Committee's report, which reads: 'although Governments were duty bound to submit reports, the Committee could accept their national indicators as a general criterion for international assessment': UN Doc. E/1990/23, *supra*, n. 66, at 68, para. 271.

[74] For the role of alternative information in the supervision process, *see above*, Ch. 2, text accompanying nn. 316–76.

[75] This was the conclusion of the Committee in its General Comment No. 1. *Supra*, n. 8, at 88, para. 4.

Governments were not entitled to content themselves with making a vague general commitment to take steps to ensure that their people did not suffer from hunger, but should be obliged to adopt a precise programme for the implementation of all the rights.[76]

The establishment of such a programme or policy should also include bench-marks to provide a 'conceptual framework' in which the progress made towards the full realization of the rights can be evaluated.[77] It has also been suggested that, like the terms of article 14, a timetable should be established for the implementation of such a policy.[78]

2 Substantive Concerns

The perspective of the Committee in developing the substantive obligations incumbent upon States parties has been dominated by four related issues: participation, disadvantagement, privatization, and State organization.[79] The question of participation has been foreseen to some extent by the explicit recognition of democratic principles in the Covenant itself. Article 1(1), for example, proclaims the right of all peoples to self-determination and 'by virtue of that right they *freely determine their political status* and freely pursue their social and cultural development' (emphasis added). This 'internal' aspect of self-determination[80] is also foreseen in article 21(3) of the Universal Declaration which more explicitly states that 'the will of the people shall be the basis of the authority of government'.[81] That the Covenant conceives of democracy as a concept inherent in the rights is further emphasized by references to 'democratic society' in article 8(1)(a) and (c), and by the agreement that education 'shall enable all persons to participate effectively in a free society'.[82]

Such a reading of the Covenant coincides with the central role of participation in the development process.[83] Not only is the individual posited as

---

[76] Alston, E/C.12/1987/SR.4, at 3, para. 6. *See also* Concluding observations on report of Nicaragua, E/C.12/1993/14, at 3, para. 11.

[77] *See* Sparsis, E/C.12/1989/SR.8, at 10, para. 58. It may be noted that the full realization of some rights may of itself be progressive in nature in which case the requirement of progress is continuous.

[78] *Ibid.*

[79] These issues are by no means the only concerns of the Committee; they merely represent areas in which the Committee seems to have expressed a continuing interest. Participation and impoverishment are issues that have derived from current development approaches. *See* Friedman J., *Empowerment: The Politics of Alternative Development* (1993).

[80] *See* Cassese A., 'The Self-Determination of Peoples' in Henkin L. (ed.), *The International Bill of Rights* (1981), 92.

[81] This is reflected in art. 25(b) ICCPR which provides for the right to vote. The interdependence of the rights within the two Covenants is foreseen in their preambles.

[82] Art. 13(1).

[83] *See e.g.* Report of the Secretary-General, *Concrete Proposals for the Effective Implementation and Promotion of the Declaration on the Right to Development*, UN Doc. E/CN.4/1993/16, at 3–4, paras. 7–14 (1993); Türk D., *The Realization of Economic, Social and Cultural*

the primary subject of development,[84] but common emphasis is placed upon 'empowerment' or 'self-reliance' as an objective.[85] Thus the development process is conceived of as being an 'enabling' process whereby structural impediments (both social and economic, on a micro and macro scale) are lifted to allow the individual to define and fulfil his or her material and non-material needs.[86]

The Committee has emphasized the symbiotic relationship between democratic participation and the enjoyment of economic, social, and cultural rights.[87] As one member commented:

Even if the responsibility to ensure observance of the right to an adequate standard of living lay ultimately with the state, efforts should be made to see to it that individuals could exercise their right to participate in the achievement of the country's development objectives.[88]

Similarly, the Committee has indirectly emphasized the importance of participation in its requirement that governments undertake promotional and publicity strategies with respect to the Covenant. States are expected to publicize the text of the Covenant,[89] seek the participation of NGOs in the drafting of the State reports,[90] and disseminate those reports as widely as possible.[91] As a State representative noted, the role of the government in

---

Rights, Final Report, UN Doc. E/CN.4/Sub.2/1992/16, at 46–7, paras. 177–81 (1992); Barsch R., 'The Global Consultation on the Right to Development' (1993) 13 *Hum. Rts. Q* 322.

[84] If individuals were seen merely as the 'object' of development, their rights would then subsist merely at the level of entitlements to delivery of specific goods and services, or the fulfilment of certain 'needs'. The notion of the individual as a 'subject' of development envisages an emphasis on self-reliance, empowerment, and participation in the development process which accords more closely to the concept of human dignity. *See e.g.* Tomasevski, *supra*, n. 18, at 155. Art. 2(1) of the Declaration on the Right to Development thus states: 'The human person is the central subject of development and should be the active participant and beneficiary of the right to development': GA Resn. 41/128 (4 Dec. 1986), 41 UN GAOR, Resns. Supp. (No. 53), at 186 (1986).

[85] Shepherd G., 'The Power System and Basic Human Rights: From Tribute to Self-Reliance' in Shepherd G. and Nanda V. (eds.), *Human Rights and Third World Development* (1985), 13; Friedman, *supra*, n. 79.

[86] Conroy describes an ideal development model in which: 'the necessary incentives for private enterprise do not involve an immediate worsening of the conditions in which the poorest sectors of the population usually live. Such a development model might include public investments, both direct and through subsidies, in food, health, education and housing, for the purpose of immediately eliminating the suffering of the poor, restoring their human dignity and offering them the necessary opportunities so that they can play an active and dignified part not only in the process of economic growth, but also in all spheres of social life': Conroy H., *On the Relation between Development and the Enjoyment of All Human Rights. Recognizing the Importance of Creating the Conditions Whereby Everyone may Enjoy these Rights*, UN Doc. A/CONF.157/PC/60/Add.2, at 19, para. 113 (1993).

[87] Statement to the World Conference, in UN Doc. E/1993/22, 82, at 83–4, para. 9.

[88] Konate, E/C.12/1987/SR.10, at 2, para. 2.

[89] *See e.g.* Taya, E/C.12/1988/SR.12, at 13, para. 72.

[90] *See e.g.* Alston, E/C.12/1988/SR.12, at 15, para. 72.

[91] General Comment No. 1. The primary purpose of dissemination at the reporting stage is to facilitate public scrutiny of government policies and engender a constructive dialogue on the national level, *Supra*, n. 8, at 88, para. 5.

educating and encouraging participation is central to 'increasing the will of the people to implement social change'.[92]

Democratic participation also has a subsidiary aim of ensuring that all sectors of the population are taken into account in any human rights strategy. This relates to the second issue, namely, the position of the vulnerable and disadvantaged sectors of society.[93] The Committee has consistently required that governments pay particular attention to the position of such social groups within States. Accordingly, just as much as the use of aggregate national statistics is criticized, so also State policies that are centered solely upon general economic growth have been considered to be inadequate for securing the rights of marginalized sectors of the population.[94] The emphasis placed upon such groups by the Committee suggests that its approach has been marked by considerations of equality and non-discrimination.[95]

The Committee's concern with the position of the vulnerable and disadvantaged has been brought into sharpest relief in the context of the worldwide trend towards *laissez-faire* market economics and the privatization of State properties.[96] In its statement to the World Conference, the Committee commented that:

The increasing emphasis being placed on free market policies brings with it a far greater need to ensure that appropriate measures are taken to safeguard and promote economic, social and cultural rights. Even the most ardent supporters of the free market have generally acknowleged that it is incapable, of its own accord, of protecting many of the most vulnerable and disadvantaged members of society.[97]

The perceived problem is that if public services are privately operated and open to market forces, access to them becomes a correlate of income distribution in which the poorer sectors of the population have to fend for themselves in an increasingly unequal society.[98] In such circumstances the Committee has emphasized the need for adequate social safety nets, which should cover the whole range of the rights and 'be formulated in terms of rights rather than charity or generosity'.[99] Even then, it has been recognized

---

[92] Ruiz Cañañas (Mexico), E/1986/WG.1/SR.8, at 8, para. 43.

[93] *See e.g.* Alston, E/C.12/1987/SR.3, at 3, para. 10; *ibid.*, 1990/SR.31, at 3, para. 10; Simma, E/C.12/1990/SR.15, at 3, para. 7. Van Boven comments: 'If a human rights programme has any relevance to people, it should first and foremost be concerned with the vulnerable, the weak, the oppressed, the exploited': Van Boven T., *People Matter: Views on International Human Rights Policy* (1982), 74.

[94] *See* Sparsis, E/C.12/1989/SR.16, at 17, para. 92; Rattray, *ibid.*, SR.17, at 17, para. 90.

[95] *See below*, Ch. 4.

[96] *See generally* Ghai D., *The IMF and the South: The Social Impact of Crisis and Adjustment* (1991), at 5.

[97] E/1993/22, 82, at 84, para. 10. *See also* Türk, *supra*, n. 83, at 26–8, paras. 97–105.

[98] *See e.g.* Concluding observations on report of Italy, E/1993/22, at 50, para. 190.

[99] Statement to the World Conference, *supra*, n. 87, at 84, para. 10, For criticism of the reach of 'targeted subsidies' *see* Türk (final) Report, *supra*, n. 83, at 28, para. 104.

that the private provision of public services may result in long delays being experienced between the time when a problem was identified and the possible intervention of the State.[100]

On a theoretical level, by replacing a public service with the market principle the State appears to delegate its responsibility for that service to the private sector. This, as one commentator has argued, 'undermines the very notion of government obligations in the area'.[101] Although the Committee has tended to look critically upon associated elements of privatization, such as reductions in the proportion of government spending set aside for health and welfare services, it has not gone so far as to declare the process as being incompatible with the obligations under the Covenant. This is conditioned primarily by its approach to the question of State organization.

It is commonly assumed, partly as a result of the politicization of human rights, that economic, social, and cultural rights require a 'socialist' or 'centrally planned' form of government. Although a proposal to make the realization of the rights dependant upon the 'organization' of the State was narrowly rejected in the drafting of the Covenant,[102] it was made clear that the Covenant itself did not prefer any particular system of organization despite arguments to that effect.[103] The Committee, for its own part, has made clear that:

the undertaking 'to take steps . . . by all appropriate means including particularly the adoption of legislative measures' neither requires nor precludes any particular form of government or economic system being used as the vehicle for the steps in question, provided only that it is democratic and that all human rights are thereby respected. Thus, in terms of political and economic systems the Covenant is neutral and its principles cannot accurately be described as being predicated exclusively upon the need for, or the desirability of, a socialist or a capitalist system, or a mixed, centrally planned, or *laissez-faire* economy, or upon any other particular approach. In this regard, the Committee reaffirms that the rights recognized in the Covenant are susceptible of realization within the context of a wide variety of economic and political systems, provided only that the interdependence and indivisibility of the two sets of human rights, as affirmed *inter alia* in the preamble to the Covenant, is recognized and reflected in the system in question.[104]

The Committee has followed this policy in admitting no preference for any particular form of State structure. It appears to concur with the assertion that 'successes and failures have been registered in both market and non-

---

[100] Alston, E/C.12/1989/SR.15, at 7, para. 40.
[101] Tomasevski, *supra*, n. 18, at 170.   [102] E/CN.4/SR.233, at 22 (1951).
[103] *See* Alston and Quinn, *supra*, n. 5, at 181–3. Indeed it was stated: 'The Commission . . . was not concerned with the organization or the Constitution of a State but merely with the guarantee of human rights by the State. The Covenant would lay down the obligation: how that obligation would be fulfilled may vary from State to State': Chile, E/CN.4/SR.271, at 7 (1952).
[104] General Comment No. 3, *supra*, n. 4, at 85, para. 8.

market economies, in both centralized and de-centralized political structures'.[105] Accordingly it could be concluded that there is 'no single road' to the full realization of the rights.[106]

However, whereas the Covenant does not prescribe the precise form of organization required, it does nevertheless require that the State possess certain general attributes. Thus, article 8 would seem to require that the State structure allow for the existence of more than one trade union,[107] and the non-discrimination provisions arguably require the separation of the Church and State.[108] Members of the Committee have, in this respect, been critical of certain forms of organization that do not seem capable of fulfilling the rights in the Covenant.[109] One member concluded that the Committee 'understood that questions of a general nature on wider aspects of the political or economic system of a country were not their concern except in so far as they affected the enjoyment of the rights embodied in the Covenant'.[110]

Some recognition of this fact was evident in the debate preceding the adoption of the General Comment. There, certain members suggested that reference be made to the need for 'democratic' government.[111] Although the final text does not contain any reference to democratic government, there appears to have been agreement as to that interpretation.[112] Indeed, the Committee's emphasis on participation lends weight to the argument that some form of democracy is a prerequisite to the implementation of the rights within the Covenant.[113] However, even if the Committee does view democracy as being a prerequisite for the fulfilment of the rights within the Covenant, it has not defined what it understands by that term, nor has it ever challenged a State upon that basis.

---

[105] Limburg Principle 6. *Supra*, n. 46, at 124, para. 6. Falk comments generally that 'the human rights records of both socialism and capitalism are so poor in the Third World at this point that it is quite unconvincing to insist that one approach is generically preferable to the other'. Falk R., 'Comparative Protection of Human Rights in Capitalist and Socialist Third World Countries'(1979) 1 *Uni. HR* 3, at 5.

[106] *See e.g.* Badawi El Sheikh, E/C.12/1987/SR.12, at 2, para. 1.

[107] An example is the criticism of Rwanda whose allowance for only a single general trade union seemed to violate art. 8 of the Covenant. Texier, E/C.12/1989/SR.12, at 4, para. 18.

[108] *See e.g.* discussion on application of 'Mudawwana' (code on status of women) in Morocco, E/C.12/1994/SR.8, at 4–6 and 8–10, paras. 15–25 and 40–5.

[109] Particular criticism was aimed at the equation of 'citizen' with 'activist in the People's Movement' in Zaïre. *See e.g.* Alvarez Vita. E/C.12/1987/SR. 19, at 3, para. 9. For an analysis of the compatibility of certain 'idealized States' with the notion of human rights *see* Lukes S., 'Five Fables about Human Rights' in Shute S. and Hurley S. (eds.), *On Human Rights* (1993), 19.

[110] Badawi El Sheikh, E/C.12/1987/SR.19, at 4, para. 15.

[111] *See e.g.* Marchan Romero, E/C.12/1990/SR.46, at 7, para. 35.

[112] *See* Alston, E/C.12/1990/SR.48, at 8, para. 41.

[113] *Cf.* art. 4, which refers to 'democratic society'. This does not necessarily exclude single party states however. At the Butare Colloquium on Human Rights it was generally agreed that 'the one party state was not necessarily less democratic or more likely to give rise to violations

V. 'INCLUDING PARTICULARLY THE ADOPTION OF LEGISLATIVE MEASURES'

Although it has commonly been asserted that the enactment of legislation is essential to the implementation of economic, social, and cultural rights on the domestic plane,[114] the *travaux préparatoires* make clear this was not intended to be the case. The original wording of article 2(1) which required that States take steps 'by legislative as well as other means' was specifically amended on the understanding that legislation would not be obligatory.[115] It was noted that:

The ratification of a treaty entailed, for the States Parties to it, no more than the fulfilment of the obligations expressed in the treaty, whether by legislation, administrative action, common law, custom or otherwise.[116]

As the International Law Commission has since recognized, the reference to legislative action in article 2(1), although indicating a preferred method of implementation, did not alter the fundamental principle of State discretion in the choice of means to undertake its obligations under the Covenant.[117]

In general, the main focus of the Committee has been on the practical experience of implementation rather than with the presence or absence of legislation.[118] It has been noted, however, that although the Covenant did not automatically imply that legislation was an indispensable component of government policy, 'if that were the interpretation adopted by Governments, the burden of proof would lie with those Governments, which would therefore be expected to show that the non-legislative measures that they had taken effectively ensured . . . [the rights concerned] and that it was not essential to take legislative measures'.[119] In fact the Committee has shown particular concern as to the recognition and status of economic, social, and cultural rights in domestic law.[120]

---

of human rights than a multiparty system'. Hannum H., 'The Butare Colloquium on Human Rights and Economic Development in Francophone Africa: A Summary and Analysis' (1979) 1 *Uni. HR* 63, at 75. Indeed it has been considered that minorities can be better protected in such systems: ICJ, *Human Rights in a One-Party State* (1978), at 110.

[114] *See* Sviridov, E/C.12/1987/SR.6, at 4, para. 14. Equally, during the drafting process, Nikolaeva (USSR) argued that 'legislative measures were absolutely essential to ensure respect for rights stated in the Covenant': A/C.3/SR.1184, at 251, para. 31 (1962).

[115] *See* UK objections to the original phrase, UN Doc. A/2910/Add.1, at 4, 10 UN GAOR, Annexes (Ag. Item 28), Pt. 1 (1955). *Also* comment of Sharp (New Zealand), A/C.3/SR.1181, at 238, para. 33 (1962).

[116] UN Doc. E/CN.4/SR.427, at 10 (1954).   [117] *See above*, text accompanying nn. 1–3.

[118] *See e.g.* Simma, E/C.12/1989/SR.15, at 2, para. 3; cf. Concluding observations on report of Iran, E/C.12/1993/7, at 1, para. 2.   [119] Alston, E/C.12/1987/SR.6, at 3, para. 8.

[120] *See e.g.* Concluding observations on report of Kenya, E/C.12/1993/6, at 3, para. 10; and Canada, E/C.12/1993/5, at 4, para. 25. *See also* discussion on implementation of Covenant in Iceland, E/C.12/1993/SR.30, at 4–5, paras. 10–18.

There are a number of situations in which legislation could be said to be essential. The existence of a law contravening the provisions of the Covenant would oblige the State concerned to take the necessary action to annul its effectiveness.[121] Likewise, legislation might also be appropriate if alternative measures such as education or persuasion were manifestly ineffective,[122] or where there was a need to protect individuals from third party violations.[123] As the Committee has noted in its General Comment:

in many instances legislation is highly desirable and in some cases may even be indispensable. For example, it may be difficult to combat discrimination effectively in the absence of a sound legislative foundation for the necessary measures. In fields such as health, the protection of children and mothers, and education, as well as in respect of the matters dealt with in articles 6 to 9, legislation may also be an indispensable element for many purposes.

Even so, it is apparent that the need for further legislation will turn upon a number of factors such as the adequacy of existing legislation or other legal guarantees and the appropriateness of adopting a 'legal' approach to implementation where social or economic measures might be more effective.

The Committee has been quick to point out, however, that although legislation certainly forms an important part of the implementation process, it was 'by no means exhaustive of the obligations of States parties'.[124] This conclusion is forced by the fact that in a number of cases the existence of certain social structures or resources will be a precondition to the effective realization of the rights by means of legislation. For example, it would be simply meaningless for the State to guarantee every individual a house, yet do nothing to ensure that there was sufficient housing available. In such a situation the adoption of legislative measures is only one element of a series of economic and social activities needed to give effect to the rights in the Covenant. Moreover, even in the case of those rights that are not dependent for their implementation upon State resources (such as the right to form and join a trade union in article 8), legislation alone will not be sufficient if not accompanied by effective and accessible enforcement procedures.[125]

---

[121] Concluding observations on report of Senegal, E/C.12/1993/18, at 3, para. 12, *Cf.* Limburg Principle 18, *supra*, n. 46, at 125.

[122] This was noted during the drafting of the Covenant. Pico (Argentina), A/C.3/SR.1184, at 250, para. 16 (1962).

[123] *e.g.* the necessity of legislation in the field of industrial safety and health measures. Sparsis, E/C.12/1988/SR.6, at 5, para. 33.

[124] General Comment No. 3, *supra*, n. 4, at 84, para. 4. For the same point in the *travaux préparatoires, see* Representative of the USSR, E/CN.4/SR. 272, at 10 (1952). The representative of the USA dropped the use of the word 'ensure' in its amendments to art. 2(1) for fear that it might imply that legislation alone is enough to secure the rights: E/CN.4/SR.271, at 12 (1952).

[125] A similar position exists with regard to the ICCPR. In its General Comment No. 3(13) the Human Rights Committee recognized that 'implementation does not depend solely on

Two questions thus present themselves to the Committee in analysing the adequacy of legislative measures in a particular situation: first, whether the economic and social conditions are compatible with the legislative enforcement of the right; secondly, whether the existing enforcement procedures are adequate to secure the right in practice. Thus the Committee has often pointed out that a description of legislative provisions in a given State is meaningless[126] if not accompanied by information on the progress made in the practical implementation of the rights.[127]

To a large extent, the Committee expects that where legislation has been enacted to implement the rights, there is a need for recourse procedures.[128] These have their parallel in the administrative or other recourse mechanisms that run outside the ambit of the legal system. As the Committee stressed in its General Comment:

Among the measures which might be considered appropriate, in addition to legislation, is the provision of judicial remedies with respect to rights which may, in accordance with the national legal system, be considered justiciable. The Committee notes, for example, that the enjoyment of the rights recognized, without discrimination, will often be appropriately promoted, in part, through the provision of judicial or other effective remedies. Indeed those States parties which are also parties to the International Covenant on Civil and Political Rights are already obligated (by virtue of arts. 2 (paras. 1 and 3) 3 and 26 of that Covenant) to ensure that any person whose rights or freedoms (including the right to equality and non-discrimination) recognized in that Covenant are violated, 'shall have an effective remedy' (art. 2(3)(a)).[129]

The Committee goes on to state that it considers a number of provisions within the Covenant that 'would seem to be capable of immediate application by judicial and other organs in many national legal systems'.[130] These include articles 3, 7(a)(i), 8, 10(3), 13(2)(a), 13(3), 13(4), and 15(3).[131]

constitutional or legislative enactments, which in themselves are often not *per se* sufficient': 5th Annual Report of to the General Assembly. UN Doc. A/36/40, Annex VII, 36 UN GAOR, Supp. (No. 40) (1981).

[126] *See e.g.* criticism of the Canadian report E/C.12/1989/SR.8. In particular Simma commented that: 'When reports focused too narrowly on legal aspects, the suspicion naturally arose that there might be some gap between law and practice': E/C.12/1989/SR.8, at 8, para. 42.

[127] *e.g.* Concluding observations on report of Canada, E/C.12/1993/5, at 2, para. 6. Too much emphasis on theoretical implementation as opposed to practice has also been criticized, Neneman, E/C.12/1988/SR.2, at 4, para. 17.

[128] Alston comments that in order to determine whether rights were realized the Committee 'looked for a degree of entrenchment in a legal instrument such as a constitution and for "justiciability"': E/C.12/1990/SR.7, at 2, para. 6.

It has been noted that although economic, social, and cultural rights are to be found in the constitutions of many countries, there was little inclination on the part of national courts to enforce them. *See* Simma, E/C.12/1990/SR.3, at 11, para. 68. With respect to Canada, *see* Vandycke R., 'La Charte constitutionelle et les droits économiques, sociaux et culturels' (1989–90) *Can. HRY*, 167.

[129] General Comment No. 3, *supra*, n. 4, at 84, para. 5.   [130] *Ibid.*   [131] *Ibid.*

The specification, by the Committee, of the provisions that may be open to immediate application by judicial organs, is in part a response to the common assertion that economic, social, and cultural rights are not justiciable. According to that view, economic, social, and cultural rights are considered too vague for violations of their provisions to be effectively determined.[132] A distinction, however, has to be drawn between international and domestic enforcement of the rights. At the international level, the focus of judicial concern is the degree to which the State has acted in conformity with its obligations; it is here that 'justiciability' is a difficult issue in that it requires a careful assessment of performance taking into account resource availability. At the domestic level, however, judicial remedies focus upon the enforcement of existing legislative or administrative measures taken with regard to the economic and social climate in the State concerned.[133] An insistence on judicial remedies at the domestic level is merely to ensure that the measures taken towards the full realization of the rights are not purely superficial and vacuous.

VI. 'FULL REALIZATION'

Whatever the intricacies of the implementation process, it would appear that the ultimate objective of the Covenant is the 'full realization' of the rights. During the drafting of the Covenant the words 'full realization' were included to replace the term 'implementation' 'in order to strengthen rather than to weaken the objective set before future contracting parties'.[134] Its effect is to emphasize that the State conduct referred to in article 2(1) is to be directed at this particular result. States therefore cannot make do with rights 'on the cheap'.[135]

The Committee itself has noted that the principal obligation of result in article 2(1) is the 'full realization' of the rights.[136] That this objective is conditioned by the phrase 'progressive realization' is merely a recognition of the fact that 'the full realization of all economic, social, and cultural rights will generally not be able to be achieved in a short period of time'.[137] Although reference has occasionally been made to the need to establish

---

[132] Vierdag E., 'The Legal Nature of the Rights Guaranteed by the International Covenant on Economic, Social and Cultural Rights' (1978) 9 *Neth. ILR* 69. Similarly the representative of Colombia asserted before the Committee that economic, social, and cultural rights 'were too vague for their infringement to give rise to legal action': E/C.12/1990/SR.14, at 6, para. 31. *Contra*, Van Hoof, *supra*, n. 13, at 104.

[133] A caveat may be that the rights could be entrenched in a constitution without substantial change in form. The rights have been enforced in practice on occasions, *e.g.* Canada, E/C.12/1989/SR.10, at 12, para. 42; Netherlands, E/C.12/1989/SR.14, at 3, para. 8.

[134] Cassin (France), E/CN.4/SR.223, at 8 (1951).   [135] *Ibid.* E/CN.4/SR.237, at 7 (1952).

[136] General Comment No. 3, *supra*, n. 4, at 85, para. 9.   [137] *Ibid.*

an understanding of the 'ideal situation',[138] the Committee has generally concentrated upon the process rather than the result of implementation. It is assumed, even in the case of developed countries, that the full realization of the rights has not been achieved. Hence the Committee requires that all States, not merely developing ones, show the 'progress made' and the 'difficulties encountered' in the realization of the rights. The Committee has not, on the other hand, established a clear understanding of what it envisages to be the ultimate result to be achieved.

That there may be some difficulty in establishing concrete objectives is apparent from the fact that certain rights were intended to be dynamic standards. During the drafting of the Covenant, it was commented that the introduction of the word 'progressively' 'introduced a dynamic element, indicating that no fixed goal had been set',[139] and that 'the realization of those rights did not stop at a given level'.[140] This is reflected particularly in article 11 which refers to 'the continuous improvement of living conditions'.[141] Here the result to be achieved becomes merged with the desired conduct.

To assert that the objectives of the Covenant are dynamic in nature is not to suggest that they are deprived of value. Although it is necessary for the rights to be given sufficient detail such that it is possible to predict, with reasonable accuracy, whether or not a State has achieved that objective, any definition will have to be given enough flexibility to take into account the differing nature of each State's social and economic systems, and the need for the provision to stand the test of time. For example, it would not be appropriate for a precise figure to be given as a definition of 'fair wages' in article 7(a)(i). Other human rights bodies have similarly asserted the dynamic nature of human rights obligations.[142] Having said that, at present many of the provisions within the Covenant remain vague and ill-defined. The main problem that faces the Committee is to define those standards in a way that ensures a balance between predictability and flexibility.

VII. 'PROGRESSIVE ACHIEVEMENT'

The dominant characteristic of obligations concerning economic, social, and cultural rights must be their 'progressive' nature. Although more re-

---

[138] Taya, E/C.12/1990/SR.4, at 2, para. 2.

[139] Sørensen (Denmark), E/CN.4/SR.236, at 21 (1951).

[140] Mr Whitlam (Australia), E/CN.4/SR.237, at 5 (1951).

[141] One member of the Committee has commented with regard to this art. that 'the individual was entitled not only to "well-being", but to "better-being", and thus the right to play a part in determining living conditions': Konate, E/C.12/1987/SR.11, at 11, para. 54.

[142] With regard to the ECHR *see Tyrer Case*, Eur. Ct. HR, Series A, Vol. 26, judgment of 25 Apr. 1978 (1979–80) 2 EHRR 1.

cently such rights have been included in the African Charter on the same basis as civil and political rights,[143] they are generally considered to be incapable of immediate implementation owing to the considerable expense involved in their realization. All major instruments relating to economic, social, and cultural rights provide, therefore, for implementation in a piecemeal fashion.[144]

The requirement in the ICESCR that the rights be realized progressively can be contrasted with the undertaking in the ICCPR to 'respect and to ensure' the rights recognized in the Covenant.[145] It is important, nevertheless, not to overstate this difference. There has been considerable debate about whether the obligation in the ICCPR is in itself immediate;[146] emphasis has been placed, in particular, upon the economic consequences of implementation of civil and political rights. Alston and Quinn comment in this vein:

the reality is that the full realization of civil and political rights is heavily dependent both on the availability of resources and the development of the necessary societal structures. The suggestion that realization of civil and political rights requires only abstention on the part of the state and can be achieved without significant expenditure is patently at odds with reality.[147]

It would appear, in fact, that the implementation of the ICCPR is to be undertaken 'at the earliest possible moment'.[148] It is arguable that the same comment may be made about the implementation of the ICESCR, notwithstanding the reference to available resources.

Concern was expressed during the drafting of the ICESCR that reference to progressive achievement would allow States to postpone the realization

---

[143] African Charter on Human Rights and Peoples' Rights (1981), 21 ILM 59.

[144] Art. 1 of the Additional Protocol to the Inter-American Convention on Human Rights speaks of progressive achievement. OAS Treaty Series No. 69, 17 Nov. 1988. Art. 20 of the European Social Charter (1961), allows States parties to select which arts. (over and above a minimum) they consider themselves bound to. Some States have accepted obligations relating to all of the rights in the Charter. *See generally* Harris D., *The European Social Charter* (1984). The difference between the ESC and the ICESCR is really one of emphasis, in that the ESC concentrates upon the full realization of a selection of rights, whereas the ICESCR gives legal recognition to steps being taken towards the full realization of all the rights.

[145] *See* Buergenthal, *supra*, n. 16.

[146] With the view that civil and political rights are resource-dependent themselves and therefore capable only of progressive implementation, *see* Jhabvala F., 'Domestic Implementation of the Covenant on Civil and Political Rights' (1985) 32 *Neth. ILR* 461. *Contra* Schwelb E., 'Notes on the Early Legislative History of the Measures of Implementation of the Human Rights Covenants' in *1 René Cassin Amicorum Discipulorumque* (1969), 301; Schachter O., *supra*, n. 72, at 324. A debate on this issue is to be found in correspondence in the *Hum. Rts. Q*: Humphrey J., 'Letter to the Editor' (1984) 6 *Hum. Rts. Q* 539; Jhabvala F., 'Letter to the Editor' (1985) 7 *Hum. Rts. Q* 242 (1985); Iwasawa Y., 'Letter to the Editor' (1985) 7 *Hum. Rts. Q* 565.

[147] Alston and Quinn, *supra*, n. 5, at 172.

[148] UN Doc. A/5655, para. 23, 18 UN GAOR, 5655 mtg. (1963).

of the rights indefinitely[149] or entirely avoid their obligations.[150] The majority, however, did not agree with this view; it was argued that implementation should be continued 'without respite'[151] so that full realization could be achieved 'as quickly as possible'.[152] These concerns have been reflected by the Committee in its General Comment No. 3, where it states:

the fact that realization over time, or in other words progressively, is foreseen under the Covenant should not be misinterpreted as depriving the obligation of all meaningful content. It is on the one hand a necessary flexibility device, reflecting the realities of the real world and the difficulties involved for any country in ensuring full realization of economic, social and cultural rights. On the other hand, the phrase must be read in the light of the overall objective, indeed the *raison d'être*, of the Covenant which is to establish clear obligations for States parties in respect of the full realization of the rights in question. It thus imposes an obligation to move as expeditiously and effectively as possible towards that goal.[153]

Thus, far from viewing the phrase 'progressive realization' as a let-out clause, the Committee has sought to give it a meaning that supplements the meaning of other phrases within article 2(1). According to its analysis, States may not delay in their efforts to realize the rights,[154] and indeed they must take the course which would achieve that objective in the shortest possible time.

The obligation outlined above would appear to require a continuous improvement of conditions over time without backward movement of any kind—in what may be described as a form of 'ratchet effect'. The Committee comments in this regard:

any deliberately retrogressive measures ... would require the most careful consideration and would need to be fully justified by reference to the totality of the rights provided for in the Covenant and in the context of the full use of the maximum of available resources.[155]

Notably the Committee does not present retrogressive measures as *prima facie* violations of the Covenant, even where they are deliberate. It does,

---

[149] UN Doc. A/2929, *supra*, n. 53, at 20, para. 23.

[150] Chile, E/CN.4/SR.273, at 8 (1952). The Eastern European countries were concerned that the references to resources and progressive achievement in art. 2(1) created 'so many restrictions and exceptions that its entire significance would evaporate': Ukraine, E/CN.4/SR.233, at 9 (1951).

[151] Egypt, E/CN.4/SR.233, at 10 (1951). The replacement of the words 'by stages' with 'progressive' during the drafting was thought to have this effect on the meaning of the art.

[152] Volio (Costa Rica), A/C.3/SR.1202, at 338, para. 27 (1962). It should be noted however that the Costa Rican amendment for the establishment of a general time limit for implementation of the rights was rejected. Opponents felt that States should be entitled to proceed according to a time scale determined by their own resources. *See* Diaz Casanueva (Chile), A/C.3/SR.1181, at 237, para. 26 (1962).

[153] General Comment No. 3, *supra*, n. 4, at 85.

[154] *See also* Alston, E/C.12/1990/SR.21, at 7, para. 21.

[155] General Comment No. 3, *supra*, n. 4, at 85, para. 9.

however, suggest that any retrogressive step would need to be 'fully justi-fied'. Two forms of justification appear to be envisaged by the Committee. First, where the State is suffering an economic crisis such that, even by utilizing 'the maximum of available resources', a deterioration of the situation is inevitable. Secondly, where a retrogressive measure is taken for the purpose of improving the situation with regard to the 'totality of the rights in the Covenant'.

The second point, which appears to legitimize 'trade-offs' between rights, is particularly controversial. It might be open for a State, for example, deliberately to increase the number of unemployed if the benefits were better wages and a higher standard of living for the majority of workers. Such an approach conflicts with a number of principles that underpin the Covenant. First, any retrogressive measure would represent a 'limitation' on the enjoyment of the rights and accordingly should be justified in relation to article 4. This requires, *inter alia*, that limitations must be 'determined by law' and must promote the 'general welfare in a democratic society'. Secondly, despite the wording of article 4, the Covenant was principally intended for the protection of the rights of the individual. As such, it cannot be governed solely by strict utilitarian principles. Indeed the Committee itself has often stressed that the Covenant is a vehicle for the protection of the vulnerable and disadvantaged groups in society.

Certainly some adverse effects may flow from well-intentioned measures, but where retrogressive measures were the result of deliberate policy, the Committee would do better to consider it a *prima facie* violation of the Covenant in the absence of further justificatory evidence. It would then be for the State concerned to show that there were sound reasons for adopting the policy at issue. Admittedly the Committee comes close to this position but does so in an excessively tentative and ambiguous manner.

It is apparent from the terms of the Covenant that the principal, but not exclusive, constraint upon the immediate realization of the rights will be the lack of economic resources.[156] As a counterpoint, where circumstances permit, States should achieve the rights immediately. This is evident not only in the case of those rights whose realization is not resource-dependant, but also where the State concerned has sufficient resources at its disposal to take the relevant steps. Such an approach was apparent in the drafting of article 2(1). There, fear that article 2(1) would become an escape clause for developed States[157] was countered by the argument that each State should ensure the rights 'except in circumstances where retarded economic development made that impossible'.[158] Although economic considerations will

---

[156] In addition, States will have to take into account matters such as existing structural impediments and social prejudice.

[157] *e.g.* Lebanon, E/CN.4/SR.271, at 11 (1952).

[158] Yugoslavia, E/CN.4/SR.233, at 5 (1951). Alston and Quinn have noted that supporters of the idea of progressive achievement 'viewed it not as an escape hatch for states whose

always play a part in any calculation relating to the implementation of the rights, the presumption is that developed States are under an obligation to implement the provisions of the Covenant immediately, the progressive nature of the obligation applying only to those States that lack sufficient resources to do so themselves.[159]

The Committee, however, has not taken the view that developed States should be bound to implement the obligations immediately. It has recognized that even developed States have specific problems, such as the high cost of welfare institutions,[160] ageing populations,[161] and rising unemployment,[162] which may undermine their ability to implement the rights.[163] The dynamic approach of the Committee as to the objectives in the Covenant[164] has led it to require information on the 'progress made'[165] and the problems encountered in the realization of the rights even with respect to developed countries.[166] Indeed it has been unwilling to accept statements of government representatives claiming that the rights are fully implemented in their country.[167]

Whereas failure to take any action at all may clearly be identified as a breach of State obligations, in the majority of cases it will be particularly difficult for the Committee to evaluate whether or not a State has taken the appropriate course of action. Beyond the difficulties of measuring progressive achievement,[168] whether or not a situation improves will not be

performance failed to match their abilities . . . [but] simply as a necessary accommodation to the vagaries of economic circumstances': *supra*, n. 5, at 175.

[159] This is the view of Kartashkin V., 'Covenants on Human Rights and Soviet Legislation' (1977) 10 *HRLJ* 97, at 98–9. In this vein the UK representative commented rather ambiguously that the word 'progressively' 'did not in any way mean that States whose social development was adequate would not be bound by the obligations laid on them in the Covenant': E/CN.4/SR.237, at 10 (1951).

[160] The Committee expressed some concern over the expense of social welfare institutions in Sweden. E/C.12/1988/SR.9.

[161] This was the reason given by the Polish representative as the main obstruction to the implementation of Poland's new social policy in 1989. E/C.12/1989/SR.5 at 2, para. 5.

[162] *See* Sparsis, E/C.12/1987/SR.14, at 9, para. 30.

[163] *e.g.* Sparsis, E/C.12/1988/SR.10, at 4, para. 13.

[164] *See below*, text accompanying nn. 139–42.

[165] Art. 16 requires that States submit reports on the measures adopted and the progress made in achieving observance of the rights in the Covenant. The notion of progress is central to the obligations of States under the Covenant. Sparsis, E/C.12/1989/SR.8, at 10, para. 58.

[166] *See* Alston, E/C.12/1988/SR.8, at 6, para. 22; Neneman, E/C.12/1988/SR.20, at 5, para. 21.

[167] See the Committee's reaction to the Austrian representative's statement that its domestic situation was fully in conformity with the Covenant. E/C.12/1988/SR.4, at 2, para. 3.

[168] The Committee has spent much time considering the possibilities of using statistical indicators to measure State performance, *see* UN Docs. E/C.12/1991/SR.20–1. The problems involved in the use of statistics weigh heavily on the work of the Committee. As Tomasevski has noted: 'Quantified results (data, indicators, tables) do not reflect reality but theoretical assumptions of reality, and they cannot be interpreted without an insight into the underlying assumptions': Tomasevski K., 'Human Rights Indicators: The Right to Food as a Test Case' in Alston P. and Tomasevski K. (eds.), *The Right to Food* (1985), 135, at 136. *See also Report of the Seminar on Appropriate Indicators to Measure Achievements in the Progressive Realization of Economic, Social and Cultural Rights*, UN Doc. A/CONF.157/PC/73 (1993); Türk D., *The*

conclusive as regards State responsibility. If the situation deteriorates (for example, with an increase in the number of homeless families), that has to be directly attributable to State action or inaction for its responsibility to be invoked. Even where the State was directly responsible, the Committee suggests that it will not necessarily find a violation of the Covenant. On the other hand, if the situation improves, it is not necessarily the case that the State will have taken the appropriate path. For example, it may have been able to achieve more in the given circumstances. To intervene at this stage, it is clear that the Committee will have to consider the possible alternative courses of action open to the State (including the allocation of resources) and weigh up the competing priorities. Here it is particularly difficult for the Committee to evaluate State action without becoming entirely prescriptive as to the course of action to be taken.

VIII. 'RIGHTS RECOGNIZED'

On a strict reading of the Covenant, the terms of article 2(1) should apply only to those 'rights recognized' in the Covenant. This presents problems in so far as a certain number of substantive provisions do not contain the word 'recognize'. Articles 3 and 8 refer to an undertaking to 'ensure'; articles 13(3) and 15(3) to an undertaking to 'respect'; and article 2(2) requires States to 'guarantee' the exercise of the rights without discrimination. By not mentioning the word 'recognize' these provisions appear to operate independently of the specific terms of article 2(1). Indeed, the terminology employed (to 'respect' and 'ensure'), corresponding as it does to that of article 2(1) of the ICCPR, implies that those articles should be implemented immediately.[169] Having said that, although it was recognized during the drafting of the Covenant that article 8 was to be implemented immediately, it was less clear whether this was also intended to be the case for article 13(3), 15(3), or 2(2).[170]

New International Economic Order and the Promotion of Human Rights: Realisation of Economic, Social and Cultural Rights, UN Doc. E/CN.4/Sub.2/1990/19, at 3–37 (1990); Goldstein R., 'The Limitations of Using Quantitative Data in Studying Human Rights Abuses' (1986) 8 *Hum. Rts. Q* 607; Stohl M., Carleton D., Lopez G., and Samuels S., 'State Violation of Human Rights: Issues and Problems of Measurement' (1986) 8 *Hum. Rts. Q* 592; Claude R. and Jabine P., 'Editors' Introduction' (1986) 8 *Hum. Rts. Q* 551.

[169] At the same time it is universally recognized that the obligation to 'guarantee' suggests an undertaking considerably more stringent than that found in art. 2(1) ICESCR. The term was rejected in the drafting of art. 2(1) ICESCR as being 'too onerous in the circumstances', Nissot (Belgium), E/CN.4/SR.272, at 10 (1952).

[170] Denmark (Mr Sørensen) commented that only trade union rights were of immediate application. E/CN.4/SR.236, at 21 (1951). A Chilean amendment (E/CN.4/L.62/Rev. 2) for the immediate application of art. 7(a)(i) providing for equal remuneration for work of equal value was rejected. E/CN.4/SR.281, at 14 (1952).

The Committee has referred to the immediate realization *inter alia* of articles 3, 8, 13(3), and 15(3).[171] To a large extent, these provisions would appear to be capable of immediate realization. Whether or not article 2(1) is said to apply to these provisions, it is submitted that priority has to be given to the specific terminology within the substantive articles themselves. Accordingly, it would not be open to States to rely upon the terms of article 2(1) to delay the application of those provisions.

A similar concern relates to articles 10 and 14 which make no reference to 'rights'.[172] Article 14, on the one hand, is a contingency provision that specifies a time period within which States should adopt a plan for the progressive implementation of the principle of compulsory primary education. There is no room in this case for the provision to be implemented in a progressive fashion. Article 10, on the other hand, refers to special protection that 'should' exist for the family, mothers, and children. It is arguable that the use of the word 'should' imposes nothing more than a moral obligation upon States. This is unlikely, however, given the intention to create binding legal obligations. It cannot be assumed that the Covenant's provisions do not possess legal force unless there are overriding indications otherwise.[173] Given the legal nature of such an obligation, the immediacy of implementation is particularly clear in relation to article 10(1) and (3). These provisions, relating to the protection of the family and of children, are particularly reminiscent of articles 23 and 24 of the ICCPR and should perhaps be treated in a similar manner. Article 10(2), however, seems to be the exception. It refers to the provision of paid leave or social security benefits for working mothers during childbirth, and thus requires State financial input, placing it within the category of rights that were intended to be implemented progressively.

The mere fact that article 10 makes no specific reference to 'rights' does not prevent those provisions being treated in the same way as the other provisions in the Covenant. The Committee has considered it appropriate to infer the existence of a 'right' from the terms. It refers, in its reporting guidelines, to 'rights' in article 10, [174] and specifically to the right to enter into marriage with full and free consent.[175] It should be assumed that as article 2(1) was intended to outline State obligations with respect to all the

---

[171] General Comment No. 3, *supra*, n. 4, at 84, para. 5.

[172] These arts. reflect the great emphasis placed upon obligations in the terms of the Covenant. The representative of the ILO noted during the drafting that the ICESCR reflected a middle road between the citation of a number of rights on the one hand and the establishment of government obligations on the other. E/C.14/AC.14/SR.1, at 32 (1951).

[173] *See* Bernhardt R., 'Treaties' in *Encyclopedia of Public International Law* (1984), Vol. 7, 459, at 460.

[174] Reporting Guidelines, UN Doc. E/1991/23, Annex IV, 98–9, UN ESCOR, Supp. (No. 3) (1991).

[175] *Ibid.* 97.

substantive articles, it must also apply to article 10 notwithstanding the lack of specific reference to 'rights'. This does not mean, however, that all its terms should be implemented in a progressive manner; where the realization of rights is not impeded by lack of resources, they should be put into effect immediately.

IX. 'TO THE MAXIMUM OF ITS AVAILABLE RESOURCES'

Perhaps the most overstated characteristic of economic, social, and cultural rights is their reliance upon economic resources. It has been the major reason for differentiating between economic, social, and cultural rights and civil and political rights, and was the primary justification both for allowing States to implement the rights in a progressive manner and for having a reporting system as the means of supervision. As noted above, the fact that the implementation of the rights was considered to be contingent upon economic resources did not, in the drafters' eyes, constitute an excuse for States to delay in the realization of the rights.[176] It was merely a recognition of the fact that many States did not have sufficient resources to undertake the large-scale action required by the Covenant immediately.

On a general level the Committee has shown that the economic situation of a country will be taken into consideration in its evaluation of State reports.[177] In particular it has found itself bound to use different yardsticks to judge the efforts of States with varying economic circumstances.[178] It has thus resorted to the use of national bench-marks as an initial indicator of State compliance with the obligations in the Convention.[179] As such, States

---

[176] *See above*, text accompanying n. 149.

[177] This has been referred to as a 'contextual approach', Badawi El Sheikh, E/C.12/1989/SR.7, at 4, para. 13; Texier, E/C.12/1989/SR.12, at 4, para. 18.

[178] *See* Texier, E/C.12/1988/SR.8, at 3, para. 5; Konate, E/C.12/1988/SR.17, at 6, para. 36. Rather ambiguously Texier has also commented that 'the Committee did in fact use the same criteria to evaluate the efforts made by countries, but it took account of their levels of development': E/C.12/1988/SR.23, at 11, para. 103.

A differentiation could be made between qualitative and quantitative criteria. Whereas it is possible to evaluate State performance on the same qualitative criteria of homelessness, e.g., the quantitative aspect will vary considerably according to the social and economic position of the country concerned. However it is particularly difficult to separate the two forms of data, particularly as quantitative criteria are dependent upon qualitative assumptions. Moreover it is difficult to imagine that a particular set of considerations can be used universally, for example to describe the notion of poverty. In reality the Committee has not stipulated the use of particular qualitative criteria, but it is assumed that a certain amount of comparison will be made between countries on whatever measure of assessment that a State chooses. For human rights studies using such data *see e.g.* Park H., 'Human Rights and Modernization: A Dialectical Relationship' (1980) 2 *Uni. HR* 85; Dasgupta P., 'Well-Being and the Extent of its Realization in Poor Countries' (1990) 100 *The Economic Rev.*, No. 400, Conference Supplement, 1.

[179] *See e.g.* Rattray, E/C.12/1989/SR.19, at 7, para. 41.

are given a margin of discretion in the assessment of what resources are available.[180] This does not mean, however, that the Committee will defer entirely to State assessments of the situation, or that it has no right to express opinions on the adequacy of governmental budgetary appropriations.[181]

It was apparent even in the drafting of the Covenant that a State's resources were not limited merely to those which it provided for the purpose.[182] The evaluation of what resources are considered to be available was thus an objective one. The non-absolute nature of a State's discretion in this regard has been underscored by the Committee's willingness to consider issues of government expenditure.[183] Indeed, certain members of the Committee have sought to evaluate State performance by reference to the proportion of GNP or GDP spent on public services.[184] That this requires a careful evaluation of the various demands for public expenditure has meant that the Committee as a whole has been reluctant to adopt this approach.[185] It has, however, been critical of cases in which the proportion of a particular State's GDP spent on social and economic services has declined.[186] It has questioned the increase in spending in other sectors such as defence[187] and has implied that where there is no apparent justification for a reduction in expenditure the State may be considered to have violated its obligations under the Covenant.[188] Although this may be an appropriate

---

[180] *See above*, n. 51.

[181] Such a view has been criticized by Alston and Quinn, *supra*, n. 5, at 178–9.

[182] A US proposal (E/CN.4/L.54/Rev. 1) was to include the words 'for their purpose' after 'maximum of available resources', to stress that a State is only expected to use 'the maximum which could be expended for a particular purpose without sacrificing essential services': Roosevelt (USA), E/CN.4/SR.271, at 3 (1952). The amendment was rejected primarily because of its narrow scope in that it might give governments room to argue that minimal allocations are sufficient. *See e.g.* Santa Cruz (Chile), E/CN.4/SR.271, at 4 (1952).

[183] That the Committee has not made any really clear statement on this point is perhaps due to the extremely sensitive nature of the issue. As the Danish representative said in the drafting of the Covenant, 'It would be unrealistic to attempt to dictate to States how they should allocate their resources in that respect'. E/CN.4/SR.236, at 20 (1951).

[184] *e.g.* one member of the Committee intimated that he felt that an expenditure of only 5% of a State's GNP on social security was inadequate. Neneman, E/C.12/1988/SR.12, at 11, para. 52. Comparative analysis is often used to assess the adequacy of expenditure. *See e.g.* Neneman, E/C.12/1989/SR.8, at 9, para. 51; *ibid.*, E/C.12/1990/SR.44, at 11, para. 51.

[185] *But see* Concluding observations on report of Canada, E/C.12/1993/5, at 4, para. 20. Elsewhere it was suggested by an expert from UNDP that if a State allocated 20% of its budget to military expenditure and only 5% to education, there were grounds for thinking that there was a violation of the Covenant, Schulenburg (United Nations Development Programme), E/C.12/1991/SR.21, at 11, para. 56. Indeed the UNDP stresses in its 1990 report that 'many countries spend a high proportion of their budgets and GDPs on defence, offering great potential for switching resources towards the social sectors': UNDP, *Human Development Report 1990* (1990), at 76. Committee members have suggested that this is an area in which the Committee might progress in future: Alston, E/C.12/1991/SR.21, at 11, para. 56.

[186] *See e.g.* Concluding observations on report of Kenya, E/C.12/1993/6, at 4, para. 17.

[187] *See e.g.* Alston, E/C.12/1988/SR.13, at 2, para. 25.

[188] *Ibid*. That the Committee is unlikely to accept the argument that a government wishes to

approach, it must be stressed that evaluating State performance solely by input would be misconceived as it fails to take account of the extent to which it was received by the needy.

When assessing the amount of money available it is clear that the Committee is prepared to take into account not only domestic resources but also any international resources that may be used by the State concerned.[189] Indeed, in times of crisis, the State is under an obligation to seek international assistance.[190] The issue remains nonetheless as to the circumstances in which a State may refuse international aid.

The Committee however has been careful not to allow States to overplay the problems of development.[191] It has adopted the philosophy that economic hardship should bring considerations of economic, social, and cultural rights into particular focus. This approach has been forcefully argued by one member of the Committee:

> The Covenant had sometimes been described as a 'good weather instrument' which was a product of the exaggerted optimism of the 1960s about the possibility of sustained economic growth. It was stated to be losing importance because of current world-wide economic conditions. That attitude was based on false reasoning: just as conditions of political unrest constituted the decisive test for the relevance of the International Covenant on Civil and Political Rights, so, in time of economic crisis, the International Covenant on Economic, Social and Cultural Rights should assume its most important function—that of a last ditch defence for the most vulnerable.[192]

As such the Committee has stressed that debt-servicing problems,[103] austerity programmes,[194] economic recession,[195] or simple poverty,[196] although to be considered, cannot exempt a State from its obligations under the Covenant. Such an approach has been characterized by two main principles. First, as was stated by the Committee in its General Comment:

> even where the available resources are demonstrably inadequate, the obligation remains for a State party to strive to ensure the widest possible enjoyment of the relevant rights under the prevailing circumstances.[197]

decrease public expenditure to improve the economy might well lead it into collision course with governments that espouse such a philosophy.

[189] *See e.g.* Alston, E/C.12/1990/SR.7, at 3, para. 7; Simma, *ibid.*, SR. 11, at 3, para. 11. This conforms to para. 26 of the Limburg Principles which states: '"Its available resources" refers to both the resources within a State and those available from the international community through international cooperation and assistance': *supra*, n. 46, at 26.

[190] *See e.g.* Badawi El Sheikh, E/C.12/1988/SR.17, at 9, para. 55. Alston argues that this is particularly the case where widespread starvation would otherwise occur. Alston P., 'International Law and the Human Right to Food', in Alston P. and Tomasevski K. (eds.), *The Right To Food* (1984), 9, at 43.

[191] *See e.g.* Marchan Romero, E/C.12/1990/SR.46, at 8, para. 36.

[192] Simma, E/C.12/1990/SR.15, at 3, para. 7.

[193] *See e.g.* Texier, E/C.12/1990/SR.21, at 9, para. 33.

[194] *See e.g.* Alston, E/C.12/1990/SR.17, at 7, para. 31.

[195] *See e.g.* Sparsis, E/C.12/1990/SR.15, at 3, para. 10.

[196] E/1990/3, at 52, para. 211, UN ESCOR, Supp. (No. 3), (1990).

[197] General Comment No. 3, *supra*, n. 4, at 86, para. 11.

The assumption that underlies such a position is that, in cases such as these, there still remains scope to improve the position of the disadvantaged by more effective and equitable use of existing resources.[198] Thus members of the Committee have advocated methods such as taxation[199] and agrarian reform[200] to combat poverty in countries experiencing economic hardship.[201] Indeed one member of the Committee argued that a State could only absolve itself from its responsibility for improving the well-being of the disadvantaged by claiming special circumstances and invoking article 4.[202] Short of achieving substantive progress, the Committee still expects States, as a minimum, to undertake the basic procedural obligations of monitoring the situation, and devising strategies and programmes for the realization of the rights as provided for in General Comment No. 1.[203] Undertaking such basic obligations has been considered necessary to demonstrate good faith on the part of the State concerned.[204]

This principle reflects a particular approach to the question of economic development. It seems to be the position of the majority of the Committee that the process of economic growth should be combined with the realization of human rights.[205] The idea that certain 'trade-offs' can be made is implicitly rejected.[206] For example, in the process of development it is held

---

[198] The Committee has expressed significant interest in the question of equality as one of the objectives of the Covenant. *See e.g.* Sparsis, E/C.12/1988/SR.12, at 12, para. 63; E/C.12/1990/SR.18, at 13, para. 75.   [199] *See* Butragueno, E/C.12/1990/SR.13, at 9, para. 43.

[200] *See* Texier, E/C.12/1990/SR.13, at 9, para. 33.

[201] The question of redistribution on a large scale is quite controversial. As a method for realization of economic, social, and cultural rights on its own it is criticized in that it 'might produce disincentives to production and attendant dislocations to the point where the position of the least advantaged might in fact be lowered instead of raised towards the full-scale implementation of socio-economic rights.' Andreassen B.-A., Skalnes T., Smith A., and Stokke H., 'Assessing Human Rights Performance in Developing Countries: The Case for a Minimum Threshold Approach to the Economic and Social Rights' in Andreassen B.-A. and Eide A. (eds.), *Human Rights in Developing Countries 1987/88* (1988), 333 at 342. Other commentators, recognizing the political sensitivity of full scale redistribution, have argued for a hybrid strategy of redistribution during growth to be implemented in an incremental fashion. *See* Donnelly J., 'Human Rights and Development: Complementary or Competing Concerns?' in Shepherd G. and Nanda V. (eds.), *Human Rights and Third World Development* (1985), 27, at 42–4.

[202] He continued to remark that the implementation of an austerity programme could not 'exempt the government from its responsibility to promote the well-being of the poorest'. Alston, E/C.12/1990/SR.17, at 7, para. 31.

[203] General Comment No. 3, *supra*, n. 4, at 86, para. 11.

[204] *See* Alston, E/C.12/1989/SR.3, at 3, para. 7. Under-development is not the only cause for special treatment, other cases can be natural disasters and wars. Fofana, E/C.12/1989/SR.4, at 5, para. 22.

[205] A certain number of the Committee have however questioned whether the protection of economic, social, and cultural rights is indeed compatible with economic development. One member, e.g., commented that: 'The solutions designed to ensure that States fulfilled their obligations under the Covenant were not always suited to the needs of individual countries: in some cases, for instance, the over-protection of economic rights might make the debt problem even worse': Muterahejuru, E/C.12/1989/SR.2, at 5, para. 20, *Cf. also* Rattray, E/C.12/1989/SR.17, at 17, para. 90.

[206] Donnelly identifies 'needs', 'equality', and 'liberty' trade-offs. Simply speaking, the

that economic, social, and cultural rights cannot be sacrificed in favour of economic growth.[207] That the Committee has adopted much of this thinking is evident in its statement to the World Conference on Human Rights where it remarked that:

full realization of human rights can never be achieved as a mere by-product, or fortuitous consequence, of some other developments, no matter how positive. For that reason, suggestions that the full realization of economic, social and cultural rights will be a direct consequence of, or will flow automatically from, the enjoyment of civil and political rights are misplaced. Such optimism is neither compatible with the basic principles of human rights nor is it supported by empirical evidence. The reality is that every society must work in a deliberate and carefully structured way to ensure the enjoyment by all of its members of their economic, social and cultural rights.[208]

Thus, States should make particular efforts to ensure that the protection of economic, social, and cultural rights is 'built in' to all relevant development programmes and policies, particularly in the case of structural adjustment.[209] According to this approach, it is indefensible that the poorer segments of society should suffer most during economic crises.[210] It does operate on the assumption, however, that economic growth can be achieved without such sacrifices.[211]

'needs trade-off' is one which justifies high levels of absolute poverty in the short run to minimize the economic and human cost in the long run. The 'equality trade-off' recognizes the economic benefits of maintaining income inequality during periods of growth. Finally the 'liberty trade-off' sees the suspension of various civil and political rights as being helpful to the establishment of an effective development policy. He argues that such 'categorical trade-offs of the conventional wisdom are not merely unnecessary but often harmful to both development and human rights'. Donnelly J., *supra*, n. 201, at 27–9. *See also* Goodin R., 'The Development-Rights Trade-Off: Some Unwarranted Economic and Political Assumptions' (1979) 1 *Uni. HR* 31.

[207] The idea that benefits from greater growth might 'trickle down' to the disadvantaged sectors of the population has been generally dismissed. *See e.g.* McChesney A., 'Promoting the General Welfare in a Democratic Society: Balancing Human Rights and Development' (1980) 27 *Neth. ILR* 283; Tomasevski, *supra*, n. 18, at 153; Türk, *supra*, n. 83, at 24–6, paras. 91–6; Conroy, *supra*, n. 86, at 17–23, paras. 101–45.
    The Committee noted in its General Comment No. 2 (1990) that 'no specific development co-operation activity can automatically be presumed to constitute a contribution to the promotion of respect for economic, social and cultural rights. Many activities undertaken in the name of 'development' have subsequently been recognized as ill-conceived and even counter productive in human rights terms' in E/1990/23, Annex III, 86, at 87 (1990).
    [208] Statement to the World Conference, *supra*, n. 87, at 82, para. 3.
    [209] General Comment No. 2, *supra*, n. 207. *See also* Concluding observations on report of Nicaragua, E/C.12/1993/14, at 3, para. 14.
    [210] *See e.g.* Sparsis, E/C.12/SR.15, at 3, para. 10.
    [211] *See* Cornea G., Jolly R., and Stewart F. (eds.), *Adjustment with a Human Face, Protecting the Vulnerable and Promoting Growth* (1987). Others suggest that although participatory development may incur short-term economic costs, in the long term, growth will be greater and more sustainable, *e.g.* Conroy, *supra*, n. 86, at 19, paras. 110–5.
    The Committee also implicitly denies the need for a 'liberty trade-off'. Its recognition of the interdependence of the two categories of rights would lead one to assume that it is no more

The second basic principle underlined by the Committee, which relates closely to the first, is that States are required to provide, as a minimum, for the basic needs of the population.[212] In its General Comment No. 3, the Committee stated:

the Committee is of the view that a minimum core obligation to ensure the satisfaction of, at the very least, minimum essential levels of each of the rights is incumbent upon every State party. Thus, for example, a State party in which any significant number of individuals is deprived of essential foodstuffs, of essential primary health care, of basic shelter and housing, or of the most basic forms of education is, *prima facie*, failing to discharge its obligations under the Covenant.[213]

It is apparent that this 'minimum threshold approach'[214] does not entail the division of the rights according to their priority,[215] but rather that each right should be realized to the extent that provides for the basic needs of every member of society.[216] These minimum standards should be achieved by all States, irrespective of their economic situation, at the earliest possible moment.[217] All available means should be utilized including, if necessary, international assistance.[218]

What is less clear is whether these standards are international or State-specific.[219] The universal nature of the rights in the Covenant suggests that

justifiable to sacrifice civil and political rights for the purpose of development. Thus in its General Comment No. 2 it stressed that UN agencies involved in development issues should 'do their utmost to ensure that their activities are fully consistent with the enjoyment of civil and political rights'. For an analysis of the role of civil and political rights in development *see* Howard R., 'The Full-Belly Thesis: Should Economic, Social and Cultural Rights Take Priority Over Civil and Political Rights? Evidence From Sub-Saharan Africa' (1983) 4 *Hum. Rts. Q* 467.

[212] Sparsis has commented that 'no State could use its low level of economic and social development as a pretext for failing to respond to the basic necessities of its population'. E/C.12/1987/SR.4, at 2, para. 3. For the relationship between human rights and basic needs, *see* Alston P., 'Human Rights and Basic Needs: A Critical Assessment' (1979) 12 *HRLJ* 19; Muchlinski P., '"Basic Needs" Theory and "Development Law"' in Snyder F. and Slynn P. (eds.), *International Law of Development: Comparative Perspectives* (1987), 237.

[213] General Comment No. 3, *supra*, n. 4, at 86, para. 10.

[214] *See generally* Andreassen B.–A. *et al.*, *supra*, n. 201, at 340. Eide A., 'Realization of Social and Economic Rights and the Minimum Threshold Approach' (1989) 10 *HRLJ* 35, at 43–7. For the similar notion of a 'minimum core content' *see* Alston P., 'Out of the Abyss: The Challenges Confronting the New United Nations Committee on Economic, Social and Cultural Rights' (1987) 9 *HRQ* 352.

[215] There has been some opposition within the Committee to establishing a category of rights that relate to basic needs on the ground that it undermines the interdependence of civil and political and economic, social, and cultural rights. *See e.g.* Konate, E/C.12/1990/SR.4, at 5, para. 19.

[216] *See* Mratchkov, E/C.12/1990/SR.46, at 8, para. 37.

[217] Alston has endorsed para. 25 of the Limburg Principles which reads: 'States parties are obligated, regardless of the level of economic development, to ensure respect for minimum subsistence rights for all': E/C.12/1987/SR.19, at 8, para. 40.

[218] *See* Taya, E/C.12/1990/SR.46, at 9, para. 42.

[219] Neneman, e.g., remarked that 'it was rather out of place to speak of water, heating, and electricity in relation to Masai huts in Africa' and as such it was not possible to have universal

a common core should be established for application internationally.[220] The current practice of the Committee, in requiring States to establish benchmarks of poverty, for example, and to identify the disadvantaged sectors of the population, suggests that in the short term at least, State-specific minima are the only viable options.[221] There is some evidence, however, that the Committee intends to establish international standards in future.[222]

In its General Comment No. 3, the Committee implies that failure to provide for the basic subsistence needs of the population may be considered a *prima facie* violation of the Covenant. This points to an interesting and as yet unexplored aspect of article 2(1).[223] The availability of resources has been seen alternatively as a limit on the obligation of the State to implement the rights in full,[224] or as a conditional factor in determining what the State is obliged to achieve.[225] This is of considerable importance with regard to the question where the 'burden of proof' lies in determining whether or not a State has violated its international obligations.[226] The former view conceives of the non-realization of the rights as a *prima facie* violation for which a defence of lack of resources could be pleaded. The latter sees the obligation itself as being contingent upon State resources such that a violation can only be said to have occurred if the State has not taken measures consistent with its resources.

The general approach of the Committee, with its utilization of national benchmarks and its reluctance to establish actual violations,[227] has been to view the fulfilment of the obligations as contingent upon the presence of resources. It would appear that this approach has been radically revised by

---

indicators when speaking of economic, social, and cultural rights. E/C.12/1990/SR.21, at 10, para. 42. Andreassen *et al.* speak of country-specific thresholds 'measured by indicators measuring nutrition, infant mortality, disease frequency, life expectancy, income, unemployment, and underemployment etc.': *supra*, n. 201, at 341.

[220] *See* Tomasevski, *supra*, n. 18, at 151.   [221] *See above*, text accompanying nn. 73–4.

[222] *See e.g.* Sparsis, E/C.12/1990/SR.4, at 9, para. 43.

[223] *See also* Muterahejuru, E/C.12/1990/SR.46, at 11, para. 51.

[224] *See* Fofana, E/C.12/1989/SR.4, at 5, para. 22. Badawi El Sheikh, E/C.12/1987/SR.6, at 9, para. 35. Alston commented in this vein that the ICESCR 'could be ratified and enter into force even at a time when the government was not fully in compliance with the obligations laid down therein'. E/C.12/1988/SR.13, at 5, para. 19.

[225] Alston and Quinn have remarked that 'it is the state of a country's economy that most vitally determines the level of its obligations as they relate to any of the enumerated rights under the Covenant': *supra*, n. 5, at 177.

[226] The difficulties in assessing the realization of the rights has been recognized by Tomasevski. She maintains that they have increased 'by the blurring of the distinction between the *inability* of a government to implement its human rights obligations, and its *breach* of them': *supra*, n. 18, at 137.

[227] One member of the Committee has commented in this respect that 'The Committee had not yet established any objective yardstick for determining in respect of any particular country whether or not there had been violations of the Covenant': Rattray, E/C.12/1990/SR.15, at 5, para. 21.

the idea of 'minimum core obligations' which apply irrespective of resource considerations. However, in its General Comment, the Committee goes on to state that 'any assessment as to whether a State has discharged its minimum core obligation must also take account of resource constraints applying within the country concerned'.[228] This seems to imply that the question of resources enters into the discussion at the point of determining whether or not the minimum core obligation has been satisfied. Indeed, the debate within the Committee clearly showed that there was no intent to establish a 'presumption of guilt'.[229]

It is submitted that there is no way of reading the General Comment (in the light of the preceding debate) as anything but contradictory upon this point. The General Comment clearly mentions the fact that failure to provide for the basic needs of the population would amount to a *prima facie* violation of the Covenant. It goes on to state that:

In order for a State party to be able to attribute its failure to meet at least its minimum core obligations to a lack of available resources it must demonstrate that every effort has been made to use all resources that are at its disposition in an effort to satisfy, as a matter of priority, those minimum obligations.[230]

This must be read as establishing a 'presumption of guilt' independent of resource considerations. If otherwise, it becomes pointless to speak of either minimum core obligations or *prima facie* violations.

The clear appeal of this approach is that it becomes possible to speak of the widespread violation of economic, social, and cultural rights in a technical legal sense instead of merely as a moral injunction.[231] As far as the Committee is concerned, it avoids the problems of measuring progress against resource availability, of speculating as to alternative courses of action, or of acquiring evidence of State responsibility. In cases where significant numbers of people live in poverty and hunger, it is for the State to show that its failure to provide for the persons concerned was beyond its control.

Nevertheless there are a number of problems associated with the Committee's approach that have not yet been explored. First, there is the obvious problem of establishing minimum thresholds for the rights that may be operated on an international basis. It remains to be seen whether the Committee has the ability to produce standards of sufficient precision and flexibility. Secondly, in placing the emphasis on 'minimum' core obligations

---

[228] General Comment No. 3, *supra*, n. 4, at 86, para. 10.

[229] *See* Alston, E/C.12/1990/SR.48, at 9, para. 43.

[230] General Comment No. 3, *supra*, n. 4, at 86, para. 10.

[231] The Committee has recently commented: 'The fact that one fifth of the world's population is afflicted by poverty, hunger, disease, illiteracy, and insecurity is sufficient grounds for concluding that the economic, social and cultural rights of those persons are being denied on a massive scale': statement to the World Conference, *supra*, n. 87, at 3, para. 8.

for the fulfilment of what might be termed 'basic needs', the Committee will primarily direct its attention to the actions of developing States. That the developing States will be treated differently from the developed States may open the Committee to the criticism that it is not being entirely even-handed. Finally, this approach may obscure the fact that much of the responsibility for poverty and deprivation in the world lies with the developed States' approach to international trade and the economic order. In that sense, responsibility should be placed upon the international community and not merely confined to the 'victim State'.

X. 'INDIVIDUALLY AND THROUGH INTERNATIONAL ASSISTANCE AND CO-OPERATION, ESPECIALLY ECONOMIC AND TECHNICAL'

As noted above, the need for international assistance is already foreseen to some extent by the idea that 'available resources' in article 2(1) refers not merely to national resources but also international ones.[232] There seems to be a general understanding that the full realization of economic, social, and cultural rights in developing countries is to some extent dependent upon the provision of international assistance.[233] Although the primary obligation must be seen to be upon the State to do everything within its power to realize the rights within the Covenant,[234] it is recognized that lack of re-

---

[232] At a textual level this has parallels with arts. 11(1), (2), 22, and 23. Art. 11(1) provides that States recognize the importance of international co-operation based on free consent in the realization of the rights to adequate food, clothing, housing, and the continuous improvement of living conditions. Art. 11(2) requires that States take measures individually and through international co-operation towards the realization of the right to be free from hunger. Art. 22, although primarily a procedural provision, recognizes the role of United Nations organs and specialized agencies in the provision of technical assistance to States parties. Finally art. 23 provides that the States parties agree that the achievement of the rights recognized in the Covenant includes *inter alia* the furnishing of technical assistance.

Such provisions specify little beyond the requirements for co-operation and technical assistance referred to in art. 2(1). As noted earlier, the reiteration of passages from art. 2(1) in the substantive arts. following has no specific consequence. On a broad reading of art. 2(1) then, it would follow that these references add little to the existing State obligations.

[233] This seems to have been the concern of the drafters in including the provision on international co-operation. Cassin commented in this respect that: 'by providing for recourse to international co-operation instead of allowing the enjoyment of certain rights to be put off, it filled the gap between what States could in fact do and the steps they would have to take to meet their obligations under the Covenant': E/CN.4/SR.216, at 6 (1951).

[234] The Mexican representative noted during the drafting of the Covenant that: 'Economic development had to be based above all on the rational and efficient use of a country's own resources and on the hard work of the people; international economic assistance could only be supplementary and was mainly a means of counter-acting economic maladjustments arising from external causes': Mexico (Mr De Santiago Lopez), E/CN.4/SR.1204, at 346, para. 20 (1962).

sources might oblige some States to look to the international community for assistance to that end.[235]

Although there seems to be agreement that the rights in the Covenant are contingent, to a degree, on the provision of international assistance, the nature, scope, and obligatory nature of such assistance is unclear. The Committee addresses the issue in its General Comment No. 3, but does little in the way of elaborating upon the content of the obligation. It states:

The Committee wishes to emphasise that in accordance with Articles 55 and 56 of the Charter of the United Nations, with well-established principles of international law, and with the provisions of the Covenant itself, international co-operation for development and thus for the realization of economic, social and cultural rights is an obligation of all States. It is particularly incumbent upon those States which are in a position to assist others in this regard. The Committee notes in particular the importance of the Declaration on the Right to Development adopted by the General Assembly in its Resolution 41/128 of 4 December 1986 and the need for States parties to take full account of all of the principles recognized therein. It emphasises that, in the absence of an active programme of international assistance and co-operation on the part of all those States that are in a position to undertake one, the full realization of economic, social and cultural rights will remain an unfulfilled aspiration in many countries.[236]

Article 55 of the UN Charter specifies as one of the purposes of the United Nations the promotion of 'higher standards of living, full employment, and conditions of economic and social progress and development'.[237] Under article 56, member States pledge themselves 'to take joint and separate action in co-operation with the organization' to this end. These principles have been further expanded in the 'Declaration on Principles of International Law Concerning Friendly Relations and Co-operation Among States in Accordance with the Charter of the United Nations'.[238] Not only is the Charter vague as to the meaning of international co-operation, but the Declaration does not seem to elucidate much further.[239] All that might be

---

[235] The mere lack of international assistance, however, does not absolve a State from its obligation to take steps towards the realization of the rights. The Chilean representative in the drafting of the Covenant, while noting that international assistance might be necessary for accelerated development, added that States were 'obliged to take steps individually—whether or not international assistance was forthcoming': E/CN.4/SR.1203, at 342, para. 11 (1962).

[236] General Comment No. 3, *supra*, n. 4, at 87, para. 14.

[237] Art. 1(3) of the Charter similarly states that one of the main purposes of the United Nations is 'to achieve international cooperation in solving international problems of an economic, social and cultural or humanitarian character'.

[238] GA Resn. 2625 (XXV) (24 Oct. 1970), 25 UN GAOR, Resns. Supp. (No. 28) (1970).

[239] Although expanding in greater detail the areas in which co-operation is required, including in particular human rights, it does not elucidate the nature or the scale of co-operation envisaged. Arangio-Ruiz comments that the provisions in the Declaration are purely 'reiterations in different words of the statement that States should co-operate': Arangio-Ruiz G., *The UN Declaration on Friendly Relations and the System of the Sources of International Law* (1979), at 143. Alston and Quinn conclude that the Declaration 'attests implicity to the absence

concluded from the provisions of the Charter is that 'there is a clear commitment to do something for the achievement of the purposes mentioned in article 55; there is certainly no right to do nothing'.[240]

It is apparent from the discussion prior to the adoption of the General Comment that it was felt mention should be made of the Declaration on the Right to Development[241] as reflecting the context in which economic, social, and cultural rights are to be achieved.[242] The Committee would thus appear to be concerned about the international structural constraints that impede the full realization of all human rights, and recognizes the existence of a link between the requirement of international assistance in the Covenant, and the demands for a New International Economic Order.[243] As was remarked by one member of the Committee, 'such phenomena as extreme poverty were not produced in a vacuum but reflected a particular international economic situation'.[244] However, beyond being a broad indication of the Committee's general approach, the reference to the Right to Development does little to elucidate the precise obligations incumbent upon States parties pursuant to the duty to co-operate internationally.

Article 2(1) speaks of 'international assistance and co-operation, especially economic and technical'. It is not clear whether the terms 'assist-

of any consensus among States as to the precise meaning of the duty to co-operate': Alston and Quinn, *supra*, n. 5, at 188.

[240] Verwey W., *The Establishment of a New International Economic Order and the Realization of the Right to Development and Welfare* (1980), at 22. *See also* Van Hoof F., 'Problems and Prospects with Respect to the Right to Food' in Van Dijk P. *et al.* (eds.), *Restructuring the International Economic Order: The Role of Law and Lawyers* (1987), 107, at 117.

[241] *See* The Declaration on the Right to Development, GA Resn. 41/128 (4 Dec. 1986). For recent studies on the right to development *see* Van Boven T., 'Human Rights and Development—Rhetorics and Realities', in Nowak M., Steurer D., and Tretter H. (eds.), *Festschrift für Felix Ermacora* (1988), 575; Türk D., 'The Human Right to Development' in Van Dijk P., Van Hoof F., Koers A., and Mortelmans K. (eds.), *Restructuring the International Economic Order: The Role of Law and Lawyers* (1986), 85; Rich R., 'The Right to Development: A Right of Peoples?' in Crawford J., *The Rights of Peoples* (1988), 39; Alston P., 'Revitalizing United Nations Work on Human Rights and Development' (1991) 18 *Mel. Uni. LR* 216; O'Manique J., 'Development, Human Rights and Law', (1992) 14 *Hum. Rts. Q* 383; *The Realization of the Right to Development: Global Consultation on the Right to Development as a Human Right* (1991); Report of the Working Group on the Right to Development, E/CN.4/1994/21; Barsch, *supra*, n. 83.

[242] *See e.g.* Mratchkov, E/C.12/1990/SR.46, at 8, para. 39.

[243] The Mexican representative commented, e.g., during the drafting process, that what was required of international co-operation was 'permanent international machinery for preventing sudden and excessive fluctuations in the prices of primary commodities, which could be disastrous for the developing countries': Santiago Lopez (Mexico), E/CN.4/SR.1204, at 346, para. 20 (1962). *See generally* Ferrero R., *The New International Economic Order and the Promotion of Human Rights*, E/CN.4/Sub.2/1983/24/Rev. 1.

Paragraph 3 of the Declaration on the Establishment of a New International Economic Order reads: 'The political, economic, and social well-being of present and future generations depends more than ever on co-operation between all the members of the international community on the basis of sovereign equality and the removal of the disequilibrium that exists between them': GA Resn. 3201 (S–VI) (1 May 1974).

[244] Konate, E/C.12/1990/SR.21, at 4, para. 3.

ance' and 'co-operation' have discrete meanings. Neither is it obvious whether the terms 'economic and technical' refer to both forms of international action or merely to 'co-operation'. The Committee has not attempted to explain the phrase. It is submitted that 'co-operation' is the wider term providing for mutual action directed towards a common goal (including mutual assistance), whereas 'assistance' implies the provision or transfer of some 'good' from one State to another. Action, whether co-operation or assistance, in the economic and technical fields would appear to be desirable but does not rule out the possibility of other forms of international co-operation.

Article 23 provides an indicative definition of the international action foreseen by article 2(1). It includes 'the conclusion of conventions, the adoption of recommendations, the furnishing of technical assistance and the holding of regional meetings and technical meetings for the purpose of consultation and study'.[245] Although all these matters are of relevance to article 2(1) (especially the need for technical assistance), there is no mention of the most fundamental form of action, namely economic assistance. Indeed it is arguable that a duty to provide economic assistance would run counter to the terms of article 25 of the Covenant which provides that '[n]othing in the present Covenant shall be interpreted as impairing the inherent right of all peoples to enjoy and utilize fully and freely their natural wealth and resources'. That article, however, was merely intended to prevent article 2(1) from being 'invoked in support of the imperialist policies and practices tending to control the economy of developing countries and to impair thereby their political independence'.[246] It should not be read to detract from an obligation to provide assistance inferrable from other provisions in the Covenant.

The precise nature of the obligations in this field may be usefully analysed by reference to the tripartite typology shown above.[247] It may be seen that the obligations to respect, protect, and ensure operate at the international level just as they do at the national level.[248] Thus States could be said to have an initial duty to restrain themselves from any action that might impede the realization of economic, social, and cultural rights in other countries.[249] The Committee has underlined such an obligation,[250]

---

[245] Other references to international action may be found in arts. 11(2) and 23.

[246] UN Doc. A/6546, 21 UN GAOR, Annexes (Ag. Item 62), at 18, para. 98 (1966).

[247] *See above*, text accompanying nn. 11–38.   [248] Eide, *supra*, n. 12, at 40.

[249] This might operate at the level of respecting the self-determination of other peoples and their sovereignty over natural resources. Eide also includes respect for shared resources and access to a global pool of scientific endeavour. *Ibid.* 41–2.

[250] A duty to respect the realization of the rights in other countries was mentioned by Mr Eide in his address to the Committee at its 3rd session. E/C.12/1989/SR.20, at 10, para. 41. It was endorsed by at least one member of the Committee. *See e.g.* Alvarez-Vita, E/C.12/1989/SR.21, at 8, para. 30.

particularly in relation to the work of the international lending agencies. Thus, in its General Comment No. 2, the Committee addressed itself to the issue of the adverse effects of structural adjustment programmes, imposed by the international lending agencies, on the realization of human rights. In particular it commented in paragraph 9 that 'international measures to deal with the debt crisis should take full account of the need to protect economic, social, and cultural rights through, *inter alia*, international co-operation'.[251] In so far as the international community as a whole has an obligation to take cognizance of human rights in its interactions, it is axiomatic that States parties have a similar duty to respect the realization of the rights in other countries.

With regard to the duty to protect, States would have a duty to ensure that all other bodies subject to their control respect the enjoyment of rights in other countries. Thus it has been suggested that States have a duty to regulate the action of domestically based corporations to ensure respect for the rights in other countries.[252] Although the Committee has paid little attention to the activities of such corporations,[253] it has recognized this form of obligation as regards the international lending agencies. In its General Comment No. 2, where the Committee stressed the need for lending agencies to respect the basic rights of the population, it addressed not just the lending agencies themselves, but also the States parties to the Covenant that participate in and support the work of those agencies.[254] Similarly, in its reporting guidelines, the Committee requests States to indicate whether any effort is made to ensure that, when participating in development co-operation, it is used to promote the realization of economic, social, and cultural rights.[255]

By far the most controversial issue with regard to the issue of international co-operation is that which relates to the obligation to fulfil. This is often posited in terms of whether there is an obligation on the part of the more wealthy States to provide aid to less affluent countries. During the drafting of the Covenant, Chile claimed that 'international assistance to under-developed countries had in a sense become mandatory as a result of commitments assumed by States in the United Nations'.[256] This was almost universally challenged by the other representatives of all the groupings

---

[251] General Comment No. 2, *supra*, n. 207, at 88–9, para. 9. On the question of structural adjustment *see generally* Cornia G., Jolly R., and Stewart F., *Adjustment with a Human Face* (1987), Vol. 1, 1–127; Skolgy S., 'Structural Adjustment and Development: Human Rights and an Agenda for Change' (1993) 15 *Hum. Rts. Q* 751.

[252] Alston, *supra*, n. 190, at 44. For the effect of such corporations *see* Andersen-Speekenbrink C., 'The Legal Dimension of Socio-Cultural Effects of Private Enterprise' in De Waart P., Peters P., and Denters E. (eds.), *International Law and Development* (1988), 283.

[253] *But see* Wimer Zambrano, E/C.12/1989/SR.21, at 8, para. 32.

[254] General Comment No. 2, *supra*, n. 207.   [255] Reporting Guidelines, *supra*, n. 174.

[256] E/CN.4/SR.1203, at 342, para. 10 (1962).

involved.[257] The general consensus was that developing States were entitled to ask for assistance but not claim it as a legal right.[258] The text of article 11 bears out this conclusion. In recognizing the role of international co-operation in the realization of the rights, it stipulates that it should be based upon 'free consent'.[259]

Nevertheless, members of the Committee have stressed that it was not enough for States to refrain from action that injured other States, they should also make positive efforts to promote the realization of economic, social, and cultural rights.[260] This does not mean that developed States are required to meet the needs of the poorer States,[261] but rather that they are under a duty to provide some form of assistance to the developing world.

In practice, questions have been asked of Sweden,[262] Norway,[263] the Netherlands,[264] and Czechoslovakia[265] as to the extent of their co-operation with other countries. Members of the Committee have also questioned the adequacy of some aid programmes.[266] There is no evidence, however, that the Committee expects a specific form of aid to be given, nor does it prescribe to whom that aid should go.[267] More attention seems to have been placed

---

[257] *e.g.* Greece, UN Doc. A/C.3/SR.1204, at 346, para. 14 (1962); USSR, UN Doc. A/C.3/SR.1203, at 342, para. 14 (1962); Saudi Arabia, UN Doc. A/C.3/SR.1203, at 341, para. 5 (1962); France, UN Doc. A/C.3/SR.1205, at 352, para. 12 (1962). A similar debate arose over the Declaration on the Right to Development. Many of the Western States voted against or abstained from voting *inter alia* because of the implication that development was to be achieved through the transfer of resources from the developed to the developing world. *See e.g.* statement of the UK on behalf of the European Community: 'While the circumstances of the developing countries have prompted many aid initiatives on their behalf, this does not at present confer to them a "right" in the strict sense of the word. Instruments such as the international development strategy provide a framework for international action but constitute guidelines rather than legally binding obligations': UN Doc. A/41/536, at 16, para. 13 (1986).

[258] Para. 33 of the Limburg Principles maintains that international co-operation and assistance should be based on the sovereign equality of States.

[259] There is sound reasoning behind this position. On the one hand it would be a breach of sovereignty on the part of the wealthy State to be required to provide aid to a particular country. On the other hand the recipient State should not be obliged to accept aid if the aim of the donor country was to exploit the relationship to its own economic advantage. This point was made by the representative of the Congo during the drafting of the Covenant. UN Doc. A/C.3/SR.1181, at 237, para. 30 (1962).

[260] *See* Alvarez Vita, E/C.12/1989/SR.21, at 8, para. 30.

[261] *See* Alston, E/C.12/1990/SR.22, at 14, para. 87; Muterahejuru, E/C.12/1990/SR.46, at 11, para. 52.

[262] *See* Muterahejuru, E/C.12/1988/SR.10, at 7, para. 28.

[263] *See* Alston, E/C.12/1988/SR.13, at 12, para. 69.

[264] *See* Muterahejuru, E/C.12/1989/SR.14, at 15, para. 62.

[265] *See* Muterahejuru, E/C.12/1987/SR.14, at 12, para. 38.

[266] *See e.g.* Muterahejuru, E/C.12/1989/SR.12, at 12, para. 67.

[267] Shelton argues, however, by reference to human rights instruments and general principles of law that there is a duty on States to provide famine assistance and contribute to a global food reserve system in the long run. Shelton D., 'The Duty to Assist Famine Victims' (1984–5) 70 *Iowa LR* 1279. Cf. MacCalister-Smith P., *International Humanitarian Assistance* (1985), 67–9.

upon the utilization of aid once it is received.[268] Indeed the reporting guide-lines merely request information as to the role of international assistance in the full realization of the rights (with the exception of article 8).[269]

It is apparent that the current practice in the provision of aid to develop-ing countries is quite unsatisfactory from the point of view of the realization of economic, social, and cultural rights. First, in terms of the quality of aid, considerable proportions of world aid go to middle- and high-income coun-tries; many 'aid programmes' have a tenuous link with development; and much aid is 'tied' to the donor country either in the sense of being condi-tional upon the operation of a trade agreement or being linked to the donor country's own firms and exporters.[270] Secondly, in terms of the quantity of aid, few developed States have actually achieved the widely accepted ODA target of 0.7 per cent of GNP. In fact in a number of developed countries official aid is less than half that figure.

While there would appear to be considerable scope for strengthening States' external obligations in the light of these facts, it is an area in which States are unlikely, in the foreseeable future, to agree to specific demands on the amount or distribution of aid to third countries. It is considered, nevertheless, that the Committee should begin by looking in more detail at the amount of aid provided, and at the manner in which it is distributed. It does not have to do so with a view to setting immediate standards but rather as an indication of its concern. If it does wish to start imposing indicative criteria as to the amount of aid that should be provided by developed states, note could be made of the comments of the World Bank in its 1990 report:

Real growth in aid of only 2 percent a year is an unacceptably weak response to the challenge of global poverty. The international community needs to do better—much better. At a minimum, it should ensure that aid does not fall as a proportion of the donors' GNP.[271]

Indeed, even given the vague nature of the obligation to co-operate inter-nationally, it would be a clear signal to the Committee that a State was not committed to its obligation to assist other States if the amount of aid it provided to other States declined over a number of years.

XI. CONCLUSION

Article 2(1) was adopted principally as a compromise proposal satisfying those who wished to establish binding State obligations as regards the

---

[268] *See e.g.* Taya, E/C.12/1990/SR.46, at 9, para. 42.
[269] Reporting guidelines, *supra*, n. 174, at 91, 94, 96, 99, 103, 106, 107, 108, and 110.
[270] World Bank (IBRD), *World Development Report 1990* (1990), 127–8.
[271] *Ibid.* 136.

economic, social, and cultural rights in the Covenant, while having the necessary flexibility to take into account the resource constraints that might impede the immediate full realization of the rights. It is, however, a fairly unsatisfactory article, with its convoluted phraseology in which clauses and sub-clauses are combined together in an almost intractable manner, making it virtually impossible to determine the precise nature of the obligations. It is hardly surprising that most commentators focus merely upon the phrase 'with a view to achieving progressively the full realization of the rights', while ignoring for the most part the other phrases that accompany it.

However, given that article 2(1) is central to the definition of State obligations with respect to the rights in the Covenant, it is the key, not only to the implementation of the substantive articles but also to the role of the Committee as a supervisory body. Any progress made by the Committee in developing the value of the Covenant as a human rights guarantee is conditional upon a clear understanding of the precise nature of the State obligations found in article 2(1). The Committee was quick to recognize this fact and fairly early on, with the assistance of the influential Limburg Principles, came to an understanding as to the broad obligations found in article 2(1). This interpretation, which has been encapsulated in its General Comment No. 3, has provided the framework for all its work since. The general comment states a number of important principles upon which State action should be based.

In summary, the Committee has considered that States are required to take immediate, deliberate, concrete, and targeted steps towards the realization of the rights. While legislation is often highly desirable and sometimes indispensable, it is not sufficient in itself to dispose of State obligations with respect to the Covenant. In particular, emphasis should be placed upon the provision of judicial remedies at the national level. States will, however, be given a degree of discretion in deciding what steps are deemed to be appropriate. Notwithstanding the progressive nature of the obligation, States are required to ensure the satisfaction of, at the very least, minimum essential levels of each of the rights. Similarly, in times of resource scarcity, States are under an obligation to strive for the widest possible enjoyment of the relevant rights with particular emphasis upon the position of vulnerable members in society. Finally the Committee has emphasized the obligation upon States to co-operate internationally towards the full realization of the rights.

While the General Comment provides a useful textual analysis and draws a conceptual picture of the State's obligations as regards the rights in the Covenant, the principles remain generalized and require considerably more detail for it to be possible to predict, in a given situation, whether or not a State is complying with its obligations under the Covenant. It is clear that the Committee should not be unduly prescriptive, but it needs to be in a position whereby it is able to evaluate whether or not a State has taken the appropriate course of action, and whether it has done so to the utmost extent of its resources.

Particular problems that are immediately apparent are those of defining and enforcing the minimum core content of the rights and determining when a State has taken sufficient measures to dispose of its obligations under the Covenant. First, as regards the minimum core content of the rights, it remains to be seen whether the Committee has the ability to produce standards of sufficient precision and flexibility to take into account the different situations world-wide. It might also be questioned whether instituting such a standard will not, in fact, serve to focus the Committee's attention on the activities of the less affluent countries while at the same time ignoring the position of the wealthy States.

Secondly, the Committee faces considerable technical difficulties in evaluating whether or not a State has taken the appropriate course of action. Not only does it have to find a way of accurately measuring progress as regards the enjoyment of the rights (particularly at the individual level), but it also has to determine whether or not that progress was adequate. It is clear that to intervene at this stage the Committee will have to consider the possible alternative courses of action open to the State (including the allocation of resources) and weigh up the competing priorities without becoming entirely prescriptive.

4
Non-Discrimination and Equality

Article 2(2)
The States Parties to the Present Covenant undertake to guarantee that the rights enunciated in the present Covenant will be exercised without discrimination of any kind as to race, colour, sex, language, religion, political or other opinion, national or social origin, property, birth or other status.

Article 3
The States Parties to the present Covenant undertake to ensure the equal right of men and women to the enjoyment of all economic, social and cultural rights set forth in the present Covenant.

I. INTRODUCTION

As a human rights instrument, the clear purpose of the Covenant is to protect the fundamental rights of every person without exception. That human rights are seen to adhere to every human being by virtue of their humanity means that they are possessed by every person to an equal extent. As the Preamble stresses, the Covenant is based upon an idea of the 'equal and inalienable rights of all members of the human family'. The concept of 'equal rights' is confirmed in the Covenant in a general manner by the fact that the rights pertain to 'everyone', and more specifically in article 3 which makes express reference to the equal rights of men and women. The idea of equality may also be found in a number of other provisions in the Covenant. Article 7 refers to 'equal remuneration for work of equal value', to 'equal pay for equal work', and to 'equal opportunity for everyone to be promoted'. Similarly, article 13 provides that 'higher education shall be made equally accessible to all'. However, it follows from the structure of the Covenant that the most important provision as regards the promotion of equality or of equal rights within the Covenant is article 2(2). In that provision, recognition of a concept of equality is to be discovered in a negative formulation prohibiting discrimination.

It could be said that the dual concepts of non-discrimination and equality deriving from article 2(2) 'constitute the dominant single theme of the

Covenant'.[1] Not only are equality issues relevant to the implementation of all the rights in the Covenant, but the prohibition on discrimination also provides a useful and specific focus for claims relating to economic, social, and cultural rights which otherwise might be dismissed as long-term objectives.

II. THE CONCEPTS OF NON-DISCRIMINATION AND EQUALITY

The idea of equality has been peculiarly resistant to definition and, over the centuries, has been given all forms of meanings and characteristics. It is common enough to find references to 'equality of treatment', 'equality of access', 'equality of result or achievement', 'equality of opportunity', 'absolute equality', 'relative equality', 'precise equality', 'formal equality', '*de facto* equality', and '*de jure* equality'.[2] Despite the inconsistencies in terminological usage and the continuing disputes over certain peripheral issues, a number of basic principles are generally accepted.

The idea of human rights assumes that all human beings have some basic, commonly shared characteristics, and that as a result they should be viewed and judged as members of the human race rather than as members of a particular group. The recognition of these shared qualities gives rise to a principle of equality which requires that all persons be treated with equal respect. Thus 'certain forms of state and governmental behaviour which consistently exploit or degrade men and deny both the possession of the shared qualities and "the moral claims that arise (therefrom)" by certain groups while conceding and indeed recognizing them in the case of others should be excluded'.[3]

Recognition has to be paid to the fact that, although people have certain common characteristics, they nevertheless possess independent attributes and qualities (whether innate or assumed) which may legitimately be taken into account in the distribution of goods, services, and advantages. It is

---

[1] Ramcharan B., 'Equality and Nondiscrimination' in Henkin L. (ed.), *The International Bill of Rights* (1981), 246. In saying this he was referring to the ICCPR; as we shall see however this is also true for the ICESCR.

[2] For an account of three different forms of equality *see* Galloway D., 'The Models of (In)Equality' (1993) 38 *McGill LJ* 64.

[3] Polyviou P., *The Equal Protection of the Laws* (1980), 11. Sieghart comments in this vein: 'The primary characteristic which distinguishes "human" rights from other rights is their universality: according to the classical theory, they are said to "inhere" in every human being by virtue of his humanity alone. It must necessarily follow that no particular feature or characteristic attaching to any individual, and which distinguishes him from others, can affect his entitlement to his human rights, whether in degree or in kind, except where the instruments specifically provide for this for a clear and cogent reason—for example, in restricting the right to vote to adults, or in requiring special protection for women and children': Sieghart P., *The International Law of Human Rights* (1985), 75.

frequently asserted that equality demands that those who are equal be treated in an equal manner,[4] and that those who are different should be treated differently.[5] The fundamental question remains, however, as to the circumstances in which people can be said to be equal or different,[6] and to the considerations which may form legitimate justifications for differential treatment.

One commentator has usefully categorized justifications for differential treatment into two groups: differentiations based upon 'character and conduct imputable to the individual' (such as industriousness, idleness, lawfulness, merit, and carelessness[7]); and differentiations based upon individual qualities which are relevant to social values (such as physical and mental capacities and talent).[8] However, these criteria do not exhaust all the possible justifications for differential treatment in every circumstance.

The achievement of an equitable balance between identical and differential treatment, however, may be approached from either a positive or a negative vantage point. In positive terms, the principle would require that everyone be treated in the same manner unless some alternative justification is provided. In negative terms the principle might be restated to allow differences in treatment unless they are based upon a number of expressly prohibited grounds.

The principle of non-discrimination approaches the matter of equality from the negative standpoint.[9] It is primarily a legal technique employed to counteract unjustified inequality.[10] The concept of non-discrimination is,

---

[4] Ramcharan commented in this light: 'Equality . . . means equal treatment for those equally situated'. Ramcharan, *supra*, n. 1, at 252. *Cf.* also Tawney R., *Equality* (1931), at 47. Vickers J., 'Majority Equality Issues of the Eighties' (1980) *Can. HRY* 47.

[5] Aristotle, *Nicomachean Ethics*, Bk. 5 (trans. Ross W., 1925). *See also* Dworkin, who distinguishes between 'equal treatment' and 'treatment as an equal': Dworkin R., *Taking Rights Seriously* (1977), p. xii. Vierdag notes however that an essential element of proportionality exists in determining the extent of different treatment. He therefore concludes that non-discrimination requires: 'Equal treatment of equals and unequal treatment of unequals in proportion to the inequality': Vierdag E., *The Concept of Discrimination in International Law* (1973), 7.

[6] Moon R., 'Discrimination and its Justification: Coping with Equality Rights Under the Charter' (1988) 26 *Osgood HLJ* 673, at 682. This has led some to argue that the idea of equality is an empty and tautological concept: 'It tells us to treat like people alike; but when we ask who "like people" are, we are told they are "people who should be treated alike"': Westen P., 'The empty idea of Equality' (1982) 95 *Harv. LR*, 537, at 547.

[7] *e.g.* convicted criminals may legitimately be denied the enjoyment of certain rights on the basis that they have disqualified themselves through their actions.

[8] Ramcharan, *supra*, n. 1, at 253. These have been termed by another commentator as 'natural endowments'. Raphael D., *Justice and Liberty* (1980), 48.

[9] The most coherent discussion of the notion of discrimination in legal terms is to be found in Judge Tanaka's dissenting opinion in the *South West Africa Cases (Second Phase)*, (1966) *ICJ Rep.* 6 at 284–316.

[10] Partsch comments that the creation of the legal norm of non-discrimination was primarily aimed at avoiding the uncertainties of the notion of equality. He goes on to say: 'The basic consideration in favour of this negative approach is to achieve a higher degree of clarity and

however, only a limited means to pursue equality. First, it operates upon the presumption that differential treatment is legitimate unless based upon a proscribed ground. Even in such a case, differential treatment is only *prima facie* discriminatory. Secondly, the concept of non-discrimination is merely a procedural principle (or an obligation of conduct[11]) governing the treatment of people as equals.[12] It may be conditioned by, but certainly does not recognize itself, a wider concept of equality that may take cognizance of factual social inequalities.[13] In short, non-discrimination tends to concentrate upon the prohibition of differential treatment rather than identifying those forms of action that are necessary to achieve substantive equality.[14]

The notion that people are 'equal' may give rise to claims to different forms of equality. At one extreme, it might be interpreted as 'equality of consideration', recognizing that everyone should have their claims to equal treatment taken into account.[15] Essentially this is no more than saying that those claims exist. At the other extreme, equality can be seen as 'equality of result',[16] in which there should be a numerically equal distribution of goods, services, and advantages. This is universally recognized as being neither desirable nor possible.[17]

Between these two extremes may be found claims of 'equality of opportunity'. In a weak sense this may be interpreted as allowing everyone to develop their capabilities and pursue their interests without unjustified restrictions. A stronger sense of equality of opportunity, however, requires that opportunity be made meaningful and effective through, in particular,

certainty in arriving at equality': Partsch K., 'Fundamental Principles of Human Rights: Self-Determination, Equality and Non-Discrimination' in Luard E., *The International Protection of Human Rights* (1957), at 69. Similarly the PCIJ commented in the *Minority Schools in Albania Case* (1935) *PCIJ* Ser. A/B, no. 64: 'Equality in law precludes discrimination of any kind; whereas equality in fact may involve the necessity of different treatment in order to attain a result which establishes an equilibrium between different situations'.

[11] *Cf.* Moon, *supra*, n. 6. at 694.

[12] Some commentators see the object of the non-discrimination clauses as being the promotion of 'equality of treatment'. *See e.g.* Klerk Y., 'Working Paper on Article 2(2) and Article 3 of the International Covenant on Economic, Social and Cultural Rights' (1987) 9 *Hum. Rts. Q* 250, at 255.

[13] *Cf.* Meron T., 'The Meaning and Reach of the International Convention on the Elimination of All Forms of Racial Discrimination' (1985) 79 *AJIL* 283, at 286. For the view that equality and non-discrimination are merely positive and negative formulations of the same idea *see* Dinstein Y., 'Discrimination and International Human Rights' (1985) 15 *Isr. YHR* 11, at 19; Bayefsky A., 'The Principle of Equality or Non-Discrimination in International Law' (1990) 11 *HRLJ* 1, at 1–2.

[14] *Cf.* MacKinnon C., *Feminism Unmodified—Discourses on Life and Law* (1987), 32–45. For a critique of the 'formal' and 'substantive' notions of equality *see* McIntyre S., 'Backlash against Equality: The Tyranny of the "Politically Correct" ' (1993) 38 *McGill LJ* 1, at 26–32.

[15] Polivou, *supra*, n. 3, at 12; Raphael, *supra*, n. 8, at 51.

[16] Also referred to as absolute equality, material equality, or equality of satisfaction.

[17] If this approach was taken then the policy of maintaining reasonable differentiations between people in terms of merit or virtue, e.g., is untenable. *See* Flew A., *Equality in Liberty and Justice* (1989), 177.

the removal of external barriers that affect the acquisition of benefits and distribution of social 'goods', and through the positive promotion of maximum opportunity (for example by education and training[18]). The notion of equality here demands differential treatment on the basis of initial *de facto* inequality.[19] Efforts to maximize equality of opportunity have commonly involved the imposition of redistributionalist taxation policies to finance social welfare programmes for the advancement of vulnerable and disadvantaged groups in society. Although this form of equality of opportunity appears to envisage a form of equality of outcome, it is apparent that 'there is no single correct distribution which is discoverable and which satisfies the right to equality'.[20]

III. EQUALITY IN THE COVENANT

A The Text of the Covenant

It is very much apparent that a notion of equality runs through the heart of the Covenant. The Covenant assumes the creation or maintenance of State

[18] An example of the necessity of different treatment is the provision of special access facilities for the physically disabled in educational facilities. Clearly if they were to be treated 'equally' there would be no grounds for building special ramps or lifts. This would effectively deprive them of access to educational opportunities that are open to others. Vickers comments in this respect: 'If we interpret equal treatment as identical treatment regardless of the different needs of individuals, few equality goals will be realized and most equality rights will exist simply on paper': Vickers, *supra*, n. 4, at 58.

[19] The question of different treatment is particularly problematic with regard to minorities. On the one hand the social disadvantagement of such groups might require a long term integrationalist stance emphasizing equality of treatment. On the other hand, notions of cultural independence and self-determination argue in favour of different treatment. Schachter distinguishes between races and ethnic groups: 'In respect of race, one should follow a "universalist–integrationalist" policy (eliminating distinctions) whereas in regard to ethnic groups a pluralist solution, based on the separate but equal doctrine, can be justified and achieved': Schachter O., 'How Effective are Measures against Racial Discrimination?' (1971) 4 *HRJ* 293, at 296.

Capotorti argues that the essential difference between the protection of minorities and non-discrimination is that the former requires the maintenance of certain differential treatment to allow them to continue developing their own characteristics. Capotorti F., *Study on the Rights of Persons Belonging to Ethnic, Religious and Linguistic Minorities*, E/CN.4/Sub.2/384/Rev.1, at 41, para. 242 (1979). However he seems not to recognize that failure on the part of the State to protect the right to cultural identity of minorities is also a question of discrimination.

Indeed, Sigler confounds the argument further by asserting that the definition of a minority as: 'any group category of people who can be identified by a sizable segment of the population as objects for prejudice or discrimination or who, for reasons of deprivation, require the positive assistance of the State. A persistent nondominant position of the group in political, social, and cultural matters is the common feature of the minority': Sigler J., *Minority Rights: A Comparative Analysis* (1983), 5.

[20] Moon, *supra*, n. 6, at 696. *Cf.* Majury D., 'Strategizing in Equality' in Fineman M. and Thomadsen N. (eds.), *At the Boundaries of Law—Feminism and Legal Theory* (1991), 320, at 323–4.

welfare institutions and social safety nets (for example, the provision of housing, food, clothing, and social security), and as such is openly re-distributionalist. Certainly the Covenant does not envisage an absolute equalization of result in the sense of achieving an equal distribution of material benefits to all members of society, but it does recognize a process of equalization in which social resources are redistributed to provide for the satisfaction of the basic rights of every member of society.[21] As an ideal then, an uneven distribution of material benefits is only tolerable in so far as the satisfaction of the basic economic, social, and cultural rights of every member of society is already achieved.[22] On a broad view, the objectives of the Covenant are conditioned by the idea of equality of opportunity in its strongest sense.

Both the text of the Covenant and the intentions of the drafters appear to bear out this conclusion. The idea of equality of opportunity is specifically recognized in articles 7(c) and 13(2)(c). Article 7(c), in particular, specifies that the only legitimate considerations in achieving equality of opportunity for promotion are seniority and competence.[23] States would appear to be under an obligation to eliminate all other barriers to promotion that might exist both *de jure* and *de facto*. In particular this might require the adoption of positive measures to promote the opportunities of groups in society that are under-represented in higher management positions. That positive measures may (and indeed should) be taken on behalf of certain groups in society is confirmed by the text of article 10(2) and (3) of the Covenant which provides for special measures of protection to be accorded to mothers before and after childbirth and to children especially in the workplace.

Article 3 itself is not so clear in this respect. It provides for the 'equal right' of men and women to the enjoyment of all rights in the Covenant. This might be interpreted as saying no more than that men have no greater claim to the enjoyment of the rights than women. However, it is clear that the drafters intended the provision to have more substance. Although article 3 did not require absolute equality of treatment or result,[24] there was

---

[21] As Raphael stated: 'differential distribution according to need implies a belief in a right to a certain kind of equality. The man who is said to be in need falls below a level of benefits which is taken to be the right of all. When special provision is made for him, this is an attempt to bring him, so far as possible, up to the level of what is due equally to all': Raphael, *supra*, n. 8, at 85.

[22] The term 'basic' is used in the sense of an identifiable 'minimum core content' of the rights which is to be achieved irrespective of resource considerations. *See above*, Ch. 3, text accompanying nn. 212–26.

[23] Art. 13(2)(c) requires that higher education be 'equally accessible to all, on the basis of capacity'. It is not as specifically stated here that capacity should be the only consideration.

[24] McKean comments: 'Some representatives considered that the paragraph might be taken to decree an "absolute" or "precise" equality or "identity of treatment" but others urged that what was being sought was an effective equality in fact—not the abolition of differences between the roles of men and women in marriage, but rather the equitable distribution of

certainly a feeling that factual equality should be increased. As the USSR representative commented, the Third Committee was 'elaborating principles of *de jure* equality; from these principles would arise the *de facto* equalization of human rights'.[25] He continued, 'equality of rights went further than mere non-discrimination; it implied the existence of positive rights in all the spheres dealt with in the draft Covenant'.[26]

It might be argued from the presence of article 3 that the concept of equal rights only applies in relation to the position of women. It would be inappropriate, however, to approach article 3 in such a restrictive manner. Not only is the scope of the non-discrimination provision considerably wider, the presence of article 3 merely reflects the preoccupation of the United Nations at the time of drafting with the issue of sexual equality.[27]

B The Approach of the Committee

The approach of the Committee towards the realization of the rights in the Covenant is marked by its insistence upon a process of equalization. As an initial step towards the realization of the rights in the Covenant States are required to identify the disadvantaged sectors of the population.[28] Those groups should be the focus of positive State action aimed at securing the full realization of their rights. That the Committee considers action should be prioritized in favour of vulnerable and disadvantaged groups in society affirms its belief that the full realization of the rights will not be achieved merely through economic growth,[29] but rather that direct action must be taken to ensure a more equal (or equivalent) enjoyment of the rights.[30] Indeed, to the extent that the Committee relies upon State-specific benchmarks or indicators, the definition of disadvantagement becomes a relative, as opposed to a universal, or absolute, definition. In such a case, measures to combat disadvantagement are inevitably redistributionalist.

If a process of equalization is considered to be a means by which States should achieve the full realization of the rights, it becomes difficult to assess the degree to which the Committee is really concerned with the question of equality itself. For example, if a State builds special homes for persons with physical disabilities, such a step may alternatively be seen as a step towards the realization of the right to housing, or as a measure aimed at achieving

---

rights and responsibilities': McKean W., *Equality and Discrimination under International Law* (1983), 182.

[25] USSR, UN Doc. A/C.3/SR.1183, para. 10 (1962).

[26] *Ibid.*   [27] Klerk, *supra*, n. 12, at 256.

[28] This is stated as being one of the aims of the reporting process. *See* General Comment No. 1, UN Doc. E/1989/22, Annex III, at 87, UN ESCOR, Supp. (No. 4) (1989).

[29] *See above*, Ch. 3, text accompanying nn. 205–11.

[30] For a criticism of such an approach *see* Flew, *supra*, n. 17, at 182–209. He argues instead for the issue of poverty, for example, to be dealt with through a process of economic growth.

real equality of access to adequate housing. Nevertheless, the concept of equality is relevant outside the achievement of specific levels of enjoyment of economic, social, and cultural rights. Thus, even where the 'minimum core content' of the rights is achieved for all persons, the State may be seen to be under an obligation to ensure that everyone has equality of opportunity or access to higher levels of enjoyment of the rights concerned.[31]

In addition to its action in relation to discrimination, which will be dealt with below, members of the Committee have made numerous references to equality of access and opportunity.[32] In doing so, Committee members have tended to rely upon the factual situation in dealing with the question of discrimination.[33] They have further enquired as to State policies designed to remedy situations of *de facto* inequality,[34] and have looked for improvements in the position over time.[35]

It is arguable that determining the extent of equality of opportunity in terms of the result achieved confuses the notion of equality of opportunity with that of equality of result.[36] As Nickel comments:

Success in providing equal opportunities will have to be judged in ways that . . . require reference to the presence of quality programs to educate and protect against discrimination. Statistical measures of outcomes may be useful as practical guides, but they will not serve as criteria of success.[37]

Accordingly, equality of opportunity should be measured by indicators that take into account the possible choices taken by those concerned.

The Committee has been clear that it does not countenance the creation of a situation of absolute equality of result. It has emphasized, for example, the necessity of some autonomy for ethnic minorities to ensure the enjoyment of their own culture.[38] As one member stated:

---

[31] This is relevant to the discussion of whether art. 2(2) is subordinate or autonomous, *see below*, text accompanying nn. 158–75.

[32] *See e.g.* Concluding observations of report of Iran, E/C.12/1993/7, at 4, para. 8; Alston, E/C.12/1990/SR.31, at 3, para. 10; Rattray, E/C.12/1991/SR.11, at 8, para. 45.

[33] *e.g.* it was commented that a higher proportion of unemployed women in a State suggested a certain amount of inequality in education and training, *see e.g.* Muterahejuru, E/C.12/1987/SR.5, at 10, para. 4; Neneman, E/C.12/1988/SR.3, at 7, para. 29. Similar concern has been expressed over situations where the number of girls in education is lower than that of boys, *see e.g.* Texier, E/C.12/1988/SR.14, at 7, para. 40; Alston, E/C.12/1988/SR.17, at 8, para. 48; Rattay, E/C.12/1990/SR.31, at 4, para. 13; Jimenez Butragueno, E/C.12/1991/SR.3, at 11, para. 51.

[34] *See e.g.* Sviridov, E/C.12/1987/SR.20, at 2, para. 2; Alston, E/C.12/1990/SR.31, at 3, para. 10.

[35] *See e.g.* Jimenez Butragueno, E/C.12/1988/SR. 11, at 2, para. 5.

[36] Some commentators have taken the view that the full realization of equality of opportunity is to be determined by whether 'the allocation of the good in question in fact works out unequally or disproportionately between different sections of society; if the unsuccessful sections are under a disadvantage which could be removed by further reform or social action'. Williams B., 'The Idea of Equality', in Williams B. (ed.), *Problems of the Self* (1973).

[37] Nickel J., 'Equal Opportunity in a Pluralistic Society' in Paul E., Miller F., Paul J., and Ahrens J. (eds.), *Equal Opportunity* (1987), 115.

[38] *See e.g.* Alvarez Vita, E/C.12/1991/SR.11, at 10, para. 54.

'Full' realization of the economic, social and cultural rights recognized in the Covenant did not mean equalling out for all persons in the areas concerned but the fact that everyone was entitled, *de facto*, to the equal opportunity to enjoy his rights with dignity.[39]

At the same time, it seems unavoidable that statistical evidence of 'results' will be used as a measure of equality of opportunity, if only to ensure the effectiveness of any action taken. This does not mean that the Committee is necessarily looking towards a numerical distribution of goods among groups in society, but rather that the measures taken to achieve equality of opportunity are not merely formal and empty of content. As has been noted, equality of opportunity is concerned with the outcome of policies 'so that it results in a fairer and more balanced distribution of social benefits'.[40]

IV. ARTICLE 2(2): NON-DISCRIMINATION

The only precise indication as to the meaning of non-discrimination in the drafting of the Covenant was provided by a discussion over whether the term 'discrimination' or the term 'distinction' should be used.[41] There, an overwhelming majority[42] endorsed a three-power amendment (Argentina, Italy, and Mexico) to replace the word 'distinction' with the word 'discrimination'.[43] The stated purpose was to confirm that certain distinctions may be justified to promote the position of certain backward and under-privileged sectors of the population.[44] The word discrimination seemed to convey more accurately the requirement that the distinction be of an un-justified nature or arbitrary.[45]

That this decision should not be over-emphasized, however, is made clear by the fact that during the drafting of the ICCPR the term distinction was retained, it being confirmed that not all distinctions would be forbidden.[46]

---

[39] Taya, E/C.12/1990/SR.46, at 9, para. 42.   [40] Moon, *supra*, n. 6, at 699.

[41] For an analysis of the *travaux préparatoires* concerning art. 2(2), *see* Klerk, *supra*, n. 12, at 251–3.

[42] 76–2, 13 abstentions, UN Doc. A/5365, at 22, 17 UN GAOR, Annex (Ag. Item 43) (1962).

[43] UN Doc. A/C.3/L.1028/Rev. 2 (1962).

[44] There were also fears that the guarantee of rights without distinction would also prevent States from placing any restrictions *inter alia* on the rights of aliens to take up employment in a country. The replacement of the word distinction by discrimination was intended to avoid such ambiguity. UN Docs. A/C.3/SR.1182, at 241 (1962); A/C.3/SR.1202, at 338 (1962); and A/C.3/SR.1203, at 341 (1962).

[45] Similarly in the drafting of art. 3 it was made clear that not all differences of treatment would be illegitimate. McKean, *supra*, n. 24, at 182.

[46] UN Doc. A/C.3/SR.1258, paras. 244–5 (1963); UN Doc. A/C.3/SR.1259, para. 249 (1963). *See also* Klerk, *supra*, n. 12, at 252. McKean comments that the change in attitude from that taken with regard to the ICESCR was largely due to the change in composition of the Committee in the intervening time. McKean, *supra*, n. 24, at 149. The use of the word 'distinction' is also surprising considering that art. 4 ICCPR refers to 'discrimination'.

Similarly, in the *Belgian Linguistic Case*,[47] despite the fact that the French text of article 14 used the term *distinction*, the European Court of Human Rights held that the article 'does not forbid every difference in treatment in the exercise of the rights and freedoms recognized'.[48]

The only other indication as to the intended meaning of non-discrimination in the Covenant is to be found in the references to 'discrimination in its classical juridical meaning'[49] and to 'discrimination . . . in international usage'.[50] It appears to have been suggested that there was a specific and identifiable juridical meaning of the term 'discrimination'.[51] It is possible that reference was being made to the ILO Convention Concerning Discrimination in Respect of Employment and Occupation (ILO No. 111)[52] and the UNESCO Convention Against Discrimination in Education,[53] both of which contain definitions of discrimination. Certainly, if a clear international test for discrimination in all fields were established, it would have considerable relevance to the interpretation of article 2(2).[54]

An important exchange of views took place over the meanings of 'distinction' and 'discrimination' with regard to art. 26 ICCPR (draft art. 24). It was pointed out that the law was justified in making reasonable differentiations in the treatment of certain groups of individuals such as minors, aliens, or persons of unsound minds. *See* UN Docs. A/C.3/SR.1097–1102 (1962). Discrimination in this sense did not mean distinctions of a favourable kind (positive discrimination), nor did it include private individual preferences. McKean, *supra*, n. 24, at 139–40.

McKean comments that art. 2(1) ICCPR 'does not prevent the drawing of distinctions on the grounds of merit or capacity, nor does the equality principle require identical treatment for all, or forbid relevant and reasonable distinctions'. Indeed art. 25 ICCPR seems to recognize that it is only 'unreasonable restrictions' that qualify as discrimination. Similarly, objections to the phrase 'equality before the law' in art. 26 ICCPR were dispelled by the argument that it was a procedural and not substantive equality that was sought, which did not preclude reasonable differentiations between individuals or groups of individuals.

[47] *Case 'Relating to certain aspects of the laws on the use of languages in education in Belgium'* (Merits), Eur. Ct. HR, Series A, Vol. 6, judgment of 23 July 1968 (1979–80) 1 EHRR 252.
[48] *Ibid.* at 284.   [49] Pakistan, A/C.3/SR.1102, para. 4 (1961).
[50] Argentina, A/C.3/SR.1184, para. 7 (1962).
[51] Ramcharan argues with regard to the provisions of the ICCPR that the status of the concept of non-discrimination in international law has effect both as to the permissibility of derogations from the principle in the Covenant, but also to the determination of State compliance with its obligations under the Covenant. Ramcharan, *supra*, n. 1, at 250.
[52] Adopted 25 June 1958, entered into force 15 June 1960, 362 UNTS 32. Art. 1(1) reads: 'For the purposes of this Convention the term "discrimination" includes any distinction, exclusion or preference made on the basis of race, colour, sex, religion, political opinion, national extraction or social origin, which has the effect of nullifying or impairing equality of opportunity or treatment in employment or occupation.'
[53] Adopted 14 Dec. 1960, entered into force 22 May 1962, 429 UNTS 93. Art. 1(1) reads: 'For the purposes of this Convention the term "discrimination" includes any distinction, exclusion, limitation or preference which, being based on race, colour, sex, language, religion, political or other opinion, national or social origin, economic condition or birth, has the purpose or effect of nullifying or impairing equality of treatment in education.'
[54] This is particularly so if the principle of non-discrimination is thought to have the status of customary international law.
In the *Barcelona Traction Case*, the ICJ included among the obligations of States *erga omnes* 'the principles and rules concerning the basic rights of the human person including protection

The definitions of discrimination provided in the above-mentioned Conventions may also be compared with those in the International Convention on the Elimination of All Forms of Racial Discrimination (ICERD)[55] and the Convention on the Elimination of All Forms of Discrimination Against Women (Conv. EDAW).[56] Their similarities have led certain commentators to conclude that a universal 'composite concept' of discrimination can be discerned in the various instruments characterized by the following elements:

(1) a difference in treatment,
(2) which is based upon certain prohibited grounds,
(3) and has a certain purpose or effect,
(4) in selective fields.[57]

The Committee on Economic, Social, and Cultural Rights, however, has not as yet established its own definition of the term 'discrimination' in a General Comment. The only definition to be found in its work is in the reporting guidelines on the subject of article 6. There, the Committee requests States to provide it with information as to:

any distinctions, exclusions, restrictions or preferences, be it in law or in administrative practices or in practical relationships, between persons or groups of persons, made on the basis of race, colour, sex, religion, political opinion, nationality or social

from slavery and racial discrimination': (1970) *ICJ Rep.* 3, at 33–4. Similarly in its Advisory Opinion on *Namibia* (1971) the ICJ stated that 'to establish . . . and to enforce distinctions, exclusions, restrictions, and limitations exclusively based on grounds of race, colour, descent, or national origin . . . constitutes a denial of fundamental human rights' and 'is a flagrant violation of the purposes of the Charter': Advisory Opinion (1971) *ICJ Rep.* 3, at 57.

Reference to other international instruments is also suggested in para. 41 of the Limburg Principles which states: 'In the application of art. 2(2) due regard should be paid to all relevant international instruments including the Declaration and Convention on the Elimination of all Forms of Racial Discrimination': (1987) 9 *Hum. Rts. Q* 122, at 127.

[55] Adopted 21 Dec. 1965, entered into force 4 Jan. 1967, 660 UNTS 195. Art. 1(1) reads: 'In this Convention, the term "racial discrimination" shall mean any distinction, exclusion, restriction or preference based on race, colour, descent, or national of ethnic origin which has the purpose or effect of nullifying or impairing the recognition, enjoyment or exercise, on an equal footing, of human rights and fundamental freedoms in the political, economic, social, cultural or any other field of public life.'

[56] Adopted 18 Dec. 1979, entered into force 3 Sept. 1981. GA Resn. 34/180, 34 UN GAOR, Resns., Supp. (No. 46) at 193 (1980), 1249 UNTS 243. Art. 1 reads: 'For the purposes of the present Convention, the term "discrimination against women" shall mean any distinction, exclusion or restriction made on the basis of sex which has the effect or purpose of impairing or nullifying the recognition, enjoyment or exercise by women, of human rights and fundamental freedoms in the political, economic, social, cultural, civil or any other field.'

[57] Schwelb E., 'The International Convention on the Elimination of All Forms of Racial Discrimination' (1966) 15 *ICLQ* 996, at 1001. The outline of such a definition has been accepted by the HRC in its General Comment on art. 2(1) ICCPR where it stated that the term discrimination: 'should be understood to imply any distinction, exclusion, restriction or preference which is based on any ground such as race, colour, sex, language, religion, political or other opinion, national or social origin, property, birth or other status, and which has the purpose or effect of nullifying or impairing the recognition, enjoyment or exercise by all persons, on an equal footing, of all rights and freedoms': General Comment No. 18 (37), UN Doc. A/45/40, at 174, para. 7, 45 UN GAOR, Supp. (No. 40) (1990).

origin, which have the effect of nullifying or impairing the recognition, enjoyment or exercise of equality of opportunity or treatment in employment or occupation.[58]

The similarity between this definition and that adopted in other human rights contexts suggests that the Committee will approach the question of discrimination in the same manner. The four elements of discrimination will be dealt with separately below.

A Differential Treatment

The Committee utilizes the common terms to describe differential treatment, namely 'distinctions', 'exclusions', 'restrictions', or 'preferences'. Clearly any one of these terms would suffice to establish an action for the purpose of discrimination. The inclusion of the term 'preferences' suggests that the action does not necessarily have to be directed against the group alleging discrimination, but may be effected through unreasonable promotion of one group at the expense of others.[59] Indeed the Committee noted in the case of Vietnam that there was evidence of discrimination 'on the basis of preferences in favour of persons from certain groups'.[60] The crucial aspect of this, and the other terms, is that they are all relative, presuming a standard of treatment from which that action is differentiated. As one commentator has noted, 'the discriminatory or equal treatment of one person must be measured by the relative treatment of somebody else'.[61]

As was established during the drafting of the Covenant, differential treatment, although a prerequisite, is not in itself sufficient to establish a case of discrimination. The Committee's definition goes on to speak of actions that have the effect of 'nullifying or impairing the recognition, enjoyment, or exercise of equality of opportunity'.[62] However, defining 'discrimination' in terms of 'equality of opportunity' does little to clarify the complex of issues. In the context of employment, for example, it has to be accepted that certain job requirements may indirectly limit the access to employment of certain groups (such as women in jobs that require heavy manual labour). Similarly in some cases, preference may legitimately be given to members of specific racial groups for the purpose of authenticity.[63]

This matter has been underlined in other human rights fora. In the *Mauritian Women's Case*[64] the Human Rights Committee, in finding a

[58] Reporting Guidelines, UN Doc. E/1991/23, Annex IV, at 91, para. 3, UN ESCOR, Supp. (No. 3) (1991).

[59] It has to be pointed out that from the point of view of equality of opportunity, differential treatment may actually be required in certain circumstances. It is particularly in this respect that the principle of non-discrimination falls short of providing for equality.

[60] Concluding observations on report of Vietnam, E/C.12/1993/8, at 2, para. 8.

[61] Dinstein, *supra*, n. 13, at 11.   [62] *Supra*, n. 58.

[63] *e.g.* a theatrical production might require an actor of a specific racial background.

[64] HRC Resn. 9/35, UN Doc. A/36/40, at 134, 36 UN GAOR, Supp. (No. 40) (1981).

violation of articles 2(1) and 3 of the ICCPR, considered that a distinction based on sex was not in itself conclusive. The determining factor was that no 'sufficient justification' had been given for such a distinction.[65] Similarly, the European Court of Human Rights found in the *Belgian Linguistic Case* that the principle of equality of treatment is violated 'if the distinction has no objective and reasonable justification'.[66] Any such justification would be assessed in relation to the aim and effects of the measure with regard being had to the 'principles which normally prevail in democratic societies'. There must also be a 'reasonable relationship of proportionality between the means employed and the aim sought to be realized'.[67] That consideration is given to 'principles that normally prevail in democratic societies' is underlined by the margin of appreciation given to States in the determination of 'to what extent differences in otherwise similar situations justify a different treatment in law'.[68] The Court has commented in this respect that 'the scope of this margin will vary according to the circumstances, the subject-matter, and its background'.[69]

As far as the Committee is concerned, it has not readily addressed such issues. It has found violations of articles 2(2) and 3 in a number of cases, but has not undertaken to assess whether or not there was sufficient justification for the measures in question. Thus in the case of Iran, the Committee merely declared that the exclusion of women from studying a large number of subjects at university and the need for them to obtain the permission of their husbands to work or travel abroad were incompatible with the obligations under the Covenant.[70] It may well be considered that such situations are sufficiently clear in themselves not to have to consider alternative justifications, but the Committee needs to establish a clear understanding of its approach to questions of discrimination in order to give its pronouncements credibility.

B Purpose or Effect

The Committee's definition of discrimination, like the ILO Convention, refers to the 'effect' of that differential treatment.[71] The Racial Discrimination Convention refers, in addition, to discrimination that has the 'purpose' of impairing or nullifying the enjoyment of the rights concerned.[72]

---

[65] *Ibid.* para. 9.2(b) 2(ii) 3.   [66] *Supra*, n. 47.   [67] *Ibid.*

[68] Van Dijk P. and Van Hoof G., *Theory and Practice of the European Convention on Human Rights* (4th ed., 1991), 396.

[69] *Inze* v. *Austria*, Eur. Ct. H.R., Series A, Vol. 126, judgment of 28 Oct. 1987, (1988) 10 EHRR 394, para. 41. However there has been little articulation of what constitutes those circumstances, subject-matters, or backgrounds in which the margin of appreciation will operate. Bayefsky, *supra*, n. 10, at 18.

[70] Concluding observations on report of Iran, E/C.12/1993/7, at 3, para. 6.

[71] *See above*, text accompanying n. 58.   [72] *Supra*, n. 55.

Although the Committee makes no reference to 'purpose' this does not affect State responsibility for intentional but ineffective discriminatory measures.[73] Thus the presence of discriminatory legislation would amount to a breach of the Covenant even if it were not enforced. Accordingly, members of the Committee criticized legal provisions in Zaïre and Iran which required women to seek the permission of their husbands in order to work outside the home[74] or to travel.[75] Similarly, an order prohibiting the employment of members of the Baha'i community in Iran were considered to be contrary to the terms of the Covenant.[76]

In practice, the actual intention of the State concerned seems to be of little importance.[77] It is clear that in the majority of States some form of discrimination is inherent in the civil, political, social, economic, and cultural traditions of the country. A particular government at any given juncture cannot be considered to have willed that situation, whether expressly or impliedly.[78] The necessity of eliminating discrimination requires that the government take action to remedy circumstances for which it is not itself responsible. This is particularly clear in so far as States are obliged to eliminate discrimination between private individuals. Thus, although discriminatory intention might be determined merely by the existence of discriminatory policies and legislation,[79] the Committee has not refrained from criticizing governments on the basis of the *de facto* situation alone.[80]

The emphasis on the 'effect' of policies rather than their intention also means that neutral measures will be considered 'discriminatory' if in fact they negatively affect a group in society that has been singled out for protection. As Judge Tanaka commented in the *South West Africa Cases (Second Phase), 1966*[81] with regard to racial discrimination:

---

[73] As regards the ICCPR, there is some evidence that the practice of the Human Rights Committee suggests that a notion of forseeability has been incorporated in which some results would not be considered as the true consequences of discriminatory rules. Bayefsky, *supra*, n. 13, at 10.

[74] *See* Alvarez Vita, E/C.12/1988/SR.17, at 2, para. 3.

[75] *See* Vysokayova, E/C.12/1994/SR.11, at 3, para. 9.

[76] *See* Simma, E/C.12/1993/SR.7, at 10, para. 41.

[77] For the problems associated with the need to prove an 'intent' to discriminate, *see* Moon, *supra*, n. 6, at 687–8.

[78] For problems relating to the US doctrine of 'state action', *see* Black C., 'Forward: State Action, Equal Protection and California's Proposition 14' (1967) 81 *Harv. LR* 69.

[79] This is not conclusive in itself however as discrimination may operate as an unfortunate side-effect of a piece of legislation. In such a case a test of forseeability would have to be made to impute discriminatory intention. In this respect, it is difficult to concur with Meron's assertion that discriminatory intention is easy to establish. Meron, *supra*, n. 13, at 287.

[80] *See e.g.* Simma, E/C.12/1990/SR.16, at 7, para. 32. The PCIJ advocated a similar conclusion in its advisory opinion relating to *German Settlers in Poland* (1923), PCIJ Ser. B, No. 6: 'There must be equality in fact as well as ostensible legal equality in the sense of the absence of discrimination in the words of the law.'

[81] *Supra*, n. 9.

The arbitrariness which is prohibited, means the purely objective fact and not the subjective condition of those concerned. Accordingly, the arbitrariness can be asserted without regard to . . . motive or purpose.[82]

This form of discrimination, as found in certain jurisdictions,[83] has often been termed 'indirect discrimination'.[84] Although a certain amount of recognition has been paid by Committee members to the notion of indirect discrimination,[85] no effort has been made to define the concept as yet. As a general principle, however, indirect discrimination is not established if only one person is adversely affected by the provision concerned; it must affect the group concerned proponderately or in a disproportionate manner.

An emphasis on the discriminatory 'effect' of policies and programmes does raise two important points about the Committee's approach. First, it places some emphasis upon what might be termed 'equality of result' as opposed to procedural equality. In effect, the principle of non-discrimination has been given a broad interpretation to embody ideas of equality of opportunity. Secondly, to the extent that indirect discrimination may be established by reference to effects upon a particular group (for example a racial group), it might be said to give rise to a notion of collective rights.[86]

C Grounds upon which Discrimination is Prohibited

Most non-discrimination provisions proscribe discrimination on a specified number of grounds, such as sex, race, or ethnic origin 'to make clear that certain factors are unacceptable as grounds for distinction'.[87] As seen above, this does not mean that all distinctions drawn upon those grounds will necessarily be discriminatory; rather that they are 'suspect classifications'. At most, distinctions drawn upon these suspect grounds could be said to amount to *prima facie* discrimination, depending upon whether or not there is any reasonable justification.

[82] *Ibid.* 293.

[83] It has been defined and most fully developed in the USA following the case of *Griggs* v. *Duke Power Co.*, 401 US 424 (1971). In the UK *see* Race Relations Act 1976, s. 1(1)(b), Sex Discrimination Act 1975 s. 1(1)(b).

[84] *See* CERD General Recommendation XIV (42), UN Doc. A/48/18, at 115, 48 UN GAOR, Supp. (No. 18) (1993), where it was stated: 'In seeking whether an action has an effect contrary to the Convention, it will look to see whether that action has an unjustifiable disparate impact upon a group distinguished by race, colour, descent, or national or ethnic origin.' A similar concept is that of 'constructive discrimination' defined by one commentator as 'when an act of the state adds to the disadvantage of an already disadvantaged group': Moon, *supra*, n. 6, at 697.

[85] *See e.g.* Simma, E/C.12/1989/SR.8, at 8, para. 46; Alston, E/C.12/1994/SR.3, at 6, para. 30.

[86] It cannot be said to be a fully-fledged 'collective right' however, as the group identity merely acts as a condition for the protection of the individual. It does not, e.g., give rise to claims for a specific benefit to be granted to that group.

[87] Ramcharan, *supra*, n. 1, at 252.

The list of 'prohibited' or 'suspect' grounds tends to vary from one treaty to another. It might be the purpose of the treaty, for example, to deal with a specific type of discrimination, in which case, the grounds on which discrimination is prohibited are more restricted.[88] It is clear that the ICESCR, in containing a list of ten prohibited grounds ('race, colour, sex, language, religion, political or other opinion, national or social origin, property, birth, or other status') was not intended to be limited in such a way. Nevertheless, the question whether the enunciated grounds are the only ones on which distinctions are prohibited is not specifically addressed.

1 Exhaustive or Illustrative

The ten prohibited grounds for discrimination parallel those found in the UDHR. They are not the only grounds to be found in international human rights treaties; others include 'association with a national minority',[89] 'ethnic origin',[90] and 'disability'.[91] It is arguable that the exclusionary principle, *expressio unius est exclusio alterius*, limits the prohibited grounds to those specifically enumerated in the Covenant. Indeed, that the reference to discrimination 'of any kind' (found in the UDHR) was omitted during the drafting of article 2(2) has led one commentator to conclude that the list of grounds was intended to be exhaustive.[92]

Nevertheless, during the drafting of the ICCPR, proposals to specify additional grounds of discrimination were deemed unnecessary because they fell into the ambit of the expressions 'discrimination on any ground' and 'other status'.[93] It would be logical to read the term 'other status' in the ICESCR as having a similarly open-ended meaning.[94] Moreover, it has been asserted that, even though a three-power amendment replaced the words 'such as' with the phrase 'as to', the lack of discussion that took place over the change indicates that the enumeration was intended to remain merely illustrative.[95]

[88] Examples of this type of treaty are the Racial Discrimination Convention which is limited to distinctions drawn on the basis of 'race, colour, descent, or national or ethnic origin', and the Discrimination against Women Convention which relates to distinctions 'on the basis of sex'.

[89] Art. 14, European Convention on Human Rights (1950), 213 UNTS 221. It is unlikely that this adds much to the prohibition of discrimination on the ground of national origin. *See e.g.* Dinstein, *supra*, n. 13, at 12.

[90] Art. 2(1) Convention on the Rights of the Child, 28 ILM 1448 (1989).

[91] *Ibid.*   [92] Bayefsky, *supra*, n. 13, at 5.

[93] UN Doc. A/2929, para. 181, 10 UN GAOR, Annexes (Ag. Item 28), pt. II (1955).

[94] It should be noted that the Spanish text of the ICESCR and the ICCPR speak of *otra condición social* (other social status) which would limit the type of additional ground for discrimination.

[95] Klerk, *supra*, n. 12, at 256. For the opinion that art. 2 UDHR is illustrative *see* Verdoot A., *Naissance et significance de la déclaration universelle des droits de l'homme* (1964), 95.

If the grounds for discrimination are not exhaustive, it is possible that any distinction may require reference to the non-discrimination principle.[96] If that were the case, the Committee would have to develop a rationale to justify under what circumstances and on what grounds differential treatment is legitimate.[97] Although the Committee has not gone so far as to establish an all-embracing rationale with respect to discrimination, it has extended its scrutiny of differential treatment to grounds other than those specifically enumerated. It has specifically stated, for example, that the requirement that rights be exercised 'without discrimination of any kind', 'clearly applies to discrimination on the grounds of disability' despite the fact that 'disability' is not mentioned as one of the prohibited grounds.[98]

In addition to asking questions on the status of ethnic minorities,[99] natural children,[100] women,[101] and men,[102] or discrimination on the basis of religious belief,[103] alternative political philosophies,[104] and class bias,[105] it has

[96] This was the position adopted by the European Court of Human Rights in *Rasmussen* v. *Denmark* Eur. Ct. HR, Series A, Vol. 87, judgment of 28 Nov. 1984. The Human Rights Committee does not seem to have adopted this approach with regard to art. 26 however. Bayefsky, *supra*, n. 13, at 6–7.

[97] This could involve a form of 'minimal scrutiny' as that operated in the US, *see Allied Stores of Ohio* v. *Bowers Tax Commission of Ohio*, 358 US 522, at 530 (1959).

[98] *See* Draft General Comment on Persons with Disabilities, E/C.12/1993/WP.26, at 2, para. 5.

[99] *e.g.* Muterahejuru, E/C.12/1990/SR.18, at 13, para. 78; Simma, E/C.12/1994/SR.11, at 4, para. 15; Neneman, E/C.12/1992/SR.2, at 6, para. 31. *Cf.* Concluding observations on report of New Zealand, E/C.12/1993/13, at 3, para. 17; Australia, E/C.12/1993/9, at 2, para. 8. This could be seen to include indigenous populations, cf. Konate, E/C.12/1990/SR.7, at 4, para. 13; Bonoan-Dandan, E/C.12/1991/SR.3, at 10, para. 44; Alvarez Vita, E/C.12/1994/SR.11, at 6, para. 26.

[100] *e.g.* Fofana, E/C.12/1987/SR.7, at 8, para. 39; Badawi El Sheikh, E/C.12/1988/SR.8, at 2, para. 3; Bonoan-Dandan, E/C.12/1994/SR.4, at 7, para. 35; Ceausu, E/C.12/1994/SR.10/Add.1, at 3, para. 9.

[101] The Committee has asked numerous questions as to the position of women. As regards the legal situation of women *see e.g.* legal prohibition against discrimination against women, Jimenez Butragueno, E/C.12/1987/SR.7, at 6, para. 23; *de jure* and *de facto* differences between men and women, Alvarez Vita, E/C.12/1987/SR.8, at 7, para. 29.; equality under the law, Jimenez Butragueno, E/C.12/1987/SR.8, at 8, para. 33; different marriageable ages for men and women, Rattray, E/C.12/1987/SR.9, at 9, para. 41; legislative measures to prevent dismissal of pregnant women, Mrachkov, E/C.12/1988/SR.10, at 6, para. 25; differences between men and women in family law, Simma, E/C.12/1994/SR.8, at 8, para. 38.

[102] Especially in relation to paid leave to look after children, *e.g.* Jimenez Butragueno, E/C.12/1987/SR.12, at 4, para. 14. Texier, E/C.12/1987/SR.19, at 10, para. 47; or the enjoyment of parental benefits, Jimenez Butragueno, E/C.12/1988/SR.18, at 3, para. 12. Also in respect to widower's pension, *e.g.* Alvarez Vita, E/C.12/1993/SR.10, at 8, para. 44. Unlike the Discrimination against Women Convention, the prohibited ground of 'sex' is not confined to the position of women. The presence of arts. 3 and 10 confirms, however, that the position of women is of primary importance.

[103] *e.g.* Simma, E/C.12/1987/SR.11, at 10, para. 48.

[104] *e.g.* Konate, E/C.12/1987/SR.11, at 12, para. 58. This includes the expression of opposition to the established political views, Simma, E/C.12/1987/SR.13, at 8–9, para. 40; Alston, E/C.12/1987/SR.19, at 9, para. 45. *Cf.* Concluding observations on report of Germany, E/C.12/1993/17, at 2, para. 8.

[105] Rattray, E/C.12/1990/SR.7, at 5, para. 16.

directed itself to the situation of those in particular regional areas,[106] aliens,[107] (including the stateless,[108] migrant workers,[109] and refugees[110]) unmarried couples, and parents,[111] people with AIDS,[112] or physical[113] and mental disabilities,[114] homosexuals,[115] the poor,[116] and the elderly.[117]

It has to be borne in mind, however, that by asking questions on the situation with regard to such groups, the Committee is not necessarily attempting to discover elements of discrimination. It may instead merely be assessing the enjoyment of economic, social, and cultural rights. Thus *de facto* differences in the enjoyment of rights between different regions would not normally be considered a matter of discrimination. Nevertheless, in centering its attention on these social groups, the Committee appears to consider that possible additional grounds exist under which discrimination is prohibited, such as health, nationality, disability, poverty, age, and sexual orientation.

Of these possible grounds, there would seem to be little reason to object to the inclusion of grounds such as health,[118] disability,[119] or age.[120] Clearly,

[106] *e.g.* The treatment of populations in overseas and dependent territories: Daudi, E/C.12/1987/SR.5, at 4, para. 15 (Netherlands Antilles); Badawi, E/C.12/1988/SR.8, at 2, para. 3 (Greenland and Faroe Islands); Mrachkov, E/C.12/1989/SR.12, at 13, para. 73 (French Overseas Territories). The position of rural populations: Mratchkov, E/C.12/1988/SR.7, at 6, para. 43; Sparsis, E/C.12/1988/SR.7, at 2, para. 2; Muterahejuru, E/C.12/1990/SR.2, at 11, para. 67. Poor urban populations: Texier, E/C.12/1989/SR.12, at 10, para. 50.

[107] *See below*, text accompanying nn. 126–45.

[108] *e.g.* Texier, E/C.12/1988/SR.10, at 12, para. 66; Badawi El Sheikh, E/C.12/1988/SR.11, at 3, para. 15.

[109] *e.g.* Mratchkov, E/C.12/1987/SR.6, at 12, para. 61; Simma, E/C.12/1990/SR.34, at 4, para. 22; Konate, E/C.12/1992/SR.14, at 3, para. 10.

[110] *e.g.* Taya, E/C.12/1988/SR.3, at 6, para. 27; Texier, E/C.12/1989/SR.8, at 5, para. 22; Texier, E/C.12/1990/SR.7, at 2, para. 5; Texier, E/C.12/1992/SR.18, at 9, para. 51.

[111] *e.g.* Wimer Zambrano, E/C.12/1987/SR.11, at 12, para. 60; Texier, E/C.12/1989/SR 14, at 16, para. 70; Muterahejuru, E/C.12/1987/SR.12, at 3, para. 8.

[112] *e.g.* Rattray, E/C.12/1987/SR.20, at 3, para. 10; Alston, E/C.12/1988/SR.9, at 5, para. 25; Texier, E/C.12/1990/SR.2, at 10, para. 56; Simma, E/C.12/1990/SR.34, at 5, para. 25.

[113] *e.g.* Deaf children, Jimenez Butragueno, E/C.12/1990/SR.8, at 11, para. 52. *See generally* Draft General Comment on Persons with Disabilities, E/C.12/1993/WP.26.

[114] *See e.g.* Jimenez Butragueno, E/C.12/1987/SR.20, at 4, para. 13.

[115] *e.g.* Simma, E/C.12/1989/SR.16, at 18, para. 95.

[116] *e.g.* Neneman, E/C.12/1988/SR.3, at 9, para. 43; Texier, E/C.12/1990/SR.16, at 9, para. 44.

[117] *e.g.* Butragueno, E/C.12/1988/SR.14, at 3, para. 13; Simma, E/C.12/1988/SR.6, at 4, para. 18; Jimenez Butragueno, E/C.12/1990/SR.40, at 5, para. 71; Jimenez Butragueno, E/C.12/1992/SR.14, at 2, para. 4.

[118] Reaction to the discovery of HIV/AIDS has entailed many instances of discrimination in the field of economic, social, and cultural rights. It is considered that denials of education, marriage, social services, and employment go far beyond those measures necessitated by the nature of the infection. *See e.g.* UN Doc. E/CN.4/Sub.2/1990/9, at 6–8, paras. 30–40; 'AIDS and Discrimination' (1988) 41 *ICJ Rev.* 35–49; Center for Human Rights, *Report of an International Consultation on AIDS and Human Rights* (1989).

[119] *See generally* Standard Rules on the Equalization of Opportunities for Persons with Disabilities, GA Resn. 48/96 (20 Dec. 1993), 48 UN GAOR, Supp. (No. 49) (1993). Despouy L., *Human Rights and Disability*, UN Doc. E/CN.4/Sub.2/1991/31.

[120] Vickers, *supra*, n. 4, at 52. *See also* UN Doc. E/C.12/1993/WP.21; and the discussion: E/C.12/1993/SR.12.

this does not mean that all differences in treatment based upon such grounds are discriminatory. For example, it is accepted in a number of States that the elderly may be deprived of their right to work through compulsory retirement.[121] It does mean that differences justified on such grounds will be subjected to a stricter level of scrutiny than others.

On the other hand, the posited grounds of sexual orientation, poverty, and nationality all present difficulties with respect to their inclusion which will be discussed below:

(a) Sexual Orientation

The acceptance of equality with regard to those with alternative sexual orientations is clearly subject to a great deal of controversy. Although homosexuality, for example, is tolerated in a number of countries, there remain a number of others in which it is a criminal offence.[122] Indeed, even in the most tolerant of States, there often remain considerable elements of both public and private discrimination against homosexuals.[123]

In principle, there is no reason why the extent of a person's enjoyment of economic, social, or cultural rights should depend upon their sexual orientation. The problem for the Committee, as with other human rights bodies,[124] is whether there is sufficient moral consensus within which it may locate its position. This is not merely a trivial question as it is ultimately for the States parties themselves to decide the meaning of the terms within the Covenant. On a 'pragmatic' approach, if the Covenant were treated as a 'living instrument' with standards reflecting the current moral and legal developments among the States parties,[125] sexual orientation might be established as a prohibited ground for discrimination at some stage in the future. It is considered, nevertheless, that the Committee should take a principled approach and operate a strict level of scrutiny as regards all distinctions based upon sexual orientation on the basis that that consideration is not relevant to the enjoyment of economic, social, and cultural rights.

---

[121] On this point *see* Alston, E/C.12/1991/SR.9, at 6, para. 24. ILO Recommendation No. 166 (1982) para. 5 (a) states that age alone cannot constitute a valid reason for termination of employment 'subject to national law and practice regarding retirement'.

[122] The European Court of Human Rights however has recognized an increased tolerance of homosexual behaviour in the European context. Accordingly, it found the imposition of criminal sanctions to be in breach of the right to privacy under art. 8 of the ECHR. *Dudgeon* v. *United Kingdom*, Eur. Ct. HR, Series A, Vol. 45, judgment of 22 Oct. 1981 (1981) 4 EHRR 149; *Norris* v. *Ireland*, Eur. Ct. HR, Series A, Vol. 142, judgment of 26 Oct. 1988 (1988), (1991) 13 EHRR 186.

[123] *See* Helfer L., 'Lesbian and Gay Rights as Human Rights: Strategies for a United Europe' (1991) 32 *VJIL* 157.

[124] *See* Girard P., 'The Protection of the Rights of Homosexuals under International Law of Human Rights: European Perspectives' (1986) *Can. HRY* 3.

[125] Cf. *Tyrer* v. *United Kingdom*, Eur. Ct. HR, Series A, Vol. 26, judgment of 25 Apr. 1978 (1979–80) 2 EHRR 1.

(b) Nationality

With regard to nationality as a prohibited ground for discrimination, it should be noted that article 2(2) rules out discrimination on the ground of national origin but not on the basis of nationality.[126] Indeed article 2(3) specifically allows limitations to be placed upon the enjoyment of the rights of non-nationals in the case of developing States.[127] Lillich draws the conclusion that the ICESCR 'does not embody a general norm of non-discrimination against aliens'.[128]

However, an interesting 'interpretative declaration' was made by Belgium upon ratification:

With respect to article 2, paragraph 2, the Belgian Government interprets non-discrimination as to national origin as not necessarily implying an obligation on States automatically to guarantee to foreigners the same rights as to their nationals. The terms should be understood to refer to the elimination of any arbitrary behaviour but not of differences in treatment based on objective and reasonable considerations, in conformity with the principles prevailing in democratic societies.[129]

While overtly intended to limit the scope of obligations as regards non-nationals, the declaration in fact confirms that the term 'national origin' may plausibly be read in a wide sense to include non-nationals. It then merely reiterates the idea that not all differences in treatment will necessarily amount to discrimination.

[126] Whereas 'nationality' refers to the position of aliens and migrant workers, 'national origin' seems to relate to the ethnic or racial origin of the individual irrespective of their nationality. For a discussion of the differences between the terms *see* comments of Lord Simon in *Ealing London Borough Council* v. *Race Relations Board* [1972] AC 342, at 362–3. *Cf.* Kartashkin V., 'Economic, Social and Cultural Rights' in Meron T. (ed.), *Human Rights in International Law* (1985) 111, at 131. Schwelb concurs in this view in commenting that 'national origin' relates to present and past 'nationality' in an ethnographic sense. He also comments that with respect to the term 'nationality' in its legal sense, only previous nationality is a prohibited ground for discrimination. Schwelb, *supra*, n. 57, at 1007.

[127] It might be argued on the basis of art. 2(3) that this does not entitle developed countries to discriminate in such a manner and that in any case differentiations may not be made with regard to non-economic rights, Lillich R., *The Human Rights of Aliens in Contemporary International Law*, (1981) 47.

The definition of economic rights in itself is unclear. It is assumed that they are rights 'that enable a person to earn a living or that relate to that process'. Dankwa E., 'Working Paper on Article 2(3) of the International Covenant on Economic, Social and Cultural Rights' (1987) 9 *Hum. Rts. Q* 230, at 240. Similarly, as McKean notes: 'the term "developing country" is not defined, and the language used is unconscienably vague. It must therefore be regarded as an unfortunate inclusion in a covenant of this nature and likely to cause invidious and unreasonable distinctions to be made against aliens on the ground of their foreign nationality': McKean, *supra*, n. 24, at 201.

[128] Lillich continues however: 'It must be emphasised that this conclusion is not tantamount to stating that international law now authorises discrimination against aliens in these areas. All one may conclude is that this particular instrument is not in and of itself the source of such a general norm of non-discrimination': *ibid*. 48.

[129] Multilateral Treaties Deposited with the Secretary-General as of 31 Dec. 1991. UN Doc. ST/LEG/SER.E/10, at 123 (1991).

Some members of the Committee have tended to assume that any differentiation in treatment between nationals and non-nationals is principally illegitimate.[130] One member's interpretation of article 2(3) reinforces the view that the only exception to this rule is to be found in relation to economic rights in developing countries.[131] At times individual Committee members have limited their attention to the provision of social benefits, health care, and education,[132] but often they have gone further to include employment rights.[133]

Criticism of such differential treatment has gone to the extent of finding violations in a number of cases. For example with regard to the French report, one member considered that the fact that a disabled adults allowance was only payable to French nationals was contrary to article 2.[134] Similarly, in the case of Costa Rica, it was considered that the restrictions upon the trade union rights of non-nationals constituted a violation of the Covenant.[135] Although these cases only represented the views of individual members,[136] the Committee as a whole has since expressed its concern about foreign workers being barred from holding trade union office in Senegal.[137]

The reluctance of the Committee to be unequivocal in its defence of the equal treatment of aliens would seem to be a result of the force of State practice.[138] For example, many States reporting to the Committee operate different systems of social security in relation to non-nationals,[139]

---

[130] General Guidelines, E/C.12/1991/1, at 2.

[131] It was commented with respect to a provision in the Austrian report (E/1984/6/Add.17, para. 49(b)) that if foreigners in Austria did not receive the same benefits as nationals, it would be contrary to art. 2(3) as it was not a developing country. Alvarez Vita, E/C.12/1988/SR.3, at 4–5, para. 13; Badawi El Sheikh, E/C.12/1988/SR.4, at 8, para. 45.

[132] *See e.g.* Texier, E/C.12/1987/SR.12, at 5, para. 16.

[133] One member commented thus that measures taken under Jordanian law to restrict the employment of foreigners were contrary to the non-discrimination clauses of the Covenant. Konate, E/C.12/1987/SR.7, at 10, para. 51.

[134] Alvarez Vita, E/C.12/1989/SR.12, at 12, para. 61. This conclusion in itself was somewhat suspect given the French declaration on ratification regarding restrictions on aliens' rights to social security and employment. It was argued that the provision should be considered in the light of arts. 9 and 2 read together; as there was no declaration in respect to art. 2, there was a breach of the provisions of the Convention. Alvarez Vita, E/C.12/1989/SR.13, at 9, para. 38. That this did not represent the view of the Committee as a whole is reflected in the Committee's concluding observations which merely state that 'the observation was made'. UN Doc. E/1989/22, at 35, para. 160 (1989).

[135] *See* Alvarez Vita, E/C.12/1990/SR.40, at 12, para. 52.

[136] This was made particularly clear in the case of Costa Rica. Alston, E/C.12/1990/SR.50, at 4, para. 28.

[137] Concluding observations on the report of Senegal, E/C.12/1993/18, at 2, para. 8.

[138] It might also be noted that the Committee on the Elimination of Racial Discrimination has tended to allow the differential treatment of non-nationals. Meron, *supra*, n. 13, at 312. Similarly, during the drafting of art. 26 ICCPR, States were not ready to accept that aliens should have equal rights as citizens. *See* Ramcharan, *supra*, n. 1, at 263.

[139] *See e.g.* Netherlands, E/C.12/1989/5, E/1989/22, at 4; Luxembourg, E/C.12/1990/CRP.4/Add.4, at 5, para. 16.

particularly where reciprocal agreements are in force.[140] In addition it is somewhat unlikely that States would consider themselves bound by a provision forcing them to eliminate any restrictions on the employment of aliens.[141]

However, these facts alone do not necessarily imply that the application of the principle of non-discrimination is totally irrelevant. For example, in the majority of cases, differential treatment is justified on the basis of economics.[142] It is open to the Committee to determine the validity of the differential treatment of aliens by assessing whether it is motivated by sound economic reasons or mere prejudice.[143] In this respect one member of the Committee commented that the Jordanian report:

seemed to indicate that foreigners were penalized solely because they were foreigners, rather than because they threatened the employment opportunities of Jordanian nationals—in short, that foreigners were the object of discrimination.[144]

If this approach is adopted by the Committee, it could be said that even though equality of treatment is not necessarily prescribed, discrimination on the basis of nationality is by no means legitimate. The question for the Committee is to what extent differential treatment is legitimate.

Moreover, even if non-nationals are not entitled to equal treatment in all respects, it is important to stress that this does not deprive them of all rights under the Covenant. Certainly, in so far as the Covenant establishes the rights of 'everyone', non-nationals would have a right to the enjoyment of the minimum core content of those rights. Thus, in practice, the Committee will censure situations where aliens enjoy few rights and are the object of exploitation.[145]

---

[140] *Cf.* Mahalic D. and Mahalic J., 'The Limitation Provisions of the International Convention on the Elimination of All Forms of Racial Discrimination' (1987) 9 *Hum. Rts. Q* 74, at 78. It might be difficult to establish then that a State must not discriminate against a particular nationality even if that were to be considered inequitable. *See contra*, Lerner N., *The Convention on the Elimination of All Forms of Racial Discrimination* (1980), 30.

[141] However, immigration policies have not been above criticism, *see* Grissa, E/C.12/1993/SR.24, at 12, para. 49. In this regard the Limburg Principles state that 'as a general rule the Covenant applies equally to nationals and non-nationals'. Limburg Principles, *supra*, n. 54, at 127, para. 42.

Whereas restrictions are usually accepted on the employment of aliens, this is not so with respect to the conditions of employment. A number of ILO Conventions operate in this area: *e.g.* the Migration for Employment Convention (Revised) of 1949 (No. 97), 120 UNTS 71; and the Migrant Workers (Supplementary Provisions) Convention of 1975 (No. 143), 1120 UNTS 77. It might be noted that art. 1(2) of the Racial Discrimination Convention provides that its non-discrimination provisions do not apply to distinctions, exclusions, or restrictions made by a State party between citizens and non-citizens.

[142] *See* Lillich, *supra*, n. 127, at 123.

[143] It is by no means axiomatic that aliens are prejudicial to the economy of a State. *See* Konate, E/C.12/1987/SR.7, at 2, para. 2. Meron comments in this light: 'It can perhaps be argued that economic constraints may justify limiting some entitlements (such as welfare or health care) to citizens, but limiting employment-related benefits would not be supportable under this rationale': Meron, *supra*, n. 13, at 312.

[144] Konate, E/C.12/1987/SR.7, at 2, para. 2.

[145] Members of the Committee expressed great concern over the position of Haitian workers

(c) Wealth

The general limitations upon the poor to equality of access or opportunity with regard to employment, education, culture, or housing have led some commentators to regard 'wealth' as an additional ground upon which discrimination is prohibited. Hence the Czechoslovakian representative commented before the Committee that:

The fact that some persons might be prevented from enjoying certain rights because they did not have the means to do so could be regarded as *de facto* discrimination.[146]

The Committee does seem to be concerned about extreme inequalities in wealth[147] and inadequate action being taken on behalf of the poor.[148] Recognition has also been made of the particular disadvantage of the poor in the area of access to culture.[149] Some members have occasionally made an express recognition of the link between poverty and discrimination.[150]

The major problem with regard to positing 'wealth' as an independent ground of discrimination is that the majority of cases of such discrimination will involve a simultaneous violation of article 2(2) and one of the substantive articles of the Convention. The independent utility of the non-discrimination provision becomes apparent only when the State has gone further than it is obliged to under the provisions of the Covenant.[151] A case in point might be the establishment of special schools for the academically gifted. If access to such a school were restricted to males only or members of a minority ethnic group, article 2(2) would quite legitimately be invoked. However, to restrict access to the wealthy by the requirement of fee payment would rarely be considered discriminatory.[152] The fact that access to many higher social 'goods' often depends upon economic wealth suggests that 'wealth' itself is often a legitimate ground for differential treatment and for that reason could hardly be considered 'suspect'.[153] One possible

---

on sugar plantations in the Dominican Republic. *See e.g.* Texier, E/C.12/1990/SR.44, at 13, para. 54.

[146] E/C.12/1987/SR.12, at 10, para. 40.

[147] Sparsis, E/C.12/1988/SR.12, at 12, para. 63; Sparsis, E/C.12/1989/SR.16, at 17, para. 92; Simma, E/C.12/1990/SR.8, at 10, para. 43. Simma commented in relation to the Columbian report that the Committee had to address itself to the underlying causes of difficulties, mentioning 'in particular the lack of equality . . . and the apparent lack of concern of the upper classes for the problems of the most vulnerable': E/C.12/1990/SR.13, at 11, para. 47.

[148] *See e.g.* Alston, E/C.12/1990/SR.11, at 5, para. 24.

[149] *See e.g.* Texier, E/C.12/1990/SR.16, at 9, para. 44.

[150] One member thus commented in regard to the vast disparities in wealth, that 'Santiago is a city of apartheid'. Texier, E/C.12/1988/SR.12, at 10, para. 50.

[151] Assuming that the right is 'autonomous' in nature. *See below*, text accompanying nn. 158–75.

[152] This is a case of indirect discrimination. Were the discrimination to be direct i.e. on the basis of parental income irrespective of ability to pay (e.g. through a scholarship), there would be more grounds for objection. Additionally, if the establishment of such a school drew finances away from projects that were aimed at the relief of poverty and disadvantagement, the State might be criticized for confusing its priorities.

[153] With respect to wealth classifications in the US *see* Polivou, *supra*, n. 3, at 437–44.

justification for this could be that, unlike sex, age or race, wealth is not an immutable or inherent attribute of the human person and therfore may be excluded under the *eiusdem generis* principle.

2 *The Suspect Nature of Classifications*

Given the emphasis that race,[154] sex,[155] and religion[156] have been accorded on the international plane, it may be argued that, in assessing the legitimacy of differential treatment, actions based upon such grounds should be given stricter scrutiny.[157] This may be appropriate given the extraordinary prominence given to racial discrimination in international case law,[158] and the emphasis on sexual discrimination in the Covenant.[159]

As far as the Committee is concerned the position of women has been given by far the most consideration. Questions are invariably asked about equality before the law,[160] equal rights,[161] and factual differences in the

[154] For evidence of the international community's interest in racial discrimination *see* The International Convention on the Suppression and Punishment of the Crime of Apartheid, GA Resn. 3068, 28 UN GAOR, Supp. (No. 30), at 166, UN Doc. A/9030 (1973), 1015 UNTS 243; The Declaration on the Elimination of All Forms of Racial Discrimination, GA Resn. 1904, 18 UN GAOR, Supp. (No. 15), at 35, UN Doc. A/5515, (1964); The Convention on the Elimination of all Forms of Racial Discrimination, *supra*, n. 55.

[155] For evidence of the interest of the international community in the status of women *see* The Convention on the Political Rights of Women, GA Resn. 640, 7 UN GAOR, Supp. (No. 20), at 27, UN Doc. A/2361 (1952), 193 UNTS 135 (1953); The Convention on the Nationality of Married Women (1957), 309 UNTS 65; The Declaration on the Elimination of All Forms of Discrimination Against Women, GA Resn. 2263, 22 UN GAOR, Supp. (No. 16), at 35, UN Doc. A/6716, (1967); The Convention on the Elimination of all Forms of Discrimination Against Women, *supra*, n. 56.

[156] Bayefsky, *supra*, n. 13, at 19. *See generally* Benito E., *Elimination of All Forms of Intolerance and Discrimination Based on Religion and Belief* (1989).

[157] For the US practice as regards levels of scrutiny *see* Moon, *supra*, n. 6, at 688–9. For the position under the ECHR *see Abdulaziz, Cabales and Balkandali* v. *United Kingdom*, Eur. Ct. HR, Series A, vol. 94, judgment of 28 May 1985 (1985) 7 EHRR 471, where the court stated (para. 78): 'the advancement of the equality of the sexes is today a major goal in the member States of the Council of Europe. This means that very weighty reasons would have to be advanced before a difference of treatment on the grounds of sex could be regarded as compatible with the Convention.'

[158] Judge Tanaka commented in the *South West Africa Cases* that 'we consider that the norm of non-discrimination or non-separation on the basis of race has become a rule of customary international law', *supra*, n. 9, at 293. Moreover in its advisory opinion in the *Namibia Case* the ICJ stated 'to enforce distinctions, exclusions, restrictions and limitations exclusively based on grounds of race, colour, descent, or national or ethnic origin which constitute a denial of fundamental human rights is a flagrant violation of the purposes and principles of the Charter.' *Legal Consequences for States of the Continued Presence of South Africa in Namibia (South West Africa) Notwithstanding Security Council 276 (1970)*, Advisory Opinion (1971) *ICJ Rep.* 3, at 57. Similarly the ICJ has indicated that rules concerning racial discrimination have a force *erga omnes. Barcelona Traction Light and Power Case*, (1970) *ICJ Rep.* at 3, paras. 33–4.

[159] In addition to the mention of discrimination on the grounds of sex in art. 2(2), art. 3 mentions the equal rights of women, and art. 7(a)(i) the right of women to equal conditions of work.   [160] *See* above, n. 79.

[161] *See e.g.* the right of women to chose their own spouse, Rattray, E/C.12/1987/SR.8, at 7,

position of women in relation to men.[162] In a number of cases the Committee as a whole has expressed its concern over the position of women.[163] To this extent, the Committee could be said to exercise a particularly strict test as to differentiations *de jure* and *de facto* on the basis of sex.

The main failing of the Committee thus far is that it has not established any clear test for evaluating differences in treatment upon the grounds enumerated in article 2(2). It is submitted that in so far as the list of prohibited grounds is open-ended, virtually any difference in treatment is open to scrutiny by the Committee. The virtue of having specifically stated grounds, however, is not to prevent review of differentiations on other grounds, but rather to establish that certain classifications are *prima facie* suspect and therefore will be subject to more detailed scrutiny. As an initial step, then, it would be necessary for the Committee to establish what classifications it sees as falling within the realm of article 2(2), and the test by which State action will be reviewed.

D The Scope of the Non-Discrimination Provision

Some guarantees of non-discrimination only operate in relation to specific, narrowly defined areas, as in the ILO or UNESCO Conventions (which relate to employment and education). Article 2(2) of the ICESCR, in contrast, applies to a much broader range of rights. It provides that the guarantee of non-discrimination should operate in relation to all the economic, social, and cultural rights in the Covenant. However, by specifically referring to the rights in the Covenant, article 2(2) would appear to be a partially subordinate provision, prohibiting discrimination only in so far as it relates to matters covered by those rights.[164] Indeed, there is little

para. 26; Kouznetsov, E/C.12/1990/SR.2, at 12, para. 72.; the authority to start a business or open a bank account, Jimenez Butragueno, E/C.12/1989/SR.9, at 6, para. 24; differential retirement ages, Sviridov, E/C.12/1987/SR.6, at 5, para. 18. Simma, E/C.12/1988/SR.3, at 3, para. 8; the right to administer their own assets, Jimenez Butragueno, E/C.12/1987/SR.8, at 8, para. 33; restrictions on the employment of women, Alvarez Vita, E/C.12/1987/SR.6, at 11, para. 53; the right to travel abroad, Vysokayova, E/C.12/1994/SR.11, at 3, para. 9.

[162] *See e.g.* the number of women unemployed, Rattray, E/C.12/1987/SR.6, at 12, para. 66. Neneman, E/C.12/1987/SR.7, at 7, para. 29; access of women to social security, Rattray, E/C.12/1987/SR.6, at 13, para. 69; the proportion of women receiving technical training, Konate, E/C.12/1987/SR.7, at 2, para. 3; the percentage of women employed in the public sector, Muterahejuru, E/C.12/1987/SR.7, at 3, para. 7; the proportion of women in higher education, Jimenez Butragueno, E/C.12/1988/SR.3, at 8, para. 36; the percentage of women in management positions, Simma, E/C.12/1994/SR.8, at 8, para. 38; the existence of training and support for women's cooperatives, Simma, E/C.12/1989/SR.6, at 10, para. 45.

[163] *See e.g.* Concluding observations on report of Iran, E/C.12/1993/7, at 3, para. 6.

[164] Art. 3 similarly relates to 'all economic, social and cultural rights set forth in the present Covenant'. As a matter of comparison, it is thought that the ICCPR non-discrimination clause is limited to those rights recognized by that Convention. Ramcharan, *supra*, n. 1, at 257. This is also the practice of the European Court of Human Rights. Thus in the *Sunday Times Case*, Eur. Ct. HR, Series A, Vol. 30, judgment of 26 Apr. 1979 (1979–80) 2 EHRR 245, the Court

evidence to suggest that article 2(2) was intended to be wholly 'free-standing' or 'autonomous', in the sense of article 26 of the ICCPR.[165]

According to the traditional definition of discrimination adopted by a number of international treaties, the test for whether an action is discriminatory can be determined by whether it has a negative effect on the realization of the rights protected. For discrimination to have occurred, the difference in treatment must have the effect of 'nullifying' or 'impairing'[166] the recognition, enjoyment, or exercise[167] of human rights. To the extent that breach of the non-discrimination provision will inevitably involve a simultaneous violation of one of the substantive articles, the provision could be said to be superfluous.[168]

Three arguments mitigate against such a conclusion. First, even though there is often distinct correlation between covert discriminatory situations and general social stratification of power, wealth, prestige, and education, it is important to recognize that discrimination is not merely a consequence of that stratification, but also a cause.[169] As such the recognition and elimination of discrimination is central to the improvement of the well-being of such groups. Secondly, recognition of historical discrimination can serve to justify and even require positive and affirmative action programmes.[170] Finally, to the extent that the principle of non-discrimination may give rise to claims to positive State action in the realization of equality of

reaffirmed that 'Article 14 safeguards individuals, or groups of individuals, placed in comparable situations, from all discrimination in the enjoyment of the rights and freedoms set forth in the other normative provisions of the Convention and Protocols'.

[165] Art. 26 ICCPR has been interpreted as operating as an 'autonomous right' whose application was 'not limited to those rights which are provided for in the Covenant', *see* General Comment 18/37, *supra*, n. 57, para. 12. Thus, in practice, the HRC has dealt with matters outside the strict context of civil and political rights, *see e.g. Broeks* v. *Netherlands*, 2 Selected Decisions HRC, 196 (1987). *Cf.* Scott C., 'The Interdependence and Permeability of Human Rights Norms: Towards a Partial Fusion of the International Covenants on Human Rights', (1989) 27 *Osg HLJ* 769, at 851–9; Opsahl T., 'Equality in Human Rights Law with Particular Reference to Article 26 of the International Covenant on Civil and Political Rights', in Nowak M., Steurer D., and Tretter H. (eds.), *Progress in the Spirit of Human Rights* (1988), 51.

[166] ILO Convention, the Racial Discrimination Convention, and the Discrimination against Women Convention. The UNESCO Convention only includes the term 'impairing'. On the basis that 'nullifying' is the narrower term, meaning not merely a restriction on the enjoyment of a right, but the total denial of that right, 'impairment' can be said to cover the same field.

[167] The meaning of all of these three terms is unclear, particularly as to any differences between them. It is presumed that 'recognition' refers to the legal enactment of individual rights. Any de jure differentiation on a suspect ground would be discriminatory under this leg of the definition. 'Enjoyment' can be said to refer to the *de facto* realization of the rights in the Covenant. Finally 'exercise' perhaps relates most closely to the ability of each individual to enforce their rights through judicial or administrative remedies.

[168] Flew argues in this respect that the relief of poverty cannot be achieved through the promotion of equality but solely through growth and the production of wealth. Equality and non-discrimination thus retain little justification in his view. Flew A., *supra*, n. 17, at, 182–9.

[169] Schachter, *supra*, n. 19, at 296.   [170] *Ibid.* 295.

opportunity, the fulfilment of basic needs alone would not necessarily sufficiently dispose of State obligations with respect to disadvantaged groups.

The position under the European Convention is interesting in this regard. That a violation can occur merely by the discriminatory exercise of a particular right has been recognized by the European Court in the *Belgian Linguistic Case*[171] where it held with respect to the ECHR:

Article 6 of the Convention does not compel States to institute a system of appeal courts. A State which does set up such courts consequently goes beyond its obligations under Article 6. However it would violate that Article, read in conjunction with Article 14, were it to debar certain persons from these remedies without a legitimate reason while making them available to others in respect of the same type of actions.[172]

The Court appears to want to give the non-discrimination provision a degree of independence without implying that it operates outside the realm of the rights contained within the Convention.[173] Certainly, the Court has not been willing to deal with economic, social, and cultural rights for example.

There is evidence to suggest that article 2(2) is a strictly 'subordinate' non-discrimination clause. As a provision that lies in Part II of the Covenant, it may be viewed not as a right in itself, but rather a 'service provision', outlining obligations in relation to the substantive articles in Part III. Moreover, as it refers to the 'rights enunciated in the present Covenant', it may be limited in that respect.[174] However, neither of these factors

---

[171] *Supra*, n. 47.

[172] This passage has been interpreted variously by commentators. Dinstein argues that the court implied that the non-discrimination provision was free standing—that there could be a violation of art. 14 without there being a corresponding violation of any other art. Dinstein, *supra*, n. 13. On the other hand Bayefsky comments that this case underlines the fact that the discrimination clause has no independent existence in that the violation only occurred in conjunction with the substantive arts. Bayefsky, *supra*, n. 13, at 4.

It is interesting to note the view of Judge Fitzmaurice in the *National Union of Belgian Police Case*, Eur. Ct. HR, Series A, Vol. 19, Judgment of 27 Oct. 1975 (1979–80) 1 EHRR 578, where he argued that art. 14 was subordinate in that it only applied in so far as it related to a State obligation under the ECHR.

[173] This is underlined by its decision in *Inze* v. *Austria*, where it stated: 'Art. 14 complements the other substantive provisions of the Convention and its protocols. It has no independent existence, since it has effect solely in relation to the "rights and freedoms" safeguarded by those provisions. Although the application of art. 14 does not presuppose a breach of one or more of such provisions—and to this extent it is autonomous—there can be no room for its application unless the facts of the case fall within the ambit of one or more of the latter': *supra*, n. 69, para. 36.

[174] In its General Comment No. 18 (37) b/, c/, the Human Rights Committee implies that art. 2(1) ICCPR is indeed subordinate. In referring to art. 26 it states that it 'does not merely duplicate the guarantee already provided for in art. 2 but provides in itself an autonomous right.' As a result 'the principle of non-discrimination contained in art. 26 is not limited to those rights which are provided for in the Covenant': *supra*, n. 57, at 175, para. 12.

establishes whether or not the rather looser form of subordination adopted by the European Court will operate in the case of article 2(2).

Despite references to articles 2(2) and 3 as independent rights,[175] there is little evidence to suggest that the Committee views article 2(2) as fully autonomous in the sense of article 26 of the ICCPR.[176] Indeed any reference to violations of civil and political rights has been justified by their impact on economic, social, and cultural rights.[177] Given the more extensive supervisory mechanisms of the HRC, it would be unnecessary and duplicitous for the CESCR to enter into a review of discrimination in the field of civil and political rights.

On the other hand, several considerations suggest that the Committee is not ready to assign a strictly subordinate role to article 2(2). First, in dealing with questions of discrimination the Committee has not confined itself to rights explicitly laid down in the Covenant.[178] Secondly, it has clearly interpreted the notion of non-discrimination as one which calls for equality of access and opportunity.[179] It is this notion of equality, as noted above,[180] that has coloured the Committee's general approach to the implementation of the rights. To see non-discrimination as an objective as opposed to a procedural principle is to confer upon it an individual status.

The approach of the Committee would seem to be close to that of the European Court. While it will not concern itself with matters that do not fall within the general scope of economic, social, and cultural rights, it will not confine itself to combatting discrimination only in those areas where a violation of the substantive rights occurs. It is submitted that this is a suitable and balanced approach. To extend the scope of the provision beyond economic, social, and cultural rights would not only lead to possible conflicts with other human rights organs, but would impose too great a burden of work upon the Committee. On the other hand, to restrict

---

[175] This might be the inferred from the grouping of such provisions together with the substantive rights in General Comment No. 3, ESCOR, Supp. 3, Annex III, at 84, para. 5, UN Doc. E/C.12/1990/8 (1991).

[176] Members of the Committee have, however, asked questions relating to civil and political rights, *see* Simma, E/C.12/1994/SR.8, at 6, para. 27.

[177] *See e.g.* Simma, E/C.12/1990/SR.42, at 12, para. 57.

[178] *e.g.* the Committee has considered questions such as: the authority of women to start a business or open a bank account, Jimenez Butragueno, E/C.12/1989/SR.9, at 6, para. 24; differential retirement ages, Sviridov, E/C.12/1987/SR.6, at 5, para. 18, Simma, E/C.12/1988/SR.3, at 3, para. 8; the right of men to paid leave to look after children, Jimenez Butragueno, E/C.12/1987/SR.12, at 4, para. 14, Texier, E/C.12/1987/SR.19, at 10, para. 47; persecution of the Baha'is, Alvarez Vita, E/C.12/1990/SR.42, at 11, para. 56.

[179] In the Committee's guidelines, reference is made to equality of opportunity in relation to art. 6, and equality of access with regard to arts. 11 and 13. *Supra*, n. 58.

Meron comments that the Committee on the Elimination of Racial Discrimination has dealt with distinctions on the grounds of race in a similar manner. He concludes that 'the "common law" of the Convention is based on the notion of equality, rather than on its definition of racial discrimination'. Meron, *supra*, n. 13, at 291.

[180] *See above*, text accompanying nn. 28–31.

the provision to a subordinate status would deprive it of any substantive value.

V. STATE OBLIGATIONS

A Immediate or Progressive Implementation?

Whereas the obligation under article 2(1) of the ICESCR is progressive in nature, this does not seem to be the case with regard to article 2(2). The fact of its physical separation from article 2(1) and the inclusion of the word 'guarantee' draw one to the conclusion that States are under an obligation to eliminate discrimination immediately.[181] This was the interpretation advocated during the drafting of the Covenant,[182] and has been endorsed in the Limburg Principles,[183] and in the practice of the Committee. The Committee expressly stated that it considered articles 2(2) and 3 as being 'capable of immediate application by judicial and other organs in many national legal systems'.[184]

It would seem quite apparent that States are capable of eliminating most *de jure* discrimination immediately. There is certainly little justification for introducing new legislation or administrative practices that are discriminatory.[185] The most important factor appears to be the contention that the elimination of *de jure* discrimination does not involve significant economic expenditure. Thus in the case of Zaïre, which was criticized for having a law that required women to ask permission from their husbands to work outside the home, it was felt that the question of economic development was irrelevant.[186] Klerk argues that, even in times of economic crisis, 'the introduction or the continuation of discriminatory practices can never be "compatible with the nature of these rights"'.[187] Accordingly, the promotion of the general welfare cannot be achieved at the expense of one section of

---

[181] Klerk argues this point from the fact that the progressive implementation provision of art. 2(1) only applies to the substantive art. in part III. Art. 2(2) is not subordinate to the other provisions in Part II. Klerk, *supra*, n. 12, at 261.

[182] The Lebanese proposal to include the word 'guarantee' was preferred to that of the representative of France, which provided for progressive implementation. 8 UN ESCOR (274th mtg), at 13, UN Doc. E/CN.4/SR.274, (1952). A proposal to amalgamate the first two para. of art. 2 (UN Doc. A/C.3/L.1054 and Add.1, (1962)) was considered unacceptable in the Third Committee. 17 UN GAOR, C.3, (1206th mtg), paras. 10–13, 11 UN Doc. A/C.3/SR.1206 (1962).

[183] Para. 35 reads: 'Art. 2(2) calls for immediate application and involves an explicit guarantee on behalf of the States parties. It should, therefore, be made subject to judicial review and other recourse procedures': *supra*, n. 54, at 127.

[184] General Comment No. 3, *supra*, n. 175, at 4, para. 5.

[185] Klerk, *supra*, n. 12, at 262; This was also the conclusion of the Third Committee, 17 UN GAOR, Annex, (Ag. Item 43), para. 64, UN Doc. A/ 5365 (1962).

[186] *See* Texier, E/C.12/1988/SR.17, at 6, para. 36.   [187] Klerk, *supra*, n. 12, at 263.

society. 'Non-discrimination is not a favour that can be granted only in a time of a growing economy.'[188]

However, it would be wrong to suggest that the elimination of discrimination will always be capable of being achieved immediately. First, it is undoubtedly true that certain forms of corrective action will inevitably involve considerable financial expenditure. For example, the elimination of discrimination as regards retirement ages or remuneration in employment[189] may involve employees being paid more for longer periods of time. Secondly, whereas *de jure* discrimination may be eliminated by the creation and enforcement of relevant legislation, the existence of *de facto* discrimination, as evidenced through material inequalities and individual prejudice, is a matter that necessitates longer-term social and educational programmes aimed eliminating discrimination in a progressive manner.[190] It is relevant to note here that the specialized instruments on discrimination all imply that States are entitled to eliminate discrimination gradually.[191] This conclusion is more evident in so far as States are required to combat discrimination by third parties, and to achieve equality of opportunity.

B The Type of Action Required

As regards *de facto* discrimination,[192] legislative action must be considered a necessary first step in any policy. Members of the Committee have looked towards legislative measures as evidence of a State's commitment to eliminating discrimination.[193] Thus one member commented that:

The Covenant did not automatically imply that legislation was an indispensable component of a policy designed to eliminate discrimination in employment, for example. However, it was evident that, if that were the interpretation adopted by Governments, the burden of proof would lie with those Governments, which would therefore be expected to show that the non-legislative measures that they had taken

---

[188] Klerk, *supra*, n. 12, at 264.   [189] *See below*, Ch. 6.

[190] Cohen has drawn a similar distinction. He sees action to eliminate elements of discrimination in policies, programmes, procedure, and criteria as 'corrective action'; whereas action to give disadvantaged groups equal standing with the majority he calls 'compensatory action'. Cohen C., 'Affirmative Action and the Rights of the Majority', in Fried L., *Minorities: Community and Identity* (1983), 353, at 355.

[191] ILO Convention, art. 2; UNESCO Convention arts. 3 and 4; and Conv. EDAW, art. 2. ICERD art. 2(1) also appears to allow for progressive implementation, but in art. 5 requires States parties to 'guarantee' equality before the law. Cf. *Yilmaz-Dogan* v. *Netherlands*, CERD Report, 43 UN GAOR, Supp. (No. 18), at 59 (1988).

[192] Action to combat *de jure* discrimination merely involves repealing the offending legislation or administrative directive. *See e.g.* Jimenez Butragueno, E/C.12/1990/SR.42, at 16, para. 86.

[193] Questions have been asked as to the legal prohibition of discrimination against women, Jimenez Butragueno, E/C.12/1987/SR.7, at 6, para. 23; and legislative measures taken to prevent dismissal of pregnant women, Mrachkov, E/C.12/1988/SR.10, at 6, para. 25.

effectively ensured the elimination of discrimination and that it was not essential to take legislative measures.[194]

It is evident that any legislative measures taken, to be effective, should be accompanied by judicial remedies.[195] The provision of such remedies seems to be particularly appropriate given the duty to 'guarantee' the exercise of the rights without discrimination.

Although legislation is certainly important, it will not necessarily be completely effective. As suggested above, those aspects of discrimination which relate to social attitudes cannot be eliminated immediately merely through the enforcement of relevant legislation. Here, other measures, particularly educational and social, are more appropriate.[196] It has been suggested in the Committee that States are expected to undertake pro-grammes to combat the discriminatory attitudes and prejudices of the popu-lation.[197] In particular, action should be directed towards the elimination of stereotypes whether racial, religious, sexual, or other.[198]

The need to take measures beyond legislative action is particularly evid-ent in the pursuit of equality of opportunity. Inequality of opportunity is often the result of inequality in the economic condition of various groups in society, of social and cultural expectations that affect potential develop-ment, or of differences that result from the education and training received. Thus action in favour of real equality of opportunity calls for extensive measures in the whole field of economic, social, and cultural rights, particu-larly as regards education, vocational training, and social promotion and protection.[199] As one member of the Committee recognized:

There was . . . a need to transcend the formal approach to equality in order to gain insight into the obstacles to equality in daily life, and the arrangements made through education, for instance, to make sure that equality really was achieved.[200]

---

[194] Alston, E/C.12/1987/SR.6, at 3, para. 8. In its draft General Comment on Persons with Disabilities the Committee comments that 'comprehensive anti-discrimination legislation in relation to disability would seem to be indispensable in virtually all States parties', *supra*, n. 98, at 5, para. 16.

[195] Members of the Committee have thus asked *inter alia*: what penalties are provided for violations of non-discrimination laws in employment, Simma, E/C.12/1989/SR.15, at 2, para. 3; how many decisions have been made regarding discrimination in housing, Rattray, E/C.12/1990/SR.2, at 11, para. 63; What effective remedies exist in the courts for women, Jimenez Butragueno, E/C.12/1988/SR.19, at 4, para. 12.

[196] A memorandum of the Secretary-General recognized that: 'It is clear that forms of discrimination which deny legal rights may and should be fought by legal measures, while those which comprise merely social treatment must chiefly be fought by education and by other social measures': UN Doc. E/CN.4/Sub.2/8, at 2 (1947).

[197] *See e.g.* Alvarez Vita, E/C.12/1988/SR.14, at 6, para. 32.

[198] *See e.g.* Jimenez Butragueno, E/C.12/1990/SR.16, at 8, para. 37. *See also* Valticos N., *International Labour Law* (1979), 111.

[199] *See e.g.* Concluding observations on report of Iceland, E/C.12/1993/15, at 3, para. 8.

[200] Rattray, E/C.12/1987/SR.16, at 9, para. 40.

This requires not only the removal of any impediments that way stand in the way of equality of opportunity,[201] but also that certain positive steps are taken to promote the position of vulnerable and disadvantaged groups in society. The degree to which such affirmative action is necessary will be discussed below. It is clear nevertheless that legislative measures alone will not be sufficient in such cases.[202]

C Affirmative and Protective Action

1 The Legitimacy of Affirmative Action

The concept of discrimination in international law, while requiring strict scrutiny of any differential treatment based upon a suspect classification, does not automatically prohibit differential treatment if justified by some socially relevant objective.[203] Affirmative action programmes,[204] involving the adoption of special measures to benefit socially, economically, or culturally deprived groups, may therefore be considered legitimate in so far as they are aimed at promoting the social well-being of such groups.[205] Further, the principle of equality of opportunity in its strong sense may actually be seen to require preferential treatment for groups which currently suffer from *de facto* inequality.[206]

Despite no reference to affirmative action in the text of the Covenant, it is clear from the *travaux préparatoires* that such measures were not intended to be considered discriminatory. During the drafting of the Covenant, India suggested that an explanatory paragraph should be included in

---

[201] *See e.g.* Jimenez Butragueno, E/C.12/1991/SR.4, at 13, para. 67.

[202] *See e.g.* Texier, E/C.12/1989/SR.10, at 8, para. 43.

[203] *See* Mckean, *supra*, n. 24, at 288.

[204] Other terms for the same concept are 'reverse discrimination' or 'positive discrimination'. The term 'affirmative action' is preferred, as technically, such measures do not amount to discrimination as defined in this work.

[205] Moon comments that classifications which benefit disadvantaged groups should not be precluded as they are 'not motivated by prejudice which is what the test of strict scrutiny is designed to detect'. *Supra*, n. 6, at 691. On the justification for affirmative action *see* Dworkin R., *Taking Rights Seriously* (1977), 227–9; Nickel J., 'Discrimination and Morally Relevant Characteristics' in Gross B., *Reverse Discrimination* (1977), 288; Tur R., 'Justifications of Reverse Discrimination' in Stewart M., *Law, Morality and Rights* (1979), 259.

[206] *See above*, text accompanying nn. 18–20. Goldstein argues that 'even in the unusual cases in which equality requires differential treatment, it is still limited to that: i.e., differential, not preferential, treatment is required.' Goldstein S., 'Reverse Discrimination—Reflections of a Jurist' (1985) 15 *Isr. YHR* 28, at 30. It is unclear exactly what he means by such a distinction as it might be argued that any difference in treatment involves some form of preference. A more valid distinction could be drawn between differences in treatment that are intended to promote a vulnerable group in a general sense and those that aspire to achieving some numerical representation. The latter aspires to a form of absolute equality, whereas the former may be so constructed to allow for the intercession of individual choice, presenting less of a restriction upon the rights of members of the majority.

the text of article 2 specifying that: 'Special measures for the advancement of any socially and educationally backward sections of society shall not be construed as 'distinction' under this article'.[207] It was explained that the principle of non-discrimination:

raised certain problems in the case of the particularly backward groups still to be found in many under-developed countries. In his country, the constitution and the laws provided for special measures for the social and cultural betterment of such groups; measures of that kind were essential for the achievement of true social equality in highly heterogeneous societies. He felt certain that the authors of the draft Covenant had not intended to prohibit such measures, which were in fact protective measures. . . . He therefore thought it essential to make it clear that such protective measures would not be construed as discriminatory within the meaning of the paragraph.[208]

The proposal was finally withdrawn, it having been made clear that the three-power amendment implicitly included this understanding.[209] On an analysis of the *travaux préparatoires* of both the ICESCR and the ICCPR, Thornberry concludes that 'the concept of affirmative action . . . is not contrary to the law of the Covenants'.[210] He goes on to point out that since article 1(4) of ICERD and article 4(1) of Conv. EDAW[211] do contain explicit statements about the legitimacy of affirmative action measures, a contrary interpretation in the context of the Covenants would display an 'extraordinary lack of congruence'.[212]

Even if the *travaux préparatoires* do recognize the legitimacy of affirmative action, there is little indication outside the scope of article 3[213] that such positive measures are in fact required. Facing a similar situation as regards the ICCPR the Human Rights Committee has made a positive statement in

---

[207] UN Doc. A/C.3/SR.1182, para. 17 (1962). As an alternative he sought the insertion of an explanatory statement in the report.

Similarly, a Belgian proposal (UN Doc. A/C.3/L.1030 (1962)) to add a clause to art. 2(2), explaining that the prohibition did not extend to protective measures taken on the basis of age and sex, was withdrawn on the basis that this was understood in the terms of the three-power amendment. UN Doc. A/C.3/SR.1204, para. 29 (1962).

[208] UN Doc. A/C.3/SR.1183, paras. 12, 29 (1962). It was clear however in speaking of 'protective measures' the Indian representative, in commenting that such measures were essentially temporary, meant affirmative action. UN Doc. A/C.3/SR.1257, para. 18 (1963).

[209] This is the import of the discussion over the use of the term 'discrimination' as opposed to 'distinction'. *See above*, text accompanying nn. 41–5. During the drafting of art. 27 ICCPR, relating to the rights of minorities, it was recognized that differential treatment might be granted to them to ensure real equality of status with the other elements of the population. UN Doc. A/2929, *supra*, n. 93, at 181.

[210] Thornberry P., *International Law and the Rights of Minorities* (1991), 284.

[211] The Committee on the Elimination of Discrimination against Women has recommended that 'States Parties make more use of temporary special measures such as positive action, preferential treatment or quota systems to advance women's integration into education, the economy, politics and employment'. General Recommendation 5, (7th Sess. 1988), at 109, UN Doc. A/43/38 (1988).

[212] *Ibid.*   [213] *See* UN Doc. A/C.3/SR.1182, para. 11 (1962).

this regard. In its General Comment 18/37 it stated that the 'principle of equality sometimes requires States parties to take affirmative action in order to diminish or eliminate conditions which cause or help to perpetuate discrimination prohibited by the Covenant'.[214] On this basis, commentators have argued that States are indeed obliged to take affirmative action for the benefit of disadvantaged groups.[215]

The Committee has directed a number of questions towards affirmative action especially as regards people with physical disabilities[216] and ethnic or racial minorities.[217] In doing so it seems to accept the legitimacy of such action even if there has been a residual concern over its ultimate purpose.[218] Nevertheless, it has not explicitly recognized the obligatory nature of affirmative action. It could be argued that the Committee implicitly recognizes such an obligation through its requirement that States concentrate upon the situation of vulnerable and disadvantaged groups in society,[219] but this is nevertheless a matter that ideally should be made clear in a future General Comment.

2 *The Form of Affirmative Action*

A few general remarks could be made about the possible form and content of affirmative action programmes with respect to economic, social, and cultural rights. It is clear that affirmative action can take a number of different forms.[220] At one level it might merely involve the provision of special benefits to disadvantaged groups such as advice, training, housing, or food. This is quite uncontroversial; most States operate some form of redistributive process in which certain groups in society are identified as being legitimate recipients of special treatment or benefits (for example, the poor, the elderly, and the sick).[221] Indeed, as noted above, a basic level of

---

[214] General Comment 18/37, *supra*, n. 57, para. 10. *See also* ILO Convention, art. 2; UNESCO Convention, art. 4; ICERD, art. 2(2); Conv. EDAW, art. 3.

[215] *See e.g.* Ramcharan, *supra*, n. 1, at 261.

[216] *See e.g.* Jimenez Butragueno, E/C.12/1989/SR.15, at 4, para. 15; Fofana, E/C.12/1990/SR.11, at 4, para. 19; *ibid.*, E/C.12/1991/SR.4, at 12, para. 64.

[217] Questions have been asked as to: measures taken to ensure ethnic balance in schools, Badawi El Sheikh, E/C.12/1989/SR.10, at 10, para. 59; special treatment given to racial minorities in employment, Wimer Zambrano, E/C.12/1987/SR.20, at 10, para. 45; special measures taken to ensure respect for cultural life of the gipsy community, Texier, E/C.12/1988/SR.14, at 7, para. 41; Alvarez Vita, E/C.12/1991/SR.11, at 13, para. 75.

[218] *See e.g.* alarm expressed at preferential treatment given to families of war veterans in provision of scholarships, Jimenez Butragueno, E/C.12/1993/SR.10, at 8, para. 30.

[219] As noted above, this conclusion depends upon whether the action is seen to be directed towards the realization of the rights themselves or at achieving equality of opportunity. *See above*, text accompanying nn. 30–1. A more explicit statement is to be found in the Draft General Comment, *supra*, n. 98, at 5–6, paras. 17–18.

[220] *See* Gross B., *Discrimination in Reverse: Is Turnabout Fair Play?* (1978), at 18.

[221] Goldstein accedes to this which he considers as an integral part of the political process, *supra*, n. 206, at 31.

redistribution is itself necessitated by any process aimed at the realization of the rights in the Covenant.

At another level affirmative action might take the form of quota systems in public employment, education, or employment training.[222] It is argued that quota systems, which envisage the distribution of social goods on the basis of suspect classifications, discriminate against those who are deprived of employment, for example, as the result of a requirement of numerical representation.[223] They are further criticized for serving to disadvantage other vulnerable groups that have similar claims to equality of opportunity,[224] for actually contributing to hostility and resentment between social groups,[225] and for failing to take into account the fundamental element of individual choice. The operation of quota systems may be justified, however, on the basis that the advancement of a particular group is as socially relevant a reason for the distribution of social goods as, for example, capacity and merit.[226] That is does envisage a form of equality of result is itself not conclusive, as that is an inevitable element of any action directed towards the achievement of a real, rather than a merely formal, equality of opportunity.

Articles 7(c) and 13(2)(c) appear to rule out the possibility of quotas being imposed in the contexts of promotion in employment and access to higher education. Article 7(c) stipulates that everyone should have equal opportunity to be promoted in employment 'subject to no consideration other than those of seniority and competence'. Similarly, article 13(2)(c) provides that higher education shall be made equally accessible to all 'on the basis of capacity'. Both articles seem to prohibit advantages being given on other grounds, however socially desirable. A case could be made, nevertheless, for the operation of quota systems in each case on the basis that the terms of articles 7(c) and 13(2)(c) are open to 'progressive achievement'. Thus, a system in which a proportion of places in higher education is set aside for students of a particular group could be justified if it could be shown that it would ultimately contribute to the achievement of equal access on the basis of capacity at some stage in the future. Even then, that wider concerns of social utility could not be used as justificatory evidence means that the possibilities for imposing quotas with respect to higher education and employment are strictly limited.

Members of the Committee have given little indication of what forms of positive measures they consider to be legitimate. Recognition has been given to of a wide range of training and fiscal measures[227] but no objection

---

[222] *See e.g.* in the US, *Bakke* v. *Regents of the University of California*, 483 US 265 (1978).
[223] Cohen, *supra*, n. 190, at 356; Schachter, *supra*, n. 19, at 295.
[224] Goldstein, *supra*, n. 206, at 39.   [225] Schachter, *supra*, n. 19, at 305.
[226] Dworkin, *supra*, n. 205, at 227–9.
[227] Questions have been asked *inter alia* as to: subsidies to allow poor access to cultural life,

has as yet been made regarding the imposition of quotas.[228] It is submitted that the Committee should at least assess the nature and extent of any affirmative action measures by reference to the purpose for which they were instituted. Not only should such action conform to the necessity of promoting equality of opportunity, its extent should also be proportionate to the measure of existing disadvantagement. Consideration should thus be given to other possible courses of action that do not involve the apportionment of benefits on the basis of 'suspect classifications'. The imposition of quotas might be justified as a measure to remedy a particularly urgent situation of disadvantagement that is closely associated with *de facto* discrimination against one social group. It should be remembered, nevertheless, that such affirmative measures are to be instituted as a temporary expedient, and should not form part of a permanent strategy.

3 A Case of Affirmative Action: Minority Groups

The question of affirmative action is particularly problematic with regard to ethnic and racial minorities.[229] On the one hand the social marginalization of such groups may require their being integrated within, or at least not excluded from, the State-development process.[230] On the other hand, the need to maintain their cultural independence and self-determination argues in favour of positive measures to ensure development as separate entities. This tension was apparent during the drafting of article 27 of the ICCPR in a discussion on whether the obligations in respect of minorities were positive or merely negative.[231]

There is no provision within the Covenant that specifically requires States to take positive measures to protect or promote the rights of minorities.[232] It does arguably recognize the different needs of ethnic minorities particu-

---

Neneman, E/C.12/1988/SR.3, at 9, para. 43; training and support for women's co-operatives, Simma, E/C.12/1989/SR.6, at 10, para. 45.

[228] Quotas referred to have included: measures to ensure ethnic balance in schools, Badawi El Sheikh, E/C.12/1989/SR.10, at 10, para. 59; a law reserving 2 per cent of jobs for the disabled, Jimenez Butragueno, E/C.12/1989/SR.15, at 4, para. 15.

[229] Capotorti emphasizes that while the questions of non-discrimination and minority protection are distinct in that the former requires uniform treatment and the latter special treatment, they are in fact 'two aspects of the same problem: that of fully ensuring the equal rights to all persons': *supra*, n. 19, at 14. *See also* McKean, *supra*, n. 24, at 142. The HRC points out, however, that art. 27 ICCPR (relating to the rights of persons belonging to minorities) may be distinguished from the general non-discrimination clause in art. 2(1) in that the latter 'applies to all individuals within the territory': General Comment No. 23(50), UN Doc. CCPR/C/21/Rev.1/Add.5, at 2, para. 4 (1994).

[230] Cf. Muterahejuru, E/C.12/1992/SR.4, at 12, para. 54.

[231] *See also* Thornberry, *supra*, n. 210, at 178–80; Cholewinski R., 'State Duty to Ethnic Minorities: Positive or Negative?' (1988) 10 *Hum. Rts. Q* 344; Sohn L., 'The Rights of Minorities' in Henkin L. (ed.), *The International Bill of Rights* (1981), 270.

[232] Konate, E/C.12/1992/SR.17, at 3, para. 9.

larly as regards their cultural identity. Although article 15 merely states that everyone has the right to 'take part in cultural life', a recognition of legitimate differences in belief and tradition is to be found in article 13(3) and (4). Under that article, parents have the right to establish and choose schools other than those established by the public authorities. Similarly, the reference to self-determination in article 1 of the Covenant may be interpreted as implying that minorities have a right to pursue their own 'economic, social, and cultural development' without excessive interference from the authorities.[233] Although these provisions appear to stress freedom from State interference in the maintenance of an independent identity, the question remains of the extent to which the Covenant places positive obligations upon States to promote the cultural rights of minorities.

Despite the obvious pitfalls in defining 'ethnic minorities',[234] members of the Committee have endorsed the idea that they are entitled to have their independence respected.[235] It follows that ethnic groups and indigenous populations should have the right to express themselves in their own language, enjoy their own culture,[236] and establish their own educational institutions if they choose to do so.[237] In addition, members have generally been critical of attempts to assimilate such groups into the mainstream,[238]

[233] As the Human Rights Committee stated with respect to art. 27 ICCPR: 'the rights protected by art. 27 include the rights of persons, in community with others, to engage in economic and social activities which are part of the culture of the community to which they belong': UN Doc. A/45/40, Vol. II, App. A, para. 32.2 (1990).

[234] *See* Sigler and Capotorti, *supra*, n. 19. It may be noted here that the institution of positive measures in favour of ethnic minorities can be assimilated only as a group right. This is not the case for other actions under art. 2(2). A distinction may be drawn between rights that fall upon the individual as a result of his or her membership of a group, and rights that belong to the individual who is to be identified by means of a group membership. Thus one member of the Committee commented with regard to a reply of the representative of Iran: 'The delegation's statement about the definition of minorities raised an interesting legal point but failed to address the real issue. Whether or not minority rights were treated as group rights was irrelevant to the existence of the rights of individual members of those groups': Alston E/C.12/1990/SR.43, at 8, para. 42.

[235] *e.g.* Taya, E/C.12/1987/SR.16, at 4, para. 14.

[236] *See e.g.* Texier, E/C.12/1988/SR.13, at 9, para. 39.

[237] *See e.g.* Rattray, E/C.12/1990/SR.16, at 10, para. 54. Judge Tanaka commented in respect of minorities that the notion of equality before the law: 'prohibits a State to exclude members of a minority group from participating in rights, interests and opportunities which a majority population group can enjoy. On the other hand, a minority group shall be guaranteed the exercise of their own religious and education activities. This guarantee is conferred on members of a minority group, for the purpose of protection of their interests and not from the motive of discrimination itself. By reason of protection of the minority this protection cannot be imposed upon members of minority groups, and consequently they have the choice to accept it or not': *supra*, n. 7.

[238] *See* Alston, E/C.12/1988/SR.13, at 13, para. 71; Simma, E/C.12/1993/SR.15, at 7, para. 29. Recognition of certain problems have been identified however. Thus Mr Wimer Zambrano commented: 'Recognition of indigenous languages, which reflected a concern to respect the traditions and the cultural identity of different indigenous populations, nevertheless ran counter to another objective of equal importance in countries of Latin America, the desire to achieve assimilation': E/C.12/1990/SR.18, at 14, para. 89.

one member going so far as to make note of their right to self-determination.[239]

More significantly, however, and following the example of the HRC,[240] the Committee has recognized the existence of certain positive obligations with respect to minorities. In its concluding observations on the report of Mexico, the Committee expressly referred to the need for resources to be made available for indigenous groups 'to enable them to preserve their language, culture, and traditional way of life'.[241] The significance of this obligation is not so much that the States have undertaken a resource commitment, but rather the implicit assumption that the disposal of those resources should be in the hands of the groups concerned.

D Private Discrimination

In contrast to article 2(1)(d) of ICERD and article 2(b), (e), and (f) of Conv. EDAW which require the State to bring an end to racial discrimination by any persons, group, or organization, the Covenant makes no reference to discrimination between private individuals. Similarly, the *travaux préparatoires* make little specific mention of an obligation on the part of States to ensure non-discrimination between private individuals.[242] It is only possible to infer such an obligation from references to *de facto* equality.[243]

That States undertake to 'guarantee' the exercise of the rights without discrimination does suggest that the obligation in article 2(2) extends beyond mere control of public bodies. Indeed, to the extent that States are required to control private activity in relation to the substantive articles (for example to ensure the right to work[244] or safe and healthy working conditions), article 2(2) should also apply. One commentator concludes that 'under Articles 2(2) and 3 States are equally obliged to prohibit others to practise discrimination in public life'.[245]

The Committee has expressed some interest in the need to protect the rights of individuals against possible violations by other individuals,[246] and has in particular looked towards control of the private sector. No distinction

[239] *See* Konate, E/C.12/1989/SR.8, at 10, para. 52.

[240] The HRC comments with respect to art. 27 ICCPR: 'positive measures by States may also be necessary to protect the identity of a minority and the rights of its members to enjoy and develop their culture and language and to practice their religion, in community with the other members of the group': General Comment No. 23(50), *supra*, n. 229, at 3, para. 6.2. On the case law *see generally* McGoldrick D., 'Canadian Indians, Cultural Rights and the Human Rights Committee' (1991) 40 *ICLQ* 658.

[241] E/C.12/1993/16, at 3, para. 11.

[242] Klerk, *supra*, n. 12, at 266. But see the discussion in the Third Committee relating to art. 26 ICCPR, A/C.3/SR.1098–99 (1961).

[243] *See above*, text accompanying nn. 16–20.

[244] *Cf. Yilmaz Dogan* v. *The Netherlands, supra*, n. 191.   [245] Klerk, *supra*, n. 12, at 267.

[246] For the operation of the concept of *Drittwirkung, see above*, Ch. 3, text accompanying nn. 23–5.

is drawn as regards article 2(2). Although there is certainly greater concern as regards the activity of public bodies,[247] members of the Committee have thus looked towards the operation of non-discriminatory norms between private groups and individuals such as in private sector employment,[248] education,[249] and health care.[250] Only in a recent draft General Comment relating to persons with disabilities has the Committee given more concrete recognition to this question.[251]

Even if it is accepted that the obligation in article 2(2) is not restricted to public bodies, some consideration needs to be given to the extent to which States are under a duty to regulate the actions of private individuals. There is clearly a tension here between individual freedom or privacy and the demands of combating discrimination.[252] As Henkin notes:

That racial discrimination is often private discrimination means that efforts to eliminate it meet resistance from competing values of individual right which also have attractive claims in human dignity.[253]

During the drafting of article 26 of the ICCPR it was made clear that individual preferences or the exercise of individual choice were not to be subject to legal regulation.[254] However matters of everyday life, such as housing, transport, restaurants, and employment, were deemed to be capable of control by the State.[255] Ramcharan concludes rather generally that 'certain types of discrimination by individuals, other than in personal and social relationships, would violate the guarantees of the Covenant and that a state party is under an obligation to take measures against such forms of discrimination'.[256] The task is clearly one of defining the threshold between

[247] *e.g.* many questions are directed exclusively at public employment, *see e.g.* Jimenez Butragueno, E/C.12/1991/SR.3, at 11, para. 51.

[248] Questions have been directed towards: differences of retirement ages in the private sector, Jimenez Butragueno, E/C.12/1988/SR.10, at 8, para. 39; equal access of women to employment in the private sector, Simma, E/C.12/1989/SR.8, at 8, para. 46; and maternity leave for women in private sector, Mrachkov, E/C.12/1987/SR.8, at 7, para. 30.

[249] *See* Rattray, E/C.12/1993/SR.13, at 11, para. 47.

[250] *See e.g.* Rattray, E/C.12/1990/SR.2, at 10, para. 61.

[251] The Committee comments that States 'need to ensure that not only the public sphere, but also the private sphere, is, within appropriate limits, subject to regulation to ensure the full participation and equality within society for all persons with disabilities ... it is essential that private employers, private suppliers of goods and services, and other non-public entities be subject to both non-discrimination and equality norms in relation to persons with disabilities': *supra*, n. 98, at 4, para. 11.

[252] Meron interprets the right of association as restricting the scope of the principle of non-discrimination 'so as to protect strictly personal relations from its reach': Meron, *supra*, n. 13, at 294.

[253] Henkin L., 'National and International Perspectives on Racial Discrimination' (1971) 4 *HRJ* 263, at 265.

[254] Saudi Arabia, UN Doc. A/C.3/SR.1099, para. 18 (1961); Pakistan, UN Doc. A/C.3/SR.1102, para. 4 (1961).

[255] USSR, UN Doc. A/C.3/SR.1098, para. 6 (1961).

[256] Ramcharan, *supra*, n. 1, at 262–3.

the exercise of individual choice and the control of discriminatory behaviour in public life.[257]

Within the scope of the Covenant there are a number of areas in which the State might be obliged to ensure non-discrimination. For example, access to private employment or training, the rental of private accomodation, admission to trades unions or private educational establishments, access to privately owned cultural facilities (such as theatres or cinemas). While it might be said that there is a *prima facie* case for regulating the activities of all such institutions and individuals, it has to be recognized that there is also a need to protect the intimate and personal activities of individuals in their association with others. One solution is that, as Meron argues, the degree of intervention should be a function of the size and selectivity of the organization concerned.[258] In cases where discrimination is deeply engrained, however, a more far-reaching approach may be appropriate.

The Committee has not, at this stage, made any attempt to rationalize the competing demands in this area. For example, in one case the Austrian representative noted that there was a problem of discrimination in the private sector as 'wages were freely agreed between employer and employee and because of the high value attached to the independence of the social partners'.[259] Although apparently negating any State responsibility for discrimination in the sphere of private sector employment, this statement was rather superficially accepted by the Committee without comment. It is submitted that the Committee needs to address these complex problems with more precision with a view to establishing some principle to describe State obligations as regards discrimination between private individuals and bodies. As a minimum, the Committee needs to ensure that States themselves are aware of the competing principles and have laws and regulations that reflect a balanced approach.

VI. CONCLUSION

The concepts of equality and non-discrimination are arguably central to the implementation of the Covenant, and of great significance in the development of the Committee's supervisory functions. In broad terms, the essence of the Covenant may be seen to encompass an appeal to equality. This is apparent in the overtly 'welfarist' rights, such as the rights to social security,

---

[257] There has been considerable criticism by feminists of the existing division between the public and private spheres. In this context *see e.g.* Okin S., 'Gender, the Public and the Private' in Held D., *Political Theory Today* (1991), 67.

[258] Meron, *supra*, n. 13, at 295.

[259] Berchold (Austria), E/C.12/1988/SR.4, at 3, para. 11.

health, housing, and education, which are clearly founded upon a redistributionalist philosophy. The principle of non-discrimination is of importance as, in a context in which basic norms relating to economic and social
rights vary according to the economic resources of the State concerned, it is
an unchanging and universally applicable standard, which is also evidently
justiciable. Having said that, neither notion has been given the attention it
deserves in the practice of the Committee. Given the complexity and controversial nature of the issues involved, there is manifestly a need for the
Committee to make some clear statement as to its position. In particular,
attention needs to be paid to the notion of equality of opportunity in so far
as it is seen as being a relevant objective of the Covenant. This is so not
merely by virtue of the fact that it in some guises it gives rise to claims for
affirmative and protective action, but also because it poses significant problems of measurement or evaluation.

In relation to the principle of non-discrimination, the Committee appears
to have adopted a position analogous to that of other human rights bodies.
It has interpreted article 2(2) in a relatively broad manner both as to its
scope *ratione materiae* and *ratione personae*. Although the article is not
deemed to be entirely autonomous in the sense of article 26 of the ICCPR,
it covers both direct and indirect discrimination by public authorities and
private individuals and may be seen to operate even where there is no
evidence of a violation of one of the substantive articles itself. Similarly, the
article is not limited to those 'suspect' classifications specifically enumerated, but may also cover other unreasonable differentiations. For example,
the Committee has been clear in its opinion that discrimination on the
grounds of age, health status, or disability is prohibited by the terms of the
Covenant. Perhaps most importantly, the Committee views article 2(2) as
imposing obligations to be implemented immediately. As such, it represents
an important exception to the general terms of article 2(1) and is crucial to
arguments in favour of instituting an optional protocol allowing for individual and collective complaints relating to rights in the Covenant.

Even in the Committee's development of the notion of discrimination,
however, there is room for greater specificity. Although it is clearly necessary for article 2(2) to apply beyond the restricted classification of grounds
upon which discrimination is prohibited, the Committee needs to establish
what additional grounds it considers to be 'suspect' and the level of scrutiny
with which it will evaluate differentiations. Similarly, as regards regulation
of the activities of private individuals a balance has to be struck between the
demands of individual choice and freedom and the necessity of combating
discrimination in the longer term. As suggested, the Committee should look
initially to ensure that States reflect such a balance in their laws and administrative practices.

5
The Right to Work

Article 6
1. *The States Parties to the present Covenant recognize the right to work, which includes the right of everyone to the opportunity to gain his living by work which he freely chooses or accepts, and will take the appropriate steps to safeguard this right.*
2. *The steps to be taken by a State Party to the present Covenant to achieve the full realization of this right shall include technical and vocational guidance and training programmes, policies and techniques to achieve steady economic, social and cultural development and full and productive employment under conditions safeguarding fundamental political and economic freedoms to the individual.*

I. INTRODUCTION

Despite the statistical existence of unemployment in every country in the world, work continues to be 'an essential part of the human condition'.[1] For many, it represents the primary source of income upon which their physical survival depends. Not only is it crucial to the enjoyment of 'survival rights' such as food, clothing, or housing,[2] it affects the level of satisfaction of many other human rights such as the rights to education, culture, and health. Article 6, however, is not so much concerned with what is provided by work (in terms of remuneration), or the conditions of work, but rather with the value of employment itself. It thus gives recognition to the idea that work is an element integral to the maintainance of the dignity and self-respect of the individual.

II. THE *TRAVAUX PRÉPARATOIRES*

The initial idea of including an article on the right to work in the draft Covenant was discussed in the General Assembly's Third Committee in 1950.[3] There the Socialist States argued for the inclusion of such an article

---

[1] Sieghart P., *The Lawful Rights of Mankind* (1986), 123.
[2] *See* Tomes I., 'The Right to Work and Social Security' (1967–8) 8–9 *Bull. Czech. L* 192, at 196; Van der Ven J., 'The Right to Work as a Human Right' (1965) 11 *Howard LJ* 397, at 405–6.
[3] UN Docs. A/C.3/SR.289–91, 297–9, 5 UN GAOR, C.3, 289th–91st and 297th–99th mtgs. (1950).

on the basis that it formed one of the 'cornerstones of modern society'.[4] It was pointed out that the right to work gave other rights 'a foundation in reality'[5] and, in particular, was essential to a guarantee of the right to life.[6] In the following year, a number of proposals[7] were considered by the Commission on Human Rights.[8] A draft article produced by the Commission was then reviewed by the General Assembly's Third Committee in 1956 which finalized what is now article 6.[9]

A A Guarantee of the Right to Work

The initial proposals fell into three main groups: those of the Socialist States, those of the Western States, and the compromise proposals. The Socialist States proposed that States should undertake to 'guarantee' or 'ensure' the right to work.[10] In contrast, the Western States' proposals merely required States to 'promote conditions' under which the right to work might be realized.[11] The main compromise formula was for the article to include a bold statement of the right to work[12] while deferring a decision on whether or not the obligation should be progressive until the adoption of a general clause. It soon became apparent that many States would not accept an obligation to 'guarantee' the right to work in the sense of ensuring full employment or eliminating unemployment. In particular, it was feared that such a guarantee would bind States to a centralized system of government and require that all labour be under the direct control of the State.[13]

It was made clear that, in many countries, the achievement of the right to work was dependent upon the economic climate in which it operated. External constraints relating to the balance of international trade or the availability of raw materials[14] made the achievement of the right to work contingent upon international action as well as upon a particular national economic or social policy.[15] In that light it was generally considered that the right to work could only be achieved in a progressive manner.[16] Indeed,

---

[4] Hoffmeister (Czechoslovakia), A/C.3/SR.299, para. 33 (1950).
[5] Panyushkin (USSR), A/C.3/SR.297, para. 54 (1950).
[6] Afnan (Iraq), A/C.3/SR.298, para. 64 (1950).   [7] E/CN.4/AC.14/2, at 3 (1951).
[8] E/CN.4/SR.205–7 and 216–8 (1951).   [9] A/C.3/SR.709–13 (1956).
[10] *See e.g.* USSR proposal, E/CN.4/AC.14/2, at 3 (1951).
[11] *Ibid.*, proposals of USA, Denmark, and Egypt.
[12] *Ibid.*, proposal of Yugoslavia. *See also* proposal of ILO, E/CN.4/AC.14/2/Add. 1 (1951).
[13] Roosevelt (USA), E/CN.4/SR.269, at 6 (1952); Later she commented: 'it was difficult to see how democratic States could guarantee absolutely and by their own action the right to work to all persons without becoming totalitarian States': E/CN.4/SR.275, at 11 (1952).
[14] *See* Rossel (Sweden), E/CN.4/SR.216, at 6 (1951).
[15] *See* Cassin (France), E/CN.4/SR.275, at 12 (1952).
[16] *See e.g.* Bowie (UK), E/CN.4/SR.206, at 10 (1951); Sørensen (Denmark), E/CN.4/SR.207, at 10 (1951); Roosevelt (USA), E/CN.4/SR.276, at 6 (1952).

some States argued that a guarantee of the right to work was impossible at any stage.[17]

In using the stock formula in which the States parties 'recognize' the right to work the drafters clearly placed article 6 within the compass of article 2(1) which provides for the progressive realization of the right.[18] However, while rejecting the term 'guarantee', the delegates seemed to be concerned primarily with the obligation to achieve full employment. It is unclear from the drafting whether it was intended that all aspects of the article, such as the obligation to refrain from imposing forced labour, were intended to be progressively implemented.

B The Opportunity to Gain his Living

The majority of proposals that gained broad support utilized the phrase 'opportunity to gain his living by work' or its equivalent.[19] This specific wording was proposed in order to underline the fact that the individual must be able to earn a living wage.[20] It was criticized, however, because it was seen to limit the concept of work to that which generated income,[21] and because the question of remuneration fell more clearly within the scope of article 7.[22]

Although inclusion of the phrase 'opportunity to gain his living by work' did have considerable support, the main controversy lay over its precise relationship with the right to work. The original proposal, accepted at the Commission's seventh session, linked the right to work with the opportunity to gain one's living by the phrase 'that is to say'.[23] Although it was argued that the concepts in fact described two separate rights,[24] the majority felt that the opportunity to gain one's living was, in part at least, a definition of the right to work.[25] A Greek amendment to alter the phrase to read 'the fundamental right to work, which includes the right of

[17] *See e.g.* Cassin (France), E/CN.4/SR.269, at 4 (1952); Hoare (UK), E/CN.4/SR.278, at 8 (1952).

[18] That art. 6 was to be governed by the general implementation clause was the reason for the rejection of additional arts. on the implementation of the right to work. *See e.g.* UN Doc. E/2256, at 16–17, 14 UN ESCOR, Supp. (No. 4) (1952).

[19] *See e.g.* Proposal of France, E/CN.4/576; proposal of ILO, E/CN.4/AC.14/2/Add. 1.

[20] *See* Cassin (France), E/CN.4/SR.216, at 27 (1951).

[21] *See* Yu (China), E/CN.4/SR.216, at 25 (1951).

[22] *See* Azmi Bey (Egypt), E/CN.4/SR.216, at 29 (1951).

[23] Art. 20 of the draft covenant read: 'Work being the basis of all human endeavour, the States Parties to the Covenant recognize the right to work, that is to say, the fundamental right of everyone to the opportunity, if he so desires, to gain his living by work which he freely accepts': UN Doc. E/1992, Annex I, at 23, 13 UN ESCOR, Supp. (No. 9) (1951).

[24] *See* Pazhwak (Afghanistan), A/C.3/SR.709, at 137, para. 28 (1956).

[25] *See e.g.* Diaz Casanueva (Chile), A/C.3/SR.709, at 137, para. 34 (1956); Ponce (Ecuador), A/C.3/SR.711, at 148, para. 12 (1956).

everyone to the opportunity to gain his living by work'[26] was ultimately adopted,[27] it being felt that the right to work 'did not mean simply the right to remuneration but the right of every human being to do a job freely chosen by himself, one which gave meaning to his life'.[28] Although other elements within the right to work were unfortunately not spelt out,[29] the discussion implies that article 6 includes, at least, the right not to be arbitrarily deprived of work of any kind, whether remunerative or otherwise.

There was some underlying confusion as to the exact nature of State obligations implied by the right to gain a living through work. Some States considered that the opportunity to work obliged the State to provide employment for all who wished work.[30] Other States, however, interpreted the phrase as merely implying that the State should restrain itself from preventing persons from working.[31] A general reading of the debate would suggest that a position of compromise was reached that enabled the word 'opportunity' to be included by consensus.[32] Whereas market or mixed economy States would not accept an obligation to provide employment, as suggested above, they could accept a position where they were responsible for developing employment opportunities.[33] This could be achieved either directly through State employment or indirectly by developing the economic conditions for increasing private sector employment.

C Free Choice in Employment

A certain tension between a guarantee of the right to work and free choice in employment was identified in the early stages of drafting.[34] It was agreed that the State could not be expected to provide everyone with work of their own choosing. If the State was obliged to provide employment, the range of opportunities available to the individual would obviously be limited by the requirements of the country's social and economic development.[35]

[26] UN Doc. A/C.3/L.536. A similar amendment was to use the word 'as' in place of 'that is to say'. See Mufti (Syria), A/C.3/SR.709, at 137, para. 31 (1956).

[27] 42 votes to 10 with 13 abstentions. The word 'fundamental' was deleted from the final version. UN Doc. A/3525, at 4, para. 28, 11 UN GAOR, Annexes, (Ag. Item 31) (1956).

[28] Thierry (France), A/C.3/SR.709, at 138, para. 37 (1956); See also Mufti (Syria), A/C.3/SR.710, at 144, para. 42 (1956).

[29] Cf. Marriott (Australia), A/C.3/SR.711, at 150, para. 36 (1956).

[30] See e.g. Azkoul (Lebanon), E/CN.4/SR.268, para. 8 (1952); Jevremovic (Yugoslavia), E/CN.4/SR.277, para. 11 (1952).

[31] See e.g. Nisot (Belgium), E/CN.4/SR.268, para. 8 (1952); Pazhwak (Afghanistan), A/C.3/SR.710, at 141, para. 7 (1956).

[32] E/CN.4/SR.218, para. 7 (1952).

[33] See Diaz Casanueva (Chile), A/C.3/SR.710, at 144, paras. 37–8 (1956).

[34] See e.g. Jevremovic (Yugoslavia), E/CN.4/SR.205, at 11 (1951); Bowie (UK), E/CN.4/SR.206, at 10 (1951); Rossel (Sweden), E/CN.4/SR.216, at 6 (1951).

[35] See Santa Cruz (Chile), E/CN.4/AC.14/SR.3, at 15–16 (1951).

Some States accordingly suggested that the element of free choice in employment should be qualified for the purpose of maintaining full employment.[36] The majority, however, looked to the primacy of free choice over the achievement of full employment as an objective of State policy.[37]

There was considerable support for the idea that the article should contain some indication that forced labour or slavery was illegal.[38] Although it was pointed out that the prohibition of forced labour was implicit in the negative conception of a 'right to work',[39] and was already the subject of article 5 of the draft Covenant,[40] proposals were made to include the phrases 'of his own choice'[41] or 'who so desires'[42] to indicate this concern. The term 'desires' was the one chosen initially, together with the stipulation that work be freely accepted.[43] The term 'choice' was rejected on the basis that it might have implied that governments undertook to find the employment of everyone's choosing.[44] The inclusion of both the terms 'desires' and 'freely accepts' seemed to stress that people should not only be free from coercion in their choice of occupation but also be at liberty not to work at all.

However, at a later stage the position was reversed. The term 'desires' was deleted in favour of the phrase 'work which he freely chooses or accepts'.[45] One justification for the deletion of the term 'desires' was that it might be seen as a legitimization of 'social parasitism'.[46] For those States that instigated the change, work was not merely a right but also a duty.[47]

[36] *See e.g.* Valenzuela (Chile), E/CN.4/SR.206, at 23 (1951); Ahmed (Pakistan) A/C.3/SR.709, at 138, para. 39 (1956).

[37] The USSR representative objected, e.g., that free choice could be used to justify unemployment and the lack of measures to combat it. Morosov (USSR), E/CN.4/SR.218, at 7 (1951).

[38] *See e.g.* Simarsian (USA), E/CN.4/SR.216, at 18 (1951); Sender (ICFTU), E/CN.4/SR.216, at 19 (1951).

[39] *See* Jevremovic (Yugoslavia), E/CN.4/SR.216, at 20 (1951); Cassin (France), E/CN.4/SR.216, at 27 (1951). Cassin later commented: 'Article 20 [later art. 6] contained both the positive and negative aspects, like the word *droit* itself. Inherent in that word was the notion that it could be exercised voluntarily; otherwise it would be an obligation. Equally inherent was the notion of the ability to exercise the right.' He went on to argue that there was therefore no need to include the words 'opportunity' or 'desires' within the text. E/CN.4/SR.268, at 9 (1952).

[40] *See e.g.* Malik (Lebanon), E/CN.4/SR.217, at 11 (1951).

[41] *See e.g.* Mehta (India), E/CN.4/SR.216, at 24 (1951).

[42] *See e.g.* Sørensen (Denmark), E/CN.4/SR.216, at 9 (1951).

[43] UN Doc. E/1992, Annex I, at 23, *supra*, n. 23. It would seem that the inclusion of the term 'freely accepts' was similarly intended to prohibit forced labour. *See* Simarsian, E/CN.4/SR.217, at 10 (1951).

[44] *See* Myrddin-Evans (ILO), E/CN.4/SR.216, at 29 (1951).

[45] UN Doc. A/3525, *supra*, n. 27, at 3–4, paras. 25 and 28.

[46] *See* Aznar (Spain), A/C.3/SR.709, at 137, para. 30 (1956); Jaramillo Arrubla (Colombia), *ibid.* 138, para. 44; Nestor (Rumania), A/C.3/SR.712, at 153, para. 7 (1956). One member of the Third Committee felt he could not support the term 'desires' as it was at variance with his State's vagrancy laws. Rivas (Venezuela), A/C.3/SR.710, at 143, para. 21 (1956).

[47] *See e.g.* Aznar (Spain), A/C.3/SR.709, at 137, para. 30 (1956). That there might be some

Fortunately, however, the possibility that the individual might be obliged in law to take up some form of employment, as seems to be implied here, was not subject to agreement. First, a number of States emphasized that the concept of a right to work did not allow for the possibility of a co-existent duty to work. Secondly, if work must be freely accepted as article 6 requires, it is difficult to see how a duty to work could ever be enforced. It was thus the presence of the phrase 'freely accepts', which was generally considered to prohibit forced labour, that led to the deletion of the word 'desires' as being essentially redundant.[48]

The term 'chooses', far from carrying the implications assigned to it in the Commission's debate, was merely intended to strengthen the existing meaning of the article. In the final analysis it seems that the term 'chooses' covered the right to choose a trade or profession while the term 'accepts' covered the right to accept or refuse an offer of employment.[49] As such the alterations did not substantially change the meaning assigned to the original Commission version of the article.[50] Despite some opposition,[51] the article seems to have been adopted on the strength of this analysis.

D Full Employment

Although proposals for a guarantee of the right to work were rejected, there remained considerable support for the inclusion of a reference to full employment.[52] This led a contemporary commentary to conclude that the presence of paragraph 2 gave recognition to a right to be provided with work, in addition to the right not to be prevented from working.[53] However, the debate on paragraph 1 does not seem to bear this out. Any such right to employment was to be viewed in relation to the State obligation to secure full employment in a progressive manner, which in itself was conditional upon the economic development of the country concerned.

Recognizing that 'full employment' was merely a method of imple-

---

conflict between the free choice of work and the duty to work was dispelled by one member: 'the obligation to work and freedom to work were in no way incompatible. Men ought to work, but they should be free to choose their trade or profession': Jaramillo Arrubla (Columbia), A/C.3/SR.709, at 138, para. 44 (1956). How an obligation to work and a freedom not to accept work can be reconciled is unclear. This somewhat dubious reasoning was not followed in that delegate's later statements. Cf.A/C.3/SR.712, at 154, para. 14 (1956).

[48] *See e.g.* Aznar (Spain), A/C.3/SR.710, at 141, para. 4 (1956); De Almeida (Brazil), A/C.3/SR.710, at 142, para. 11 (1956).

[49] *See* Jaramillo Arrubla (Colombia), A/C.3/SR.712, at 154, para. 14 (1956).

[50] *Cf.* Cheng (China), A/C.3/SR.710, at 144, para. 35 (1952).

[51] *See e.g.* Elliot (UK), A/C.3/SR.712, at 154, para. 8 (1956).

[52] *See e.g.* Fischer (WFTU), E/CN.4/SR.217, at 4 (1951); Whitlam (Australia), E/CN.4/SR.277, at 10 (1952); *see generally* UN Doc. E/2256, para. 110, 14 UN ESCOR, Supp. (No. 4) (1952).

[53] UN Doc. A/2929, 10 UN CAOR, Annexes (Ag. Item 28), pt. II, at 103, para. 2 (1955).

mentation,[54] the question whether or not reference to it should be made in a second paragraph to article 6 became enveloped in a more general debate on whether specific implementation clauses should be included within the substantive portion of the Covenant. Even following the Commission's adoption of a second paragraph relating to full employment, certain members continued to advocate its deletion.[55] It was argued that it was better to state the principle of the right to work in general terms leaving the specifics of implementation to the ILO, the proposed reference to full employment being self-evident.[56] Additionally, it was considered illogical to insert specific implementation clauses into some articles and not others.[57]

On the other hand, most States felt that in order for the Covenant to go beyond the UDHR[58] it was necessary for the specifics of implementation, beyond those found in article 2,[59] to be spelt out where possible.[60] As far as article 6 was concerned, those standards had already been established in ILO instruments,[61] and had gained general acceptability on the international plane.[62] For the majority, then, the question was not the inclusion of a second paragraph relating to full employment, but what elements should be referred to therein. Although important,[63] the obligation to achieve full employment was only one method of securing the right to work.[64] This point was made apparent in the final version of article 6, which stipulates that the steps to ensure the right to work 'shall include' the obligation to achieve full employment. Paragraph 2 thus was intended to provide an illustrative, rather than an exhaustive, definition of the measures of implementation to be taken with respect to article 6(1).

1 Economic Development

There was general agreement that the achievement of full employment was dependant upon the structure and economic development of the country

---

[54] It was noted that full employment could either be seen as a means for ensuring the right to work or as a separate goal. *See* Azkoul (Lebanon), E/CN.4/SR.276, at 13 (1952).

[55] UK Amendment, A/C.3/L.534.

[56] *See* Elliot (UK), A/C.3/SR.709, at 137, para. 29 (1956); Shipley (Canada), *ibid.*, para. 32; Thierry (France), *ibid.* 138, para. 38.

[57] *See* Elliot (UK), A/C.3/SR.710, at 143, para. 26 (1956).

[58] It was felt that without para. 2, art. 6 would not differ substantially from the UDHR. Abdel-Ghani (Egypt), A/C.3/SR.710, at 143, para. 20 (1956). In particular some States seemed to be driven by the rather erroneous idea that without para. 2 States would not be bound *inter se* with respect to art. 6. *See e.g.* Ponce (Ecuador), A/C.3/SR.711, at 148, para. 13; Pudlak (Czechoslovakia), *ibid.*, at 149, para. 19.

[59] *See* Eustathiades (Greece), A/C.3/SR.710, at 143, para. 29 (1956).

[60] *See* Diaz Casanueva (Chile), A/C.3/SR.710, at 144, para. 38 (1956); Massoud-Ansari (Iran), A/C.3/SR.711, at 149, para. 31.

[61] *See* Vlahov (Yugoslavia), A/C.3/SR.710 at 142, para. 9 (1956).

[62] *See* Morosov (USSR), A/C.3/SR.710, at 142, para. 15 (1956).

[63] *See* Santa Cruz (Chile), E/CN.4/SR.216, at 11 (1951).

[64] *See* Hoare (UK), E/CN.4/SR.278, at 8 (1952).

concerned.[65] However, it was feared that proposals to make reference to the technical means for ensuring full employment,[66] such as the need for 'economic expansion' or 'development,'[67] might be used as an excuse by States for avoiding their obligations[68] and would duplicate and even limit article 2.[69] In support of the proposals, it was argued that reference to economic expansion or development was indeed necessary,[70] being justified by the text of articles 55 and 56 of the UN Charter.[71] That mention should be made of economic development was finally accepted by the Commission and later by the Third Committee (despite certain reservations[72]) on condition that social and cultural development should also be mentioned to give the article fuller expression.[73]

That reference to economic, social, and cultural development is made in article 6 is perhaps of limited significance given the imprecise nature of the term. At most, it serves to highlight the perceived interdependence of the articles in the Covenant and re-emphasizes that article 6 is intended, in part at least, to be progressively implemented.

2　National and International Programmes

In the light of the external considerations that bear upon a particular country's economic development, it was also proposed that article 6 should refer explicitly to 'national and international programmes' to achieve economic development.[74] Although members agreed with the intentions of the proposal,[75] concern was expressed as to the precise obligations that ensued[76] and the limitative effect they might have on article 2.[77] Delegates

---

[65] *See e.g.* it was commented that the aims of art. 6 would be achieved 'only in so far as the States provided every opportunity for employment and ensured a stable economy in which only temporary unemployment would be possible': Sender (ICFTU), E/CN.4/SR. 276, at 9 (1952). *See also* Roosevelt (US), E/CN.4/SR.276, at 6 (1952); Santa Cruz (Chile), *ibid.* 8.

[66] *See* Juvigny (France), E/CN.4/SR.276, at 11 (1952); Cassin (France), E/CN.4/SR.278, at 4 (1952).

[67] In the end the preference was for the word 'development'. *Cf.* E/CN.4/SR.278, at 13 (1952).

[68] *See* Azkoul (Lebanon), E/CN.4/SR.276, at 12 (1952); Kovalenko (USSR), E/CN.4/SR.278, at 3 (1952).

[69] *See e.g.* Rossel (Sweden), E/CN.4/SR.277, at 3 (1952).

[70] *See* Waheed (Pakistan), E/CN.4/SR.277, at 6 (1952).

[71] *See* Santa Cruz (Chile), E/CN.4/SR.277, at 3 (1952).

[72] *See e.g.* Marriott (Australia), A/C.3/SR.711, at 150, para. 34 (1956); Cheng (China), A/C.3/SR.712, at 154, para. 10 (1956).

[73] *See* Pazhwak (Afghanistan), A/C.3/SR.709, at 137, para. 28 (1956); Mufti (Syria), *ibid.*, para. 31; Ponce (Ecuador), A/C.3/SR.711, at 148, para. 12 (1956).

[74] *See* Santa Cruz, E/CN.4/SR.276, at 8 (1952).

[75] *See e.g.* Rossel (Sweden), E/CN.4/SR.277, at 3 (1952).

[76] *See* Hoare (UK), E/CN.4/SR.276, at 10 (1952); Azkoul (Lebanon), E/CN.4/SR.276, at 12 (1951).

[77] *See* Roosevelt (USA), E/CN.4/SR.277, at 7 (1952).

seem to have been satisfied finally by an assurance that, on the basis of article 2, national and international action was implicit in the proposal and therefore did not have to be explicitly mentioned.[78]

3 Productive Employment

At a number of stages during the drafting of article 6 it was submitted that work should be productive.[79] Although little discussion took place over the inclusion of this word in the final stages, it seems to have been intended to prohibit the adoption of social projects of little significance merely to draw in the unemployed for the purpose of maintaining full employment. This imputation, however, was never confirmed.

4 Fundamental Political and Economic Freedoms

A US proposal that full employment should be achieved 'under conditions ensuring fundamental political and economic freedoms to the individual' had considerable support, especially from other Western States which wanted to make clear that full employment was not an objective to be imposed through totalitarian means at the expense of democracy and freedom.[80] Some States argued that the term 'freedoms' should not be limited to fundamental ones, but should be expanded to include all political and economic freedoms.[81] It was responded, however, that the purpose was to safeguard only those freedoms which were fundamental in relation to the right to work and not just any freedoms,[82] and that to include all freedoms was too vague and might sanction abuse.[83] In retrospect, this was a meaningless debate. Nowhere was it defined what freedoms were considered to be 'fundamental', or which ones were considered to relate to the right to work. Perhaps all that could be concluded from the discussion was that the phrase

---

[78] *Ibid.* 8. Nevertheless the provision was rejected by only a very small majority of 6 votes to 5 with 7 abstentions.

[79] *See* Santa Cruz (Chile), E/CN.4/SR.216, at 24 (1951); Fischer (WFTU), E/CN.4/SR.217, at 4 (1951). This must be distinguished from the proposal that the right to work should be limited to 'socially useful' work, which was suggested as a recognition that society requires its members to undertake work that contributes to the general well-being. *See* Whitlam (Australia), E/CN.4/SR.217, at 12 (1951); Ciasullo (Uruguay), *ibid.*, at 10; Yu (China), *ibid.*, at 12. There was a certain amount of opposition to the term 'socially useful' as it was thought it might be open to abuse by States. Myrddin-Evans (ILO), E/CN.4/SR.217, at 16 (1951).

[80] *See* Azkoul (Lebanon), E/CN.4/SR.276, at 12 (1952); Rossel (Sweden), E/CN.4/SR.277, at 3 (1952). One participant suggested thus that States should seek to prevent further unemployment and achieve full employment under conditions satisfying material needs and with 'respect for freedom and the safeguarding of moral and spiritual values': Sender (ICFTU), E/CN.4/SR.276, at 10 (1952).

[81] *See* Pazhwak (Afghanistan), A/C.3/SR.709, at 137, para. 28.

[82] *See* Eustathiades (Greece), A/C.3/SR.709, at 138, para. 35.

[83] *See e.g.* Rivas (Venezuela), A/C.3/SR.710, at 143, para. 22 (1956); Diaz Casanueva (Chile), *ibid.*, 144, para. 38.

was intended to prohibit 'trade-offs' between the right to work and other civil and political rights.

5 Steps to be Taken

As suggested above,[84] there were questions over the extent to which the various proposals relating to the implementation of article 6 modified article 2(1) itself. It was made clear that the purpose of article 6(2), as evidenced by the phrase 'steps to be taken',[85] was not to limit article 2 but rather to outline and elaborate on those conditions which were required for the full attainment of the right to work.[86] Nevertheless, it should be made clear that not all the steps outlined in article 6(2) were conceived of as existing on the same theoretical level. For example, the reference to development was included only in so far as it related to the achievement of full employment. Equally, although full employment must be seen as method of implementing the right to work, it was also presented as a goal in its own right.[87]

III. THE APPROACH OF THE COMMITTEE

A A Guarantee of the Right to Work

In utilizing the term 'recognize',[88] the wording of article 6 when read in light of the *travaux préparatoires*[89] and the opinions of commentators,[90] clearly dismisses the idea that States are required to 'guarantee' the right to work. Despite this, a number of the Committee members have looked towards a legal guarantee of the right to work,[91] one member even arguing that such a guarantee should be formally enshrined in the

---

[84] *See above*, text accompanying nn. 58–64.

[85] The US proposal was accordingly amended by the Lebanese proposal to become the new joint amendment E/CN.4/L.95.

[86] *See* Roosevelt (USA), E/CN.4/SR.277, at 8 (1952).

[87] For a discussion on the interrelationship between the substance of the rights and their means of implementation *see above*, Ch. 3, text accompanying nn. 8–10.

[88] The term 'recognize' is seen as being an indication that the provision is considered to fall within the confines of art. 2(1), *see above*, Ch. 3, text accompanying nn. 169–75.

[89] *See above*, text accompanying nn. 10–18.

[90] *See e.g.* Van den Berg G. and Guldenmund R., 'The Right to Work in East and West' in Bloed A., and Van Dijk P. (eds.), *Essays on Human Rights in the Helsinki Process* (1985), 103 at 111. *See also,* with respect to the UK, Hepple B., 'A Right to Work' (1981) 10 *Ind. LJ* 65 at 73. It is also interesting to note that the International Labour Conference decided not to provide for a guarantee of the right to work, *see* Mayer J., 'The Concept of the Right to Work In International Standards and the Legislation of ILO Member States' (1985) 124 *ILR* 225 at 239.

[91] *See e.g.* Badawi El Sheikh, E/C.12/1987/SR.5, at 3, para. 10; Mratchkov, E/C.12/1989/SR.18, at 4, para. 11; Neneman, E/C.12/1990/SR.11, at 5, para. 27.

Constitution.[92] It remains difficult to envisage, however, how such a guarantee should operate.

A guarantee of the right to work would seem to imply that the State should provide a job for every person who is available for, and willing to, work. To correspond to the requirements of human dignity, such a guarantee would have to ensure that the type of work suited the skills and aptitudes of the individual worker concerned, and that the individual be given the right to refuse employment. Inevitably, the institution of such a guarantee would require considerable expenditure and necessitate close control of the labour market. It is clear that even in those States that do 'guarantee' the right to work, it is generally conditional upon the needs of society, offset by a duty to work and implemented through the political framework as opposed to law.[93] The situation is even less favourable in market economies where control of labour is insufficient, and in developing countries where lack of resources constrains the institution of such a guarantee. Thus where there is constitutional enactment of a right to work, it is frequently expressed as a long-term objective to be promoted rather than ensured.[94]

Although individual members of the Committee have occasionally referred to the need to 'guarantee' the right to work, the Committee as a whole seems to have taken a more reserved attitude. In general, the Committee has looked towards the implementation of policies and measures aimed at ensuring that there is 'work for all who are available for and seeking work'.[95] As one member noted, 'it was clear that the right to work could be implemented only if work was available';[96] the availability of work is something which States should aim to achieve over time. The clearly progressive nature of the obligation indicates that the Committee views article 6, at least as far as the obligation to secure full employment is concerned, as falling squarely within the terms of article 2(1).

B Elements of the Right to Work

Despite the fact that a guarantee of the right to work is not realistic, it would be superficial to view article 6 merely as requiring the progressive achievement of full employment. That full employment is referred to in article 6(2) as one of the steps towards the full realization of the right to

---

[92] *See* Kouznetsov, E/C.12/1990/SR.15, at 6, para. 27. The form which such an expression should take in the Constitution however was not established.

[93] *See* Hepple B., 'Security of Employment', in Blainpain R. (ed.), *Comparative Labour Law and Industrial Relations* (3rd ed., 1987), at 475.

[94] Mayer, *supra*, n. 90, at 237–8.

[95] Revised guidelines regarding the form and content of reports to be submitted by States parties under arts. 16 and 17 of the International Covenant on Economic, Social, and Cultural Rights. UN ESCOR, Supp. (No. 3), Annex IV, 88 at 90, UN Doc. E/1991/23 (1991).

[96] Sparsis, E/C.12/1987/SR.5, at 7, para. 31.

work suggests that other elements are implicit in the right which have yet to be spelt out. A right to work in a broader sense seems to encompass two general areas of concern: a right to enter employment and a right not to be unjustly deprived of employment.[97] As far as the former is concerned, it includes all matters that affect access to work such as levels of unemployment, equality of opportunity, vocational guidance and training, and education. The latter field on the other hand concerns employment security and in particular security against unfair dismissal.

Further elements of the right to work are specified in article 6, which speaks of 'the right of everyone to the opportunity to gain his living by work which he freely chooses or accepts'. The reference to the opportunity to gain one's living suggests that, as a minimum, remuneration should be consistent with the satisfaction of basic needs. This finds more precise recognition in article 7.[98] The reference to freely chosen work also appears to provide for a 'right not to work', implying a prohibition of forced labour and even perhaps legitimizing a right to strike.

In the next section, the three main elements of the right to work, namely, access to employment, freedom from forced labour, and security in employment, will be discussed in turn.

1 Access to Employment

(a) *Full Employment*

Although article 6(2) was conceived of as being an 'implementation clause' in so far as it outlined state obligations as opposed to individual rights,[99] there is no doubt that it forms an indissoluble element in the achievement of the right to work. This is more apparent if it is considered that the 'steps' outlined in the Covenant form partial definitions of the 'rights' to which they refer.[100] Whereas full employment might be posited as a precondition to the full realization of the right to work, it must be conceded that an individual's right to work is not necessarily conditional upon the existence of full employment.

It is apparent that the Committee expects there to be some degree of unemployment in every State with which it deals. Thus, considerable scepticism was expressed as to Czechoslovakia's assertion that unemployment was non-existent,[101] particularly in view of the fact that Czechoslovakia operated a system to assist the unemployed.[102] However, what appears to

---

[97] *e.g.*, the Constitution of Luxembourg provides in art. 11 for a right to work. This has been interpreted as providing for free choice of employment, free access to employment, and freedom from discrimination. *See* UN Doc. E/1990/5/Add. 1, at 2, para. 3.
[98] *See below*, Ch. 6.   [99] *See above*, text accompanying nn. 54–64.
[100] *See above*, Ch. 3, text accompanying nn. 7–10.
[101] *See e.g.* Konate, E/C.12/1987/SR.13, at 5, para. 21.
[102] *See* Simma, E/C.12/1987/SR.13, at 9, para. 41; Texier, E/C.12/1987/SR.13, at 10, para. 50.

have eluded the Committee in this case is that, in the context of economics, it is generally conceded that the notion of 'full employment' does not mean the total absence of unemployment. Forms of unemployment have traditionally been divided into three categories: frictional unemployment, cyclical (or demand-deficiency) unemployment, and structural unemployment.[103] Whereas cyclical and structural unemployment are matters of serious public concern,[104] frictional unemployment represents the number of people between jobs and as such is not a reflection of the inadequacy of the labour market, but rather of employment mobility. Given that a measure of unemployment (in a general sense) is inevitable, it is surely appropriate for the Committee to define what it understands by the term 'full employment' and the extent to which it considers it to be a realistic objective.[105]

Here the text of article 6 is instructive. In outlining the steps to be taken to achieve the realization of the right to work, article 6(2) does not speak merely of full employment, but rather of 'policies and techniques to achieve . . . full and productive employment'. The achievement of full employment, then, is not something that the article actually requires. Rather, what is required is a policy that directs itself towards that end.

It is clear from the Committee's comments upon article 2(1) that an essential precondition to the formulation of precise and effective policies is an accurate evaluation of the present situation.[106] Thus, according to the Committee's guidelines, States are required to produce information on the 'situation, level and trends of employment, unemployment, and underemployment'.[107] In practice members of the Committee have also expected States to offer some form of explanation for the current level of unemployment[108] and further information on the nature of the unemployment (for example the amount of long-term unemployment).[109] In addition, information is requested as to the level of unemployment with respect to specific categories of workers, and it has offered as examples 'women, young per-

---

[103] *See e.g.* Scott M. and Laslett R., *Can We Get Back to Full Employment?* (1978), 10–11. Other definitions also include seasonal unemployment, *see* Worswick G., 'Summary', in Worswick G. (ed.), *The Concept and Measurement of Involuntary Unemployment* (1976), 305.

[104] 'Cyclical unemployment' is generally considered to be a result of deficiency of demand for labour; 'structural unemployment' is unemployment that results from imperfections in the labour market (such as a mismatch between training and labour demand).

[105] It was traditionally considered that an unemployment level of about 3% was consonant with full employment. For a discussion of 'target rates' of unemployment, *see* Blackaby F., 'The Target Rate of Unemployment' in Worswick G. (ed.), *The Concept and Measurement of Involuntary Unemployment* (1976), 279. *Cf.* ESC, art. 1 which speaks of 'high and stable' levels of employment.   [106] *See above*, Ch. 3, text accompanying nn. 62–5.

[107] Reporting guidelines, *supra*, n. 95, at 90.

[108] *See* Texier, E/C.12/1987/SR.5, at 6, para. 23; Sviridov, E/C.12/1987/SR.6, at 5, para. 16.

[109] *See* Texier, E/C.12/1989/SR.6, at 5, para. 20.

sons, older workers, and disabled workers'.[110] This corresponds to the obligation to identify vulnerable or disadvantaged persons, groups, regions, or areas with regard to employment.[111] Such areas of concern will clearly vary from country to country and the State will have considerable discretion in identifying them. Nevertheless members of the Committee have generally looked for information on the employment situation of each of the above groups and occasionally on the situation of particular ethnic groups.[112] Any information provided should be placed in the context of the situation both five and ten years previously.[113]

Accurate and useful measurement of unemployment, however, is subject to serious difficulties. Whereas unemployment may be estimated with relative ease in developed States,[114] in developing States, which have a smaller percentage of the working population in wage-earning employment (many being self-employed) and have less well-developed social security systems, unemployment is considerably more difficult to measure. In addition, in developing States, the figures of unemployment are likely to disguise serious under-employment (in the sense of employees having insufficient work).[115] Although the Committee has begun to tackle the question of statistical indicators in general, it has not as yet done so in the context of full employment.

As noted above, on the basis of their evaluation of the situation, States are expected to pursue a policy with the aim of ensuring that there is work for all who are available for and seeking work.[116] The precise nature of such a policy has not been specifically provided for by the Committee although reference is made to ILO standards in this area, particularly the Employment Policy Convention of 1964 (No. 122).[117] One member has commented that the mere identification of four objectives of public policy was not a sufficient indication that an employment policy as envisaged by Convention

---

[110] Reporting guidelines, *supra*, n. 95, at 90. *Cf.* Report of the Committee's Seventh Session, E/1993/22, at 44, para. 160.   [111] *Ibid.*

[112] The following questions are exemplary: what was Jamaica doing to reduce the high unemployment rate, particularly in the case of women? Neneman, E/C.12/1990/SR.11, at 5, para. 27. What measures was Canada taking to reduce the high level of unemployment especially among women and children? Mratchkov, E/C.12/1989/SR.8, at 7, para. 36. What were the trends of unemployment among young women and ethnic groups? Simma, E/C.12/1989/SR.8, at 8, para. 43; Neneman, E/C.12/1989/SR.8, at 9 para. 49.

[113] Reporting guidelines, *supra*, n. 95, at 90.

[114] Even here there do remain problems such as defining who is 'seeking work', *see* Hussmanns R., Mehran F., and Verma V., *Surveys of Economically Active Population, Employment, Unemployment and Underemployment* (1990), 97–105.

[115] *See* Squire C., *Employment Policy in Developing Countries* (1981), 58–65.

[116] Such an obligation is sometimes Constitutionally entrenched, *e.g.* Panama, E/1984/1/Add.19, at 2.

[117] *See e.g.* Sparsis, E/C.12/1990/SR.10, at 13, para. 82; Alston, E/C.12/1987/SR.6, at 3, para. 10. The reporting guidelines provide for reference to the relevant parts of ILO Convention No. 122 to avoid repetition. *Cf.* ILO Employment Policy Convention (No. 122), 1964, 569 UNTS 65.

No. 122 had been established. Such a policy 'seemed to be required if a State wished to prove that it was making every possible effort to ensure full employment'.[118] Beyond the question of the sufficiency of the policy concerned, members of the Committee have looked for both policies to combat unemployment in general[119] and policies that are directed at assisting specific vulnerable and disadvantaged groups.[120]

There is room for the Committee to expand further upon the type of policy it expects. It is submitted that States should be expected to show that they have a coherent strategy of the short, medium, and long-term which has as a central aim the achievement of full employment. In this respect it is arguable that a government policy that was directed towards the achievement of economic growth at the expense of maintaining a permanent pool of unemployed would be in conflict with that State's obligations under the Covenant.[121]

Similarly a stricter level of scrutiny should be directed at policies that relegate employment goals to long-term strategies. In this respect, those States that pursue a pure 'monetarist' philosophy where the emphasis is upon the adoption of fiscal measures to reduce inflation and encourage investment will be required to show that the short and medium-term effects are not unduly detrimental to the employment situation.[122] Although the reduction of inflation may be a precondition for the resumption of steady and stable growth, it should not be undertaken without measures to mitigate its adverse effect on employment.[123]

The Committee has, in general, paid considerable attention to the enjoyment of rights in the face of structural adjustment.[124] It has been argued in this context that those States that are suffering high levels of unemployment, whether as a result of structural adjustment or otherwise, should demonstrate that certain short-term policies are being taken with the spe-

---

[118] Alston, E/C.12/1987/SR.6, at 3, para. 10.

[119] *See e.g.* Texier, E/C.12/1990/SR.40, at 12, para. 57.

[120] *See* Texier, E/C.12/1989/SR.6, at 5, para. 20.

[121] *Cf.* art. 1(1) of the European Social Charter, *see* Conclusions I, at 13–14 (1970); Harris D., *The European Social Charter* (1984), at 23.

[122] The 'monetarist philosophy' that underlay UK and US economic policy in the 1980s was essentially a rejection of the Keynsian idea that governments could fix the level of unemployment through monetary and fiscal policies. It was asserted that such measures would lead to inflation and eventually a rise in unemployment. It was advocated instead that governments should concentrate on combatting inflation. If left alone, unemployment would settle at a 'natural rate' which was determined purely by the nature of the labour market. *See* Brittan S., *Second Thoughts on Full Employment Policy* (1975), 15–22. Although the monetarist philosophy does not prevent measures being taken to improve training and flexibility in the labour market, it does present a considerable obstacle to the idea that full employment is a matter than can be achieved through government action alone.

[123] *Cf.* Report of the ILO Director-General, 'Human Rights—A Common Responsibility' (1987) *Int. Lab. Conf. 75th Sess.* at 35.

[124] *See* General Comment No. 2 (1990), UN ESCOR, Supp. (No. 3), Annex III, at 88, para. 9, UN Doc. E/C.12/1990/3 (1990).

cific aim of reducing unemployment and which are targeted at alleviating the situation of the most vulnerable and disadvantaged and avoiding regional imbalance. A general or long-term policy in such a case would not be sufficient.[125] Further, where there is a large informal sector, States should adopt, in addition to short-term relief strategies, a policy that has as its aim the full integration of the informal sector into the formal economic and social life of the nation.

Whilst the text of article 6(2) does not require that full employment exist but rather that States pursue policies towards that end, the actual rate of unemployment will be significant in the Committee's evaluation of whether or not the State is committed to a policy to create high and stable levels of employment. There is no evidence yet that the Committee has established a 'ceiling' above which unemployment should not rise except in extreme circumstances, although it is open to it to do so. However, it is clear that the higher the level of unemployment, the stricter the scrutiny of State policy undertaken by the Committee will be. Members of the Committee have quite rightly expressed particular concern over rising levels of unemployment[126] or disproportionately high levels of unemployment within a State.[127] Although such situations do not necessarily give rise to violations of the Covenant in themselves, it is clear that they are of serious concern to the Committee when evaluating whether a State was in fact pursuing an adequate policy.

In accordance with article 6(2), the Committee has also expressed concern that employment should be productive and that measures should be adopted to this end.[128] It would appear to consider that policies merely aimed at producing high levels of employment with no apparent benefit to society are incompatible with the Convention.[129] That States should not undertake unproductive activities merely to boost employment is consonant with the principle that they should utilize their resources efficiently towards the realization of the rights in the Covenant.[130] Thus the view has been put forward within the ILO that increased productive employment is a vital factor in the realization of other basic economic and social rights (or, as the ILO puts it, the fulfilment of basic needs).[131]

---

[125] *Cf.* Mayer, *supra*, n. 90, at 240; Van den Berg and Guldenmund, *ibid.* 112.
[126] *See e.g.* Texier, E/C.12/1987/SR.5, at 6, para. 23; Sviridov, E/C.12/1987/SR.6, at 5, para. 16.
[127] Concluding observations of report of Lebanon, E/C.12/1993/10, at 2, para. 12.
[128] *See* Reporting guidelines, *supra*, n. 95, at 90.
[129] Whereas 'false employment' of this kind should be discouraged, the Committee must take heed of the ILO policy to encourage States to time the undertaking of public works in such a way as to reduce industrial fluctuations and unemployment. ILO Unemployment Recommendation (No. 1), 1 Off. Bull. 419 (1919–20); ILO Public Works (National Planning) Recommendation (No. 51), 22 Off. Bull. 86 (1937).
[130] *See above*, Ch. 3, text accompanying nn. 176–231.
[131] Valticos N., *International Labour Law* (1979), 118.

(b) The Opportunity to Gain his Living by Work

The reference to the opportunity to gain one's living by work in article 6 appears to relate most closely to the right to favourable conditions of work, and in particular the right to fair wages found in article 7(a)(i). Although the Committee does request information in its reporting guidelines as to the proportion of the working population who hold more than one job in order to secure an adequate standard of living for themselves and their family,[132] a more detailed consideration of the matter has occurred under the aegis of article 7.[133]

(c) Equal Access to Employment

The right to work in article 6, read together with the terms of article 2(2), prohibits discrimination as regards access to vocational guidance and training, access to freely chosen employment, and security of tenure in employment.[134] In fact, while adopting the ILO definition of discrimination, the Committee has addressed itself to the question of discrimination in employment as a whole. According to the reporting guidelines, the Committee is specifically concerned with 'distinctions, exclusions, restrictions, or preferences, be it in law or in administrative practices or in practical relationships, between persons or groups of persons, made on the basis of race, colour, sex, religion, political opinion, nationality, or social origin, which have the effect of nullifying or impairing the recognition, enjoyment, or exercise of equality of opportunity or treatment in employment or occupation'.[135]

It may be implied from the Committee's guidelines that equality of opportunity and treatment should be established for all individuals and groups within society. Quite clearly, any restriction that has the effect of unreasonably impairing the employment opportunities of members of a particular group would be contrary to the provisions of the Covenant. Thus, as in the cases of Iran and Zaïre, legal provisions which required women to seek the permission of their husbands in order to work outside the home have been considered to be a violation of the Covenant.[136]

It is apparent that a great number of States allow distinctions to be drawn with regard to access to employment on the grounds of sex, national origin, political opinion, religion, and sometimes race.[137] According to the general principles of non-discrimination, although many such distinctions may be considered to be 'suspect', those made as to the particular requirements of

---

[132] Reporting guidelines, *supra*, n. 95, at 91.   [133] *See below*, Ch. 6.
[134] *See generally*, above, Ch. 4.   [135] Reporting guidelines, *supra*, n. 95, at 91.
[136] *See* Alvarez Vita, E/C.12/1988/SR.17, at 2, para. 3; Concluding observations on report of Iran, E/C.12/1993/7, at 3, para. 6.
[137] *See* Blainpain R., 'Equality of Treatment in Employment' in Hepple B. (ed.), *Int. Encyclopedia of Comparative Law* (1990), Vol. XV, 'Labour Law', Ch. 10, at 17.

a job would not amount to discrimination.[138] The Committee thus requests information as to distinctions, exclusions, or preferences based on one of the stipulated conditions which are not considered to be discrimination in that country 'owing to the inherent requirements of a particular job'.[139] In addition, it has requested information on difficulties, disputes, and controversies as to the application of such conditions.[140]

Again, the Committee has not been called upon to establish the legitimacy of certain job requirements. Its approach at this stage merely seems to be to encourage debate at the national level as to the desirability of any such conditions. It is submitted that certain considerations should be borne in mind. First, such distinctions should be legitimate 'only in the case of jobs which by their very nature involve a special responsibility to contribute to the attainment of the institution's objectives',[141] or as part of a wider social commitment to the promotion of equality. Secondly, the legitimacy of such distinctions, especially as regards sex, change according to the prevailing social and moral norms of the time. In particular, measures of protection which, for example, restrict the employment of women in certain types of work (such as coal mines[142]), are now considered to be excessively paternalistic.[143]

Thirdly, whereas distinctions as to race might be legitimate for certain cultural purposes such as the employment of actors of a certain race for the purposes of 'authenticity',[144] it is doubtful whether they should be utilized otherwise. As has been stated, 'the term "race" cannot be given a very precise scientific definition, the essential point being the way in which the persons concerned consider their differences'.[145] Given the imprecise nature of such a concept and the possibilities for abuse, it would be better if any necessary distinctions, such as employment for authenticity, be made on the basis of national origin. Finally, although it is clear that restrictions will be placed upon foreign nationals and those of particular political persuasions

---

[138] *See* above, Ch. 4. *Cf. also* ILO Convention No. 111, art. 1(2). ILO Discrimination (Employment and Occupation) Convention (ILO Convention 111) 1958, 362 UNTS 31. Valticos, *supra*, n. 131, at 107.

[139] Reporting guidelines, *supra*, n. 95, at 91.   [140] *Ibid.*

[141] Rossillion C., 'ILO Standards and Actions for the Elimination of Discrimination and the Promotion of Equality of Opportunity in Employment' in Blainpain R. (ed.), *Equality and Prohibition of Discrimination in Employment* (1985) at 27.

[142] *See e.g.* ILO Night Work (Women) Convention (No. 4) 1919, 38 UNTS 67.

[143] *See*, e.g., the UK's denunciation of art. 8(4) European Social Charter which provides for the regulation of the employment of women at night and in underground mining. *See also* Polson T., 'The Rights of Working Women: An International Perspective' (1974) 14 *VJIL* 729, at 736–41.

[144] *Cf.* The exception provided for in the UK Race Relations Act 1976, s. 1(1)(b)(ii). *See e.g.* Hepple B., 'Great Britain' in Blainpain R. (ed.), *Equality and the Prohibition of Discrimination in Employment* (1985), 117.

[145] Valticos N., 'International Labour Law' in Blainpain R. (ed.), *International Encyclopaedia for Labour Law and Industrial Relations* (1977), s.246.

on employment in certain higher civil service posts, such restrictions should be limited to posts that bear some relation to the security of the State,[146] and to the extent that those persons can not reasonably be relied upon.[147]

The Committee has come to consider the legitimacy of restrictions imposed on access to employment, particularly where they are based on grounds of political affiliation.[148] Thus, in one case, a member of the Committee questioned the operation of the *Berufsverbot* laws in the FRG under which people whose political views did not reflect enough fidelity to the 'free democratic basic order' were excluded from public service. Information from an ILO report indicated that people had been excluded from access to non-security-related jobs, such as teaching, merely because they had criticized the existing economic order in Germany. Professor Alston doubted the legitimacy of those restrictions, concluding that 'economic and social rights could be effectively recognized only if individuals were free to speak out openly'.[149] In later comments on the same subject, the Committee emphasized this point in declaring that 'discrimination in employment on the ground of political opinion should be explicitly prohibited under law'.[150]

Members of the Committee have concerned themselves primarily with the position of women in the workforce.[151] Nevertheless it is clear that the Committee is also attentive to discrimination on the grounds of race, colour, sex, religion, political or other opinion, nationality, or social origin.[152] One area of growing concern appears to be the situation of the elderly.[153] One member, in particular, has been keen to ensure that those who are retired retain the right to engage in gainful employment without penalty[154] and has looked towards the possibility of retirement ages being deferred or abolished.[155] Other members of the Committee, however, have been wary about going so far. It was pointed out, in particular, that the abolition of the retirement age would conflict with other interests by blocking the employment or promotion prospects of younger people.[156]

---

[146] *Cf.* Alston, E/C.12/1987/SR.22, at 5, para. 18.

[147] *Cf.* ILO Convention No. 143. Valticos, *supra*, n. 131, at 107–8.

[148] *See e.g.* Konate, E/C.12/1991/SR.4, at 10, para. 55.

[149] Alston, E/C.12/1987/SR.19, at 9, para. 45. The matter also arose in the context of the European Convention, *see Kosiek* v. *FRG* Eur. Ct. H. R., Series A, Vol. 105, judgment of 28 Aug. 1986, (1987) 9 EHRR 328.

[150] Concluding observations on report of Germany, E/C.12/1993/4, at 2, para. 8.

[151] *See e.g.* Sviridov, E/C.12/1987/SR.6, at 5, para. 16; Rattray, E/C.12/1987/SR.6, at 12, para. 66; Jimenez Butragueno, E/C.12/1991/SR.3, at 11, para. 51; Sparsis, E/C.12/1992/SR.4, at 11, para. 50.

[152] *See above*, Ch. 4.

[153] *See e.g.* general discussion of a draft general comment on the rights of the elderly and old, E/C.12/1992/SR.8.

[154] Jimenez Butragueno, E/C.12/1992/SR.14, at 2, para. 3.

[155] *Ibid.*, E/C.12/1992/SR.4, at 12, para. 56.

[156] Simma, E/C.12/1992/SR.8, at 3, para. 16.

While the issue of retirement will be of growing importance in the developed world over the coming years, at present the Committee appears to consider it as an acceptable limitation on the individual's right to work.[157]

Another matter of interest in the context of discrimination is the degree to which aliens have a right to equal opportunity in employment.[158] It is readily accepted that foreign workers may be required to obtain special authorizations (or permits) in order to work.[159] Indeed the ILO has generally been cautious in its approach to distinctions between nationals and non-nationals.[160] However, it might be argued that the Covenant, in specifically allowing for the differential treatment of non-nationals in the case of developing countries (under article 2(3)), impliedly rules out the possibility of restrictions being imposed upon equality of access to employment in the case of developed countries.

A reservation on this specific point was entered by the UK on ratification. It reserved 'the right to interpret article 6 as not precluding the imposition of restrictions, based on birth or residence qualifications, on the taking of employment in any particular region or territory for the purpose of safeguarding the employment opportunities of workers in that region or territory'.[161] France also took steps in this direction, and made a declaration to the effect that article 6 is 'not to be interpreted as derogating from provisions governing the access of aliens to employment'.[162]

It is open to question whether the French interpretative declaration is in fact a 'mere interpretative declaration' or rather a 'qualified interpretative declaration' that might be assimilated to a reservation.[163] Arguably, France was in fact relying upon its declaration as a condition for its acceptance of the obligations under article 6 in which case the declaration would have the force of a reservation. This appears to have been the view of the French delegation when addressing the subject before the Committee. There, a member of the Committee had raised the question of the compatibility of a French law that restricted the payment of disability benefits to French nationals with article 2(2) of the Covenant.[164] In reply the French delegate

---

[157] This does not mean that any dismissal on the basis of age will necessarily be legitimate. As ILO Recommendation No. 166 (1982) provides (para. 5(a)), age cannot constitute a valid reason for termination of employment 'subject to national law and practice regarding retirement'.

[158] *See above*, Ch. 4.

[159] Blainpain, *supra*, n. 137, at 26. An important exception is found in art. 48 EEC Treaty.

[160] Dao (ILO), E/C.12/1989/SR.18, at 5, para. 28.

[161] *See* UN Doc. ST/LEG/SER.E/10, at 127 (1992).   [162] *Ibid.* 124.

[163] Such a distinction was utilized by the European Court of Human Rights in *Belilos* v. *Switzerland*, Eur. Ct. HR, Series A, Vol. 132, paras. 41–9, Judgment of 20 Apr. 1988, (1988) 10 EHRR 466.

[164] *See* Alvarez Vita, E/C.12/1989/SR.12, at 12, para. 61.

referred to the declaration implying that it had modified the French obligations under the Covenant.[165]

As the Covenant makes no reference to reservations it is presumed that they are legitimate in so far as they conform to the rules of customary international law, which can be taken to be those in article 19 of the Vienna Convention.[166] Neither reservation appears to be incompatible with the object or purpose of the Covenant, nor has any State objected to them. The effect of the UK and French reservations, which may be said to be tacitly approved, are to modify the obligations of those States under the Covenant in relation to other States parties.[167] They do not imply, however, that the provisions of the Covenant in general allow for such an interpretation.

In so far as the UK and France considered it necessary to rely upon reservations to modify their obligations under the Covenant, it might be assumed that the Covenant otherwise prohibits discrimination against aliens with respect to employment. Given general State practice, however, this would be a difficult position to maintain. Members of the Committee have paid little attention to the complexities of the issues involved. Questions have been asked as to the employment possibilities of foreign workers (including refugees[168]) in the same manner as for other groups.[169] However, when it comes to deal with the question in more detail the Committee might well find it difficult to adopt an interpretation that might prejudice the immigration policies of the States concerned.

It is possible that article 4 might be utilized to some effect here. According to that article, States are required to show that any restrictions they impose on the employment opportunities of foreign workers are determined by law and are 'solely for the purpose of promoting the general welfare in a democratic society'. Although this would not prohibit discrimination as regards aliens wishing to work in the country concerned, it would mean that any restrictions imposed should be extraordinary and justified on the basis of the general welfare.[170]

---

[165] *See* de Gouttes (France), E/C.12/1989/SR.13, at 10, para. 42. At a later stage France submitted a piece of 'additional information' in which it specifically utilized the language of art. 19(c) of the Vienna Convention in stating that the declaration 'cannot be seen as contrary to the object and purpose of the Covenant': E/1989/5/Add.1, at 6, para. 25.

[166] Vienna Convention on the Law of Treaties 1969, 1155 UNTS. 331.

[167] Arts. 20–1 Vienna Convention, *ibid*. An interpretative declaration, on the other hand, does not purport to modify the obligations under the Covenant but rather establishes an understanding of the relevant provision's meaning. Such a declaration, with the tacit acceptance of other States parties, might be seen to be an instrument indicating the general interpretation of art. 6 in accordance with art. 31(2)(b) of the Vienna Convention.

[168] *See* Taya, E/C.12/1988/SR.3, at 6, para. 22; Texier, E/C.12/1990/SR.40, at 12, para. 56.

[169] *See e.g.* Taya, E/C.12/1987/SR.6, at 6, para. 23.

[170] The European Court of Human Rights has not deferred entirely to State immigration policies that might affect the enjoyment of the rights of non-nationals. *See Berrehab* v. *Netherlands*, Eur. Ct. HR, Series A, Vol. 138, judgment of 21 June 1988, (1989) 11 EHRR 322.

Whereas article 6 is generally progressive in nature, the prohibition of discrimination is to be implemented immediately.[171] In theory then, a State will be obliged to ensure that whatever stage in the realization of article 6 it has achieved, there should be no vestiges of discrimination. It is clear that the State is obliged to take the necessary legislative and administrative action (whether through enacting new measures or repealing old inconsistent ones) to ensure equality of treatment as to employment and the related spheres of education, vocational guidance, and training. Although article 2(1) specifically leaves States with a certain amount of discretion as to what measures are appropriate, members of the Committee have placed a high priority on legislation in the field of discrimination.[172]

In addition, it is clear that the Committee expects States to take appropriate action to ensure observance of the principles of non-discrimination with respect to employment and vocational guidance under private control.[173] Various methods could be employed to achieve this end such as making the receipt of funds or licences dependent upon the observance of such principles. Committee members have also placed some emphasis upon the establishment of appropriate agencies to promote the application of the policy and provide for appropriate remedies.[174]

A point of some interest is the extent to which States are required to control trade union security measures (such as the closed shop), that might effectively limit access to employment through a requirement of union membership. It is possible to argue that such arrangements, despite being discriminatory, have a legitimate purpose in ensuring the effectiveness of the trade unions concerned. Although the Covenant itself, like other international instruments,[175] does not expressly prohibit closed shop agreements, the Committee has suggested that they are incompatible with the right not to join trade unions which it has read into article 8.[176] It has made no comment with respect to the effect of such agreements on an individual's right to work.

In accordance with its approach to non-discrimination generally,[177] the Committee has looked towards the achievement of *de facto* equality of

However, it is doubtful whether it would take such a position in the delicate area of employment.

[171] *See above*, Ch. 4, text accompanying nn. 181–4.

[172] *See e.g.* Sviridov, E/C.12/1987/SR.6, at 4, para. 14; Alston, E/C.12/1987/SR.6, at 3, para. 8.

[173] *See e.g.* Simma, E/C.12/1989/SR.8, at 8, para. 46; Muterahejuru, E/C.12/1987/SR.5, at 10, para. 46.

[174] For the ILO position, *see* Valticos, *supra*, n. 131, at 110.

[175] In the case of the European Social Charter, the text itself is neutral on the question of closed-shop agreements. The Committee of Independent Experts, however, has found union security agreements to be incompatible with art. 5. *See* Conclusions XI-1, at 78 (1989).

[176] *See below*, Ch. 7, text accompanying nn. 163–73.

[177] *See above*, Ch. 4, text accompanying nn. 28–35.

opportunity.[178] Thus members of the Committee have expressed interest both as to the level and type of employment in different social groups.[179] There does appear to be some expectation that States take specific measures to develop the employment prospects of disadvantaged groups. As with the ILO,[180] it would seem that any such differences aimed at promoting equality of opportunity and treatment would not be considered discriminatory. The ILO additionally has considered that specific quotas in employment are not necessarily discriminatory if their effect is to 'secure an equilibrium between the different communities and ensure protection of minorities, or to compensate for discrimination against the economically less advanced population group'.[181] Although it might be possible to infer from the Committee's general approach that affirmative action measures are legitimate, the necessity of taking those measures in the context of employment has not been clearly established.

(d) Employment Services

In contrast to the European Social Charter (article 1(3)), the Covenant does not specifically provide for the establishment and maintenance of employment agencies, nor has the Committee made mention of such an obligation in its reporting guidelines. Indeed individual members have only mentioned the matter infrequently.[182] However, there is little doubt that the provision of placement services is crucial not only to the full exercise of the individual's right to freely chosen work of an appropriate nature, but is important as far as the effective use of human resources is concerned. That the State stands to gain from the maximization of its human potential suggests that a right to employment placement services could be inferred from the obligation to achieve steady economic, social, and cultural development and full and productive employment.[183]

(e) Occupational Training

Article 6(2) provides that the steps taken to achieve the full realization of the right to work shall include 'technical and vocational guidance and training programmes'. The reference to technical and vocational training might more naturally have formed part of the right to education in article 13 rather than the right to work. In so far as article 6 provides for an individual

[178] *See e.g.* Simma, E/C.12/1988/SR.3, at 3, para. 8.

[179] *See e.g.* Muterahejuru, E/C.12/1987/SR.5, at 10, para. 46; Texier, E/C.12/1989/SR.6, at 5, para. 24; Sparsis, E/C.12/1992/SR.4, at 11, para. 48.

[180] *See* art. 5 ILO Discrimination (Employment and Occupation) Convention (No. 111) 1958, 362 UNTS 31.

[181] Valticos, *supra*, n. 131, at 108.

[182] *See e.g.* Texier, E/C.12/1989/SR.10, at 8, para. 40; Jimenez Butragueno, E/C.12/1987/SR.14, at 11, para. 32.

[183] The standards on the organization of a public employment service are found in the ILO Employment Service Convention (No. 88) 1948, 70 UNTS 85.

right to technical and vocational guidance and training, like article 13, it is logically of a progressive character.[184] The ultimate objective is clearly for every individual to be given the opportunity for appropriate guidance and training with regard to their personal capacity and relevant employment opportunities. Such a service should be free or financially assisted in appropriate cases.

At this early stage, the Committee has limited itself to requesting information as to the mode of operation and practical availability of such training programmes. Information is requested specifically on the situation with respect to persons according to their race, colour, sex, religion, and national origin.[185] Members of the Committee have also been concerned with the financing of such schemes.[186] Although private training establishments were to be accommodated, it was felt that there should also be a central authority for evaluating the needs of industry[187] and co-ordinating the activities of the public and private training schemes.[188]

2 Free Choice in Employment

Article 6 provides that the right to work includes the opportunity to gain one's living by work which is freely chosen or accepted. Members of the Committee have stressed the need for free choicc in employment,[189] but little has been said about how it should be ensured in practice. The Committee's guidelines merely suggest that there should be relevant national provisions ensuring freedom of choice.[190]

In theory, the concept of freely chosen employment extends to ensuring the fullest opportunity for each worker to use his or her skills in a suitable job.[191] There is a possible tension here between absolute individual choice and the limited options that might be open to him or her in the employment market.[192] It is not realistic to suggest, for example, that the State has to create work opportunities that correspond entirely to the wishes of

---

[184] Although the right to occupational training is to be implemented immediately under art. 10 of the European Social Charter, it would probably be too burdensome for many developing States.

[185] Reporting guidelines, *supra*, n. 95, at 91.

[186] *See e.g.* Badawi El Sheikh, E/C.12/1987/SR.5, at 3, para. 11.

[187] *See* Sparsis, E/C.12/1987/SR.5, at 7, para. 31.

[188] *See* Jimenez Butragueno, E/C.12/1988/SR.3, at 4, para. 9. For the ILO position in this area, *see*, General Survey of the Committee of Experts, *Human Resources Development: Vocational Guidance and Training, Paid Educational Leave* (1991), ILC 78th Sess., Report III (Pt. 4B).

[189] *See e.g.* Badawi El Sheikh, E/C.12/1987/SR.13, at 7, para. 30; Alvarez Vita, E/C.12/1987/SR.21, at 12, para. 54; Rattray, E/C.12/1987/SR.13, at 6, para. 24.

[190] Reporting guidelines, *supra*, n. 95, at 90.

[191] *See* Konate, E/C.12/1987/SR.7, at 2, para. 2.

[192] *See* Badawi El Sheikh, E/C.12/1987/SR.22, at 2, para. 2.

individuals seeking work.[193] As the Austrian representative stressed before the Committee:

The right to work, understood as a right to a job or a specific job, was not included in the Austrian legal order, and it was impossible for the State to guarantee a certain job to a certain person in a certain place. Employment opportunities clearly depended on the economic situation. What could be guaranteed was the right to help in finding a new job and in overcoming the difficulties associated with unemployment.[194]

An obligation to ensure freedom of choice can only imply that the State should provide appropriate employment training, guidance, and placement services. These have already been dealt with above.[195]

However, as was made clear in the drafting of article 6, the reference to freely chosen and accepted employment was also considered to entail a prohibition of forced labour.[196] Such a conclusion may also be drawn from the term 'opportunity' and indeed from the idea that a right to work implies simultaneously a right not to work. The ILO has dealt extensively with the question of forced labour particularly in Convention No. 29 of 1930[197] and Convention No. 105 of 1957.[198] The latter Convention deals with various matters that are of relevance to the application of the right to work within the Covenant. It prohibits *inter alia* the use of forced labour as a method of using labour for purposes of economic development and as a means of labour discipline (specifically for having participated in a strike).

The Committee as a whole has not made any specific references to the question of forced labour and does not make it a matter for general response in its reporting guidelines. Although this may reflect a desire not to impinge upon the work of the Human Rights Committee with respect to article 8 of the ICCPR, individual members of the Committee have not considered themselves to be so constrained. In particular, in the case of the Dominican Republic, great concern was expressed as to the position of Haitian workers where there was evidence to show that they had been recruited by force and compelled to work for the entire sugar-cane harvest season.[199]

---

[193] *See* Sieghart P., Ziman J., and Humphrey J., *The World of Science and the Rule of Law* (1986), 71.

[194] Berchtold (Austria), E/C.12/1988/SR.4, at 3, para. 13. Similarly, as the Director-General of the ILO noted: 'While this [freedom of choice] does not mean that work must be made available in accordance with individual preferences irrespective of a need for the services concerned, it implies the development of programmes to foster skills for the use of which opportunities can reasonably be expected to exist': Report of the ILO Director-General, *supra*, n. 123, at 33.

[195] *See above*, text accompanying nn. 182–8.

[196] *See above*, text accompanying nn. 45–51.

[197] ILO Forced Labour Convention (No. 29) 1930, 39 UNTS 55.

[198] ILO Forced Labour Convention (No. 105), 1957, 320 UNTS 291.

[199] *See* Texier, E/C.12/1990/SR.44, at 12, para. 54.

While article 6(2) stipulates that among the steps to be taken to realize the right to work, States should create policies and techniques to achieve steady economic, social, and cultural development, it is clear that the right to choose employment prohibits the adoption by States of measures such as the compulsory requisitioning of labour to achieve economic growth or full employment.[200] It is arguable, nevertheless, that States may rely upon the provisions of article 4 to justify compulsory labour in cases of emergency where the 'general welfare' so demands.[201] Thus some States allow a certain amount of compulsion in employment in cases of *force majeure*.[202] However, any such exception would clearly have to be 'determined by law' and proportionate to the emergency faced.

Whereas the ILO has considered that compulsory employment training programmes or 'youth schemes' are contrary to the prohibition of forced labour[203] (with certain limited exceptions[204]), article 6 does not seem to cover them to the same extent. In particular, free choice of employment appears to be confined to cases of remunerative work alone, excluding those schemes that have no direct form of remuneration. In absence of an unambiguous provision to this effect, however, it is open for the Committee to interpret free choice in employment as applying to all forms of employment whether remunerative or otherwise, but in doing so it would have to consider how far it wishes to extend the scope of the Covenant. For example, this would bring in questions such as the legitimacy of forced labour as part of penal service.[205] There is a case for arguing that, as other instruments already deal with such questions,[206] it would be better for the Committee to confine itself to issues of work as a remunerative activity.

In considering the report of Zaïre, it was noted that the ILO Committee of Experts had commented on the requisitioning of medical practitioners and graduates and had emphasized the need to bring all legislation concerning civic service into conformity with the Forced Labour Convention (No. 29) 1930.[207] Members of the Committee relied upon this information to enquire into the general situation of forced labour in

---

[200] *See* Valticos, *supra*, n. 131, at 98.

[201] This would broadly cover the exception found in art. 8(c)(iii) ICCPR.

[202] Vallaro (Panama), E/C.12/1991/SR.5, at 2, para. 5.

[203] *See* Abolition of Forced Labour—General Survey by the Committee of Experts on the Application of Conventions and Recommendations, 65th Sess. (1979), ILO II.65/3 (4B), at 41.

[204] Special Youth Schemes Recommendation 1970 (No. 136), para. 7(2)(a) and (b), in ILO, *International Labour Conventions and Recommendations (1919–1981)* (1982), at 81.

[205] This question did arise in the case of Panama, but only following the comments of the ILO representative, *see* Swepston (ILO), E/C.12/1991/SR.3, at 5, para. 21; Ucros (Panama), E/C.12/1991/SR.3, at 13, para. 61.

[206] *See e.g.* art. 8(3)(c)(ii) ICCPR.

[207] *See* Dao (ILO), E/C.12/1988/SR.17, at 9, para. 59. One of the exceptions to the prohibition of youth schemes relates to obligations of service that have been accepted as a condition of training. The Committee of Experts has considered that such an exception may operate only where there is full compliance with the forced labour conventions.

Zaïre.[208] Following an assurance by Zaïre that such requisitioning had been discontinued, the matter went no further. One might infer that the Committee will concern itself with issues of civic service[209] (and presumably military service), but in the absence of its own detailed standards, the Committee will initially draw upon those of the ILO in its interpretation of the Covenant.[210] This was apparently accepted by Zaïre in the present case.

According to the ILO, the notion of freely chosen employment also prohibits the use of compulsory labour as a means of labour discipline either to ensure the performance of a contract or as a punishment for breaches of labour discipline. Unlike the question of penal labour, this would appear to fall clearly within the realm of the Covenant. The Committee has not adopted any coherent policy on such a question and individual comments have only centered on the question of the right not to work in general.[211] It is submitted that the Committee should ensure that workers have the right to terminate contracts of employment (with reasonable notice in appropriate cases). Particular care should be taken when the law provides for the enforcement of the individual labour contract, especially where it is by use of criminal law.[212]

A similar concern relates to the right to strike. Although not necessarily relating to the right to terminate employment, excessive restrictions on the right to strike may well amount to a form of coercion to work against the individual's better judgement.[213] The Committee has dealt with the question of the right to strike in the context of article 8 of the Covenant where it is specifically provided for.[214]

Perhaps the area that has concerned members of the Committee most is where States provide for a 'duty to work'. As noted above, certain members of the Committee have stressed that the right to work implies a right not to work.[215] Accordingly, a legally enforceable duty to work might well be in contravention of article 6 of the Covenant.[216] In many States, a duty to work may be Constitutionally defined,[217] yet remain merely a moral obligation

---

[208] *See e.g.* Alston, E/C.12/1988/SR.17, at 8, para. 45.

[209] For the approach of the European Commission on Human Rights in this area, *see* Nedjati Z., *Human Rights under the European Convention* (1978), 73.

[210] For the Committee's willingness to utilize ILO standards, *see* Konate, E/C.12/1990/SR.42, at 5, para. 18.

[211] *See e.g.* Rattray, E/C.12/1987/SR.21, at 13, para. 63.

[212] The enforcement of contracts of employment through criminal law has been considered to be contrary to the European Social Charter, *see* e.g. Conclusions V, at 6 (1977); Harris, *supra*, n. 121, at 27.

[213] *See* General Survey of the Committee of Experts, *supra*, n. 188, paras. 122–31; Ben-Israel R., *International Labour Standards: The Case of Freedom to Strike* (1988), at 24–5.

[214] *See below*, Ch. 7, text accompanying nn. 228–76.

[215] *See* Rattray, E/C.12/1987/SR.21, at 13, para. 63.

[216] *See* Neneman, E/C.12/1988/SR.17, at 4, para. 23.

[217] *See e.g.* Yemen, E/1990/5/Add.2, at 2, para. 3; Costa Rica (art. 7 of the Constitution), E/1990/5/Add.3, at 2, para. 6; Panama (art. 59 Constitution of 1972), E/1984/6/Add.19, at 2.

without concomitant legal sanctions.[218] Members of the Committee have inquired into the precise legal value of such provisions when they are apparent, and have warned against the possible abuses to which the obligation to work could give rise.[219] There is no evidence as yet that the mere existence of such provisions will be considered to be contrary to the provisions of the Covenant.

3 Guarantee against Arbitrary Dismissal

Although it is not mentioned specifically, it would be reasonable to conclude that one element of the right to work in article 6 should be the right not to be arbitrarily deprived of work.[220] Indeed this could be inferred from the recognition of an obligation to respect and protect the right to work. While the Committee as a whole has only indirectly made reference to such a right in the context of the right to work,[221] individual members have been strong advocates of freedom from arbitrary dismissal. Indeed one member commented that '[w]ithout a fundamental guarantee against arbitrary dismissal, the right to work would be meaningless'.[222]

The most commonly established rules on employment security provide that termination of employment should not take place unless there is a valid reason connected with the capacity or conduct of the worker or based upon the operational requirements of the undertaking concerned.[223] Members of the Committee have not indicated whether they will adopt this general principle, but have merely suggested that dismissals should not be 'arbitrary'. Members thus appear to expect the States concerned to establish their own rules governing whether or not a dismissal is 'justified',[224] but nevertheless will comment upon the adequacy of such rules. For example, in considering the report of Trinidad and Tobago it was noted that the concept of 'retirement in the public interest' appeared to involve 'a risk of arbitrariness'.[225]

In certain circumstances the dismissal of an employee for arbitrary reasons might amount to discrimination. Thus in the case of Czechoslovakia, it was noted that a report of the ILO Committee of

[218] *Cf.* General Survey on Forced Labour, *supra*, n. 188, para. 45.

[219] *See e.g.* Mratchkov, E/C.12/1990/SR.40, at 13, para. 63; *ibid.*, E/C.12/1991/SR.4, at 12, para. 66; Neneman, E/C.12/1991/SR.3, at 8, para. 41.

[220] For the *travaux préparatoires* on this point *see above*, text accompanying n. 31.

[221] *Cf.* General observations on additional information of Panama, E/1993/22, at 53, para. 197.

[222] Badawi El Sheikh, E/C.12/1987/SR.5, at 3, para. 12. *See also* Mratchkov, E/C.12/1990/SR.40, at 13, para. 63.

[223] *Cf.* ILO Termination of Employment at the Initiative of the Employer Recommendation (No. 119), 1963, in ILO, *International Labour Conventions and Recommendations (1919–1981)* (1982), at 138. *See also* Hepple, *supra*, n. 93, at 478–80.

[224] *See e.g.* Mratchkov, E/C.12/1987/SR.6, at 12, para. 62; Mratchkov, E/C.12/1987/SR.21, at 10, para. 43.

[225] Marchan Romero, E/C.12/1989/SR.17, at 17, para. 89.

Experts drew attention to fact that workers might be dismissed for short-comings related not only to their professional skills, but also to their civic engagement (non-legal social responsibilities), moral, or political qualities. The Committee pointed out that protection of workers against discrimination on the ground of political opinion should also be extended in respect of activities expressing opposition to established political principles. One member commented:

Even if the aim of the authors of Charter 77 had been to change the existing social order, in the absence of any indication that they sought to bring about that result by violent or unconstitutional means, such an aim should not constitute grounds for considering them as being beyond the protection afforded under article 2(2) of the Covenant.[226]

It appears that the termination of employment on such grounds would amount to a violation of article 2(2) in conjunction with article 6.

In the practice of a number of States, certain procedural safeguards accompany dismissal arrangements. These may include the communication of reasons for dismissal to the employee, consultation with, or notification of the fact of dismissal to, the relevant trades unions, and the provision of advance notice to the employees concerned in cases of contracts of indefinite duration. In cases of dismissal for serious misconduct, notice may not be required, but it should only take place after a hearing and then only where the employer cannot be expected to take any other course.[227] Certain members of the Committee have made reference to these principles in their questions.[228] In one notable case, a rule that the employer only had to give notice of dismissal or make redundancy payments to workers with more than ten years service was considered too restrictive.[229] However, nowhere has the Committee made reference to such principles *in toto*.

The Committee's main cause for concern seems to have been that there should be adequate safeguards to enable any worker who feels he has been unjustifiably dismissed to appeal,[230] or apply for judicial review[231] of that decision to a court or some other independent body. Thus in the case of Panama, the Committee was critical of the fact that the remedies provided in the labour code against arbitrary dismissal did not apply when political

[226] Simma, E/C.12/1987/SR.13, at 9, para. 40. *Cf.* Concluding observations on report of Germany, E/C.12/1993/17, at 2, para. 8.

[227] *See* Hepple, *supra*, n. 93, at 493–4; Kennedy T., *European Labour Relations* (1980), at 386. *See also* Valticos, *supra*, n. 131, at 169.

[228] *See e.g.* did trade unions play any role in protecting workers from arbitrary dismissal? Sviridov, E/C.12/1987/SR.6, at 4, para. 16. Did the concept of 'grievous fault' whereby workers could be dismissed without notice exist in Czechoslovakia? Texier, E/C.12/1987/SR.13, at 10, para. 49.

[229] *See* Sparsis, E/C.12/1989/SR.11, at 15, para. 66.

[230] *See e.g.* Texier, E/C.12/1987/SR.5, at 5, para. 22; Mratchkov, E/C.12/1988/SR.3, at 4, para. 10; Simma, E/C.12/1993/SR.25, at 5, para. 20.

[231] *See* Rattray, E/C.12/1987/SR.5, at 9, para. 43.

grounds were invoked.[232] Additionally, members have stressed that the individual should be provided with some form of remedy for an invalid termination of contract,[233] which might take the form of compensation[234] or reinstatement.[235]

The concept of workforce reductions may be distinguished from disciplinary dismissals in that it generally affects a larger number of employees and has more significant social and economic consequences for society as a whole.[236] As members of the Committee have only occasionally alluded to the specific nature of workforce reductions,[237] it is submitted that certain general principles may be borne in mind. First, whereas job security may be provided for it is not often of a uniform nature. As one commentator noted: 'There is a hierarchy of ranks in the labour market from whole-time secure employment through less secure forms of whole-time employment, part-time employment, and casual and temporary work to continuous unemployment.'[238] Many of the more pressing problems will relate to the less secure forms of employment. Secondly, the lack of collective bargaining power in specific sectors of employment often entails that certain groups in society such as ethnic minorities, women, and migrant workers are particularly vulnerable to unemployment. Thirdly, in the face of economic adjustment it is open for States to encourage the use of alternative methods to alleviate the pressure upon undertakings without recourse to workforce reductions. Such methods might include the reduction of the workforce through 'natural wastage' or the reduction of working time.

IV. CONCLUSION

Although it is commonly assumed that a right to work means the right to be given the job of one's choice, it is manifestly clear, both from the *travaux préparatoires* and from the approach of the Committee that this is neither realistic nor the principal utility of article 6. The Committee has not been in a position to require that States achieve full employment at any particular point in their development, nor has it come to an understanding as to the means by which unemployment might be monitored or what benchmarks might be utilized for assessing the adequacy of State performance. Rather,

[232] General observations on additional information of Panama, E/1993/22, at 53, para. 197.
[233] *See* Mratchkov, E/C.12/1987/SR.13, at 4, para. 12.
[234] *See* Mratchkov, E/C.12/1987/SR.6, at 12, para. 62.
[235] *See* Mratchkov, E/C.12/1990/SR.34, at 7, para. 47.
[236] *See* Hepple, *supra*, n. 93, at 479.
[237] *See e.g.* Texier, E/C.12/1988/SR.3, at 5, para. 15; Mratchkov, E/C.12/1988/SR.17, at 5, para. 30; Jimenez Butragueno, E/C.12/1988/SR.17, at 8, para. 52; Jimenez Butragueno, E/C.12/1989/SR.18, at 5, para. 20.
[238] Hepple, *supra*, n. 93, at 480.

the Committee's current concern has been to ensure that States establish and pursue a policy that has as its main objective the achievement of full employment and that due consideration is given to vulnerable sectors of the population.

The Committee has indicated, however, that article 6 includes a number of other elements that derive from ensuring to the individual the opportunity to work. Particular matters that have been identified by Committee members include the right of equal access to employment, the right to freedom from arbitrary dismissal, and the right to freedom from forced labour. In terms of equality of access, the Committee has been effective in identifying instances of discriminatory legislation and practice that impede access to employment for certain groups such as women or political dissidents. It has also shown an awareness of possible new areas of concern such as the rights of the elderly and people with disabilities. While these are important developments, it is apparent that the Committee needs to establish some general principles that should be used to govern access to employment in specific circumstances.

The Committee has been very clear in its understanding that the right to work includes a right not to be arbitrarily dismissed. While it has not yet established any broad principles to govern the practice of dismissals, it has consistently looked to the existence of adequate judicial or other safeguards to allow those dismissed some form of remedy. In certain cases it has gone further in criticizing specific cases of dismissals, such as those undertaken on the basis of political affiliation of the employee or of their trade union membership. These, however, remain isolated instances from which no broad policy may be inferred.

As regards free choice in employment, the Committee has recognized its importance and has in fact addressed several cases of forced labour. Nevertheless, it has worked very much on an *ad hoc* basis in the light of information received from the ILO. This may be partly explained by the fact that on a textual analysis there is no clear right not to work. Although reference is made to freely chosen work, it is made solely in the context of remunerative employment, thus apparently excluding a number of issues relating to forced labour such as penal service or compulsory training without pay. More significantly, however, it is clear that both the ILO and the Human Rights Committee have established roles as regards the elimination of forced labour, making it unnecessary for the Committee to take on that burden.

The role of the Committee as an international supervisory body in relation to matters arising out of article 6, as with articles 7, 8, and 9, will inevitably be secondary to that of the ILO. In fact, as is evident from the cases of the Dominican Republic, Czechoslovakia, and Germany, the Committee will often take its cue from the ILO. It is arguable that the Committee may have a minor role in reinforcing the supervisory processes of the ILO, but its main utility will be in addressing States that are not party to the relevant ILO Conventions, or where the Covenant standards are more strict. As such there is a pressing need for members of the Committee to have sufficient understanding and awareness of the relevant ILO norms and the degree to which article 6 duplicates or extends the protection offered by those ILO provisions. This is also appropriate, not merely because of the necessity of maintaining institutional co-operation and compatible standards, but also because those ILO standards will reflect, to a large degree, the current State practice of many of the State parties to the Covenant.

At present, such knowledge is lacking in the Committee. Given the inadequate Secretariat servicing and generally poor level of participation by the ILO, there is clearly a need for individual Committee members to develop their own expertise in the area. As an initial measure, the Committee will have to establish the general scope of article 6. For example, it will have to decide the extent to which article 6 provides for the individual right to benefit from the services of employment agencies or the right to vocational guidance and training. Further, it will have to take a position with respect to those issues that are of particular delicacy, such as the legitimacy of restrictions on the access to employment for non-nationals (whether through work permits or otherwise), or non-union members (where pre-entry closed shop agreements exist).

6
Just and Favourable Conditions of Work

Article 7
The States Parties to the present Covenant recognize the right of everyone to
the enjoyment of just and favourable conditions of work which ensure, in
particular:
  (a) Remuneration which provides all workers as a minimum with:
      (i) Fair wages and equal remuneration for work of equal value with-
      out distinction of any kind, in particular women being guaranteed
      conditions of work not inferior to those enjoyed by men, with
      equal pay for equal work;
      (ii) A decent living for themselves and their families in accordance
      with the provisions of the present Covenant;
  (b) Safe and healthy working conditions;
  (c) Equal opportunity for everyone to be promoted in his employment to
  an appropriate higher level, subject to no considerations other than
  those of seniority and competence;
  (d) Rest, leisure and reasonable limitation of working hours and periodic
  holidays with pay, as well as remuneration for public holidays.

I. INTRODUCTION

In a broad sense, the right to just and favourable conditions of work in
article 7 is an essential corollary of the right to work (found in article 6). If,
on the one hand, work is seen to be a necessary evil then humanity requires
that the conditions under which it is undertaken are as tolerable as possible.
On the other hand, if work is seen to be a productive activity entered into
as a matter of choice, then utility demands that the terms of employment
are reasonable and attractive. Notwithstanding such considerations, some
elements of article 7 are among the most controversial of all economic,
social, and cultural rights.[1] It may be questioned, for example, whether
rest and leisure are sufficiently important to be established as 'human
rights'. Equally, it is now frequently argued that the benefits to the individual of instituting a minimum wage are far outweighed by the harm it
causes to the economy in general. There are, however, a number of less
controversial elements to article 7, such as the right to equal remuneration
and the right to safe and healthy working conditions, which are undoubtedly of importance.

[1] *See* Sieghart P., *The Lawful Rights of Mankind* (1986), 129.

Although the text of article 7 defines the right to just and favourable conditions of work in more detail than article 23 of the UDHR, for example, it does so by establishing a number of other rights (such as the right to fair wages, or equal pay) each of which in turn requires further definition. As with articles 6 and 8 however, the Committee has the benefit of being able to draw upon the great experience of the ILO in developing the precise meaning of terms within article 7.

II. THE *TRAVAUX PRÉPARATOIRES*

The Commission on Human Rights discussed the provisions on conditions of work at its 218th to 222nd, and 279th to 281st meetings in 1951 and 1952.[2] The draft article 7 was then finalized following a discussion in the Third Committee at its 713th to 719th meetings in 1956.[3] The following issues were considered in the drafting process.

A Article 7: State Obligations

As with other articles in the Covenant, the principal discussion centered on the question whether the State could be said to be wholly responsible for conditions of work.[4] It was argued that the method of securing conditions of work varied according to the organization of the industrial and economic system of the State concerned. In the case of those States that operated a system of collective bargaining, it would be impossible for the State to assume responsibility for matters that were negotiated by the trade unions,[5] especially as regards the right to equal pay.[6] Thus a USSR amendment[7] to add a provision requiring States to guarantee just and favourable conditions of work to all wage earners, either through law or collective agreements, was rejected.[8]

Nevertheless it came to be accepted that the State did have some responsibility to improve conditions of work in a progressive manner,[9] especially where the State itself acted as an employer.[10] Such a responsibility was accepted, however, on the basis that States would retain

---

[2] UN Docs. E/CN.4/SR.218–22 (1951); UN Docs. E/CN.4/SR.279–81 (1952).
[3] UN Doc. A/C.3/SR.713–19 (1956).
[4] UN Doc. A/2929, 10 UN GAOR, Annexes (Ag. Item 28), pt. II, at 105, para. 10 (1955).
[5] *See* Bowie (UK), E/CN.4/SR.206, at 10 (1951); Roosevelt (USA), E/CN.4/SR.279, at 12 (1952).
[6] *See* Sørensen (Denmark), E/CN.4/SR.207, at 8 (1951); Boersma (Netherlands), A/C.3/SR.713, at 158, para. 12 (1956).
[7] E/CN.4/L.46, para. 4.   [8] It was rejected by 9 votes to 8 with 4 abstentions.
[9] *See* Thierry (France), A/C.3/SR.715, at 173, para. 45 (1956).
[10] *See* Rossel (Sweden), E/CN.4/SR.207, at 13 (1951); Bengtson (Sweden), A/C.3/SR.713, at 160, para. 31 (1956).

considerable discretion as to the means by which fair conditions of work would be ensured.[11]

B Article 7(a): Minimum Remuneration

There was considerable concern during the drafting of article 7(a) that the term 'minimum remuneration' would have a limitative effect;[12] it was feared that the phrase would be used as a 'ceiling' rather than a 'minimum' and might act as a check on further progress.[13] It was thought preferable that the level of remuneration should reflect the ideas of fairness and equality, mention of which was to be found elsewhere in the article.[14] The term 'minimum remuneration' was finally accepted, however, on the basis that it would have considerable utility in the context of less developed countries.[15] One member, in recognizing the potential usefulness of the term with regard to future implementing bodies, commented that 'it seemed difficult to disregard an aspect of the matter that might give rise to a court action'.[16]

In the Third Committee a number of States were concerned that the guarantee of minimum remuneration attached itself to the position of 'workers' which, if construed to include only industrial workers, was unduly restrictive.[17] It was explained that article 7 was not intended to cover the position of the self-employed or employers,[18] and that the term 'workers' had been advocated on the basis that protection was to be restricted to wage-earners.[19] After noting that ILO practice was to use the term 'worker' as a generic one, including both industrial and commercial employees,[20] the provision was found to be generally acceptable upon the condition it was to be seen as including all categories of workers.[21] Surprisingly enough, the precise meaning of the term remained somewhat obscure. On the basis that delegates wished to use the term in a wide sense,[22] it is assumed that it

---

[11] *See* Myrrdin-Evans (ILO), E/CN.4/SR.218, at 18 (1951); Pickford (ILO), E/CN.4/SR.279, at 14 (1952).

[12] *See* Manas (Comm. on Status of Women), E/CN.4/SR.279, at 6 (1952); Santa Cruz (Chile), *ibid.* 7 (1952); Mehta (India), *ibid.* 9 (1952); Pickford (ILO), *ibid.* 14 (1952); Payro (ILO), A/C.3/SR.714, at 164, para. 16 (1956); Marriott (Australia), *ibid.* SR.716, at 176, para. 11 (1956).

[13] *See* Sender (ICFTU), E/CN.4/SR.279, at 15 (1952).

[14] *See* Elliott (UK), A/C.3/SR.715, at 170, para. 13 (1956).

[15] *See e.g.* Ahmed (Pakistan), A/C.3/SR.716, at 177, para. 24 (1956). Rivas (Venezuela), *ibid.* 178, para. 33 (1956).

[16] Cassin (France), E/CN.4/SR.279, at 11 (1952).

[17] *See e.g.* Massoud-Ansari (Iran), A/C.3/SR.717, at 182, para. 21 (1956). Pazhwak (Afghanistan), *ibid.* 183, para. 26 (1956).

[18] *See* Cheng (China), A/C.3/SR.715, at 170, para. 23 (1956).

[19] *See e.g.* Diaz Casanueva (Chile), A/C.3/SR.717, at 183, para. 24 (1956).

[20] *See* Payro (ILO), A/C.3/SR.717, at 183, para. 27 (1956).

[21] *See* Pazhwak (Afghanistan), A/C.3/SR.718, at 185, para. 4 (1956).

[22] UN Doc. A/3525, 11 UN GAOR, Annexes, Ag. Item 31, at 6, para. 44 (1956).

includes all those who work for a living (excluding those who work merely on a voluntary basis). In addition to wage-earners, this would also appear to cover the self-employed.

C Article 7(a)(i): Fair Wages and Equal Remuneration

It was proposed that wages should be fixed both in relation to the cost of living and the profits made from the undertakings employing the workers.[23] However, it was pointed out that a reference to the profits made would pose considerable problems, especially in the context of State-owned industries.[24] It might also legitimize reductions in wages in enterprises running at a loss and result in vastly different wages for similar work across the public utilities.[25] Both proposals were ultimately rejected, although the reference to the cost of living by only a narrow margin.[26]

The main discussion centered upon the question whether specific reference should be made to women in the equal remuneration clause. It was argued that such a reference was repetitious[27] and would be 'dangerous' in that it implied that women were not covered by the original equality clauses,[28] and that there was some disadvantage in employing women.[29] A simple reference to 'workers' or 'everyone' which did not limit the principle to men and women was thought preferable.[30] Those who advocated a reference to women in the equal remuneration clause argued that most States still had a long way to go in that regard.[31] It was noted that the principle had been enshrined in the Charter of the UN and the UDHR,[32] and that both the General Assembly in Resolution 421(V)[33] and the Commission on the Status of Women[34] had specifically requested that reference be made to the equal rights of women. This was enough to convince the majority of the Commission on Human Rights.

[23] *See* Jevremovic (Yugoslavia), E/CN.4/SR.279, at 8 (1952).
[24] *See e.g.* Mehta (India), E/CN.4/SR.279, at 9 (1952).
[25] *See* Cassin (France), E/CN.4/SR.279, at 11 (1952).
[26] It was rejected by 6 votes to 5, with 7 abstentions.
[27] *See* Roosevelt (USA), E/CN.4/SR.224, at 12 (1951).
[28] *See e.g.* Bowie (UK), E/CN.4/SR.222, at 6 (1951); Mehta (India), *ibid.* 9 (1951); Bengtson (Sweden), A/C.3/SR.713, at 160, para. 31 (1956); Pazhwak (Afghanistan), A/C.3/SR.714, at 163, para. 3 (1956); Macchia (Italy), A/C.3/SR.715, at 169, para. 6 (1956).
[29] *See* Bowie (UK), E/CN.4/SR.224, at 5 (1951).
[30] *See* Bowie (UK), E/CN.4/SR.218, at 14 (1951). *Ibid.*, SR.222, at 6 (1951); Mossel (Sweden), E/CN.4/SR.279, at 9 (1952).
[31] *See e.g.* Kovalenko (Ukrainian SSR), E/CN.4/SR.280, at 11 (1952); Cheng (China), A/C.3/SR.715, at 170, para. 23 (1956); Gerlein de Fonnegra (Colombia), *ibid.* 171, para. 27 (1956); Novikova (Byelorussia SSR), *ibid.* 172, para. 41 (1956).
[32] *See* Bernadino (Dominican Republic), A/C.3/SR.714, at 164, para. 18 (1956); Paulus (India), A/C.3/SR.714, at 165, para. 31 (1956).
[33] *See* Santa Cruz (Chile), E/CN.4/SR.224, at 7 and 12 (1951).
[34] UN Doc. E/CN.6/197.

An interesting discussion was prompted by the UK's assertion that it had been forced to restrict the right to equal pay in order to combat inflation. The UK reasoned that if the principle of equal pay were instituted, purchasing power would increase, reducing the number of goods available for export and increasing the demands for imports.[35] Other States could not agree to such an argument.[36] Indeed, at a later stage one State pointed out that discrimination against women could eventually hinder the improvement of the general standard of living, through the lowering of the average wage level.[37] What became clear, however, was that States considered such economic arguments inconsistent with the nature of the provision. Action to combat inflation should not penalize one particular group in society, especially one that was already disadvantaged.

D Article 7(a)(ii): A Decent Living

At its eighth session, the Commission unanimously endorsed a proposal that remuneration should be such as to provide workers with 'a decent living for themselves and their families'. In the Third Committee some States suggested that that point had already been addressed by the notion of 'fair wages' and by the reference to an adequate standard of living in article 11.[38] For the majority, however, a specific statement to the effect that remuneration should be sufficient to provide for a decent living was necessary.[39] To some States it had the added benefit of emphasizing that the term 'remuneration' also covered matters that fell outside mere financial remuneration, such as social security benefits and cheap housing.[40] On this analysis the article seems explicitly to foresee the possibility of States supplementing low wages by State benefits to ensure reasonable living standards. If that is the case, the provision relating to 'fair wages' seems to be deprived of full effect.

E Article 7(b): Safe and Healthy Working Conditions

A reference to working conditions 'not injurious to health' was first proposed by Yugoslavia.[41] It was later taken up by the ILO[42] and found its way with little discussion into the final text.

---

[35] *See* Hoare (UK), E/CN.4/SR.280, at 6 (1952).
[36] *See e.g.* Mehta (India), E/CN.4/SR.280, at 8 (1952); Jevremovic (Yugoslavia), *ibid.* 12 (1952); Figueroa (Chile), *ibid.* 13 (1952).
[37] *See* Rivas (Venezuela), A/C.3/SR.716, at 175, para. 8 (1956).
[38] *See e.g.* Boersma (Netherlands), A/C.3/SR.713, at 158, para. 12 (1956); Macchia (Italy), A/C.3/SR.715, at 169, para. 6 (1956).
[39] *See e.g.* Eustathiades (Greece), A/C.3/SR.714, at 167, para. 41 (1956).
[40] *See* Rivas (Venezuela), A/C.3/SR.716, at 173, para. 6 (1956); Marriott (Australia), *ibid.* 176, paras. 13 and 18 (1956).
[41] UN Doc. E/CN.4/AC.14/Add.2, at 2.
[42] *See* Myrrdin-Evans (ILO), E/CN.4/SR.218, at 18 (1951).

F Article 7(c): Equal Opportunity for Promotion

During the Third Committee's discussion of the draft article, Guatemala sponsored an amendment to include a reference to equal opportunity in promotion.[43] Although certain States objected to such a provision on the basis that seniority and competence were not the only criteria on which promotion was based,[44] no other suggestions were made and the amendment was adopted by a majority decision.

G Article 7(d): Rest, Leisure, and Reasonable Limitation of Working Hours

Following a USSR amendment,[45] the general reference to rest and leisure was adopted by the Commission despite the contention that the phrase 'reasonable limitation of working hours and periodic holidays with pay' was more specific,[46] and indeed implied the notions of rest and leisure.[47]

Although a reference to limitation of working hours was generally acceptable,[48] some felt that the term 'reasonable' was too ambiguous, vague, and subjective.[49] It was proposed in the alternative that working hours should be subject to 'legal limitation'.[50] Certain States responded that legal interference in this area would be opposed by national trade unions[51] and that it would leave too great a discretion to the State concerned.[52] Additionally it was noted that legal limitations would be particularly difficult to enforce with regard to agricultural workers, small farmers working their own land, and small ships. In such cases the best method was collective bargaining.[53]

In the Third Committee Spain proposed that a reference be made to remuneration for public holidays.[54] It was argued, however, that this would give the question of public holidays undue prominence at the expense of other equally important aspects such as vocational rehabilitation, individual or collective labour contracts, and labour disputes.[55] Further, it was thought that if the right to periodic holidays with pay[56] were specifically recognized,

---

[43] UN Doc. A/C.3/L.546 and Corr. 1.

[44] *See e.g.* Mufti (Syria), A/C.3/SR.715, at 174, para. 54 (1956).

[45] UN Doc. E/CN.4/L.46, para. 3.   [46] *See* Bowie (UK), E/CN.4/SR.218, at 14 (1951).

[47] *See* Roosevelt (USA), E/CN.4/SR.279, at 12 (1952).

[48] It was considered that it was inappropriate for any precise figure to be given as a limit on the working week which was rather a matter for the implementing body to establish. Myrrdin-Evans (ILO), E/CN.4/SR.218, at 18 (1951); *ibid.* 20 (1951).

[49] *See e.g.* Diaz Casanueva (Chile), A/C.3/SR.713, at 159, para. 19 (1956).

[50] *See* Valensuela (Chile), E/CN.4/SR.218, at 16 (1951).

[51] *See e.g.* Sørensen (Denmark), E/CN.4/SR.218, at 16 (1951).

[52] *See* Myrrdin-Evans (ILO), E/CN.4/SR.218, at 18 (1951); Simarsian (USA), *ibid.* 19 (1951).

[53] *See* Sørensen (Denmark), E/CN.4/SR.218, at 21 (1951).

[54] UN Doc. A/C.3/L.538 (1950).

[55] *See* Diaz Casanueva (Chile), A/C.3/SR.713, at 159, para. 16 (1956).

[56] *See* Abdel-Ghani (Egypt), A/C.3/SR.713, at 160, para. 27 (1956); Vlahov (Yugoslavia), A/C.3/SR.714, at 166, para. 33 (1956).

it would limit the ability of trade unions to negotiate their own conditions of work.[57] Those who supported the amendment noted that public holidays were not covered by the term 'periodic holidays'.[58] The phrase seems to have been adopted on this basis.

Despite a proposal that the article should refer to 'annual' as opposed to 'periodic' holidays,[59] the latter term was finally adopted on the understanding that it meant that workers should be given consecutive holidays of not less than two weeks' duration at least once a year.[60]

III. THE APPROACH OF THE COMMITTEE

A Article 7(a): Minimum Remuneration

According to article 7(a) every worker has the right to a minimum level of remuneration[61] which provides them with 'fair wages'[62] and enough to ensure them (and their families) a decent living.[63] Although the term 'fair wages' might appear to be synonymous with the idea that remuneration should, as a minimum, provide workers and their families with a decent living, the *travaux préparatoires* show an intention to distinguish between the two.[64] Each concept will be considered in turn.

1 Fair Wages

That wages should be 'fair' suggests that they should be 'equitable' or 'just'. This goes considerably further than merely saying that wages should provide for the basic needs of all workers. The fact that the term 'fair wages' is included in a section that also specifies the right to 'equal remuneration for work of equal value' lends weight to the idea that fairness requires wage rates to be set in accordance with the real social value of the employment. This is particularly relevent to the position of women in the workforce, whose value has often been underrated.[65] However, an assessment of wages merely in terms of the productive output of a particular form of employment would not necessarily be 'fair'. Certain forms of employment may not

---

[57] *See* Macchia (Italy), A/C.3/SR.715, at 169, para. 9 (1956).
[58] *See* Mufti (Syria), A/C.3/SR.715, at 174, para. 54 (1956).
[59] Payro (ILO), A/C.3/SR.714, at 164, para. 15 (1956).
[60] Brena (Uruguay), A/C.3/SR.716, at 177, para. 29 (1956).
[61] *Cf.* UDHR, art. 23(2) and (3); European Social Charter, art. 4; ILO Minimum Wage-Fixing Machinery Convention (No. 26), 1928, 29 UNTS 3; ILO Minimum Wage-Fixing Machinery (Agriculture) Convention (No. 99) 1951, 172 UNTS 159; and ILO Minimum Wage-Fixing Convention (No. 131), 1970, 825 UNTS 77.
[62] Art. 7(a)(i).   [63] Art. 7(a)(ii).   [64] *See above*, text accompanying nn. 38–40.
[65] For the question of pay differentials between men and women *see below*, text accompanying nn. 86–108.

be intrinsically more 'valuable' than others, yet are undertaken at higher cost to the worker.

Accordingly, it is submitted that the term 'fair wages' implies that the basic level of pay for each particular occupation should reflect the nature and circumstances of the work undertaken. Certain objective criteria such as the level of skill, the amount of responsibility, the amount of disruption to family life, the value of the productive output to the economy, and the health and safety risks involved should be taken into account in determining whether the wages of a particular occupation could be said to be 'fair'. Certainly this would mean that wage-rates should reflect, to a large extent, the value of the employment undertaken, but it would also mean that workers employed in dangerous occupations or who work unsociable hours should be afforded sufficient remuneration to act as a recompense for the disruption to their family life or health.

Unfortunately, the Committee has given no indication whether it views the term 'fair wages' in this light. The reporting guidelines merely make reference to minimum wages and equal remuneration. Indeed, it is rare for Committee members to refer specifically to the right to 'fair wages' at all. It is submitted that there is little justification, either on the basis of the *travaux préparatoires* or the text of article 7(a) itself, to view the term merely as a repetition of the concept of 'minimum remuneration' for the purpose of providing a 'decent living'. As suggested above, 'fairness' requires reference to a range of socially relevant considerations over and above the economic value of the work undertaken, in the determination of the level of wages in a particular occupation.

2 Minimum Wages

Whereas ILO instruments provide for minimum 'wages', the Covenant refers to minimum 'remuneration'. It is clear from the *travaux préparatoires* that 'remuneration' was considered to be a wider concept than 'wages'.[66] It is assumed that the drafters had in mind the distinctions operated by the ILO. According to ILO practice, wages are defined as sums to be paid under a contract of employment for work done or services rendered. The term 'remuneration' includes, in addition, emoluments such as bonuses or benefits (in cash or kind) paid by the employer to the worker arising out of the worker's employment.[67] In theory this distinction means that, in calculating whether or not a worker has sufficient means to enjoy a decent life,

[66] *See above*, text accompanying n. 40.

[67] *See* General Survey of the Committee of Experts, *Minimum Wages*, ILC, 79th Sess., Report III (Pt. 4B), 7–13 (1992). Cf. art. 119(2) Treaty of Rome (1957), 298 UNTS 11. The definition in art. 119(2) has presented particular problems with respect to whether or not pensions payments form part of an employer's remuneration, *see* Shrubsall V., 'Sex Discrimination and Pensions Benefits' (1990) 19 *Ind. LJ* 244.

consideration will be given to additional benefits or bonuses that may arise from his or her employment. There is no indication that the Committee is aware of such a distinction.[68] Instead, the Committee has focused its attention almost exclusively on the level of wages and particularly upon the establishment and maintenance of a system of minimum wages.

That the Committee considers the establishment of a system of minimum wages as a priority in the realization of article 7(a) is suggested by the detailed information that is requested in its reporting guidelines.[69] The guidelines indicate that the Committee expects the creation of a system which conforms, in large part, to the ILO Minimum Wage-Fixing Convention of 1970 (No. 131)[70] to which reference is made. Accordingly it appears to be expected that a system, as extensive as possible, be established which is enforceable either in law or by means of some other sanction. Machinery should be set up to fix, monitor, and adjust the level of the minimum wage at regular intervals,[71] which should take into account the needs of the workers, their families and any relevant economic circumstances such as the cost of living and the level of inflation.[72] Finally, the system as a whole should be subject to supervision, and presumably enforcement, where necessary.

Individual members of the Committee have frequently looked to the establishment of a minimum wage to ensure the realization of the right to just and favourable conditions of work.[73] In the absence of a system of minimum wages, they have enquired as to the existence of other measures that would ensure that workers received 'equitable remuneration geared to the cost-of-living index in order to enable them to lead a decent life'.[74] It is apparent that the vast majority of States have established some form of minimum-wage legislation and, of those that have not, a number have established systems of wage protection through collective agreements.[75] Recognition is paid to the fact that wages are, and should be, to some extent determined through a process of collective bargaining, but it has been noted that 'the minimum wage was mainly applicable in sectors where trade unions did not exist or were very weak'.[76] There is no doubt that in the eyes

[68] It was argued by one member of the Committee that payment in kind 'violated a worker's freedom of choice and restricted his right to spend his salary as he so wished': Grissa, E/C.12/1994/SR.10/Add.1, at 7, para. 36. For a discussion of the economic effects of a minimum wage, *see* Craig C., Rubery J., Tarling R., and Wilkinson F., *Labour Market Structure, Industrial Organisation and Low Pay* (1982), 96–141.

[69] Reporting Guidelines, UN ESCOR, Supp. (No. 3), Annex IV, at 92, UN Doc. E/C.12/1990/8 (1991).

[70] *Supra*, n. 61.   [71] Grissa, E/C.12/1994/SR.4, at 3, para. 9.

[72] *See* Simma, E/C.12/1994/SR.28, at 4, para. 17.

[73] *See e.g.* Texier, E/C.12/1987/SR.5, at 6, para. 24; Sparsis, E/C.12/1987/SR.5, at 7, para. 32.

[74] Fofana, E/C.12/1988/SR.3, at 6, para. 23.

[75] Report of the Director-General of the ILO, *Human Rights: A Common Responsibility*, ILC, 75th Sess., at 43 (1988).

[76] Sparsis, E/C.12/1988/SR.4, at 6, para. 32.

of a number of members of the Committee, equitable remuneration is to be secured primarily through the institution of a compulsory minimum wage.[77] This suggests that, although article 7 speaks of 'workers' in a general sense, it is not deemed to apply to the self-employed or employers. The Committee, however, has made no specific comment upon this question.

As regards the operation of the system of minimum wages, members of the Committee have been concerned that there should be sufficient worker participation in the determination of standards.[78] Thus members criticized the position in Uruguay where wages were fixed unilaterally by the State.[79] Although it would be natural to expect the participation of trade unions in such a scheme, it has been pointed out that, as trade unions were not prevalent in vulnerable sectors, an independent body should be set up to advise the government.[80]

The final, and perhaps most important, issue is that the minimum wage should have sufficient enforcement. In those cases where the State itself is the employer, enforcement should not be difficult. Having said that, there is evidence to suggest that it does remain a continuing problem in some developing States.[81] In this context it is considered that the Committee should direct a certain amount of its attention to the question whether there are adequate inspection services and sufficient sanctions for breach of the minimum wage standards. The approach of the Committee with respect to the establishment of a labour inspectorate will be dealt with below.

According to article 7(a)(ii), the level of remuneration should be such as to provide for a 'decent living' for the worker and his or her family. The text indicates that the term 'decent living' is to be read in the light of the other provisions in the Covenant. Particular reference could be made to article 11 which refers to 'an adequate standard of living'. More specifically, however, the phrase 'a decent living' appears to refer to those rights that depend for their enjoyment upon personal income such as the rights to housing, food, clothing, and perhaps health, education, and culture.

Although States are expected to establish their own standards and goals with respect to the level of remuneration, the Committee is willing to intervene in certain cases. Thus in the case of Kenya, the Committee criticized the level of minimum wages which appeared 'to be far too low to even allow a very modest standard of living'.[82] Thus the minimum wage should at

---

[77] *See e.g.* Sparsis, E/C.12/1990/SR.10, at 12, para. 79; Rattray, E/C.12/1991/SR.3, at 9, para. 43.
[78] *See* Sparsis, E/C.12/1988/SR.3, at 6, para. 18.
[79] *See e.g.* Simma, E/C.12/1994/SR.4, at 3, para. 6, and E/C.12/1994/SR.6, at 7, para. 30.
[80] *See* Sparsis, E/C.12/1988/SR.4, at 6, para. 32. *See also* General Survey, *supra*, n. 67, at 65–99.
[81] *See* Report of the Director-General, *supra*, n. 75, at 43–4. Goldman A., 'Settlement of Disputes over Interests' in Blainpain R. (ed.), *Comparative Labour Law and Industrial Relations* (3rd ed., 1987), 361 at 368.
[82] Concluding observations on report of Kenya, E/C.12/1993/6, at 3, para. 12.

least be sufficient to meet the 'basic needs' of the worker. As far as the ILO is concerned, the level of minimum wages should take into account not only the needs of the workers and their families (in which reference would be made to matters such as the general level of wages, the cost of living, social security benefits), but also economic factors such as the requirement of economic development, levels of productivity, and the desirability of maintaining high levels of employment.[83] Although the Committee does refer rather generally to 'economic factors' that may be taken into consideration,[84] its position in this regard is not clear. In particular, no indication is given whether economic considerations could justify setting the level of minimum wages below that which would provide for basic needs.

As the general approach of the Committee has been to look towards a process of 'equalization' in the enjoyment of economic, social, and cultural rights, there is a possibility that it will look towards the adoption of a test similar to that operated with respect to the European Social Charter. There, the Committee of Independent Experts has established a 'decency threshold' in which the lowest permissible wage in any sector of the economy is quantified as being 68 per cent of the national average.[85] Although such a test is relatively easy to utilize it is essentially directed at equality of income distribution rather than the adequacy of income *per se*. The level of income advanced by the test, which is essentially a national standard, may well be insufficient to provide for basic needs in poorer countries and excessive in more wealthy countries. It may, nevertheless, be useful as a basic indicator when used in conjunction with other criteria.

The utilization of minimum wage-fixing machinery as the sole means for ensuring adequate remuneration may be criticized in so far as it is only an indirect and partial procedural mechanism. Although it may be open for a worker in the public sector to rely upon article 7(a)(ii) in a claim against the State as regards the inadequacy of his or her pay, the State cannot be seen to have the same responsibility for wages in the private sector. Thus for impoverished workers employed in the private sector, the principal claim against the State will be that the wage-fixing machinery has insufficient coverage. Moreover, in so far as coverage is generally determined on the basis of sectors of the workforce, the claim will have to be conditioned by the individual's membership of a particular 'vulnerable group' to which protection has been afforded. This falls considerably short of the type of protection usually associated with human rights guarantees.

---

[83] *See* General Survey, *supra*, n. 67, at 101–9. Valticos N., *International Labour Law* (1979), at 130.

[84] Reporting guidelines, *supra*, n. 69, at 92.

[85] *See* Conclusions V, at 25–26 (1977); Harris D., *The European Social Charter* (1984), 49–51. This standard is currently being reconsidered, *see* Harris, E/C.12/1994/SR.12, at 3, para. 6.

3 Equal Remuneration

Article 7(a)(i) specifies as a general principle that all workers should be provided with 'equal remuneration for work of equal value'. More specifically, however, it provides that women should be guaranteed 'equal pay for equal work'. The concept of 'equal pay for equal work' is the more restrictive of the two concepts in that it confines the comparison to workers with the same job description in the same establishment. The concept of equal remuneration for work of equal value, however, like the 'comparable worth' doctrine in the United States,[86] requires comparisons to be made between a wider range of jobs across the spectrum of the employment market.[87]

The rationale for extending the equal pay guarantee to work of equal value is that groups in society (particularly women) are generally vulnerable to low wage levels and not only as a result of direct discrimination. The problem is rather that the employment market is often segregated, with women undertaking forms of employment that are less well protected by trade unions and traditionally undervalued by society.[88] To some extent this problem may be ameliorated by action to increase access to employment for women[89] and by the protection of wages in vulnerable sectors of the labour market. However, even with the existence of a truly integrated and open employment market, there would still remain a need to ensure pay reflected the proper value of the work undertaken.

It would appear that the concept of 'equal pay for equal work' in the Covenant is narrower than that provided for in the ILO Equal Remuneration Convention of 1951[90] or in the European Social Charter,[91] both of which refer to 'equal pay for work of equal value'.[92] However, the text of article 7(a)(i) makes clear that the term 'equal pay for equal work' is merely one element of the more general concept of 'equal remuneration for work of equal value'. It has been concluded that 'the wording of the provision mandates the application of the theory of comparable worth'.[93]

[86] *See* Benson M., 'Equal Pay for Work of Equal Value' (1985) 15 *Isr. YHR* 66, at 67–70.
[87] *Cf.* Valticos, *supra*, n. 83, at 176.
[88] *See* Rubenstein M., *Equal Pay* (1984); Horrel S., Rubey J., and Burchell B., 'Unequal Jobs or Unequal Pay?' (1989), 20 *Ind. RLJ*, No. 3, 176.
[89] *Cf.* Para. 6, ILO Equal Remuneration Recommendation (No. 90), 1951, ILO, *International Labour Conventions and Recommendations (1919–1981)* (1982), at 44.
[90] ILO Equal Remuneration Convention (No. 100), 1951, 165 UNTS 303.
[91] *See* Harris, *supra*, n. 85, at 53.
[92] In the practice of the European Communities, however, the concept of equal pay for equal work has been interpreted to include work 'to which equal value is attributed'. Council Dir. 75/117, [1975] OJ L45/19. *See generally* Szyzczak E., 'Pay Inequalities and Equal Value Claims' (1985) 48 *MLR* 139, at 140; Argiros G., 'Sex Equality in the Labour Market and the Community Legal Order: An Attempt at an Appraisal' (1989) 11 *Liv. LR* No. 2, 161, at 171–4; More G., '"Equal Treatment" of the Sexes in European Community Law: What Does "Equal" Mean?' (1993) 1 *Fem. L St.* 45.
[93] Benson, *supra*, n. 86, at 71.

The requirement of equal remuneration in the Covenant is broader than that found in other instruments in two respects. First, whereas ILO Convention No. 100[94] and article 119 of the Treaty of Rome[95] provide for equal pay only in relation to men and women, article 7(a)(i) applies to 'all workers ... without distinction of any kind'. Secondly, the Covenant uses the term 'remuneration' which is arguably broader than the term 'pay'.[96] Wide though its coverage may be, the Covenant gives no further instruction as to how the concept should be realized.

Although it is evident that the 'work of equal value' concept is wider than, and includes, the concept of equal pay for equal work, the Committee has tended to deal with the matters separately.[97] The reason for this is indicated by the text of article 7(a)(i) itself. Whereas States are required to 'recognize' the right to equal remuneration for work of equal value (thus implying progressive achievement[98]), they must 'guarantee' the right of women to equal pay for equal work. Use of the term 'guarantee' implies that full enjoyment of the right should be ensured immediately. Thus the Committee's reporting guidelines request information as to 'infringements' of the principle of equal pay for equal work.[99] This interpretation also has some support in the practice of States. Both Barbados and the UK have made reservations to the effect that they postpone the application of the principle of article 7(a)(i) in so far as it concerns the provision of equal pay to men and women for equal work; in doing so, they imply that article 7(a)(i) does indeed require States immediately to guarantee the principle of equal pay for equal work.[100]

Whereas it might be assumed that the reference in article 7(a)(i) to 'equal pay for equal work' applies only to women, the Committee has requested more general information on infringements of the principle with respect to any person or group of persons. A wider operation of the principle of equal pay for equal work may be justified by the fact that it is merely a specific element of the equal value concept which is to operate 'without distinction of any kind'. It has to be noted, however, that although a general legislative provision requiring equal pay may be sufficient in overt cases, if the Committee considers that 'indirect' or 'implicit' discrimination is to be

[94] Provisions on equal remuneration and on the decrease of differentials between rates of remuneration resulting from discrimination are also contained in the ILO Social Policy (Basic Aims and Standards) Convention (No. 117) 1962, 494 UNTS 249.

[95] EEC Treaty (1957), *supra*, n. 67.

[96] For the difference between 'remuneration' and 'wages', *see above* text accompanying nn. 66–8. It is notable, however, that the European Court of Justice has interpreted 'pay' in a broad manner. *See* Argiros, *supra*, n. 92, at 169–71.

[97] *See e.g.* Reporting guidelines, *supra*, n. 69, at 92–3.

[98] *See above*, Ch. 3, text accompanying nn. 169–75.

[99] Reporting guidelines, *supra*, n. 69, at 92.

[100] UN Doc. E/C.12/1988/1, at 7 and 18 (1987).

prohibited, then the State will have to establish which groups are to be protected.

The Committee gives no indication how the right to equal pay for equal work is to be guaranteed. Although it is clear that the State may guarantee equal pay where remuneration is subject to statutory control (such as in public undertakings), effectively to guarantee the right to equal pay in other areas States will have to provide for individual remedies.[101] The form such remedies may take would depend upon the structure and form of the existing wage-fixing mechanisms within the State concerned. It is submitted that it is indispensable for the Committee to enquire as to the existence of mechanisms through which the right to equal pay for equal work may be effectively enforced.

As regards the principle of equal remuneration for work of equal value, the Committee expects States to 'promote an objective appraisal of jobs on the basis of the work to be performed'.[102] Such an appraisal should take into account differences in income distribution not only within enterprises or sectors of the employment market, but also between 'comparable jobs in the public and private sector'.[103] It is interesting to note that the Committee has rather cautiously used the term 'promote'. Clearly the establishment of such a scheme across all forms of employment in all areas would represent a monumental task, and would in any case present problems where the government does not traditionally interfere directly in the determination of wages in the private sector.[104] Although the Committee has occasionally implied that article 7(a)(i) as a whole is capable of immediate implementation,[105] the guidelines clearly suggest that any obligation to create a job evaluation scheme is merely progressive.[106]

Although the appraisal of job value should be 'objective', the Committee has not itself established any criteria which should be taken into account. It is clear from the text of article 7(a) that the social utility of a particular job is not a sufficient criterion alone. As a minimum, the level of pay should be such as to provide all workers and their families with a decent living.[107]

---

[101] An example might be the UK Equal Pay Act 1970. *See e.g.* Palmer C. and Poulton K., *Sex and Race Discrimination in Employment* (1987), 91–125; Bourn C. and Whitmore J., *Race and Sex Discrimination* (2nd ed., 1993).

[102] Reporting guidelines, *supra*, n. 69, at 93.

[103] *Ibid.* For the position of the ILO *see* ILO General Survey, *Equal Remuneration*, ILC, 72nd Sess., Report III (Part 4B), para. 22 (1986).

[104] Valticos, *supra*, n. 83, at 177. The Committee of Independent Experts of the European Social Charter has experienced certain problems in this regard, *see* Harris, *supra*, n. 85, at 54–6.

[105] *See above*, Ch. 3, text accompanying nn. 130–1.

[106] *Cf. also* Sparsis, E/C.12/1990/SR.10, at 12, para. 78.

[107] *See above*, text accompanying nn. 66–85. For a discussion of the possible conflict between needs and equal pay, *see* Källström K., 'Article 23' in Eide A. *et al.* (eds.), *The Universal Declaration of Human Rights: A Commentary* (1992), 357, at 364.

Moreover, that wages should be 'fair' suggests that other considerations of justice should be taken into account.[108] It is submitted that to the extent to which it expects States to establish job evaluation schemes, the Committee should attempt to outline the general criteria that should be applied.

B Equality in Conditions of Employment

Article 7(a)(i), in addition to providing for equal remuneration, establishes that women should be guaranteed 'conditions of work not inferior to those enjoyed by men'. It would appear, nevertheless, from the existence of article 2(2), which prohibits discrimination in the enjoyment of the rights, that such a reference is unnecessary. Indeed the Committee has not viewed the provision as either adding to or subtracting from the general non-discrimination clause in any way. Whereas the concept of non-discrimination has been dealt with in more detail elsewhere,[109] it is pertinent to note that members of the Committee have been concerned primarily with the employment conditions of women[110] and migrant workers[111] (whether legally or illegally employed[112]).

C Safe and Healthy Working Conditions

Article 7(b) provides that everyone has a right to safe and healthy working conditions. This provision overlaps with article 12 which refers to the right to health. Article 12(2) in particular provides in sub-paragraph (b) for the improvement of all aspects of environmental and industrial hygiene, and in sub-paragraph (c) for the prevention, treatment, and control *inter alia* of occupational diseases. The utility of article 7(b), with its broad and generalized terms of reference, may be questioned, especially in light of the multiplicity of ILO Conventions that deal with specific concerns in this area.[113]

The Committee in its reporting guidelines requests information as to the legal or administrative provisions that prescribe minimum conditions of occupational health and safety.[114] The Committee has not specifically defined any standards that are to apply in this area, it being left to the States themselves initially to establish their own national standards. To the extent

---

[108] *See above*, text accompanying n. 65.   [109] *See above*, Ch. 4.

[110] *See e.g.* Jimenez Butragueno, E/C.12/1987/SR.7, at 6, para. 25.

[111] *See* Jimenez Butragueno, E/C.12/1988/SR.3, at 4, para. 9; Texier, E/C.12/1989/SR.6, at 5, para. 22; Simma, E/C.12/1990/SR.34, at 4, para. 22.

[112] *See* Wimer Zambrano, E/C.12/1987/SR.7, at 7, para. 28; Simma, E/C.12/1990/SR.40, at 10, para. 44.

[113] The ILO specifically refers to 21 conventions that operate in this area excluding those corresponding to specific occupational sectors or particular categories of workers. UN Doc. E/1994/5, at 4 (1993).

[114] Reporting guidelines, *supra*, n. 69, at 93.

that the Committee refers to the ILO Occupational Safety and Health Convention 1981,[115] however, it may be concluded that the Committee expects those standards to operate with respect to the Covenant, especially as regards the obligation to formulate a 'coherent national policy'. It may well be appropriate for the Committee to clarify this question.

There is evidence to suggest that the Committee conceives of the right to safe and healthy working conditions as being open to progressive achievement. It asks specifically for information as to the categories of workers which are excluded either in whole or in part from the existing schemes, and expects the progressive reduction in occupational accidents over time.[116] In so far as article 7(b) relates to article 2(1), it can be assumed that the Committee will look to the establishment of policies directed towards the prevention of accidents and injury to health. However, while the elimination of all accidents is clearly not possible, an obligation for States to establish national policies embodied in legislation that prescribes standards which apply to all employed workers[117] could be implemented immediately. The standards themselves certainly may be improved over time, as indeed they should be, but the establishment of a coherent national policy should be a minimum requirement for all States. The financial burden upon the State, and indeed on the undertaking concerned, in enforcing such standards is far outweighed by the human and economic costs of not doing so.[118] As has been noted by the ILO, 'there is wide agreement that flexibility should have no place in standards aimed at ensuring safety and health at work'.[119]

Members of the Committee have recognized the central role of legislation and regulations in this area.[120] Like the requirement in article 4 of ILO Convention No. 155, members have asked about the extent of participation of workers in the establishment of such regulations,[121] and whether the areas of risk have been evaluated and preventive measures designed.[122] The Committee should also take note of the fact that the constant introduction of new technologies, substances, and working methods means that the situation has to be constantly under supervision.[123]

---

[115] ILO Occupational Safety and Health Convention (No. 155), 1981, Cmnd 8773.

[116] Reporting guidelines, *supra*, n. 69, at 93.

[117] The term 'employed workers' could be considered to include those self-employed who operate as independent contractors. *See* Szubert W., 'Some Considerations on Safety and Health at Work in Comparative Law' in Gamillscheg F. *et al.*, *In Memoriam: Sir Otto Khan-Freund* (1980), 701, at 713.

[118] Report of the Director-General of the ILO, *Making Work More Human: Working Conditions and the Environment*, ILC, 60th Sess., at 23 (1974).

[119] Report of the Director-General, *supra*, n. 75, at 47.

[120] *See e.g.* Texier, E/C.12/1987/SR.5, at 6, para. 25.

[121] *See e.g.* Mratchkov, E/C.12/1987/SR.7, at 5, para. 19.

[122] *See e.g.* Konate, E/C.12/1987/SR.7, at 2, para. 4.

[123] Report of the Director-General, *supra*, n. 75, at 47.

Once States have established appropriate legislation and regulations on safety and health at work, the most crucial aspect is the degree to which they are enforced and the ability of those injured in accidents to claim compensation. More often than not a labour inspectorate is mandated with the supervision of legislation regarding conditions of work and particularly safety standards. Although the Committee makes reference to the ILO Labour Inspection Convention of 1947 (No. 81) and the Labour Inspection (Agriculture) Convention of 1969 (No. 129) in its reporting guidelines,[124] no clear mention is made of an obligation to establish labour inspectorates, or of their appropriate number, size, or power, once created.[125] Given that inspectorates are often poorly organized, overworked, and limited in their powers,[126] this is an area which perhaps deserves more consideration.

Individual members of the Committee have, however, taken a certain amount of interest in the establishment and functioning of labour inspectorates, not only in the field of safety and health at work, but also with respect to general conditions of work.[127] Thus questions have been asked about the organization, size, and range of functions of the labour inspectorate concerned,[128] the number of cases taken up by the inspectorate[129] and the sanctions imposed for breach of the regulations.[130] Members have not gone so far as to lay down specific operating requirements for such inspectorates. Given that there is a need for enforcement over a whole range of issues within article 7, it might be appropriate if the Committee were to suggest that labour inspectorates be established to enforce the various regulations and assist or advise employers. Consideration could be given to the requirements laid down in ILO Convention No. 81 where inspectorates must be independent and subject to central control. The inspectors themselves should have adequate training, facilities, and powers, and be sufficient in number to undertake their work.[131]

With respect to compensation, it has been argued by one member of the Committee that ILO Conventions Nos. 42 (Workman's Compensation (Occupational Diseases) Convention 1934) and 17 (Workman's Compensation (Accidents) Convention 1925) were 'identical in spirit to article 7'. Accordingly the New Zealand Accident Rehabilitation and Compensation Insurance Act of 1992 was deemed to be 'incompatible with the spirit of article 7' in that it placed the burden of proof in compensation claims upon

---

[124] Reporting guidelines, *supra*, n. 69, at 93.

[125] The Committee has noted the absence of information on the question of labour inspectorates, Concluding observations on the report of Italy, E/1993/22, at 53, para. 10.

[126] Szubert, *supra*, n. 117, at 708.

[127] *See e.g.* Sparsis, E/C.12/1991/SR.3, at 10, para. 48.

[128] *See e.g.* Mratchkov, E/C.12/1991/SR.7, at 11, para. 46; Texier, E/C.12/1994/SR.4, at 4, para. 12.

[129] *See e.g.* Texier, E/C.12/1989/SR.6, at 5, para. 19.

[130] Texier, E/C.12/1987/SR.5, at 6, para. 25; Ider, E/C.12/1993/SR.7, at 9, para. 36.

[131] *See* Valticos, *supra*, n. 83, at 214–19.

the victim and also required victims to bear part of the cost of medical treatment.[132] It has yet to be seen whether the Committee as a whole will develop this line of thinking.

Although it is beyond the powers of the Committee to lay down specific health and safety requirements that should be established in particular forms of employment, it clearly has a role to play in ensuring that adequate mechanisms exist to enable the continued adjustment, improvement, and enforcement of standards relating to the working environment.

D Equal Opportunity for Promotion

Article 7(c) provides that everyone has the right to equal opportunity to be promoted 'subject to no considerations other than those of seniority or competence'. While being linked with the right to work in article 6 and the right of women to equal conditions of work in article 7(a)(i), the right to equal opportunity in promotion is perhaps most closely related to article 2(2), which guarantees the exercise of the rights within the Covenant without discrimination.

As has been noted elsewhere, the Committee has interpreted the general non-discrimination clause as requiring some form of *de facto* equality.[133] Accordingly the Committee's reporting guidelines require the provision of information about groups which do not currently enjoy equal opportunity in promotion. Specific steps are required to combat that situation and promote the opportunities for advancement of the disadvantaged sectors in society.[134] It is evident that the degree to which States succeed in this task will be assessed by how many persons within the disadvantaged groups enter into more responsible positions within society.[135] There is, nevertheless, some question whether quotas could legitimately be employed in this context, given that article 7(c) specifically limits the relevant considerations to those of seniority and competence.[136]

The approach of individual members of the Committee suggests that the State has an obligation to establish objective norms to govern promotion possibilities in the public sector.[137] In relation to private sector employment, members have looked towards the adoption of legislation to guarantee

[132] Simma, E/C.12/1993/SR.25, at 4, para. 17. Cf. UN Doc. E/1994/5, at 11.
[133] *See above*, Ch. 4, text accompanying nn. 32–40.
[134] Reporting guidelines, *supra*, n. 69, at 93. *Cf. also* ILO Recommendation No. 111, para. 2 which provides for equality of opportunity as to advancement in accordance with the individual's character, experience, ability, or diligence. ILO Discrimination (Employment and Occupation) Recommendation (No. 111), 1958, in ILO, *International Labour Conventions and Recommendations 1919–1981* (1982), at 49.
[135] Questions are regularly asked about the number of women occupying positions of responsibility at work, *see e.g.* Jimenez Butragueno, E/C.12/1991/SR.3, at 11, para. 52.
[136] *See above*, Ch. 4, text accompanying nn. 220–8.
[137] *See e.g.* Mratchkov, E/C.12/1987/SR.5, at 8, para. 40.

equality of promotion opportunities.[138] It might be pointed out that such legislative measures would most probably take the form of a general non-discrimination provision guaranteed by some form of individual remedy.

E Rest and Leisure

Article 7(d) provides for a general right to rest and leisure, and specific work-related aspects of that right, namely the reasonable limitation of working hours, periodic holidays with pay, and remuneration for public holidays. While it may be argued that a right to leisure implies an obligation on the State to promote or provide adequate leisure facilities,[139] the Committee has concentrated almost exclusively upon the reduction in working hours and the provision of paid holidays.

That the Committee intends initially to rely upon the ILO standards in this field is apparent from the reference in its guidelines to the Weekly Rest (Industry) Convention of 1921 (No. 14), the Weekly Rest (Commerce and Offices) Convention of 1957 (No. 106), and the Holidays with Pay Convention (Revised) of 1970 (No. 132).[140] It is particularly noticeable that in the area of remuneration for public holidays, where there is no relevant ILO Convention to apply, the Committee has made little comment. In addition to making reference to ILO Conventions, the reporting guidelines request, rather generally, information on laws and practices relating to the various rights within article 7(d), factors and difficulties that affect the degree of realization particularly on the categories of workers which are excluded in law or practice from the enjoyment of the rights, and measures taken to improve the situation.[141]

It is notable that the Committee has made no mention of the Hours of Work (Industry) Convention of 1919 (No. 1),[142] the Hours of Work (Commerce and Offices) Convention of 1930 (No. 30),[143] or the Forty-Hour Week Convention of 1935 (No. 47).[144] One reason may be the limited number of States that have ratified those treaties.[145] Whether or not the Committee considers that these ILO standards are realistic, it would be appropriate for the Committee to make some form of statement about what length of

---

[138] *See e.g.* Daoudi, E/C.12/1987/SR.5, at 4, para. 15.

[139] *See* Melander G., 'Article 24' in Eide A. *et al.* (eds.), *The Universal Declaration of Human Right: A Commentary* (1992), 379, at 380.

[140] Reporting guidelines, *supra*, n. 69, at 92. ILO Weekly Rest (Industry) Convention (No. 14), 1921, 38 UNTS 187; ILO Weekly Rest (Commerce and Offices) Convention (No. 106) 1957, 958 UNTS 324; ILO Holidays with Pay Convention (Revised) (No. 132) 1970, Cmnd 4706. [141] Reporting guidelines, *supra*, n. 69, at 93.

[142] ILO Hours of Work (Industry) Convention (No. 1), 1919, 38 UNTS 17.

[143] ILO Hours of Work (Commerce and Offices) Convention (No. 30) 1930, 39 UNTS 85.

[144] ILO Forty-Hour Week Convention (No. 47) 1935, 271 UNTS 199.

[145] *e.g.*, the Forty-Hour Week Convention (No. 47) of 1935 has been ratified by only 8 States.

working week it considers suitable as a general standard,[146] and what would be considered excessive. The only statements made to this effect by individual members indicate that States should make efforts to reduce the length of the working week[147] and that a 54-hour working week would in normal circumstances be considered excessive.[148]

It is submitted that the Committee should establish as a principle, in line with the approach of the ILO,[149] that States should attempt to reduce the working week in a progressive manner. Clearly the extent to which States are capable of shortening the working week is dependant upon their social and economic situation and the degree to which it would affect productivity, competitiveness, and the balance of trade. However, given the existing general differentials between States, a useful guideline for the Committee might well be the provisions of the ILO Reduction of Hours of Work Recommendation of 1962 (No. 116).[150] It recommends that States pursue a national policy designed to promote the principle of progressive reduction of normal hours of work with a view to attaining the standard of the 40-hour week. In the case of those States which operate an existing working week of more than forty-eight hours, immediate steps should be taken to reduce it to that level.

By referring to the Weekly Rest Conventions, the Committee seems to imply that those obligations are operative as far as article 7(d) is concerned. If that is the case, States have an obligation to ensure that employees, whether in public or private undertakings, shall enjoy a period of rest of at least twenty-four consecutive hours in every seven days. Exceptions are provided for in certain defined situations, but in such cases compensatory rest periods should be provided. Like the provision relating to the working week, it would be appropriate for the Committee to view this provision as a progressive one, such that States should attempt to increase the period of weekly rest over time. Nevertheless, as the ILO has discovered, the question of weekly rest has not generally been a serious problem.[151]

As regards the right to holidays with pay, it was made clear in the drafting of article 7 that the term 'annual holiday' was intended to mean that workers should be given, at minimum, consecutive holidays of two weeks' duration once a year.[152] Although this is less than that provided for in the

[146] For the ILO position, *see* General Survey of the Committee of Experts, *Working Time: Reduction of Hours of Work, Weekly Rest and Holidays with Pay*, ILC 70th Sess., Report III (Pt. 4B) (1984).
[147] *See* Texier, E/C.12/1989/SR.8, at 5, para. 26.
[148] *See* Mratchkov, E/C.12/1989/SR.8, at 7, para. 36. A 52-hour working week was accepted without comment in the case of Kenya, E/C.12/1993/SR.4, at 4, para. 10.
[149] General Survey, *supra*, n. 145, at 10.
[150] ILO Reduction of Hours of Work Recommendation (No. 116), 1962, in ILO, *International Labour Conventions and Recommendations (1919–1981)* (1982), at 785.
[151] *Ibid.* 185.
[152] *See above* text accompanying n. 61. Cf. art. 2(3) European Social Charter.

ILO Holidays With Pay Convention (Revised) of 1970 (which provides for a three-week holiday),[153] it should clearly be made the basic standard. The Committee has yet to give this right some meaning. In addition to stipulating what it considers to be the minimum duration of annual holiday, the Committee will also have to consider the legitimacy of qualifying periods for, or the division of, holiday entitlements, and the means by which such standards are to be enforced.

IV. CONCLUSION

The broad and general terms of article 7, while lacking the specificity found in other instruments (such as the European Social Charter), do not suffer from the inherent limitations that such definitions might offer. For example, the general right to equal remuneration for work of equal value allows for a far wider application than other guarantees which restrict comparisons to the relative position of men and women. However, that the provisions have to be given more precise and meaningful detail places a considerable burden upon the Committee. Although the Committee has certainly addressed detailed matters that have arisen under article 7, it has not yet been able to develop a coherent approach and has some way to go in terms of developing the guarantee. This is true not only of the right to safe and healthy working conditions, which remains almost entirely inchoate, but also of the right to equal remuneration which is one of the more accessible elements of article 7.

One fundamental characteristic of the right to just and favourable conditions of work is that it concerns the relationship between private individuals (or bodies). Certainly the State may have direct responsibility for such matters in so far as it is an employer itself, but in most States now conditions of work are the subject of the private employment contract and stipulations of collective agreements. The effectiveness of the rights within article 7 is thus heavily dependent upon the horizontal application of rights.[154]

As it is rarely conceded that the State should interfere in the terms and conditions of every employment contract, State obligations will primarily involve establishing a minimum 'floor' of rights (which should form the basis of every employment contract) and instituting mechanisms of enforcement. Although the Committee does face problems with establishing the exact level at which each right should be set, it does have a serious role to play in ensuring that basic procedural obligations are undertaken. For

[153] *See* General survey, *supra*, n. 146, paras. 151–259.
[154] For a discussion of the notion of *Drittwirkung*, *see above*, Ch. 3, text accompanying nn. 23–5.

example, it should at least examine the existence, coverage, and operation of minimum wage machinery, labour inspectorates, and wage evaluation schemes. Although it has taken some interest in this matter, this element of its work has so far been seriously undervalued.

Thus far, although the Committee is in the fortunate position of being able to draw upon the vast experience of the ILO in the area, it has made only a little headway in developing the substance of the guarantee found in article 7. There is clearly a need for the Committee to adopt a more sophisticated stance and focus its attention upon the various elements of article 7. Having said that, a brief glance at the number of ILO conventions and recommendations in the area (particularly with respect to health and safety at work) does give an indication of the extremely difficult task that faces the Committee in developing the normative content of the rights and assessing State reports in a meaningful manner. It is perhaps fortunate that the Committee only has to play a supportive role to the ILO in the area.

7
The Right to Form and Join Trade Unions

Article 8

1. The States Parties to the present Covenant undertake to ensure:

 (a) The right of everyone to form trade unions and join the trade union of his choice, subject only to the rules of the organization concerned, for the promotion and protection of his economic and social interests. No restrictions may be placed on the exercise of this right other than those prescribed by law and which are necessary in a democratic society in the interests of national security or public order or for the protection of the rights and freedoms of others;

 (b) The right of trade unions to establish national federations or confederations and the right of the latter to form or join international trade-union organizations;

 (c) The right of trade unions to function freely subject to no limitations other than those prescribed by law and which are necessary in a democratic society in the interests of national security or public order or for the protection of the rights and freedoms of others;

 (d) The right to strike, provided that it is exercised in conformity with the laws of the particular country.

2. This article shall not prevent the imposition of lawful restrictions on the exercise of these rights by members of the armed forces or of the police or of the administration of the State.

3. Nothing in this article shall authorize States Parties to the International Labour Organization Convention of 1948 concerning Freedom of Association and Protection of the Right to Organize to take legislative measures which would prejudice, or apply the law in such a manner as would prejudice, the guarantees provided for in that Convention.

I. INTRODUCTION

As is recognized in a number of human rights instruments, the right to join and form trade unions may be seen to derive from the more general right to freedom of association.[1] That it has been given specific legal recognition

---

[1] *Cf.* art. 22(1) ICCPR (1966); art. 11(1) ECHR (1950). The UDHR, however, provides for

over and above other forms of association[2] is a reflection of the fact that freedom of association for trade union purposes has become 'a major postulate of democratic government in an industrial society',[3] Trade unions not only form one of the most common forms of association, but they have also played a historic role in the protection of the rights and interests of workers. Identification of the instrumental value of trade unions in the realization of other economic and social rights (particularly the right to just and favourable conditions of work[4]) is reflected in the value placed upon the rights of trade unions themselves in the Covenant (articles 8(1)(b) and (c)), as opposed to the rights of the individual trade union members.

It is possible to argue that the right of trade unions to function freely may readily be inferred from the effective enjoyment of the individual right to freedom of association and indeed may have been framed in those terms. As it is, article 8 is very much a hybrid of individual and collective rights. That tensions may arise between the rights of the individual and those of the collective is apparent in the experience of the European Court of Human Rights.[5] The fact that the collective rights are specifically enumerated, as opposed to inferred, might make the resolution of such conflicts more difficult to attain.

Article 8 is of particular importance as far as the Committee is concerned, as it represents a good benchmark against which the progress of the Committee, in developing the norms within the Covenant, may be measured. It has many of the hallmarks of the rights enumerated in the ICCPR, being defined in comparable detail and being subject to immediate implementation. It has also been the subject of a certain amount of case law, both at the national and international level, which may serve as an initial guide to the work of the Committee.

II. THE *TRAVAUX PRÉPARATOIRES*

During the drafting of the Covenant,[6] there was considerable opposition to the inclusion of an article relating to trade union rights. The first, and main,

the right to freedom of association (art. 20) and the right to form and join trade unions (art. 23(4)) in two separate articles.

[2] Other forms of association may include professional associations, societies, clubs, or co-operatives.

[3] Jenks W., *Human Rights and International Labour Standards* (1960), 50.

[4] For the role of collective bargaining in the realization of the rights in art. 7, *see above*, Ch. 6, text accompanying nn. 75–6.

[5] *See e.g. Young, James and Webster Cases* Eur. Ct. HR, Vol. 44., judgment of 13 Aug. 1981, (1982) 4 EHRR 38. *Sibson* v. *UK* Eur. Ct. HR, judgment of 20 April 1993, 17 EHRR 193.

[6] Proposals for an art. on trade union rights were discussed in the Commission at its 7th and 8th sessions, and later in the General Assembly's Third Committee. *See* UN Doc. E/CN.4/SR.203–4, 206–8, 218, 224–6 (1951); UN Doc. E/CN.4/SR.298–300 (1952); UN Doc. A/C.3/

contention was that as freedom of association was already provided for in the draft Covenant (and in article 20 of the UDHR), the inclusion of an article on trade union rights was unduly repetitious.[7] It was also considered unjust to single out trade unions over and above other forms of association such as co-operative societies which might equally deserve attention.[8] In response, those in favour of trade union rights argued that the protection of freedom of association alone would be inadequate.[9] It would allow too many restrictions to be imposed on trade unions and would give them insufficient protection.[10] Trade unions were a 'necessary instrument for implementing economic, social, and cultural rights'[11] and therefore their protection was an 'essential condition' for the guarantee of economic rights in general,[12] and the right to satisfactory working conditions in particular.[13] It was noted, moreover, that the right to join and form trade unions had already been given recognition in article 23(4) of the UDHR.[14]

The second, and more fundamental, contention was that trade union rights were essentially 'prejudicial to the general conception of human rights'.[15] Such rights related to only one category of persons, and were therefore not universal,[16] and pertained to collectives rather than individuals. In response, it was pointed out that the right to form and join trade unions was in fact 'open to interpretation' as an individual right.[17] In any case, there was no problem with introducing rights that belonged to communities because they were nevertheless fundamental.[18] Indeed, as was noted in the report of the Third Committee in 1956, it was not 'fitting', 'on the one hand to grant the right to form and join trade unions and, on the other, to deprive unions of their rights to function and join in national and international federations'.[19]

The early drafts of the article were of a single paragraph, containing only an expression of the right to join and form trade unions. It was assumed that

SR.719–26 (1956). *See generally* UN Doc. A/2929, 10 UN GAOR, Annexes (Ag. Item 28), pt. II, 106–7 (1955); UN Doc. A/3525, 11 UN GAOR, Annexes (Ag. Item 31), 8–12, paras. 54–75 (1956).

[7] *See e.g.* Whitlam (Australia), E/CN.4/SR.225, at 9–10 (1951); Mehta (India), E/CN.4/SR.224, at 23 (1951).

[8] *See e.g.* Sørensen (Denmark), E/CN.4/SR.224, at 24 (1951).

[9] *See* Cassin (France), E/CN.4/SR.225, at 9 (1951); Morosov (USSR), *ibid.* 15 (1951).

[10] *See* Jevremovic (Yugoslavia), E/CN.4/SR.298, at 10 (1952). Ironically, the restrictions in the art. on freedom of association were included in the final version of art. 8.

[11] Malik (Lebanon), E/CN.4/SR.298, at 8 (1952).

[12] Jevremovic (Yugoslavia), E/CN.4/SR.298, at 9 (1952).

[13] *See* Chaudhuri (Pakistan), A/C.3/SR.719, at 199, para. 19 (1956).

[14] Santa Cruz (Chile), E/CN.4/SR.225, at 13 (1951).

[15] Sørensen (Denmark), E/CN.4/SR.224, at 24 (1951).

[16] *See e.g.* Mehta (India), E/CN.4/SR.224, at 23 (1951).

[17] *See* Malik (Lebanon), E/CN.4/SR.224, at 23 (1951).

[18] *See* Santa Cruz (Chile), E/CN.4/SR.224, at 23 (1951).

[19] UN Doc. A/3525, *supra*, n. 6, at 9, para. 66.

further detailed elaboration would be undertaken at a later stage by the ILO. However, following pressure from the Latin American and Socialist States, the article was expanded in the Third Committee, where the discussion moved from what rights should be included in article 8 to what limitations should be imposed on the rights. The final text, although subject to agreement, was not entirely satisfactory for all concerned. On the one hand a number of States clearly preferred the initial general provision drafted by the Commission.[20] On the other hand, those who looked for a more detailed article were disappointed that it be subject to so many restrictions.[21] The fact that all the proposals that remained at the voting stage were adopted reflects the concern that the article needed to be acceptable to as many States as possible. It is considered that this was achieved, however, by sacrificing the coherence of the article as a whole.

A Article 8(1): The Obligation to Ensure

It was generally agreed that 'progressive implementation could not be invoked in the case of trade union rights because no expenditure was necessary on the part of the State'.[22] The action required of States was one of self-restraint or non-interference.[23] As the UK representative commented in the Third Committee:

the Commission had decided that some of the rights in that Covenant should be the subject of an obligation which would be definite and immediate, and not progressive in character. Article 8 was such an article since it required States to 'undertake to ensure' the right. That obligation was the same as the one in article 21 of the draft Covenant on Civil and Political Rights.[24]

It was clear that in using the word 'ensure' in preference to the standard term 'recognize', the drafters intended that the article should not fall within the terms of article 2(1).

However, there was some indication among members of the Third Committee that, although immediate, the obligation was not solely negative. Mention was also made of the need for positive action by the State to promote trade unionism among workers,[25] particularly with respect to countries in which trade union organization was obstructed by low levels of development.[26]

---

[20] *See e.g.* Vlahov (Yugoslavia), A/C.3/SR.726, at 227, para. 27 (1956); Basavilbaso (Argentina), *ibid.* para. 28 (1956).
[21] *See e.g.* Castaneda (Mexico), A/C.3/SR.726, at 227, para. 30 (1956); Morosov (USSR), *ibid.* para. 33 (1956).   [22] Jevremovic (Yugoslavia), E/CN.4/SR.298, at 10 (1952).
[23] Malik (Lebanon), E/CN.4/SR.298, at 11 (1952).
[24] Hoare (UK), A/C.3/SR.720, at 197, para. 20 (1956). Draft art. 21 is now art. 22 ICCPR.
[25] *See* Diaz Casanueva, (Chile), A/C.3/SR.720, at 195, para. 3 (1956).
[26] *See* Diaz Casanueva, (Chile), A/C.3/SR.720, at 196, para. 6 (1956).

B Article 8(1)(a): The Right to Form and Join Trade Unions

1 'The Right of Everyone to Form Trade Unions . . .'

As far as the Commission was concerned, although article 8 referred to the right of 'everyone' to form trade unions, it was not intended to extend as far as employers.[27] In the Third Committee, however, this question gave rise to some debate. It was pointed out that, whereas the English, Chinese, and Russian terms for 'trade unions' were understood to refer to workers' organizations only, the French term *syndicats*, and the Spanish term *sindicatos*, both included employers' associations.[28] Notwithstanding these semantic difficulties, there was little real discussion about whether it was proper for employers' associations to be included in the definition. A number of States did indicate that the term should be read its broadest sense[29] as used in the ILO Convention of 1948,[30] under which both workers and employers would be covered.[31] It was even argued that organizations of employers were essential to economic development.[32] However, despite the unsatisfactory situation resulting from the adoption of a text which meant different things to different States,[33] a proposal that a declaration be made as to the scope of the provision was not adopted.[34]

In the absence of any clear statement about the scope of the article it would seem that the matter was intended to be left to the ratifying States.[35] Although, as noted above, some States considered that the protection extended to employers' associations, there is also evidence that a number of States voted for the provision on the understanding that it was limited to workers' organizations.[36]

2 '. . . The Trade Union of his Choice . . .'

In order to ensure that the right to form and join trade unions could be exercised freely and without coercion, it was decided that the right should be subject to the phrase 'the trade union of his choice'.[37] While this proposal

---

[27] The Secretary-General comments: 'Art. 8 was not intended to govern the rights of employers. It was stated that independent professional workers should be entitled to form professional organizations and that the rights of co-operative associations would not be prejudiced by their not being mentioned in the Covenant': UN Doc. A/2929, *supra* n. 6, at 106, para. 17 (1953).   [28] UN Doc. A/3525, *supra*, n. 6, at 10–11, para. 73.

[29] *See e.g.* Azkoul (Lebanon), A/C.3/SR.724, at 218, para. 14 (1956).

[30] *See* Diaz Casanueva (Chile), A/C.3/SR.722, at 208, para. 26 (1956).

[31] *See* Delhaye (Belgium), A/C.3/SR.722, at 208, para. 24 (1956).

[32] *See* Diaz Casanueva (Chile), A/C.3/SR.725, at 222, para. 8 (1956).

[33] *See* Diaz Casanueva (Chile), A/C.3/SR.725, at 221, para. 7 (1956).

[34] For the proposal, *see* Chairman, A/C.3/SR.723, at 215, para. 49 (1956).

[35] *See e.g.* Hoare (UK), A/C.3/SR.723, at 215, para. 50 (1956); Delhaye (Belgium), A/C.3/SR.724, at 217, para. 2 (1956).

[36] *See e.g.* Knox (Denmark), A/C.3/SR.726, at 225, para. 7 (1956); Kowalikowa (Poland), *ibid.* 226, para. 13 (1956).

[37] UN Doc. A/2929, *supra* n. 6, at 106, para. 14.

had considerable support, it was quickly pointed out that it suggested that individuals have the right to join any trade union irrespective of whether or not they have fulfilled the conditions of membership. If enforced, this would significantly limit trade unions' freedom to lay down their own organizational rules.[38] Accordingly it was suggested that the right to join a particular trade union should be specifically 'subject ... to the rules of the organization concerned'.[39] While this proposal itself was criticized as being both unnecessary[40] and potentially harmful, in that States might be prevented from legislating against inequitable trade union rules,[41] it received ultimate approval.

The adoption of the proposed wording seems to indicate that, while trade unions are free to establish their own conditions of membership, such conditions are subject to an element of State control to the extent necessary to ensure that the right with article 8 of the Covenant are respected.[42] An obvious case in point would be to ensure that such rules of entry are not discriminatory.

3 '... For the Promotion and Protection of his Economic and Social Interests'

In the Commission, the political activity of trade unions was a matter of some concern to a number of States.[43] It was considered necessary to include in article 8 a provision restricting trade union activity to the protection of workers' 'economic and social interests' so as to avoid them concerning themselves with 'purely political' matters.[44] Those who opposed the provision noted that it was 'only natural' that trade unions should have a role in the formulation of social and economic policy given their influence over the economy of the country,[45] and that they should participate in the implementation of social legislation.[46] Such a provision was 'extremely dangerous' in that it might be used as a pretext for taking measures against representative unions[47] and could mandate the formation of employer monopolies.[48] Belgium argued in particular that the right to form and join trade unions was absolute and should not be made dependent on the purpose sought by the individual.[49] On the other hand, in support of the

---

[38] *See* Bowie (UK), E/CN.4/SR.226, at 9 (1951); Chaudhuri (Pakistan), A/C.3/SR.719, at 191, para. 21 (1956).   [39] *See* Currie (Canada), A/C.3/SR.721, at 201, para. 16 (1956).

[40] *See e.g.* Bratanov (Bulgaria), A/C.3/SR.722, at 206, para. 8 (1956).

[41] *See e.g.* Serrano (Philippines), A/C.3/SR.722, at 207, para. 16 (1956).

[42] Cf. Mufti (Syria), A/C.3/SR.726, at 225, para. 9 (1956).

[43] *See e.g.* Santa Cruz (Chile), E/CN.4/SR.225, at 13–14 (1951).

[44] *See* Eggermann (IFCTU), E/CN.4/SR.225, at 18 (1951).

[45] Pattet (ICFTU), E/CN.4/SR.225, at 21 (1951).

[46] *See* Fischer (WFTU), E/CN.4/SR.225, at 25 (1951).

[47] Fischer (WFTU), E/CN.4/SR.225, at 26 (1951).

[48] *See* Jevremovic (Yugoslavia), E/CN.4/SR.298, at 9 (1952). This of course is on the assumption that the provision extends to employers.

[49] *See* Delhaye (Belgium), A/C.3/SR.722, at 208, para. 24 (1956).

proposal, Chile explained that although discussion of economic and social matters was clearly within the powers of trade unions, they should not interfere with policy-making at a regional and national level which ought to be undertaken through the normal democratic channels.[50] This disagreement was eventually resolved in the Third Committee by the inclusion of the word 'promotion' which effectively widened the range of activities envisaged for trade unions.[51]

The essence of the discussion indicates that the article was intended to allow trade unions to undertake a broad range of activities in the protection and promotion of workers' interests. The main restriction envisaged was that trade unions should not involve themselves in activities of a purely political nature. Apparently this would not exclude them from creating links with, or giving allegiance to, certain political parties, but would prohibit action that was aimed at the subversion of the democratic processes. Although providing a general understanding of the intended purport of the provision, this still leaves considerable doubt about the legitimacy of particular activities. For example, it was not fully resolved whether, or in what circumstances, strikes aimed at bringing down a government would be legitimate.

4 Restrictions

A reference to article 16 (now article 22 of the ICCPR) appeared in the early version of article 8 adopted at the Commission's seventh session.[52] Although ultimately deleted, it was argued that as article 8 was to be implemented immediately like article 22 of the ICCPR, it should be subject to the same restrictions[53] (found in article 22(2) and (3), with the exception of the reference to public health[54]). In disagreement, certain States suggested that such limitations would run counter to the provisions of ILO Convention No. 87,[55] and were rendered unnecessary by the terms of article 4.[56] However, it was pointed out that Article 4 had not yet been discussed and therefore could not be relied upon,[57] especially as it was not clear

[50] *See* Santa Cruz (Chile), E/CN.4/SR.225, at 22 (1951); Santa Cruz (Chile), E/CN.4/SR.300, at 7 (1952).
[51] The provision was finally adopted by 47 votes to 1 with 19 abstentions. UN Doc. A/3525, *supra* n. 6, at 11, para. 74.
[52] *See* UN Doc. A/2929, *supra* n. 6, at 106, para. 16.
[53] *See* Hoare (UK), A/C.3/SR.720, at 197, para. 21 (1956); Currie (Canada), A/C.3/SR.721, at 201, para. 15 (1956).
[54] *See* Hoare (UK), A/C.3/SR.719, at 191, para. 23 (1956).
[55] *See e.g.* Brena (Uruguay), A/C.3/SR.719, at 191, para. 28 (1956); Morosov (USSR), *ibid.* 192, para. 31 (1956).
[56] *See* Morozov (USSR), A/C.3/SR.719, at 192, para. 31 (1956); Diaz Casanueva (Chile), A/C.3/SR.720, at 196, para. 5 (1956); Vlahov (Yugoslavia), *ibid.* 198, para. 31 (1956).
[57] *See* Hoare (UK), A/C.3/SR.720, at 197, para. 22 (1956); Massoud-Ansari (Iran), A/C.3/SR.722, at 206, para. 9 (1956).

whether in fact it would operate with respect to article 8.[58] In any case a general limitations clause did not prohibit specific ones where appropriate.[59]

This discussion on permissible restrictions upon the right to form and join trade unions, although rather summary in nature, does give some indication of the intentions of the drafters. First, for a definition of the various terms used, such as 'national security' or 'democratic society', reference may be made to the *travaux préparatoires* of article 22 of the ICCPR. Secondly, to the extent that article 8(1)(a) is already subject to specific limitations, it appears that it is excluded from the scope of the general limitations clause in article 4. This point is fully supported by the *travaux préparatoires* of article 4, which reiterate that interpretation.[60]

C Article 8(1)(b): The Right to Federate

A proposal was put forward in the Commission establishing the right of trade unions to federate in 'local, regional, and international spheres'.[61] However, fear that international federations of trade unions might interfere in the internal politics of individual States[62] meant that no right to federate was included in the Commission's final draft. Instead the right to join trade unions was extended to 'local, national, and international trade unions'.[63]

Different considerations governed the debate in the Third Committee. There it was argued that a 'right to federate' as such was out of place in the Covenant because it did not relate to the rights of individuals but rather to the rights of trade unions themselves.[64] In response it was argued that the mere fact that the provision related to a group right was of itself not crucial. In order effectively to guarantee the right to form and join trade unions, trade unions themselves had to be guaranteed the right to act, which included the right to federate.[65]

It is submitted that, as a matter of textual consistency, the Commission draft was preferable to that of the Third Committee. It is submitted that although collective rights are not always incompatible with individual rights, and indeed might be required to ensure the full protection of the individual in certain circumstances,[66] in this case they are unnecessary. The

---

[58] *See* Azkoul (Lebanon), A/C.3/SR.721, at 201, para. 21 (1956).
[59] *See* Brena (Uruguay), A/C.3/SR.723, at 214, para. 46 (1956).
[60] *See* UN Doc. A/2929, *supra*, n. 6, at 25, para. 50.
[61] Azmi Bey (Egypt), E/CN.4/SR.224, at 24 (1951).
[62] *See* Ciasullo (Uruguay), E/CN.4/SR.225, at 7 (1951).
[63] UN Doc. E/2256, 14 UN ESCOR, Supp. (No. 4), at 21–2 (1952).
[64] *See e.g.* Hamilton (Australia), A/C.3/SR.723, at 213, para. 30 (1956).
[65] *See e.g.* Kowalikowa (Poland), A/C.3/SR.720, at 196, para. 13 (1956); Bratanov (Bulgaria), A/C.3/SR.722, at 205, para. 6 (1956).
[66] *See e.g.* Brownlie I., 'The Rights of Peoples in Modern International Law', in Crawford J. (ed.), *The Rights of Peoples* (1988), 1, at 3.

right to federate internationally could easily have been posited as a principle deriving from the effective enjoyment of the right to form and join trade unions. The crucial difference would be that in cases of conflict between individual and collective interests, the provision would necessarily have to be decided in favour of the individual.

D Article 8(1)(c): The Right of Trade Unions to Function Freely

As stated above, the right of trade unions to function freely was considered to be a necessary corollary of the right to form and join trade unions and was adopted as such by the Third Committee.[67] As an independent provision, it would appear to include, over and above the right to strike and the right to federate (both of which are themselves specifically recognized), the right of trade unions to operate freely and call conferences and meetings without interference, and the right to collective bargaining.[68] Nevertheless, the precise scope and meaning of this provision was left undefined.

In the Third Committee the original draft provided that the right of trade unions to function freely should be restricted only 'for the protection of the rights and freedoms of others.'[69] Although this phrase was rejected as being too vague, limitative,[70] and unnecessary,[71] a later draft providing that the right could be limited in the interests of 'public order' or the 'security of the State'[72] was ultimately accepted,[73] despite considerable opposition.[74]

Given the fact that a limitation clause was considered necessary, the right to function freely should properly be interpreted in a wide sense. That the exact functions of trade unions were left undefined may be because mention had already been made of the right of trade unions to establish and enforce their own organizational rules,[75] and that they could exercise those functions necessary for the protection and promotion of their members' interests.[76] In addition, provisions were on the table relating to the right to strike and the right to federate. Indeed it later became apparent during the debate on the right to strike, that the right to function freely includes, at least, a right to collective bargaining.

---

[67] UN Doc. A/3525, *supra*, n. 6, at 11, para. 74(j) (1956).

[68] *See* Sender (ICFTU), E/CN.4/SR.225, at 10 (1951); Pickford (ILO), E/CN.4/SR.299, at 5 (1952).

[69] UN Doc. A/C.3/L.552/Rev. 1.

[70] *See* Bratanov (Bulgaria), A/C.3/SR.722, at 206, para. 6 (1956).

[71] *See* Serrano (Philippines), A/C.3/SR.722, at 207, para. 15 (1956).

[72] *See* Azkoul (Lebanon), A/C.3/SR.721, at 201, para. 22 (1956). Cf. Amendment of Netherlands and the United Kingdom: UN Doc. A/C.3/L.555.

[73] UN Doc. A/3525, *supra* n. 6, at 10, para. 70.

[74] *See e.g.* Townsend Ezcurra (Peru), A/C.3/SR.721, at 202, para. 28 (1956).

[75] *See above* text accompanying nn. 38–42.

[76] *See above* text accompanying nn. 43–51.

E Article 8(1)(d): The Right to Strike

There was considerable debate both in the Commission and in the Third Committee over whether it was appropriate to include within the Covenant a provision guaranteeing the right to strike.[77] Those opposed to such a provision argued: (i) the right to strike was often not subject to State regulation and thus should be left to the State concerned;[78] (ii) the right to strike was subject to a number of restrictions and therefore could not be considered to be a truly universal right;[79] (iii) the right to strike was merely a means to implement trade union rights and not a proper right in itself;[80] (iv) the right to strike was a collective right and thus was out of place in a Covenant dealing with individual rights;[81] (v) the right to strike was not a primary right but only a right of 'last resort'[82] to be exercised following other attempts at conciliation and only when other rights were endangered;[83] (vi) the proposed article had no corresponding provision in the UDHR, and therefore there was no justification for including it in the Covenant.[84]

Such arguments effectively prevented the inclusion of a right to strike in the early Commission drafts. However, in the Third Committee, the majority opinion was that the right to strike was essential for the protection of the economic and social interests of workers[85] to the extent that it was meaningless to try to guarantee trade union rights without a right to strike.[86] It was pointed out that the right to strike was mentioned in the legislation of many countries,[87] and had become a social reality that had to be recognized.[88] Interestingly enough, for one State at least, the right to strike was associated with the right not to be forced to work which already had recognition in the Covenant.[89]

Although a number of States agreed to the inclusion of a right to strike, they argued that, given the effect of strikes on the economy,[90] reference

[77] *See generally* Ben-Israel R., *International Labour Standards: The Case of Freedom to Strike* (1988), 72–83.
[78] *See e.g.* Azmi Bey (Egypt), E/CN.4/SR.224, at 24 (1951); Juvigny (France), E/CN.4/SR.300, at 4 (1952). [79] *See* Mehta (India), E/CN.4/SR.225, at 25 (1951).
[80] *See* Rossel (Sweden), E/CN.4/SR.300, at 9 (1952); Azmi Bey (Egypt), E/CN.4/SR.225, at 21 (1951). [81] *See* Hamilton (Australia), A/C.3/SR.723, at 213, para. 32 (1956).
[82] Beaufort (Netherlands), A/C.3/SR.721, at 202, para. 25 (1956).
[83] *See* Rajan (India), E/CN.4/SR.299, at 11 (1952).
[84] *See* Juvigny (France), E/CN.4/SR.300, at 4 (1952). Ben-Israel notes that the absence of a right to strike in ILO Conventions was also an important factor in its exclusion in the early drafts of art. 8. Ben-Israel, *supra* n. 77, at 73.
[85] *See e.g.* Morosov (USSR), E/CN.4/SR.298, at 8 (1952).
[86] *See e.g.* Bracco (Uruguay), E/CN.4/SR.229, at 3 (1952); Brena (Uruguay), A/C.3/SR.719, at 191, para. 25 (1956); Townsend Ezcurra (Peru), *ibid.* 193, para. 40 (1956).
[87] *See* Townsend Ezcurra (Peru), A/C.3/SR.721, at 202, para. 29 (1956).
[88] *See* Chaudhuri (Pakistan), A/C.3/SR.723, at 212 para. 15 (1956).
[89] *See* Jevremovic (Yugoslavia), E/CN.4/SR.225, at 6 (1951).
[90] Concern was expressed particularly for the position of developing countries in which it

should be made to the fact that it was a 'last resort' following conciliation.[91] It was suggested, however, that in some cases it might be necessary to call a strike without resorting to conciliation procedures.[92] Moreover, conciliation was a complex process in which it was not always clear when negotiations had broken down—often they continued as long as the strike lasted.[93] In the same vein, some States argued that it was wrong to mention the right to strike without the other methods of dispute settlement,[94] or other activities of trade unions,[95] such as the right to picket.[96] Whatever their merit, such remarks had little effect upon the final wording adopted.

At most stages of the debate, there was dispute over the extent to which the right to strike should be subject to limitations. In the Commission it was argued that strikes should be limited where the vital interests of the State were at stake.[97] In response, it was pointed out that this would leave the door open to abuse as the State alone could judge its own security considerations[98] and that any such limitation would encourage governments to attack trade union rights.[99] Indeed Yugoslavia argued that, given the financial constraints on strikes, unjustified strike action was extremely unlikely.[100] However, although not explicitly stated, it would seem that the limitations laid down in article 8(1)(c) (that the right may be limited in the interests of national security or public order or the rights and freedoms of others) would similarly apply to the right to strike—it being clear that initiating strikes is one of the functions of trade unions.

The limitation finally adopted in article 8(1)(d) was proposed as a compromise, and gave much away to those who opposed the inclusion of the

was considered necessary that new industries be protected from irresponsible trade union action, Massoud-Ansari (Iran), A/C.3/SR.722, at 206, para. 11 (1956). Nevertheless it was explained that one reason for introducing the right to strike was 'to protect the workers in under-developed countries against the reactionary tendencies of the dictatorships to which they so frequently succumbed precisely because of the backwardness and instability of the economies of such countries. Another reason was that the under-developed countries were the first to suffer in an economic crisis, and the workers in those countries were usually the hardest hit': Ayala Mercado (Bolivia), A/C.3/SR.722, at 207, para. 19 (1956).

[91] *See e.g.* Roosevelt (USA), E/CN.4/SR.225, at 12 (1951); Eggermann (IFCTU), *ibid.* 18 (1956); Azmi Bey (Egypt), *ibid.* 22 (1951); Cheng Paonan (China), E/CN.4/SR.299, at 15 (1952); Diaz Casanueva (Chile), A/C.3/SR.721, at 203, para. 36 (1956); Ayala Mercado (Bolivia), A/C.3/SR.722, at 207, para. 19 (1956).

[92] *See* Sender (ICFTU), E/CN.4/SR.299, at 8 (1952).

[93] *See* Whitlam (Australia), E/CN.4/SR.300, at 8 (1952); Hoare (UK), *ibid.* 11 (1952).

[94] *See e.g.* Hoare (UK), A/C.3/SR.720, at 198, para. 26 (1956); Vlahov (Yugoslavia), *ibid.* para. 30 (1956).

[95] *See* Aman (Sweden), A/C.3/SR.722, at 205, para. 3 (1956).

[96] *See* Serrano (Philippines), A/C.3/SR.722, at 207, para. 15 (1956).

[97] *See* Azmi Bey (Egypt), E/CN.4/SR.225, at 22 (1951). An amendment was proposed to that effect, UN Doc. E/CN.4/595.

[98] *See* Fischer (WFTU), E/CN.4/SR.225, at 26 (1951); Jevremovic (Yugoslavia), E/CN.4/SR.226, at 5 (1951).

[99] *See* Morosov (USSR), E/CN.4/SR.299, at 13–14 (1952).

[100] *See* Jevremovic (Yugoslavia), E/CN.4/SR.298, at 10 (1952).

provision.[101] Although the limitation made the provision generally accept-able, some states were concerned that making the right subject to the laws of the particular country could render it virtually inoperable.[102] This was not enough to dissuade the vast majority of States from voting in favour of the proposal.[103]

F Article 8(2): Members of the Armed Forces, Police, and the Administration of the State

A provision allowing the imposition of restrictions on the trade union rights of workers in the public services was proposed in the Commission.[104] These were later encapsulated in the joint amendment proposed by the Nether-lands and the United Kingdom, apparently inspired by the terms of the ECHR,[105] which legitimized the imposition of restrictions on members of the police, armed forces, and those concerned with the administration of the State.[106]

A number of States argued that, although restrictions on the armed forces and the police were legitimate, that was not the case with respect to members of the administration of the State.[107] ILO practice did not allow restrictions upon the trade union rights of all public officials—only those in the army and police, and then only to an extent determined by law.[108] Moreover, to allow limitations upon the right to strike in the public service was open to abuse as the concept of a public service was a flexible one.[109] In that sense it would be unduly prejudicial in the case of States with large nationalized sectors.[110] It might also be a retrograde step for those States where the right to strike was denied only to workers in essential services.[111]

The UK responded that the terms of the ILO Convention referring to the armed forces and police were merely declaratory,[112] and in any case they did not stipulate that there should be such restrictions but only foresaw their

[101] UN Doc. A/3525, *supra* n. 6, at 10, para. 68.
[102] *See e.g.* Hoare (UK), A/C.3/SR.722, at 209, para. 33 (1956); Hamilton (Australia), A/C.3/SR.723, at 214, para. 32 (1956); Stabel (Norway), A/C.3/SR.725, at 221, para. 4 (1956).
[103] UN Doc. A/3525, *supra* n. 6, at 11, para. 74(m).
[104] *See* Ciasullo (Uruguay), E/CN.4/SR.225, at 7 (1951); Rajan (India), E/CN.4/SR.299, at 11 (1952).
[105] *See* ECHR, Art. 11(2).   [106] UN Docs. A/C.3/L.550 and A/C.3/L.555.
[107] *See e.g.* Dupont Willemin (Guatemala), E/CN.4/SR.225, at 8 (1951); Sender (ICFTU), E/CN.4/SR.299, at 8 (1952); Shoham-Sharon (Israel), A/C.3/SR.722, at 208, para. 31 (1956).
[108] *See e.g.* Santa Cruz (Chile), E/CN.4/SR.299, at 11 (1952); Brena (Uruguay), A/C.3/SR.719, at 191, para. 28 (1956); Morozov (USSR), *ibid.* 192, para. 31 (1956).
[109] *See* Juvigny (France), E/CN.4/SR.300, at 4 (1952); Bratanov (Bulgaria), A/C.3/SR.722, at 206, para. 7 (1956).
[110] *See* Eustathiades (Greece), A/C.3/SR.721, at 200, para. 6 (1956); Thierry (France), A/C.3/SR.721, at 200, para. 11 (1956).
[111] *See* Juvigny (France), E/CN.4/SR.300, at 4 (1952).
[112] *See* Hoare (UK), A/C.3/SR.720, at 197, para. 24 (1956).

possibility.[113] It would seem that States' acceptance of this provision was conditioned to some extent by their assumption that the ILO would play a significant part in the supervision of the Covenant. It could be inferred from the discussion that restrictions imposed would be considered legitimate only in so far as they comply with the ILO standards in the area. That this seems to have been the intention of the drafters is made clear by the inclusion of sub-paragraph 3 which makes reference to the ILO Freedom of Association Convention.

G Article 8(3): The ILO Convention of 1948

Considerable misgivings were expressed about the inclusion of a reference to ILO Convention No. 87[114] as proposed by the Netherlands and the UK.[115] States argued that such a reference was unclear in its meaning and unnecessary.[116] Not only was it of legally negligible value in that the obligations in the ILO Convention could not be derogated from on the basis of the Covenant,[117] but it also implied that the obligations in other conventions were not similarly protected.[118] Moreover, no such cross-reference had been made in articles 6 and 7.[119] There were few coherent arguments put forward in favour of the paragraph beyond a statement that the paragraph would avoid any future conflicts between the Convention and the Covenant. The paragraph was adopted by a small majority in the Third Committee, perhaps as a matter of maintaining support for the article as a whole.[120]

III. THE APPROACH OF THE COMMITTEE

The Committee has not as yet produced a general comment, or undertaken a general discussion on article 8. The only indication of its approach to article 8 is to be found from its reporting guidelines and the comments and questions of individual members. It is a provision, however, in respect of which Committee members have been critical of the performance of a

---

[113] *See* Hoare (UK), A/C.3/SR.722, at 209, para. 33 (1956).
[114] ILO Freedom of Association and Protection of the Right to Organize Convention (No. 87), 9 July 1948, 68 UNTS. 17.
[115] A/C.3/L.550 and L.555. *See* Hoare (UK), A/C.3/SR.719, at 191, para. 23 (1956).
[116] *See e.g.* Brena (Uruguary), A/C.3/SR.719, at 192, para. 29 (1956).
[117] *See* Eustathiades (Greece), A/C.3/SR.721, at 200, para. 6 (1956); Mufti (Syria), A/C.3/SR.726, at 225–6, para. 10 (1956).
[118] *See* Serrano (Philippines), A/C.3/SR.722, at 207, para. 18 (1956); Shoham-Sharon (Israel), A/C.3/SR.722, at 208, para. 29 (1956).
[119] *See* Kowalikowa (Poland), A/C.3/SR.720, at 196, para. 14 (1956).
[120] The para. was adopted by 19 votes to 14 with 35 abstentions. UN Doc. A/3525, *supra*, n. 6, at 11, para. 74(p).

number of States, reflecting a greater confidence in the precise level of protection offered by the Covenant.

A Article 8: The Obligation to Ensure

As was noted during the drafting of the Covenant, the right to join and form trade unions is an integral part of the general right to freedom of association found in article 22 of the ICCPR.[121] As the rights within the ICESCR are generally subject to progressive implementation under article 2(1), in contrast to the ICCPR (in which States undertake to 'ensure' the rights), the contradictory position might have arisen in which the same rights were to be implemented immediately under one Covenant and progressively under the other. This possibility is specifically negatived in article 8 which, as was intended during the drafting,[122] uses the term 'ensure' to make clear that it is to be implemented in an immediate manner.

Some commentators have argued that article 2(1) of the ICESCR applies only to those rights that are specifically 'recognized' in the terms of the article.[123] Although there is no indication in the drafting that this was intended to be the case,[124] such an interpretation has some textual coherence. Even if this interpretation is not acceptable, however, it is clear that as the realization of the rights in article 8 is not wholly contingent upon the availability of economic resources, they should be ensured within a reasonable time.

The Committee has made clear that it considers that article 8 'would seem to be capable of immediate application by judicial and other organs in many national legal systems'.[125] That the enjoyment of the rights within article 8 is primarily a matter for legal regulation is reflected in the questions in the Committee's reporting guidelines which are directed primarily at legal and administrative conditions and restrictions that govern the exercise of trade union rights.[126] This approach seems justified to the extent that a number of States that have come before the Committee have noted that the right to join trade unions is to be found in their respective

---

[121] *See above* text accompanying n. 7. The HRC, however, has been reluctant to read into art. 22 other rights that are associated with the right to form and join trade unions such as the right to strike. *See J.B. et al.* v. *Canada* (1986) 2 Selected Decisions HRC 34.

[122] *See above* text accompanying nn. 22–6.

[123] Alston P. and Quinn G., 'The Nature and Scope of States Parties' Obligations under the International Covenant on Economic, Social and Cultural Rights' (1987) 9 *Hum. Rts. Q* 156, at 185.

[124] *See above* Ch. 3, text accompanying n. 170.

[125] General Comment No. 3 (1990), UN ESCOR, Supp. (No. 3), Annex III, at 84, para. 5, UN Doc. E/1991/23 (1991).

[126] Reporting Guidelines, UN ESCOR, Supp. (No. 3), Annex IV, at 94, UN Doc. E/1991/23 (1991).

constitutions.[127] However, as was noted in the Committee's General Comment, constitutional enactment alone is not necessarily sufficient in itself to ensure that a right will be guaranteed in practice.[128]

That the right is to be ensured immediately does not, however, mean that the obligation is strictly negative. States are also expected to take action to promote and protect the right to form and join trade unions. Thus the Committee has been keen to ensure that anti-trade union activities are prohibited[129] and that trade unionism is generally encouraged. As a reflection of this concern, questions are frequently asked about the number and structure of trade unions[130] and the proportion of the workforce that is unionized.[131] Nevertheless, the Committee could go further; given the important role of trade unions in securing just and adequate conditions of work, it might be considered desirable for States to assist workers in unorganized sectors, particularly through educational measures, to form effective trade unions.

B Article 8(1)(a): The Right to Form and Join the Trade Union of his Choice

1 The Right of 'Everyone'

Article 8 provides that 'everyone' has the right to form and join trade unions. Unlike article 7(a), its scope *ratione personae* is not limited to 'workers'. Despite the unresolved nature of the controversy apparent in the *travaux préparatoires*,[132] the fact that the French text refers to *syndicats* and the Spanish to *sindicatos*, both of which have a broader meaning than the English term 'trade unions', suggests that employers' organizations should also fall within the terms of article 8.[133] Although the Committee has not

---

[127] *See e.g.* Rhenan Segura (Costa Rica), E/C.12/1990/SR.40, at 6, para. 22; Weitzel (Luxembourg), E/C.12/1990/SR.33, at 5, para. 15. *See also* Panama, E/1984/6/Add.19, at 17; Afghanistan, E/1990/5/Add.8, at 7, para. 22; Syria, E/1990/6/Add.1, at 8, para. 28; Rwanda, E/1984/7/Add.29, at 15.

[128] General Comment No. 3, *supra*, n. 125, at 84, para. 28. *See generally* Craven M., 'The Domestic Application of the International Covenant on Economic, Social and Cultural Rights' (1993) 40 *Neth. ILR* 367, at 377–81.

[129] *See e.g.* Simma, E/C.12/1994/SR.9, at 9, para. 33; Bonoan-Dandam, E/C.12/1994/SR.10/Add.1, at 2, para. 1.

[130] Reporting guidelines, *supra*, n. 126, at 95.

[131] *See e.g.* Mratchkov, E/C.12/1988/SR.17, at 5, para. 30; Ider, E/C.12/1993/SR.7, at 8, para. 34.

[132] *See above* text accompanying nn. 27–36.

[133] This interpretation would bring the Covenant in line with ILO Convention No. 87 which provides that both workers and employers shall have the right to establish and join trade unions 'without distinction whatsoever'. Valticos N., *International Labour Law* (1979), at 82; The Committee of Experts on the Application of Conventions and Recommendations' General Survey on Freedom of Association and Collective Bargaining, 69th Sess. (1983), ILO II: 69/3 (4B), paras. 100–2 (1983).

made clear its view on this question, it is not of utmost importance as most problems in the area relate to employees' trade unions.[134]

A related question of some interest in light of the Committee's position on closed shop agreements[135] is whether the article extends to professional associations established by public law that fulfil a legal duty or form part of a public institution. As far as the ECHR is concerned, the European Court of Human Rights has found that such bodies are not associations within the meaning of Article 11 (the right to freedom of association).[136] Accordingly there is no right not to join those organizations where they operate a closed-shop agreement. If the Committee does consider such associations to be 'trade unions' for the purposes of article 8, it will have to bear in mind their legitimate regulatory functions when applying the right not to join trade unions.

Notwithstanding the general application of article 8, certain restrictions appear to be legitimized by the Covenant. Article 8(2), in particular, provides that the article 'shall not prevent the imposition of lawful restrictions on the exercise of these rights by members of the armed forces or of the police or of the administration of the State'. Whereas article 9 of ILO Convention No. 87 allows for restrictions to be placed upon the trade union rights of members of the armed forces and the police, unlike article 8 of the ICESCR no such restrictions are allowed in relation to members of the administration of the State.[137]

As article 8(3) confirms, those States parties that are also party to ILO Convention No. 87 would still be bound by the provisions of that Convention. Indeed, article 8(3) requires that for States parties to the ILO Convention the terms of article 8(1) and (2) should be read subject to the provisions of that Convention. Accordingly, a State that imposed wholesale restrictions on the ability of public servants to join or form trade unions would be in violation not only of the ILO Covention but also of the Covenant.[138]

---

[134] Jenks W., *The International Protection of Trade Union Freedom* (1957), at 173. He notes earlier that the decision to include employers' organizations was due to a recognition that the collective regulation of conditions of employment required strong and free workers' and employers' organizations. *Ibid.* 24–5.

[135] *See below* text accompanying nn. 163–73.

[136] *See Le Compte, Van Leuven and De Meyère* v. *The Netherlands*, Eur. Ct. HR, judgment of 23 June 1981, Series A, No. 43, p. 27, para. 65, (1982) 4 EHRR 1.

[137] *Supra*, n. 114. Cf. General Survey, *supra*, n. 133, para. 87. The ILO Freedom of Association Committee has been particularly critical of the UK as regards restrictions imposed upon the right of civil servants employed at GCHQ to join organizations of their own choosing. *See generally* Ewing K., *Britain and the ILO*, (1989) 11–14, 31–7. The European Commission of Human Rights, however, did not consider the restrictions to be in breach of art. 11 ECHR. *See CCSU* v. *United Kingdom* (1987), 20 DREComHR 228, (1988) 10 EHRR 269. Cf. Fredman S. and Morris G., 'Union Membership at GCHQ' (1988) 17 *Ind. LJ* 105.

[138] Whereas the terms of art. 8(3) will modify the existing obligations under the terms of art. 8, it is open to question whether this means that the wider terms of the ILO Convention should be given general effect under the Covenant. This interpretation was expressly negatived by the

Similarly, as article 5(2) makes clear, limitations cannot be invoked merely on the pretext that the Covenant offers less protection than that already provided in domestic law.[139]

In contradistinction, those States not party to the ILO Convention might be entitled to rely upon article 8(2) as justification for restrictions upon the trade union activity of public servants in general, which would represent a significant loophole as far as international standards are concerned. As commentators have noted, some of the major problems as regards freedom of association have arisen with respect to the position of public servants.[140]

The only occasion on which members of the Committee actually confronted this issue was in a discussion about the extent to which civil servants in the Dominican Republic enjoyed freedom of association.[141] It was pointed out by the ILO representative that certain legislation within the Dominican Republic allowed the authorities to dissolve public employee associations and therefore seemed to be in conflict with the right to freedom of association.[142] The Committee did not address this point directly, but concentrated instead upon the right to strike of public employees. In that context, it appears that the Committee is not willing to accept general restrictions upon the right, but will investigate the necessity for such restrictions. It is assumed that as article 8(2) applies to all sections of article 8(1), the Committee will also scrutinize limitations imposed upon the right of public servants to form and join trade unions.[143]

If the Committee does take the view that broad restrictions on the rights of public employees to exercise their rights to form and join trade unions are of doubtful legitimacy, it will have to explain its position at a textual level. This will involve making some important decisions as to the meaning and relative scope of the various limitation clauses that might be seen to operate in relation to article 8(1)(a). It will also mean defining what categories of employees are considered to fall within the scope of the term 'members of the administration of the State'. For example, it might be open to define that term in a narrow manner to include only those working in emergency services or otherwise involved in the security of the State. This

HRC as regards the identical provisions of art. 22(3) in *J.B. et al.* v. *Canada, supra,* n. 121, at 38, para. 6.5.

[139] Art. 5(2) reads: 'No restriction upon or derogation from any of the fundamental human rights recognized or existing in any country in virtue of law, conventions, regulations or custom shall be admitted on the pretext that the present Covenant does not recognize such rights or that it recognizes them to a lesser extent.'

[140] Pankert A., 'Freedom of Association' in Blainpain R. (ed.), *Comparative Labour Law and Industrial Relations* (3rd ed., 1987), 173 and 178; Jenks, *supra* n. 117, at 178.

[141] UN Doc. E/1991/23, UN ESCOR, Supp. (No. 3), at 58, para. 226 (1991).

[142] Dao (ILO), E/C.12/1990/SR.44, at 8, para. 38.

[143] It might also be noted that as far as ILO standards are concerned, more restrictions will be tolerated as regards the right to strike than the right to form and join trade unions.

would not allow general restrictions being placed upon the rights of civil servants or public employees.

It is considered that there is good reason to deny the possibility of limiting the right of members of the administration of the State to form and join trade unions. As is evident from the *travaux préparatoires*, the intention of article 8(2) was not to provide for such restrictions but merely to make them possible in certain circumstances.[144] In particular, the purpose appears to have been to bring article 8(1) into line with article 22 of the ICCPR,[145] which, in outlining the right to form and join trade unions, does not allow the imposition of restrictions upon the rights of members of the administration of the State. It is considered that, in the light of article 22 of the ICCPR and ILO standards,[146] the real intention of the drafters was to allow restrictions *vis-à-vis* the armed forces and the police in relation to the whole of article 8(1), but to allow for restrictions as regards members of the administration of the State only in the case of the right to strike.[147] Unfortunately this is not clear in the text, which remains open to interpretation otherwise.

Although the terms of article 8 are generally obscure, it is arguable that use of the term 'lawful' restrictions in article 8(2) was intended to refer to the criteria laid down in article 8(1)(a) to govern the imposition of restrictions on the right to form and join trade unions. Accordingly, any restrictions imposed upon the right to form and join trade unions should be 'prescribed by law' and 'necessary in a democratic society in the interests of national security or public order or for the protection of the rights and freedoms of others'.[148] If this were the case, it would be difficult to justify a general restriction upon the right of public servants to join or form trade unions irrespective of the type of work that they undertake.

Another area that has attracted the attention of the Committee is the extent to which non-nationals are allowed full participation in trade unions. In the cases of Costa Rica and Panama, individual members of the Committee expressed the view that the restrictions placed upon the right of foreigners to take part in trade union activities might be incompatible with the Covenant.[149] While in neither case did the Committee as a whole adopt

---

[144] *See above* text accompanying n. 113.   [145] *See above* text accompanying n. 53.

[146] Those contained in ILO Convention No. 87, *supra*, n. 114.

[147] For the situation with respect to the right to strike, *see below* text accompanying nn. 228–77.

[148] For a discussion of limitations generally, *see below* text accompanying nn. 180–90.

[149] *See* Alvarez Vita, E/C.12/1990/SR.40, at 11, para. 52; Texier, E/C.12/1990/SR.40, at 12, para. 56. As far as the ILO is concerned, art. 6(1)(a)(ii) of the ILO Migration for Employment Convention (Revised) of 1949 (No. 97), 120 UNTS 71, provides for equal treatment regarding membership of trade unions for foreign workers. This has been supplemented by art. 10 of the ILO Migrant Workers (Supplementary Provisions) Convention of 1975 (No. 143), 1120 UNTS 323. *Cf.* art. 19, European Social Charter 1961; UN Convention on the Protection of the Rights of All Migrant Workers and Members of their Families (1990).

this position, it has since expressed its 'concern' over the existence of such a bar in the case of Senegal.[150]

2 *Subject to the Rules of the Organization Concerned*

Article 8(1)(a) provides for the right to join the trade union of one's choice 'subject only to the rules of the organization concerned'. As the *travaux préparatoires* make clear, this provision was included to protect the right of trade unions to establish internal rules and maintain control over their own membership.[151] The ILO has noted that the free determination of the structure and membership of trade unions is an essential element of the right to form and join trade unions.[152] The need to protect unions from State interference already has some recognition in article 8(1)(c) which refers to their right to function freely. Article 8(1)(a), however, appears to centre upon the dynamic between the interests of the individual and those of the organization.

The only occasion on which this issue came to be discussed was in the case of the Democratic People's Republic of Korea. Members of the Committee raised questions over a statement to the effect that the right to join trade unions was acknowledged only if individuals 'recognize the programme and rules of the Korean trade unions and strive to implement them'.[153] One member went so far as to say that this seemed to be an 'extremely restrictive provision'.[154] Unfortunately the Committee members did not take the opportunity to establish what principles they considered were involved.

Although it is not appropriate for the State to lay down conditions for trade union membership, it is reasonable to expect the right to join trade unions to be subject to the internal membership rules of the organization concerned. If otherwise, the very purpose of the trade union could be easily defeated. However, the State does have a residual responsibility in ensuring that trade unions do not abuse their position of power through the exercise of unreasonable or arbitrary rules, such as ones that discriminate against women or racial groups.

3 *The Trade Union 'of his Choice'*

The right to form and join the trade union 'of his choice' would seem to provide for a right not to be compelled to join a particular trade union. While simple in principle, the matter is clouded in cases where there is only

---

[150] Concluding observations on report of Senegal, E/C.12/1993/18, at 2, para. 8.
[151] *See above* text accompanying nn. 39–42.
[152] General Survey, *supra*, n. 133, para. 121.
[153] E/1984/6/Add.7. para. 66.   [154] Konate, E/C.12/1987/SR.22, at 3, para. 6.

one trade union, or where a union security agreement is in operation. Each of these matters will be dealt with in turn.

(a) Trade Union Diversity

While the reporting guidelines neutrally request information as to the 'number and structure of trade unions established',[155] members of the Committee have taken a stronger line in arguing that 'plurality of trade unions formed part of the notion of freedom of trade union rights'.[156] Accordingly in cases where only a single trade union[157] or a single federation[158] exists in the whole country, the Committee has considered the States concerned to be in violation of the Covenant.[159]

The position adopted by the Committee is not necessarily inevitable. Although there is clearly a need to protect union activity from State interference, it might well be to the advantage of workers, particularly in small developing countries, to avoid trade union multiplicity. This would certainly be the case as far as collective bargaining was concerned. Thus the formation of a single trade union or federation might in itself be a matter of choice as far as the workers are concerned. It could not possibly be the case that the State is required itself to establish new trade unions to cater for individual choice. It is submitted that in cases where a single trade union exists the Committee should direct its attention to whether it emerged as a result of the free will of the workers concerned,[160] and whether workers still retain the right to form new trade unions. The State here has an obligation to refrain from action that would institutionalize the single trade union in law.[161] The essential question then is not whether or not trade union diversity exists, but whether that diversity remains a possibility.[162]

(b) Union Security Agreements

It is clear that when a worker takes up employment in an undertaking where a union security clause (whether pre- or post-entry[163]) is in operation,

---

[155] Reporting Guidelines, *supra*, n. 126, at 95.

[156] Konate, E/C.12/1987/SR.13, at 5, para. 22.

[157] *See* Texier, E/C.12/1989/SR.12, at 4, para. 18.

[158] *See* Sparsis, E/C.12/1988/SR.4, at 6, para. 32.

[159] *See* Concluding observations on report of Vietnam, E/C.12/1993/8, at 2, para. 9.

[160] This point has occasionally been made by members of the Committee, *see e.g.* Mrachkov, E/C.12/1991/SR.7, at 11, para. 47.

[161] An interesting point, taken up by only one member, was the general federation of agricultural workers in Syria that 'had been established under Decree No. 127/1964' and that two other organizations had been merged by decree (No. 21/1974), Khoury (Syria), E/C.12/1991/SR.7, at 5, para. 16. *Cf.* General Survey, *supra*, n. 133, para. 137. This does raise serious questions about the legitimacy of the closed shop however, *see below*, text accompanying nn. 163–73.

[162] Jenks, *supra*, n. 134, at 180; Valticos, *supra*, n. 133, at 82.

[163] A post-entry closed shop agreement is sometimes referred to as an 'open shop agreement', *see* Pankert, *supra*, n. 140, at 182. There are, in addition to the two forms of closed shop

he or she is effectively obliged to join the union concerned.[164] In such a situation, the restriction upon freedom of choice is often justified as a necessary means for securing union bargaining power.[165] Although article 20(2) of the UDHR provides that '[n]o one may be compelled to belong to an association', other international instruments display more caution in this respect. Article 2 of ILO Convention No. 87 leaves it open to the States concerned whether union security agreements are considered to be legitimate. Similarly, proposals to insert provisions guaranteeing the negative freedom of association into both the ICCPR[166] and the ECHR[167] were rejected. Certainly there was no real discussion of the matter during the drafting of the ICESCR.

As far as the Covenant is concerned, there are two issues. First, whether the right to join the trade union of one's choice includes a right not to join a particular trade union. Secondly, whether dismissal resulting from failure to join the union concerned could amount to a violation of the right to work in article 6.[168] In both cases there is clearly a tension between the rights of the individual and the right of trade unions to function freely and effectively.

To some extent, the terms of the Covenant point to the legitimacy of closed shop agreements. Unlike the ECHR and the ICCPR the right to join trade unions is not placed in the context of 'freedom of association' and thus arguably does not bear the same connotations of negativity.[169] Moreover, in specifically outlining the rights of trade unions the Covenant appears to demand that the relative interests of trade unions should not be dismissed out of hand. Indeed, just as much as the right of trade unions to function freely may be subject to limitations 'for the protection of the rights and freedoms of others',[170] that is also the case as regards the individual right to

agreements, agency shop agreements under which workers, while not being required to become union members, are obliged to pay dues to the union concerned.

[164] In post-entry closed shop agreements there is of course the theoretical possibility of the worker terminating his or her employment before entry into the Union.

[165] Pankert identifies 4 main objectives of trade union security agreements: (i) to enable unions to control access to jobs; (ii) to strengthen the position of the unions in a hostile environment; (iii) to force outsiders to share the financial burden of the operation of the trade union; and (iv) to strengthen trade unions as an indispensable partner for the effective operation of the industrial relations system: Pankert, *supra*, n. 140, at 182.

[166] *Ibid.* 181–2.

[167] *See* Shea C., 'The Case of Young, James and Webster: British Labour Law and the European Convention on Human Rights' (1982) 15 *Cornell ILJ* 489, at 506; Lewis-Anthony S., *The Right to Freedom of Peaceful Assembly and to Freedom of Association as Guaranteed by Article 11 of the European Convention on Human Rights* (1992), at 16.

[168] For the extent to which art. 6 protects the individual worker from arbitrary dismissal, *see above*, Ch. 5, text accompanying nn. 120–238.

[169] For a discussion of the implications of 'rights' and 'freedoms' in the context of the closed shop, *see* von Prondzynski F., 'Freedom of Association and the Closed Shop: The European Perspective' (1982) 41 *CLJ* 256, at 263–4.

[170] Art. 8(1)(c).

join trade unions.[171] It is quite possible to interpret the 'rights of others' in article 8(1)(a) as including the rights of trade unions. Far from outlawing closed shop agreements, the text of the Covenant suggests that the position is to be determined on a case-by-case basis and justified by reference to the appropriate limitation clauses found in article 8.

In a recent case, however, the Committee has indicated that it does consider closed shop agreements to be inconsistent with the individual's right to join and form trade unions of his or her choice. In its comments upon the additional information supplied by Zaïre, the Committee included the following statement:

The Committee would like to draw the attention of the Government of the Republic of Zaïre to the fact that the provisions of Zaïrian law concerning automatic membership of permanent staff of the State public services in the National Union of Zaïrian Workers (Ordinance No. 73–223 of 25 July 1973) seems to be inconsistent with the obligations under article 8 of the Covenant, which guarantees the freedom of the individual to join the trade union of his choice.[172]

The Committee has thus adopted a stance similar to that of the Committee of Independent Experts to the European Social Charter in prohibiting both the pre- and post-entry closed shop on the basis that the right to join a trade union implicitly includes a right not to join a trade union.[173] As suggested above, this was not necessarily the only conclusion that the Committee could have drawn from the text of article 8, and was perhaps unduly strict on the point. It is considered that it would have been better to leave such matters to be determined by the State in conjunction with the unions concerned.

4 Conditions

The Committee, in its reporting guidelines, requests States to supply information upon the substantive and formal conditions which must be fulfilled

---

[171] Art. 8(1)(a).

[172] UN Doc. E/1992/23, UN ESCOR, Supp. (No. 3), at 78, para. 328 (1992).

[173] The Committee of Independent Experts has taken the following position: 'Considering that freedom to join trade unions, guaranteed by Article 5 of the Charter, necessarily implies the absence of any sort of obligation to become or remain a member of a trade union, the Committee held that the absence of adequate protection of such freedom in national law (either through lack of appropriate statutes through case law validating practices conflicting with freedom to organize) cannot be considered as consistent with Article 5 of the Charter'; Conclusions XI–I, at 78 (1989).

The European Court of Human Rights has similarly found, on the particular facts of the case, that the dismissal of employees for failing to join a trade union under a closed shop agreement that was imposed during their employment was a violation of the ECHR, *see Young, James and Webster Case*, *supra*, n. 5. Cf. Shea, *supra*, n. 167; von Prondzynski, *supra*, n. 169; Forde M., 'The European Convention on Human Rights and Labour Law' (1983) 31 *AJCL* 301; Van Hoof G., *Theory and Practice on the European Convention on Human Rights*

in order to form trade unions.[174] It seems to have in mind provisions that require a minimum level of membership for an organization to gain the status of a trade union, or restrict membership to those working in specific trades.[175] The Committee has not as yet expressed any opinion over what conditions it feels are acceptable, but it is implicit in its approach that the need to impose certain conditions on the establishment of trade unions should not be such as to impair the effective exercise of that right. Certainly members of the Committee have been particularly wary of State involvement in the creation of trade unions.[176] It is considered, nevertheless, that the Committee faces a difficult task in determining the borderline between legitimate regulation and unlawful restriction.[177]

Reference could be made here to ILO standards. As far as the ILO is concerned, although formalities for the formation of trade unions may be prescribed by law, they must not be equivalent to prior authorization nor constitute an obstacle amounting to a prohibition.[178] More specifically, where registration is necessary to gain legal personality, the conditions should not be such as to restrict the right freely to establish such organizations.[179]

5 Restrictions

The Committee, quite appropriately, directs most of its attention to the imposition of restrictions upon the right to form and join trade unions. Thus in its reporting guidelines it asks for information about any legal restrictions that are placed upon this right and their application over time.[180] Individual members have often pursued such questions themselves.[181]

The text of the Covenant is by no means clear as to the relevant provisions that govern the imposition of restrictions upon the right to form and join trade unions. Although article 8(1)(a) contains its own outline of the general criteria that govern the imposition of lawful restrictions, it is subject to the terms of article 8(2) which provides that the article as a whole should

---

(2nd ed., 1990), 428–40. The question whether the pre-entry closed shop agreement is incompatible with art. 11 ECHR is still a matter of debate, Lewis-Anthony, *supra*, n. 167, at 17.

[174] Reporting guidelines, *supra*, n. 126, at 94.

[175] For the ILO position on these matters, *see* Pankert, *supra*, n. 140, at 179.

[176] *See e.g.* Texier, E/C.12/1994/SR.9, at 7, para. 26. *See above*, text accompanying nn. 155–8.

[177] *See* von Prondzynski F., *Freedom of Association and Industrial Relations: A Comparative Study* (1987), 25.

[178] General Survey, *supra*, n. 133, para. 105. Valticos, *supra*, n. 133, at 82.

[179] Art. 7, Freedom of Association Convention. *See generally*, General Survey, *supra*, n. 133, paras. 106–17.

[180] Reporting Guidelines, *supra*, n. 126, at 94.

[181] *See e.g.* Badawi El Sheikh, E/C.12/1987/SR.22, at 2, para. 3; Texier, E/C.12/1987/SR.5, at 6, para. 26; Simma, E/C.12/1987/SR.13, at 9, para. 44.

not prevent the imposition of lawful restrictions upon members of the police, armed forces, or members of the administration of the State. Further, the legality of restrictions imposed upon rights within article 8 is also more generally governed by the terms of article 4 which outlines the characteristics of permissible limitations upon all the rights in the Covenant. As mentioned above, the position is particularly unclear as regards the legitimacy of restrictions upon the right to form and join trade unions of members of the administration of the State.[182]

The Committee has not, as yet, undertaken to clarify either the meaning or the relative scope of the limitation clauses. It is considered that in order to give article 8 some meaningful content the Committee will have to begin by untangling the knot of limitation clauses that serves to obscure the level of protection offered by the rights. As an initial point it is clear that article 4 was only intended to apply with respect to those articles that were not already subject to limitations.[183] Indeed, the limitations in article 8(2) were created on the basis that article 4 would not apply to article 8.[184] The legality of restrictions should, therefore, initially be determined by the specific terms of article 8(1)(a).

According to article 8(1)(a), restrictions should be 'prescribed by law'[185] and be 'necessary in a democratic society in the interests of national security or public order or for the protection of the rights and freedoms of others'.[186] Such terms are identical to those found in article 22 of the ICCPR and have been the subject of consideration by the European Court of Human Rights.[187] The European Court has stipulated, *inter alia*, that the law concerned must both be accessible and enable the individual to foresee the legal consequences of his or her actions.[188] That the action taken must be 'necessary' has been interpreted as meaning that it should be more than merely 'reasonable' or 'desirable', but should conform to a 'pressing social need'.[189] In addition, the Court has invoked a principle of proportionality in

---

[182] *See above* text accompanying nn. 140–8.

[183] *See* UN Doc. A/2929, *supra*, n. 6, at 25, para. 50.

[184] *See above* text accompanying nn. 58–60.

[185] The French text in contrast uses the term 'provided by law' (*prévues par la loi*).

[186] The French text makes clear that the term 'necessary' is to apply separately to each of the four justifications: *L'exercice de ce droit ne peut faire l'objet que des seules restrictions prévues par la loi et qui constituent des mesures nécessaires, dans une société démocratique, dans l'intérêt de la sécurité nationale ou de l'ordre public, ou pour protéger les droits et les libertés d'autrui.*

[187] *See generally* Jacobs F., 'The "Limitation Clauses" of the European Convention on Human Rights', in de Mestral *et al.* (eds.), *The Limitation of Human Rights in Comparative Constitutional Law* (1986), 21, at 30–4. *See also* Kiss A., 'Permissible Limitations on Rights' in Henkin L. (ed.), *The International Bill of Rights* (1981), 290; Lockwood B., Finn J., and Jubinsky G., 'Working Paper for the Committee of Experts on Limitation Provisions' (1985) 7 *Hum. Rts. Q* 35.

[188] *Sunday Times* v. *United Kingdom*, Eur. Ct. HR, Series A, Vol. 30, judgment of 26 Apr. 1979, para. 49 (1979–80) 2 EHRR 245.

[189] *Handyside Case*, Eur. Ct. HR, Series A, Vol. 24, judgment of 7 Dec. 1976, para. 48 (1979–80) 1 EHRR 737. It is clear, however, that the European Court will allow States a 'margin of

determining whether or not the action taken was justified by the aim pursued.[190] If the Committee were to follow the European Court's interpretation of these terms, it would immediately have a good framework for evaluating the legitimacy of limitations.

It is considered that the Committee should be circumspect about the application of article 8(2) to the right to form and join trade unions in article 8(1)(a). As suggested above, the scope of limitations that it seems to legitimize is far greater than that provided by either the ILO or the ICCPR.[191] As a general provision it would appear to require that all the terms of article 8(1) are read in such a way as to allow for restrictions to be placed upon the rights of members of the armed forces, police, and the administration of the State. Nevertheless, article 8(2) does state that any such restrictions should be 'lawful'. It would not deprive that article of all meaning if the term 'lawful' were read to mean 'in accordance with the specific requirements laid down for the imposition of restrictions within the terms of article 8(1)'. Such an interpretation would allow the Committee a certain degree of control over the imposition of restrictions under the terms of article 8(2).

C Article 8(1)(b): The Right to Federate

The right of trade unions to establish national federations or confederations and for the latter to join international trade union organizations is clearly related to the right of trade unions to function freely as established in article 8(1)(c). At the same time, many of the provisions that relate to the establishment of trade unions within a given country (governed by article 8(1)(a)), will also apply to national federations.

According to the reporting guidelines, the Committee expects States to provide information on how the right to federate and affiliate internationally is secured and any restrictions that have been placed upon its enjoyment. This reflects the established practice of the individual members.[192] Although not specifically established, it would seem appropriate for the Committee to provide that the same rights and guarantees apply to federations as to trade unions themselves.[193] Thus far it could only be said

---

appreciation' in determining whether or not a limitation is 'necessary'. For the operation of the margin of appreciation doctrine, *see* MacDonald R., 'The Margin of Appreciation in the Jurisprudence of the European Court of Human Rights', in *International Law and the Time of its Codification: Essays in Honour of Robert Ago* (1987), 187; O'Donnell T., 'The Margin of Appreciation Doctrine: Standards in the Jurisprudence of the European Court of Human Rights' (1982) 4 *Hum. Rts. Q* 474.

[190] *Sunday Times Case, supra,* n. 188, paras. 62, 67.

[191] *See above,* text accompanying n. 137.

[192] Questions have included: did trade unions have the right to form confederations in Jordan? Konate, E/C.12/1987/SR.7, at 3, para. 5. Were trade unions freely allowed to affiliate internationally in Korea? Sparsis, E/C.12/1987/SR.21, at 9, para. 40.

[193] *Cf.* arts. 6 and 7 ILO Convention No. 87, *supra,* n. 114.

that the right to federate should not be subject to undue State control. Accordingly in the case of Jordan, members of the Committee were critical of the need for approval from the Minister for Social Affairs and Labour for trade unions to join an international organization.[194] Such requirements have also been criticized by the ILO Committee on Freedom of Association.[195]

It is interesting to note that the United Kingdom, upon signature, reserved the right 'not to apply sub-paragraph (b) of paragraph 1 in Hong Kong, in so far as it may involve the right of trade unions not engaged in the same trade or industry to establish federations or confederations'.[196] On ratification the government went further in reserving the right not to apply article 8(1)(b) at all in Hong Kong.[197] No objections have been made as to the legitimacy of this reservation.

D Article 8(1)(c): The Right of Trade Unions to Function Freely

The free functioning of trade unions could be said to include *inter alia* the right to federate and affiliate internationally and, to a lesser degree, the right to strike (or perhaps to organize strikes), both of which stand as separate rights within the Covenant. The utility of the right to function freely would seem to be in its protection of the internal organization of trade unions, the right to organize and take action short of strikes, the right to bargain collectively, and the protection of trade unions from dissolution or suspension.

1 The Internal Organization of Trade Unions

If trade unions are to be given the right to function freely they must have the ability to draw up their constitutions and rules, to elect their own representatives and organize their administration and policies. This is confirmed by article 8(1)(a) which makes the right to join trade unions subject to 'the rules of the organization concerned'.[198] The Committee has not given a clear indication of the extent to which the State may control the internal affairs of trade unions. It has, however, been critical of States where government involvement appears to be excessive. Thus in one case the existence of a Government Office created to 'monitor' trade unions was criticized.[199] Similarly, in the case of Kenya, the Committee expressed concern about the domination of the central trade union organization by KANU, the single party that governed the country.[200]

---

[194] *See* Sparsis, E/C.12/1987/SR.6, at 10, para. 45; Alvarez Vita, E/C.12/1987/SR.6, at 11, para. 50.
[195] Pankert, *supra*, n. 140, at 185.   [196] UN Doc. E/C.12/1988/1, at 17 (1987).
[197] *Ibid.* 18.   [198] *Cf.* art. 3(1) ILO Convention No. 87, *supra*, n. 114.
[199] *See* Mratchkov, E/C.12/1990/SR.40, at 13, para. 63.
[200] *See* Simma, E/C.12/1993/SR.4, at 5, para. 13.

A more difficult problem is raised by rules relating to trade union executive positions. A number of States have rules disqualifying certain kinds of person from election as union officers, such as those engaged in occupations other than those which they wish to represent, foreign nationals, and those convicted of crimes which suggest that they are untrustworthy.[201] The ILO Committee of Experts has noted that in such cases there is a real risk of arbitrary and improper interference in trade union affairs by the State but has often given States the benefit of the doubt.[202] As noted above,[203] the Committee has been critical of cases where non-nationals are barred from holding executive positions in trade unions. Most recently in the case of Senegal, this led the Committee to express its concern in its Concluding Observations.[204]

Unfortunately, the Committee has not yet attempted to outline those activities of trade unions that are protected by their right to function freely or the degree to which those activities may be subject to legal regulation. Certainly in so far as the free functioning of trade unions implies the right of trade unions to organize their own administration, they should be protected from excessive control of their finances or interference with their premises and correspondence. Additionally, as the ILO has noted,[205] trade unions should also have the right to organize their activities and formulate programmes. Clearly, however, not every activity undertaken by trade unions will be so protected.

During the drafting of the Covenant considerable concern was expressed about the possible political activities of trade unions. Accordingly, the purposes for which a person might join or form a trade union were specifically limited to 'the promotion and protection of his economic and social interests'.[206] However, to prohibit trade unions from all activities of a political nature would be unduly restrictive. As has been noted, general questions of economic and social policy that form a large part of the political diet in most countries do have an effect on the workers' interests.[207] Indeed in Western Europe, it is commonplace for a close association to exist between trade unions and political parties.[208] It might be argued that restrictions on the political activities of unions should only extend as far as ensuring that the means employed had sufficient relation to the immediate objective of promoting the workers' interests, and should not be such as to compromise the continuance of the trade union movement. It would be

---

[201] Pankert, *supra*, n. 140, at 186–7.   [202] General Survey, *supra*, n. 133, at 178–9.

[203] *See above* text accompanying nn. 149–50.

[204] Concluding observations on report of Senegal, E/C.12/1993/8, at 2, para. 8.

[205] General Survey, *supra*, n. 133, at 180–226.

[206] *See above* text accompanying nn. 43–51.   [207] General Survey, *supra*, n. 133, at 195.

[208] Bean R., *Comparative Industrial Relations* (1985), at 22. It has been noted by the ILO Committee of Experts that States should not attempt to interfere with the normal functions of trade unions merely because of their freely established relationship with a political party. *See* Report of the Director-General, *Human Rights: A Common Responsibility*, ILC, 75th Sess., at 17 (1988).

difficult to justify, for example, trade union action being taken to protest against a government's commitment to nuclear weapons or its maintenance of diplomatic relations with certain other States.

2 *Collective Bargaining*

Whereas an analysis of the variety of forms and functions of the collective agreement is outside the scope of this present study,[209] it is sufficient to note that they may serve the functions *inter alia* of preventing industrial conflict, increasing worker participation in decision-making, and forming the basis for standard conditions of employment.

That article 8(1)(c) was intended to protect the right of trade unions to bargain collectively was apparent in the drafting of the Covenant.[210] Members of the Committee have also identified collective bargaining as being implicit in the concept of freedom of association.[211] The Committee specifically mentions the question of collective bargaining in its reporting guidelines and requests States to indicate the measures being taken to 'promote free collective bargaining'.[212] In implying that States have an obligation to promote collective bargaining, the Committee probably had in mind ILO Convention No. 98[213] to which it refers in its guidelines. Article 4 of that Convention provides that measures should be taken to promote the full development and utilization of collective bargaining 'with a view to the regulation of terms and conditions of employment by means of collective agreements'.[214]

This interpretation of article 8 has not been universally accepted. The representative of New Zealand, in explaining the terms of the new Employment Contracts Act, noted that ratification of ILO Convention No. 98 posed a problem in that emphasis was placed upon collective bargaining in the negotiation of employment contracts (which under the Act was a matter of free choice for the parties concerned). He went on to argue that ratification of Convention No. 98 was not necessary 'in order fully to comply with the provisions of article 8'.[215] While it is undoubtedly true that article 8 does

---

[209] *See generally* Schmidt F. and Neal A., 'Collective Agreements and Collective Bargaining' in Hepple B. (ed.), *Labour Law* (1984), Ch. 12, Vol. XV; Cordova E., 'Collective Bargaining' in Blainpain R. (ed.), *Comparative Law and Industrial Relations* (3rd ed., 1987), 307; Kahn-Freund O. (ed.), *Labour Relations and the Law: A Comparative Study* (1965), 21–124; Bean, *supra*, n. 208, at 70–99; Prondzynski, *supra*, n. 177, at 39–58.

[210] *See above* text accompanying n. 68.

[211] *See* Sparsis, E/C.12/1988/SR.3, at 6, para. 18.

[212] Reporting guidelines, *supra*, n. 126, at 94.

[213] ILO Right to Organize and Collective Bargaining Convention (No. 98), 1 July 1949, 96 UNTS 257.

[214] This has been supplemented by Recommendation (No. 91) of 1951 which leaves it to the States parties themselves to establish 'machinery appropriate to the conditions existing in each country'. ILO Collective Agreements Recommendation (No. 91), 1951, in ILO, *International Labour Conventions and Recommendations (1919–1981, 1982)*, at 205.

[215] Beeby (New Zealand), E/C.12/1993/SR.25, at 6, para. 30.

not require ratification of ILO Convention No. 98, if problems are perceived as to the compatibility of the act with that Convention, it does signal potential problems with article 8 to the extent that the standards in the two treaties are the same. Thus the Committee noted in its concluding observations that the reforms introduced by the New Zealand Act 'raise questions of compatibility in relation to the rights recognized in articles 7 and 8 of the Covenant'.[216] It therefore requested New Zealand to review the statute and eliminate any conflicts identified,[217] and recommended ratification of ILO Convention No. 98.[218] It seems to be established that there is considerable concurrence in the standards under ILO Convention No. 98 and the Covenant.

In utilizing the term 'promote' the Committee makes clear that it does not expect States to guarantee to every trade union the right to bargain collectively. It is common practice in a number of States to allow employers to limit the number of trade unions with whom they conclude collective agreements. Often only the 'most representative' union within a particular bargaining unit has the right to consultation and negotiation in the collective bargaining process.[219] Certainly it would appear that the Committee requires, at least, that trade unions generally have the 'freedom' to bargain collectively.[220] The principal question is, however, the degree to which the Committee will consider as justifiable restrictions upon the right of particular trade unions to participate in the bargaining process.

Obligations incidental to the promotion of collective bargaining appear to be the encouragement of trade unionism, the establishment of mechanisms for dispute settlement, and the extension of collective agreements to other categories of workers. Members of the Committee have emphasized the importance of worker participation in the establishment of standards relating to conditions of work. In particular questions have been asked about the extent of worker participation in management,[221] in the creation of legislation,[222] and the conclusion of collective agreements.[223] In addition, members have expected States to refrain from interfering in the conclusion of collective agreements,[224] and have looked to the establishment of

---

[216] Concluding observations on report of New Zealand, E/C.12/1993/13, at 3, para. 13.

[217] *Ibid.* 3, para. 19.   [218] *Ibid.* 3, para. 20.

[219] *See* Pankert, *supra*, n. 140, at 180. In the context of the ECHR, *see National Union of Belgian Police Case*, Eur. Ct. HR, Series A, Vol. 19, judgment of 27 Oct. 1975, (1980) 1 EHRR 578; *Swedish Engine Drivers Case*, Eur. Ct. HR, Series A, Vol. 20, judgment of 6 Feb. 1976, (1980) 1 EHRR 617. *See generally* Forde, *supra*, n. 173.

[220] *Cf.* Mratchkov, E/C.12/1992/SR.13, at 12, para. 45. This is currently the position under the ECHR, *see* Van Hoof, *supra*, n. 173, at 436.

[221] *See e.g.* Mratchkov, E/C.12/1987/SR.13, at 4, para. 14.

[222] *See e.g.* Sparsis, E/C.12/1987/SR.5, at 7, para. 32.

[223] *See e.g.* Sparsis, E/C.12/1987/SR.5, at 7, para. 32.

[224] *See e.g.* Sparsis, E/C.12/1987/SR.6, at 10, para. 42; Sparsis, E/C.12/1988/SR.3, at 6, para. 18.

minimum standards through legislation in the absence of strong workers' organizations.[225]

It is notable, however, that ILO Convention No. 98 does not apply to the armed forces, police, or public servants engaged in the administration of the State. This is reflected in the specific wording of article 8(2) of the Covenant. The ILO Committee of Experts has drawn a distinction between officials engaged in administration of the State who might be excluded from the protection of that convention and persons employed in public enterprises who should enjoy the right to free collective bargaining.[226] At the present stage it would seem that the Committee, by referring to Convention No. 98, has taken up a position analogous to that of the ILO. This is equally apparent from its reference in the reporting guidelines to the ILO Labour Relations (Public Service) Convention (No. 151),[227] which provides for the establishment and operation of public employees' organizations with procedures for the determination of conditions of work and settlement of disputes. That special conditions are considered to exist in relation to civil servants has been recognized by individual members of the Committee.[228]

3 Protection from Dissolution or Suspension

The third and final element of the right to function freely is the protection of trade unions from dissolution and suspension. Although the Committee has not expressed any opinion on this matter, it is clearly implicit in the terms of article 8 that trade unions should not be arbitrarily prevented from functioning freely. In cases where unions have been suspended or dissolved, the State concerned will have to justify its action on the basis of national security, public order, or the protection of the rights of others. In addition, it will have to be shown that the action taken was strictly necessary. As dissolution is the most extreme form of measure to be taken in this context, it is submitted that attention should be paid to whether it was strictly proportionate to the intended aim.

E Article 8(1)(d): The Right to Strike

In expressly providing for the right to strike, the Covenant stands out in relation to other international instruments (with the exception of the

---

[225] *See e.g.* Sparsis, E/C.12/1987/SR.6, at 10, para. 42.
[226] Dao (ILO), E/C.12/1988/SR.17, at 9–10, para. 60.
[227] ILO Labour Relations (Public Service) Convention (No. 151), 27 June 1978, UKTS 33 (1981). Reporting guidelines, *supra*, n. 126, at 94.
[228] *See e.g.* Sparsis, E/C.12/1990/SR.10, at 13, para. 81; Sparsis, E/C.12/1990/SR.34, at 7, para. 51.

European Social Charter[229]). The ILO in particular has been forced to infer a right to strike from article 3 of ILO Convention No. 87 under which trade unions have the right to formulate their programmes and organize their activities.[230] However, the fact that a right to strike may be inferrable from the prohibition of forced labour in article 6(1), the right to form and join trade unions 'for the promotion and protection of his economic and social interests' in article 8(1)(a),[231] and from the right of trade unions to function freely in article 8(1)(c), would suggest that even for those States that have made reservations with respect to article 8(1)(d),[232] a general prohibition on strikes would be inconsistent with the provisions of the Covenant as a whole. This would seem to be the position of certain members of the Committee who have stressed that the right to strike was central to the ability of unions to conduct collective bargaining.[233] Indeed one member asserted that the possibility of conducting meaningful collective bargaining without the right to strike was 'an exercise in futility'.[234]

Despite the fact that the right to strike is generally exercised as a form of collective action taken by trade unions, it is framed as an individual right in the Covenant. This is significant in so far as it indicates that protection in the case of strikes should not merely be afforded to the Union concerned but also to the individual who should, in particular, be protected from dismissal on this ground.[235] The terms of article 8(1)(d) are also significant in so far as no mention is made of the purposes for which strike action might be taken.[236] Whereas under article 8(1)(a) the right to form and join trade unions is specifically restricted to the 'promotion and protection of his economic and social interests', no such condition is to be found in article 8(1)(d). Although this might imply that all strikes are to be protected, irrespective of their purpose, such a position would be difficult to sustain in

---

[229] Art. 6(4) European Social Charter provides for both a right to strike and a right to lock-out: 'the right of workers and employers to collective action in cases of conflicts of interest, including the right to strike, subject to obligations that might arise out of collective agreements previously entered into'.

[230] *Cf.* Ben-Israel, *supra*, n. 77, at 93.

[231] The HRC faced this question in the case of *J.B. et al.* v. *Canada, supra*, n. 121. The majority decided (erroneously in the author's opinion), that, as the ICESCR specifically included the right to strike in art. 8(1)(d), it could not be considered to be an implicit element in the right to form and join trade unions.

[232] In addition to the reservations dealt with below, the following States have made reservations or declarations with respect to art. 8(1)(d): France, Mexico, the Netherlands, New Zealand, and Norway. UN Doc. ST/LEG/SER.E/10, at 124 and 126 (1992).

[233] *See e.g.* Konate, E/C.12/1990/SR.11, at 6, para. 37.

[234] Sparsis, E/C.12/1988/SR.4, at 6, para. 32.

[235] For the importance of the individual aspect of the right to strike in the UK, *see* Ewing K., 'The Right to Strike' (1986) 5 *Ind. RL* 143, at 158.

[236] *Cf.* art. 6(4) of the European Social Charter (1961) which restricts the right to take collective action to cases of 'conflicts of interests'.

light of current State practice.[237] For example, even in States where the constitution explicitly or indirectly guarantees the right to strike, political strikes are generally considered unlawful.[238]

The Committee has yet to establish an understanding of what form of action is protected by article 8(1)(d). In addition to the traditional form of strike (characterized by the complete stoppage of work) and its variants (such as the wildcat and sympathy strikes), there are several other forms of industrial action that might also be included in the definition, such as the partial stoppage of work, the go-slow, the work to rule, the sit-down strike, and the repeated walk-out.[239] It is submitted that a wide definition be adopted but a certain flexibility given to States as to the restrictions imposed on the various forms. The fundamental consideration should be whether or not the action taken is in pursuit of the economic and social interests of the workers concerned.

The Committee has looked to the establishment of the right to strike as a legal or constitutional right in the States concerned.[240] Recognition is given, however, to the fact that some countries may secure the right through different legal approaches. This reflects the approach of the ILO Committee of Experts which considers that the right to strike may be recognized either implicitly or explicitly in legislation.[241] Nevertheless, certain members of the Committee have been unhappy about situations where there is stated to be no right to strike but merely a freedom to strike.[242]

The matter arose in the context of the Jamaican report where the situation was explained:

The Supreme Court had come to the decision, based on some English common law decisions, that there was in fact no right to strike as such . . . Since it was an infringement of common law for a person to be compelled to work, slavery having been abolished, there must therefore be a freedom not to work. But if the consequences of exercising that freedom was that one withdrew services for which provision had been made in the contract, a case could arise where there was a breach of the

---

[237] Schermers uses this particularly as a reason for concluding that the right to strike is not properly a human right at all. Schermers H., 'Is there a Fundamental Human Right to Strike?' (1989) 9 *Yrbk. Eur. L* 225.

[238] Birk R., 'Industrial Conflict: The Law of Strikes and Lock-outs' in Blainpain R. (ed.), *Comparative Labour Law and Industrial Relations* (3rd ed., 1987), 401, at 415. For the ILO position, *see* Ben-Israel, *supra*, n. 77, at 93–8.

[239] *See* Ben-Israel, *supra*, n. 77, at 93.   [240] Reporting guidelines, *supra*, n. 126, at 95.

[241] Dao (ILO), E/C.12/1988/SR.4, at 8, para. 43.

[242] Birk explains these concepts: 'Freedom of strike means that the strike is legally permitted but no special privileges are granted. In this case the strike does not need special rules. The legal *limits* of the freedom to strike are hence a consequence of the *general legal order*. The strike is tolerated but not privileged . . . The right to strike differs from the freedom to strike when the legal order evaluates the pursuit of collective interests more highly than the opposed individual obligations of the employment contract. The strike is therefore privileged. If the right to strike is guaranteed the legal order of a state must hence take precautions to ensure the exercise of this right and not to impede it': Birk, *supra*, n. 238, at 406–7.

contract of employment. From that it was inferred that there was a freedom to strike, but not the right to strike.[243]

Members of the Committee were critical of this arrangement—it was suggested that 'mere freedom to strike was not sufficient'[244] and that the right to strike should be integral to the contract of employment.[245] Accordingly, it was suggested that Jamaica should consider amending its legislation to bring it into line with the article 8(1)(d) of the Covenant.[246]

It is considered that the Committee members were taking an excessively strict line on this question. Whereas certain States have a constitutionally protected right to strike,[247] others ensure the right through statutory immunity from civil liability. What should be of concern to the Committee is not whether the law expressly provides for a freedom or a right to strike, but whether employees are able in practice, without legal penalty, to participate in strike action.[248] This means that in countries such as the UK or Jamaica, statutory immunity from liability should be sufficiently extensive to ensure the operation of the right to strike, and should be bolstered by the protection of the individual worker from dismissal.[249]

Nevertheless, members of the Committee have persisted in treating cases where strikes may in principle involve a breach of contract with a certain degree of caution.[250] They seem to consider that the enactment of legislation

---

[243] Rattray, E/C.12/1990/SR.15, at 5, para. 22. It is interesting to note here that the legal situation in Jamaica had to be explained by one of the members of the Committee given the insufficient nature of the oral and written reports. *Cf.* Nembhard (Jamaica), E/C.12/1990/SR.12, at 4, para. 29.

As regards the position of strikes under the UK common law, *see* Morris G. and Archer T., *Trade Unions, Employers and the Law* (1992), 174–277; Ewing K., *The Right to Strike* (1991), 4–22. Ewing concludes: 'The legal position of the British worker engaged in a labour dispute is quite remarkable. A strike, for whatever reason, is a breach of contract; any form of industrial action short of a strike can lead to the total loss of pay; those engaged in industrial action may be dismissed with impunity (regardless of the reasons for the industrial action); there is no right to unemployment benefit; and strikers and their families are penalised by social welfare legislation, even when the dispute is the singular fault of the employer': *ibid.* 141.

[244] Jimenez Butragueno, E/C.12/1990/SR.11, at 2, para. 6.

[245] *See* Konate, E/C.12/1990/SR.15, at 6, para. 25.

[246] *See* Konate, E/C.12/1990/SR.11, at 5, para. 36.

[247] States that have declared the possession of a constitutional right to strike include: Costa Rica, E/1990/5/Add.3, at 18, para. 29; Panama, E/1984/6/Add.19, at 17, para. 24; Afghanistan, E/1990/5/Add.8, at 7, para. 24.

[248] Cf. Rattray, E/C.12/1989/SR.18, at 8, para. 42.

[249] The current legal position of the right to strike in the UK has come under much criticism from the ILO and the Committee of Independent Experts of the European Social Charter. Two main points have concerned the ILO Committee of Experts: first the lack of adequate protection of the individual from dismissal during a strike; secondly, the limited scope of immunity from civil liability. *See* ILO Observation of the Committee of Experts on Conventions Nos. 87 and 98 (1989), *cited in* Ewing, *supra*, n. 137, at 31–7. The Committee of Independent Experts has been concerned about the fact that an employer may dismiss all employees who take part in a strike. *See* Conclusions XI–I, at 90 (1989).

[250] *See e.g.* Rattray, E/C.12/1987/SR.5, at 9, para. 44; Texier, E/C.12/1988/SR.3, at 5, para. 15; Simma, E/C.12/1988/SR.4, at 7, para. 36.

to ensure the right to strike is a priority.[251] Whether or not it is always appropriate to seek legislation in this area, it is undoubtedly important that existing legislation is clear and precise[252] and does not impede the ability of employees to strike.[253] Thus the Committee has expressed concern over laws which have allowed the authorities to prohibit or restrict strikes either directly (as in the case of Morocco[254]) or indirectly through a requirement of compulsory arbitration.[255]

Beyond the question of how the right to strike is formulated in domestic law, the Committee has concerned itself with any restrictions that are placed upon the exercise of the right and special provisions that relate to certain categories of workers.[256] Article 8(1)(d) provides that the right to strike should be ensured 'provided it is exercised in conformity with the laws of the particular country', suggesting that States have considerable discretion in placing legal restrictions upon the enjoyment of the right to strike. This can be contrasted with the right to strike in ILO practice, which cannot be limited by legal provisions if they are not in conformity with the criteria laid down by the Freedom of Association Committee of the Governing Body.[257] However, as has been noted above, for those States that are party to ILO Convention (No. 87), the terms of article 8(1)(d) have to be read in conformity with the provisions of the ILO Convention. Additionally, if higher standards were already in place, States could not lower them on the grounds of the Covenant as stipulated in article 5(2). This has been dubbed the 'most-favourable-to-individual' clause.[258]

It is arguably more appropriate to interpret the phrase 'in conformity with the laws of the particular country' as legitimizing the imposition of certain procedural requirements, rather than allowing substantive limitations which are governed by article 8(2). Procedural requirements on the right to strike identified by the Committee on Freedom of Association have included the obligation to observe a certain quorum, to take the decision by secret ballot, and to provide the employer with prior notice. Additionally certain temporary restrictions might be legitimate, such as strike restrictions during conciliation and arbitration procedures, during the duration of collective agreements, and during cooling-off periods.[259]

---

[251] *See e.g.* Rattray, E/C.12/1989/SR.17, at 17, para. 90; Konate, E/C.12/1990/SR.11, at 3, para. 12.

[252] *See* Concluding observations on report of Vietnam, E/C.12/1993/8, at 2, para. 9.

[253] *Cf.* Dao (ILO), E/C.12/1989/SR.8, at 11, para. 59.

[254] *See e.g.* Texier, E/C.12/1994/SR.9, at 7, para. 25.

[255] *See* Concluding observations on report of Senegal, E/C.12/1993/18, at 3, para. 12.

[256] Reporting guidelines, *supra*, n. 126, at 95. Mratchkov, E/C.12/1992/SR.13, at 12, para. 45.

[257] Ben-Israel, *supra*, n. 77, at 87.

[258] Buergenthal T., 'To Respect and Ensure: State Obligations and Permissible Derogations' in Henkin L. (ed.), *The International Bill of Rights* (1981), 72 at 89.

[259] Ben-Israel, *supra*, n. 77, at 118–21.

Although the Committee has not as yet established any stated policy, it would seem that it will respect the imposition of procedural requirements in so far as they are reasonable and do not stand as an excessive restriction upon the enjoyment of the right to strike. On occasion members have spoken out against particularly limiting rules. Thus in the case of the Dominican Republic, a law which provided that in order to strike 60 per cent of the workers concerned needed to have voted in favour was thought to be contrary to the practice of the ILO's Committee on Freedom of Association and article 8(1)(d) itself.[260] Similarly, a requirement that all strikes be referred with twenty-one days' notice to the Minister of Labour for permission was thought to be contrary to the 'letter and spirit of the Covenant'.[261] In a further case, a provision requiring workers to notify their employer of any planned strike between fourteen and twenty-eight days in advance was considered 'unduly harsh'[262] and posed a 'serious obstacle'[263] to the exercise of that right in that it could have 'a dissuasive effect on workers wishing to strike'.[264]

In addition to procedural restriction, the Committee has made note of restrictions imposed on the right to strike of certain public servants and those working in essential services.[265] It would appear that such restrictions are legitimized under article 8(2) where a general reference is made to members of the administration of the State. Arguably any such restrictions should also conform to the general criteria laid out in article 4, namely be determined by law, compatible with the nature of the right, and be 'solely for the purpose of promoting the general welfare in a democratic society'. Reliance upon article 4 here is justified on the basis that article 8(1)(d) itself does not contain a specific limitation clause.[266] The Committee, while recognizing the lawfulness of restrictions in general, has not defined which categories of workers are to fall under each heading, nor on what basis restrictions may be imposed. In this regard individual members have merely

---

[260] *See* Mratchkov, E/C.12/1990/SR.44, at 14, para. 73.

[261] Concluding observations on report of Kenya, E/C.12/1993/6, at 4, para. 13.

[262] Art. 103, Labour Act. Alvarez Vita, E/C.12/1987/SR.6, at 11, para. 51; Simma, E/C.12/1987/SR.6, at 12, para. 59.

[263] Texier, E/C.12/1987/SR.7, at 4, para. 12. He commented that 'Most domestic legislation provided for some period of prior notification, but the time-span was usually extremely short'.

[264] Rattray, E/C.12/1987/SR.6, at 13, para. 68. It is worth noting that a rule that provided for an 8-day delay after notification was not considered to be excessive by the Committee on Freedom of Association. *See* Ben-Israel, *supra*, n. 77, at 120.

[265] This has been the subject of a reservation by Trinidad and Tobago, which states with respect to art. 8(1)(d) and 8(2) that it 'reserves the right to impose lawful and/or reasonable restrictions on the exercise of the aforementioned rights by personnel engaged in essential services under the Industrial Relations Act or under any Statute replacing same which has been passed in accordance with the provisions of the Trinidad and Tobago Constitution': UN Doc. E/C.12/1988/1, at 16 (1987).

[266] It is argued above that art. 4 does not in general apply to art. 8, *see above*, text accompanying n. 181.

made enquiries into which categories of workers are covered by the restrictions employed,[267] and what alternative forms of action are available to those denied a right to strike.[268]

Given the practice of the ILO in this area,[269] it would be appropriate for the Committee to begin to define the categories of workers whose right to strike may be restricted. Clearly, if the article were to be read restrictively, 'members of the State administration' should apply to civil servants alone. Those employed in State enterprises could not legitimately be deprived of the right to strike. This would certainly be the understanding of a number of States. Japan, for example, declared upon ratification that 'members of the police' referred to in article 8(2) should be interpreted as including the fire service personnel of Japan.[270] In doing so, it clearly assumed that the fire service personnel did not automatically fall into the category of members of the administration of the state. It is considered that States would, nevertheless, be able to rely upon the general limitations clause in article 4 to impose restrictions upon the right to strike of those working in essential services.

The question of restrictions upon the right to strike arose notably in the case of Panama. Following the comments of the ILO representative,[271] questions were asked about the nature and scope of restrictions imposed upon the right to strike in Panama.[272] It was explained that certain restrictions were placed upon the exercise of the trade union rights of members of the civil service in Panama following a demonstration which coincided with an attempted *coup d'état*. Following the refusal of a request for them to rescind their decision to strike, the government had adopted Act No. 25 authorizing the dismissal of members of the civil service who jeopardized national security by taking part in strikes or demonstrations. There was, however, provision for administrative appeal which had been utilized by some public servants following their dismissal, a number of whom were subsequently reinstated.[273]

No real discussion of the matter was undertaken by the Committee, which seemed to accept the legitimacy of the Panamanian position as explained. Certainly, no mention was made of the matter in the Committee's concluding comments. The case is interesting in so far as it appears to be a situation that would normally be governed by a derogation clause. However, unlike the ICCPR,[274] the Covenant does not contain a derogation

---

[267] *See e.g.* Alvarez Vita, E/C.12/1989/SR.10, at 7, para. 33; Simma, E/C.12/1989/SR.18, at 2, para. 2; Sparsis, E/C.12/1990/SR.44, at 12, para. 56; Texier, E/C.12/1987/SR.5, at 6, para. 26.

[268] Sparsis, E/C.12/1992/SR.13, at 11, para. 37.

[269] *See* Ben-Israel, *supra*, n. 77, at 106–14.   [270] UN Doc. E/C.12/1988/1, at 13 (1987).

[271] Swepston (ILO), E/C.12/1991/SR.3, at 6, para. 23.

[272] *See e.g.* Sparsis, E/C.12/1991/SR.3, at 10, para. 48.

[273] Ucros (Panama), E/C.12/1991/SR.3, at 13–14, para. 64.

[274] Art. 4 ICCPR provides that in time of public emergency which threatens the life of

clause. Higgins explains this on the basis that derogation clauses are only necessary where there are strong implementation provisions, which are absent in the case of the ICESCR.[275] It is clear, however, that article 8 is to be implemented in an immediate manner, and therefore does not contain the flexibility found in other articles.

The main problem, however, is that although article 8(2) does allow restrictions to be made on the right to strike of members of the administration of the State, article 5(2) appears to provide that the provisions of the Covenant cannot be used as a justification for restricting the rights of individuals as currently enjoyed under national or international law.[276] If this is the case, then restrictions are arguably valid only in so far as they are imposed before ratification, which would mean that Panama is not acting in conformity with the Covenant. Although it is clear that States are less likely to resort to derogations in the case of economic, social, and cultural rights,[277] if limitations cannot be placed upon the enjoyment of rights after ratification, States might be severely hampered from dealing with national emergencies in an effective manner. There is a case, then, for interpreting article 5(2) in a more restricted manner—perhaps subject to article 4 which provides for limitations for the purpose of promoting the general welfare in a democratic society.

Although this discussion presents no clear answers to the questions raised, it does suggest that the Committee has considerable work to do on defining the scope and application of the limitation clauses. The fact that little consideration was given to the Panamanian case is unfortunate not only because it deserved serious consideration by the Committee, but also because it provided the Committee with an opportunity to extrapolate certain principles of general application relating to the operation of limitation provisions.

IV. CONCLUSION

In a number of respects, the Committee's task in evaluating State reports with respect to article 8 is considerably easier than for other articles. First,

the nation, States parties may take measures derogating from their obligations under the Covenant. On the operation of this provision, *see* Hartman J., 'Working Paper for the Committee of Experts on Article 4' (1985) 7 *Hum. Rts. Q* 89; Meron T., *Human Rights Law-Making in the United Nations* (1986), 86–100; McGoldrick D., *The Human Rights Committee* (1991), 301–27.

[275] Higgins R., 'Derogations under Human Rights Treaties' (1976–7) 48 *BYIL* 281, at 286. *See also* Kiss, *supra*, n. 187, at 291.

[276] *See* Buergenthal, *supra*, n. 258, at 89.

[277] *See* Green L., 'Derogations of Human Rights in Emergency Situations' (1978) 16 *Can. YIL*, 92, at 103.

[278] Forde, *supra*, n. 173, at 332.

article 8 is confined to a relatively small area of State activity and is comparatively specific. Secondly, it is in general not subject to progressive implementation and therefore offers the Committee greater ease of assessment and evaluation of State performance. Thirdly, as with articles 6, 7, and 9, it is a subject area covered by the work of the ILO which has a plethora of standards that may readily be utilized by the Committee in developing the norms within the Covenant. Finally, the Committee has the opportunity of drawing upon the experience of other human rights supervisory bodies (such as the Committee of Independent Experts of the European Social Charter, the European Court of Human Rights, and the HRC) in so far as they deal with the right to form and join trade unions or the right to freedom of association in general. In the light of these considerations, the Committee's treatment of article 8 is a good indicator of how well the Committee has developed its role as a human rights supervisory body.

The Committee has got to the stage of establishing the broad nature of the obligations in article 8 and has taken a position on several important questions. In particular, one might note its opinion that a closed shop agreement operated in Zaïre was in violation of article 8 which guarantees the freedom of the individual to join the trade union of his or her choice. One might also note its opinion that legal provisions requiring advance authorization for strikes, or making them conditional upon arbitration procedures, are incompatible with article 8. That these are but a few examples of the many cases in which Committee members have spoken out against States parties shows a willingness to enforce the standards within the Covenant and indicates that the Committee is receiving a certain amount of pertinent information. The Committee has clearly been assisted in this regard by the representatives of the ILO, who have pointed out areas that have been of concern to ILO supervisory bodies. Indeed the information provided by the ILO has often served to 'trigger' the interest of the Committee.

Whether or not the Committee will rely directly upon ILO standards it is clear that there is need for greater awareness and understanding of those standards and the general practice of States. As appeared from the Committee's approach to the question of non-nationals holding executive positions in trade unions, little attention was paid to the delicate manner in which the ILO generally approached the question. Similarly, their approach to the issue of trade union diversity reflected a lack of sophistication that was out of place in the context of a complex and sensitive issue. That the Committee should be aware of the need for greater delicacy is exemplified by Forde's comments on the European Court of Human Rights:

The principal question . . . is the appropriateness of judges, many of whom possess relatively little industrial relations expertise, laying down common standards for collective bargaining systems of great complexity that often differ fundamentally from each other. Especially at the international level, there is a grave danger of amateurs, no matter how eminent they may be as jurists, tinkering with arrangements they do not fully understand, and tending to impose standards that may work in their countries upon the entirely different labour market systems of other States.[278]

Although premised by the perceived anti-union stance of the European Court, Forde's comments serve as a warning to the Committee.

To some extent the ability of the Committee to develop an understanding of article 8 is restricted by the lack of sufficient information and the general nature of the reporting procedure, but many of the faults of the system could be overcome by careful and considered questions both in the reporting guidelines and within the Committee itself. That article 8 is relatively detailed suggests that close attention should be paid to the specific wording of the provisions. In particular, an effort should be made to define the relative scope and meaning of the various limitation clauses. For example, consideration should be given to the term 'members of the administration of the State' in article 8(2), and to the extent to which that provision as a whole overrides the specific terms of article 8(1)(a). As the terms of the constructive dialogue give little opportunity for discussion of the specific working of article 8, it is clear that the Committee will need to adopt a General Comment on the question before any real headway is made.

8
The Right to an Adequate Standard of Living

Article 11

1. The States Parties to the present Covenant recognize the right of every-one to an adequate standard of living for himself and his family, includ-ing adequate food, clothing and housing, and to the continuous improvement of living conditions. The States Parties will take appropri-ate steps to ensure the realization of this right, recognizing to this effect the essential importance of international co-operation based on free consent.

2. The States Parties to the present Covenant, recognizing the fundamental right of everyone to be free from hunger, shall take, individually and through international co-operation, the measures, including specific programmes, which are needed:

(a) To improve methods of production, conservation and distribu-tion of food by making full use of technical and scientific knowl-edge, by disseminating knowledge of the principles of nutrition and by developing or reforming agrarian systems in such a way as to achieve the most efficient development and utilization of natural resources.

(b) Taking into account the problems of both food-importing and food exporting countries, to ensure an equitable distribution of world food supplies in relation to need.

I. INTRODUCTION

Article 11 is one of the most wide-ranging and general of the articles in the Covenant, encompassing a host of concerns that are usually addressed in the context of State 'development'. There is no doubt that the right to an adequate standard of living, including the rights to food, housing, and clothing is of paramount importance not least because at minimum levels it represents a question of survival. It is also true to say that the right to an adequate standard of living has been violated 'more comprehensively and systematically than probably any other right'.[1] That the realization of the right is overlaid by issues of economic development, agrarian reform, principles of nutrition, international trade, and aid (to name but a few) poses a challenge to the Committee that may serve as an acid-test of its effectiveness as the principal supervisory body to the Covenant.

Thus far the Committee has not shied away from addressing questions related to article 11. At its third and fourth sessions it conducted general discussions on rights contained within article 11, and at its sixth session adopted a General Comment on the right to housing. It would not be wrong to suggest that article 11 is the area in which the Committee's practice is most developed. Indeed, the growing confidence of the Committee in the area is highlighted by its willingness to take a strong stance on the question of housing with respect to a number of States.

II. THE *TRAVAUX PRÉPARATOIRES*

A Introduction

The Commission on Human Rights considered proposals relating to article 11 at its seventh session in 1951[2] and again at its eighth session in the following year.[3] The result of its deliberations was two articles, the first recognizing 'the right of everyone to adequate food, clothing, and housing', and the second recognizing 'the right of everyone to an adequate standard of living and the continuous improvement of living conditions'.[4] The Third Committee then took over consideration of article 11.[5] After some discussion, the matter was referred to a Working Party, established for the purpose of drafting a compromise text. After only one meeting the Working Party produced a report[6] and its proposals were subsequently adopted in their entirety (with only two minor additions) and now form the text of article 11(1).[7] The text of article 11(2) was not adopted until eight years

---

[1] Alston P., 'International Law and the Human Right to Food' in Alston P. and Tomasevski K. (eds.), *The Right to Food* (1984), 9–68, at 9. He speaks specifically about the right to food, but his comment would also seem to apply more generally to the right to an adequate standard of living.

[2] UN Docs. E/CN.4/SR.203–4, 218, 222–3, 13 UN ESCOR, CN.4 (203–4, 218, 222–3 mtgs.) (1951).

[3] UN Docs. E/CN.4/SR.294–5, 14 UN ESCOR, CN.4 (294–5 mtgs.) (1952). *See generally* UN Doc. A/2929, at 109–11, paras. 29–32 (1955), 10 UN GAOR, Annexes (Ag. Item 28), Pt. II (1955).

[4] UN Doc. E/2573, Annex IA, 18 UN ESCOR, Supp. (No. 7) (1954).

[5] UN Docs. A/C.3/SR.739–43, 11 UN GAOR, C.3 (739–43 mtgs.), at 293–311 (1957). *See generally* UN Doc. A/3525, at 17–19, paras. 120–44, 11 UN GOAR, Annexes (Ag. Item 31) (1957).

[6] UN Doc. A/C.3/L.586, 11 UN GAOR, C.3 (1957).

[7] UN Doc. A/3525, *supra* n. 5, at 19, para. 144.

later when, in 1963, the Third Committee came to discuss the matter again following the receipt of a number of relevant proposals.[8]

B Article 11(1)

1 Two Separate Articles

In its first detailed discussion of proposals for article 11, the Commission was divided on whether or not the right to housing should be dealt with separately from the right to an adequate standard of living. Although there was no doubt that the right to housing fell within the concept of the right to an adequate standard of living, the question was one of formulation. On the one hand, it was argued that the main objective was to draft a provision on the right to an adequate standard of living. To single out housing as a separate provision would give it undue prominence,[9] especially in the light of the fact that other elements such as health, clothing, food, and transport were also relevant.[10] On the other hand it was pointed out that it would be extremely difficult to draft a provision outlining the general concept of an adequate standard of living;[11] it would be easier to enunciate the elements of that standard in separate, specific, and obligatory provisions.[12] Moreover, to provide for the right to an adequate standard of living alone was insufficient,[13] particularly as it might be limited merely to the fulfilment of immediate needs.[14] In the end, the Commission did adopt a separate provision on the right to housing even though it was clear that some States continued to oppose its inclusion.[15]

In the Third Committee, it was decided, following the suggestion of the Swedish delegate, that articles 11 and 12 as drafted by the Commission should be discussed together.[16] It was argued that the rights to food, housing, and clothing could be seen as 'illustrations' of the right to an adequate standard of living[17] or as 'component elements'.[18] Although China objected

---

[8] UN Docs. A/C.3/SR.1232, 1264, 1267–9, 18 UN GAOR, C.3 (1232, 1264, 1267–9 mtgs.) (1963). *See generally* UN Doc. A/5655, at 20–3, paras. 86–108, 18 UN GAOR, Annexes (Ag. Item 48) (1963).

[9] *See e.g.* Bowie (UK), E/CN.4/SR.222, at 18 (1951); Whitlam (Australia), E/CN.4/SR.222, at 20 (1951); Mehta (India), *ibid.* The UK later argued that the concept was already implicit in other arts. that related to conditions of work, standards of living, and standards of health, and was therefore unnecessary and duplicitous, Hoare (UK), E/CN.4/SR.294, at 5 (1952).

[10] *See* Yu (China), E/CN.4/SR.222, at 17 (1951).

[11] *See e.g.* Valenzuela (Chile), E/CN.4/SR.222, at 19 (1951).

[12] *See* Morosov (USSR), E/CN.4/SR.222, at 18 (1951).

[13] *See e.g.* Morosov (USSR), E/CN.4/SR.294, at 6 (1952); Mehta (India), E/CN.4/SR.294, at 8 (1952).

[14] *See* Azkoul (Lebanon), E/CN.4/SR.294, at 11 (1952).

[15] *See e.g.* Roosevelt (USA), E/CN.4/SR.222, at 23 (1951).

[16] A/C.3/SR.739, at 293, paras. 1–8 (1957).

[17] Brena (Uruguay), A/C.3/SR.739, at 293, para. 11 (1957).

[18] Hoare (UK), A/C.3/SR.740, at 299, para. 26 (1957).

that the right to an adequate standard of living was broader than these three rights and should stand alone,[19] the majority quickly decided to combine the two articles.[20] As the Indonesian representative noted, an adequate standard of living could not be achieved without adequate food, clothing, and housing.[21]

2 The Right to Housing

At its seventh session in 1951, the Commission had two draft articles before it: one from the USSR referring to a right to living accommodation,[22] and the other from the USA providing for a right to adequate housing. The USSR amendment was rejected because it placed too great an emphasis on the role of the State[23] and insufficient attention to the role of international co-operation.[24] The USA proposal, on the other hand, was adopted by a large margin.[25]

At the following session, the USSR proposed a further amendment to the effect that States parties would undertake to adopt 'all necessary measures, particularly by legislation, to ensure to everyone a dwelling consistent with human dignity'.[26] The purpose of the amendment was to make clear, by use of the phrase 'all necessary measures', that State obligations included, not merely the building of houses, but also measures such as subsidies, tax exemptions, loans, and the provision of the requisite materials on favourable terms.[27] The amendment was ultimately rejected on the basis that it duplicated the terms of article 2(1) (which outlines the State's obligations), and would therefore destroy the balance of the Covenant.[28] It was also noted that the phrase 'dwelling consistent with human dignity' appeared to be narrower than the term 'adequate housing'[29] and would therefore provide an insufficient guarantee.[30] It is notable, nevertheless, that there is no indication that the measures of implementation outlined in the discussion would not be applicable in relation to the implementation of the right to housing as it now stands.

[19] *See* Tsao (China), A/C.3/SR.739, at 295, para. 32 (1957).

[20] A/C.3/SR.739, at 295, para. 38 (1957).

[21] *See* Sutanto (Indonesia), A/C.3/SR.740, at 298, para. 23 (1957).

[22] UN Doc. E/CN.4/AC.14/2/Add.3, Sect. VI, at 4, (1951). The proposal read: 'The State shall take the necessary legislative measures, to ensure to everyone living accommodation worthy of man.'

[23] *See e.g.* Cassin (France), E/CN.4/SR.222, at 21 (1951).

[24] Roosevelt (USA), E/CN.4/SR.222, at 19 (1951).

[25] 12 votes to 0 with 6 abstentions. E/CN.4/SR.222, at 23 (1951).

[26] UN Doc. E/CN.4/L.48 (1952).

[27] *See* Boratynski (Poland), E/CN.4/SR.294, at 7–8 (1952).

[28] *See e.g.* Juvigny (France), E/CN.4/SR.294, at 9 (1952); Azkoul (Lebanon), E/CN.4/SR.294, at 11 (1952).

[29] Azkoul (Lebanon), E/CN.4/SR.294, at 12 (1952).

[30] Bowie (UK), E/CN.4/SR.294, at 10 (1952).

3 Food and Clothing

Until the Commission's eighth session, no reference to clothing or food had been agreed upon. At that session however, China proposed the inclusion of the words 'food, clothing, and . . .' before 'housing'.[31] It was explained that although housing might be more important for industrialized countries, the need for food and clothing came first in countries with a rural economy, especially 'under-developed countries'.[32] The proposal gained a wide range of support[33] and was finally adopted. At a later stage, the term 'adequate' was included before 'food, clothing, and housing', to clarify the text[34] and to introduce the idea that those components of the standard of living should be maintained at a certain level.[35]

4 An Adequate Standard of Living

In 1951 Australia proposed the inclusion of a provision relating to 'the right to an adequate standard of living'. It was intended to be both 'concise and inclusive' and would represent the 'kernel' of the concept ready to be expanded in later international agreements.[36] Although critics pointed out that the proposed right was 'a very vague concept defying all attempts at definition',[37] and that in some circumstances it might serve to prejudice economic and social development,[38] it retained considerable support within the Commission.[39]

China argued that the right to an adequate standard of living should be defined, mentioning in particular the rights to 'housing, health, clothing, food, and means of transport'.[40] It was initially pointed out that the question of health was to be dealt with at a later stage,[41] and that transport could not be seen to be 'a first essential in an adequate standard of living'.[42] Later, however, the Chinese proposal was rejected in its entirety.[43] The UK explained that there was a 'general understanding of all that was implied

---

[31] UN Doc. E/CN.4/L.57, 14 UN ESCOR, CN.4 (1952).

[32] Cheng Paonan (China), E/CN.4/SR.294, at 5 (1952).

[33] *See e.g.* Hoare (UK), E/CN.4/SR.294, at 10 (1952).

[34] *See* Mahmud (Ceylon), A/C.3/SR.742, at 306, para. 35 (1957).

[35] *See e.g.* Hoare (UK), A/C.3/SR.742, at 303, para. 10 (1957).

[36] *See* Whitlam (Australia), E/CN.4/SR.223, at 4 (1951).

[37] Valenzuela (Chile), E/CN.4/SR.222, at 19 (1951).

[38] *Ibid.*

[39] *See e.g.* Bowie (UK), E/CN.4/SR.222, at 18 (1951). The proposal was preferred to that of the USA, which merely recognized the right to 'improved standards of living': Roosevelt (USA), E/CN.4/SR.222, at 16 (1951).

[40] Yu (China), E/CN.4/SR.222, at 17 (1951).

[41] *See* Chairman, E/CN.4/SR.222, at 18 (1951).

[42] Whitlam (Australia), E/CN.4/SR.223, at 4 (1951). *See also* Mehta (India), E/CN.4/SR.223, at 6 (1951).

[43] 7 votes to 3 with 5 abstentions. E/CN.4/SR.223, at 8 (1951).

by adequate standards of living'[44] and that the Commission should avoid entering into an 'interminable and fruitless discussion' in attempting to define it.[45]

At the Commission's seventh session, a certain number of States noted that the concept of an adequate standard of living related to virtually all of the economic, social, and cultural rights under discussion. In addition to the rights to food, housing, and clothing, particular mention was made of the rights to work,[46] fair wages,[47] health,[48] and education.[49] Given the broad scope of the concept of an adequate standard of living, several States suggested that it should perhaps be placed as a general article or 'understanding' before the other rights.[50] The matter was not discussed further, it being decided that the order of the articles would be dealt with at a later stage.[51] Unfortunately, no process of rationalization ever took place.

Although it became apparent in the Third Committee that the rights to food, clothing, and housing were to be considered at least as a partial definition of the right to an 'adequate standard of living', the latter term was again subject to criticism. It was noted that the concept of an adequate standard of living varied considerably between countries and over time,[52] and accordingly, 'the range of meaning covered by the term, which was very vague at the national level, was even harder to determine at the international level'.[53]

The majority of the Third Committee, however, considered that 'an adequate standard of living' was a 'generally understood and accepted concept'.[54] Not only had a Committee of Experts already defined some components of an adequate standard of living,[55] it was also a notion understood by the inhabitants of every country.[56] Additionally, the inclusion of the phrase was considered necessary to 'impress upon States that the raising

[44] Bowie (UK), E/CN.4/SR.222, at 18 (1951).
[45] Bowie (UK), E/CN.4/SR.223, at 7 (1951).
[46] *See* Cassin (France), E/CN.4/SR.223, at 7 (1951).
[47] *See* Valenzuela (Chile), E/CN.4/SR.223, at 5 (1951).
[48] *See* Yu (China), E/CN.4/SR.222, at 17 (1951). Later in the Third Committee, it was noted that art. 11 had some relation to art. 12, especially in as far as an adequate standard of living related to a person's 'physical, mental, and social well-being' mentioned in the latter art. Hoare (UK), A/C.3/SR.739, at 294, para. 14 (1957).
[49] *See* Mehta (India), E/CN.4/SR.223, at 6 (1951).
[50] *See* Cassin (France), E/CN.4/SR.222, at 23 (1951); Valenzuela (Chile), E/CN.4/SR.223, at 5 (1951). A similar proposal was that the provisions should begin with an affirmation that human beings had the fundamental right to food and life, Cassin (France), E/CN.4/SR.223, at 7 (1951).
[51] *See* Chairman, E/CN.4/SR.223, at 5 (1951).
[52] *See* Hamilton (Australia), A/C.3/SR.743, at 310, para. 16 (1957).
[53] Baroody (Saudi Arabia), A/C.3/SR.739, at 293, para. 4 (1957).
[54] Brena (Uruguay), A/C.3/SR.742, at 303, para. 9 (1957).
[55] Diaz Casanueva (Chile), A/C.3/SR.739, at 294, para. 20 (1957).
[56] *See* Diaz Casanueva (Chile), A/C.3/SR.739, at 294, para. 21 (1957).

of the standard of living should be one of their constant preoccupations',[57] and to bring article 11 into line with article 25 of the UDHR.[58]

It was proposed to replace the word 'adequate' with the word 'decent' in order to clarify the meaning of the right,[59] and make it conform with article 7 which spoke of a 'decent living'.[60] The term 'decent' was also considered to be more appropriate in that it connoted a higher standard of living than a merely adequate one, which could be interpreted as covering only the bare necessities of life.[61] The majority, however, did not think that replacing the term 'adequate' with 'decent' would make the matter any clearer.[62] The term 'adequate' related to the physical, moral, and mental development of the individual and linked the article with article 12 as regards health standards. Moreover the term 'adequate standard of living' had 'clear and well-understood implications' and was to be found in article 25 of the UDHR.[63]

Given the broad definition of the concept of a standard of living, it is considered that there was questionable value in its being placed as a separate right in itself. The Commission (and the Third Committee) would have done better either to adopt the proposal of the USSR and leave it out entirely while enacting its component parts as rights in the Covenant,[64] or to adopt a form of the French proposal and include it as a general principle (perhaps in the preamble).[65] Either way it might have avoided the somewhat anomalous position of its being a right which appears to have little independent substance.

5 For Himself and his Family

A joint amendment proposed by El Salvador, the Dominican Republic, and Ecuador[66] aimed at harmonizing the text of article 11 with article 25 of the UDHR by including a reference to the 'well-being of the individual and his family'.[67] A number of States considered this proposal unnecessary as the idea of the family was already taken care of by the use of the word 'everyone'.[68] Moreover, certain States felt that the proposal would raise questions

---

[57] Diaz Casanueva (Chile), A/C.3/SR.739, at 294, para. 21 (1957).
[58] *See* Brena (Uruguay), A/C.3/SR.742, at 303, para. 9 (1957).
[59] Brena (Uruguay), A/C.3/SR.739, at 294, para. 12 (1957).
[60] *See* Brillantes (Philippines), A/C.3/SR.739, at 295, para. 24 (1957). For the drafting of the term 'decent living' in art. 7, *see above* Ch. 6, text accompanying nn. 38–40.
[61] *See* Brillantes (Philippines), A/C.3/SR.740, at 299, para. 28 (1957).
[62] *See e.g.* Baroody (Saudi Arabia), A/C.3/SR.739, at 295, para. 36 (1957).
[63] *See e.g.* Brena (Uruguay), A/C.3/SR.740, at 299, para. 29 (1957).
[64] *See above* text accompanying n. 12.   [65] *See above* text accompanying n. 50.
[66] UN Doc. A/C.3/L.583, 12 UN GAOR, C.3 (1957).
[67] *See* Lima (El Salvador), A/C.3/SR.740, at 299, para. 31 (1957).
[68] *See e.g.* Tsao (China), A/C.3/SR.742, at 303, para. 4 (1957).

about the scope of the provision[69] especially as regards individuals without families.[70]

The majority of the Third Committee, however, voted for the inclusion of the phrase. It appears that States considered that the provision would be made clearer with a reference to the family,[71] and that it would have the advantage of stressing the fact that wages and salaries should be such as to afford a decent standard of living not only to the workers themselves, but also to their families.[72] A suggestion that the phrase should be followed by the words 'if any' to stress that it did not exclude those without families[73] was not taken up. The assumption seems to have been that they would nevertheless be included under the term 'everyone'.

6 The Continuous Improvement of Living Conditions

At the Commission's seventh session, Yugoslavia proposed that the original Australian text providing for the right to an adequate standard of living should be amended to include the phrase 'and the continuous improvement of living conditions' in order to give the provision a 'dynamic character'.[74] Although it was argued that such a dynamic element would be better placed in a general clause rather than a substantive article,[75] the amendment was ultimately adopted by the Commission.[76] The Third Committee later endorsed the phrase with little discussion. It was considered to be entirely consistent with the principle of the progressive realization of economic and social rights,[77] and appropriate given the fundamental nature of the right concerned.[78]

One important objection was raised with respect to the proposed right to the 'continuous improvement of living conditions'. The Belgian representative argued that 'the primary aim should be to improve the living conditions of the most under-privileged; persons outside that category could hardly claim, at the current stage, to have a "right" to "continuous improvement"' of their living conditions.[79] The difficulties of this term, as implied by the criticism, were generally overlooked. Certainly, the inclusion of the phrase 'the continuous improvement of living conditions' does confirm that the standards are dynamic and State-specific rather than universal, but that

---

[69] *See* Delhaye (Belgium), A/C.3/SR.743, at 310, para. 9 (1957).
[70] *See e.g.* Brillantes (Philippines), A/C.3/SR.742, at 303, para. 7 (1957).
[71] *See* Bernadino (Dominican Republic), A/C.3/SR.742, at 303, para. 5 (1957).
[72] *See* Castaneda (Mexico), A/C.3/SR.742, at 304, para. 27 (1957).
[73] *See* Eustathiades (Greece), A/C.3/SR.742, at 304, para. 19 (1957).
[74] Jevremovic (Yugoslavia), E/CN.4/SR.223, at 5 (1951).
[75] *See* Whitlam (Australia), E/CN.4/SR.223, at 6 (1951).
[76] 6 votes to 5 against, with 7 abstentions. E/CN.4/SR.223, at 8 (1951).
[77] *See* Baroody (Saudi Arabia), A/C.3/SR.739, at 293, para. 4 (1957).
[78] *See* Radic (Yugoslavia), A/C.3/SR.743, at 310, para. 10 (1957).
[79] Delhaye (Belgium), A/C.3/SR.743, at 309, para. 8 (1957).

much might have been inferred from the concept of an 'adequate standard of living'. It does raise questions as to the individual nature of the right, however, if it is conceded that only the poor have a right to the 'continuous improvement of living conditions'.

7 Appropriate Steps to Ensure the Realization of the Right

The general intention of States in the drafting process was that the rights in article 11 should be implemented in a progressive manner in accordance with the provisions of article 2(1). This is evidenced not only by specific statements to that effect,[80] but also by the fact that a considerable proportion of the discussion centered upon the compatibility of the draft article with specific elements of article 2(1). However, it was noted by several States that the wording of the second sentence of paragraph 1, which speaks of the obligation 'to ensure' the realization of the right, suggests that the implementation of article 11 should be immediate.[81] On close examination, it would appear that most States considered that the immediacy of the obligation referred to the 'steps' to be taken rather than the full realization of the rights.[82] It was particularly evident, for example, that States considered the realization of the rights to be dependent upon resources.[83] Indeed, there was an explicit intention on the part of a number of States that article 11 be bound by the terms of article 2(1) as regards progressive realization of the rights.[84]

In formulating the terms of implementation, a number of States argued that 'it was not intended that States should be directed to do anything specific'.[85] Rather, States would be under a duty to develop general conditions through which the rights in question might be secured to individuals.[86] An Afghan amendment[87] to that effect, however, was criticized for concen-

---

[80] *See e.g.* Hamilton (Australia), A/C.3/SR.743, at 310, para. 16 (1957).

[81] *See e.g.* Afnan (Iraq), A/C.3/SR.743, at 311, para. 32 (1957); Juvigny (France), A/C.3/SR.742, at 304, para. 14 (1957).

[82] *e.g.* Iraq rather controversially commented: 'Art. 2 provided that States were to take steps progressively, whereas the steps referred to in art. 11 were to be taken immediately': Afnan (Iraq), A/C.3/SR.743, at 311, para. 32 (1957). It is currently considered however that art. 2(1) does require steps to be taken immediately. *See above* Ch. 3, text accompanying nn. 39–46.

[83] *See e.g.* Diaz Casanueva (Chile), A/C.3/SR.739, at 294, para. 21 (1957); Tsuruoka (Japan), A/C.3/SR.740, at 299, para. 25 (1957).

[84] *See e.g.* Castaneda (Mexico), A/C.3/SR.742, at 305, para. 26 (1957); Hamilton (Australia), A/C.3/SR.743, at 310, para. 16 (1957). It might be noted, however, that, even if a right is bound by the terms of art. 2(1), there is room to argue for the immediate implementation of a right which involves minimal resource commitments. *See above* Ch. 3, text accompanying nn. 176–230.

[85] *See* Quan (Guatemala), A/C.3/SR.739, at 293, para. 9 (1957).

[86] *See* Tsuruoka (Japan), A/C.3/SR.740, at 299, para. 25 (1957); Pazhwak (Afghanistan), A/C.3/SR.739, at 295, para. 27 (1957).

[87] UN Doc. A/C.3/L.578, 12 UN GAOR, C.3 (1957).

trating on the 'object' of the right rather than the right itself[88] and was subsequently withdrawn. In rejecting an approach that centered upon the State playing a 'facilitative' role, it would seem that the intention was for States to have a more positive role in the realization of the rights to food, housing, and clothing. One particular example was cited by a member of the Third Committee in which she argued that where private undertakings did not have sufficient capital to build houses for low-income groups it was for the State to sponsor such housing.[89]

8 International Co-operation

The most controversial element in the drafting of article 11 was the second sentence of article 11(1) drafted by the working party, which provided that 'States Parties will take appropriate steps to ensure the realization of this right, recognizing to this effect the essential importance of international co-operation based on free consent'.[90] Those who opposed the provision maintained that it was unnecessary, as reference to international co-operation was better dealt with in article 2(1)[91] and in Part IV of the Covenant.[92] The repetition of such an obligation might in turn detract from the general obligation[93] and imply that article 11 was more important than other rights.[94] Moreover, international co-operation was only one of several factors which governments would have to consider when they came to apply article 11,[95] and it might discourage States from taking independent action to implement the article.[96]

On the other hand it was argued that the reference to international co-operation 'in no way' conflicted with the general provisions on the subject,[97] and was 'essential'[98] given the fundamental importance of the rights in article 11[99] and the need to impose precise obligations upon States.[100] Indeed the Greek representative commented that article 11 was 'so basic and far-reaching that all the other rights might be regarded as specific aspects of

---

[88] *See* Tsao (China), A/C.3/SR.739, at 295, para. 33 (1957).

[89] *See* Afnan (Iraq), A/C.3/SR.739, at 295, para. 30 (1957).   [90] *Supra*, n. 6.

[91] *See e.g.* Hoare (UK), A/C.3/SR.742, at 304, para. 11 (1957); Shoham-Sharon (Israel), A/C.3/SR.742, at 304, para. 16 (1957).

[92] *See e.g.* Tsao (China), A/C.3/SR.742, at 303, para. 3 (1957).

[93] *See* Hamilton (Australia), A/C.3/SR.743, at 310, para. 16 (1957); Paulus (India), A/C.3/SR.742, at 306, para. 41 (1957).

[94] *See e.g.* Brillantes (Philippines), A/C.3/SR.743, at 309, para. 5 (1957).

[95] *See* Castaneda (Mexico), A/C.3/SR.742, at 304, para. 26 (1957).

[96] *See* Brillantes (Philippines), A/C.3/SR.742, at 303, para. 8 (1957).

[97] *See* Brena (Uruguay), A/C.3/SR.742, at 305, para. 22 (1957).

[98] Montero (Chile), A/C.3/SR.742, at 305, para. 24 (1957).

[99] *See e.g.* Ahmed (Pakistan), A/C.3/SR.742, at 305, para. 32 (1957); Tsuruoka (Japan), A/C.3/SR.742, at 306, para. 39 (1957).

[100] *See* Radic (Yugoslavia), A/C.3/SR.743, at 310, para. 10 (1957).

it or as applying to certain categories of persons; there was therefore every justification for stressing international co-operation in that particular article'.[101] The provision was eventually adopted by a majority,[102] it having been made clear that international co-operation should be 'based on free consent'.[103]

One interesting point that became clear during the debate was that a number of members of the Third Committee appeared to consider that the rights in article 11 were 'more fundamental' than other rights in the Covenant.[104] Ostensibly, this was the reason given for including a reference to international co-operation. However, it is not clear whether it was intended that those rights should be afforded any form of priority, whether in terms of public expenditure or otherwise.

C Article 11(2)

In 1963 the Director-General of the FAO submitted an informal amendment to the Third Committee proposing the inclusion of a draft article relating to the right to be free from hunger which would follow the existing article 11.[105] The proposal provided for the 'right of everyone to be free from hunger' which States undertook to achieve 'within the shortest possible time'. National and international action to that end should pay attention to the sharing of world food supplies in an equitable manner, increasing food production, the adaptation of systems of land tenure and land use, and the improvement of methods of production, conservation, and distribution of food.[106] This suggestion came to be reflected in the proposal of Saudi Arabia[107] and in the combined proposal of Chile, Colombia, Ecuador, and Uganda.[108] A further proposal was put forward by a working group specifically set up to produce a non-controversial text that could command unanimity.[109] The various proposals and amendments were considered by the Third Committee at a series of meetings in 1963.[110]

---

[101] Eustathiades (Greece), A/C.3/SR.742, at 304, para. 18 (1957).
[102] 31 votes to 14 with 17 abstentions. *See* UN Doc. 3525, *supra*, n. 5, at 19, para. 143.
[103] *See* Mufti (Syria), A/C.3/SR.742, at 306, para. 33 (1957).
[104] *e.g.*, the Japanese representative commented: 'article 11 had a place distinct from other articles, for it was concerned with life and death; for example, education and hygiene were not as essential to survival, as food, clothing and housing were': Tsuruoka (Japan), A/C.3/SR.742, at 306, para. 39 (1957).
[105] Sen (FAO), A/C.3/SR.1232, at 93–4, paras. 4–10 (1963). *See generally* Alston, *supra* n. 1, at 30–1.
[106] UN Doc. A/C.3/SR.1232, at 94, para. 10 (1963).
[107] UN Doc. A/C.3/L.1172, 18 UN GAOR, C.3 (1963).
[108] UN Doc. A/C.3/L.1175, 18 UN GAOR, C.3 (1963).
[109] UN Doc. A/C.3/L.1177, 18 UN GAOR, C.3 (1963).
[110] UN Docs. A/C.3/SR.1264–5, 1267–9, 18 GAOR, C.3 (1264–5, and 1267–9 mtgs.) (1963). *See generally* UN Doc. A/C.3/5655, *supra* n. 8, at 20–3, paras. 86–108.

1 The Right to Freedom from Hunger

The FAO proposal was made primarily with the aim of clarifying State obligations in relation to the elimination of hunger.[111] A large number of States recognized the 'paramount importance' of the right;[112] as the Australian representative noted, 'no human right was worth anything to a starving man'.[113] Nevertheless, questions were raised about the appropriateness of including such provisions in a legal instrument such as the draft Covenant.[114] Indeed the Philippines commented that 'it was hard to predict what practical effect a provision of that kind would have, but it was bound at least to draw national attention to the problem and offer some hope of relief to the hungry of the world'.[115]

Opponents of the proposals argued that the draft Covenants should be restricted to outlining the fundamental human rights and the basic principles that underlay them. Although freedom from hunger was an important principle, the Covenant should not contain any specific measures of implementation.[116] Not only would measures to ensure freedom from hunger differ from country to country, questions such as increasing world food supplies and ensuring their equitable distribution, or reforming systems of land tenure, were properly subjects to be dealt with by the General Assembly's Second Committee and by specialized agencies.[117] Further, it was considered that the provisions were unfortunately 'vague and general', capable of different interpretations,[118] and reflected considerations that would be more suited to inclusion in a separate declaration on the question.[119]

Much as the arguments against the provisions suggest that there was a considerable division within the Third Committee on the matter, ultimately not a single State voted against the proposals. This is perhaps a testament to the delicate phraseology of the final text which, while outlining certain principles, did not prejudice the development of more specific policies by international agencies or the State concerned. As the Australian representative commented:

[111] Sen (FAO), A/C.3/SR.1232, at 94, para. 10 (1963).
[112] *See e.g.* Yapou (Israel), A/C.3/SR.1264, at 271, para. 7 (1963).
[113] Gilchrist (Australia), A/C.3/SR.1267, at 287, para. 8 (1963).
[114] *See e.g.* Gilchrist (Australia), A/C.3/SR.1267, at 287, para. 8 (1963).
[115] Quiambao (Philippines), A/C.3/SR.1267, at 287, para. 6 (1963).
[116] *See* Ataullah (Pakistan), A/C.3/SR.1264, at 271, para. 4 (1963); A/C.3/SR.1269, at 300, para. 9 (1963).
[117] *See* Ataullah (Pakistan), A/C.3/SR.1264, at 271, para. 4 (1963); Beaufort (Netherlands), A/C.3/SR.1266, at 285, para. 60 (1963); Alatas (Indonesia), A/C.3/SR. 1268, at 293, para. 4 (1963).
[118] *See* Monod (France), A/C.3/SR.1269, at 300, para. 7 (1963).
[119] *See* Beaufort (Netherlands), A/C.3/SR.1266, at 285, para. 62 (1963); Herndl (Austria), A/C.3/SR.1268, at 294, para. 9 (1963).

While it would have been unwise of the Third Committee to act as a body of economic experts or put forward detailed proposals on the economic means of achieving the realization of the right in question, it was quite fitting that it should indicate the general areas in which Governments much take action.[120]

The crucial characteristic of article 11(2) appears to have been that although certain objectives and methods of implementation were outlined, they were considered sufficiently general not to bind a State to any particular course of action.

2 The Fundamental Right of Everyone

The word 'fundamental' is first to be found in the joint proposal drafted by the working group. There, States parties recognized the 'fundamental importance of the right of everyone to be free from hunger'. It was later pointed out that there was a difference between recognizing a right and recognizing the importance of a right—the latter being a far weaker obligation.[121] It was accordingly suggested that the paragraph be amended so as to refer to 'the fundamental right of everyone to be free from hunger'.[122] This became the final revised text which was adopted by the Third Committee.

Much as the right to be free from hunger is the only right in either Covenant that is explicitly referred to as 'fundamental', the *travaux préparatoires* give no indication that it be given any pre-eminence among the range of human rights. In the absence of explanation, it is to be assumed that the drafters did not intend to invest in the word 'fundamental' any particular legal significance.

3 Measures and Specific Programmes

A number of States, in order to emphasize the optional nature of the obligations in the final paragraphs of article 11(2),[123] proposed the inclusion of the word 'necessary' before the word 'measures'.[124] This suggestion was strongly opposed on the basis that such an amendment would weaken the text by implying that the need for measures was merely hypothetical rather than absolute.[125] All States, irrespective of their situation, are under an obligation to take appropriate measures and specific programmes within the areas stipulated. The form of those measures and programmes however

---

[120] Gilchrist (Australia), A/C.3/SR.1267, at 287, para. 8 (1963).

[121] Kabbani (Syria), A/C.3/SR.1268, at 293, para. 1 (1963).

[122] Eluchans (Chile), A/C.3/SR.1268, at 294, para. 12 (1963).

[123] *See* Mantzoulinos (Greece), A/C.3/SR.1268, at 294, para. 10 (1963).

[124] *See e.g.* Capotorti (Italy), A/C.3/SR.1268, at 294, para. 18 (1963). An earlier amendment initially suggested the replacement of the words 'which are needed' with 'if and where needed': Mantzoulinos (Greece), A/C.3/SR.1268, at 294, para. 10 (1963).

[125] *See* Eluchans (Chile), A/C.3/SR.1268, at 294, para. 13 (1963).

would be determined by the social and economic context within the country concerned.[126]

4 Paragraph (a)

The debate in the Third Committee rarely touched upon the main elements of paragraph (a) apart from the question of agrarian reform. It was generally accepted that food production, conservation, and distribution were objectives of fundamental importance with a view to ensuring freedom from hunger. Specific comments merely stressed the importance of agricultural self-reliance[127] and of adequate modern systems of marketing of agricultural produce.[128]

As regards agrarian reform, the original five-power amendment used the phrase 'adapting or reforming existing systems of land tenure and land use and systems for the exploitation of natural resources'.[129] This was then rationalized by the working party to its current form. Following a request for an explanation of the phrase, Chile explained that in paragraph (a) the sponsors 'wished to point out suitable measures to be taken by States parties in order to implement the right to be free from hunger'.[130] The representative continued:

Among those measures was the development or reform of agrarian systems, with a view to improving the use of agricultural resources. States Parties were given an alternative: they could either develop or reform agrarian systems, depending on their needs. Moreover, 'agrarian systems' implied both improved techniques of land exploitation and legal questions, such as those of ownership.[131]

If a just agrarian system existed then the State was not obliged to undertake land reform—in such cases only the improvement of farming methods would be required.[132]

This interpretation was supported by a large number of States whose main concern seemed to be that they should not be bound to undertake land reform. Two unsuccessful proposals were made to introduce the phrase 'if necessary' before the reference to land reform.[133] Their rejection did not so much reflect the idea that land reform was essential in all cases, rather that the existing text already sufficiently provided for alternative approaches. The amendments would merely have complicated the provision.[134]

---

[126] *See e.g.* Alatas (Indonesia), A/C.3/SR.1268, at 293, para. 5 (1963).

[127] *See e.g.* Herrera (Costa Rica), A/C.3/SR.1269, at 299, para. 3 (1963).

[128] *See e.g.* Zalamea (Colombia), A/C.3/SR.1267, at 288, para. 11 (1963).

[129] *Supra* n. 108.　　　[130] Eluchans (Chile), A/C.3/SR.1267, at 287, para. 3 (1963).

[131] *Ibid.*　　　[132] *Ibid* para. 4.

[133] *See* Aujay de la Dure (France), A/C.3/SR.1267, at 288, para. 18 (1963); Mantzoulinos (Greece), A/C.3/SR.1268, at 294, para. 10 (1963).

[134] *See* Eluchans (Chile), A/C.3/SR.1268, at 294, para. 13 (1963).

The general agreement thus appears to have been that each country should find the approach to agrarian reform best suited to its conditions,[135] and that it should be carried out 'wherever necessary, desirable, and acceptable to the majority of those to be affected'.[136] Although this suggests that priority should be given to democratic participation in the formulation and implementation of land reform programmes, ultimately it would be for the States themselves to determine whether, and to what extent, agrarian reform was necessary. This interpretation appears to deprive the article of much of its substance. As one State noted, given that the measures laid down were 'perfectly well known to even the most backward country', paragraph (a) was essentially unnecessary.[137]

5 Paragraph (b)

Both the original proposals for article 11(2) referred to the sharing of the world food supplies on a rational and equitable basis.[138] In order to clarify the notion of sharing resources, it was proposed that reference be made to 'the interests of both food producers and consumers'.[139] This concern was taken up in the joint proposal which stressed that States take into account the problems of both food-importing and food-exporting countries. Chile argued that the term 'problem' was preferable to that of 'interests' because 'the distribution of food supplies should be based not solely on the interests of the countries involved or on purely economic grounds, but also on social and humanitarian considerations which were implicit in the word "problems"'.[140] Moreover, it was pointed out that freedom from hunger should not be interpreted as freedom to dispose of agricultural surpluses to the detriment of the economies of the less developed countries.[141]

III. THE APPROACH OF THE COMMITTEE

A An Adequate Standard of Living

As was made clear in the *travaux préparatoires*, the concept of an adequate standard of living[142] was intended to have a broad and general meaning.

---

[135] *See e.g.* Mendez (Guatemala), A/C.3/SR.1267, at 288, para. 12 (1963).
[136] Attlee (UK), A/C.3/SR.1267, at 287, para. 5 (1963).
[137] U Myat Tun (Burma), A/C.3/SR.1267, at 288, para. 14 (1963).
[138] *Supra*, nn. 107–8.
[139] *See* U Myat Tun (Burma), A/C.3/SR.1264, at 271, para. 6 (1963).
[140] *See* Eluchans (Chile), A/C.3/SR.1268, at 294, para. 16 (1963).
[141] *See* U Myat Tun (Burma), A/C.3/SR.1267, at 288, para. 15 (1963).
[142] Cf. art. 25(1) UDHR. *See* Eide A., 'Article 25' in Eide A. *et al.* (eds.), *The Universal Declaration of Human Rights: A Commentary* (1992), 395.

Although the rights to food, clothing, and housing expressly form a partial definition of the right, mention was also made to the rights to health, education, and transport. States, however, showed great reluctance to define the right in any greater detail relying *inter alia* upon the argument that the right to an adequate standard of living was a term whose meaning was generally understood.[143]

It is clear, however, that the Committee, in assessing the progress of States in realizing the right to an adequate standard of living, cannot rely merely upon an intuitive understanding of the notion. Some attempt has to be made to define it in more detail if only for the purpose of measurement. Whether or not the Committee manages to give the provision substantial meaning will be the most significant test of its capabilities, not least because, as Sen notes, the notion of a standard of living is 'full of contrasts, conflicts and even contradictions'.[144]

An important consideration for the Committee is the degree to which the right to an adequate standard of living actually contributes to the protection offered by the Covenant. If, as the *travaux préparatoires* indicate, the right is primarily an agglomeration of other economic, social, and cultural rights, it will have little utility as an independent human right. If, on the other hand, it is read to include concerns that are not already addressed by other rights, it might usefully extend the scope of the Covenant.

Thus far, the Committee has not assigned to the right to an adequate standard of living a meaning that substantially extends the protection offered by other rights. In discussing article 11, little mention is ever made of an adequate standard of living *per se*; the Committee has instead concentrated on the rights to adequate housing and food. Moreover, when dealing specifically with the right to an adequate standard of living, Committee members have generally concentrated upon questions relating to social security,[145] unemployment,[146] and income levels.[147] In doing so, they have appeared to duplicate much of the work undertaken in relation to articles 6 to 9 of the Covenant.

Even where questions have been asked specifically on the standard of living, they have been general and unfocused. The main practice of

---

[143]   *See above* text accompanying nn. 54–8.

[144]   Sen A., *The Standard of Living* (1985), at 1.

[145]   *See e.g.* Sparsis, E/C.12/1988/SR.5, at 6, para. 24; Badawi El Sheikh, E/C.12/1988/SR.18, at 4, para. 17.

[146]   *See e.g.* Texier, E/C.12/1988/SR.12, at 10, para. 49; Sparsis, E/C.12/1988/SR.13, at 14, para. 85; Jimenez Butragueno, E/C.12/1989/SR.12, at 13, para. 71; Fofana, E/C.12/1990/SR.7, at 3, para. 8.

[147]   *See e.g.* Texier, E/C.12/1987/SR.9, at 7, para. 28; Simma, E/C.12/1988/SR.5, at 7, para. 30; Sparsis, E/C.12/1988/SR.10, at 10, para. 55.

the Committee has been to call upon States to establish benchmarks to define an adequate standard of living[148] (such as a 'poverty-line'[149]), pinpoint and direct action in favour of the disadvantaged,[150] ensure non-discrimination,[151] increase equality,[152] and establish legal remedies where appropriate.[153]

In the Committee's reporting guidelines, however, it is possible to identify a number of questions which appear to relate particularly to the right to an adequate standard of living. There, information is requested about the current standard of living of the population, both in the aggregate and as to different groups within the population. In addition, States are required to indicate the per capita GNP of the poorest 40 per cent of the population and their Physical Quality of Life Index (PQLI).[154]

It is notable that the Committee does not stipulate how the standard of living of the population is to be measured, but rather leaves it to the State concerned to adopt its own criteria for evaluation. Moreover, the indicators referred to by the Committee do not give a great deal of insight into the content of the right. First, the PQLI is a composite indicator intended to 'measure the performance of the world's poorest countries in meeting the most basic needs of people'.[155] It uses as measurements infant mortality, life expectancy, and literacy. Quite apart from the technical limitations of the PQLI,[156] it has serious shortcomings in terms of its utility to the Committee. It was designed to be a macro-economic indicator measuring the physical welfare of the total population, not individual welfare or social and psychological welfare. Moreover the components, which roughly concentrate upon the degree of enjoy-

---

[148] *See e.g.* Sparsis, E/C.12/1987/SR.16, at 12, para. 56; Rattray, E/C.12/1989/SR.19, at 7, para. 41; Sparsis, E/C.12/1990/SR.44, at 12, para. 58.

[149] *See* Alston, E/C.12/1988/SR.16, at 7, para. 29; Alston, E/C.12/1990/SR.2, at 10, para. 64; Alston, E/C.12/1990/SR.7, at 3, para. 7.

[150] *See* Konate, E/C.12/1987/SR.19, at 12, para. 58; Alston, E/C.12/1988/SR.13, at 13, para. 71; Badawi El Sheikh, E/C.12/1989/SR.5, at 11, para. 65; Texier, E/C.12/1989/SR.16, at 14, para. 66.

[151] *See* Texier, E/C.12/1989/SR.5, at 9, para. 51; Jimenez Butragueno, E/C.12/1990/SR.44, at 13, para. 61.

[152] *See* Texier, E/C.12/1988/SR.12, at 10, para. 50; Sparsis, E/C.12/1988/SR.12, at 12, para. 63; Alston, E/C.12/1988/SR.13, at 6, para. 25.

[153] *See e.g.* Sparsis, E/C.12/1987/SR.9, at 10, para. 49; Sparsis, E/C.12/1987/SR.20, at 5, para. 18.

[154] Reporting guidelines, UN Doc. E/1991/23, UN ESCOR, Supp. (No. 3), Annex IV, at 11 (1991). For the PQLI *see* Morris M., *Measuring the Conditions of the World's Poor: The Physical Quality of Life Index* (1979).

[155] Morris, *ibid.* 34.

[156] For a discussion on the relative value of the PQLI as a human rights indicator, *see* Türk D., *The New International Economic Order and The Promotion of Human Rights: Realization of Economic, Social and Cultural Rights*, UN Doc. E/CN.4/Sub.2/1990/19, at 27, para. 83 (1990).

ment of the rights to health and education, were chosen primarily for their utility as indicators rather than the degree to which they encompassed the range of concerns that fall within the notion of 'quality of life'.[157]

Secondly, the UNICEF indicator (the per capita GNP of the poorest 40 per cent of the population) is considered to be a broad measure of poverty.[158] The use of this indicator, together with its request that States establish a 'poverty line',[159] suggests that the Committee defines the deprivation of an adequate standard of living in terms of poverty.[160] However, identifying the relationship between two concepts does little to rectify the present problem. Poverty is as resistant to precise definition as is an adequate standard of living.[161]

The indicators to which the Committee refers will provide it with an insight into the general welfare of the population as a whole. At a State level, the PQLI, like the Human Development Index of United Nations Development Programme (UNDP),[162] will rank countries according to their aggregate level of 'social development'. Their primary utility is in providing a comparative picture of social development between countries with a view to managing economic growth 'in the interest of the people'.[163] Such indicators do not provide information about specific human rights nor are they oriented to the position of the individual. If viewed in this light, the right to an adequate standard of living becomes merely a right of the State (or the people) to social and economic development.[164]

The Committee appears to be content to leave the precise definition of an adequate standard of living to the State concerned. While it is entirely appropriate for States to establish their own quantitative bench-marks of 'adequacy' taking into account their current level of economic and social development,[165] the Committee itself should specify the qualitative matters that comprise the notion of a 'standard of living'. Following the Commit-

---

[157] Morris, *supra* n. 154, at 34–5, and 94.

[158] *See* Türk, *supra*, n. 156, at 28.   [159] Reporting guidelines, *supra*, n. 154, at 99.

[160] The World Bank clearly defines poverty as 'the inability to attain a minimal standard of living': IBRD (World Bank), *World Development Report 1990* (1990), at 26.

[161] For a discussion of the notions of absolute and relative poverty, *see* United Nations Development Programme, *Human Development Report 1990* (1990), 106–8.

[162] *Ibid.* 9–16.   [163] *Ibid.* 10.

[164] As McChesney commented: 'The comprehensive right to an "adequate standard of living" under ICESCR Art. 11 invokes the essence of development, and . . . would appear to justify almost any action in the name of economic progress': McChesney A., 'Promoting the General Welfare in a Democratic Society: Balancing Human Rights and Development' (1980) 27 *Neth. ILR* 283, at 289.

[165] It is worth noting that the World Bank utilizes country-specific poverty lines. It reasons: 'The perception of poverty has evolved historically and varies tremendously from culture to culture. Criteria for distinguishing poor from non-poor tend to reflect specific national priorities and normative concepts of welfare and rights. In general, as countries become wealthier, their perception of the acceptable minimum level of consumption—the poverty line—changes': IBRD, *supra*, n. 160, at 27.

tee's discussion on statistical indicators,[166] it may be assumed that the Committee will at some stage in the future specify particular rights-oriented indicators for use by States that will, to some degree, outline what the Committee perceives to be the content of the right.

As suggested above, there is a need for the Committee to explain the utility of the right to an adequate standard of living from the point of view of how it extends the protection offered by the Covenant.[167] One possibility with much to recommend it is for the Committee to interpret the concept as encompassing, as a minimum, the 'basic needs' of the individual.[168] The 1976 World Employment Conference of the ILO defined basic needs in the following manner:

First, they include certain minimum requirements of a family for private consumption: adequate food, shelter and clothing, as well as certain household equipment and furniture. Second, they include essential services provided by and for the community at large, such as safe drinking water, sanitation, public transport and health, educational and cultural facilities.[169]

Some of these concerns (such as food, clothing, and housing) are already specifically enumerated by the Covenant itself. The category of basic needs, however, also includes matters that do not fall easily within the compass of the enumerated human rights, such as 'safe drinking water', 'public transport',[170] and 'sanitation'.[171] It would be entirely appropriate for the Committee to concentrate upon these matters under the heading of an adequate standard of living in so far as they are not dealt with elsewhere. It remains to be seen, however, whether the Committee does adopt such a methodology.

---

[166] *See* UN Doc. E/1992/23, UN ESCOR, Supp. (No. 3), at 81–6, paras. 332–51 (1992). *Cf.* E/C.12/1991/SR.20–21.

[167] *See above* text accompanying n. 144.

[168] On basic needs theory, *see* Doyal L. and Gough I., *A Theory of Human Need* (1991); Braybrooke D; *Meeting Needs* (1987). On the developmental aspect of 'basic needs', *see* International Labour Office, *Employment, Growth and Basic Needs: A One World Problem* (1976); Ghai D. and Alfthan T., 'On the Principles of Quantifying and Satisfying Basic Needs', in Ghai D. *et al.* (eds.), *The Basic-Needs Approach to Development: Some Issues Regarding Concepts and Methodology* (1978), 19; Hopkins M. and Van Der Hoeven R., *Basic Needs in Development Planning* (1983). For the legal and human rights aspects of basic needs, *see* Alston P., 'Human Rights and Basic Needs: A Critical Assessment' (1979) 12 *HRJ* 19; Green R., 'Basic Human Rights/Needs: Some Problems of Categorical Translation and Unification' (1981) 26 *ICJ Rev.* 53; Trubeck D., 'Economic, Social and Cultural Rights in the Third World: Human Rights Law and Human Needs Programs' in Meron T. (ed.), *Human Rights in International Law* (1984), 205; Muchlinski P., ' "Basic Needs" Theory and "Development Law" ' in Snyder F. and Slinn P., *International Law of Development: Comparative Perspectives* (1987), 237; Stewart F., 'Basic Needs Strategies, Human Rights, and The Right to Development' (1989) 11 *Hum. Rts. Q* 347.

[169] International Labour Office, *Target Setting for Basic Needs* (1982), at 2.

[170] It is relevant to note that 'transport' was one of the rights proposed for inclusion in art. 11 but was not considered important enough to be given specific recognition. *See above* text accompanying n. 40.

[171] *See* Alston, *supra*, n. 168, at 36.

B The Right to Adequate Food

1 Introduction

The right to adequate food[172] in article 11(1) emanates from, and forms part of, the more general right to an 'adequate standard of living'. As such, action taken towards the realization of the right to food has to be viewed from the perspective of how it contributes to the realization of the right to an adequate standard of living. This would seem to require an approach in which action in favour of providing adequate food, over and above the fulfilment of basic needs, would have to be balanced with competing priorities such as housing or water. In cases where resource allocation is not driven by the fulfilment of basic needs, a State would be required to assess the most effective utilization of resources to achieve the general realization of an adequate standard of living. This might mean, for example, that preference be given to housing rather than food.

2 Freedom from Hunger

The general notion of the right to food would seem to have more explicit recognition in article 11(2), which provides for a right 'to be free from hunger'. It is not clear in what way this provision relates to the right to adequate food or indeed the right to an adequate standard of living. The Committee, by the construction of its general guidelines, appears to consider that the elements of article 11(2) relate to the achievement of the right to food.[173] Indeed it draws no clear distinction between the right to food and the right to freedom from hunger (the latter notion not even being mentioned).

However, some members of the Committee do appear to recognize the existence of a distinction between the right to food and the right to freedom from hunger;[174] far from being synonymous concepts, the right to freedom from hunger is considered to be merely a 'sub-norm'. Whereas freedom from hunger implies freedom from starvation, or the fulfilment of basic needs necessary for survival, the right to food is a more extensive concept requiring a level and type of food that is consonant with human dignity.

---

[172] *See* UDHR, art. 25(1); Geneva Convention Relative to the Treatment of Prisoners of War (1949), arts. 26 and 51; Geneva Convention Relative to the Protection of Civilians in Time of War (1949), arts. 23 and 55; Protocol Additional to the Geneva Conventions of 12 Aug. 1949 and Relating to the Protection of Victims of International Armed Conflicts (Protocol I), arts. 54, 69, and 70; Protocol Additional to the Geneva Conventions of 12 Aug. 1949, and Relating to the Protection of Victims of Non-International Armed Conflicts, arts. 14 and 15.

[173] *See* Reporting guidelines, *supra*, n. 154, at 12–13.

[174] *See e.g.* Simma, E/C.12/1989/SR.20, at 7, para. 26.

One reason for maintaining a distinction between freedom from hunger and the right to food is that the former is specifically referred to as 'fundamental'. No other right in either of the two Covenants is referred to in this manner. It has been suggested in the Committee that the term 'fundamental' implies that the State, assisted if necessary by the international community, has an obligation (of an immediate as opposed to a progressive nature) to avoid starvation. Further, as freedom from starvation is so closely linked to the right to life (as found in article 6 of the ICCPR), it should be respected under all circumstances.[175]

However, there are a number of arguments against giving the provision priority. First, despite the inclusion of the term 'fundamental', the *travaux préparatoires* do not demonstrate an intention to give the provision any form of priority.[176] Secondly, much as famines are often presented as essentially man-made phenomena, it is as yet unrealistic to consider the obligation to prevent starvation as one open to immediate implementation. Finally, it is legally incorrect to assume that a provision is non-derogable merely because it resembles a non-derogable right in another treaty.[177]

Thus, on a strictly legal level, although the right to freedom from hunger is said to be 'fundamental' there is little justification for interpreting it as having any form of priority over other rights. This does not mean, however, that the right is not important. Certainly, as commentators have pointed out, at one level at least, the right to food is a 'basic right' upon which the enjoyment of other rights depends. As Shue noted:

Any form of malnutrition, or fever due to exposure, that causes severe and irreversible brain damage, for example, can effectively prevent the exercise of any right requiring clear thought and may, like brain injuries caused by assault, profoundly disturb personality. And, obviously, any fatal deficiencies end all possibility of the enjoyment of rights as firmly as an arbitrary execution.[178]

It is clear that the fundamental nature of the right to freedom from hunger relates to its association with survival. In this sense it might be distinguished from a right to 'adequate food' that extends beyond basic needs. The term 'fundamental' then, would appear to require that action taken towards the realization of the right to adequate food (in its widest sense) should be directed primarily towards the enjoyment of minimum levels of subsistence.

---

[175] *See* Dobbert (FAO), E/C.12/1989/SR.20, at 6, para. 18.

[176] *See above* text accompanying nn. 121–2.

[177] This matter is of little practical importance, however, given the lack of a derogation clause in the ICESCR.

[178] Shue H., *Basic Rights: Subsistence, Affluence and US Foreign Policy* (1980), 24–5. *See also* Konate, E/C.12/1989/SR.21, at 2, paras. 6–7. It was noted in the Committee that in 1982 the Human Rights Committee had expressed the link between the right to life and malnutrition in its general comment on art. 6. Eide, E/C.12/1989/SR.21, at 5. *See* HRC General Comment 6(16), UN Doc. A/37/40, at 93 (1982).

In other words, action should be prioritized in favour of the realization of the 'minimum core-content' of the right to food.[179]

3 The Meaning of 'Adequate Food'

As has been implied above,[180] the right to adequate food would seem to extend beyond that which is required for survival. Some commentators have suggested that adequacy should be measured not merely by what is necessary for survival, but by a person's health or by their ability to pursue a normal, active existence.[181] It is clear, however, that whatever criterion against which adequacy is to be measured will itself have to be defined. For example, the notion of 'health' as a reference criterion 'is limited by our inability to define a state of health which an adequate nutrient intake should sustain'.[182]

In addition to the quantitative sufficiency of the food supply, it has also been considered that the notion of adequacy introduces a qualitative element,[183] namely that food should be culturally acceptable and healthy (or in other words, safe).[184] An effort has thus been made to endow the concept of adequate food with a broad definition that extends beyond merely an analysis of calorific intake. Accordingly, the mere presence or absence of malnutrition would not in itself be the sole determinant of whether a State was complying with its obligations.

In its guidelines, the Committee has not attempted to define what it considers to be adequate food. It requests States merely to provide information about the extent to which the right to adequate food has been realized.[185] It could be assumed, then, that it expects States to form their own national benchmarks of what amounts to 'adequate food'.[186] The Committee does, however, refer to 'malnutrition' which would seem to suggest that it understands the concept of adequate food to mean more than mere freedom from starvation.[187] Committee members themselves have frequently looked to measures of calorie intake as a means of assessing the adequacy of the food supply.[188] In doing so they have often requested

---

[179] *See above* Ch. 3, text accompanying nn. 212–26.

[180] *See above* text accompanying n. 174.

[181] Alston, *supra*, n. 1, at 22–3. Similar criteria are often used as definitions of malnutrition.

[182] Pacey A. and Payne P., *Agricultural Development and Nutrition* (1985), at 23.

[183] It should be noted that this 'qualitative' and 'quantitative' distinction is not entirely watertight. The concept of adequate food for the maintainance of health not only requires a minimum calorific intake but also a certain balance of nutrients.

[184] Alston, *supra*, n. 1, at 33; Eide, E/C.12/1989/SR.21, at 6, para. 18; Eide A., *Right to Adequate Food as a Human Right* (1989), 27.

[185] Reporting guidelines, *supra*, n. 154, at 12.

[186] *See e.g.* Muterahejuru, E/C.12/1989/SR.17, at 16, para. 86.

[187] Reporting guidelines, *supra*, n. 154, at 12.

[188] *See e.g.* Neneman, E/C.12/1988/SR.6, at 4, para. 22.

disaggregated statistics according to vulnerable groups and individuals.[189] In particular, concern has often been expressed about declines in the average calorie intake over a period of time,[190] and occasionally in cases where the calorie intake seems excessively high.[191]

Despite considerable agreement during the Committee's general discussion[192] that 'the right to receive food was not simply a question of calories but adequate nutrition',[193] Committee members seem to have concentrated rather heavily on calorific intake as a measure of adequate food. Such an approach may be subject to criticism. First, it has been pointed out that estimates of calorific intake suffer from personal, inter-personal, and inter-temporal variations as measures of food adequacy.[194] Secondly, calorific intake may give an indication of 'undernourishment' (defined as an inadequate intake of calories), but is insufficient as a measure of 'malnourishment' which is defined more widely as a lack of essential nutrients (such as vitamins),[195] and wholly fails to accommodate a wider sense of food 'adequacy' that might be seen as relating to individual capabilities.[196]

That Committee members have only rarely requested information about the nutritional status of the population,[197] or about food quality and safety,[198] may be criticized as being unduly cautious. However, the Committee does face considerable problems in assessing the level of enjoyment of the right to food even in so far as it relates merely to malnutrition. Whereas a consumption survey would be the ideal method, it poses prohibitive logistical and financial obstacles.[199] Physical indicators of health are thought to offer 'much promise' as measurements of malnutrition,[200] but even here there are difficulties in establishing that a restricted food intake is entirely responsible for the apparent health problems. It is clear that whatever form of measurement is adopted, it is likely to display only a 'probabilistic picture' of nutritional deprivation.[201]

---

[189] *See e.g.* Alston, E/C.12/1988/SR.10, at 11, para. 59. *See also* Eide, E/C.12/1989/SR.20, at 11, para. 46.

[190] *See e.g.* Neneman, E/C.12/1988/SR. 17, at 4, para. 25; Simma, E/C.12/1989/SR.6, at 10, para. 47; Neneman, E/C.12/1988/SR.12, at 11, para. 55.

[191] *See e.g.* Alston, E/C.12/1988/SR.18, at 2, para. 3.

[192] *See generally* UN Doc. E/1989/22, at 68–72, paras. 310–26 (1989).

[193] *Ibid.* 71, para. 320. *Cf.* Simma, E/C.12/1989/SR.20, at 7, para. 26.

[194] Drèze J. and Sen A., *Hunger and Public Action* (1989), 37–41.

[195] Huddleston B., 'Approaches to Quantifying the World Food Problem', in Clay E. and Shaw J. (eds.), *Poverty, Development and Food* (1987), 1 at 11.

[196] *See above* text accompanying nn. 181–2.

[197] *See e.g.* Texier, E/C.12/1989/SR.9, at 7, para. 30; Neneman, E/C.12/1989/SR.20, at 8, para. 34.

[198] *See e.g.* Taya, E/C.12/1988/SR.8, at 6, para. 26; Simma, E/C.12/1989/SR.16, at 18, para. 95; Alvarez Vita, E/C.12/1987/SR.19, at 13, para. 69.

[199] Huddleston, *supra*, n. 195, at 10.   [200] *Ibid.* 11.

[201] *See* Drèze and Sen, *supra*, n. 194, at 41.

4 The Realization of the Right to Food

Article 11(1) makes reference to the obligation of States to 'take appropriate steps to ensure the realization', *inter alia*, of the right to food, while recognizing 'the essential importance of international co-operation based on free consent'. This seems to parallel the obligation in article 2(1) with the exception of the use of the word 'ensure'. As was apparent in the drafting of the Covenant, there was no clear intention to oblige States to achieve the realization of the rights in article 11 immediately.[202] Unsurprisingly the Committee has taken a similar viewpoint. In its guidelines the Committee specifically asks for information on the extent to which the right to adequate food has been realized in that country—the implication being that it is acceptable for full realization not to have been achieved for the time being.[203]

The modalities of implementation were debated in the Committee's general discussion on the right to food. The report of the discussion states:

Some members of the Committee considered that every country should take immediate steps to ensure the realization of the right to food; that ultimate realization at the fullest acceptable level may in the circumstances of some countries be achieved progressively but the national and international obligations arising under the Covenant meant that with co-ordinated efforts a meaningful start could be made immediately in all States, whilst it was generally agreed that the primary responsibility for ensuring the right to food rested with the individual.[204]

Although only being the opinion of 'some members', the form of obligation underlined here largely conforms to the Committee's general approach with respect to article 2(1).[205] One interesting point, however, is the statement that the 'primary responsibility' for ensuring the right to food lay with the individual. Although individuals are certainly responsible for buying or growing food for themselves and their families under normal conditions, to say that they have 'primary responsibility' in times of famine is to understate the State's obligations with respect to food.

It is considered that the Committee members intended to stress the importance of individual access to food rather than the provision of food by the State. As the general discussion shows, '[i]t was generally agreed that the right to food was much more extensive than the right to stand in line for food'.[206] The role of the State, then, is one of ensuring that the external conditions are such that individuals have the ability to feed themselves.[207] In

---

[202] *See above* text accompanying nn. 80–4.
[203] Reporting guidelines, *supra*, n. 154, at 99.
[204] General discussion, *supra*, n. 192, at 71, para. 321.   [205] *See above*, Ch. 3.
[206] General discussion, *supra*, n. 192, at 71, para. 320.
[207] *See* Tomasevski K., 'Human Rights: The Right to Food' (1985) 70 *Iowa LR* 1321, at 1325. As Christensen comments: 'the emphasis lies, *not* on 'feeding' or 'maintaining' people, but on creating a social and economic environment which fosters development and hence need not depend upon charity': Christensen C., *The Right to Food: How to Guarantee* (1978), at 33.

particular it might be said that the principal State obligation 'is not, at least initially, to give food to others. Instead, it is a duty not to restrict unduly the right of others to obtain an adequate diet'.[208]

People's access to food quite clearly depends upon a number of factors relating to their own social and economic situation (such as their income) and upon 'external' factors such as the availability of necessary foodstuffs and their prices. One well-known approach has been to assess a person's command over food through an analysis of his or her 'entitlements'.[209] Members of the Committee have rightly recognized the importance here of income,[210] especially as it might be secured through the rights to work and to social security.[211] However, in the case of small food producers (who are particularly vulnerable to famine), access to food is more closely related to trade-based and production-based considerations (such as a decline in crop yield).[212] In those circumstances, indicators relating to work, to income, or social security are not likely to provide a sufficient indication of access to food.[213] In so far as the individual's access to food is dependant upon his or her control over resources, there is clearly a need for decisions, strategies, and policies affecting resources to be taken with the active participation of those affected.[214] As has been noted in the Committee, the realization of the right to food is thus also dependent upon participatory rights such as the right to organize[215] and the right to self-determination.[216]

In the context of malnutrition, however, commentators have gone considerably further in linking the right to food with a whole range of other rights.[217] In particular, it has been commented that 'a person's capability to avoid undernourishment may depend not merely on his or her intake of food, but also on the person's access to health care, medical facilities, elementary education, drinking water, and sanitary facilities'.[218] The fulfilment of other basic needs would also seem to be necessary in order to

---

[208] Brockett C., 'The Right to Food and United States Policy in Guatemala' (1984) 6 *Hum. Rts. Q* 366, at 367.

[209] Sen A., *Poverty and Famines: An Essay on Entitlements and Deprivation* (1981). Sen identifies four categories of entitlements: trade-based, production-based, own-labour based, and inheritance and transfer entitlements. A person may be reduced to starvation by failures in either the endowment component (i.e. crop failure) or in the exchange component (i.e. food price rise) of these entitlements (at 2–8). The benefit of such an approach is that it concentrates on individual demand for food rather than just its supply, and may explain famines which occur during 'boom' periods. For criticisms of this approach, *see* Devereux S., *Theories of Famines* (1993), 76–81.

[210] *See e.g.* Neneman, E/C.12/1989/SR.20, at 9, para. 36.

[211] *See e.g.* Simma, E/C.12/1989/SR.20, at 7, para. 26.

[212] *See* Devereux, *supra*, n. 209, at 74–6.

[213] *See* Alston, *supra*, n. 1, at 17; Kassahun Y., 'The Food Questions Within the Prism of International law of Development' (1985) 38 *Oklahoma LR* 863, at 882.

[214] Devereux, *supra*, n. 209, at 80–1.

[215] This would seem to be the case particularly in respect to agricultural workers.

[216] *See e.g.* Simma, E/C.12/1989/SR.20, at 7, para. 26.

[217] Alston, *supra*, n. 1, at 10. *See also* Tomasevski, *supra*, n. 207, at 1324–5.

[218] Drèze and Sen, *supra*, n. 194, at 13.

realize the right to food not only because of the physiological interrelationships between them (for example, between health and nutrition[219]) but
because they are mutually interdependent for their realization.[220] This
has led one commentator to the conclusion that 'a compartmentalised
approach to the right to food is both empirically unworkable and theoretically unacceptable'.[221]

The recognition of an interlinkage between the right to food and other
rights is inevitable given the impracticability of assessing the enjoyment of
the right to food without taking into consideration the enjoyment of other
rights (such as the right to work or social security). It may, however, lead to
the conclusion that the enjoyment of the right to food is entirely dependent
upon the enjoyment of other rights and therefore need not be referred to
directly itself. There is some evidence that the Committee has taken such an
approach. Although the guidelines require the same information to be
provided by every State, the Committee has generally only concentrated on
the question of the right to food in relation to poorer developing countries.[222] With regard to the more wealthy States, the Committee seems to
concentrate on the questions of employment, income, and social security,
reflecting the assumption that if these rights are fully provided for, the
individual will have no problem with access to food. Thus, no questions
were asked about the right to food in the consideration of the report of
Luxembourg,[223] and even in the case of Costa Rica, few direct questions
were asked.[224] The margin of discretion given to such States seems to reflect
the assertions of many Western States which maintain that the central
problem relating to food in those countries is over-consumption rather than
under-consumption.[225] In those States, efforts are concentrated on encour-

---

[219] Christensen cites a number of examples of the interdependence between food and
health: physical and mental health depend upon adequate nutrition (especially in the case of
children); malnourished adults have a greater susceptibility to disease; illness diminishes the
physiological benefits of 'adequate' food supplies, may increase the body's nutrient requirements, and may deplete the body's nutrient supply. Christensen, *supra*, n. 207, at 31–2.

[220] Lustig comments e.g. that households would not necessarily use the extra income (that
was intended for food) to eliminate malnutrition, but to fulfil other subsistence needs. Lustig
N., 'Direct and Indirect Measures to Ensure Access to Food Supplies' in *World Food Security:
Selected Themes and Issues* (1985), 38 at 46.

[221] Alston, *supra*, n. 1, at 19. Christensen gives three supporting arguments: 'First, there are
physiological interrelationships which limit the effectiveness of efforts that fulfill only one
physical need while bypassing others. Second, a right to food may be more sustainable if it is
part of a 'package' of subsistence rights which provides minimal guarantees of economic
security. Third, common duties are associated with the provision of all subsistence rights.
Violations of one right are likely to generate difficulties with regard to others as well':
Christensen, *supra*, n. 207, at 31.

[222] One notable exception was the case of Canada in which the Committee extensively
considered the question of access to food. Some responsibility for this may be put down to the
forceful intervention of a NGO.

[223] *See* E/C.12/1990/SR.33–6.   [224] *See* E/C.12/1990/SR.38, 40, 41, and 43.

[225] *See e.g.* Steel (UK), E/C.12/1989/SR.16, at 9, para. 43; Walkate (Netherlands), E/C.12/

aging people to eat more healthily, through *inter alia* the provision of public information as to diets and fitness regimes.[226] Unfortunately, beyond the requirement that States disseminate knowledge of the principles of nutrition, the Committee has not developed an understanding of the manner in which the right to food applies to wealthy States with well-developed social security systems.

In its general approach to the realization of rights in the Covenant, the Committee looks in particular at the legal regulation of the rights and the degree to which monitoring and targeted policy-making has been undertaken.[227] These matters will be considered individually in the context of the right to food.

(a) Legal Regulation

Although it is not immediately clear how a legal system may affect an individual's access to food, it is apparent that a number of States do recognize a right to food in their constitutions.[228] In addition, those States that have adopted or incorporated the Covenant into their domestic law will also have an expression of the right in their legal systems.[229] These moves find support with a number of commentators who consider that the most effective or direct route to secure the right to food is through constitutional enactment or specific legislation.[230]

This approach has not been evident in the work of the Committee. There, the role of law in the realization of that right has been given a relatively low profile. In contrast to the right to housing, the guidelines do not ask for detailed information on legal provisions that may affect a person's access to food,[231] and only occasionally has the matter been raised at all.[232] A lack of concern with the role of law in the realization of the right to food is also reflected in the State reports. For example, it was noted in the UK report to the Committee that 'there are no laws, regulations or agreements, nor court

---

1989/SR.14, at 9, para. 36. It has been maintained, however, that inadequate food remains a problem in Canada, *see* Concluding observations on report of Canada, E/C.12/1993/5, at 3, para. 16. *See generally* Robertson R., 'The Right to Food: Canada's Broken Covenant' (1989–90) 6 *Can. HRY* 185, at 191–4.

[226] *See e.g.* Opdahl (Norway), E/C.12/1988/SR.15, at 6, para. 22; Willers (FRG), E/C.12/1987/SR.20, at 10, para. 41.

[227] *See above* Ch. 3, text accompanying nn. 61–78.

[228] *See e.g.* Ecuador, UN Doc. E/1986/3/Add. 14, at 11, para. 55 (1986); Netherlands, UN Doc. E/1986/4/Add. 24, at 1, para. 2 (1986). Ganji cites in addition: Pakistan, Turkey, Uruguay, and Yemen. Ganji M., 'The Realization of Economic, Social and Cultural Rights: Problems and Perspectives', UN Docs. E/CN.4/1108/Rev. 1, and E/CN.4/1131/Rev. 1, at 16 (1975).

[229] On the incorporation of the Covenant into Domestic law, *see generally* Craven M., 'The Domestic Applicability of the International Covenant on Economic, Social and Cultural Rights' (1993) 40 *Neth. ILR* 367.

[230] *See e.g.* Alston, *supra*, n. 1, at 16; Robertson, *supra*, n. 225, at 215.

[231] *See* Reporting guidelines, *supra*, n. 154, at 12.

[232] E/C.12/WG/1991/CRP.2, at 3, para. 22.

decisions bearing on the right of everyone to adequate food in the United Kingdom'.[233]

It is considered that the Committee is wrong to overlook the relationship between law and the realization of the right to food. Even in the absence of a specific legal recognition of a right to food, it is clear that the legal framework will condition the access of individuals and groups to the resources necessary to feed themselves.[234] As has been noted in the context of famines:

> The legal system that precedes and survives through the famine may not, in itself, be a particularly cruel one. The standardly accepted rights of ownership and exchange are not . . . authoritarian extravaganzas . . . [t]hey are, rather, parts of the standard legal rules of ownership and exchange that govern people's lives in much of the world. But when they are not supplemented by other rights (e.g. social security, unemployment insurance, public health provisions), these standard rights may operate in a way that offers no chance of survival.[235]

According to the general requirements for the implementation of the Covenant, States are obliged to ensure that no laws or regulations exist which operate to deprive people of their rights in the Covenant.[236] This would be clear in cases where, for example, a State discriminated against certain groups as regards access to State-subsidized food. Greater attention, however, needs to be paid to cases where the existing system of exchange and ownership serves to impede the access of individuals to adequate food.[237]

(b) Monitoring Malnutrition

As outlined in its general comment, the Committee has placed considerable emphasis on the importance of monitoring the extent of realization of the rights.[238] Thus in its reporting guidelines it requests States to provide information on the general realization of the right to food with reference to sources 'including nutritional surveys and other monitoring arrangements'.[239] In addition it asks for information about the extent of hunger and malnutrition in the country concerned, with specific reference to the situation of vulnerable and disadvantaged groups, and for the establishment of time-related goals and nutritional bench-marks for measuring achievements in guaranteeing access to food by vulnerable groups and sectors or within worse-off regions.[240] Individual members of the Committee have

---

[233] UN Doc. E/1980/6/Add.16, at 2 (1980).   [234] *See* Alston, *supra*, n. 1, at 16.

[235] Drèze and Sen, *supra*, n. 194, at 23.

[236] *See above* Ch. 3, text accompanying nn. 16–21.

[237] For an analysis of the influence of land law on the right to food, *see* Plant R., 'The Right to Food and Agrarian Systems: Law and Practice in Latin America' in Alston P. and Tomasevski K. (eds.), *The Right to Food* (1984), 187.

[238] General Comment No. 1, UN ESCOR, Supp. (No. 4), Annex III, at 88, para. 3, UN Doc. E/1989/22 (1989). *Cf. also* Eide, *supra*, n. 184, at 51, paras. 257–61.

[239] Reporting guidelines, *supra*, n. 154, at 12.   [240] *Ibid.*

consistently asked for information on the incidence of hunger and malnutrition[241] and their possible causes.[242] Despite the general tendency to ignore the food situation in developed countries,[243] members have occasionally insisted upon the need for monitoring such countries to ensure that there was no significant amount of malnutrition, and have criticized States where they have failed to do so.[244]

As noted above, nowhere does the Committee define what it means by either 'adequate food' or 'malnutrition', nor does it request specific indicators.[245] It is assumed that in the process of monitoring and evaluation States will have to define these matters for themselves. Currently, the statistical information provided to the Committee by States is partial and generalized, indicating no regular pattern of monitoring. In its discussion on the use of indicators, there would appear to be an intention on the part of the Committee to establish a list of indicators that should be utilized in monitoring.[246] It is submitted that this would considerably increase the Committee's control and supervision of State compliance with their obligations.

(c) *Vulnerable Groups*

The guidelines require States to provide information on the extent of hunger and malnutrition in that country with particular reference to the vulnerable or disadvantaged groups in society. It stipulates that information should at least cover the position of landless peasants, marginalized peasants, rural workers, rural unemployed, urban unemployed, urban poor, migrant workers, indigenous populations, children, elderly people, and other 'especially affected groups'. It should also address whether there is any significant difference in the situation of men and women in the above groups, and requires information about changes over the past five years for each group.[247] This general concern for vulnerable and disadvantaged groups has been reflected in the questions of the pre-sessional working group.[248] In addition, members of the Committee have looked at the disparities in the relative positions of those in rural and in urban districts.[249]

In so far as the effectiveness of the guidelines has not truly been tested, it is as yet too early to say whether States will be able or willing to provide the amount of disaggregated data required by the Committee. Thus far,

---

[241] *See e.g.* Alston, E/C.12/1988/SR.17, at 8, para. 46; Alston, E/C.12/1988/SR.10, at 5, para. 19; Texier, E/C.12/1990/SR.2, at 9, para. 55; Alston, E/C.12/1990/SR.2, at 10, para. 64.

[242] *See e.g.* Alston, E/C.12/1988/SR.17, at 8, para. 46.

[243] *See above* text accompanying nn. 223–6.

[244] *See e.g.* Concluding observations of report of New Zealand, E/C.12/1993/13, at 3, para. 15.

[245] *See above* text accompanying nn. 185–8.

[246] *See* General Discussion, *supra*, n. 192.

[247] Reporting guidelines, *supra*, n. 154, at 12.

[248] E/C. 12/WG/1991/CRP.1, at 4, para. 24(a); E/C.12/WG/1991/CRP. 4, at 6, para. 37.

[249] *See* Alston, E/C.12/1987/SR.22, at 6, para. 21; E/C.12/WG/1991/CRP. 4, at 6, para. 36.

States have rarely volunteered information on the position of particular disadvantaged groups. The statistical information provided generally relates to the aggregate position of the population as a whole. It is important to note, however, that the emphasis on vulnerable groups is of primary importance for the adoption of targeted and considered policies. It will not necessarily be the case that all the specified groups will have insufficient access to food. What is important, however, is that the State identify those groups in society that are vulnerable in this respect.

5 Specific State Obligations

Although article 11 as a whole was intended to be governed by the general obligation clauses in article 2(1), under which States parties are obliged to take steps to achieve progressively the full realization of the rights,[250] it was decided nevertheless to include certain specific obligations in article 11(2) relating to the right to food. Those obligations were not intended to detract from the general State obligations found in article 2(1), but merely provided a more detailed outline of the measures to be taken and the objectives to be achieved in the context of the right to food. However, as a result of the uneven, over-hasty, and badly co-ordinated drafting process, article 11(2) appears to be a 'relatively confused and by no means all-embracing mixture of means and ends'.[251] Three objectives seem to be specifically outlined, namely to improve methods of production, conservation, and distribution of food, to achieve the most efficient development and utilization of natural resources,[252] and to ensure an equitable distribution of world food supplies in relation to need.[253] Whereas the first two objectives are national ones, the third relates to the international plane.[254]

States are under an obligation to take the necessary measures and programmes, both individually and through international co-operation, to achieve these objectives. Specifically however, with respect to the two national objectives (in article 11(2)(a)), States should make full use of technical and scientific knowledge, disseminate knowledge of the principles of nutrition, and develop or reform their agrarian systems. Given the general obligation to take the necessary measures to achieve the stated objectives, there is no reason to consider that the measures specifically enumerated are exhaustive.[255]

---

[250] *See above* text accompanying nn. 80–4.　　　　[251] Alston, *supra*, n. 1, at 34.

[252] Art. 11(2)(a).　　　　[253] Art. 11(2)(b).

[254] Kassahun, however, reads sub-paras. (a) and (b) together. He argues that the objectives in sub-para. (a) are to be read in the light of the limits imposed by the problems of food-importing and food-exporting States, and comes to the conclusion that 'the formulation of art. 11 appears to maintain the *status quo* in terms of food production'. Kassahun, *supra*, n. 213, at 888.

[255] *See* Alston, *supra*, n. 1, at 34.

It is unclear whether the specified measures are intended to relate to the right to food as a whole, or merely to the right to be free from hunger. However, on the basis that the right to be free from hunger acts as a 'sub-norm' of the right to food as a whole, progress made in achieving the subsidiary ends in article 11(2) must always be judged against the objective of realizing everyone's right to adequate food and ultimately their right to an adequate standard of living.[256] It would not be sufficient, for example, to argue that agrarian reform was not necessary merely because no-one was dying of hunger.

(a) The Subsidiary Objectives

In dealing with the questions of production, conservation, and distribution, the Committee seems to confine itself to assessing the degree of realization of the right to food and ensuring that a policy has been adopted to alleviate the position of the poor and disadvantaged.[527] It has not entered into an analysis of the relative merits of the programmes undertaken, nor has it undertaken to make recommendations as to specific courses of action even on a State-by-State basis.

(i) *Production*. In order for everyone to have adequate supplies of food, it is clear that food production should be increased to keep pace with population growth.[258] Although article 11(2) speaks of an improvement in 'methods' of production, rather than an increase in production itself, it would seem obvious that the provision was intended to be directed towards the latter concern. The Committee's guidelines do nothing to resolve this question and make rather a bland reference to the objective in asking what measures had been taken to improve methods of food production.[259]

There are clearly a great number of ways in which food production may be increased and improved, such as through improving access to agricultural inputs (high yield crops, fertilisers, pesticides, and machinery), increasing the area of arable land, providing farmers and fishermen with incentives for production, undertaking soil conservation and improve-

---

[256] *Ibid.*

[257] Reporting guidelines, *supra*, n. 154, at 12; Fofana, E/C.12/1991/SR.7, at 13, para. 54.

[258] In areas such as sub-Saharan Africa, the population growth and increasing urbanization have placed considerable strain on food resources to the extent that an increase in food production is vital. *See e.g.* Christensen C. and Hanrahan C., 'African Food Crisis: Short-, Medium-, and Long-Term Responses' (1985) 70 *Iowa LR* 1293, at 1294–5; Kumar G., 'Ethiopian Famines 1973–1985: A Case Study' *WIDER Working Paper No. 26* (1987); Green R., 'Sub-Saharan Africa: Poverty of Development, Development of Poverty' in Clay E. and Shaw J. (eds.), *Poverty Development and Food* (1987), 78, at 87–8. However, for the view that access to food is one of distribution not production, *see* George S., *How the Other Half Dies* (1986), 53–68; Devereux, *supra*, n. 209, at 57–63.

[259] Reporting guidelines, *supra*, n. 154, at 12.

ment, and increasing agricultural research and the transfer of technology,[260] to name but a few.[261] Clearly, the measures taken will depend upon the agricultural and economic situation in the country concerned.

Members of the Committee have rarely entered into a discussion of the policies pursued in this direction and have generally looked only to the existence of such policies.[262] Occasionally comments have been made about the type of policy undertaken. One member, for example, argued that large-scale State food subsidies often led to insufficiently profitable output and hence to lower food production and that it was therefore essential to provide sufficient incentives to make food production profitable, thus ensuring that there was enough food on the market.[263] However in no way can it be presumed that the Committee has formulated any coherent policy in this regard.

In terms of food production it has often been considered that States should have as their objective food self-sufficiency. It is clear that a number of States have set food self-sufficiency as a target for achieving the realiz-ation of the right to food and, to a large extent, members of the Committee have endorsed such an objective.[264] The Committee has not gone so far as to analyse whether 'self-sufficiency' in terms of producing all the food for domestic consumption is a realistic or indeed a desirable proposition. Indi-vidual members of the Committee have occasionally noted that, given their dependence on international trade, poorer agricultural countries were of-ten unable to ensure self-sufficiency,[265] and that it would at any rate involve a certain amount of agricultural protectionism.[266] Indeed it is not at all clear that food self-sufficiency would necessarily guarantee food security given the vulnerability of some developing economies to domestic surpluses and deficits.[267] In fact a great number of States that are not self-sufficient do not suffer from serious food shortages. This has led some to argue that food 'self-reliance' (which involves the import of a cerain amount of food to be paid for by exports) through diversification is a more stable and effective method of securing sustained access to food for all.[268] Although self-reliance would generally appear to be a more realistic objective, as one com-mentator has noted, 'political uncertainties are such that preferring imports

---

[260] See Boerma A., A Right to Food (1976), 87–97.

[261] See Huddleston, supra, n. 195, at 18; Christensen, supra, n. 207, at 6–17.

[262] See e.g. Badawi El Sheikh, E/C.12/1988/SR.5, at 4, para. 15; Texier, E/C.12/1989/SR.5, at 9, para. 50; E/C.12/WG/1991/CRP. 2, at 3 para. 23.

[263] See Neneman, E/C.12/1989/SR.20, at 9, para. 35.

[264] See e.g. Alston, E/C.12/1988/SR.17, at 8, para. 46; Muterahejuru, E/C.12/1989/SR.6, at 12, para. 60; Dobbert (FAO), E/C.12/1989/SR.21, at 10, para. 41.

[265] See Muterahejuru, E/C.12/1989/SR.21, at 2, para. 4.   [266] Ibid. para. 1.

[267] Mangahas M., 'Relative Emphasis on Food Self-Sufficiency and Trade-Oriented Self-Reliance', World Food Security: Selected Themes and Issues (1985), 1 at 16.

[268] Ibid. 13; Drèze and Sen, supra, n. 194, at 165–76.

of food over unstable local production merely exchanges one set of vulnerabilities and risks for another'.[269]

Whereas the availability of sufficient food resources is clearly important, it is by no means clear that alone it is enough to guarantee access to food. As one member rightly pointed out 'it was not unusual for individuals to go hungry even though food production was high'.[270] The essential question is the extent to which an individual has an adequate 'command' over food, which has to be assessed through an analysis of both the supply and consumption of food.[271]

(ii) *Conservation.* The term 'conservation' in the context of article 11(2)(a) is specifically confined to the preservation of foodstuffs before they reach the market place. The term seems to have been included to remedy the problem of loss and deterioration of food that has been particularly apparent in developing countries.[272] Although given a passing comment in the Committee's guidelines, the issue of conservation of foodstuffs has not been the subject of any specific comment by the Committee or individual members. Given the role that conservation could have in increasing food self-reliance (by decreasing the need for food imports), in improving nutritional standards (by preventing nutritional deterioration), and in contributing to the effective use of human and physical resources, it would surely be worth more detailed consideration.

(iii) *Distribution.* The term 'distribution' in article 11(2)(a) would seem to relate to the distribution of food within the territorial limits of each country in contrast with article 11(2)(b) which refers primarily to international distribution. The area of State action covered by the term 'distribution' would seem to include marketing arrangements (such as the transport infrastructure[273]), price controls, rationing, food subsidies,[274] and direct food or cash relief. Clearly the objective of 'improving' the distribution of food should be read in the light of the need to ensure access to food for everyone, and its effectiveness may ultimately be measured by consumption levels.

As with the question of production, the Committee has not endeavoured to discuss or analyse specific distributional methods, and clearly lacks the

---

[269] Devereux, *supra*, n. 209, at 167.

[270] Alston, E/C.12/1987/SR.12, at 9, para. 35. *See also* Drèze and Sen, *supra*, n. 194, at 27–8.

[271] Eide, *supra*, n. 184, at 27.

[272] *See* Dobbert J., 'The Right to Food', *Academie de Droit International, Colloque* (1978), 184, at 200.

[273] Kumar G., *Ethiopian Famines 1973–1985: A Case Study* (1987), 57.

[274] The World Bank notes that a number of forms of food subsidy are used by developing countries including: general food price subsidies, food rations, food stamps, food distribution policies, and food supplementation schemes. IBRD, *supra*, n. 160, at 92–6.

necessary knowledge and technical expertise to do so. It has rather enquired how measures taken to improve distribution have 'contributed towards, or have impeded the realization of the right to adequate food'[275] particularly as regards vulnerable groups in society.[276]

(b) Development and Utilization of Natural Resources

Although the efficient development and utilization of natural resources appears to relate solely to agrarian development, commentators have generally considered that, despite the absence of a comma, it should be read to relate to the whole of article 11(2)(a).[277] The Committee appears to have adopted this interpretation in asking what effect the measures of implementation have had on the protection and conservation of food producing resources.[278] In addition, however, the Committee has laid an emphasis on the phrase that perhaps was not envisaged at the time of drafting. The drafters, in making reference to the development and utilization of natural resources, were arguably concerned merely that resources should be utilized to their maximum extent without unnecessary wastage. The Committee however, in line with more recent environmental awareness, has stressed 'ecological sustainability' and the 'protection and conservation of food producing resources'.[279] At a very general level, the Committee seems to be concerned that the utilization of natural resources should be consistent with their future, long-term, sustainability.[280]

In its questions to States, however, the Committee has not pursued such environmental issues. It would be open for the Committee to enquire into action being taken to ensure that such concerns enter into the planning debate, particularly as regards the regeneration of living resources, the productivity of soils (including action to combat desertification), the effective use of water resources, and the control of silviculture.[281]

---

[275] Reporting guidelines, *supra*, n. 154, at 12.

[276] E/C.12/WG/1991/CRP. 2, at 3, para. 23.

[277] Dobbert considers that this is the necessary implication of a teleological interpretation given that the development and utilization of natural resources are a concomitant of methods of production, distribution, and conservation of food. Dobbert, *supra*, n. 272, at 193. *See also* Alston, *supra*, n. 1, at 35.

[278] Reporting guidelines, *supra*, n. 154, at 12.

[279] *Cf.* Declaration of the United Nations Conference on the Human Environment, Stockholm 1972, 11 ILM 1416 (1972). Principle 13 states: 'In order to achieve a more rational management of resources and thus to improve the environment, States should adopt an integrated and co-ordinated approach to their development planning so as to ensure that development is compatible with the need to protect and improve the environment for the benefit of their population.'

[280] For the notion of sustainable development, *see* World Bank (BRD), *World Development Report* (1992); Brundtland Commission, *Our Common Future* (Oxford: Oxford University Press, 1987).

[281] The clearance of forest land for agricultural purposes perhaps illustrates most poignantly the competing concerns of food production and environmental protection. In many such cases

6 Specified Measures

(a) Science and Technology

Scant mention is made within the Committee of the requirement that 'full use' be made of 'technical and scientific knowledge'. It has been given a passing reference in the guidelines and has only rarely been mentioned by members of the Committee.[282] While the provision would appear to require, at minimum, the institution of national education and training programmes and research to engender the effective utilization of existing expertise, it has been noted that the provision could also be seen to have an international dimension.[283] Specifically, it might be interpreted as obliging States to co-operate internationally in the dissemination of such knowledge, whether through the auspices of the FAO or through the transfer of technology to developing countries.[284]

(b) Principles of Nutrition

The requirement in article 11(2)(a) that States 'disseminate knowledge of the principles of nutrition' has been expressly taken up by the Committee in its guidelines.[285] In addition, the Committee requests information on whether 'any significant groups or sectors within society seem to lack such knowledge'.[286] This would seem to be principally an educational objective aimed at enabling people to feed themselves in a healthy manner. Members of the Committee have taken up such educational questions particularly with regard to developed countries, where problems often relate to over-consumption.

A related field, not directly covered by the express terms of the Covenant, is the establishment and enforcement of food standards.[287] It is clear that there is a considerable potential State role in ensuring food safety. Legislative standards could be enacted to ensure that food production and marketing are undertaken in a safe and healthy manner, and that the food available is free from adverse alien substances.[288] Moreover, a system of inspection and control could be established at the national level to enforce such standards. Although the Covenant makes no reference to food quality, or measures to control it, it would be natural to infer from the concept of 'adequate food' a qualitative element. Similarly, it is clear that the measures

---

it would seem that the short-term benefits of increased food-production are outweighed by the far more drastic environmental problems that ensue.

[282] *See e.g.* Muterahejuru, E/C.12/1988/SR.17, at 6, para. 34.

[283] There are, however, objections to importing into a provision that deals primarily with national obligations that operate on the international level.

[284] Dobbert, *supra*, n. 272, at 196–7.   [285] Reporting guidelines, *supra*, n. 154, at 13.

[286] *Ibid.*   [287] *See* Dobbert, *supra*, n. 272, at 198–200.

[288] *See* Eide, *supra*, n. 184, at 27, para. 133. On the international plane *cf.* FAO/WHO Codex Alimentarius Commission.

envisaged in article 11(2) are not exhaustive and therefore could not be said to exclude an obligation to take action as regards food quality. Unfortunately, although a number of members have made reference to food quality issues, the Committee as a whole has not taken up this question in any coherent manner.

(c) *Agrarian Reform*

According to the *travaux préparatoires*, it was not intended that every State should undertake a programme of agrarian reform, but only in cases where the existing land tenure system required it.[289] For those States that did not need to undertake agrarian reform, it seems to have been considered that they should nevertheless 'develop' their agrarian systems. This distinction is not immediately apparent in the Committee's guidelines; no mention is made of the development of agrarian systems—merely their reform. Although it might be inferred that all countries are required to reform their agrarian systems to ensure the right to food, such a conclusion would be unreasonable. What the Committee has to establish is an idea of the type of agrarian system that is adequate from the point of view of realizing the right to food.

Some Committee members do seem to have been concerned with attempting to evaluate whether or not agrarian reform is necessary. Principally they have directed their attention towards the existing system of land tenure and the number of peasant farmers without their own land.[290] Although it has been asserted that any developing country which has not carried out agrarian reform would automatically be considered to have violated the Covenant,[291] there have been no occasions in which members have expressly stated that land reform is necessary.

The purpose of agrarian reform in the context of the right to food is not always clear. The *travaux préparatoires* make clear that it was deemed necessary to improve the utilization of agricultural resources.[292] More indirectly, however, existing inequalities in land distribution can contribute to social marginalization, poverty, unemployment, homelessness, and may increase rural–urban migration. Given that malnutrition (and even starvation) have significant links with poverty, all these factors would have significant effects on the enjoyment of the right to food.

The Committee, in its guidelines, requests information on the measures of agrarian reform that have been taken to ensure that 'the agrarian system is efficiently utilized in order to promote food security at household level

---

[289] *See above* text accompanying nn. 135–7.

[290] *See e.g.* Muterahejuru, E/C.12/1989/SR.9, at 6, para. 19; Fofana, E/C.12/1991/SR.7, at 13, para. 54.

[291] *See* Texier, E/C/.12/1990/SR.22, at 13, para. 81.

[292] *See above* text accompanying n. 130. For the utility of agrarian reform, *see* IBRD, *supra*, n. 160, at 64–6; Brockett, *supra*, n. 208, at 369; McChesney, *supra*, n. 164, at 315.

without negatively affecting human dignity both in rural and urban settings taking into account articles 6 and 8 of the Covenant'.[293] In addition, it wishes to know what measures have been taken to legislate, enforce, and to monitor in this regard.[294] The Committee quite rightly appears to consider that agrarian reform is only relevant in so far as it is related to the enjoyment of the right to food—it is not sufficient on its own. As one Committee member commented, 'agrarian reform might be sweeping yet result in severe deprivation of food for a significant part of the population'.[295] In referring to human dignity (and particularly articles 6 and 8 of the Covenant), the Committee would seem to stress the necessity of ensuring access to food in a manner that does not conflict with the satisfaction of other rights or needs. As one study argues:

Food procurement should be possible for all without conflicting with the satisfaction of other material and non-material basic human needs. Otherwise food procurement may not be viable over time for the household concerned, whose members will choose their final strategies based on a range of priorities.[296]

While the reference to article 6 would seem to stress the need to ensure employment prospects in rural areas during reform, article 8 probably relates to the desirability of popular participation in rural development activities in general. As has been commented elsewhere:

Rural development strategies can realize their full potential only through the motivation, active involvement and organization at the grass-roots level of rural people, with special emphasis on the least advantaged, in conceptualizing and designing policies and programmes and in creating administrative, social and economic institutions, including cooperative and other voluntary forms of organization for implementing and evaluating them.[297]

Questions of individual members have occasionally centered upon the level of participation in measures designed to promote the right to adequate food,[298] but none have done so in relation to agricultural reform *per se*.

7 Article 11(2)(b)

Little comment has been made by the Committee on the purport of article 11(2)(b) which refers to the achievement of 'an equitable distribution of world food supplies in relation to need'. The guidelines blandly ask States to 'describe and evaluate' the measures taken to ensure an equitable

---

[293] Reporting guidelines, *supra*, n. 154, at 13.
[294] *Ibid*. On the importance of law in this area, *see* Plant, *supra*, n. 237, at 187.
[295] Alston, E/C.12/1987/SR.19, at 8, para. 43.   [296] Eide, *supra*, n. 184, at 27, para. 134.
[297] Programme of Action, World Conference on Agrarian Reform and Rural Development, Rome 12–20 July 1979. *See also* Alston, *supra*, n. 1, at 20.
[298] *See e.g.* Sparsis, E/C.12/1989/SR.7, at 2, para. 2; Simma, E/C.12/1989/SR.16, at 18, para 95.

distribution of world food supplies in relation to need.[299] It is unlikely that the Committee will receive any useful information until the text is explained, and the breadth of State obligations outlined. As was noted in the general discussion, paragraph 2(b) appeared to refer not only to programmes financed by voluntary funds but also to 'international commodity arrangements under the auspices of the Committee on Commodity Problems, consultations within the Sub-Committee on Surplus Disposal and even GATT or UNCTAD negotiations on agricultural commodities'.[300] The scope of article 11(2)(b) is potentially enormous.

The assumption of the Committee, and certain commentators, has been that sub-paragraph (a) deals with national obligations and sub-paragraph (b) with the relevant international measures that have to be taken in order to achieve the fulfilment of the right to be free from hunger (and more generally the right to food).[301] Although reference is made in sub-paragraph (b) to international problems and 'world' food supplies, there is no reason why the obligation to ensure an equitable distribution of food in relation to need should not also have a national element. As an objective, it applies equally well on the domestic level as on the international level. By the same token, the principle of international co-operation is to be found in the first paragraph of article 11(2) and should be read as applying to both sub-paragraphs.

Such an approach benefits from the fact that the reference to 'need' does not have to be interpreted in terms of 'State need' but more appropriately in terms of 'individual need'. This would conform more closely to the individual nature of human rights in general and avoid placing the 'State' in a duplicitous position as the agent for realization and the co-beneficiary of human rights provisions. What it does mean is that States would have both domestic and international obligations (or internal and external obligations) to ensure that the malnourished and starving world-wide have sufficient food.[302]

This question was raised in the Committee's general discussion. One member suggested that the duty to provide for international co-operation might lead to a point at which it could be asserted that the world's surplus food resources were the 'common heritage of mankind' for meeting the

---

[299] Reporting guidelines, *supra*, n. 154, at 101.

[300] Dobbert (FAO), E/C.12/1989/SR.20, at 6, para. 21.

[301] *See e.g.* Alston, *supra*, n. 1, at 34.

[302] It is worthy of note here that the Covenant does not have any territorial restrictions on the obligations of States. It could be argued that, in principle, every State is responsible for the position of every individual with respect to the right to food. This would in effect be a step towards seeing food resources as the common heritage of mankind. However, the implication of art. 29 of the Vienna Convention on the Law of Treaties is that in the absence of a specific provision otherwise 'a treaty is binding upon each party in respect of its entire territory', and only that territory. Indeed, it is extremely unlikely that States would admit such an obligation, not least in so far as it might affect their own sovereignty.

needs of the hungry and impoverished.[303] That member, while admitting the proposal was 'excessive', considered that it was the 'only way in which an international legal obligation could be imposed upon States under the Covenant'.[304] On a more realistic level, Mr Eide (the Special *Rapporteur* to the Sub-Commission) asserted that 'it was increasingly possible to claim that States had external obligations at least to the extent of allowing other peoples in other countries to survive'.[305]

Article 11(2)(b) refers specifically to the problems of food-importing and food-exporting countries. It has been asserted that such a reference was included to reflect the fear of grain-exporting States that the FAO Freedom From Hunger Campaign might interfere with the operation of the international grain markets, and as such is anachronistic today.[306] Nevertheless, the Committee refers to the phrase in its reporting guidelines without attempting to explain its meaning. Despite the unsatisfactory nature of the wordings, probably the best interpretation today, given the fact that food-importing and food-exporting countries exist in both the developed and developing worlds, is to read the provision in light of the need to ensure an 'equitable distribution of world food supplies'. This would mean focusing particularly upon the position of developing countries of either category.[307] Although every State could claim to have some form of trade problems, the problems that are relevant here are those that directly relate to the ability of the State to ensure every individual access to adequate food.

The reference to exports and imports in article 11(2)(b) clearly relates to the terms of international trade. The Committee, however, refers in its guidelines to the need for an equitable distribution of world food supplies in terms of 'both production and trade'.[308] Two main issues appear to be of concern to the Committee: first, that the location of greatest production of food resources (the developed world), does not coincide with the location of greatest need (the developing world). There is clearly a need for greater food production in developing countries and a transfer of human and material resources out of the agricultural sector in the developed world.[309] Secondly, the protectionist farm trade policies of the developed world, accompanied by an increasing number of tariff and non-tariff barriers, have served to reduce the export earnings of developing countries, have endangered developing countries' food security through destabilizing food prices, and have obstructed agricultural development in developing

---

[303] *See* Rattray, E/C.12/1989/SR.20, at 11, para. 48.   [304] *Ibid.*
[305] Eide, E/C.12/1990/SR.20, at 10, para. 41.   [306] Alston, *supra*, n. 1, at 43.
[307] *See* Dobbert, *supra*, n. 272, at 194. This would avoid the criticism of Kassahun that the art. does not address the question of 'agribusiness' which 'allows global food production for global markets that causes the hungry country to be a food-exporting state': Kassahun, *supra*, n. 213, at 888.
[308] Reporting guidelines, *supra*, n. 154, at 101.   [309] Boerma, *supra*, n. 260, at 75–86.

countries.[310] Although such problems are commonly accepted, it is not entirely agreed that developing countries would reap significant benefits from agricultural trade liberalization.[311]

It is notable, however, that the Committee members, in speaking of the question of international co-operation, rarely refer to trade issues. In the general discussion mention was made of the inequitable terms of trade between primary producers of agricultural products and producers of manufactured products, particularly in terms of prices. 'It was therefore an important part of the solution of the problem of the right to food that there should be an adjustment in the terms of trade as called for by the new international economic and social order.'[312] The Committee has not taken it upon itself to suggest the forms of adjustment that should be undertaken.

At the international level, although a great number of measures have been taken to stabilize food prices and the volume of trade, and to create buffer stocks where necessary, it is not apparent that in the short or medium term a distribution of food supplies according to need would be provided by trade alone. This concern was expressly raised in the drafting of article 11. There, in rejecting the use of the word 'interests' in place of 'problems' in the drafting of article 11(2)(b), the States concerned wished to stress social and humanitarian considerations as opposed to merely economic ones.[313] This would mean that an international strategy to achieve more equitable distribution should not be a narrow trade-oriented one, but should seek to ensure that access to food is a reality for all members of the population concerned.[314] It is an implication that the provision of food aid would be highly desirable in some circumstances.

[310] *See e.g.* Carlson J., 'Hunger, Agricultural Trade Liberalisation, and Soft International Law: Addressing the Legal Dimensions of a Political Problem' (1985) 70 *Iowa LR*, 1187, 1209–20; IBRD, *supra*, n. 160, at 121–3.

[311] Carlson argues that 'liberalizing the agricultural trade policies of developed nations is widely recognised as a critical international goal particularly important in the battle against hunger and underdevelopment': *ibid.* 1209. Similarly the World Bank claims that developing countries will reap 'substantial gains' from trade liberalization, IBRD, *supra*, n. 160, at 123. However, sceptics have argued otherwise. Christensen concludes that 'attempts to remove these limitations within the present 'rules of the game' are likely to achieve only marginal results. Liberalizing agricultural trade, for example, would be largely ineffective. It would not significantly alter the underlying distribution of wealth which such a structure demands.' Christensen, *supra*, n. 207, at 31.

[312] General discussion, *supra*, n. 192, at 72, para. 325. On the New International Economic Order and Human rights generally, *see* Ferrero R., 'The International Economic Order and the Promotion of human Rights', UN Doc. E/CN.4/Sub.2/1983/24/Rev. 1 (1983); Baxi U., 'The New International Economic Order, Basic Needs and Rights: Notes Towards Development of the Right to Development' (1983) 23 *Ind JIL* 225. Van Hoof F., 'Problems and Prospects with Respect to the Right to Food' in van Dijk P. *et al.* (eds.), *Restructuring the International Economic Order: The Role of Law and Lawyers* (1987), 107.

[313] *See above* text accompanying n. 140.   [314] Alston, *supra*, n. 1, at 43.

8 International Co-operation and Assistance

Article 11 refers to international co-operation specifically on two occasions and implicitly on a third. First, article 11(1) provides that States parties shall take measures to realize the right to an adequate standard of living (and therefore the right to food) 'recognizing to this effect the essential importance of international co-operation based on free consent'. In merely providing that States 'recognize' the importance of international co-operation, the provision does not seem to set out a binding legal obligation. It should perhaps be seen as drawing attention to the correlative obligation found in article 2(1) of the Covenant.

The phrase 'based on free consent', it might be assumed, was inserted as a safety provision against any assumption that food-surplus States have an automatic responsibility to make transfers to food-deficient States. It might also be read as requiring that food aid should only be provided with the consent of the recipient State.[315] Either way, given its hortatory nature, it cannot be interpreted as making co-operation entirely optional, nor can it defeat the general obligation in article 2(1).

Article 11(2), however, specifically provides that States should take 'individually and through international co-operation' the measures necessary to achieve the objectives in sub-paragraphs (a) and (b). In so far as it merely repeats the general clause in article 2(1), this provision cannot be seen to add anything substantive to the existing State obligations. Indeed the fact that it refers only to the two sub-paragraphs rather than the right to food itself suggests that its scope is considerably less wide. In addition, article 11(2) does not refer to 'international assistance' but merely 'co-operation'. No attempt has been made to distinguish these two concepts as far as the Covenant is concerned, either in the *travaux préparatoires* or in subsequent practice. It would seem from an ordinary reading of the terms that co-operation is the broader concept, including not merely a positive duty to assist, but also a negative duty not to obstruct the realization of the rights.

Finally, a duty to co-operate internationally may be inferred from article 11(2)(b) which refers to the duty to ensure an equitable distribution of world food supplies in relation to need. As noted above, this provision does not necessarily refer exclusively to external obligations, but may also give rise to certain domestic obligations relating to distribution. If the domestic and international obligations are seen as complementary, there is no need to determine whether or not a State 'qualifies' for international assistance.[316] Thus the failure of a State to undertake the necessary distributional measures to ensure that everyone has access to adequate food, although

---

[315] *Ibid.* 40.   [316] *Ibid.* 36.

potentially signifying a violation of the Covenant, would not necessarily disqualify it from receiving aid. This is apparent not only because effective distribution may be an expensive and time-consuming goal, but also because the need relates to the individual, not the State.

As noted above, the concept of international co-operation does not exclusively relate to the obligation to assist. In addition, it might be argued that States have a duty to desist from action that may impede the realization of the right to food in other countries. More specifically, this could involve restraining itself from 'dumping' food surpluses on developing countries where they may have the effect of undermining domestic food production, and also perhaps the control of transnational agribusiness corporations.[317] Only scant reference has been made by the Committee to either of these obligations.[318]

With respect to the question of international assistance, there are clearly a large number of areas and fora in which this may take place, many of which have been referred to elsewhere. The most obvious concern would seem to be the provision of international aid. Recently there has been a move away from the provision of large, long-term aid programmes, which have been thought to increase dependence upon assistance,[319] impair domestic production, and reinforce existing inequalities within the recipient States.[320] However, there are still a number of arguments in favour of the provision of food aid. One commentator has noted that food aid can: (i) provide States with the ability to maintain nutritional and consumption status of the population; (ii) relieve the impact of fluctuations in food supplies and build the necessary administrative capacity; and (iii) allow for broad-based employment-orientated development strategies to increase food production.[321] In addition, there are clearly ways to prevent food aid diminishing the demand for local produce, for example by providing supplementary, not replacement, foodstuffs.[322]

Members of the Committee have however been wary of advocating the provision of food aid. They have stressed in particular the need for international co-operation to focus on assisting the production,[323] conservation,

---

[317] *See* George, *supra*, n. 258, at 158–91; Kassahun, *supra*, n. 213, at 864–8.

[318] With respect to trans-national corporations, *see* Wimer Zambrano, E/C.12/1989/SR.21, at 8, para. 32. As regards 'dumping' of unsafe food, *see* Alvarez Vita, E/C.12/1987/SR.19, at 13, para. 69.

[319] Friedmann H., 'The Origins of Third World Food Dependence' in Bernstein *et al.* (eds.), *The Food Question* (1990), 16; George, *supra*, n. 258, at 192; Eide, E/C.12/1989/SR.20, at 10, para. 44.

[320] Alston, *supra*, n. 1, at 11 and 41.

[321] Mellor J., 'Effective Food Aid for Effective Food Security' in *World Food Security: Selected Themes and Issues* (1985), 18 at 30; and 'Food Aid for Food Security and Economic Development', in Clay E. and Shaw J. (eds.) *Poverty, Development and Food* (1987), 173.

[322] Dobbert (FAO), E/C.12/1989/SR.21, at 10, para. 39.

[323] *See e.g.* Neneman, E/C.12/1989/SR.20, at 9, para. 38; Eide, E/C.12/1989/SR.20, at 10, para. 44.

and distribution[324] of food at the domestic level. It has occasionally been suggested that the Committee should enquire into the extent to which States have contributed through international co-operation towards the realization of the right to adequate food.[325] The Committee's guidelines, however, merely require information on measures taken to ensure an equitable distribution of food supplies,[326] and the Committee members' questions have been general and infrequent.[327]

As has been noted, although there may be a duty to co-operate internationally, it is likely that 'States will insist on a right to retain absolute discretion in determining the level of their contribution to world welfare requirements'.[328] Nevertheless, it is considered that the Committee might benefit from distinguishing between claims for the provision of food aid in the case of chronic malnutrition and claims that relate to a situation of famine. In the latter case, there is a more perceptible moral obligation on the part of developed States to provide immediate assistance to the victims. Such a moral obligation could be assimilated to the 'minimum core' of an obligation to provide international assistance and might more readily be susceptible to enforcement by the Committee.[329]

C The Right to Housing

1 Introduction

The Committee has dedicated more attention to the right to housing[330] than to any other right. By the end of 1993, the Committee had undertaken a general discussion, adopted a general comment, and had found a number of States to be in violation of their obligations with respect to the right to housing. Its prominent concern with the right to housing has been driven to some extent by the active participation in the Committee's work of housing-oriented NGOs. At the same time the right to housing, unlike the right to food, is subject to extensive legal regulation at the domestic

---

[324] *See* Sparsis, E/C.12/1989/SR.20, at 12, para. 52.
[325] *See* Dobbert (FAO), E/C.12/1989/SR.20, at 7, para. 22; Simma, E/C.12/1989/SR.20, at 8, para. 28.
[326] Reporting guidelines, *supra*, n. 154, at 13.
[327] *See e.g.* Alvarez Vita, E/C.12/1987/SR.19, at 13, para. 69; Muterahejuru, E/C.12/1989/SR.12, at 12, para. 64; E/C.12/WG/1991/CRP.2, at 3, para. 24.
[328] Bard R., 'The Right to Food' (1985) 70 *Iowa LR* 1279, at 1289.
[329] *Cf.* Shelton D., 'The Duty to Assist Famine Victims' (1985) 70 *Iowa LR* 1309.
[330] *See generally* Leckie S., 'The UN Committee on Economic, Social and Cultural Rights and the Right to Adequate Housing: Towards an Appropriate Approach' (1989) 11 *Hum. Rts. Q* 522, at 534–5; Leckie S., *From Housing Needs to Housing Rights: An Analysis of the Right to Adequate Housing Under International Human Rights Law* (1992); Sachar R., *Working Paper on the Right to Adequate Housing*, UN Doc. E/CN.4/Sub.2/1992/15 (1992); Sachar R., *The Right to Adequate Housing: Progress Report*, UN Doc. E/CN.4/Sub.2/1993/15 (1993).

level[331] and therefore is more susceptible to monitoring and quasi-judicial supervision.

The right to adequate housing, although found in other international instruments, has its broadest and clearest recognition in the Covenant.[332] Like the right to food, it is a component of the right to an adequate standard of living and, as the Committee has noted, 'is integrally linked to other human rights and to the fundamental principles upon which the Covenant is premised'.[333] The Committee has stressed, in particular,[334] that the rights to freedom of expression,[335] freedom of association,[336] freedom to take part in public decision-making,[337] freedom to choose one's residence,[338] and freedom from arbitrary and unlawful interference with one's privacy, family, home, or correspondence,[339] are all important for the full enjoyment of the right to housing. In addition, it might be argued that the rights to work,[340] to minimum remuneration,[341] and to social security,[342] also have an important influence upon the degree to which the right to housing is enjoyed.[343]

2 Progressive Realization

Although everyone has a right to housing, States are not under an obligation to eliminate homelessness immediately. The Committee has recognized that 'the steps required to be taken by States parties in order to promote realization of the right to adequate housing will often be time-consuming, complex, and costly'.[344] Thus, even in the case of wealthy States, the right to housing is not expected to be achieved overnight.[345] This would be particularly apparent where the government takes on direct responsibility for the provision of housing. As will be seen below, the Committee

---

[331] Leckie S., *From Housing Needs to Housing Rights*, Appendix 1, 80–6 (1992).

[332] *See also* at the universal level, art. 25(1) UDHR, art. 5(e)(iii) of the Convention on the Elimination of All Forms of Racial Discrimination (1965), art. 14(2) of the Convention on the Elimination of All Forms of Discrimination Against Women (1975), art. 27(3) of the Convention on the Rights of the Child (1989), art. 21 of the Convention Relating to the Status of Refugees (1951), and art. 43(1) of the Migrant Workers Convention (1990). *See also* ILO Recommendation No. 115 on Workers' Housing (1961), Vancouver Declaration on Human Settlements (1976).

[333] General Comment No. 4 (1991), UN ESCOR, Supp. (No. 3), Annex III, at 115, para. 7, UN Doc. E/1992/23, (1992).

[334] *Ibid.* 117, para. 9.   [335] Art. 19(2) ICCPR.   [336] Art. 22(1) ICCPR.

[337] Art. 25 ICCPR.   [338] Art. 12(1) ICCPR.   [339] Art. 17(1) ICCPR.

[340] Art. 6 ICESCR.   [341] Art. 7 ICESCR.   [342] Art. 9 ICESCR.

[343] *See* Sparsis, E/C.12/1990/SR.23, at 8, para. 30; Dao (ILO), E/C.12/1990/SR.22, at 7, para. 36.

[344] General Comment No. 4, *supra*, n. 333, at 117, para. 10. The Special Rapporteur on the Right to Housing points out that recognizing a right to housing does not imply that the State has to build housing for all the population, or that it should be provided free of charge to all, or that all aspects of the right be fulfilled immediately. *See* Sachar (progress report), *supra*, n. 330, at 12, para. 39.

[345] *Cf.* criticism of Canada, Bonoan-Dandan, E/C.12/1993/SR.5, at 19, para. 92; Muterahejuru, E/C.12/1993/SR.5, at 19, para. 94.

does not expect States to take such a central role in the provision of housing. All States have to show is that the measures being taken are sufficient 'to realize the right of every individual in the shortest possible time in accordance with the maximum of available resources'.[346]

In its General Comment No. 4, the Committee has reiterated its general rationale as regards the implementation of the Covenant. It stresses that to the extent that States are required to restrain themselves from action that obstructs access to housing, or are required to 'facilitate self-help', they should implement such obligations immediately.[347] States are thus under an obligation, for example, to refrain from action that either arbitrarily deprives people of their own housing or prevents them from finding or building their homes themselves. The Committee also comments that where these immediate obligations are beyond the powers of the State concerned, it should request international assistance.[348]

Taking into consideration the notion of progressive achievement, the Committee has opined that 'a general decline in living and housing conditions, directly attributable to policy and legislative decisions by States parties, and in the absence of accompanying compensatory measures, would be inconsistent with the obligations found in the Covenant'.[349] It is interesting to note that a general decline in living and housing conditions alone does not invoke State responsibility, only where it is 'directly attributable' to State policies and where no 'compensatory measures' are taken. For example, if a State were to find itself in an economic recession which had a negative effect on the housing market, it would not automatically be considered to be in violation of article 11.

The question of attribution is particularly interesting in so far as it is conditioned by the degree to which the State undertakes to provide housing through public as opposed to private channels. If a State which traditionally provide large amounts of public housing were forced to cut spending in an economic recession, thereby instituting a decline in housing conditions, it would be forced to take compensatory measures to alleviate the adverse effects. If, on the other hand, housing were generally controlled by the private sector which experienced a recession, the State would no longer be considered directly responsible[350] and therefore would not have to provide

---

[346] *Ibid.*

[347] In the Committee's general discussion, one expert argued that States should undertake the following immediately: (a) acknowledge that the right to housing was a human right; (b) adopt legislation to prohibit all forms of discrimination; (c) ensure that individuals and organizations were able to participate effectively in housing planning; (d) annul or amend laws which prevented or hampered the implementation of the right to housing; (e) grant all citizens equal rights in housing matters; (f) change housing policies to take into account the needs of the most underprivileged groups. Leckie (International Habitat Coalition), E/C.12/1990/SR.22, at 9, para. 55.

[348] General Comment No. 4, *supra*, n. 333, at 117, para. 10.   [349] *Ibid.* 117, para. 11.

[350] There is the possibility that the government concerned may be considered to be

compensatory measures. This is surely wrong; even where housing provision is generally undertaken by the private sector, States must retain
ultimate responsibility for shortfalls in housing or deteriorating housing
conditions. Thus where there is a decline in housing conditions, States
should take appropriate remedial action even if they cannot be held to be
directly responsible for that decline.

It is clear that States should take steps to the 'maximum of available
resources' in accordance with article 2(1). Accordingly the Committee requests information about financial measures taken by the State 'including
details of the budget of the Ministry of Housing'.[351] Although an aggregate
figure of expenditure is in itself unhelpful, where public expenditure on
housing has declined appreciably Committee members have been quick
to criticize the State concerned.[352] While the Committee clearly expects
government expenditure to be at a reasonable level,[353] it does not generally
attempt to stipulate how that money should be spent.[354]

3 Monitoring and Policy Formulation

In accordance with its approach to all rights in the Covenant, the Committee has outlined certain procedural obligations as part of States' duty to
take appropriate steps. In particular the Committee considers that States
have an obligation to undertake appropriate monitoring and policy formulation immediately. As regards monitoring, a State is required to take
'whatever steps are necessary, either alone or on the basis of international
co-operation, to ascertain the full extent of homelessness and inadequate
housing within its jurisdiction'.[355]

In its guidelines, the Committee has attempted to outline this obligation
in more detail. Information is requested about the housing situation of
those groups in society that are vulnerable and disadvantaged. As a minor
technical point here, it is unclear whether the Committee wants information
about the housing position of all 'vulnerable and disadvantaged groups'
defined in a broad sense by their social and economic status, or rather to
pinpoint those groups that are vulnerable and disadvantaged as regards

responsible for the economic recession. However, except in the most obvious cases this would
be virtually impossible to establish.

[351] Reporting Guidelines, *supra*, n. 154, at 15.

[352] *e.g.*, one member questioned whether Zaïre was in compliance with its obligations under
the Covenant in cutting expenditure on housing from 2% to 0.6% between 1972 and 1985. *See*
Alston, E/C.12/1988/SR.17, at 7, para. 44.

[353] *e.g.*, the Committee was concerned that expenditure on social housing in Canada was
merely 1.3% GNP, Concluding observations on report of Canada, E/C.12/1993/5, at 4, para. 20.

[354] In the case of Mexico, however, the Committee did go so far as specifically to recommend
the increased construction of rental housing, Concluding observations on report of Mexico, E/
C.12/1993/16, at 3, para. 13.

[355] General Comment No. 4, *supra*, n. 333, at 118, para. 13.

housing specifically. Although the definition of 'vulnerable or disadvantaged group' varies from country to country, in relation to article 2(2) the Committee has outlined certain groups that are characteristically discriminated against. It might be appropriate for the Committee to request, as a minimum, information as to the housing situation of such groups.

In addition, the guidelines require information about the number of homeless individuals and families, the number of individuals and families inadequately housed, the number of persons living in 'illegal' settlements, the number of persons evicted in the last five years (and those currently lacking protection against arbitrary eviction), the number of persons whose housing expenses are classified as unaffordable, the number of persons on waiting lists for accommodation, and the number of persons in different types of housing tenure.[356] Such considerations have been reflected in the questions of individual members of the Committee which have been directed primarily at ascertaining the extent of homelessness[357] (or the size of the housing shortage[358]), the amount of sub-standard housing,[359] and the percentage of people living in rented accomodation.[360]

As a corollary to the monitoring strategy, States are expected to develop a policy directed at the relief of the situation of those most disadvantaged. According to the Committee's General Comment, this will 'invariably require the adoption of a national housing strategy which, as stated in the Global Shelter Strategy, "defines the objectives for the development of shelter conditions, identifies the resources available to meet these goals and the most cost-effective way of using them, and sets out responsibilities and time-frame for the implementation of the necessary measures"'.[361] Moreover it appears that in drawing up this strategy States should consult those affected, including the homeless and the inadequately housed.[362]

Although the Committee presents these procedural conditions as 'obligations', they are not strictly enforced by the Committee. On no occasion has the Committee found a State to be in violation of the Covenant for failing to monitor effectively or to draw up a coherent policy with relevant participation. It has occasionally criticized States for failing to do so how-

---

[356] Reporting guidelines, *supra*, n. 154, at 13–14.

[357] *See e.g.* Texier, E/C.12/1989/SR.6, at 12, para. 62; Konate, E/C.12/1987/SR.10, at 2, para. 3; Alston, E/C.12/1989/SR.15, at 7, para. 41; Alston, E/C.12/1989/SR.17, at 7, para. 31; Rattray, E/C.12/1991/SR.3, at 12, para. 62; Rattray, E/C.12/1987/SR.16, at 9, para. 39.

[358] *See e.g.* Muterahejuru, E/C.12/1988/SR.8, at 5, para. 16; Alston, E/C.12/1988/SR.18, at 2, para. 3.

[359] *See e.g.* Rattray, E/C.12/1987/SR.16, at 9, para. 39; Simma, E/C.12/1989/SR.16, at 17, para. 94; Rattray, E/C.12/1990/SR.34, at 6, para. 43.

[360] *See e.g.* Jimenez Butragueno, E/C.12/1987/SR.9, at 9, para. 44.

[361] General Comment No. 4, *supra*, n. 333, at 118, para. 12.

[362] *Ibid*. The Special Rapporteur recommends that States develop a national resettlement policy, a draft code of conduct on forced evictions, a national urbanization policy, and a hierarchy of policy statements based on 'issue-related principles', Sachar (progress report), *supra*, n. 330, at 24, para. 97.

ever. In the case of Panama, for example, the Committee criticized the government for not having an accurate estimate of the number of persons affected by the bombing of El Chorillo during the US intervention.[363]

4 'Everyone'

Although the Covenant provides that 'everyone' has a right to housing, it appears to be qualified by the phrase 'for himself and his family'. It is possible that this might be interpreted as excluding female-headed households and those without families. The Committee, in line with the *travaux préparatoires*,[364] has explicitly refuted such an interpretation in stating that the phrase 'himself and his family' 'cannot be read today as implying any limitations upon the applicability of the right to individuals or to female-headed households or other such groups'.[365] Indeed it considers that the phrase merely 'reflects assumptions as to gender roles and economic activity patterns commonly accepted in 1966 when the Covenant was adopted'.[366] Thus when considering the report of Mexico, members of the Committee criticized a Constitutional provision that posited the right to housing as a right of 'families', and not of the individual.[367]

5 Adequate Housing

A right to housing would appear to require in general that every member of the population has access to some form of accommodation. On a broad scale this could be determined by an analysis of the size of the housing stock in relation to the population size. On a more individually oriented level, it would require an assessment of whether the distribution and availability of housing is sufficient to ensure every individual ready access to accommodation. Factors that might affect such access include the nature of ownership and affordability of the accommodation, its location and size, and the terms of policies or practices that govern distribution (for example, whether or not they are discriminatory). In addition to a right of access, the right to housing may be interpreted to include a right not to be arbitrarily deprived of housing.

In view of the fact that the right to housing is a sub-norm of the right to an adequate standard of living, the concept of 'adequacy' would seem to

[363] UN ESCOR, Supp. (No. 3), at 32, para. 135, UN Doc. E/1992/23, (1992). *See also* concluding observations on report of Canada, E/C.12/1993/5, at 4, para. 19.

[364] *See above* text accompanying nn. 66–73.

[365] General Comment No. 4, *supra*, n. 333, at 115, para. 6.   [366] *Ibid.*

[367] However, it was asserted that although the Constitution recognized the right to housing as a family right, in practice it was an individual right. Gonzales Martinez (Mexico), E/C.12/1990/SR.6, at 7, para. 37.

import into the right a qualitative element that might otherwise have been absent.[368] The Committee has commented in this regard that:

the right to housing should not be interpreted in a narrow or restrictive sense which equates it with, for example, the shelter provided by merely having a roof over one's head. Rather it should be seen as the right to somewhere to live in security, peace and dignity.[369]

Although the precise nature of adequate housing may be determined to an extent by climatic, sociological, and other factors, the Committee has found there to be certain elements that should be taken into account at all time, such as security of tenure, availability of services, affordability, habitability, accessibility, location, and cultural adequacy.[370]

(a) Access to Housing

(i) *The Provision of Housing.* In looking at the number of homeless in each country, the Committee seems to place the primary obligation for ensuring the provision of housing upon the State. However, this does not mean that the State has to act as the sole provider of housing itself. In accordance with the provisions of article 2(1), States have a certain amount of discretion as to the means of realizing the right to housing. The precise solution adopted will depend upon the economic, social, cultural, and political situation of the country concerned. In a sense, the main concern of the Committee is with the results of that policy.

Although a number of governments have undertaken to provide all housing themselves, it is clear that the Committee does not expect this to be the case in all States. Accordingly, in its General Comment, the Committee notes that:

Measures designed to satisfy a State party's obligations in respect of the right to adequate housing may reflect whatever mix of public and private sector measures considered appropriate. While in some States public financing of housing might most usefully be spent on direct construction of new housing, in most cases, experience has shown the inability of Governments to fully satisfy housing deficits with publicly built housing.[371]

In cases where the State does have a central role in the provision of housing, members of the Committee have been concerned about the conditions for the allocation of such housing[372] and the extent of choice over its

---

[368] *See* Leckie (International Habitat Coalition), E/C.12/1990/SR.22, at 8, para. 51.

[369] General Comment No. 4, *supra*, n. 333, at 115, para. 7.

[370] While the Committee inferred all of these elements from the notion of 'adequacy', it was not necessary to do so.

[371] General Comment No. 4, *supra*, n. 333, at 118, para. 14.

[372] *See e.g.* Mratchkov, E/C.12/1987/SR.21, at 10, para. 44; Rattray, E/C.12/1987/SR.16, at 9, para. 39.

location.[373] In addition, questions have been asked whether there was a variety of types of housing available,[374] and whether legal remedies were available in disputes over allocation.[375]

In taking a balanced view of the question of the provision of housing, the Committee requests information about measures taken by the State to build housing units itself and to increase 'other construction' of affordable rental housing. In particular, it places an emphasis on 'enabling strategies' whereby local community-based organizations and the 'informal sector' are encouraged to build houses themselves,[376] or are provided with resources to do so.[377] Given the emphasis on such 'enabling strategies' it would seem that it is not sufficient for the government concerned merely to build houses itself; it must also take positive steps to encourage private housing construction. This is supported by comments of individual Committee members,[378] who have also stressed the fact that private individuals or groups should be able to construct houses themselves[379] without excessive conditions being placed upon them.[380] Private house construction not only promotes the construction of appropriate housing, but can also be seen as an economic activity which contributes to the growth and development of the country concerned.[381]

On the other hand, it would not be legitimate for States to absolve themselves entirely from responsibility for the provision of housing. Chile, for example, was criticized by members of the Committee following a sharp reduction in government low-cost-housing construction projects. In particular concern was expressed over the fact that Chile appeared to leave the housing problem entirely in the hands of the private sector.[382] One member commented that by encouraging private ownership of property the Government of Chile was ignoring the position of the poor.[383] Italy has similarly been criticized for the shortage of low income housing and the insufficiency of its housing construction plan even though it was clear that much privately-owned property remained unoccupied.[384]

---

[373] *See e.g.* Rattray, E/C.12/1987/SR.12, at 8, para. 31; Taya, E/C.12/1987/SR.9, at 11, para. 52. An NGO representative argued that individuals should have ultimate choice over the kind of house and the location in which they will live. Leckie (International Habitat Coalition), E/C.12/1990/SR.22, at 10, para. 60.

[374] *See* Rattray, E/C.12/1987/SR.9, at 9, para. 42.

[375] *Ibid.*

[376] Reporting guidelines, *supra*, n. 154, at 15.

[377] *See* concluding observations on report of Mexico, E/C.12/1993/16, at 3, para. 13.

[378] *See e.g.* Mratchkov, E/C.12/1988/SR.5, at 6, para. 26, and E/C.12/1988/SR.10, at 11, para. 58.

[379] *See* Mratchkov, E/C.12/1987/SR.12, at 4, para. 12; Muterahejuru, E/C.12/1987/SR.19, at 11, para. 54.

[380] *See* Marchan Romero, E/C.12/1988/SR.5, at 7, para. 32.

[381] *See* Lugvigsen (UNCHR), E/C.12/1990/SR.22, at 6, para. 33; Barsch (Four Directions Council), E/C.12/1990/SR.23, at 3, para. 11.

[382] *See e.g.* Marchan Romero, E/C.12/1988/SR.12, at 10–11, para. 52.

[383] *See* Neneman, E/C.12/1988/SR.12, at 11, para. 56.

[384] Concluding observations on report of Italy, E/1993/22, at 50, para. 192.

In the provision of housing, the State is clearly obliged to take into account the qualitative aspects of housing detailed below. It is also obliged to enforce similar requirements on the construction and provision of housing by private individuals and companies. Accordingly, the Committee expects to receive information about legislation concerning building codes, regulations, and standards.[385]

(ii) *Discrimination and Disadvantaged Groups.* Article 11, when read in conjunction with article 2(2), prohibits discrimination as regards all elements of the right to housing. Although article 2(2) is indicative of the groups likely to be discriminated against, it is clearly not exhaustive.[386] Thus in its General Comment, the Committee specifically mentions the elderly, children, those with physical disabilities or terminal illnesses, individuals who are HIV-positive, persons with persistent medical problems, and those with mental illness, as categories of people that should be afforded 'some degree of priority consideration in the housing sphere'.[387] While not maintaining that all these groups are discriminated against in all cases or that they represent the only disadvantaged groups, the Committee appears to consider that States should at least be aware of the relative position of such groups.

In addition to refraining from discrimination itself, States are expected to enforce non-discrimination provisions with regard to private individuals.[388] In its guidelines, the Committee expects information on 'legislation prohibiting any and all forms of discrimination in the housing sector, including groups not traditionally protected'.[389] In referring to the 'groups not traditionally protected', the Committee implies that States should reconsider their discrimination laws with a view to widening their scope to include those groups specifically disadvantaged in relation to housing. As a minimum, however, States should consider explicitly prohibiting discrimination against those groups identified by the Committee in its General Comment.

States are obliged to take positive action to alleviate the position of disadvantaged groups whether or not they are the objects of discrimination.[390] In particular, the Committee has stressed that such groups should be given 'priority consideration' and that housing law and policy should take fully into account the special housing needs of those groups.[391] Indi-

---

[385] Reporting guidelines, *supra*, n. 154, at 14.
[386] *See above* Ch. 4, text accompanying nn. 89–153.
[387] General Comment No. 4, *supra*, n. 333, at 116, para. 8(e).
[388] *See above* Ch. 3, text accompanying nn. 243–57.
[389] Reporting guidelines, *supra*, n. 154, at 14.
[390] It has to be questioned whether people such as low wage-earners could be said to be discriminated against merely because they do not have the same access to housing as other, more wealthy members of society.
[391] General Comment No. 4, *supra*, n. 333, at 116, para. 8(e).

vidual Committee members have specifically looked to the housing situation of non-nationals,[392] the elderly,[393] displaced persons,[394] and women,[395] and have requested information regarding cases of such discrimination that have been taken to court.[396] More frequently however, concern is expressed about the position of those on low incomes,[397] including the unemployed,[398] in respect to whom States are expected to undertake some form of targeted action.

(iii) *Affordability*. The cost of housing clearly has a significant impact upon each individual's access to adequate housing, their ability to continue living in their current residence and their standard of living in general. Indeed as the Committee noted: 'Personal or household financial costs associated with housing should be at such a level that the attainment and satisfaction of other basic needs are not threatened or compromised.'[399] Whereas it is not necessary for States to fix all rents at a specified rate, it is clearly a priority to ensure that enough low-cost housing exists in order to cater for the needs of the whole population and in particular the poor and disadvantaged. The Committee appears to expect States to establish a 'limit of affordability' based upon ability to pay or as a ratio of income, and to assess the number of persons whose housing expenses are higher than that limit.[400] For those unable to obtain affordable housing, the State is required to establish housing subsidies and to make available 'forms and levels of housing finance which adequately reflect housing needs'.[401] Although it would be beyond the means of many States to undertake such programmes of State support immediately, it is important for the ultimate fulfilment of the right that such a long-term objective is spelt out.

Equally importantly, the Committee expects States to exercise some control over rent levels in the private sector. Tenants should be protected from rent levels or rent increases 'by appropriate means'.[402] Individual members of the Committee have similarly regularly requested information as to the means of rent control,[403] but have refrained from stipulating any

[392] *See e.g.* Alvarez Vita, E/C.12/1988/SR.17, at 2, para. 8; Badawi El Sheikh, E/C.12/1988/SR.8, at 2, para. 4.

[393] *See e.g.* Jimenez Butragueno, E/C.12/1993/SR.16, at 6, para. 23.

[394] *See* Texier, E/C.12/1993/SR.14, at 6, para. 28.

[395] *See e.g.* Alston, E/C.12/1989/SR.15, at 7, para. 41.

[396] *See e.g.* Rattray, E/C.12/1990/SR.2, at 10, para. 63.

[397] *See e.g.* Concluding observations on report of Mexico, E/C.12/1993/16, at 3, para. 13; Rattray, E/C.12/1991/SR.3, at 12, para. 62; Sparsis, E/C.12/1989/SR.16, at 17, para. 91; Alston, E/C.12/1990/SR.11, at 5, para. 24.

[398] *See e.g.* Fofana, E/C.12/1991/SR.7, at 12, para. 53.

[399] General Comment No. 4, *supra*, n. 333, at 116, para. 8(c).

[400] Reporting guidelines, *supra*, n. 154, at 13.

[401] General Comment No. 4, *supra*, n. 333, at 116, para. 8(c).   [402] *Ibid.*

[403] *See* Mratchkov, E/C.12/1988/SR.6, at 6, para. 46; Simma, E/C.12/1989/SR.15, at 3, para. 8; Fofana, E/C.12/1989/SR.18, at 3, para. 9; Rattray, E/C.12/1991/SR.3, at 12, para. 62.

specific means by which it should be achieved.[404] The Committee has been particular critical of moves to abolish or limit existing rent control by the State.[405] Thus in the case of Italy the Committee criticized an Act which appeared to restrict the *equo canone* (the system of fair rent).[406] It would seem that even where such a measure was designed to increase the amount of rented accommodation available members were still concerned about the effect the legislation would have on those living on low incomes.[407]

(b) Security of Tenure and Evictions

Much as there is variety in forms of tenure such as owner-occupation, rented accommodation, co-operative housing, and other informal settlements, there is variety in the degree of security offered to the occupier. The Committee requires that 'notwithstanding the type of tenure, all persons should possess a degree of security of tenure which guarantees legal protection against forced eviction, harassment, and other threats'.[408] Given that the Committee speaks of 'a degree of security of tenure', it leaves open the extent of protection required. While protection of tenants against harassment and threats is quite appropriate, an absolute protection against forced eviction[409] would not be sustainable in any legal system. By the nature of a lease, there must be the possibility of reversion to the owner (for example at the effluxion of time or for non-payment of rent), and in certain circumstances this may have to be carried out through forcible eviction. The object of law in such a situation is not to prevent eviction from occurring at all but rather to ensure that it occurs only in strictly defined circumstances and follows appropriate procedures to minimize the possibility of abuse. As such, it looks to strike a balance between the right of the tenant to a place to live and the right of the lawful owner to maintain control over the premises.

It might be argued that the Covenant itself does not provide for such a balance of individual interests. No specific limitations on the right to housing are foreseen by the terms of article 11, and article 4 merely provides that the rights may be subject to such limitations as are 'determined by law only in so far as this may be compatible with the nature of those rights and solely for the purpose of promoting the general welfare in a democratic society'. This might conceivably justify evictions for the purpose of protecting the

---

[404] One member rather ambiguously asked why regulation of rent increases had been entrusted to the judiciary. It was unclear, however, whether it was felt that this was inappropriate. *See* Muterahejuru, E/C.12/1990/SR.2, at 11, para. 67.

[405] *See e.g.* Simma, E/C.12/1989/SR.16, at 18, para. 94.

[406] Concluding observations on report of Italy, E/1993/22, at 50, para. 192.

[407] *Ibid.*   [408] General Comment No. 4, *supra*, n. 333, at 115, para. 8(a).

[409] On the question of forced evictions, *see generally* Analytical Report on Forced Evictions, UN Doc. E/CN.4/1994/20. Forced eviction has been described by both the Commission and its Sub-Commission as a 'gross violation of human rights, in particular the right to adequate housing', *see e.g.* Commission Resolution 1993/77 (1993).

environment, or in the interests of public health or public order, but does not necessarily take into account individual property interests (it being clear that there is no right to property in either Covenant). Even if the protection of property were assimilated to a 'general interest', the right to housing remains the primary concern and any limitations on the enjoyment of that right would have to be strictly justified.

The Committee appears to have adopted some of this thinking. In its General Comment, it provides that forced evictions 'are *prima facie* incompatible with the requirements of the Covenant and could only be justified in the most exceptional circumstances, and in accordance with the relevant principles of international law'.[410] Although not ruling out the possibility of evictions, the Committee is clear in asserting the priority of the right to housing over competing interests, including those in property. Members of the Committee do, however, take cognizance of property interests in their questions and comments.[411] Most of their attention has been directed to ensuring that a system for the protection of tenants does exist and is operated in practice.[412] In particular, attention has been focused upon legal forms of protection[413] and means of dispute settlement.[414] Certain members have looked to the existence of protective measures specifically in cases of termination of leases,[415] eviction for the purposes of repairs,[416] and eviction for non-payment of rent.[417] In the case of Italy, the Committee as a whole expressed its concern over the 'precarious nature of leases' especially in light of the fact that one family in three had been evicted.[418]

On occasions members have taken a more radical stance in addressing the competing interests and have looked towards the reform of the law of property.[419] Such an approach would appear to be particularly appropriate in those countries where the unequal ownership of land presents a significant problem for the realization of the right to housing,[420] especially as far as 'illegal settlements' are concerned. Having said that, it is probably more appropriate for the Committee to look to State action in the form of rent

[410] Commission Resolution 1993/77 (1993), 119, para. 18. A question may be raised as to what the Committee meant in referring to 'the relevant principles of international law', *see below* n. 442.

[411] *See* Texier, E/C.12/1990/SR.22, at 13, para. 83.

[412] *See* Mratchkov, E/C.12/1988/SR.10, at 7, para. 27; Fofana, E/C.12/1989/SR.18, at 3, para. 9; Simma, E/C.12/1990/SR.40, at 10, para. 46; Neneman, E/C.12/1991/SR.3, at 9, para. 41.

[413] *See e.g.* Simma, E/C.12/1990/SR.38, at 3, para. 15; Fofana, E/C.12/1988/SR.6, at 7, para. 51.

[414] *See e.g.* Texier, E/C.12/1988/SR.13, at 14, para. 83.

[415] *See* Mratchkov, E/C.12/1988/SR.6, at 6, para. 46.

[416] *See* Fofana, E/C.12/1989/SR.15, at 5, para. 23.

[417] *See* Texier, E/C.12/1989/SR.14, at 16, para. 72.

[418] Concluding observations on report of Italy, E/1993/22, at 51, para. 192.

[419] *See* Muterahejuru, E/C.12/1990/SR.23, at 9, para. 37. The Committee has also spoken of the 'regularization' of the law of property, *see* Concluding observations on report of Nicaragua, E/C.12/1993/14, at 2, para. 7.

[420] *See* Leckie (International Habitat Coalition), E/C.12/1990/SR.22, at 10, para. 67.

control, compulsory land purchase, and expropriation, than undermining the concept of property *per se*.

Although the Committee does attend to evictions undertaken by private individuals or organizations, the cases of greatest concern have involved the public authorities. The first and perhaps most important case of this kind arose with respect to the Dominican Republic. After considering its report, the Committee found it to be in violation of its obligations under article 11 of the Covenant. According to NGO sources, the Dominican Republic authorities had adopted plans for remodelling a number of cities, including Santiago and San Domingo, which had led to the eviction of nearly 15,000 families from their homes. These facts themselves were not disputed. In its concluding comments, the Committee made the following statement:

The information that had reached members of the Committee concerning the massive expulsion of nearly 15,000 families in the course of the last five years, the deplorable conditions in which the families had had to live, and the conditions in which the expulsions had taken place were deemed sufficiently serious for it to be considered that the guarantee in article 11 of the Covenant had not been respected.[421]

It is clear from the statement that the violation of the right to housing was not established solely by the fact of eviction. The Committee, in addition, refers to two factors: first, that following the evictions many of the families had been forced to live in 'deplorable conditions'.[422] The summary records show that although alternative accommodation was available, it was 'very costly'.[423] Secondly, the Committee was concerned with the 'conditions in which the expulsions had taken place'. Here the summary records show that although there was an established eviction procedure involving a concili-ation meeting in the presence of a lawyer, with a right to appeal to a tribunal and from there to the State Attorney, it had not been followed.[424] Nor had the evicted tenants been given any legal assistance.[425] It is likely that factors contributing to the Committee's finding were the scale of the evictions, the fact that it was the public authorities undertaking the evictions, and that the overt purpose was to hide the people affected from public view rather than come to their assistance.

It is unclear whether each of the two specified factors constituted indi-vidual and separate violations of the Covenant, or only in so far as they were taken together. Perhaps the most crucial factor for this case was that the evictions had taken place in violation of domestic law. To the extent that the Covenant requires the establishment of a system for the protection

---

[421] UN ESCOR, Supp. (No. 3), at 64, para. 249, UN Doc. E/C.12/1990/8 (1991).
[422] *See* Simma, E/C.12/1990/SR.44, at 10, para. 48.
[423] Texier, E/C.12/1990/SR.44, at 11, para. 53.
[424] *Ibid.*
[425] *See* Simma, E/C.12/1990/SR.44, at 10, para. 48.

of tenants, failure to comply with existing domestic mechanisms must be considered a *prima facie* violation of the Covenant.

It might be questioned whether these evictions would have amounted to a violation had they taken place with due legal process. Given that the State is under an obligation to realize the right to housing for everyone, it is possible to argue that public authorities should show a legitimate purpose in undertaking the evictions and should provide appropriate alternative accommodation. The fact that neither of these was provided suggests that the Dominican Republic did not have the interests of the population at heart in this case, and thus was not fulfilling its obligations under the Covenant. This would seem to be the position of one member who commented:

The Dominican Republic had put itself in an entirely different position than other countries which, for their part, were unable to ensure observance of the right to housing because they did not have the means. The Dominican Republic was deliberately flouting the provisions of the Covenant.[426]

In so far as evictions represent a step away from the full realization of the right to housing, public authorities should show an overriding justification for their action and should provide appropriate alternative accommodation where possible.[427]

The second principal case of forced evictions arose in the context of the Panamanian report. Questions were asked on the basis of information from non-governmental organizations[428] on the destruction of half of El Chorillo[429] and the forced expulsion of people from their homes in Tucmen, San Miguelito, and Panama Viejo,[430] following the US invasion of Panama.[431] Although the destruction of El Chorillo seems to have been accepted by the Committee as an inevitable aspect of the invasion, the forced expulsion of families from the other 'Barrios' was not. Among other criticisms the Committee expressed the following opinion:

the justification for the actions carried out by Panamanian and United States forces in Tocumen, San-Miguelito and Panama Viego in early 1990, which affected over 5,000 persons, was unacceptable under the terms of the Covenant as a ground for forcibly removing people from their homes. During the actions concerned, a large number of houses were demolished, in spite of the affected persons having lived in

[426] Simma, E/C.12/1990/SR.44, at 10, para. 48.
[427] It is to be noted that none of these considerations necessarily applies to the case of evictions by private landowners.
[428] *See* UN Doc. E/CN.4/1991/NGO/34, which was widely available in the Committee's meeting.
[429] *See e.g.* Simma, E/C.12/1991/SR.3, at 7, para. 31.
[430] *See* Simma, E/C.12/1991/SR.3, at 7, para. 32; Wimer Zambrano, E/C.12/1991/SR.3, at 8, para. 38; Rattray, E/C.12/1991/SR.8, at 2, para. 6.
[431] For details of the invasion and analyses of the legal position, *see* Quigley J., 'The Legality of the United States Invasion of Panama' (1990) 15 *Yale JIL* 276; Henkin L., 'The Invasion of Panama Under International Law: A Dangerous Precedent' (1991) 29 *Colum. J Trans. L* 293.

the area for more than two years. Additionally these evictions had not been accompanied by legal eviction orders. The Committee was of the view that evictions carried out in this way not only infringed upon the right to adequate housing but also on the inhabitants' rights to privacy and security of the home.[432]

From the summary records it is not clear what justification was offered by the Panamanian representative for the action of the combined forces. Reference is only made to El Chorillo. However, the comment suggests that, in certain circumstances (with sufficient justification), evictions may be legitimate under the Covenant. The main objection of the Committee appears to have been to the manner in which the evictions took place. Like the case of the Dominican Republic, the Committee expressed particular concern over the illegitimacy of the evictions in domestic law, and the inadequacy of alternative accommodation arrangements.[433]

In its more recent sessions, the Committee has continued to address the question of forced evictions, albeit in less detail.[434] In 1991, in continuing its scrutiny of the situation in the Dominican Republic, the Committee commented that new eviction plans that had been brought to its attention gave rise to 'serious concern'.[435] Although the evictions had been authorized by presidential decree and therefore seemed to have some legal basis, the Committee was concerned to note that the 12,000 families of La Cienaga and Los Guandules would be housed in different places according to their 'education, living habits, and social level', and that the area from which they were evicted would only be used for recreational purposes.[436] Similarly, in the case of Mexico, the Committee expressed its concern at the 'prevalence of forced evictions' and the 'lack of adequate protection' for those threatened with eviction,[437] and with respect to Kenya, it noted with concern the widespread practice of forced eviction 'without consultation, compensation, or adequate resettlement'.[438]

Given that in all of these three cases the Committee has been given considerable information from NGO sources and (on several occasions at

---

[432] UN Doc. E/1992/23, UN ESCOR, Supp. (No. 3), at 32, para. 135(c) (1992). For the view that forced eviction amounts to a violation of the right to respect for private life, *see Cyprus* v. *Turkey*, Eur. Comm. HR Cases 6780/74 and 6950/75, (1982) 4 EHRR 482.

[433] In its concluding observation the Committee noted that it 'had received information which pointed to many complaints by the residents that had received alternative accommodation and which concerned the distance which now had to be travelled to and from places of employment on relatively expensive public transportation and the overall poor quality of the housing in the resettlement sites. Moreover, two years after the invasion, a large number of persons had yet to be rehoused.' *Ibid.* 32, para. 135(b).

[434] *See e.g.* Concluding observations on report of Mexico, E/C.12/1993/16, at 3, para. 10; Concluding observations on report of Kenya, E/C.12/1993/6, at 4, para. 16; Concluding observation on report of Nicaragua, E/C.12/1993/14, at 2, para. 9.

[435] UN Doc. E/1992/23, at 79, para. 330, UN ESCOR, Supp. (No. 3) (1992).

[436] *See* Simma, E/C.12/1991/SR.19, at 4, para. 15.

[437] Concluding observations on report of Mexico, E/C.12/1993/16, at 3, para. 10.

[438] Concluding observations on report of Kenya, E/C.12/1993/6, at 4, para. 16.

least) has had the opportunity to discuss the matters with the States concerned, it is unfortunate that it has not developed its approach more clearly. The Committee might have taken the opportunity to establish certain principles that operate, for example, as regards the type of procedural mechanisms that should be put in place, or as to what objectives may or may not serve to justify forcible evictions. What needs to be considered, in such cases, is the desirability of establishing precise rules so a State may assess in advance whether its proposed action would be in conflict with the obligations under the Covenant, especially in so far as the Committee is intending to adopt a 'quasi-judicial' approach to supervision.[439] In addition, as the view of the Committee is that forced evictions are a *prima facie* violation of the Covenant, it might well consider making suggestions as to what alternative strategies are open to States to deal with the perceived problems.[440]

The current position of the Committee, however, could be described as follows. The legality of an eviction will be determined initially by reference to domestic law. The relevant procedures and safeguards established to protect the rights of inhabitants must be complied with and those affected must be fully consulted.[441] However, even in cases where the relevant procedures are carried out, eviction may still be illegitimate under the Covenant if no sufficient and overriding justification is given for the action or if no provision is made for alternative accommodation (or, where appropriate, compensation[442]). Purposes such as keeping a city clean[443] or hiding people from public view[444] do not constitute sufficient justification.[445]

(c) Qualitative Aspects of Adequate Housing

As mentioned above, the Committee has addressed itself primarily to questions concerning access to housing and security of tenure. Less attention has been focused upon the notion of 'adequacy' in so far as it relates to the quality of housing. Individual members of the Committee have frequently looked to the qualitative aspects of the right to adequate housing[446] in the creation of national bench-marks,[447] and in ascertaining the number of

---

[439] *See below* Ch. 2, text accompanying nn. 177–83.

[440] These might include land-sharing or buy-out options, *see generally* Analytical Report, *supra*, n. 409, at 38–43, paras. 148–76.

[441] It might also be added that where evictions take place minimum force should be used. *Cf.* Texier, E/C.12/1993/SR.33, at 13, para. 70.

[442] The principles of 're-housing' and 'compensation' may be seen to reflect the principles of international law to which the Committee refers in its general comment, *see* Texier, E/C.12/1993/SR.33, at 13, para. 70. On the different forms of compensation, *see* Analytical Report, *supra*, n. 409, at 43–5, paras. 177–85.

[443] *See* Simma, E/C.12/1993/SR.4, at 6, para. 17.

[444] *See above* text accompanying n. 425.

[445] One member suggested that evictions for strategic, ecological, or cultural purposes might be justified: Texier, E/C.12/1993/SR.33, at 13, para. 70.

[446] *See* Rattray, E/C.12/1987/SR.12, at 8, para. 31.

[447] *See* Muterahejuru, E/C.12/1989/SR.12, at 12, para. 64, and E/C.12/1989/SR.17, at 16, para. 86; Simma, E/C.12/1989/SR.16, at 17, para. 94; Rattray, E/C.12/1990/SR.34, at 6, para. 43.

persons housed in inadequate dwellings.[448] However, they have been less willing to establish what are the common elements of adequate housing. The approach seems to have been rather that the notion of adequacy differs from country to country.[449]

As a whole, however, the Committee has been more positive in its approach. In its guidelines, it requests information on the 'number of individuals and families currently inadequately housed and without ready access to basic amenities such as water, heating (if necessary), waste disposal, sanitation facilities, electricity, postal services, etc.' (in so far as those amenities are relevant in the country concerned).[450] In addition information is requested about the number of persons living in 'over-crowded, damp, structurally unsafe housing or other conditions which affect health'.[451] The Committee has further defined its notion of 'adequacy' in its General Comment No. 4. In addition to the aspects already referred to above, it specifies that States should take into account the availability of services, and the habitability, location, and cultural adequacy of the housing.[452]

(i) *Availability of Services*. According to the Committee 'an adequate house must contain certain facilities essential for health, security, comfort, and nutrition. All beneficiaries of the right to adequate housing should have sustainable access to potable piped drinking water, sanitation, and washing facilities, food storage, refuse disposal, site drainage, and emergency services.'[453] It would seem clear that several other services could also be included in this list such as postal services, fuel or energy for cooking, eating, and lighting (for example electricity). The fact that these were not included in the General Comment (although to be found in the Reporting Guidelines) is not to be interpreted as if the Committee does not consider them to be important. Rather, the matters outlined are merely illustrative—the concept of adequate housing is in the final analysis to be determined at the domestic level.[454]

It would seem very clear that the realization of the objectives outlined is a long-term aim. In many countries, the State does not have sufficient resources to provide much more than potable drinking water.[455] In such cases it would be appropriate for States to draw up intermediate objectives such as ensuring the provision of potable drinking water everywhere before the introduction of piped water. The type of prioritization undertaken will have to depend upon the circumstances prevailing within the State concerned (for example in colder countries the provision of electricity for heat and light may be a priority), taking into account the fundamental necessity

---

[448] *See* Rattray, E/C.12/1987/SR.16, at 9, para. 39; Texier, E/C.12/1990/SR.38, at 6, para. 37.
[449] *See e.g.* Sparsis, E/C.12/1987/SR.9, at 10, para. 49.
[450] Reporting guidelines, *supra*, n. 154, at 13.   [451] *Ibid.*
[452] General Comment No. 4, *supra*, n. 333, at 116–7, para. 8.
[453] *Ibid.* 116, para. 8(b).   [454] *Ibid.*
[455] *See* Muterahejuru, E/C.12/1990/SR.23, at 9, para. 36.

of providing for the basic needs of all members of the population at the earliest possible time.

(ii) *Habitability*. The Committee states that housing must be habitable 'in terms of protecting the inhabitants from cold, damp or other threats to health, structural hazards, and disease vectors'.[456] To a certain extent the requirement of habitability coincides with the provision of services (such as electricity for heating), but it also relates to the physical structure of the building. In so far as inadequate and deficient housing often contributes to higher mortality and morbidity rates, this is a priority.

The State should take a number of forms of action with respect to habitability beyond the provision of services. For example, it should ensure that all public housing conforms to adequate standards as regards habitability. This would mean that all new housing construction projects should automatically take such considerations into account, and that renewal operations should be undertaken to improve old, unsatisfactory housing.

It is apparent that there is a role for legislation in enforcing such standards on the construction of private housing. Although this is certainly appropriate where construction firms are operating in the private sector for profit, it is not necessarily so where housing is built by local communities, or by the individuals for themselves. In such cases, excessively stringent conditions may serve to dissuade people from building their own homes and therefore contribute to a continued shortage of housing generally.

(iii) *Location*. According to the Committee's General Comment, housing 'must be in a location which allows access to employment options, health care services, schools, and other social facilities ... , Similarly, housing should not be built on polluted sites nor in immediate proximity to pollution sources that threaten the right to health of the inhabitants'.[457] Location of housing thus is of importance not only in so far as it has an effect on the ability of people to carry on normal lives, but also to the extent that it may prejudice the health of the inhabitants.

A major consideration for the Committee seems to be that governments should not build large, low-cost housing settlements far from centres of population merely because land is cheap. In any case, in the long run this would be a false economy given State obligations to provide accessible health care, education, and full employment. The Committee took up the question of location in its criticism of Panama. In its concluding observation the Committee noted *inter alia* that it 'had received information which pointed to many complaints by the residents that had received alternative accommodation and which concerned the distance which now had to be

---

[456] General Comment No. 4, *supra*, n. 333, at 116, para. 8(d).
[457] *Ibid.* 116–7, para. 8(f).

travelled to and from places of employment on relatively expensive public transportation and the overall poor quality of the housing in the resettlement sites'.[458] As noted above, this was one of the considerations taken into account in finding Panama to be in violation of its obligations under the Covenant. The Committee's strict line in this case is undoubtedly due to the fact that the housing in question was for the purposes of resettlement following forcible eviction. It is unlikely that the Committee would adopt such a strong position otherwise.

(iv) *Cultural Adequacy*. In its General Comment the Committee states that 'the way housing is constructed, the building materials used and the policies supporting these must appropriately reflect the culture in which they are undertaken'.[459] The rationale for this is not immediately apparent from the General Comment itself, and it may seem at face value to be a matter of lesser importance. However, traditional housing in each country often reflects the form and nature of social interactions. Failure to take such concerns into account in the provision of housing may contribute to the alienation and disruption of community life and thence undermine the traditional forms of community support.

6 The Role of Law and Legislation

Unlike the right to food, the right to housing may be found in the Constitutions of a number of States.[460] Although not often subject to judicial remedies, such constitutional entrenchment suggests quite rightly that housing as an issue does warrant a certain amount of legislative intervention.[461] The Committee, in its guidelines, foresees the existence of a panoply of legislation relating to land use and distribution, security of tenure, housing finance, building codes and regulations, discrimination in housing, prevention from eviction, property speculation, and environmental health and planning.[462]

Although clearly desirable, the Committee does not specifically expect the right to housing to be provided for by the Constitution,[463] or that any specific legislative measure should be enacted.[464] Its approach has rather

---

[458] UN ESCOR, Supp. (No. 3), at 32, para. 135(b), UN Doc. E/1992/23 (1992).

[459] General Comment No. 4, *supra*, n. 333, at 117, para. 8(g).

[460] *See e.g.* Mexico, UN Doc. E/1986/3/Add.13, at 14, para. 57; Ecuador, UN Doc. E/1986/3/Add.14, at 11, para. 55; Netherlands, UN Doc. E/1986/4/Add.24, at 1, para. 2.

[461] *See* Sachar (progress report), *supra*, n. 330, at 24–33.

[462] Reporting guidelines, *supra*, n. 154, at 14.

[463] *Contra see* Von der Weid (Antenna Internationale), E/C.12/1990/SR.23, at 5, para. 18.

[464] However, as one commentator noted, failure to repeal legislation which was clearly incompatible with the provisions of the Covenant or the non-application of legislation could amount to a violation. Leckie (International Habitat Coalition), E/C.12/1990/SR.22, at 10, para. 63.

been directed to the practical experience in each country concerned and the provision of domestic remedies in case of violation of the right.[465] In its General Comment, the Committee has outlined a number of areas in which domestic legal remedies might be provided:

(a) legal appeals aimed at preventing planned evictions or demolitions through the issuance of court-ordered injunctions; (b) legal procedures seeking compensation following an illegal eviction; (c) complaints against illegal actions carried out or supported by landlords (whether public or private) in relation to rent levels, dwelling maintainance, and racial or other forms of discrimination; (d) allegations of any form of discrimination in the allocation and availability of access to housing; and (e) complaints against landlords concerning unhealthy or inadequate housing conditions. In some legal systems it might also be appropriate to explore the possibility of facilitating class action suits in situations involving significantly increased levels of homelessness.[466]

Although the Committee appears not to require the institution of such legal remedies, in a number of cases, such as discriminatory action by landlords, failure to provide remedies (whether legal or otherwise) would seem to be a major obstacle to the full realization of the right.

7 *International Co-operation*

In addition to the general obligation in article 2(1) to take measures both domestically and through international co-operation to realize the rights in the Covenant, article 11(1) specifically provides that States should 'recognize the essential importance of international co-operation based on free consent'. As is apparent from the *travaux préparatoires*, there is no reason to suppose that this provision either adds to, or detracts from, the more general obligation.[467] Indeed, in using the term 'recognize' there is room to argue that the obligation in article 11(1) is hortatory rather than one conferring binding legal obligations.

The Committee, in noting that traditionally less than 5 per cent of all international assistance has been directed at housing, calls upon States parties that are both 'recipients and providers' of aid to 'ensure that a substantial portion of financing is devoted to creating conditions leading to a higher number of persons being adequately housed'.[468] To that end, the guidelines require the provision of information on the role of international assistance in the full realization of the rights in article 11, and that measures be taken to ensure that such assistance is used 'to fulfil the needs of the most

---

[465] General Comment No. 4, *supra*, n. 333, at 119, para. 16; *see also* Alston, E/C.12/1987/SR.9, at 5, para. 22; Rattray, E/C.12/1987/SR.12, at 8, para. 31.
[466] *Ibid.* 119, para. 17.   [467] *Ibid.* 119, para. 17.
[468] General Comment No. 4, *supra*, n. 333, at 119, para. 19.

disadvantaged'.[469] The more specific concern of the Committee has been to monitor the effects of structural adjustment programmes initiated at the behest of the international financial institutions. In General Comment No. 2, the Committee calls upon international agencies to 'scrupulously avoid involvement in projects which . . . involve large-scale evictions or displacement of persons without the provision of all appropriate protection and compensation'.[470] It reiterates this more generally in its later General Comment which provides that the international financial institutions should ensure that structural adjustment measures 'do not compromise the enjoyment of the right to housing'.[471]

D The Right to Clothing

The right to clothing, although specifically included in the Covenant, has had little attention either from the Committee or independent commentators. As far as the Committee is concerned, no reference to clothing is to be found in the reporting guidelines, and only the occasional question has been asked of States by individual members. The impression given is that clothing is not a matter in which the State may exercise a great deal of control, nor one that the Committee feels is of great importance.

IV. CONCLUSION

In comparison to other articles, the Committee has spent a considerable amount of its time addressing issues within article 11. Two of its general discussions have been on the subject of rights within article 11, and the third on the related issue of statistical indicators. In addition, it has adopted its first right-oriented General Comment on the right to housing. The prominence given to article 11 is a reflection of a number of considerations. First, article 11 contains rights that are closely associated with the 'basic needs' of the individual. The enjoyment of a minimum level of the rights to food, housing, and clothing is a necessary condition for survival, and therefore warrants detailed consideration. Secondly, article 11 includes rights that are peculiar to the Covenant. Unlike the situation in respect of articles 6–9, there is no other body equivalent to the ILO that has dealt with matters such as food and housing on an individual level or has established detailed legal standards that may be applied by the Committee. Article 11 thus

---

[469] Reporting guidelines, *supra*, n. 154, at 15.
[470] General Comment No. 2, UN DOC. E/1990/23, UN ESCOR, Supp. (No. 3), 86, at 87, para. 6 (1990).
[471] General Comment No. 4, *supra*, n. 333, at 119, para. 19.

presents itself as an area in which the Committee has considerable work to do and in which its work is innovative and particularly valuable.

Finally, a related point is that article 11 is often viewed as being the epitome of economic, social, and cultural rights. The rights are phrased in very general terms; they are accompanied by broad policy objectives and are clearly dependent for their realization upon the economic resources of the State concerned. The extent to which the Committee deals effectively with article 11 will either sustain or destroy the criticisms of legal obligations in respect of economic, social, and cultural rights in general. Article 11, to a large degree, is an acid test of the Committee's effectiveness and of the fundamental utility of the Covenant.

The Committee has made headway in a number of areas. Its most significant achievement must be the General Comment on the right to housing. In its General Comment No. 4, the Committee has clearly outlined the parameters of the right to adequate housing and has usefully described the qualitative considerations that must be taken into account in the realization of the right. According to the Committee, a right to housing means more than a right to a roof over one's head. Rather, it should be seen as the right to somewhere to live in 'security, peace, and dignity' which is governed by considerations such as security of tenure, affordability, habitability, accessibility, location, and cultural adequacy.

The Committee's General Comment on housing is a success not only in its development of the norms within article 11 but also because it was produced with considerable collaboration by NGO representatives both in the previous general discussion and in the drafting of the Comment itself. It is considered that this was an essential element in ensuring that the General Comment adequately reflected the interests and concerns of the disadvantaged worldwide.

The input of NGOs has also been significant in a number of cases, particularly those of the Dominican Republic and Panama, in which the Committee has found States to be in violation of their obligations under article 11 of the Covenant. In most cases, the Committee was only able to come to that opinion on the basis of the vast amount of material supplied by the NGO concerned. The significance of the decisions is not merely in the fact that it signals a development in the role of the Committee itself, but that it clearly shows the justiciable nature (from an international point of view) of the rights in article 11. One matter of concern, however, is that in contrast to the Dominican Republic and Panamanian cases, the more recent observations relating to forced evictions have lacked the same detail and provide less of an indication of the principles upon which the Committee came to its view. This may be something that the Committee will address as it develops its methodology with respect to the concluding observations.

Outside the specific question of the right to housing the Committee has made less headway. In particular, it has failed to give substantial meaning to the right to clothing and has yet to adopt an appropriate methodology with respect to the right to an adequate standard of living. It has been suggested that the Committee should attempt to identify those elements of the right that are not already covered by other articles in the Covenant like, for example, access to land, water, or transport.

As regards the right to food, the Committee has undertaken a useful general discussion which has generated awareness of a variety of issues which have occasionally arisen in its consideration of State reports. Nevertheless, there is clearly a need for more detailed consideration of the issues, with an emphasis upon the precise obligations to which States are bound. Three main areas may be identified in which further work is necessary. First, the Committee will have to establish a means by which those persons without adequate food may be identified. This will require the establishment of qualitative criteria which define adequacy and the stipulation of means by which they may be measured. The Committee began to address the latter question at its sixth session, when it held a discussion of the use of statistical indicators; this area of work needs to be developed. Secondly, although the method by which the rights are progressively realized is primarily within the discretion of the State, it would be useful for the Committee to identify the extent to which the State can be considered directly responsible for a lack of adequate food. There are undoubtedly circumstances where the lack of food is not merely a matter of resource scarcity. Thirdly, more consideration should be given to the general question of international co-operation both as regards the role of the international agencies and bilateral assistance programmes. For example, whereas developed States will not generally accept an obligation to provide a specific form of assistance to specific States, there may be room for strengthening obligations in the case of famines or other 'natural' disasters.

9
Conclusions

It is something of a paradox that the Covenant on Economic, Social, and Cultural Rights, which was intended to form part of the new world order following the Second World War, is now, forty-nine years later, only in the early stages of its development. An unduly lengthy and complex drafting process followed by a slow process of ratification meant that the Covenant only entered into force in 1976. It suffered a false start with the abortive supervision system operated by the working group, such that its development as an effective human rights treaty essentially started in 1987 with the creation of the Committee on Economic, Social, and Cultural Rights.

That the emergence and development of the Covenant have been a painfully slow process may be put down, to a large extent, to the political and ideological forces that have used human rights as a battleground. Economic, Social, and Cultural Rights were long championed by the Socialist States which, while ensuring their inclusion in a human rights treaty, were not prepared to accept strong implementation (or rather supervision) procedures. Western States, on the other hand, in making generalized and excessively categorical claims about the nature of economic, social, and cultural rights ensured that they were separated from their civil and political counterparts in a different instrument. The resulting Covenant on Economic, Social, and Cultural Rights was a poor relation of the Covenant on Civil and Political Rights, suffering in particular from a weaker implementation procedure.

The political or ideological conflict continued into the mid-1980s and effectively ensured that the already weak supervision system created for the Covenant on Economic, Social, and Cultural Rights would have little real force. The revitalization of the Covenant, under the auspices of the Committee, may be indirectly attributed to the end of the ideological confrontation between East and West, the democratization process in former Socialist States, and the strengthening of international co-operation.

The emergence of the Committee may also be appreciated as a response to the increasing interest in, and concern with, economic, social, and cultural welfare which accompanied the political 'enlightenment' of the 1980s. Despite the resolutely free-market philosophies of the UK and the USA, it had become evident in the context of development at least that attention needed to be paid to the economically and socially vulnerable, and that sustainable development was not to be achieved merely by reliance upon economic growth and the 'trickle down' effect as advocated in the early 1970s. More recently, development organizations such as the World Bank and UNDP have begun to place emphasis upon the notion of 'good governance' (broadly speaking the range of civil, political, social, economic, and cultural rights) and have noted the importance of basic needs in the development process.

While there is increasing awareness of and concern about the economic, social, and cultural welfare of populations, this has not, as yet, been entirely transposed into the context of human rights. On the one hand, there remains considerable resistance on the part of legal commentators to the acceptance of economic, social, and cultural rights on the same basis as civil and political rights. The rights in the Covenant continue to be characterized as 'non-justiciable' or 'programmatic'. On the other hand, development organizations have been wary of adopting a rights-based stance, which is seen as being too inflexible and confrontational. In the long run, the effectiveness with which the Committee develops the Covenant will be measured by the extent to which it disposes of such arguments in a conclusive manner.

That the Covenant has considerable potential as an international instrument for the protection of economic, social, and cultural rights is evidenced by the material scope of protection offered. Although a number of the economic rights are already the subject of international procedures under the auspices of the ILO, the Covenant does offer unparalleled protection as regards social and cultural rights. In particular, it is the only universal instrument that seeks to guarantee in general the rights to food, clothing, housing, health, and cultural life.

The unique nature of the rights to which the Covenant is addressed is, however, not without its problems. Perhaps most significant is the fact that the rights are stated in an excessively broad and general manner. This has not necessarily posed a problem for supervisory bodies in the field of civil and political rights, as they have been in the privileged position of being able to draw upon a vast array of both national and international case law generated by other human rights supervisory bodies and the various national constitutional courts that had traditionally dealt with the same, or similar, rights. However, in the case of economic, social, and cultural rights, even where they are found in the Constitutions of States, they have rarely been given legal effect by the courts concerned. Moreover, international organizations working in the field of economic, social, and cultural rights (with the exception of the ILO and, to a lesser extent, UNESCO) have resolutely refused to deal with the issues in terms of rights. This inevitably means that a considerable burden is placed upon the Covenant's supervisory body to attempt to breath some life into the provisions.

Further problems evidenced in the text of the Covenant are its confused and inconsistent structure. First, it is not clear whether the obligations clause in article 2(1) relates to all the substantive rights in Part III or only to those that are specifically recognized. Secondly, the substantive articles themselves often contain a confused mixture of rights, objectives, and implementation procedures. Thirdly, it is unclear to what extent the rights are intended to be covered by the general or specific limitation clauses to be found in the Covenant or whether indeed it is possible to derogate from them at all. Finally, and perhaps most crucially, the general State obligations are so obscure that it appears, on the face of it, to be virtually impossible to establish the extent to which a State is in compliance with its obligations under the Covenant.

Similarly, Part IV of the Covenant which outlines the supervision system is marked more by what it leaves out than by what it includes. Broadly speaking it is a reporting system to be operated under the auspices of ECOSOC. Provision is made for the participation of the specialized agencies and the Commission on Human Rights and for general reports to be submitted to the General Assembly. The text, however, does not make clear the degree to which each of the bodies mentioned should involve themselves. Although ECOSOC is mandated with the 'consideration' of the reports, the Commission on Human Rights may similarly 'study' the reports and make general recommendations. It is unclear which body has the primary responsibility for undertaking supervision. Moreover, although many assumptions could be made about the object and purpose of reporting systems in general, the Covenant only provides for the submission of reports and their consideration. The periodicity, form, and content of the reports is left open, as is the nature of the consideration that should be given to them. As a whole, the raw text of the Covenant could be said to offer considerable potential but little promise.

As at June 1994, there are 129 States parties to the Covenant which, given the date on which it entered into force, is not unreasonable. Apart from their poor record of reporting under the Covenant, which is by no means unusual for the universal human rights treaties, their participation has been consistent, if disinterested. To a large extent the unenthusiastic response of States may be put down to the unsatisfactory experience of the working group in which there was very little call for States to take their reporting responsibilities seriously. In the experience of the Committee, however, States have participated in a co-operative manner and have not found it necessary to challenge either the procedural or substantive developments in the Committee's work. In fact the Committee has largely been allowed to develop its role and practices without obstruction.

It is primarily the manner in which the Committee has transformed the supervision system that marks its work thus far. In contrast to the superficial and wholly unsatisfactory working methods of the working group, the Committee has adopted a number of useful and innovative procedural initiatives to further the efficacy of its supervisory role. In particular, one could mention the receipt of information from NGOs, the adoption of detailed State-specific concluding observations, the allocation of days to undertake general discussions, and the adoption of General Comments. While the quality of State reports still leaves a certain amount to be desired, the rewards of the reform process are beginning to show. The Committee has adopted four influential General Comments, the most recent of which was on a substantive article, and has come to the point where it was able, with reasonable certainty, to find a State in violation of its obligations under the Covenant.

Having said that, there remain a number of problems that have impeded the full development of the supervisory process in the manner desired by the Committee. First, as noted above, there is need for a considerable improvement in both the quality and timeliness of State reports. The measures taken thus far by the Committee, such as the creation of new reporting guidelines and the mobilization of technical assistance, have yet to reap rewards. Also, the most recent practice of the Committee in considering situations where the State has failed to submit a report in ten years poses problems both of a logistical and legal nature.

Secondly, despite the existence of mechanisms for the receipt of information from NGOs and specialised agencies, the response has been particularly poor. There is something of a vicious circle here. Until the Committee demonstrates itself to be an effective supervisory mechanism, giving considered and detailed analyses of State reports and making determinations as to non-compliance in appropriate cases, it will not be deemed worthy of attention by such bodies. Equally, the Committee is essentially hamstrung without adequate access to alternative sources of information. As there is a limited amount that the Committee itself may do in such circumstances, the need for greater Secretariat support and more publicity become of central importance.

The lack of proper Secretariat support has been one of the most unsatisfactory aspects of the Committee's work which, if it continues, could easily stultify the future development of the Covenant. The Secretariat has undertaken no analytical studies and has provided only a minimal amount of assistance in terms of collecting information, undertaking an initial consideration of State reports and publicizing the work of the Committee. This is particularly unfortunate in the context of the Committee's work, given its dependence upon large quantities of detailed information on the situation prevailing in the countries concerned and the urgent need for a greater understanding of the content of the norms within the Covenant.

The headway made by the Committee in terms of its procedural reforms has not been matched by its development of the substantive guarantee. It has produced useful General Comments on article 2(1) and on the right to housing in article 11, which have done much to clarify the issues involved, but it continues to be overwhelmed by the range and detail of the subjects with which it is dealing. The reporting guidelines indicate quite clearly that, whereas the Committee has formulated its general approach, it has considerable work to do before it will be able to focus effectively upon the salient issues.

In terms of its general approach, the Committee has made a number of important points about the nature of State obligations under the Covenant. In particular, it has pointed out that, despite the broad terms of article 2(1), a number of the rights and articles are capable of immediate implementation. Further, it has suggested that there is a 'core obligation' under which States are required to ensure, at least, the enjoyment of a minimum core content of each right. Failure to comply with the core obligation will amount to a *prima facie* violation of the Covenant. However, in so far as the Committee has not spelt out what it understands to be the minimum core content, or even whether it is a national or international standard, suggests that it has considerably more work to do in this area. Other significant aspects of the Committee's general approach have been the emphasis placed upon the principle of non-discrimination, and its requirement that certain rights be ensured on an inter-individual level.

As regards the specific rights themselves, however, the Committee has only undertaken an in-depth analysis of the right to housing in article 11. Otherwise, it has tended to interpret the articles in a broad manner without excessive analysis of terminology. On the one hand this has enabled the Committee to view the provisions in a dynamic manner, giving them a relevance and validity in current circumstances that they might not otherwise gain. For example, the Committee has extended the range of grounds upon which distinctions might be considered discriminatory far beyond those actually specified in article 2(2). However, on the other hand, the Committee may be criticized for being too general in its approach and for failing to address the precise terms of the articles with sufficient rigour. A particular example is article 8, which is not only considerably more detailed than other articles and encompasses issues that have been dealt with at length by other bodies, but also contains a number of questions that require clarification. Specifically, there is a need for consideration to be given to the relative scope and operation of the limitations clauses in article 8(1)(a) and (2).

Notwithstanding the generality of its approach, the Committee has made a certain amount of headway with articles 6 to 8 in terms of outlining the scope of the provisions and occasionally addressing important points of concern. For example, the Committee has interpreted the right to work in article 6 as including a right not to be arbitrarily dismissed from employment and a right not to be forced to work. Similarly, with respect to article 8, it has made important, if controversial, decisions such as viewing pre-entry closed shop agreements as being in violation of the right to join the trade union of one's choice.

In developing the substance of the rights in articles 6 to 9, it is clear that the Committee will have to make reference to the work of the ILO in this area. Not only is it necessary that there should not be any conflict in standards, but it is also apparent that excessive duplication of the supervisory process would be a waste of time and resources for all parties concerned. The main function of the Committee in this area should be to supplement the protection already offered by the ILO. This means concentrating upon the position of those States that are not party to the relevant ILO Convention or who have persistently failed to take the necessary remedial action.

Even for the Committee to undertake such a limited function, it is necessary for it to develop the necessary expertise. It is somewhat unfortunate in this respect that the participation of the ILO remains at a minimal level, despite the reformed nature of the Committee. In the absence of adequate assistance from the ILO itself, the Committee will have to adopt alternative strategies for developing the necessary expertise. It has been suggested, for example, that the Committee have greater control over the appointment of its members and that individual members should take on the responsibility for developing expertise in particular subject areas.

As suggested, some of the failings of the Committee as regards its approach to the substance of the articles may be put down to the dynamics of its operation as a supervisory body. In particular one might note the lack of technical expertise within, and available to, the Committee, the inadequate amount of time allowed to the Committee to exercise its functions in an effective manner, the lack of strong Secretariat support, and the relatively unfocused nature of the reporting procedure. It appears to be extremely difficult, under present conditions, for the Committee to concentrate upon specific issues of relevance during its consideration of a State report. What is required is some form of assistance, whether in terms of Secretariat support or time, even of a temporary nature, that might in effect generate some momentum in the implementation process as a whole.

Notwithstanding the various problems faced by the Committee, the prospects for the future are positive. The Committee has operated for a number of sessions without significant conflict, has adopted a number of important general comments and has begun to make headway in developing the normative content of the rights. In addition, it has one of the most well-developed reporting systems to be found at the universal level and has begun to receive useful assistance from NGOs. The level of confidence within the Committee is perhaps reflected in its recent discussions on the possibility of drafting an optional protocol providing for a system of individual complaints. Although the establishment of a complaints system is as yet a distant prospect, it is undoubtedly true that the operation of such a system would have a beneficial effect, not only in terms of improving the protection offered by the Covenant, but also in raising the level of international awareness of the work of the Committee.

Appendix I

The International Covenant on Economic, Social, and Cultural Rights

PREAMBLE

THE STATES PARTIES TO THE PRESENT COVENANT,

Considering that, in accordance with the principles proclaimed in the Charter of the United Nations, recognition of the inherent dignity and of the equal and inalienable rights of all members of the human family is the foundation of freedom, justice and peace in the world,

Recognizing that these rights derive from the inherent dignity of the human person,

Recognizing that, in accordance with the Universal Declaration of Human Rights, the ideal of free human beings enjoying freedom from fear and want can only be achieved if conditions are created whereby everyone may enjoy his economic, social and cultural rights, as well as his civil and political rights,

Considering the obligation of States under the Charter of the United Nations to promote universal respect for and observance of, human rights and freedoms,

Realizing that the individual, having duties to other individuals and to the community to which he belongs, is under a responsibility to strive for the promotion and observance of the rights recognized in the present Covenant,

Agree upon the following articles:

PART I

Article 1

1. All peoples have the right of self-determination. By virtue of that right they freely determine their political status and freely pursue their economic, social and cultural development.

2. All peoples may, for their own ends, freely dispose of their natural wealth and resources without prejudice to any obligations arising out of international economic co-operation, based upon the principle of mutual benefit, and international law. In no case may a people be deprived of its own means of subsistence.

3. The States Parties to the present Covenant, including those having responsibility for the administration of Non-Self-Governing and Trust Territories, shall promote the realization of the right of self-determination, and shall respect that right, in conformity with the provisions of the Charter of the United Nations.

PART II

Article 2

1. Each State Party to the present Covenant undertakes to take steps, individually and through international assistance and co-operation, especially economic and

technical, to the maximum of its available resources, with a view to achieving progressively the full realization of the rights recognized in the present Covenant by all appropriate means, including particularly the adoption of legislative measures.

2. The States Parties to the present Covenant undertake to guarantee that the rights enunciated in the present Covenant will be exercised without discrimination of any kind as to race, colour, sex, language, religion, political or other opinion, national or social origin, property, birth or other status.

3. Developing countries, with due regard to human rights and their national economy, may determine to what extent they would guarantee the economic rights recognized in the present Covenant to non-nationals.

Article 3

The States Parties to the present Covenant undertake to ensure the equal right of men and women to the enjoyment of all economic, social and cultural rights set forth in the present Covenant.

Article 4

The States Parties to the present Covenant recognize that, in the enjoyment of those rights provided by the State in conformity with the present Covenant, the State may subject such rights only to such limitations as are determined by law only in so far as this may be compatible with the nature of those rights and solely for the purpose of promoting the general welfare in a democratic society.

Article 5

1. Nothing in the present Covenant may be interpreted as implying for any State, group or person any right to engage in activity or to perform any act aimed at the destruction of any of the rights or freedoms recognized herein, or at their limitation to a greater extent than is provided for in the present Covenant.

2. No restriction upon or derogation from any of the fundamental human rights recognized or existing in any country in virtue of law, conventions, regulations or custom shall be admitted on the pretext that the present Covenant does not recognize such rights or that it recognizes them to a lesser extent.

PART III

Article 6

1. The States Parties to the present Covenant recognize the right to work, which includes the right of everyone to the opportunity to gain his living by work which he freely chooses or accepts, and will take appropriate steps to safeguard this right.

2. The steps to be taken by a State Party to the present Covenant to achieve the full realization of this right shall include technical and vocational guidance and training programmes, policies and techniques to achieve steady economic, social and cultural development and full and productive employment under conditions safeguarding fundamental political and economic freedoms to the individual.

Article 7

The States Parties to the present Covenant recognize the right of everyone to the enjoyment of just and favourable conditions of work which ensure, in particular:
   (*a*) Remuneration which provides all workers as a minimum with:
      (i) Fair wages and equal remuneration for work of equal value without distinction of any kind, in particular women being guaranteed conditions of work not inferior to those enjoyed by men, with equal pay for equal work;
      (ii) A decent living for themselves and their families in accordance with the provisions of the present Covenant;
   (*b*) Safe and healthy working conditions;
   (*c*) Equal opportunity for everyone to be promoted in his employment to an appropriate higher level, subject to no considerations other than those of seniority and competence;
   (*d*) Rest, leisure and reasonable limitation of working hours and periodic holidays with pay, as well as remuneration for public holidays.

Article 8

1. The States Parties to the present Covenant undertake to ensure:
   (*a*) The right of everyone to form trade unions and join the trade union of his choice, subject only to the rules of the organization concerned, for the promotion and protection of his economic and social interests. No restrictions may be placed on the exercise of this right other than those prescribed by law and which are necessary in a democratic society in the interests of national security or public order or for the protection of the rights and freedoms of others;
   (*b*) The right of trade unions to establish national federations or confederations and the right of the latter to form or join international trade-union organizations;
   (*c*) The right of trade unions to function freely subject to no limitations other than those prescribed by law and which are necessary in a democratic society in the interests of national security or public order or for the protection of the rights and freedoms of others;
   (*d*) The right to strike, provided that it is exercised in conformity with the laws of the particular country.
2. This article shall not prevent the imposition of lawful restrictions on the exercise of these rights by members of the armed forces or of the police or of the administration of the State.
3. Nothing in this article shall authorize States Parties to the International Labour Organization Convention of 1948 concerning Freedom of Association and Protection of the Right to Organize to take legislative measures which would prejudice, or apply the law in such a manner as would prejudice, the guarantees provided for in that Convention.

Article 9

The States Parties to the present Covenant recognize the right of everyone to social security, including social insurance.

Article 10

The States Parties to the present Covenant recognize that:

1. The widest possible protection and assistance should be accorded to the family, which is the natural and fundamental group unit of society, particularly for its establishment and while it is responsible for the care and education of dependent children. Marriage must be entered into with the free consent of the intending spouses.

2. Special protection should be accorded to mothers during a reasonable period before and after childbirth. During such period working mothers should be accorded paid leave or leave with adequate social security benefits.

3. Special measures of protection and assistance should be taken on behalf of all children and young persons without any discrimination for reasons of parentage or other conditions. Children and young persons should be protected from economic and social exploitation. Their employment in work harmful to their morals or health or dangerous to life or likely to hamper their normal development should be punishable by law. States should also set age limits below which the paid employment of child labour should be prohibited and punishable by law.

Article 11

1. The States Parties to the present Covenant recognize the right of everyone to an adequate standard of living for himself and his family, including adequate food, clothing and housing, and to the continuous improvement of living conditions. The States Parties will take appropriate steps to ensure the realization of this right, recognizing to this effect the essential importance of international co-operation based on free consent.

2. The States Parties to the present Covenant, recognizing the fundamental right of everyone to be free from hunger, shall take, individually and through international co-operation, the measures, including specific programmes, which are needed:

   (*a*) To improve methods of production, conservation and distribution of food by making full use of technical and scientific knowledge, by disseminating knowledge of the principles of nutrition and by developing or reforming agrarian systems in such a way as to achieve the most efficient development and utilization of natural resources;

   (*b*) Taking into account the problems of both food-importing and food-exporting countries, to ensure an equitable distribution of world food supplies in relation to need.

Article 12

1. The States Parties to the present Covenant recognize the right of everyone to the enjoyment of the highest attainable standard of physical and mental health.

2. The steps to be taken by the States Parties to the present Covenant to achieve the full realization of this right shall include those necessary for:

   (*a*) The provision for the reduction of the stillbirth-rate and of infant mortality and for the healthy development of the child;

(*b*) The improvement of all aspects of environmental and industrial hygiene;

(*c*) The prevention, treatment and control of epidemic, endemic, occupational and other diseases;

(*d*) The creation of conditions which would assure to all medical service and medical attention in the event of sickness.

Article 13

1. The States Parties to the present Covenant recognize the right of everyone to education. They agree that education shall be directed to the full development of the human personality and the sense of its dignity, and shall strengthen the respect for human rights and fundamental freedoms. They further agree that education shall enable all persons to participate effectively in a free society, promote understanding, tolerance and friendship among all nations and all racial, ethnic or religious groups, and further the activities of the United Nations for the maintenance of peace.

2. The States Parties to the present Covenant recognize that, with a view to achieving the full realization of this right:

(*a*) Primary education shall be compulsory and available free to all;

(*b*) Secondary education in its different forms, including technical and vocational secondary education, shall be made generally available and accessible to all by every appropriate means, and in particular by the progressive introduction of free education;

(*c*) Higher education shall be made equally accessible to all, on the basis of capacity, by every appropriate means, and in particular by the progressive introduction of free education;

(*d*) Fundamental education shall be encouraged or intensified as far as possible for those persons who have not received or completed the whole period of their primary education;

(*e*) The development of a system of schools at all levels shall be actively pursued, an adequate fellowship system shall be established, and the material conditions of teaching staff shall be continuously improved.

3. The States Parties to the present Covenant undertake to have respect for the liberty of parents and, when applicable, legal guardians to choose for their children schools, other than those established by the public authorities, which conform to such minimum educational standards as may be laid down or approved by the State and to ensure the religious and moral education of their children in conformity with their own convictions.

4. No part of this article shal be construed so as to interfere with the liberty of individuals and bodies to establish and direct educational institutions, subject always to the observance of the principles set forth in paragraph 1 of this article and to the requirement that the education given in such institutions shall conform to such minimum standards as may be laid down by the State.

Article 14

Each State Party to the present Covenant which, at the time of becoming a Party, has not been able to secure in its metropolitan territory or other territories under its jurisdiction compulsory primary education, free of charge, undertakes, within two years, to work out and adopt a detailed plan of action for the progressive implementation, within a reasonable number of years, to be fixed in the plan, of the principle of compulsory education free of charge for all.

Article 15

1. The States Parties to the present Covenant recognize the right of everyone:
     (*a*) To take part in cultural life;
     (*b*) To enjoy the benefits of scientific progress and its applications;
     (*c*) To benefit from the protection of the moral and material interests resulting from any scientific, literary or artistic production of which he is the author.
2. The steps to be taken by the States Parties to the present Covenant to achieve the full realization of this right shall include those necessary for the conservation, the development and the diffusion of science and culture.
3. The States Parties to the present Covenant undertake to respect the freedom indispensable for scientific research and creative activity.
4. The State Parties to the present Covenant recognize the benefits to be derived from the encouragement and development of international contacts and co-operation in the scientific and cultural fields.

PART IV

Article 16

1. The States Parties to the present Covenant undertake to submit in conformity with this part of the Covenant reports on the measures which they have adopted and the progress made in achieving the observance of the rights recognized herein.
2. (*a*) All reports shall be submitted to the Secretary-General of the United Nations, who shall transmit copies to the Economic and Social Council for consideration in accordance with the provisions of the present Covenant;
     (*b*) The Secretary-General of the United Nations shall also transmit to the specialized agencies copies of the reports, or any relevant parts therefrom, from States Parties to the present Covenant which are also members of these specialized agencies in so far as these reports, or parts therefrom, relate to any matters which fall within the responsibilities of the said agencies in accordance with their constitutional instruments.

Article 17

1. The States Parties to the present Covenant shall furnish their reports in stages, in accordance with a programme to be established by the Economic and Social Council within one year of the entry into force of the present Covenant after consultation with the States Parties and the specialized agencies concerned.
2. Reports may indicate factors and difficulties affecting the degree of fulfilment of obligations under the present Covenant.
3. Where relevant information has previously been furnished to the United Nations or to any specialized agency by any State Party to the present Covenant, it

will not be necessary to reproduce that information, but a precise reference to the information so furnished will suffice.

Article 18

Pursuant to its responsibilities under the Charter of the United Nations in the field of human rights and fundamental freedoms, the Economic and Social Council may make arrangements with the specialized agencies in respect of their reporting to it on the progress made in achieving the observance of the provisions of the present Covenant falling within the scope of their activities. These reports may include particulars of decisions and recommendations on such implementation adopted by their competent organs.

Article 19

The Economic and Social Council may transmit to the Commission on Human Rights for study and general recommendation or, as appropriate, for information the reports concerning human rights submitted by States in accordance with articles 16 and 17, and those concerning human rights submitted by the specialized agencies in accordance with article 18.

Article 20

The States Parties to the present Covenant and the specialized agencies concerned may submit comments to the Economic and Social Council on any general recommendation under article 19 or reference to such general recommendation in any report of the Commission on Human Rights or any documentation referred to therein.

Article 21

The Economic and Social Council may submit from time to time to the General Assembly reports with recommendations of a general nature and a summary of the information received from the States Parties to the present Covenant and the specialized agencies on the measures taken and the progress made in achieving general observance of the rights recognized in the present Covenant.

Article 22

The Economic and Social Council may bring to the attention of other organs of the United Nations, their subsidiary organs and specialized agencies concerned with furnishing technical assistance any matters arising out of the reports referred to in this part of the present Covenant which may assist such bodies in deciding, each within its field of competence, on the advisability of international measures likely to contribute to the effective progressive implementation of the present Covenant.

Article 23

The States Parties to the present Covenant agree that international action for the achievement of the rights recognized in the present Covenant includes such methods as the conclusion of conventions, the adoption of recommendations, the furnishing of technical assistance and the holding of regional meetings and technical meetings for the purpose of consultation and study organized in conjunction with the Governments concerned.

Article 24

Nothing in the present Covenant shall be interpreted as impairing the provisions of the Charter of the United Nations and of the constitutions of the specialized agencies which define the respective responsibilities of the various organs of the United Nations and of the specialized agencies in regard to the matters dealt with in the present Covenant.

Article 25

Nothing in the present Covenant shall be interpreted as impairing the inherent right of all peoples to enjoy and utilize fully and freely their natural wealth and resources.

PART V

Article 26

1. The present Covenant is open for signature by any State Member of the United Nations or member of any of its specialized agencies, by any State Party to the Statute of the International Court of Justice, and by any other State which has been invited by the General Assembly of the United Nations to become a party to the present Covenant.

2. The present Covenant is subject to ratification. Instruments of ratification shall be deposited with the Secretary-General of the United Nations.

3. The present Covenant shall be open to accession by any State referred to in paragraph 1 of this article.

4. Accession shall be effected by the deposit of an instrument of accession with the Secretary-General of the United Nations.

5. The Secretary-General of the United Nations shall inform all States which have signed the present Covenant or acceded to it of the deposit of each instrument of ratification or accession.

Article 27

1. The present Covenant shall enter into force three months after the date of the deposit with the Secretary-General of the United Nations of the thirty-fifth instrument of ratification or instrument of accession.

2. For each State ratifying the present Covenant or acceding to it after the deposit of the thirty-fifth instrument of ratification or instrument of accession, the present Covenant shall enter into force three months after the date of the deposit of its own instrument of ratification or instrument of accession.

Article 28

The provisions of the present Covenant shall extend to all parts of federal States without any limitations or exceptions.

Article 29

1. Any State Party to the present Covenant may propose an amendment and file it with the Secretary-General of the United Nations. The Secretary-General shall thereupon communicate any proposed amendments to the States Parties to the

present Covenant with a request that they notify him whether they favour a conference of States Parties for the purpose of considering and voting upon the proposals. In the event that at least one third of the States Parties favours such a conference, the Secretary-General shall convene the conference under the auspices of the United Nations. Any amendments adopted by a majority of the States Parties present and voting at the conference shall be submitted to the General Assembly of the United Nations for approval.

2. Amendments shall come into force when they have been approved by the General Assembly of the United Nations and accepted by a two-thirds majority of the States Parties to the present Covenant in accordance with their respective constitutional processes.

3. When amendments come into force they shall be binding on those States Parties which have accepted them, other States Parties still being bound by the provisions of the present Covenant and any earlier amendment which they have accepted.

Article 30

Irrespective of the notifications made under article 26, paragraph 5, the Secretary-General of the United Nations shall inform all States referred to in paragraph 1 of the same article of the following particulars:

(*a*) Signatures, ratifications and accessions under article 26;

(*b*) The date of entry into force of the present Covenant under article 27 and the date of the entry into force of any amendments under article 29.

Article 31

1. The present Covenant, of which the Chinese, English, French, Russian and Spanish texts are equally authentic, shall be deposited in the archives of the United Nations.

2. The Secretary-General of the United Nations shall transmit certified copies of the present Covenant to all States referred to in article 26.

Appendix II

General Comments of the Committee on Economic, Social, and Cultural Rights

GENERAL COMMENT NO. 1 (1989)

Reporting by States Parties

1. The reporting obligations which are contained in part IV of the Covenant are designed principally to assist each State party in fulfilling its obligations under the Covenant and, in addition, to provide a basis on which the Council, assisted by the Committee, can discharge its responsibilities for monitoring States parties' compliance with their obligations and for facilitating the realization of economic, social and cultural rights in accordance with the provisions of the Covenant. The Committee considers that it would be incorrect to assume that reporting is essentially only a procedural matter designed solely to satisfy each State party's formal obligation to report to the appropriate international monitoring body. On the contrary, in accordance with the letter and spirit of the Covenant, the processes of preparation and submission of reports by States can, and indeed should, serve to achieve a variety of objectives.

2. A *first objective*, which is of particular relevance to the initial report required to be submitted within two years of the Covenant's entry into force for the State party concerned, is to ensure that a comprehensive review is undertaken with respect to national legislation, administrative rules and procedures, and practices in an effort to ensure the fullest possible conformity with the Covenant. Such a review might, for example, be undertaken in conjunction with each of the relevant national ministries or other authorities responsible for policy-making and implementation in the different fields covered by the Covenant.

3. A *second objective*, is to ensure that the State party monitors the actual situation with respect to each of the rights on a regular basis and is thus aware of the extent to which the various rights are, or are not, being enjoyed by all individuals within the territory or under its jurisdiction. From the Committee's experience to date, it is clear that the fulfilment of this objective cannot be achieved only by the preparation of aggregate national statistics or estimates, but also requires that special attention by given to any worse-off regions or areas and to any specific groups or subgroups which appear to be particularly vulnerable or disadvantaged. Thus, the essential first step towards promoting the realization of economic, social and cultural rights is diagnosis and knowledge of the existing situation. The Committee is aware that this process of monitoring and gathering information is a potentially time-consuming and costly one and that international assistance and co-operation, as provided for in article 2, paragraph 1 and articles 22 and 23 of the Covenant, may well be an integral part of any process designed to promote accepted goals of public policy and is indispensable to the effective implementation of the Covenant, it may note that this fact in its report to the Committee

and indicate the nature and extent of any international assistance that it may need.

4. While monitoring is designed to give a detailed overview of the existing situation, the principal value of such an overview is to provide the basis of the elaboration of clearly stated and carefully targeted policies, including the establishment of priorities which reflect the provisions of the Covenant. Therefore, a *third objective* of the reporting process is to enable the Government to demonstrate that such principled policy-making has in fact been undertaken. While the Covenant makes this obligation explicit only in article 14 in cases where 'compulsory primary education, free of charge' has not yet been secured for all, a comparable obligation 'to work out and adopt a detailed plan of action for the progressive implementation' of each of the rights contained in the Covenant is clearly implied by the obligation in article 2, paragraph 1 'to take steps . . . by all appropriate means . . .'

5. A *fourth objective* of the reporting process is to facilitate public scrutiny of government policies with respect to economic, social and cultural rights and to encourage the involvement of the various economic, social and cultural sectors of society in the formulation, implementation and review of the relevant policies. In examining reports submitted to it to date, the Committee has welcomed the fact that a number of States parties, reflecting different political and economic systems, have encouraged inputs by such non-governmental groups into the preparation of their reports under the Covenant. Other States have ensured the widespread dissemination of their reports with a view to enabling comments to be made by the public at large. In these ways, the preparation of the report, and its consideration at the national level can come to be of at least as much value as the constructive dialogue conducted at the international level between the Committee and representative of the reporting State.

6. A *fifth objective* is to provide a basis on which the State party itself, as well as the Committee, can effectively evaluate the extent to which progress has been made towards the realization of the obligations contained in the Covenant. For this purpose, it may be useful for States to identify specific bench-marks or goals against which their performance in a given area can be assessed. Thus, for example, it is generally agreed that it is important to set specific goals with respect to the reduction of infant mortality, the extent of vaccination of children, the intake of calories per person, the number of persons per health care provider, etc. In many of these areas, global bench-marks are of limited use, whereas national or other more specific bench-marks can provide an extremely valuable indication of progress.

7. In this regard, the Committee wishes to note that the Covenant attaches particular importance to the concept of 'progressive realization' of the relevant rights and, for that reason, the Committee urges States parties to include in their periodic reports information which shows the progress over time, with respect to the effective realization of the relevant rights. By the same token, it is clear that qualitative, as well as quantitative, data are required in order for an adequate assessment of the situation to be made.

8. A *sixth objective* is to enable the State party itself to develop a better understanding of the problems and shortcomings encountered in efforts to realize progressively the full range of economic, social and cultural rights. For this reason, it is

essential that States parties report in detail on the 'factors and difficulties' inhibiting such realization. This process of identification and recognition of the relevant difficulties then provides the framework within which more appropriate policies can be devised.

9. A *seventh objective* is to enable the Committee, and the States parties as a whole, to facilitate the exchange of information among States and to develop a better understanding of the common problems faced by States and a fuller appreciation of the type of measures which might be taken to promote effective realization of each of the rights contained in the Covenant. This part of the process also enables the Committee to identify the most appropriate means by which the international community might assist States, in accordance with articles 22 and 23 of the Covenant. In order to underline the importance which the Committee attaches to this objective, a separate general comment on those articles will be discussed by the Committee at its fourth session.

GENERAL COMMENT NO. 2 (1990)

International Technical Assistance Measures (Article 22 of the Covenant)

1. Article 22 of the Covenant establishes a mechanism by which the Economic and Social Council may bring to the attention of relevant United Nations bodies any matters arising out of reports submitted under the Covenant 'which may assist such bodies in deciding, each within the field of competence, on the advisability of international measures likely to contribute to the effective progressive implementation of the . . . Covenant'. While the primary responsibility under Article 22 is vested in the Council, it is clearly appropriate for the Committee on Economic, Social and Cultural Rights to play an active role in advising and assisting the Council in this regard.

2. Recommendations in accordance with Article 22 may be made to any 'organs of the United Nations, their subsidiary organs and specialized agencies concerned with furnishing technical assistance'. The Committee considers that this provision should be interpreted so as to include virtually all United Nations organs and agencies involved in any aspect of international development co-operation. It would therefore be appropriate for recommendations in accordance with Article 22 to be addressed, *inter alia*, to the Secretary-General, subsidiary organs of the Council such as the Commission on the Status of Women, other bodies such as UNDP, UNICEF and CDP, agencies such as the World Bank and IMF, and any of the other specialized agencies such as ILO, FAO, UNESCO and WHO.

3. Article 22 could lead either to recommendations of a general policy nature or to more narrowly focused recommendations relating to a specific situation. In the former context, the principal role of the Committee would seem to be to encourage greater attention to efforts to promote economic, social and cultural rights within the framework of international development co-operation activities undertaken by, or with the assistance of, the United Nations and its agencies. In this regard the Committee notes that the Commission on Human Rights, in its resolution 1989/13 of 2 March 1989, invited it 'to give consideration to means by which the various United Nations agencies working in the field of development could best integrate measures

designed to promote full respect for economic, social and cultural rights in their activities'.

4. As a preliminary practical matter, the Committee notes that its own endeavours would be assisted, and the relevant agencies would also be better informed, if they were to take a greater interest in the work of the Committee. While recognizing that such and interest can be demonstrated in a variety of ways, the Committee observes that attendance by representatives of the appropriate United Nations bodies at its first four sessions has, with the notable exceptions of ILO, UNESCO and WHO, been very low. Similarly, pertinent materials and written information had been received from only a very limited number of agencies. The Committee considers that a deeper understanding of the relevance of economic, social and cultural rights in the context of international development co-operation activities would be considerably facilitated through greater interaction between the Committee and the appropriate agencies. At the very least, the day of general discussion on a specific issue, which the Committee undertakes at each of its sessions, provides an ideal context in which a potentially productive exchange of views can be undertaken.

5. On the broader issues of the promotion of respect for human rights in the context of development activities, the Committee has so far seen only rather limited evidence of specific efforts by United Nations bodies. It notes with satisfaction in this regard the initiative taken jointly by the Centre for Human Rights and UNDP in writing to United Nations Resident Representatives and other field-based officials, inviting their 'suggestions and advice, in particular with respect to possible forms of co-operation in on-going projects [identified] as having a human-rights dimension or in new ones in response to a specific Government's request'. The Committee has also been informed of longstanding efforts undertaken by ILO to link its own human rights and other international labour standards to its technical co-operation activities.

6. With respect to such activities, two general principles are important. The first is that the two sets of human rights are indivisible and interdependent. This means that efforts to promote one set of rights should also take full account of the other. United Nations agencies involved in the promotion of economic, social and cultural rights should do their utmost to ensure that their activities are fully consistent with the enjoyment of civil and political rights. In negative terms this means that the international agencies should scrupulously avoid involvement in projects which, for example, involve the use of forced labour in contravention of international standards, or promote or reinforce discrimination against individuals or groups contrary to the provisions of the Covenant, or involve large-scale evictions or displacement of persons without the provision of all appropriate protection and compensation. In positive terms, it means that, wherever possible, the agencies should act as advocates of projects and approaches which contribute not only to economic growth or other broadly-defined objectives, but also to enhanced enjoyment of the full range of human rights.

7. The second principle of general relevance is that development co-operation activities do not automatically contribute to the promotion of respect for economic, social and cultural rights. Many activities undertaken in the name of 'development' have subsequently been recognized as ill-conceived and even counter-productive in human rights terms. In order to reduce the incidence of such problems, the whole

range of issues dealt with in the Covenant should, wherever possible and appropriate, be given specific and careful consideration.

8. Despite the importance of seeking to integrate human rights concerns into development activities, it is true that proposals for such integration can too easily remain at a level of generality. Thus, in an effort to encourage the operationalization of the principle contained in article 22 of the Covenant, the Committee wishes to draw attention to the following specific measures which merit consideration by the relevant bodies:

(*a*) As a matter of principle, the appropriate United Nations organs and agencies should specifically recognize the intimate relationship which should be established between development activities and efforts to promote respect for human rights in general, and economic, social and cultural rights in particular. The Committee notes in this regard the failure of each of the first three United Nations Development Decade Strategies to recognize that relationship and urges that the fourth such strategy, to be adopted in 1990, should rectify that omission;

(*b*) Consideration should be given by United Nations agencies to the proposal, made by the Secretary-General in a report of 1979,[1] that a 'human rights impact statement' be required to be prepared in connection with all major development co-operation activities;

(*c*) The training of briefing given to project and other personnel employed by United Nations agencies should include a component dealing with human rights standards and principles.

(*d*) Every effort should be made, at each phase of a development project, to ensure that the rights contained in the Covenants are duly taken into account. This would apply, for example, in the initial assessment of the priority needs of a particular country, in the identification of particular projects, in project design, in the implementation of the project, and in its final evaluation.

9. A matter which has been of particular concern to the Committee in the examination of the reports of States parties is the adverse impact of the debt burden and of the relevant adjustment measures on the enjoyment of economic, social and cultural rights in many countries. The Committee recognizes that adjustment programmes will often be unavoidable and that these will frequently involve a major element of austerity. Under such circumstances, however, endeavours to protect the most basic economic, social and cultural rights become more, rather than less, urgent. States parties to the Covenant, as well as the relevant United Nations agencies, should thus make a particular effort to ensure that such protection is, to the maximum extent possible, built-in to programmes and policies designed to promote adjustment. Such an approach, which is sometimes referred to as 'adjustment with a human face' or as promoting 'the human dimension of development' requires that the goal of protecting the rights of the poor and vulnerable should become a basic objective of economic adjustment. Similarly, international measures to deal with the debt crisis should take full account of the need to protect economic,

---

[1] 'The international dimensions of the right to development as a human right in relation to other human rights based on international co-operation, including the right to peace, taking into account the requirements of the new international economic order and the fundamental human needs' (E/CN.4/1334, para. 314).

social and cultural rights through, *inter alia*, international co-operation. In many situations, this might point to the need for major debt relief initiatives.

10. Finally, the Committee wishes to draw attention to the important opportunity provided to States parties, in accordance with article 22 of the Covenant, to identify in their reports any particular needs they might have for technical assistance or development co-operation.

GENERAL COMMENT NO. 3 (1990)

The Nature of States Parties' Obligations
(Article 2, Paragraph 1, of the Covenant)

1. Article 2 is of particular importance to a full understanding of the Covenant and must be seen as having a dynamic relationship with all of the other provisions of the Covenant. It describes the nature of the general legal obligations undertaken by States parties to the Covenant. Those obligations include both what may be termed (following the work of the International Law Commission) obligations of conduct and obligations of result. While great emphasis has sometimes been placed on the difference between the formulations used in this provision and that contained in the equivalent article 2 of the International Covenant on Civil and Political Rights, it is not always recognized that there are also significant similarities. In particular, while the Covenant provides for progressive realization and acknowledges the constraints due to the limits of available resources, it also imposes various obligations which are of immediate effect. Of these, two are of particular importance in understanding the precise nature of States parties' obligations. One of these, which is dealt with in a separate General Comment, and which is to be considered by the Committee at its sixth session, is the 'undertaking to guarantee' that relevant rights 'will be exercised without discrimination . . .'.

2. The other is the undertaking in article 2(1) 'to take steps', which in itself, is not qualified or limited by other considerations. The full meaning of the phrase can also be gauged by noting some of the different language versions. In English the undertaking is 'to take steps', in French it is 'to act' (*s'engage à agir*) and in Spanish it is 'to adopt measures' (*a adoptar medidas*). Thus while the full realization of the relevant rights may be achieved progressively, steps towards that goal must be taken within a reasonably short time after the Covenant's entry into force for the States concerned. Such steps should be deliberate, concrete and targeted as clearly as possible towards meeting the obligations recognized in the Covenant.

3. The means which should be used in order to satisfy the obligation to take steps are stated in article 2(1) to be 'all appropriate means, including particularly the adoption of legislative measures'. The Committee recognizes that in many instances legislation is highly desirable and in some cases may even be indispensable. For example, it may be difficult to combat discrimination effectively in the absence of a sound legislative foundation for the necessary measures. In fields such as health, the protection of children and mothers, and education, as well as in respect of the matters dealt with in articles 6 to 9, legislation may also be an indispensable element for many purposes.

4. The Committee notes that States parties have generally been conscientious in

detailing at least some of the legislative measures that they have taken in this regard. It wishes to emphasize, however, that the adoption of legislative measures, as specifically foreseen by the Covenant, is by no means exhaustive of the obligations of States parties. Rather, the phrase 'by all appropriate means' must be given its full and natural meaning. While each State party must decide for itself which means are the most appropriate under the circumstances with respect to each of the rights, the 'appropriateness' of the means chosen will not always be self-evident. It is therefore desirable that States parties' reports should indicate not only the measures that have been taken but also the basis on which they are considered to be the most 'appropriate' under the circumstances. However, the ultimate determination as to whether all appropriate measures have been taken remains one for the Committee to make.

5. Among the measures which might be considered appropriate, in addition to legislation, is the provision of judicial remedies with respect to rights which may, in accordance with the national legal system, be considered justiciable. The Committee notes, for example, that the enjoyment of the rights recognized, without discrimination, will often be appropriately promoted, in part, through the provision of judicial or other effective remedies. Indeed, those States parties which are also parties to the International Covenant on Civil and Political Rights are already obligated (by virtue of arts. 2 (paras. 1 and 3), 3 and 26 of that Covenant) to ensure that any person whose rights or freedoms (including the right to equality and non-discrimination) recognized in that Covenant are violated, 'shall have an effective remedy' (art. 2(3)(a)). In addition, there are a number of other provisions in the International Covenant on Economic, Social and Cultural Rights, including articles 3, 7(a)(i), 8, 10(3), 13(2)(a), (3) and (4) and 15(3) which would seem to be capable of immediate application by judicial and other organs in many national legal systems. Any suggestion that the provisions indicated are inherently non-self-executing would seem to be difficult to sustain.

6. Where specific policies aimed directly at the realization of the rights recognized in the Covenant have been adopted in legislative form, the Committee would wish to be informed, *inter alia*, as to whether such laws create any right of action on behalf of individuals or groups who feel that their rights are not being fully realized. In cases where constitutional recognition has been accorded to specific economic, social and cultural rights, or where the provisions of the Covenant have been incorporated directly into national law, the Committee would wish to receive information as to the extent to which these rights are considered to be justiciable (i.e. able to be invoked before the courts). The Committee would also wish to receive specific information as to any instances in which existing constitutional provisions relating to economic, social and cultural rights have been weakened or significantly changed.

7. Other measures which may also be considered 'appropriate' for the purposes of article 2(1) include, but are not limited to, administrative, financial, educational and social measures.

8. The Committee notes that the undertaking 'to take steps . . . by all appropriate means including particularly the adoption of legislative measures' neither requires nor precludes any particular form of government or economic system being used as the vehicle for the steps in question, provided only that it is democratic and that all

human rights are thereby respected. Thus, in terms of political and economic systems the Covenant is neutral and its principles cannot accurately be described as being predicated exclusively upon the need for, or the desirability of a socialist or a capitalist system, or a mixed, centrally planned, or *laissez-faire* economy, or upon any other particular approach. In this regard, the Committee reaffirms that the rights recognized in the Covenant are susceptible of realization within the context of a wide variety of economic and political systems, provided only that the interdependence and indivisibility of the two sets of human rights, as affirmed *inter alia* in the preamble to the Covenant, is recognized and reflected in the system in question. The Committee also notes the relevance in this regard of other human rights and in particular the right to development.

9. The principal obligation of result reflected in article 2(1) is to take steps 'with a view to achieving progressively the full realization of the rights recognized' in the Covenant. The term 'progressive realization' is often used to describe the intent of this phrase. The concept of progressive realization constitutes a recognition of the fact that full realization of all economic, social and cultural rights will generally not be able to be achieved in a short period of time. In this sense the obligation differs significantly from that contained in article 2 of the International Covenant on Civil and Political Rights which embodies an immediate obligation to respect and ensure all of the relevant rights. Nevertheless, the fact that realization over time, or in other words progressively, is foreseen under the Covenant should not be misinterpreted as depriving the obligation of all meaningful content. It is on the one hand a necessary flexibility device, reflecting the realities of the real world and the difficulties involved for any country in ensuring full realization of economic, social and cultural rights. On the other hand, the phrase must be read in the light of the overall objective, indeed the *raison d'être*, of the Covenant which is to establish clear obligations for States parties in respect of the full realization of the rights in question. It thus imposes an obligation to move as expeditiously and effectively as possible towards that goal. Moreover, any deliberately retrogressive measures in that regard would require the most careful consideration and would need to be fully justified by reference to the totality of the rights provided for in the Covenant and in the context of the full use of the maximum available resources.

10. On the basis of the extensive experience gained by the Committee, as well as by the body that preceded it, over a period of more than a decade of examining States parties' reports the Committee is of the view that a minimum core obligation to ensure the satisfaction of, at the very least, minimum essential levels of each of the rights is incumbent upon every State party. Thus, for example, a State party in which any significant number of individuals is deprived of essential foodstuffs, of essential primary health care, of basic shelter and housing, or of the most basic forms of education is, *prima facie*, failing to discharge its obligations under the Covenant. If the Covenant were to be read in such a way as not to establish such a minimum core obligation, it would be largely deprived of its *raison d'être*. By the same token, it must be noted that any assessment as to whether a State has discharged its minimum core obligation must also take account of resource constraints applying within the country concerned. Article 2(1) obligates each State party to take the necessary steps 'to the maximum of its available resources'. In order for a State party to be able to attribute its failure to meet at least its minimum core

obligations to a lack of available resources it must demonstrate that every effort has been made to use all resources that are at its disposition in an effort to satisfy, as a matter of priority, those minimum obligations.

11. The Committee wishes to emphasize, however, that even where the available resources are demonstrably inadequate, the obligation remains for a State party to strive to ensure the widest possible enjoyment of the relevant rights under the prevailing circumstances. Moreover, the obligations to monitor the extent of the realization, or more especially of the non-realization, of economic, social and cultural rights, and to devise strategies and programmes for their promotion, are not in any way eliminated as a result of resource constraints. The Committee has already dealt with these issues in its General Comment No. 1 (1989).

12. Similarly, the Committee underlines the fact that even in times of severe resource constraints whether caused by a process of adjustment, of economic recession, or by other factors the vulnerable members of society can and indeed must be protected by the adoption of relatively low-cost targeted programmes. In support of this approach the Committee takes note of the analysis prepared by UNICEF entitled 'Adjustment With a Human Face: Protecting the Vulnerable and Promoting Growth',[2] the analysis by UNDP in its *Human Development Report 1990*[3] and the analysis by the World Bank in the *World Development Report 1990*.[4]

13. A final element of article 2(1), to which attention must be drawn, is that the undertaking given by all States parties is 'to take steps, individually and through international assistance and co operation, especially economic and technical . . .'. The Committee notes that the phrase 'to the maximum of its available resources' was intended by the drafters of the Covenant to refer to both the resources existing within a State and those available from the international community through international co-operation and assistance. Moreover, the essential role of such co-operation in facilitating the full realization of the relevant rights is further underlined by the specific provisions contained in articles 11, 15, 22 and 23. With respect to article 22 the Committee has already drawn attention, in General Comment No. 2 (1990), to some of the opportunities and responsibilities that exist in relation to international co-operation. Article 23 also specifically identifies 'the furnishing of technical assistance' as well as other activities, as being among the means of 'international action for the achievement of the rights recognized . . .'.

14. The Committee wishes to emphasize that in accordance with Articles 55 and 56 of the Charter of the United Nations, with well-established principles of international law, and with the provisions of the Covenant itself, international co-operation for development and thus for the realization of economic, social and cultural rights is an obligation of all States. It is particularly incumbent upon those States which are in a position to assist others in this regard. The Committee notes in particular the importance of the Declaration on the Right to Development adopted by the General Assembly in its resolution 41/128 of 4 December 1986 and the need for States parties to take full account of all of the principles recognized therein. It emphasises that, in the absence of an active programme of international assistance

---

[2] Cornia G., Jolly R., and Stewart F. (eds.) (Oxford: Clarendon Press, 1987).
[3] (Oxford, Oxford University Press, 1990).
[4] (Oxford, Oxford University Press, 1990).

and co-operation on the part of all those States that are in a position to undertake one, the full realization of economic, social and cultural rights will remain an unfulfilled aspiration in many countries. In this respect, the Committee also recalls the terms of its General Comment No. 2 (1990).

GENERAL COMMENT NO. 4 (1991)

The Right to Adequate Housing (Article 11(1) of the Covenant)

1. Pursuant to article 11(1) of the Covenant, States parties 'recognize the right of everyone to an adequate standard of living for himself and his family, including adequate food, clothing and housing, and to the continuous improvement of living conditions'. The human right to adequate housing, which is thus derived from the right to an adequate standard of living, is of central importance for the enjoyment of all economic, social and cultural rights.

2. The Committee has been able to accumulate a large amount of information pertaining to this right. Since 1979, the Committee and its predecessors have examined 75 reports dealing with the right to adequate housing. The Committee has also devoted a day of general discussion to the issues at each of its third (see E/1989/22, para. 312) and fourth sessions (E/1923, paras. 281–285). In addition, the Committee has taken careful note of information generated by the International Year of Shelter for the Homeless (1987) including the Global Strategy for Shelter to the Year 2000 adopted by the General Assembly in its resolution 42/191 of 11 December 1987.[5] The Committee has also reviewed the relevant reports and other documentation of the Commission on Human Rights and the Sub-Commission on Prevention of Discrimination and Protection of Minorities.[6]

3. Although a wide variety of international instruments address the different dimensions of the right to adequate housing[7] article 11(1) of the Covenant is the most comprehensive and perhaps the most important of the relevant provisions.

4. Despite the fact that the international community has frequently reaffirmed the importance of full respect for the right to adequate housing, there remains a disturbingly large gap between the standards set in article 11(1) of the Covenant and the situation prevailing in many parts of the world. While the problems are often particularly acute in some developing countries which confront major resource and other constraints, the Committee observes that significant problems of

---

[5] *Official Records of the General Assembly, Forty-third Session, Supplement No. 8*, addendum (A/43/8/Add.1).

[6] Commission on Human Rights resolutions 1986/36 and 1987/22; reports by Mr Danilo Türk, Special *Rapporteur* of the Sub-Commission (E/CN.4/Sub.2/1990/19, paras. 108–20; E/CN.4/Sub.2/1991/17, paras. 137–9); see also Sub-Commission resolution 1991/26.

[7] See, e.g., art. 25(1) of the Universal Declaration on Human Rights, art. 5(e)(iii) of the International Convention on the Elimination of All Forms of Racial Discrimination, art. 14(2) of the Convention on the Elimination of All Forms of Discrimination Against Women, art. 27(3) of the Convention on the Rights of the Child, art. 10 of the Declaration on Social Progress and Development, section III (8) of the Vancouver Declaration on Human Settlements 1976 (*Report of Habitat: United Nations Conference on Human Settements* (United Nations publication, Sales No. E.76.IV.7 and corrigendum), ch. I), art. 8(1) of the Declaration on the Right to Development and the ILO Recommendation Concerning Workers' Housing 1961 (No.115).

homelessness and inadequate housing also exist in some of the most economically developed societies. The United Nations estimates that there are over 100 million persons homeless worldwide and over 1 billion inadequately housed.[8] There is no indication that this number is decreasing. It seems clear that no State party is free of significant problems of one kind or another in relation to the right to housing.

5. In some instances, the reports of States parties examined by the Committee have acknowledged and described difficulties in ensuring the right to adequate housing. For the most part, however, the information provided has been insufficient to enable the Committee to obtain an adequate picture of the situation prevailing in the State concerned. This General Comment thus aims to identify some of the principal issues which the Committee considers to be important in relation to this right.

6. The right to adequate housing applies to everyone. While the reference to 'himself and his family' reflects assumptions as to gender roles and economic activity patterns commonly accepted in 1966 when the Covenant was adopted, the phrase cannot be read today as implying any limitations upon the applicability of the right to individuals or to female-headed households or other such groups. Thus, the concept of 'family' must be understood in a wide sense. Further, individuals, as well as families are entitled to adequate housing regardless of age, economic status, group or other affiliation or status and other such factors. In particular, enjoyment of this right must, in accordance with article 2(2) of the Covenant, not be subject to any form of discrimination.

7. In the Committee's view, the right to housing should not be interpreted in a narrow or restrictive sense which equates it with, for example, the shelter provided by merely having a roof over one's head or views shelter exclusively as a commodity. Rather it should be seen as the right to live somewhere in security, peace and dignity. This is appropriate for at least two reasons. In the first place, the right to housing is integrally linked to other human rights and to the fundamental principles upon which the Covenant is premised. Thus 'the inherent dignity of the human person' from which the rights in the Covenant are said to derive requires that the term 'housing' be interpreted so as to take account of a variety of other considerations, most importantly that the right to housing should be ensured to all persons irrespective of income or access to economic resources. Secondly, the reference in article 11(1) must be read as referring not just to housing but to adequate housing. As both the Commission on Human Settlements and the Global Strategy for Shelter to the Year 2000 have stated: 'Adequate shelter means . . . adequate privacy, adequate space, adequate security, adequate lighting and ventilation, adequate basic infrastructure and adequate location with regard to work and basic facilities—all at a reasonable cost'.

8. Thus the concept of adequacy is particularly significant in relation to the right to housing since it serves to underline a number of factors which must be taken into account in determining whether particular forms of shelter can be considered to constitute 'adequate housing' for the purposes of the Covenant. While adequacy is determined in part by social, economic, cultural, climatic, ecological and other factors, the Committee believes that it is nevertheless possible to identify certain

---

[8] See n. 1.

aspects of the right that must be taken into account for this purpose in any particular context. They include the following:

(a) *Legal Security of Tenure*. Tenure takes a variety of forms, including rental (public and private) accommodation, cooperative housing, lease, owner-occupation, emergency housing and informal settlements, including occupation of land or property. Notwithstanding the type of tenure, all persons should possess a degree of security of tenure which guarantees legal protection against forced eviction, harrassment and other threats. States parties should consequently take immediate measures aimed at conferring legal security of tenure upon those persons and households currently lackng such protection, in genuine consultation with affected persons and groups;

(b) *Availability of Services, Materials, Facilities and Infrastructure*. An adequate house must contain certain facilities essential for health, security, comfort and nutrition. All beneficiaries of the right to adequate housing should have sustainable access to natural and common resources, safe drinking water, energy for cooking, heating and lighting, sanitation and washing facilities, means of food storage, refuse disposal, site drainage and emergency services;

(c) *Affordability*. Personal or household financial costs associated with housing should be at such a level that the attainment and satisfaction of other basic needs are not threatened or compromised. Steps should be taken by States parties to ensure that the percentage of housing-related costs is, in general, commensurate with income levels. States parties should establish housing subsidies for those unable to obtain affordable housing, as well as forms and levels of housing finance which adequately reflect housing needs. In accordance with the principle of affordability, tenants should be protected by appropriate means against unreasonable rent levels or rent increases. In societies where natural materials constitute the chief sources of building materials for housing, steps should be taken by States parties to ensure the availability of such materials;

(d) *Habitability*. Adequate housing must be habitable, in terms of providing the inhabitants with adequate space and protecting them from cold, damp, heat, rain, wind or other threats to health, structural hazards, and disease vectors. The physical safety of occupants must be guaranteed as well. The Committee encourages States parties to comprehensively apply the *Health Principles of Housing*[9] prepared by WHO which view housing as the environmental factor most frequently associated with conditions for disease in epidemiological analyses; i.e. inadequate and deficient housing and living conditions are invariably associated with higher mortality and morbidity rates;

(e) *Accessibility*. Adequate housing must be accessible to those entitled to it. Disadvantaged groups must be accorded full and sustainable access to adequate housing resources. Thus, such disadvantaged groups as the elderly, children, the physically disabled, the terminally ill, HIV-positive individuals, persons with persistent medical problems, the mentally ill, victims of natural disasters, people living in disaster-prone areas and other groups should be ensured some degree of priority consideration in the housing sphere. Both housing law and policy should take fully into account the special housing needs of these groups. Within many States parties

---

[9] (Geneva, World Health Organisation, 1990).

increasing access to land by landless or impoverished segments of the society should constitute a central policy goal. Discernible governmental obligations need to be developed aiming to substantiate the right of all to a secure place to live in peace and dignity, including access to land as an entitlement;

(f) *Location.* Adequate housing must be in a location which allows access to employment options, health-care services, schools, child-care centres and other social facilities. This is true both in large cities and in rural areas where the temporal and financial costs of getting to and from the place of work can place excessive demands upon the budgets of poor households. Similarly, housing should not be built on polluted sites nor in immediate proximity to pollution sources that threaten the right to health of the inhabitants;

(g) *Cultural Adequacy.* The way housing is constructed, the building materials used and the policies supporting these must appropriately enable the expression of cultural identity and diversity of housing. Activities geared towards development or modernization in the housing sphere should ensure that the cultural dimensions of housing are not sacrificed, and that, *inter alia*, modern technological facilities, as appropriate are also ensured.

9. As noted above, the right to adequate housing cannot be viewed in isolation from other human rights contained in the two International Covenants and other applicable international instruments. Reference has already been made in this regard to the concept of human dignity and the principle of non-discrimination. In addition, the full enjoyment of other rights—such as the right to freedom of expression, the right to freedom of association (such as for tenants and other community-based groups), the right to freedom of residence and the right to participate in public decision-making—is indispensable if the right to adequate housing is to be realized and maintained by all groups in society. Similarly, the right not to be subjected to arbitrary or unlawful interference with one's privacy, family, home or correspondence constitutes a very important dimension in defining the right to adequate housing.

10. Regardless of the state of development of any country, there are certain steps which must be taken immediately. As recognized in the Global Strategy for Shelter and in other international analyses, many of the measures required to promote the right to housing would only require the abstention by the Government from certain practices and a commitment to facilitate 'self-help' by affected groups. To the extent that any such steps are considered to the beyond the maximum resources available to a State party, it is appropriate that a request be made as soon as possible for international cooperation in accordance with articles 11(1), 22 and 23 of the Covenant, and that the Committee be informed thereof.

11. States parties must give due priority to those social groups living in unfavourable conditions by giving them particular consideration. Policies and legislation should correspondingly not be designed to benefit already advantaged social groups at the expense of others. The Committee is aware that external factors can affect the right to a continuous improvement of living conditions, and that in many States parties overall living conditions declined during the 1980s. However, as noted by the Committee in its General Comment No. 2 (1990) (E/1990/23, annex III), despite externally caused problems, the obligations under the Covenant continue to apply

and are perhaps even more pertinent during times of economic contraction. It would thus appear to the Committee that a general decline in living and housing conditions, directly attributable to policy and legislative decisions by States parties, and in the absence of accompanying compensatory measures, would be inconsistent with the obligations under the Covenant.

12. While the most appropriate means of achieving the full realization of the right to adequate housing will inevitably vary significantly from one State party to another, the Covenant clearly requires that each State party take whatever steps are necessary for that purpose. This will almost invariably require the adoption of a national housing strategy which, as stated in paragraph 32 of the Global Strategy for Shelter, 'defines the objectives for the development of shelter conditions, identifies the resources available to meet these goals and the most cost-effective way of using them and sets out the responsibilities and time-frame for the implementation of the necessary measures'. Both for reasons of relevance and effectiveness, as well as in order to ensure respect for other human rights, such a strategy should reflect extensive genuine consultation with, and participation by, all of those affected, including the homeless, the inadequately housed and their representatives. Furthermore, steps should be taken to ensure coordination between ministries and regional and local authorities in order to reconcile related policies (economics, agriculture, environment, energy, etc.) with the obligations under article 11 of the Covenant.

13. Effective monitoring of the situation with respect to housing is another obligation of immediate effect. For a State party to satisfy its obligations under article 11(1) it must demonstrate, *inter alia*, that it has taken whatever steps are necessary, either alone or on the basis of international cooperation, to ascertain the full extent of homelessness and inadequate housing within its jurisdiction. In this regard, the revised general guidelines regarding the form and contents of reports adopted by the Committee (E/C.12/1991/1) emphasize the need to 'provide detailed information about those groups within . . . society that are vulnerable and disadvantaged with regard to housing'. They include, in particular, homeless persons and families, those inadequately housed and without ready access to basic amenities, those living in 'illegal' settlements, those subject to forced evictions and low-income groups.

14. Measures designed to satisfy a State party's obligations in respect of the right to adequate housing may reflect whatever mix of public and private sector measures considered appropriate. While in some States public financing of housing might most usefully be spent on direct construction of new housing, in most cases, experience has shown the inability of Governments to fully satisfy housing deficits with publicly built housing. The promotion by States parties of 'enabling strategies', combined with a full commitment to obligations under the right to adequate housing, should thus be encouraged. In essence, the obligation is to demonstrate that, in aggregate, the measures being taken are sufficient to realize the right for every individual in the shortest possible time in accordance with the maximum of available resources.

15. Many of the measures that will be required will involve resource allocations and policy initiatives of a general kind. Nevertheless, the role of formal legislative and administrative measures should not be underestimated in this context. The

Global Strategy for Shelter (paras. 66–67) has drawn attention to the types of measures that might be taken in this regard and to their importance.

16. In some States, the right to adequate housing is constitutionally entrenched. In such cases the Committee is particularly interested in learning of the legal and practical significance of such an approach. Details of specific cases and of other ways in which entrenchment has proved helpful should thus be provided.

17. The Committee views many component elements of the right to adequate housing as being at least consistent with the provision of domestic legal remedies. Depending on the legal system, such areas might include, but are not limited to: (a) legal appeals aimed at preventing planned evictions or demolitions through the issuance of court-ordered injunctions; (b) legal procedures seeking compensation following an illegal eviction; (c) complaints against illegal actions carried out or supported by landlords (whether public or private) in relation to rent levels, dwelling maintenance, and racial or other forms of discrimination; (d) allegations of any form of discrimination in the allocation and availability of access to housing; and (e) complaints against landlords concerning unhealthy or inadequate housing conditions. In some legal systems it would also be appropriate to explore the possibility of facilitating class action suits in situations involving significantly increased levels of homelessness.

18. In this regard, the Committee considers that instances of forced eviction are *prima facie* incompatible with the requirements of the Covenant and can only be justified in the most exceptional circumstances, and in accordance with the relevant principles of international law.

19. Finally, article 11(1) concludes with the obligation of States parties to recognize 'the essential importance of international cooperation based on free consent'. Traditionally, less than 5 per cent of all international assistance has been directed towards housing or human settlements, and often the manner by which such funding is provided does little to address the housing needs of disadvantaged groups. States parties, both recipients and providers, should ensure that a substantial proportion of financing is devoted to creating conditions leading to a higher number of persons being adequately housed. International financial institutions promoting measures of structural adjustment should ensure that such measures do not compromise the enjoyment of the right to adequate housing. States parties should, when contemplating international financial cooperation, seek to indicate areas relevant to the right to adequate housing where external financing would have the most effect. Such requests should take full account of the needs and views of the affected groups.

Appendix III

States Parties to the International Covenant on Economic, Social, and Cultural Rights as at 30 June 1994

Afghanistan, Albania, Algeria, Angola, Argentina, Armenia, Australia, Austria, Azerbaijan, Barbados, Belarus, Belgium, Benin, Bolivia, Bosnia and Herzegovina, Brazil, Bulgaria, Burundi, Cambodia, Cameroon, Canada, Cape Verde, Central African Republic, Chile, Colombia, Congo, Costa Rica, Côte d'Ivoire, Croatia, Cyprus, Czech Republic, Democratic People's Republic of Korea, Denmark, Dominica, Dominican Republic, Ecuador, Egypt, El Salvador, Equatorial Guinea, Estonia, Ethiopia, Finland, France, Gabon, Gambia, Georgia, Germany, Greece, Grenada, Guatemala, Guinea, Guinea-Bissau, Guyana, Honduras, Hungary, Iceland, India, Iran (Islamic Republic of), Iraq, Ireland, Israel, Italy, Jamaica, Japan, Jordan, Kenya, Latvia, Lebanon, Lesotho, Libyan Arab Jamahiriya, Lithuania, Luxembourg, Macedonia (The former Yugoslav Republic of) Madagascar, Mali, Malta, Mauritius, Mexico, Mongolia, Morocco, Nepal, Netherlands, New Zealand, Nicaragua, Niger, Nigeria, Norway, Panama, Paraguay, Peru, Philippines, Poland, Portugal, Republic of Korea, Republic of Moldova, Romania, Russian Federation, Rwanda, Saint Vincent and the Grenadines, San Marino, Senegal, Seychelles, Slovakia, Slovenia, Solomon Islands, Somalia, Spain, Sri Lanka, Sudan, Suriname, Sweden, Switzerland, Syrian Arab Republic, Togo, Trinidad and Tobago, Tunisia, Uganda, Ukraine, United Kingdom of Great Britain and Northern Ireland, United Republic of Tanzania, Uruguay, Venezuela, Vietnam, Yemen, Yugoslavia, Zaïre, Zambia, Zimbabwe.

[Total: 129. The following states have signed, but not ratified the Covenant: Liberia, United States of America.]

Bibliography

BOOKS AND ARTICLES

AKEHURST M., 'Custom as a source of international law' (1972–3) 46 *BYIL* 4.

ALKEMA E. A., 'The Application of Internationally Guaranteed Human Rights in the Municipal Order' in Kalshoven F., Kuyper P. J., and Lammers J. G. (eds.), *Essays on the Development of the International Legal Order* (Alphen aan den Rijn: Sijthoff and Noordhoff, 1980), 181.

ALSTON P., 'Human Rights and Basic Needs: A Critical Assessment' (1979) 12 *HRJ* 19.

—— 'The UN Specialised Agencies and Implementation of the International Covenant on Economic, Social and Cultural Rights' (1979) 18 *Colum. J Trans. L* 79.

—— 'UNESCO's Procedures for Dealing with Human Rights Violations' (1980) 20 *Santa Clara LR* 665.

—— 'Prevention Versus Cure as a Human Rights Strategy' in International Commission of Jurists, *Development, Human Rights and the Rule of Law* (Oxford: Pergamon Press, 1981), 31.

—— 'A Third Generation of Solidarity Rights: Progressive Development or Obfuscation of International Human Rights Law?' (1982) 29 *Neth. ILR* 307.

—— 'The Universal Declaration at 35' (1983) 31 *ICJ Rev.* 60.

—— 'International Law and the Human Right to Food' in Alston P. and Tomasevski K. (eds.), *The Right to Food* (The Hague: Martinus Nijhoff, 1984), 9.

—— and QUINN G., 'The Nature and Scope of States Parties' Obligations under the International Covenant on Economic, Social and Cultural Rights' (1987) 9 *Hum. Rts. Q* 156.

—— and SIMMA B., 'First Session of the UN Committee on Economic, Social and Cultural Rights' (1987) 81 *AJIL* 747.

—— 'Out of the Abyss: The Challenges Confronting the New U.N. Committee on Economic, Social and Cultural Rights' (1987) 9 *Hum. Rts. Q* 332.

—— 'Implementing Economic, Social and Cultural Rights: The Functions of the Reporting Obligations' (1989) *Bull. HR* 5.

—— 'US Ratification of the Covenant on Economic, Social and Cultural Rights: The Need for an Entirely New Strategy' (1990) 84 *AJIL* 365.

—— 'Revitalizing United Nations Work on Human Rights and Development' (1991) 18 *Mel. Uni. LR* 216.

—— 'The Committee on Economic, Social and Cultural Rights' in Alston P. (ed.), *The United Nations and Human Rights: A Critical Appraisal* (Oxford: Clarendon Press, 1992), 473.

—— 'Appraising the United Nations Human Rights Regime' in Alston P. (ed.), *The United Nations and Human Rights: A Critical Appraisal* (Oxford: Clarendon Press, 1992), 1.

—— and SIMMA B., 'Second Session of the UN Committee on Economic, Social and Cultural Rights' (1988) 82 *AJIL* 603.

AMERASINGHE C. F., *State Responsibility for Injury to Aliens* (Oxford: Clarendon Press, 1967).

ANDERSEN-SPEEKENBRINK C., 'The Legal Dimension of Socio-Cultural Effects of Private Enterprise', in De Waart P., Peters P., and Denters E. (eds.), *International Law and Development* (Dordrecht: Nijhoff, 1988), 283.

ANDREASSEN B.-A., SKALNES T., SMITH A. G., and STOKKE H., 'Assessing Human Rights Performance in Developing Countries: The Case for a Minimum Threshold Approach to the Economic and Social Rights' in Andreassen B.-A. and Eide A. (eds.), *Human Rights in Developing Countries 1987/88* (Copenhagen: Academis Ferlag, 1988), 333.

ANKER P., *The Mandates System* (LN Publ. 1945. VI. A.1).

ARANGIO-RUIZ G., *The UN Declaration on Friendly Relations and the System of the Sources of International Law* (Alphen aan den Rijn: Sijthoff and Noordhoff, 1979).

ARGIROS G., 'Sex Equality in the Labour Market and the Community Legal Order: An Attempt at an Appraisal' (1989) 11 *Liv. LR* 161.

ARISTOTLE, *Nicomachean Ethics* (Oxford: Oxford University Press, 1980).

AZCARATE P. DE, *League of Nations and National Minorities, An Experiment* (trans. Brooke E. E.) (Washington: Carnegie Endowment, 1945).

BAILEY S., *The General Assembly of the United Nations. A study of Procedure and Practice* (Westport, Conn.: Greenwood Press, 1978).

BARD R., 'The Right to Food' (1985) 70 *Iowa LR* 1279.

BARSCH R., 'The Global Consultation on the Right to Development' (1993) 13 *Hum. Rts. Q* 322.

BAXI U., 'The New International Economic Order, Basic Needs and Rights: Notes Towards Development of the Right to Development' (1983) 23 *Ind. JIL* 225.

BAY C., 'A Human Rights Approach to Transnational Politics' (1979) 1 *Uni. Hum. Rts.* 29.

—— 'Self-Respect as a Human Right: Thoughts on the Dialectics of Wants and Needs in the Struggle for Human Community' (1982) 4 *Hum. Rts. Q* 53.

BAYEFSKY A. F., 'The Principle of Equality or Non-Discrimination in International Law' (1990) 11 *HRLJ* 1.

BEITZ C., 'Human Rights and Social Justice' in Brown P. and MacLean D. (eds.), *Human Rights and US Foreign Policy* (Lexington, Mass.: Lexington Books, 1979), 45.

BEN-ISRAEL R., *International Labour Standards: The Case of Freedom to Strike* (Deventer: Kluwer, 1988).

BENN S., 'Human Rights—for Whom and for What?' in Kameneka E. and Tay A. E.-S. (eds.), *Human Rights* (London: Edward Arnold, 1978), 59.

BENSON M., 'Equal Pay for Work of Equal Value' (1985) 15 *Isr. YHR* 66.

BERENSTEIN A., 'Economic and Social Rights: Their Inclusion in the ECHR—Problems of Formulation and Interpretation' (1981) 2 *HRLJ* 257.

BERLIN I., 'Two Concepts of Liberty' in *Four Essays on Liberty* (Oxford: Oxford University Press, 1969).

BERNARD-MAUGIRON N., '20 Years After: 38th Session of the Committee on the Elimination of Racial Discrimination' (1990) 8 *NQHR* 395.

BERNHARDT R., 'Treaties' in *Encyclopedia of Public International Law* (Amsterdam/

New York/Oxford: North Holland, 1984), Vol. 7, 459.
—— 'Domestic Jurisdiction of States and International Human Rights Organs' (1986) 7 *HRLJ* 205.

BILDER R., 'Rethinking International Human Rights: Some Basic Questions' (1969) 2 *HRJ* 557.

BIRK R., 'Industrial Conflict: The Law of Strikes and Lock-outs' in Blainpain R. (ed.), *Comparative Labour Law and Industrial Relations* (Deventer: Kluwer Law, 3rd ed., 1987), 401.

BLACKABY F., 'The Target Rate of Unemployment' in Worswick G. D. N. (ed.), *The Concept and Measurement of Involuntary Unemployment* (London: Allen and Unwin, 1976), 279.

BLAINPAIN R., 'Equality of Treatment in Employment' in Hepple B. (ed.), *International Encyclopedia of Comparative Law* (Dordrecht/Boston/Lancaster: Martinus Nijhoff, 1990), Vol. XV Labour Law, Ch. 10.

BLAUSTEIN J., 'Human Rights: A Challange to the United Nations and to our Generation' in Cordier A. W. (ed.), *The Quest For Peace* (New York: Columbia University Press, 1967), 315.

BOERMA A. H., *A Right to Food* (Rome: Food and Agriculture Organization, 1976).

BORCHARD E. M., *The Diplomatic Protection of Aliens Abroad* (N.Y.: Banks Law Publishing Co., 1915).

BOSSUYT M. J., 'La Distinction juridique entre les droits civils et politiques et les droits economiques, sociaux et culturels' (1975) 8 *HRLJ* 783.

—— *L'Interdiction de la discrimination dans le droit international des droits de l'homme* (1976), 193–202.

—— 'The Direct Applicability of International Instruments on Human Rights' (1980) 15 *RBDI* 317.

—— 'Human Rights and Non-Intervention in Domestic Matters' (1985) 35 *ICJ Rev.* 45.

BOWETT D. W., 'Problems of Self-Determination and Political Rights in Developing Countries' (1966) *Proc. Am. Soc. IL* 134.

BRAR P., 'The Practice and Procedures of the Human Rights Committee under the Optional Protocol of the International Convention on Civil and Political Rights' (1985) 25 *Ind. JIL* 506.

BRAYBROOKE D., *Meeting Needs* (Princeton, New Jersey: Princeton University Press, 1987).

BRIERLY J. L., *The Law of Nations* (Oxford: Clarendon Press, 6th ed., 1963), 62.

BRITTAN S., *Second Thoughts on Full Employment Policy* (Chichester: Rose, 1975).

BROCKETT C., 'The Right to Food and United States Policy in Guatemala' (1984) 6 *Hum. Rts. Q* 366.

BROWNLIE I., 'The Rights of Peoples in Modern International Law' in Crawford J. (ed.), *The Rights of Peoples* (Oxford: Clarendon Press, 1988), 1.

—— *Principles of Public International Law* (Oxford: Clarendon Press, 4th ed., 1990).

BRUDNER A., 'The Domestic Enforcement of International Covenants on Human Rights: A Theoretical Framework' (1985) 35 *Uni. Toronto LJ* 219.

BUCHHEIT L., *Secession—The Legitimacy of Self-Determination* (New Haven, Conn.: Yale University Press, 1978).

BUERGENTHAL T., 'Implementing the UN Racial Convention' (1977) 12 *Tex. ILJ* 187.

—— 'To Respect and Ensure: State Obligations and Permissible Derogations' in Henkin L. (ed.), *The International Bill of Rights: The Covenant on Civil and Political Rights* (New York: Columbia University Press, 1981), 72.

—— 'The US and International Human Rights' (1988) 9 *HRLJ* 141.

BURKE K., COLIVER S., DE LA VEGA C., and ROSENBAUM S., 'Application of International Human Rights Law in State and Federal Courts' (1983) 18 *Tex. ILJ* 291.

BYRNES A., 'The "Other" Human Rights Treaty Body: The Work of the Committee on the Elimination of Discrimination Against Women' (1989) 14 *Yale JIL* 1.

—— 'CEDAW's Tenth Session' (1991) 3 *NQHR* 340.

CANCADO TRINIDADE A. A. C., 'Co-existence and Co-ordination of Mechanisms of International Protection of Human Rights' (1987) 202 *Hague Recueil* 9.

CAPOTORTI F., 'The International Measures of Implementation Included in the Covenants on Human Rights' in Eide A. and Schou A. (eds.), *International Protection of Human Rights* (New York: Interscience, 1968), 131.

CARLSON J., 'Hunger, Agricultural Trade Liberalisation, and Soft International Law: Addressing the Legal Dimensions of a Political Problem' (1985) 70 *Iowa LR* 1187.

CASSESE A., 'Political Self-Determination—Old Concepts and New Developments' in Buergenthal T. (ed.), *Human Rights, International Law and the Helsinki Accord* (Montclair, New Jersey: Allanheld, Osmun, 1977), 137.

—— 'The Self-Determination of Peoples' in Henkin L. (ed.), *International Bill of Rights: The Covenant on Civil and Political Rights* (New York: Columbia University Press, 1981), 92.

CHEN L.-C., 'Self Determination as a Human Right' in Reisman W. L. and Weston B. H., *Towards World Order and Human Dignity* (New York: The Free Press, 1976), 198.

CHIANG P., *Non-Governmental Organisations at the United Nations* (New York: Praeger, 1981).

CHOLEWINSKI R., 'State Duty to Ethnic Minorities: Positive or Negative?' (1988) 10 *Hum. Rts. Q* 344.

CHRISTENSEN C., *The Right to Food: How to Guarantee* (New York: Institute for World Order, 1978).

—— and HANRAHAN C., 'African Food Crisis: Short-, Medium-, and Long-Term Responses' (1985) 70 *Iowa LR* 1293.

CLAPHAM A., *Human Rights in the Private Sphere* (Oxford: Clarendon Press, 1993).

CLAUDE R. P. and JABINE P., 'Editors' Introduction' (1986) 8 *Hum. Rts. Q* 551.

COHN C., 'The Early Harvest: Domestic Legal Changes Related to the Human Rights Committee and the Covenant on Civil and Political Rights' (1991) 13 *Hum. Rts. Q* 295.

CORDOVA E., 'Collective Bargaining' in Blainpain R. (ed.), *Comparative Law and Industrial Relations* (Deventer: Kluwer Law, 3rd ed., 1987), 307.

CORNEA G.A., JOLLY R., and STEWART F. (eds.), UNICEF, *Adjustment with a Human Face, Protecting the Vulnerable and Promoting Growth* (Oxford: Clarendon Press, 1987).

CRAIG C., RUBERY J., TARLING R., and WILKINSON F., *Labour Market Structure, Industrial Organisation and Low Pay* (Cambridge: Cambridge University Press, 1982).

CRAIG M. D., 'The International Covenant on Civil and Political Rights and U.S. Law: Department of State Proposals for Preserving the Status Quo' (1978) 19 *ICLQ* 845.

CRANSTON M., 'Human Rights Real and Supposed' in Raphael D. D. (ed.), *Political Theory and the Rights of Man* (London: Macmillan Press, 1967), 43.

CRANSTON R., 'Rights in Practice' in Sampford C. and Galligan D. J. (eds.), *Law, Rights and the Welfare State* (London: Macmillan Press, 1986), 1.

CRAVEN M., 'The Domestic Application of the International Covenant on Economic, Social and Cultural Rights' (1993) 40 *Neth. ILR* 367.

DANKWA E. V. O., 'Working Paper on Article 2(3) of the International Covenant on Economic, Social and Cultural Rights' (1987) 9 *Hum. Rts. Q* 230.

DAS K., 'United Nations Institutions and Procedures Founded on Conventions on Human Rights and Fundamental Freedoms' in Vasak K. and Alston P. (eds.), *The International Dimensions of Human Rights* (Westport, Conn.: Greenwood Press, 1982), 303.

DASGUPTA P., 'Well-Being and the Extent of its Realization in Poor Countries' (1990) 100 *The Economic Rev.* No. 400, Conference Supplement, 1.

DEL PRADO J., 'United Nations Conventions on Human Rights: The Practice of the Human Rights Committee and the Committee on the Elimination of Racial Discrimination in Dealing with Reporting Obligations of States Parties' (1985) 7 *Hum. Rts. Q* 492.

DEVEREUX S., *Theories of Famines* (New York: Harvester Wheatsheat, 1993).

DINSTEIN Y., 'Collective Human Rights of Peoples and Minorities' (1976) 25 *ICLQ* 102.

—— 'Discrimination and International Human Rights' (1985) 15 *Isr. YHR* 11.

DOBBERT J. P., 'The Right to Food', *Academie de Droit International, Colloque* 184 (1978).

DOMMEN C. and CRAVEN M., 'Making Way for Substance: The Fifth Session of the Committee on Economic, Social and Cultural Rights' (1991) 9 *NQHR* 93.

DONNELLY J., 'Human Rights as Natural Rights' (1982) 4 *Hum. Rts. Q* 399.

—— 'Cultural Relativism and Universal Human Rights' (1984) 6 *Hum. Rts. Q* 400.

—— 'Human Rights and Development: Complementary or Competing Concerns?' in Shepherd G. W. Jr. and Nanda V. P. (eds.), *Human Rights and Third World Development* (Westport, Conn.: Greenwood Press, 1985), 27.

—— *The Concept of Human Rights* (London: Routledge, 1985).

—— *Universal Human Rights in Theory and Practice* (Ithaca: Cornell University Press, 1989).

DONOHO D., 'Relativism Versus Universalism in Human Rights: The Search for Meaningful Standards' (1991) 27 *Stan. JIL* 345.

DORMENVAL A., 'UN Committee against Torture: Practice and Perspectives' (1990) 8 *NQHR* 26.

DOWRICK F. E., 'Introduction' in Dowrick F. E. (ed.), *Human Rights—Problems, Perspectives, and Texts* (Farnborough, Hants.: Saxon House, 1979), 1.

DOYAL L. and GOUGH I., *A Theory of Human Need* (Basingstoke: Macmillan Education, 1991).

DRAPER G., 'The Geneva Conventions of 1949' (1965) 114 *Hague Recueil* 63.

DRÈZE J. and SEN A., *Hunger and Public Action* (Oxford: Clarendon Press, 1989).

DRZEMCZEWSKI A., *European Human Rights Convention in Domestic Law: A*

Comparative Study (Oxford: Clarendon Press, 1983).

DWORKIN R., *Taking Rights Seriously* (London: Duckworth, 1977).

EIDE A., 'Developmentalism and Human Rights—Toward a Merger? Some Provisional Reflections' in Rehof L. A. and Gulmann C. (eds.), *Human Rights in Domestic Law and Development Assistance Policies of the Nordic Countries* (1989), 69.

—— 'Realization of Social and Economic Rights and the Minimum Threshold Approach' (1989) 10 *HRLJ* 35.

—— 'Article 25' in Eide A., Alfredsson G., Melander G., Rehof L. A., Rosas A., and Swinehart T. (eds.), *The Universal Declaration of Human Rights: A Commentary* (Oslo: Scandinavian University Press, 1992), 395.

EMERSON R., *From Empire to Nation: The Rise to Self-Assertion of Asian and African Peoples* (Cambridge, Mass.: Oxford University Press, 1960).

—— 'Self Determination' (1966) 60 *Proc. Am. Soc. IL* 135.

ENTRÈVES A. (d), *Natural Law: An Introduction to Legal Philosophy* (London: Hutchinson, 1970).

ERMACORA F., 'Human Rights and Domestic Jurisdiction' (1968) 124 *Hague Recueil* 371.

EVANS A. E., 'Self-Executing Treaties in the United States of America' (1953) 30 *BYIL* 178.

EWING K., 'The Right to Strike' (1986) 5 *Ind. RL* 143.

—— *Britain and the ILO* (London: Institute of Employment Rights, 1989).

—— *The Right to Strike* (Oxford: Clarendon Press, 1991).

FALK R. A., 'The Quasi-Legislative Competence of the General Assembly' (1966) 60 *AJIL* 782.

—— 'Comparative Protection of Human Rights in Capitalist and Socialist Third World Countries' (1979) 1 *Uni. HR* 3.

—— 'Ideological Patterns in the United States Human Rights Debate: 1945–1978' in Hevener N. K. (ed.), *The Dynamics of Human Rights in US Foreign Policy* (New Brunswick, New Jersey: Transaction Books, 1981), 29.

—— 'The Rights of Peoples' in Crawford J. (ed.), *The Rights of Peoples* (Oxford: Clarendon Press, 1988), 17.

FARER T. J., 'The United Nations and Human Rights: More Than A Whimper Less Than A Roar' (1987) 9 *Hum. Rts. Q* 553.

FAWCETT J. E. S., 'Human Rights and Domestic Jurisdiction' in Luard E. (ed.), *The International Protection of Human Rights* (New York: Praeger, 1967), 286.

FERGUSON C., 'The United Nations Human Rights Covenants: Problems of Ratification and Implementation' (1968) 62 *Proc. Am. Soc. IL* 83.

FIELDS B. and WOLF-DEITER N., 'Human Rights as a Wholistic Concept' (1992) 14 *Hum. Rts. Q* 1.

FINNIS J., *Natural Law and Natural Rights* (Oxford: Clarendon Press, 1980), 34–41.

FISCHER D., 'International Reporting Procedures' in Hannum H. (ed.), *Guide to International Human Rights Practice* (London: Macmillan Press, 1984), 165.

FLEW A., *Equality in Liberty and Justice* (London/New York: Routledge, 1989).

FOLLOWS J. W., *The Antecedents of the International Labour Organisation* (Oxford, Clarendon Press, 1951).

FORDE M., 'The European Convention on Human Rights and Labour Law' (1983) 31 *AJCL* 301.

FREDMAN S. and MORRIS G., 'Union Membership at G.C.H.Q.' (1988) 17 *Ind. LJ* 105.

FRIED C., *Right and Wrong* (Cambridge, Mass.: Harvard University Press, 1978), 108–113.

FRIEDMANN J., *Empowerment: The Politics of Alternative Development* (Cambridge, Mass.: Blackwell, 1992).

FRIEDMANN H., 'The Origins of Third World Food Dependence' in Bernstein H., *et al.* (eds.), *The Food Question* (London: Earthscan Publications, 1990), 16.

FRÖWEIN J., 'Federal Republic of Germany' in Jacobs F. G. and Roberts S. (eds.), *The Effect of Treaties in Domestic Law* (London: Sweet and Maxwell, 1987), 63.

GAER F., 'First Fruits: Reporting by States under the African Charter on Human and Peoples' Rights' (1992) 10 *NQHR* 29.

GALEY M., 'International Enforcement of Women's Rights' (1984) 6 *Hum. Rts. Q* 463.

GALLOWAY D., 'The Models of (In)Equality' (1993) 38 *McGill LJ* 64.

GEORGE S., *How the Other Half Dies* (Harmondsworth: Penguin, 1986).

GEWIRTH A., *Human Rights: Essays on Justification and Applications* (Chicago, Ill.: University of Chicago Press, 1982), 7.

GHAI D. P., and ALFTHAN T., 'On the Principles of Quantifying and Satisfying Basic Needs' in Ghai D. P. *et al.* (eds.), *The Basic-Needs Approach to Development: Some Issues Regarding Concepts and Methodology* (Geneva: International Labour Organisation, 1978), 19.

GHANDI P. R., 'The Human Rights Committee and the Right of Individual Petition' (1986) 57 *BYIL* 201.

GHEBALI V.-Y., *The International Labour Organisation: A Case Study on the Evolution of UN Specialised Agencies* (Dordrecht: Martinus Nijhoff, 1989).

GIRARD P., 'The Protection of the Rights of Homosexuals under International Law of Human Rights: European Perspectives' (1986) *Can. HRY* 3.

GOLDMAN A., 'Settlement of Disputes over Interests' in Blainpain R. (ed.), *Comparative Labour Law and Industrial Relations* (Deventer: Kluwer Law, 3rd ed., 1987), 361.

GOLDSTEIN R. J., 'The Limitations of Using Quantitative Data in Studying Human Rights Abuses' (1986) 8 *Hum. Rts. Q* 607.

GOLDSTEIN S., 'Reverse Discrimination—Reflections of a Jurist' (1985) 15 *Isr. YHR*, 28.

GOOD M., 'Freedom From Want: The Failure of United States Courts to Protect Subsistence Rights' (1984) 6 *Hum. Rts. Q* 335.

GOODIN R. E., 'The Development-Rights Trade-Off: Some Unwarranted Economic and Political Assumptions' (1979) 1 *Uni. HR*, 31.

GRAEFRATH B., 'How Different Countries Implement International Standards on Human Rights' (1984/5) *Can. HRY* 3.

GREEN J. F., *United Nations and Human Rights* (Washington, DC: Brookings Institution, 1956).

—— 'Changing Approaches to Human Rights: The United Nations, 1954 and 1974' (1977) 12 *Tex. ILJ* 223.

GREEN L. C., 'Derogations of Human Rights in Emergency Situations' (1978) 16 *Can. YIL* 92.

GREEN R. H., 'Basic Human Rights/Needs: Some Problems of Categorical Translation and Unification' (1981) 26 *ICJ Rev.* 53.

—— 'Sub-Saharan Africa: Poverty of Development, Development of Poverty' in Clay E. and Shaw J. (eds.), *Poverty, Development and Food* (London: Macmillan Press, 1987), 78.

GROSS B., *Reverse Discrimination* (1977).

GROS ESPIEL H. 'The Evolving Concept of Human Rights: Western, Socialist and Third World Approaches' in Ramcharan B. G. (ed.), *Human Rights Thirty Years after the Universal Declaration* (The Hague: Martinus Nijhoff, 1979), 41.

HAIGHT G., 'Human Rights Covenants' (1968) 62 *Proc. Am. Soc. IL* 96.

HALL W. G., *A Treatise on International Law* (Oxford: Clarendon Press, 4th ed., 1895).

HARRIS D., *The European Social Charter* (Charlottesville, Va.: Virginia University Press, 1984).

—— 'Commentary by the Rapporteur on the Consideration of States Parties' Reports and International Co-operation' (1987) 9 *Hum. Rts. Q* 147.

—— 'A Fresh Impetus for the European Social Charter' (1992) 41 *ICLQ* 659.

HART H., 'Are there any Natural Rights?' in Waldron J. (ed.), *Theories of Rights* (1984), 77.

HARTMAN J., 'Working Paper for the Committee of Experts on Article 4' (1985) 7 *Hum. Rts. Q* 89.

HAYEK F. A., *The Constitution of Liberty* (London: Routledge and Kegan Paul, 1960), 230–2.

HEINZ W. S., *Indigenous Populations, Ethnic Minorities and Human Rights* (Berlin: Quorum Verlag und Druck GmbH, 1988).

HELFER L., 'Lesbian and Gay Rights as Human Rights: Strategies for a United Europe' (1991) 32 *Virg. JIL* 157.

HENKIN L., '"International Concern" and the Treaty Power of the United States' (1969) 63 *AJIL* 272.

—— 'National and International Perspectives in Racial Discrimination' (1971) 4 *HRJ* 263.

—— 'Human Rights and "Domestic Jurisdiction"' in Buergenthal T. (ed.), *Human Rights, International Law and the Helsinki Accord* (Montclair New Jersey: Allanheld, Osmun, 1977), 21.

—— *The Rights of Man Today* (London: Stevens, 1979).

—— 'Introduction' in Henkin L. (ed.), *International Bill of Rights: The Covenant on Civil and Political Rights* (New York: Columbia University Press, 1981), 1.

—— 'Economic-Social Rights as "Rights": A United States Perspective' (1981) 2 *Hum. Rts. LJ* 223.

—— 'The International Bill of Human Rights: The Universal Declaration and the Covenants', in Bernhardt R. and Jolowicz J. A. (eds.), *International Enforcement of Human Rights* (Berlin: Springer-Verlag, 1987), 1.

—— 'The Invasion of Panama under International Law: A Dangerous Precedent' (1991) 29 *Colum. J Trans. L* 293.

HEPPLE B. A., 'A Right to Work' (1981) 10 *Ind. LJ* 65.

—— 'Great Britain' in Blainpain R. (ed.), *Equality and the Prohibition of Discrimination in Employment* (Deventer: Kluwer, 1985), 117.

—— 'Security of Employment' in Blainpain R. (ed.), *Comparative Labour Law and*

Industrial Relations (Deventer: Kluwer, 3rd ed., 1987), 475.

HERINGA A. W., 'Social Rights in the Dutch Legal Order' (1991) Conference Working Paper.

HIGGINS R., *The Development of International Law through the Political Organs of the United Nations* (Oxford: Oxford University Press, 1963), 103.

—— 'The United Nations and Lawmaking: The Political Organs' (1970) 64 *Proc. Am. Soc. IL* 38.

—— 'Derogations under Human Rights Treaties' (1976–77) 48 *BYIL* 281.

—— 'United Kingdom' in Jacobs F. G. and Roberts S. (eds.), *The Effect of Treaties in Domestic Law* (London: Sweet & Maxwell, 1987), 123.

—— 'Some Thoughts on the Implementation of Human Rights' (1989) *Bull. H.R.* 60.

—— 'The United Nations: Still a Force for Peace' (1989) 52 *MLR* 1.

HOLLOWAY K., *Modern Trends in Treaty Law* (London: Stevens, 1967).

HONEYBALL S., *Sex Employment and the Law* (Oxford: Blackwell Law, 1991).

HOPKINS M. and VAN DER HOEVEN R., *Basic Needs in Development Planning* (Aldershot: Gower, 1983).

HORREL S., RUBEY J., and BURCHELL B., 'Unequal Jobs or Unequal Pay?' (1989) 20 *Ind. RLJ* 176.

HOVET T., and HOVET E., *A Chronology and Fact Book of the United Nations 1941–1985* (New York: Oceana, 7th ed. 1986).

HOWARD R., 'The Full-Belly Thesis: Should Economic, Social and Cultural Rights Take Priority over Civil and Political Rights? Evidence from Sub-Saharan Africa' (1983) 4 *Hum. Rts. Q* 467.

HOWELL J., 'Socioeconomic Dilemmas of US Human Rights Policy' (1981) 3 *Hum. Rts. Q* 78.

HUDDLESTON B., 'Approaches to Quantifying the World Food Problem' in Clay E. and Shaw J. (eds.), *Poverty, Development and Food* (London: Macmillan Press, 1987), 1.

HUDSON M. O., 'Integrity of International Instruments' (1948) 42 *AJIL* 105.

HUMPHREY J. P., 'The UN Charter and the Universal Declaration of Human Rights' in Luard E. (ed.), *The International Protection of Human Rights* (New York: Praeger, 1967), 39.

—— 'The Universal Declaration of Human Rights: Its History, Impact and Juridical Character' in Ramcharan B. G. (ed.), *Human Rights Thirty Years after the Universal Declaration* (The Hague: Martinus Nijhoff, 1979).

—— *Human Rights and the United Nations—A Great Adventure* (Dobbs Ferry, New York: Transnational Publishers, 1984).

—— 'Letter to the Editor' (1984) 6 *Hum. Rts. Q* 539.

IBRD (World Bank), *World Development Report 1990* (Oxford: Oxford University Press, 1990).

INTERNATIONAL COMMISSION OF JURISTS, 'Human Rights Committee: Commentary' (1978) 20 *ICJ Rev.* 25.

—— 'Implementation of the International Covenant on Economic, Social and Cultural Rights: ECOSOC Working Group' (1981) 27 *ICJ Rev.* 26.

—— 'Human Rights Committee: Commentary' (1984) 33 *ICJ Rev.* 39.

IWASAWA Y., 'Letter to the Editor' (1985) 7 *Hum. Rts. Q.* 565.

—— 'The Doctrine of Self-Executing Treaties in the United States: A Critical

Analysis' (1986) 26 *VJIJ* 627.

JACOBS F. G., 'The Extension of the European Convention on Human Rights to Include Economic, Social and Cultural Rights' (1978) 3 *Hum. Rts. Rev.* 166.

—— 'The "Limitation Clauses" of the European Convention on Human Rights' in de Mestral A., Cotler I., Birks S., Klinck D., Bothe M., and Morel A. (eds.), *The Limitation of Human Rights in Comparative Constitutional Law* (Cowansville: Yvon Blais, 1986), 21.

—— 'Introduction' in Jacobs F. G. and Roberts S. (eds.), *The Effect of Treaties in Domestic Law* (London: Sweet & Maxwell, 1987), at xxiv–xxvi.

—— 'The Convention and the English Judge' in Matscher F. and Petzold H. (eds.), *Protecting Human Rights in the European Dimension* (Köln: Heymanns, 1988), 273.

JENKS C. W., *The International Protection of Trade Union Freedom* (London: Stevens, 1957).

—— *Human Rights and International Labour Standards* (New York: Praeger, 1960).

—— 'The International Protection of Trade Union Rights' in Luard E. (ed.), *The International Protection of Human Rights* (New York: Praeger, 1967).

JENNINGS I., *The Approach to Self-Government* (Cambridge: Cambridge University Press, 1956).

JHABVALA F., 'On Human Rights and the Socio-Economic Context' (1984) 31 *Neth. ILR* 149.

—— 'Letter to the Editor' (1985) 7 *Hum. Rts. Q* 242.

—— 'The Soviet-Bloc's View of the Implementation of Human Rights Accords' (1985) 7 *Hum. Rts. Q* 461.

—— 'Domestic Implementation of the Covenant on Civil and Political Rights' (1985) 32 *Neth. ILR* 461.

JOHNSON M. G., 'The Contributions of Eleanor and Franklin Roosevelt to the Development of International Protection for Human Rights' (1987) 9 *Hum. Rts. Q* 19.

KAHN-FREUND O. (ed.), *Labour Relations and the Law: A Comparative Study* (London: Stevens, 1965).

KÄLLSTRÖM K., 'Article 23' in Eide A., Alfredsson G., Melander G., Rehof L. A., Rosas A., and Swinehart T. (eds.), *The Universal Declaration of Human Rights: A Commentary* (Oslo: Scandinavian University Press, 1992), 357.

KAMENEKA E., 'Human Rights: People's Rights' in Crawford J. (ed.), *The Rights of Peoples* (Oxford: Clarendon Press, 1988), 130.

KARTASHKIN V., 'Covenants on Human Rights and Soviet Legislation' (1977) 10 *HRLJ* 97.

—— 'The Socialist Countries and Human Rights' in Vasak K. and Alston P. (eds.), *The International Dimensions of Human Rights* (Westport, Conn.: Greenwood Press, 1982), 631.

—— 'Economic, Social and Cultural Rights', in Vasak K. and Alston P. (eds.), *The International Dimensions of Human Rights* (Westport, Conn.: Greenwood Press, 1982), 111.

KASSAHUN Y., 'The Food Questions within the Prism of International law of Development' (1985) 38 *Oklahoma LR* 863.

KAUFMAN N. and WHITEMAN D., 'Opposition of Human Rights Treaties in the

US Senate: The Legacy of the Bricker Amendment' (1988) 10 *Hum. Rts. Q* 309.

KELSEN H., *The Law of the United Nations* (New York: Holt, Rinehart and Winston, 1966).

—— *Principles of International Law* (New York: Johns Hopkins Press, 2nd ed. 1967).

KENNEDY T., *European Labour Relations* (Lexington, Mass.: Lexington Books, 1980).

KISS A., 'Permissible Limitations on Rights' in Henkin L. (ed.), *The International Bill of Rights: The Covenant on Civil and Political Rights* (New York: Columbia University Press, 1982), 290.

KLERK Y., 'Working Paper on Article 2(2) and Article 3 of the International Covenant on Economic, Social and Cultural Rights' (1987) 9 *Hum. Rts. Q* 250.

KOROWICZ M., 'Protection and Implementation of Human Rights within the Soviet Legal System' (1959) 53 *Proc. Am. Soc. IL* 248.

KUMAR G., *Ethiopian Famines 1973–1985: A Case Study* (Wider Working Papers No. 26, 1987).

KUNZ J. 'The United Nations Declaration of Human Rights' (1949) 43 *AJIL* 316.

LACHS M., 'The Law in and of the United Nations—Some Reflections on the Principle of Self-Determination' (1960–1) 1 *Ind. JIL* 429.

LANDY E. A., *The Effectiveness of International Supervision; Thirty Years of ILO Experience* (London: Stevens & Sons, 1966).

LA PERGOLA A. and DEL DUCE P., 'Community Law, International Law and the Italian Constitution' (1985) 79 *AJIL* 598.

LASOK D. and BRIDGE J. W., *Law and Institutions of the European Communities* (London: Butterworths, 4th ed. 1987).

LAUTERPACHT H., *International Law and Human Rights* (London: Stevens & Sons, 1950).

—— 'Lessons from the Experience of the International Labour Organisation' in Alston P. (ed.), *The United Nations and Human Rights: A Critical Assessment* (Oxford: Clarendon Press, 1992), 580.

LEARY V., *International Labour Conventions and National Law* (The Hague/Boston/London: Martinus Nijhoff, 1982).

LECKIE S., 'The Inter-State Complaint Procedure in International Human Rights Law: Hopeful Prospects or Wishful Thinking?' (1988) 10 *Hum. Rts. Q* 249.

—— 'The UN Committee on Economic, Social and Cultural Rights and the Right to Adequate Housing: Towards an Appropriate Approach' (1989) 11 *Hum. Rts. Q* 522.

—— 'An Overview and Appraisal of the Fifth Session of the UN Committee on Economic, Social and Cultural Rights' (1991) 13 *Hum. Rts. Q* 539.

—— *From Housing Needs to Housing Rights: An Analysis of the Right to Adequate Housing Under International Human Rights Law* (London: International Institute for Environment and Development, 1992).

LERNER N., *The Convention on the Elimination of All Forms of Racial Discrimination* (Alphen aan den Rijn: Sijthoff and Noordhoff, 1980), 30.

LEWIS J., 'On Human Rights' in UNESCO, *Human Rights Comments and Interpretations* (London: Wingate, 1949), 54.

LILLICH R. B., 'Forcible Self-Help to Protect Human Rights' (1967) 53 *Iowa LR* 325.
—— *The Human Rights of Aliens in Contemporary International Law* (Manchester: Manchester University Press, 1981).
LIPPMAN M., 'Human Rights Revisited: The Protection of Human Rights under the International Covenant on Civil and Political Rights' (1980) 10 *Cal. West ILJ* 450.
LOCKWOOD B., FINN J., and JUBINSKY G., 'Working Paper for the Committee of Experts on Limitation Provisions' (1985) 7 *Hum. Rts. Q* 35.
LOMASKY L., *Persons, Rights and the Moral Community* (New York: Oxford University Press, 1987).
LOOPER R., 'Federal State Clauses in Multilateral Instruments' (1955–6) 32 *BYIL* 163.
LUARD E., 'The Origins of International Concern over Human Rights' in Luard E. (ed.), *The International Protection of Human Rights* (New York: Praeger, 1967).
LUKES S., 'Five Fables about Human Rights' in Shute S. and Hurley S. (eds.), *On Human Rights* (New York: Basic Books, 1993), 19.
LUSTIG N., 'Direct and Indirect Measures to Ensure Access to Food Supplies' in FAO, *World Food Security: Selected Themes and Issues* (Rome: Food and Agriculture Organization, 1985), 38.
MACBRIDE S., 'The Strengthening of International Machinery for the Protection of Human Rights' in Eide A, and Schou A, (eds.), *International Protection of Human Rights* (New York: Interscience, 1968).
MACCALISTER-SMITH P., *International Humanitarian Assistance* (Dordrecht: Martinus Nijhoff, 1985).
MCCHESNEY A., 'Should the US Ratify the Covenants? A Question of Merits, not of Constitutional Law' (1969) 62 *AJIL* 912.
—— 'Promoting the General Welfare in a Democratic Society: Balancing Human Rights and Development' (1980) 27 *Neth. ILR* 283.
MACDONALD M., 'Natural Rights' in Waldron J. (ed.), *Theories of Rights* (Oxford: Oxford University Press, 1984), 21.
MACDONALD R. St. J., 'The Margin of Appreciation in the Jurisprudence of the European Court of Human Rights' in *International Law and the Time of its Codification. Essays in Honour of Robert Ago* (Milan: 1987), 187.
—— 'The United Nations Charter: Constitution or Contract' in MacDonald R. St. J. and Johnstone D. M. (eds.), *The Structure and Process of International Law* (Dordrecht: Nijhoff, 1983), 889.
MCDOUGAL M. St., LASSWELL H. D., and CHEN L. C., *Human Rights and World Public Order* (New Haven, Conn.: Yale University Press, 1980).
MCGOLDRICK D., *The Human Rights Committee* (Oxford: Clarendon Press, 1991).
—— 'Canadian Indians, Cultural Rights and the Human Rights Committee' (1991) 40 *ICLQ* 658.
MCINTYRE S., 'Backlash against Equality: The Tyranny of the "Politically Correct"', (1993) 38 *McGill LJ* 1.
MCKEAN W., *Equality and Discrimination under International Law* (Oxford: Clarendon Press, 1983).
MCKEON R., 'The Philosophical Bases and Material Circumstances of the Rights of Man' in UNESCO Symposium, *Human Rights Comments and Interpretations* (London: Wingate, 1949), 37.

MacKinnon C., *Feminism Unmodified—Discourses on Life and Law* (Cambridge, Mass.: Harvard University Press, 1987).

Macpherson C., *The Political Theory of Possessive Individualism* (Oxford: Oxford University Press, 1962).

—— 'Natural Rights in Hobbes and Locke', in Raphael D. D. (ed.), *Political Theory and the Rights of Man* (London: Macmillan Press, 1967), 4.

Mahalic D. and Mahalic J. G., 'The Limitation Provisions of the International Convention on the Elimination of All Forms of Racial Discrimination' (1987) 9 *Hum. Rts. Q* 74.

Majury D., 'Strategizing in Equality' in Fineman M. and Thomadsen N. (eds.), *At the Boundaries of Law—Feminism and Legal Theory* (New York: Routledge, 1991), 320.

Mangahas M., 'Relative Emphasis on Food Self-Sufficiency and Trade-Oriented Self-Reliance' in FAO, *World Food Securiity: Selected Themes and Issues* (Rome: Food and Agriculture Organization, 1985), 1.

Mann F. A., *Foreign Affairs in English Courts* (Oxford: Clarendon Press, 1986).

Maresceau M., 'Belgium' in Jacobs F. G. and Roberts S. (eds.), *The Effect of Treaties in Domestic Law* (London: Sweet & Maxwell, 1987), 1.

Marie J.-B., 'Les Pactes internationaux relatifs aux droits de l'homme confirment-ils l'Inspiration de la déclaration universelle?' (1970) 3 *HRJ* 397.

—— 'Relations between Peoples' Rights and Human Rights: Semantic and Methodological Distinctions' (1986) 7 *HRLJ* 195.

Maritain J., 'Introduction' in UNESCO Symposium, *Human Rights Comments and Interpretations* (London: Wingate, 1949), 9.

Marks S., 'UNESCO and Human Rights: The Implementation of Rights Relating to Education, Science, Culture and Communication' (1977) 13 *Tex. ILJ* 35.

—— 'Emerging Human Rights: A New Generation for the 1980s' (1981) 33 *Rutgers L Rev.* 435.

Marshall T., *Class, Citizenship, and Social Development* (New York: 1964).

Marx K., 'On the Jewish Question' in *Collected Works III* (London: Lawrence and Wishart, 1975).

Mayer J., 'The Concept of the Right to Work In Intenational Standards and the Legislation of ILO Member States' (1985) 124 *Ind. LR* 225.

Melander G., 'Article 24' in Eide A., Alfredsson G., Melander G., Rehof L. A., Rosas A., and Swinehart T. (eds.), *The Universal Declaration of Human Rights: A Commentary* (Oslo: Scandinavian University Press, 1992), 379.

Mellor J., 'Effective Food Aid for Effective Food Security' in FAO, *World Food Security: Selected Themes and Issues* (Rome: Food and Agriculture Organization, 1985), 18.

—— 'Food Aid for Food Security and Economic Development' in Clay E. and Shaw J. (eds.), *Poverty, Development and Food*, (London: Macmillan Press, 1987) 173.

Meron T., 'The Meaning and Reach of the International Convention on the Elimination of All Forms of Racial Discrimination' (1985) 79 *AJIL*.

—— *Human Rights Law-Making in the United Nations* (Oxford: Clarendon Press, 1986).

Minogue K., 'The History of the Idea of Human Rights' in Laquer W. and Rubin B. (eds.), *The Human Rights Reader* (New York: New American Library, 1989) 3.

Moon R., 'Discrimination and its Justifications: Coping with Equality Rights under the Charter' (1988) 26 *Osgood HLJ*, 673.

MORE G., '"Equal Treatment" of the Sexes in European Community Law: What does "Equal" Mean?' (1993) 1 *Fem. L St.* 45.

MORGENSTERN F., 'Judicial Practice and the Supremacy of International Law' (1950) 27 *BYIL* 42.

MORGENTHAU H. J., *Politics Among Nations* (New York: Knopf, 5th ed., 1973), 290.

MORPHET S., 'Article 1 of the Human Rights Covenant: Its Development and Current Significance' in Hill D. (ed.), *Human Rights and Foreign Policy: Principles and Practice* (Basingstoke: Macmillan Press, 1989), 67.

MORRIS G. and ARCHER T., *Trade Unions, Employers and the Law* (Oxford: Blackwell Law, 1992).

MORRIS M., *Measuring the Conditions of the World's Poor: The Physical Quality of Life Index* (New York: Pergamon Press, 1979).

MORSINK J., 'The Philosophy of the Universal Declaration' (184) 6 *Hum. Rts. Q* 309.

MOWER A. G., 'The Implementation of the UN Covenant on Civil and Political Rights' (1977) 10 *HRJ* 271.

—— 'Organizing to Implement the UN Civil/Political Rights Covenant: First Steps by the Committee' (1978) 3 *Hum. Rts. Rev.* 122.

—— *International Cooperation for Social Justice* (Westport, Conn.: Greenwood Press, 1988).

MUCHLINSKI P. L., '"Basic Needs" Theory and "Development Law"' in Snyder F. and Slinn P. (eds.), *International Law of Development: Comparative Perspectives* (Abingdon: Professional Books, 1987), 237.

MYJER E., 'Dutch Interpretation of the European Convention: A Double System?' in Mastscher F. and Petzold H. (eds.), *Protecting Human Rights in the European Dimension* (Köln: Heymanns, 1988), 421.

NEDJATI Z., *Human Rights under the European Convention* (Amsterdam: North Holland Publishing Co., 1978).

NICKEL J. W., 'Equal Opportunity in a Pluralistic Society' in Paul E. F., Miller F. D. J., Paul J., and Ahrens J. (eds.), *Equal Opportunity* (Oxford: Blackwell, 1987), 115.

NOWAK M., 'UN Human Rights Committee: Survey of Decisions Given up till 1984' (1984) 5 *HRLJ* 199.

—— 'UN Human Rights Committee: Comment' (1990) 11 *HRLJ* 139.

NOZICK R., *Anarchy, State and Utopia* (Oxford: Blackwell, 1974).

O'DONNELL T., 'The Margin of Appreciation Doctrine: Standards in the Jurisprudence of the European Court of Human Rights' (1982) 4 *Hum. Rts. Q* 474.

OKIN S. M., 'Liberty and Welfare: Some Issues in Human Rights Theory' in Pennock J. and Chapman J. (eds.), *Human Rights, Nomos XXIII* (New York: New York Press, 1981), 242.

—— 'Gender, the Public and the Private' in Held D. (ed.), *Political Theory Today* (Cambridge: Polity Press, 1991), 67.

O'MANIQUE J., 'Universal and Inalienable Rights: A Search for Foundations' (1990) 12 *Hum. Rts. Q* 465.

—— 'Development, Human Rights and Law' (1992) 14 *Hum. Rts. Q* 383.

OPSAHL T., 'Human Rights Today: International Obligations and National Implementation' (1979) 23 *Scand. Stu. L* 149.

OPSAHL T., 'Equality in Human Rights Law with Particular Reference to Article 26 of the International Covenant on Civil and Political Rights' in Nowak M., Steurer D., and Tretter H. (eds.), *Progress in the Spirit of Human Rights* (Kehl/Strasbourg/Arlington: Engel Verlag, 1988), 51.

PACEY A. and PAYNE P., *Agricultural Development and Nutrition* (London: Hutchinson, 1985).

PALLEY C., *The United Kingdom and Human Rights* (London: Stevens & Sons/Sweet & Maxwell under the auspices of the Hamlyn Trust, 1991).

PALMER C. and POULTON K., *Sex and Race Discrimination in Employment* (London: Legal Action Group, 1987).

PANKERT A., 'Freedom of Association' in Blainpain R. (ed.), *Comparative Labour Law and Industrial Relations* (Deventer: Kluwer Law, 3rd ed. 1987), 173.

PARK H. S., 'Human Rights and Modernization: A Dialectical Relationship' (1980) 2 *Uni. HR* 85.

PARSCH K. J., 'Fundamental Principles of Human Rights: Self-Determination, Equality and Non-Discrimination' in Luard E., *The International Protection of Human Rights* (New York: Praeger, 1967), at 69.

PAUST J. J., 'Self-Executing Treaties' (1988) 82 *AJIL*, 760.

PECES-BARBA G., 'Reflections on Economic, Social and Cultural Rights' (1981) 2 *HRLJ*, 281.

PESCATORE P., 'Conclusion' in Jacobs F. G. and Roberts S. (eds.), *The Effect of Treaties in Domestic Law* (London: Sweet & Maxwell, 1987), 282.

PETERSEN M. J., *The General Assembly in World Politics* (Boston, Mass.: Allen and Unwin, 1986).

PLANT R., 'The Right to Food and Agrarian Systems: Law and Practice in Latin America' in Alson P. and Tomasevski K. (eds.), *The Right to Food* (The Hague: Martinus Nijhoff, 1984), 187.

—— *Modern Political Thought* (Oxford: Blackwell, 1991).

POLSON T. E., 'The Rights of Working Women: An International Perspective' (1974) 14 *VJIL* 729.

POLYVIOU P. G., *The Equal Protection of the Laws* (London: Duckworth, 1980).

POMERANCE M., *Self-Determination in Law and Practice* (The Hague: Nijhoff, 1982).

PROUNIS O. A., 'The Human Rights Committee: Toward Resolving the Paradox of Human Rights Law' (1985/6) 17 *Col. HRLR* 103.

PRZETACZNIK F., 'The Socialist Concept of Human Rights: Its Philosophical Background and Political Justification' (1977) 13 *RBDI* 238.

QUIGLEY J., 'The Legality of the United States Invasion of Panama' (1990) 15 *Yale JIL* 276.

RAMCHARAN B. G., 'Implementing the International Covenants on Human Rights' in Ramcharan B. G. (ed.), *Human Rights: Thirty Years after the Universal Declaration* (The Hague: Nihjoff, 1978), 159.

—— 'Equality and Nondiscrimination' in Henkin L. (ed.), *The International Bill of Rights* (New York: Columbia University Press, 1981), 246.

RAPHAEL D. D., 'Human Rights Old and New' in Raphael D. D. (ed.), *Political Theory and the Rights of Man* (London: Macmillan Press, 1967), 57.

—— *Justice and Liberty* (London: Athlone Press, 1980), 48.

RAZ J., 'Right-Based Moralities' in Waldron J., *Theories of Rights* (Oxford: Oxford University Press, 1992), 182.

REES A., 'The Soviet Union' in Vincent R. J. (ed.), *Foreign Policy and Human Rights* (Cambridge: Cambridge University Press, 1986), 61.

REISENFELD S. A., 'The Doctrine of Self-Executing Treaties and GATT: A Notable German Judgment' (1971) 65 *AJIL* 548.

RENTELN A., 'The Unanswered Challenge of Relativism and the Consequences for Human Rights' (1985) 7 *Hum. Rts. Q* 514.

RICH R., 'The Right to Development: A Right of Peoples?' in Crawford J., *The Rights of Peoples* (Oxford: Clarendon Press, 1988), 39.

ROBERTSON A. H., 'The Implementation System: International Measures' in Henkin L. (ed.), *The International Bill of Rights: The Covenant on Civil and Political Rights* (New York: Columbia University Press, 1981).

—— and Merrills J. G., *Human Rights in the World* (Manchester: Manchester University Press, 3rd ed., 1992).

ROBERTSON R., 'The Right to Food: Canada's Broken Covenant' (1989–90) 6 *Can. HRY* 185.

ROODT C., 'National Law and Treaties: An Overview' (1987/8) 13 *SAYIL* 72.

ROOSEVELT, *The Public Papers and Addresses of Franklin D.: War and Aid to Democracies, 1940,* (New York: Macmillan Press, 1941).

ROSSILLION C., 'ILO Standards and Actions for the Elimination of Discrimination and the Promotion of Equality of Opportunity in Employment' in Blainpain R. (ed.), *Equality and Prohibition of Discrimination in Employment* (Deventer: Kluwer, 1985), at 27.

ROUSSEAU C., 'Droits de l'Homme et Droit des Gens' in Cassin R. (ed.), *Amicorum Discipulorumque, Liber* (Paris: International Institute for Human Rights and Pedone, 1969), IV, 315.

RUBENSTEIN M., *Equal Pay for Work of Equal Value* (London: Macmillan Press, 1984).

RUSSELL R. B., *A History of the United Nations Charter* (Washington, DC: The Brookings Institute, 1958).

SABA H., 'UNESCO and Human Rights' in Vasak K. and Alston P. (eds.), *The International Dimensions of Human Rights* (Westport, Conn.: Greenwood Press, 1982), 401.

SAMSON K., 'Human Rights Co-ordination within the UN System' in Alston P. (ed.), *The United Nations and Human Rights: A Critical Appraisal* (Oxford: Clarendon Press, 1992), 620.

SCHACHTER O., 'The Charter and the Constitution: The Human Rights Provisions in American Law' (1951) 4 *Vand. LR* 643.

—— 'How Effective are Measures against Racial Discrimination?' (1971) 4 *HRJ* 293.

—— 'The Obligation to Implement the Covenant in Domestic Law' in Henkin L. (ed.), *The International Bill of Rights: The Covenant on Civil and Political Rights* (New York: Columbia University Press, 1981), 311.

SCHERMERS H. G., 'Netherlands' in Jacobs F. G. and Roberts S. (eds.), *The Effect of Treaties in Domestic Law* (London: Sweet & Maxwell, 1987), at 109.

SCHERMERS H. G., 'Is there a Fundamental Human Right to Strike?' (1989) 9 *Yrbk. Eur. L.*, 225.

SCHMIDT F. and NEAL A. C., 'Collective Agreements and Collective Bargaining' in Hepple B. A. (ed.), *Labour Law* (The Hague/Boston/London: Martinus Nijhoff, 1984), Ch. 12, Vol. XV.

SCHOENBERG H. O., 'The Implementation of Human Rights by the United Nations' (1977) 7 *Isr. YHR* 22.

SCHWARZENBERGER G., *Power Politics—A Study of World Society* (London: Stevens & Sons, 3rd ed., 1964).

SCHWELB E., 'The International Convention on the Elimination of All Forms of Racial Discrimination' (1966) 15 *ICLQ* 996.

—— 'Some Aspects of the International Covenants on Human Rights of December 1966' in Eide A. and Schou A. (eds.), *International Protection of Human Rights* (New York: Interscience, 1968), 103.

—— 'Some Aspects of the Measures of Implementation of the International Covenant on Economic, Social and Cultural Rights' (1968) 1 *HRJ* 363.

—— 'Notes on the Early Legislative History of the Measures of Implementation of the Human Rights Covenants' in *1 René Cassin Amicorum Discipulorumque* (Paris: Pedone, 1969), 301.

—— 'The United Kingdom Signs the Covenants in Human Rights' (1969) 18 *ICLQ* 457.

—— 'The International Court of Justice and the Human Rights Clauses of the Charter' (1972) 66 *AJIL* 372.

SCOTT C., 'The Interdependence and Permeability of Human Rights Norms: Towards a Partial Fusion of the International Covenants on Human Rights' (1989) 27 *Osgood HLJ* 769.

SCOTT M. and LASLETT R., *Can We Get Back to Full Employment?* (London: Macmillan Press, 1978).

SEIDL HOHENVELDERN I., 'Transformation or Adoption of International Law into Municipal Law' (1963) 12 *ICLQ* 88.

SEN A., *Poverty and Famines: An Essay on Entitlements and Deprivation* (Oxford: Clarendon Press, 1981).

—— *The Standard of Living* (Cambridge: Cambridge University Press, 1985).

SHAPIRO I., *The Evolution of Rights in Liberal Theory* (1986).

SHEA C., 'The Case of *Young, James and Webster*: British Labour Law and the European Convention on Human Rights' (1982) 15 *Cornell ILJ* 489.

SHELTON D., 'The Duty to Assist Famine Victims' (1985) 70 *Iowa LR* 1309.

SHEPHERD G. W., JR., 'The Power System and Basic Human Rights: From Tribute to Self-Reliance' in Shepherd G. W., Jr. and Nanda V. P. (eds.), *Human Rights and Third World Development* (Westport, Conn.: Greenwood Press, 1985), 13.

SHESTACK J., 'The Jurisprudence of Human Rights' in Meron T. (ed.), *Human Rights in International Law* (Oxford: Clarendon Press, 1984), 69.

SHUE H., 'Rights in the Light of Duties' in Brown P. and Maclean D. (eds.), *Human Rights and U.S. Foreign Policy* (Lexington, Mass.: Lexington Books, 1979), 65.

—— *Basic Rights: Subsistence, Affluence and US Foreign Policy* (Princeton: Princeton University Press, 1980).

—— 'The Interdependence of Duties' in Alston P. and Tomasevski K. (eds.), *The*

Right To Food (The Hague: Martinus Nijhoff, 1984), 85.

SIEGEL R., 'Socioeconomic Human Rights: Past and Future' (1985) 7 *Hum. Rts. Q* 255.

SIEGHART P., *The International Law of Human Rights* (Oxford: Clarendon Press, 1983).

—— *The Lawful Rights of Mankind* (Oxford: Oxford University Press, 1986).

—— ZIMAN J. and HUMPHREY J., *The World of Science and the Rule of Law* (Oxford: Oxford University Press, 1986).

SIMMA B., 'The Implementation of the International Covenant on Economic, Social and Cultural Rights' in Matscher F. (ed.), *The Implementation of Economic, Social and Cultural Rights* (Strasbourg: Engle Verlag, 1991), 75.

SINHA S. P., 'Is Self-Determination Passé?' (1973) 12 *Colum. J Trans. L* 260.

SKOGLY S., 'Structural Adjustment and Development: Human Rights—an Agenda for Change' (1993) 15 *Hum. Rts. Q* 751.

SLOAN B., 'General Assembly Resolutions Revisited' (1987) 58 *BYIL* 39.

SOHN L. B., 'A Short History of United Nations Documents on Human Rights' in the 18th Report of the Commission to Study the Organisation of Peace, *The United Nations and Human Rights* (Dobbs Ferry: Oceana, 1968), 59.

—— 'The Human Rights Law of the Charter' (1977) *Tex. ILJ* 129.

—— 'The Rights of Minorities' in Henkin L. (ed.), *International Bill of Rights: The Covenant on Civil and Political Rights* (New York: Columbia University Press, 1981), 270.

—— 'The Role of the United Nations Organs in Implementing the International Covenant on Economic, Social and Cultural Rights', *Background Paper* (1985).

—— and BUERGENTHAL T., *International Protection of Human Rights* (New York: Bobbs-Merrill, 1973).

SØRENSEN M., 'Obligations of a State Party to a Treaty as Regards its Municipal Law' in Robertson A. H. (ed.), *Human Rights in National and International Law* (Manchester: Manchester University Press, 1968), 11.

SQUIRE L., *Employment Policy in Developing Countries* (New York: Oxford University Press, 1981).

STARCK C., 'Europe's Fundamental Rights in their Newest Garb' (1982) 3 *HRLJ* 103.

STARR R., 'International Protection of Human Rights and the United Nations Covenants' (1967) 4 *Wisc. LR* 862.

STEINER H., *Diverse Partners: Non-Governmental Organisations in the Human Rights Movement* (Cambridge, Mass.: Harvard Law School, 1991).

STEWART F., 'Basic Needs Strategies, Human Rights, and the Right to Development' (1989) 11 *Hum. Rts. Q* 347.

STOHL M., CARLETON D., LOPEZ G., and SAMUELS S., 'State Violation of Human Rights: Issues and Problems of Measurement' (1986) 8 *Hum. Rts. Q* 592.

SWAN G., 'Self-Determination and the UN Charter' (1982) 22 *Ind. JIL* 264.

SZABO I., 'Historical Foundations of Human Rights and Subsequent Developments' in Vasak K. and Alston P. (eds.), *The International Dimensions of Human Rights* (Westport, Conn.: Greenwood Press, 1982), 11.

SZUBERT W., 'Some Considerations on Safety and Health at Work in Comparative Law' in Gamillscheg F. *et al.*, *In Memoriam: Sir Otto Kahn-Freund* (München: Beck, 1980), 701.

SZYZCZAK E., 'Pay Inequalities and Equal Value Claims' (1985) 48 *MLR* 139.

TARDU M. E., *Human Rights: The International Petition System* (New York: Oceana, 1985).

TEDIN K., 'The Development of The Soviet Attitude Toward Implementing Human Rights Under the UN Charter' (1972) 5 *HRJ* 399.

TESON F., 'International Human Rights and Cultural Relativism' (1985) 25 *VJIL* 868.

—— *Humanitarian Intervention* (Dobbs Ferry, New York: Transnational Publisher, 1988).

THORNBERRY P., 'Self-Determination, Minorities, Human Rights: A Review of International Instruments' (1989) 38 *ICLQ* 867.

—— *International Law and the Rights of Minorities* (Oxford: Clarendon Press, 1991).

TOLLEY H., *The UN Commission on Human Rights* (Boulder: Westview, 1987).

TOMASEVSKI K., 'Human Rights Indicators: The Right to Food as a Test Case' in Alston P. and Tomasevski K. (eds.), *The Right to Food* (The Hague, Martinus Nijhoff, 1984), 135.

—— 'Human Rights: The Right to Food' (1985) 70 *Iowa LR* 1321.

—— *Development Aid and Human Rights* (London: Pinter, 1989).

TOMES I., 'The Right to Work and Social Security' (1967–8) 8–9 *Bull. Czech L* 192.

TOMUSCHAT C., 'National Implementation of International Standards on Human Rights' (1984/5) *Can. HRY* 31.

TRIGGS G., 'Peoples' Rights and Individual Rights: Conflict or Harmony?' in Crawford J. (ed.), *The Rights of Peoples* (Oxford: Clarendon Press, 1988), 141.

TRUBECK D., 'Economic, Social and Cultural Rights in the Third World: Human Rights Law and Human Needs Programs' in Meron T. (ed.), *Human Rights in International Law* (Oxford: Clarendon Press, 1984), 205.

TUCK R., *Natural Rights Theories: Their Origin and Development* (Cambridge, Mass.: Cambridge University Press, 1979).

TUMANOV V. A., 'International Protection of Human Rights: Soviet Report' in Bernhardt R. and Jolowicz J. A. (eds.), *International Enforcement of Human Rights* (Berlin/Heidelberg/New York: Springer-Verlag, 1985), 21.

TUNKIN G. I., *Theory of International Law* (trans; Butler, 1974) (Cambridge: Harvard University Press, 1974).

TUR R., 'Justifications of Reverse Discrimination' in Stewart M., *Law, Morality and Rights* (Dordrecht: Reidel, 1983), 259.

TÜRK D., 'The Human Right to Development' in Van Dijk P., Van Hoof F., Koers A., and Mortelmans K. (eds.), *Restructuring the International Economic Order: The Role of Law and Lawyers* (Deventer: Kluwer Law, 1986), 85.

TYAGI Y., 'Third World Response to Human Rights' (1981) 21 *Ind. JIL* 119.

UMOZURIKE U., *Self-Determination in International Law* (Hamden, Conn.: Archon Books, 1972), 185.

UNESCO SECRETARIAT, 'UNESCO and the Challenges of Today and Tomorrow: Universal Affirmation of Human Rights' in Ramcharan B. G. (ed.), *Human Rights Thirty Years after the Universal Declaration* (The Hague: Martinus Nijhoff, 1979), 197.

UNITED NATIONS DEVELOPMENT PROGRAMME, *Human Development Report 1990* (Oxford: Oxford University Press, 1990).

VALTICOS N., *International Labour Law* (Deventer: Kluwer, 1979).

—— 'The Role of the ILO: Present Action and Future Perspectives' in Ramcharan B. G. (ed.), *Human Rights Thirty Years After the Universal Declaration* (The Hague: Martinus Nijhoff, 1979), 211.

—— 'The International Labour Organisation' in Vasak K. and Alston P. (eds.), *The International Dimensions of Human Rights* (Westport, Conn.: Greenwood Press, 1982), 363.

—— 'International Labour Law' in Blainpain R. (ed.), *Comparative Labour Law and Industrial Relations* (Deventer: Kluwer Law, 3rd ed., 1985), 77.

VAN BOVEN T., *People Matter: Views on International Human Rights Policy* (Amsterdam: Meulendoff Nederland, 1982).

—— 'The Relations Between Peoples' Rights and Human Rights in the African Charter' (1986) 7 *HRLJ* 183.

—— 'Human Rights and Development—Rhetorics and Realities' in Novak M., Steurer D., and Tretter H. (eds.), *Progress in the Spirit of Human Rights* (Kehl: Engel, 1988), 575.

VAN DEN BERG G. P. and GULDENMUND R. M. A., 'The Right to Work in East and West' in Bloed A. and Van Dijk P. (eds.), *Essays on Human Rights in the Helsinki Process* (Dordrecht: Martinus Nijhoff, 1985), 103.

VAN DER VEN J. J. M., 'The Right to Work as a Human Right' (1965) 11 *Howard LJ* 397.

VAN DIJK P. and VAN HOOF G. J. H., 'Domestic Status of Human-Rights Treaties and the Attitude of the Judiciary—The Dutch Case' in Nowak M., Steurer D., and Tretter H. (eds.), *Progress in the Spirit of Human Rights* (Kehl: Engel, 1988), 634.

—— and —— *Theory and Practice of the European Convention on Human Rights* (Deventer: Kluwer, 1990).

—— and ROOD J., 'Function and Effectiveness of Supervision in an Economically Interdependent World' in Van Dijk P., Van Hoof F., Koers A., and Mortelmans K. (eds.), *Restructuring the International Economic Order: The Role of Law and Lawyers* (Deventer: Kluwer Law, 1987), 135.

VAN HOOF G. J. H., 'The Legal Nature of Economic, Social and Cultural Rights: A Rebuttal of Some Traditional Views' in Alston P. and Tomasevski K. (eds.), *The Right To Food* (The Hague: Martinus Nijhoff, 1984), 97.

—— and TAHZIB B., 'Supervision with Respect to the Right to Food and the Role of the World Bank' in de Waart P., Peters P., and Denters E. (eds.), *International Law and Development* (Dordrecht: Nijhoff, 1988), 317.

VAN HOOF F., 'Problems and Prospects with Respect to the Right to Food' in Van Dijk P., Van Hoof F., Koers A., and Mortelmans K. (eds.), *Restructuring the International Economic Order: The Role of Law and Lawyers* (Deventer: Kluwer Law, 1987), 107.

VANDYCKE R., 'La Charte Constitutionelle et les Droits Économiques, Sociaux et Culturels' (1989–90) *Can. HRY* 167.

VASAK K., 'The Distinguishing Criteria of Institutions' in Vasak K. and Alston P. (eds.), *The International Dimensions of Human Rights* (Westport, Conn.: Greenwood Press, 1982), 215.

VERDOOT A., *Naissance et Signification de la Déclaration Universelle des Droits de l'Homme* (Louvin: Warny, 1964).

VERHOEVEN J., 'Traités—applicabilité directe' (1991) 24 *RBDI* 306.

VERWEY W., *The Establishment of a New International Economic Order and the Realization of the Right to Development and Welfare* (Geneva: United Nations, 1980).

VICKERS J. M., 'Majority Equality Issues of the Eighties' (1980) *Can. HRY* 47.

VIERDAG E. W., *The Concept of Discrimination in International Law* (The Hague: Nijhoff, 1973).

—— 'The Legal Nature of the Rights Granted by the International Covenant on Economic, Social and Cultural Rights' (1978) 9 *Neth. ILR* 69.

VINCENT R. J., *Human Rights and International Relations* (Cambridge: Cambridge University Press, 1986).

VLASTOS G., 'Justice and Equality' in Waldron J. (ed.), *Theories of Rights* (Oxford: Oxford University Press, 1984).

VON PRONDZYNSKI F., 'Freedom of Association and the Closed Shop: The European Perspective' (1982) 41 *CLJ* 256.

—— *Freedom of Association and Industrial Relations: A Comparative Study* (London: Mansell, 1987).

WALDRON J., 'Natural Rights in the Seventeenth and Eighteenth Centuries' in Waldron J. (ed.), *Nonsense upon Stilts* (London and New York: Methuen, 1987), 7.

—— *Liberal Rights* (Cambridge: Cambridge University Press, 1993).

WALLINGTON P. and McBRIDE J., *Civil Liberties and a Bill of Rights* (London: Cobden Trust, 1976).

WASSERSTRÖM R., 'Rights, Human Rights, and Racial Discrimination' (1964) 61 *J. of Philosophy* 628.

WESTEN P., 'The Empty Idea of Equality' (1982) 95 *Harv. LR* 537.

WESTERVEEN G., 'Towards a System for Supervising States' Compliance with the Right to Food' in Alston P. and Tomasevski K. (eds.), *The Right to Food* (The Hague, Martinus Nijhoff, 1984), 119.

WESTON B., 'Human Rights' (1984) 6 *Hum. Rts. Q* 257.

WHITE R., 'Self-Determination: Time for Reassessment' (1981) 28 *Neth. ILR* 147.

WILLIAMS B., 'The Idea of Equality' in Williams B. (ed.), *Problems of the Self* (London: Cambridge University Press, 1973).

WINTER J. A., 'Direct Applicability and Direct Effect: Two Distinct and Different Concepts in Community Law' (1972) 9 *CMLR* 425.

WOLD T., 'The Right to Social Services' (1968) 9 *JICJ* 41.

WOLF F., 'Human Rights and the International Labour Organisation' in Meron T. (ed.), *Human Rights in International Law* (Oxford: Clarendon Press, 1985), 273.

WORSWICK G. D. N., 'Summary' in Worswick G. D. N. (ed.), *The Concept and Measurement of Involuntary Unemployment* (London: Allen and Unwin, 1976), 305.

ZANDER M., *A Bill of Rights?* (London: Sweet & Maxwell, 3rd ed., 1985).

ZAYAS A. DE, MÖLLER J., and OPSAHL T., 'Application of the International Covenant on Civil and Political Rights under the Optional Protocol by the Human Rights Committee' (1985) 28 *Ger. YIL* 9.

ZÖLLER A.-C., 'UN Committee against Torture' (1989) 7 *NQHR* 210.

Miscellaneous Documents

ALSTON P., *Effective Implementation of International Instruments on Human Rights, Including Reporting Obligations under International Instruments on Human Rights*, UN Doc. A/44/668, 44 UN GAOR (Ag. Item 109) (1989).

—— *Effective Implementation of International Instruments on Human Rights, Including Reporting Obligations under International Instruments on Human Rights, Interim Report*, UN Doc. A/CONF.157/PC/62/Add.11/Rev. 1 (1993).

BENITO E., *Elimination of All Forms of Intolerance and Discrimination Based on Religion and Belief* (Geneva: United Nations, 1989).

CAPOTORTI F., *Study on the Rights of Persons Belonging to Ethnic, Religious and Linguistic Groups*, UN Doc. E/CN.4/Sub.2/384/Rev. 1 (1979).

CENTRE FOR HUMAN RIGHTS, *Report of an International Consultation on AIDS and Human Rights* (Geneva: United Nations, 1989).

COMMITTEE ON ECONOMIC, SOCIAL, AND CULTURAL RIGHTS, *General Comment No. 1 (1989)*, UN Doc. E/1989/23, Annex III, UN ESCOR, Supp. (No. 4), 87 (1989).

—— *General Comment No. 2 (1989)*, UN Doc. E/1990/23, Annex III, UN ESCOR, Supp. (No. 3), 86 (1990).

—— *General Comment No. 3 (1990)*, UN Doc. E/1991/23, Annex III, UN ESCOR, Supp. (No. 3), 83 (1991).

—— *General Comment No. 4 (1991)*, UN Doc. E/1992/23, Annex III, UN ESCOR, Supp. (No. 3), 114 (1992).

—— *Towards an Optional Protocol to the International Covenant on Economic, Social and Cultural Rights*, in UN Doc. E/1993/22, Annex IV, UN ESCOR, Supp. (No. 2), 87 (1993).

—— *Statement to the World Conference on Human Rights on Behalf of the Committee on Economic, Social and Cultural Rights*, in UN Doc. E/1993/22, Annex III, UN ESCOR, Supp. (No. 2), 82 (1993).

CONROY H., *On the Relation between Development and the Enjoyment of All Human Rights, Recognizing the Importance of Creating the Conditions whereby Everyone may Enjoy these Rights*, UN Doc. A/CONF.157/pc/60/Add. 2, at 19, para. 113 (1993).

DESPOUY L., *Human Rights and Disability*, UN Doc. E/CN.4/Sub.2/1991/31 (1991).

EIDE A., *Rights to Adequate Food as a Human Right* (Geneva: United Nations, 1989).

EUROPEAN COMMISSION, Intermediate Report on Application of Directive No. 79/7 (Com. 83), 793 (1984).

FERRERO R., *The New International Economic Order and the Promotion of Human Rights*, UN Doc. E/CN.4/Sub.2/1983/24/Rev. 1 (1983).

GANJI M., *The Realization of Economic, Social and Cultural Rights: Problems and Perspectives*, UN Docs. E/CN.4/1108/Rev. 1 and E/CN.4/1131/Rev. 1, at 16 (1975).

ILO COMMITTEE OF EXPERTS, General Survey: *Abolition of Forced Labour*, ILC, 65th Sess., Report II. 65/3 (Pt. 4B) (1979).

—— General Survey: *Freedom of Association and Collective Bargaining*, ILC, 69th Sess., ILO Report II: 69/3 (Pt. 4B) (1983).

—— General Survey: *Working Time: Reduction of hours of work, weekly rest and holidays with pay*, ILC, 70th Sess., Report III (Pt. 4B) (1984).

ILO COMMITTEE OF EXPERTS, General Survey: *Equal Remuneration*, ILC, 72nd Sess., Report III (Pt. 4B) (1986).

—— General Survey: *Human Resources Development: Vocational Guidance and Training, Paid Educational Leave*, ILC, 78th Sess., Report III (Pt. 4B) (1991).

—— General Survey: *Minimum Wages*, ILC, 79th Sess., Report III (Pt. 4B) (1992).

ILO DIRECTOR-GENERAL (Report), *Making Work More Human: Working Conditions and the Environment*, ILC, 60th Sess. (Geneva: International Labour Office, 1974).

—— (Report), *Human Rights: A Common Responsibility*, ILC, 75th Sess. (Geneva: International Labour Office, 1988).

INTERNATIONAL LABOUR OFFICE, *Employment, Growth and Basic Needs: A One World Problem* (Geneva: International Labour Office, 1976).

—— *Target Setting for Basic Needs* (Geneva: International Labour Office, 1982).

—— *Impact of ILO Policies on the UN*, ILO Doc. GB.225/IO/3/3 (Geneva: International Labour Office, 1984).

LEWIS-ANTHONY S., *The Right to Freedom of Peaceful Assembly and to Freedom of Association as Guaranteed by Article 11 of the European Convention on Human Rights* (Strasbourg: Council of Europe, 1992).

SACHAR R., *Working Paper on the Right to Adequate Housing*, UN Doc. E/CN.4/Sub.2/1992/15 (1992).

—— *The right to Adequate Housing: Progress Report*, UN Doc. E/CN.4/Sub.2/1993/15 (1993).

SECRETARY-GENERAL (Report), *Concrete Proposals for the Effective Implementation and Promotion of the Declaration on the Right to Development*, UN Doc. E/CN.4/1993/16 (1993).

—— (Report), *Report of the Seminar on Appropriate Indicators to Measure Achievements in the Progressive Realization of Economic, Social and Cultural Rights*, UN Doc. A/CONF.157/PC/73 (1993).

—— (Report), *Forced Evictions*, UN Doc. E/CN.4/1994/20 (1993).

TÜRK D., *The New International Economic Order and the Promotion of Human Rights: Realization of Economic, Social and Cultural Rights*, UN Doc. E/CN.4/Sub.2/1989/19 (1989).

—— *The New International Economic Order and the Promotion of Human Rights: Realization of Economic, Social and Cultural Rights*, UN Doc. E/CN.4/Sub.2/1990/19 (1990).

—— *The New International Economic Order and the Promotion of Human Rights: Realization of Economic, Social and Cultural Rights, Final Report*, UN Doc. E/CN.4/Sub.2/1992/16 (1992).

UNDP, *Human Development Report 1990* (Oxford: Oxford University Press, 1990).

WORKING GROUP ON THE RIGHT TO DEVELOPMENT (Report), UN Doc. E/CN.4/1994/21 (1994).

WORLD BANK (IBRD), *World Development Report 1990* (Oxford: Oxford University Press, 1990).

—— *World Development Report 1992* (Oxford: Oxford University Press, 1992).

Index